**ORACLE**®   *Oracle Press*™

# Oracle Performance Tuning Tips & Techniques

**Rich Niemiec**

## Tata McGraw-Hill Publishing Company Limited
**NEW DELHI**

*McGraw-Hill Offices*
**New Delhi** New York St Louis San Francisco Auckland Bogotá
Caracas Lisbon London Madrid Mexico City Milan
Montreal San Juan Singapore Sydney Tokyo Toronto

**Tata McGraw-Hill**

*A Division of The McGraw·Hill Companies*

**Oracle Performance Tuning Tips and Techniques**

**Tata McGraw-Hill Edition 2000**

Reprinted in India by arrangement with The McGraw-Hill Companies, Inc., New York

**For Sale in India Only**

**ISBN 0-07-463775-4**

Published by Tata McGraw-Hill Publishing Company Limited, 7 West Patel Nagar, New Delhi 110 008, and printed at Sai Printo Pack, New Delhi 110 044

"Perhaps, in order for us to really become free, we have to move from struggling to hear God's voice to letting God's Voice speak through us."

Rabbi Jonathan Kraus

### To Regina, My Hero in Life!

I have been blessed immeasurably by God in life by the gift of your love. Through your love I feel a warmth and an experience that is so deep that it helps me to see and understand the depth of God's love. I stand in the warmth of life because you are near. I love you dearly! You walked into my life and elevated it to where so much of what I do is so much of who you are. It has been a wonderful journey together that has brought four wonderful children, Jacob, Lucas, Hollyann and Melissa into our lives. You never cease to amaze me as you weather every storm with fortitude.

One night, there was a terrible storm and I noticed a single rose glowing through the storm. I kept checking to see if it would blow apart and yet it continued to survive this storm. In the morning, it was more beautiful than ever with the sunlight glistening through the raindrops making the rose glow even brighter. You are like that rose. The winds come and yet you stand strong in your beliefs, the rain falls and you never waver, you endure the storm and when it's over and the morning light shines bright and I see a more beautiful person than I once knew. I see your strength, your encouragement and the depth of your love so much more than I saw before… a beauty that comes from within your heart. What a wonderful and caring heart that you share with others! You are a once in a lifetime person…and with every breath I take I will love thee. The times spent with you will forever be the greatest moments of my life…my heart only beats when you are near. The years with you continue to be the very best years of my life.

I hear the voice of God through you and the love of God through your love…you will forever be my hero in life!

Brad Brown, Rich Niemiec, and Joe Trezzo founded TUSC in 1988. In addition to TUSC's corporate office in the Chicago suburb of Lombard, Illinois, the founders have since expanded the company with additional offices in suburban Denver (Lakewood) and Detroit. Brad, Rich, and Joe are all members in the Entrepreneur Hall of Fame.

TUSC is a full-service consulting company specializing in Oracle that provides senior-level expertise for the analysis, design, development, implementation, and support of information systems. TUSC is on the Inc. 500 list of fastest-growing private firms in America for both 1997 and 1998, and is recognized as an industry leader within and outside the Oracle community.

TUSC attributes its success to its "adapt and overcome philosophy" grounded in the traits of the uncommon leader: integrity, moral courage, physical courage, self control, enthusiasm, knowledge, initiative, respect, tact, loyalty, and unselfishness. The members of TUSC believe that it's always better to give than it is to receive, the TUSC-authored books are TUSC's way of sharing its knowledge with professionals in the Oracle community. If you have any comments about the materials covered in this book or would like to share some tips of your own, fell free to drop the author a line at niemiecr@tusc.com. Or, visit our home page at www.tusc.com. Our Web site features downloadable technical papers, additional tips, white papers, and links to other sources of Oracle information.

### Rich Niemiec

Rich is the author of this book. He is recognized by his colleagues as an expert in the industry, having delivered the top presentation at international Oracle user conferences three of the past six years. Rich also is quite active in Oracle user groups, having served as executive vice-president of the International Oracle Users Group-Americas, president of the Midwest Oracle Users Group, executive editor of *Select* magazine and editor in chief of *Exploring Oracle DBMS* magazine. He was the 1998 Chris Wooldridge Award winner.

### Brad Brown

Brad is the author of *Oracle Application Server Web Toolkit Reference* published by Oracle Press. Brad has been working with management information systems for more than 15 years, including the last 10 with a focus on Oracle. He is recognized worldwide as a leading Oracle author and is quite involved with numerous organizations, having served as president and membership chair of the Rocky Mountain Oracle Users Group and executive editor of *Exploring Oracle DBMS* magazine.

### Joe Trezzo

Joe is the author of the Oracle PL/SQL Tips and Techniques book soon to be published by Oracle Press. He has been designing, developing, deploying, administering, and managing Oracle-based systems since 1985 (version 4). Joseph is a certified Oracle DBA, an accomplished author (having served as editor-in-chief of *Exploring Oracle DBMS* magazine), and a VIP presenter at international conferences. He has presented papers at the last 11 international Oracle conferences, earning Top 10 honors the last four years.

# Contents

# Foreword

In the next five years, both the private sector and public sector will experience more change in their business processes than they have in the last 60 years. The Internet will create an order of magnitude reduction in the cost and timeframe to conduct business transactions. This will change the competitive playing field beyond what most senior executives have in their current planning horizons. If the current establishment of business leaders fails to recognize this fundamental change, they will yield their present competitive position to a whole new class of *digital* competitors.

How innovative should management be? A customer order that costs $100.00 to process needs to be done for less than $10.00. An invoice and customer payment that costs $1.00 needs to be done for less than 10 cents. Unless today's physical infrastructures and distribution channels are replaced with electronic networks that provide this type of economic advantage, present leaders run the risk of being "amazoned." The key challenge for senior executives is to ascertain the velocity of electronic commerce substitution in their industry, and beat it.

Some basic precepts that form the foundation for business transactions today are likely to change, such as vertically integrated supply chains, geographic placement of manufacturing and distribution, command and control structures, linear manufacturing processes, timeframe assumptions, and physical world economics. In this new world, the customers will reign supreme. Customer loyalty will become more difficult to retain through the physical world. In the electronic world, customers will have "click" loyalty because they are able to move from supplier to supplier with browser access. The _STRUCTURE_ of companies will change from vertically integrated hierarchies that exercise command and control to confederations of strategic projects that aggregate the right partnerships to exploit network value. _BUSINESS PROCESSES_ will change as electronic networks substitute for today's labor intensive activities. Self-service will become commonplace as customers, suppliers, and employees transact themselves rather than relying on intermediaries. The very process of changing business will become a software exercise where changes can be made in a high-level business process design and can be reflected in automatically generated software the next day. The _ECONOMIC MODEL_ will shift to favor softer assets. Knowledge will become the most important asset on the balance sheet—really remarkable given that we don't even recognize knowledge on the balance sheet today. The value of networked-based companies will be manifested in their ability to collect information from their virtual supply chains, add value to it some way and redistribute that value back into their virtual networks. And finally, the _CULTURE_ of companies will change when digital kids entering the workforce demand tools and methods that are dramatically different than those that have been utilized for the last several decades. Inherent in the network company is its globality. We all become connected and are able to communicate, access information, or transact business on a global basis. All of this is no less than a fundamentally new economy in which old economics and assumptions about physical business transactions are obsolete.

So where should senior executives place their bets in this brave new world? How fast should the current infrastructure and distribution channels be transformed to the electronic world? Is competitive advantage gained by moving faster and taking greater risk, replacing current physical channels, like Egghead did when they closed all of their retail stores and opened their current business called Egghead.com? It is somewhat of a "forest and trees" conundrum and every CEO must ask, "how fast do I burn down my forest?"

Three basic principles can guide decisions in the next few years that will determine competitive outcomes for the next 20 years. First, every infrastructure decision has to pass the fundamental test of Internet economics. Will this decision, once implemented, deliver an order of magnitude change in my economic model? Or will it at least lower the cost of a business process by more than 70 percent? Secondly, does the decision acknowledge that the customer is king and must be served in a "pull"-verses-"push" supply chain? In the past, we have managed profit by forecasting our markets and have tried to match that forecast through management of our supply chains. In the future, the customer is able to give us accurate forecasts that are real-time as the supply chain recognizes that it needs to "make one" every time the channel "scans one". This pull-verses-push philosophy of supply chain management will favor those that have electronic networks that are able to react to individual end-user customer transactions. The third principle is to have more information about the end-to-end supply chain than your competition does. Business intelligence about what is going on with your customers, your manufacturing process, and the enterprise as a whole will give the advantage to companies in the electronic world. Knowledge will become our most important asset.

In the Internet business world, big is beautiful. Systems must scale and must be available all the time. As Oracle technology becomes the engine of the Internet, the most valuable skills will become those that know how to tune the critical engine upon which business will rely. Oracle's strategy is to help companies and governments transform their physical infrastructure to the electronic world. We are establishing the platform for network application development that will become the infrastructure for the way we conduct business in the next several decades. Just like electricians were critical as the world electrified and engineers were critical as the world industrialized, Oracle technicians will become critical as the world becomes networked. Rich Niemiec has created an excellent tutorial for the world's future technicians that must make electronic commerce work as well as electricity, telephony, and television work today. In the next 10 years, the Information Industry becomes the most important industry in the world. Oracle, as a leader of this industry, will become the foundation of the Internet and in no small way, Mr. Niemiec has created a part of the quilt that will make up the foundation of our digital society in the 21st century.

Ray Lane
President & Chief Operating Officer
Oracle Corporation

# Acknowledgments

Thanks to Brad Brown and Joe Trezzo who have a better understanding of both life and business than all of Harvard put together. Eventually, Harvard will catch on and start teaching business that passes the test of time. Brad is probably the fastest and best developer that I have ever seen (look for the next great Internet product to be authored by Brad) and Joe probably has the best understanding of how a long-term business *should* be run and I am happy to see Joe now sharing the *real-life* experience with colleges. Both are great friends and have always been there when I needed them. I am lucky to know both of you and all of the thanks in the world could not be enough thanks for you guys! Any many thanks to Kristen Brown and Lori Trezzo who have always been there to offer strength along the way. We couldn't possibly thank you enough!

Thanks to Tony Catalano, Dave Kaufman, Bill Lewkow, Burk Sherva, Jake Van der Vort, and Dave Ventura who at numerous times gave their own personal time to cover things for me. This gave me an opportunity that I would have never had to complete this. Thanks, you guys are the best!

Thanks to Jennifer Galloway, my technical writer, who tirelessly worked on every chapter of the book at all times of the day and night. No matter what the roadblock or change was, Jennifer would always find a way to make it happen. Her positive spirit was always a blessing to the process. Also, thanks to Cheryl Rouland who was the technical writer on the early edits of two chapters of this book.

Thanks to Sheila Reiter, the first to believe in us; the always-smiling Barb Dully who brings everyone's spirit up with her smile; and Amy L. Prevatt, Jennifer Taylor, Georganna Hathaway, the enthusiastic administration staff who makes every day at TUSC a great one! Thanks for all the smiles!

Thanks to Ray Lane who wrote an excellent forward for this book. Ray has always been one of the great visionaries of our time. His leadership at Oracle has helped take Oracle to another level that would have been unattainable without him. Ray, along with Larry, has made Oracle not only the current database leader, but they have positioned it to be the future backbone of all of Internet commerce. True visionaries! We owe them a lot along with Bob Miner, Ed Oates, Ken Jacobs, Randy Baker, Gary Bloom and all of the past and current Oracle architects that make Oracle products great and fun to use.

Thanks to Kevin Loney who was an outstanding technical reviewer! His dedicated attitude to this book helped take this book to the next level. I am greatly thankful to him for his work on this book and his unselfish sharing of knowledge.

Thanks to the team who helped make this happen! Greg Pucka who contributed a large amount of material in various sections of the book, especially the estat/bstat and beginning tuning chapter. Thanks a lot Greg! Joe Trezzo who contributed a large amount of information on the V$ view and x$ table chapters. Judy Corley and Mark Greenhalgh who contributed the bulk of the material on the UNIX utilities chapter. Jake Van der Vort who contributed a large amount of material on the Parallel Query chapter. Bob Taylor who contributed a large amount of code for the PL/SQL chapter. Roger Schrag who contributed a large amount of information on table joins. Joe Holmes who contributed the information on the mathematical analysis and the linear and quadratic equations related to tuning. Randy Swanson who tirelessly checked the init.ora parameters related to memory give-back and helped with the last minute changes for Oracle8i in the middle of the night. Sean McGuire who helped me with the Oracle8 chapter and contributed init.ora parameters. Gary Hibbard who helped with the SQLJ and Web information. Dave Hathway who contributed a large amount of material to the TRACE/EXPLAIN chapter. Thanks to Ken Morse who contributed a large amount of information to the Enterprise Manager chapter. Thanks to the entire TUSC DBA Tech Team who tested the Total Performance Index (TPI) on all of our major clients, especially Allen Peterson and Bob Yingst who helped with the Remote TUSC DBA queries.

Thanks to Scott Rogers who believed in the series and the TUSC authors along with Brandon Nordin. Thanks for believing in us Scott! Thanks to Monica Faltiss and Marlene Vasilieff who kept the dynamic schedule going. Also, thanks to the others that contributed, including Dennis Weaver, Stefany Otis, and Richard Shrout.

And also, thanks to all of the people at TUSC who enabled me to write this book and continue to make a positive difference in my life:

Brian E. Anderson, Dianna L. Anderson, Joel M. Anonick, Diane B. Ansah, Scott A. Barbarick, Gregory Bogode, Bradley D. Brown, Michael L. Butler, Patrick T. Callahan, Alain P. Campos, Anthony S. Catalano, Judy A. Corley, Janet L. Dahmen, Jennifer L. Deletzke, Susan K. DiFabio, Doug G. Dikun, Thomas J. Drew, Debra J. Dudek, Barbara J. Dully, Brett A. Feldmann, Robin N. Fingerson, David M. Fornalsky, Jennifer N. Galloway, Craig A. Gauthier, Chelsea A. Graylin, Mark A. Greenhalgh, John G. Gregory, Steve L. Hamilton, Georganna R. Hathaway, Scott V. Heaton, Michael D. Henderson, Michael J. Holder, Mohammad M. Jamal, Raymond H. Jensen, David S. Kaufman, Lori A. Kelley, Prabhjot Khurana, Andrea R. Kummer, Jean M. Kuzniar, Felix M. Lacap, Ron E. Lemanske, William J. Lewkow, Lawrence C. Linnemeyer, Antonia Lopez, Matthew T. Malcheski, Daniel A. Martino, Sean P. McGuire, Michael W. McIntyre, James E. Michel, Kevin E. Morgan, Donald Paul Murray, Karen B. O'Donoghue, Michael P. O'Mara, Mark A. Pelzel, Allen L. Peterson, James T. Pianki, Dennis W. Pieniazek, Barry W. Prescott, Amy L. Prevatt, Heidi E. Ratini, Robert S. Reczek, Sheila L. Reiter, Mark E. Riedel, Kathleen L. Rinker, Christopher J. Rizzo, Kim A. Ross, Becky R. Russell, Chad J. Scott, Larrel C. Scott, Kevin A. Sheahan, Burkhard R. Sherva, Chi Son, Jack R. Stein, Kathleen M. Sumpter, Randall A. Swanson, Linda B. Talacki, Jennifer L. Taylor, Robert

W. Taylor Jr., Christopher B. Thoman, Cheryl J. Thomas, John M. Thompson, Don H. Tornquist, Joseph C. Trezzo, Joseph S. Tseng, Jake M. Van der Vort, Vince Vazquez, David S. Ventura, Jon A. Vincenzo, Jack L. Wachtler, James J. Walsh, Kimberly A. Washington, Charles L. Wisely, Daniel G. Wittry, Thomas J. Wood, and Robery B. Yingst.

And thanks to all the people below who have made a positive difference in my life either directly or indirectly (in addition to those above):

Floyd Adams, Georgia Adams, Michael Abbey, Rusty Able, Steve and Becky Adams, Bill Aikman, Dan Andejeski, Debbie Applebaum, Barry Ariko, Eyal Aronoff, Michael Ault, Kim Austin, Pastor James C. Austin, Randy Baker, Richard Barker, John Bell, Jason Bennett, Ronny Billen, Gary Bloom, Melanie Bock, Kirk and Louise Bolt, Judy Boyle, Don Brett, J. Birney and Julia Brown, Mike Broulette, Rhonda Bruner, Sam Bruner, Sam Buchbinder, Jeremy Burton, Leona Caffey, Dave Cagigal, Dan Cameron, Joe Carbonara, Monty Carolan, Cindy Cendrowski, Joan Clark, Ray J. Clark, Rich Clough, Dr. Ken Coleman, Larry Collins, Mike Corey, Peter Corrigan, Stephen Covey, Sharon Daley, Tom Davidson, Tony DeMeo, Marilynn Deacy, Jose DiAvilla, Bill and Barbara Dinga, Sergeant Donates, Dr. Paul Dorsey, Joe Dougherty Jr., Carlos Duchicelli, Carl Dudley, Pat Dwyer, Allen Earls, Albert Einstein, Larry Ellison, Lisa Elliot, Buff Emslie, Dan Erickson, Dr. Charles "Chick" Evans, Dr. Tony Evans, Kirstin Farella, Tony Feisel, Steven Feurenstein, Charlene Fiene, Ted and Joan File, Charlie Fishman, Jan Fleming, Tim Fleming, Andrew "Flip" Filipowski, John Foley, Henry Ford, Chris Gain, Karen Gainey, Bob Galvin, Larry Galvin, Mike Gangler, Len Geshan, Karen Gilbert, Geoff Girvin, Danny Glover, Mark Gokman, Laverne Gonzales, Dennis Gottlieb, Joe Graham Jr., Tony Granato, Allen Greenspan, Paul Groot, Mark Gurry, Mike Hagan, Mrs. Hall, Mark Hammond, Simon Heyes, Gary Hibbard, Bob Hill, Alicia Hoekstra, Ed Honor, Bill Hopkins, Napoleon Hopper Jr., Rich Horbaczewski, Dan Hotka, Frederick L. Hovde, Brian Innes, Diane Ingalls, Gerald B. Jackson, Ken Jacobs, Nancy Jahnke, Tony Jambu, Alex Jankowskus, Mark Jarvis, Mr. and Mrs. Jaskulski, Tony Jedlinski, Jim Jones, Michael Jordan, Dan Keller, Robert Kennedy, Dr. Martin Luther King Jr., George Koch, Peter Koletzke, Richard G. Kramer, Paul C. Krause, Mark Krefta, Ron Krefta, Dave Kreines, Mark Kroll, Mark Kwasni, Paul Lam, Marva Land, Ray Lane, Brian Laskey, Rich Levine, Ari Likki, Terry McCarthy, Donna McConnell, Mac McGuigan, Rev. Terry McReynolds, Christi Maines, Og Mandino, Tom Manzo, Tom Marquardt, Hector Matienzo, John Matuzak, Stacy Mezzetta-de Cossio, Kathy Michalek, Amy Miller, Ron Miller, Billy Mills, Bob Miner, Jal Mistri, John Molinaro, Cecilia Moran, Kim Moskin, Minelva Munoz, Scott Nelson, Barbara Niemiec, Cindy Niemiec, Donald Niemiec, Tony Niemiec, Merrilee Nohr, Eric Nolke, Julie O'Brian, Jon O'Connell, Tom O'Connor, Ed Oates, Chee-Mun Ong, Rita Palanov, Jeri Palmer, Korosh Parizadeh, Arlene Patton, Shannon Pauley, Don Peppers, Gail Peterson, Dr. Mary Peterson, Terry Prasad, John Prescott, Bill Pribyl, Helen Ramos, John Ramos, Gary Raymond, Suresh Reddy, Theresa Repznecki, Frank Ress, Arnold Ridgel, John Robertson, John Rogers, Charlie Rose, Rev. Timothy Rossow, Gene Rubalcaba, Steve Rubin, Mr. Ruff, Doug Russell, Joseph P. Russell, Kimberlee Schmahl, Don Schneck, Bill Schott, Robert Schuller, Tom Sheridan, George Shinn, Steve Silver, Julie Silverstein, Shari Simon, Dr. Austin Shelly, Anthony Speed, Bert Spencer, Jeff Spicer, Bill Spinuzzi, Leslie Steere, Bob Stodola, Bob Strube Sr., Bob Strube Jr., Katherine Suchy, Cyndie Sutherland, Burt and Dianna Summerfield, Nancy Taslitz, Mark Tanaka, Garland Taylor, Emery Taylor, Maurice Taylor, Eugene (Egbar) and Adrienne (the Sky's the Limit) Trezzo, Eileen Trnka, Tom Trybus, Tom Trynka, David Tuson, Paul Virtue, Monica Walters, Oleg Wasynczuk, Jim Weber, Dr. Erich Wessner, Steve Wilkinson, John Wilmott, Oprah Winfrey, Don Wischmeyer, Marcia Wood, Chris Wooldridge, Don

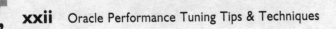

Woznicki, Tom Wycoff, Janet Yingling, Nancy Yonker, Carl Zetie, Tony Ziemba, Edward Zhu, Chris Zorich and of course Dr. Ted Niemiec, Rob Niemiec, Dianne Innes, Donna Ackerman, Dr. Dave Niemiec, Andrea Niemiec, and Mike Niemiec; ...and probably numerous other people that I've forgotten. And (put your name here) _____ for buying this book or if I forgot you.

Very special thanks to Jacob Niemiec, Lucas Niemiec, Hollyann Niemiec and Melissa Niemiec. Very special thanks to my grandmother, who gave me the money to buy my first $5 suit (I still wear it at times) and she *still* asks me if I need any money; and to my grandfather who taught me the power of God before he died; my father who made sure that I never missed church and taught me sales before he died; and most of all my mother who did everything within her means to keep us as a family going; she was and is incredible and one of my heros in life!

# Introduction

"Life is only worth living if you live it for others."
Albert Einstein

## Hurry Up and Live Before You Die!

The best way to describe the world today is to "Hurry up and Live before you Die!" The speed of technology has had a profound effect on how we live today. I spent some time asking some of the older generation when the world started moving faster and also when it started moving at this somewhat unbearable pace. Since I've always moved at this pace, I was wondering when everyone else began to move this quickly (I wanted to ensure that it wasn't my fault). Before I look to the future that I think is evolving, I'd like to cover a few of the quotes that some of these older folks passed on. One of the quotes that I heard most often was, "Things started moving faster when the first PC came out." Nobody (from the older crowd) could put their finger on when the PC came out, but they were sure that it was the culprit (my personal opinion is that it started with the medium called the television). Others were sure, "Things started moving faster when highways started connecting everyone." Everyone got in a hurry to go places and just forgot to take the time to stop and talk to each other. Maybe the connection on the Internet (akin to the connection on the highways) is making this more of an issue and providing striking parallels between the industrial revolution and the Internet revolution. The recent speed of business has increased to jet airplanes and cross-country sales calls. The Internet makes the East Coast just a click away from the West coast. Larger companies will fail as a result of the Internet revolution. Amazon.com was certainly the predecessor of what one company can do to take the market from another company. Those companies that don't keep pace will surely fall into the downward spiral of being the fodder of a feeding frenzy among their competitors.

Another insightful comment was, "Things started moving faster when women began to work." This may be one of the most accurate reasons for people not having the time that they used to. While this certainly took time away from many families, it was certainly an inevitable change (yet to be experienced in other countries). For women who never had the opportunity to work in the world, or for women who had no choice and had to work (like my own mother), this is one thing that isn't going to change back. Maybe the only missing piece of this movement was an understanding between those women who chose to work (and rightfully so) and those who chose not to work (and rightfully so as well). This gap is beginning to close and a needed mutual respect is beginning to form in this arena. Once again, the Internet can serve as the medium for this social change.

Another very common statement from retired seniors was, "People are moving so darn fast and they don't even realize they aren't going anywhere." This is the sentiment of many senior citizens. Their point is that they do realize that we are progressing faster and doing more (they don't think that we know that they know this), but they point out that we are not moving any faster or closer to the things that are truly important in life. Listen to the wisdom of the older generation! They believe that we are bringing future technologies closer more rapidly but at a cost to our own personal well-being, and that we're making "a large number of mistakes along the way." They say that the things that are important in life are those that come with taking your time and stopping to really have a conversation with another person and getting to know those around us. Hurrying up so that we have time to live is not the solution that will bring us happiness, in their opinion.

Many also blame the negative changes on the '60s and early '70s and the Woodstock Generation. Certainly the devastating effect of losing friends and leaders in Vietnam and living through the monumental loss of Dr. Martin Luther King Jr., Robert Kennedy, and John F. Kennedy have taken an immeasurable toll on a portion of all generations. I believe that had Robert Kennedy lived to become President, things would have turned out differently for many of those living through this point in history (and life would have been different for many of us today). But this generation did not "fade to black" as many purport but are alive and well in society (many are driving the current technology), and the few who didn't shine through initially are re-emerging with the Internet movement. I believe that the Internet has pulled many of those lost and forgotten back to the surface by providing a medium to connect and work out those issues left undone. I believe that we will not see the full impact of this generation until the Internet is fully realized as a medium for the masses. I believe that the Internet will be medium that makes this happen for the leaders still "missing in action" from this generation as opposed to conventional wisdom which makes the Internet a medium for the young to excel. The Internet will be as much of a medium for social change as it is for business change.

As much as Vietnam has impacted all or our lives, perhaps the unfinished business of the Civil War has lingered on longer. It's staggering to consider that we lost more Americans in the Civil War than in all other wars combined (Civil War > WWI + WWII + Korea + Vietnam +…etc.), and yet this loss still didn't bring all men and women to equality. Today we still suffer as a result of the unfinished business of the Civil War. Perhaps the impeachment of Andrew Johnson and forcing the true equality of people then, would have eliminated today's injustice of racial inequality. Likewise, perhaps the impeachment of William Clinton would have lessened the cost on morality that our future generations will suffer (or is the forgiveness of Clinton a positive growth step toward greater understanding of the flaws each of us has…accepting, forgiving, and correcting the person without approving the action). Every nation in time stands in belief of something that becomes the foundation of future generations. We currently have a class struggle (poverty is the real culprit) disguised as a race struggle and many who want to prolong it so that they can live off of it. Yet many types of discrimination continue to plague America. The assassination of Abraham Lincoln cost us the first chance to fix this error of our nation's forefathers, the assassinations of John F. Kennedy, Dr. Martin Luther King, and Robert Kennedy cost us the second chance to fix the error. I haven't seen a leader effectively bridge this gap since Robert Kennedy (1968 forever being a turning point in US history). The error lingers on, yet could a leader or movement on the Internet drive home a final closing in this horrible chapter in American history, one beginning to repeat in other countries?

Everything changes with the Internet. The color of your skin, your gender, or even the nation that you are born in will no longer matter once the Internet drives past fruition. The DBAs and developers of the world will make the systems that run this future world (many are being built now). Perhaps the future discrimination will be those of intellectual or genetic nature (similar to that in the movie *Gattica*) and the puzzle will once again be distorted by those who don't understand that America (and the world) is a song that sounds best when we sing it together. One of the hopes in 1900 was that world hunger would be solved by the year 2000. Here we are 100 years later even farther away from the goal than when we started the century. I don't see this changing; if anything, it will be more prevalent in the first century of the new millennium (read Jeremy Rifkin's, *The End of Work*). Perhaps the Internet and short-term labor shortage will allow us to embrace this issue before the real Internet wave hits. As Michael Bloomberg put it, "In America, if you lose your job you get another one; in Malaysia, if you lose your job your family starves." Perhaps the Malaysia reality is not further than 10 years away from happening in America as world markets begin to merge. Or, are our leaders strong enough to ensure that the American reality is one that will become common in Malaysia.

As for the future, I think that Kurt Vonnegut, Jr. probably showed the worst side of this potential future in the book *Player Piano* where there was a consolidation of technology into the hands of a few companies that ruled the world for the most part. The underlying point of the book was that we didn't even have time to play the piano (the player piano was perhaps the preface to the current age). This is certainly one possible future as we see the battle between the entrepreneurs and the big companies that gobble them up. Also, instead of the entrepreneurs of the past who had ideas that they believed in, we see people starting companies with the single goal of selling out and becoming rich. The dedicated entrepreneurs, built on character of the past, are few and far between in today's fast-paced world.

In the early part of the century it was the J.P. Morgans that believed in a cold, big-business attitude of running a company. There was also his rival, Henry Ford, who believed in making a difference and whose credo was, "If something is morally wrong it is wrong for business." Larry Ellison said in a Smithsonian interview that Henry Ford's greatest contribution wasn't the Ford Foundation and all of the good works that it does, but rather the Ford Motor Company and all of the people that it positively affects. I agree with Larry, the bigger impact was made with the Ford Motor Company. But, I also believe that Henry Ford would not have succeeded with the Ford Motor Company without the "make a difference" attitude of the Ford Foundation. If you set out to make a difference in the lives of others, all of the great things that have a mass positive impact will follow. I believe that Ford's belief in sharing with others is what attracted those bright people to his company that eventually built the automobiles that impacted the world and made such a large difference in history. The battle between Larry Ellison (the modern day James Dean) and Bill Gates (the modern day J.P. Morgan…so far) is only the predecessor of the real battles that will consume much larger companies and test the fortitude of world values.

As we look to the future, we must also consider the ties back to the industrial revolution and many parallels of the '20s with today. These include a stock market that defies conventional valuations for stocks (current stocks are priced at well over 100% of Gross Domestic Product) and the replacement of the industrial millionaires (who originally replaced the land barons and railroad tycoons) with the technology billionaires. This current growth cycle is far from over, but when you start seeing men wearing hats (*en masse* as in the '20s) with their suits, you may want to look for that major stock market adjustment. The stock market may hiccup prior to Y2K (due to problems in other countries), but the end of this growth wave has certainly not played out yet. As the Internet revolution hits its stride, the effects of this sleep-deprived nation will certainly take its toll. If you don't take time now to live, you'll find yourself looking back forgetting where you spent your life. If you take time to experience the conversations with other people, you'll also get a lot more done that matters most and your work will stand the test of time as Henry Ford's does. Ford is still a hero today who we can learn from and look up to while J.P. Morgan is just another rich guy who's dead. I believe Henry Ford died a much happier man, but more importantly lived a much more fulfilling and joyful life. The future will be what we collectively make it; it will either be the cold business world or a song filled with fortitude. I prefer fortitude.

In 1978 the Cray supercomputer was priced at $20M. In 1995, the Sony PlayStation processed three times more instructions per second than that original Cray at a price of $199. The future is here now! Oracle's Java-enhanced 8i database will lead the way as the best and most versatile database powering the Internet (they currently power the top 10 Internet databases). What distinguishes the company that will succeed in the coming decade and the one that will fail is the education of its developers and DBAs. The DBA will be the guardian of the company's information and will dictate the speed of access to that information on the Internet. The speed of your company's Internet database will depend on how well the Oracle queries are tuned by developers and how well the database is tuned by your DBA. Read this book before you run out of time!

If you read and understand this entire book, I guarantee that it will change your life. When this knowledge is applied, it will give you incredible joy in life as you take reports from hours to seconds. You'll experience people who bring the report back to you because they think that it has an error in it (they can't believe that it actually completed that fast). I have been greatly blessed with many of these tips and went through incredible pain with only one purpose—to make a difference in your life. Don't miss this opportunity—read the entire book! The book has been separated into logical areas of tuning with the first chapter serving as the Cliff's Notes for the entire book. The topics covered include

- Chapter 1 is for people like me who think they don't have time to read an entire book. It is the Cliff's Notes to the rest of the book and the 90% answer to tuning.
- Chapter 2 is for beginners who have little previous experience with tuning.
- Chapter 3 focuses on tuning Disk I/O.
- Chapter 4 is a detailed look at the init.ora parameters and those I find most crucial for tuning.
- Chapter 5 is a look at Oracle's Enterprise Manager and related tools used for tuning.
- Chapter 6 focuses on TKPROF and EXPLAIN PLAN.
- Chapter 7 covers the most important hints used in tuning.
- Chapter 8 covers basic to intermediate query tuning.
- Chapter 9 covers advanced tuning, including table joins, distributed queries. and mathematical techniques.
- Chapter 10 investigates tuning related to PL/SQL and PL/SQL that can help in tuning efforts.
- Chapter 11 looks at the gains that parallel query can give and how to implement this powerful option.
- Chapter 12 looks at overall changes and advancement in Oracle8.
- Chapter 13 covers specific tuning advancements in Oracle8 and Oracle8i (8.1).
- Chapter 14 takes an in-depth look at the V$ views and queries that can be advantageous.
- Chapter 15 takes an in-depth look at accessing x$ tables that give more precise tuning information.
- Chapter 16 covers UNIX utilities that are needed for operating system information.
- Appendix A covers the init.ora that are both documented and undocumented.
- Appendix B shows all of the v$ views in versions 7 and 8.
- Appendix C shows all of the x$ tables.

People ask how it was growing up for me. So this will be my one and only time that I will give a picture of it. I have buried it deep in the introduction so that only those who read this far will discover it. Personally, I rarely look back, only forward. I never have regrets regarding the past as it is the past that builds our character that allows us to embrace a more challenging and exciting future.

I remember growing up on the *really* south side of Chicago in various south-side towns extending into the steel mill counties of Northwest Indiana in an indescribable place known as

"The Region" (I always called it "Teenage Wasteland" after the song by The Who). My dad started as a steel worker at Bethlehem Steel in the day and was a college student (he never graduated) and drummer in a band by night. Eventually, my parents split up and life began to change. My father always came to see us *every* Sunday, and this made a very big difference in all of our lives.

Keep in mind that for me at the time, this was a normal life that I thought everyone experienced. I remember the embarrassment of taking welfare coupons to the store to buy groceries (but only when nobody I knew was around) and skipping lunch because I couldn't take the embarrassment of people knowing I needed a welfare token to get my lunch. I remember going to caddy at the golf course to earn money for college (I was eleven at the time). I also had a job at my uncle's dry cleaners at the time. I also remember sitting on a Dunkin Donuts dumpster with my brother Dave eating the donuts that had been thrown out the day before on our way to work at the golf course. The unthinkably part is that we were in heaven because we were hungry and the donuts were an incredible treat (even though you had to tear off the moldy parts). I used to buy to pumpkin pies and day-old donuts with the money I didn't put toward college (my mother forced me to save some for college), and Dave used to always buy pork chops (we didn't have meat very often growing up). I also remember wading through the dumpsters of McDonalds with Dave to find those Olympic coupons they had as a special. It was a give-away at the time where you could get an entire meal if the U.S. Olympic team won the gold (Big Mac), Silver (Coke) and Bronze (Fries). People used to throw away the coupons of the events that hadn't happened yet and we would dig them out of the garbage (when we weren't chased off) and save them until the event happened. I can say we owe a lot to the archery, swimming, and weightlifting teams that "pulled through for us" and helped us to take our entire family to McDonalds for special night out for dinner several times that summer. Dave and I also used to go garbage picking (my wife once told me that I probably shouldn't bring this up in life but she doesn't get to read the preface until it's printed) and find all kinds of great stuff. My mother would severely scold us for doing this, but then would allow us to keep any of the non-bug infested stuff (we furnished a lot of the house this way).

Dave and I would both eventually win Evans Scholarships (it didn't cover everything but it helped a lot), a caddy scholarship set up by Chick Evans. Chick Evans was an amateur golfer who wanted to make a difference in the life of others less fortunate. He certainly made a difference in our lives (Dave is now a dentist in Indiana). My mother worked various jobs to keep the family going back then. I even remember various relatives (especially my Uncle John and Aunt Janet) surprising us with groceries from time to time (great food versus the normal Kraft Macaroni and Cheese that it felt like I had every night). It's not that we didn't have *any* food, we just didn't have any *real* food (especially if you didn't know how to cook) and if you didn't wake up early enough in the morning (before the milk was gone), there wasn't anything for breakfast unless you could talk your sister into making something with Bisquick (always the last thing left on the shelf).

I remember my mother working midnights at a hotel on the Hammond-Gary border and talking about the shooting or robbery the night before. This job used to really scare me. I used to think that we all would end up as orphans and get separated one day. My mother did all this so her family of eight would survive. Of my seven brothers and sisters, there is a doctor in Munster, a manager of a motor company in Racine, a hotel general manager in Atlanta, a nursing student in Detroit, a head server (and entrepreneur in the making) in Detroit, a dentist in Indiana, and an Oracle developer in Chicago (hey, I tried to make him a DBA). In college, I remember giving blood, refereeing basketball games, waxing storage doors, doing numerous other odd jobs to make money, and also serving tables at a sorority to earn my meals…how could this piece of paper (degree) possibly be worth all of this…or so I thought at the time. And then one day my life changed…my future wife would say, "If you are a homeless man on the streets of Chicago, I'll be the homeless wife by your side with every step you take." I knew then that I would marry her. That sentence changed my life (I've carried it every day of my life in my wallet), because the weight of the world, the weight to succeed, the weight to achieve, the weight of expectations, the weight of what you *should* do in life, all were lifted from my shoulders. I could now be myself for the rest of my life and had a wife by my side that would be there for me. What a change that made. Life was forever different and only then was I able to let my light shine through. I got that piece of paper, and an improbable journey to make a difference began…

But the journey wasn't easy. One battle ends and another begins. After a job designing microchips, I had a job designing skyscrapers with a computer system built on something called Oracle (Version 4 at the time). I went out for lunch and most improbably met someone I had seen in the Marine Reserves on the busy streets of Chicago. That person said that I *must* come to work for this company called Oracle. I did. I remember one of my first weeks at Oracle, "Hey Rich, have you ever heard of Oracle*Forms?" (Never heard of it, only worked with the database.) "Well, you're a former Marine, you'll figure it out, you're teaching it on Thursday and Friday." I stayed up three nights straight to learn and teach this class and with rave reviews (maybe the worst thing that could have happened). I remember another week at Oracle, "Hey Rich, have you ever heard of SQL*Loader?" (ODL was the loader at the time.) "Of course you haven't, it just came out. You're teaching the course this week, and oh by the way, you'll have to write the class as well since there isn't one yet. See if you can get a copy of the product from Belmont." Oracle has come a long way since then, yet still continues to blaze the trail toward better technology. I barely even knew anyone at the office or where anything was…I was becoming completely overwhelmed. Last week worked out well, but is this how it was going to be *every* week? This company was moving so fast it was unbelievable. Then a guy came over to my cube and said hey, let me show you around and introduce you to some people. The first friendly face and first person who took the time to say hello—it was Joe Trezzo. Then, the next week, everything changed again. "You two whiz kids over there (he was referring to Joe and me), I want you guys to hook up with the other whiz kid in the office to build a multi-million dollar proposal to get us into this major client." The other whiz kid was of course, Brad Brown. The three of us would eventually go on to build the first client-server application on Oracle in the late '80s.

The "Three Musketeers" would reunite later in our careers and the creation of TUSC and a new journey would begin. We were set on doing our small part to help Oracle become even stronger by educating and striving to make a difference in the world of Oracle from the outside looking in. We were quite dedicated to building the Oracle User Groups in the Midwest to the levels that Joe had experienced on the East Coast. The goal was to educate, give back, and do our part to elevate this incredible product where it deserved to be. After writing this entire book, I can see more of the incredible product that Bob Miner, Larry Ellison, and Ed Oates once built. The database is absolutely bottomless beyond belief and incredibly powerful. It is exactly what you make it; Oracle has given you the infinitely versatile tool.

With the inception of TUSC was a new battle that was even tougher yet. The calls would come at midnight to save the latest corrupted database. I would go to tune a database and it would be 5PM thinking I was going to be done at 6PM, but somehow when I was done and I looked up at the clock, it was 6AM the next morning. Thirteen hours went by in the blink of an eye. A mile-high battle to build a company with character with only Brad, Joe, our wives, and me to do all of the consulting work, selling, administration, financials, and everything else. A guy at the stock exchange (we were doing a job there) used to say, "If it couldn't be done, TUSC could do it." He told everyone on the floor that they better look out when the TUSC IPO (Initial Public Offering) comes. Another person told us that we should hire every warm body we could find and sell the world every promise like everyone else does so that we could sell out the company fast on an IPO and retire rich. Sounded nice, but this is not what we believed in, nor was it what made the Henry Fords and Ford Motor Companies of the world. Instead, we took our time to build a company on character, doing things the right way, with honesty and fortitude. It was well worth it! And now, a decade later, TUSC is over 100 people with offices in Chicago, Denver, and Detroit—people who believe in character, and TUSC is company that *will* stand the test of time. How lucky I have been in life to be blessed with Brad and Joe, who are two wonderful partners dedicated to character.

Through all of this, there has never been a complaint from my wife Regina, who continued to help me with everything and endure every new challenge with me. She has never let me down in life. She was with me from the beginning when we didn't have anything (we actually *rented* flowers for our wedding). Every conference was a nightmare as it was additional work added to everything else I was barely getting done. I would stay up for three days straight (I can never get past the third day) trying to build the next presentation, the goal to make a symphony (the perfectionist in me was both a blessing and a curse), and then rush out the door at the last second as the presentation was printing the final copy to make the plane in time…yet no complaints (she even bought me a faster printer). And finally the nightmare of this book. Why did I ever do this book?! A pain that I could never express in words. Wanting to give back all that I've ever learned in life so that people may feel the same exhilaration of that I've been lucky to experience. Remembering the pain of not knowing the answers and fighting to find the solutions (usually while listening to music on hold with *you know who*). It was so that people could see what I've been able to see. In the beginning, I thought that I could take all of my prior presentations and get this book done in a weekend or two (I probably could have but this wouldn't have been the result). It turned out to be over a year. What a painful year it has been. My wife, after all that she had been through, continued to be my shining star through it all— by my side until this the final sentences are complete. How lucky I have been in life to be blessed with a hero by my side like Regina!

This is a one in a million book—make sure that you read it all! And, of course, strive every day to making a difference for others and improve toward being an uncommon leader. The uncommon leader traits are Integrity, Moral Courage, Physical Courage, Self Control, Enthusiasm, Knowledge, Initiative, Respect, Tact, Loyalty, Unselfishness, and Humility. The goal of the uncommon leader are fortitude (the strength of mind to endure pain or adversity with courage and character) and making a difference in the lives of others. I try to improve each day.

I wanted this picture (the one at the top of this introduction) to be on the cover of this book as I believe that I have only been given the chance to live and experience the joy of life through the strength and touch of God's hand. God often seeks out the unlikely—I was definitely the most unlikely for this improbable journey.

# References

*Player Piano*, Kurt Vonnegut Jr.

*Marketing 1:1*, Don Peppers and Martha Rogers

*Blur; The Speed of Change in the Connected Economy*, Christopher Meyer and Stan Davis

*Direct from Dell; Strategies that Revolutionized an Industry*, Michael Dell and Catherine Fredman

*The End of Work*, Jeremy Rifkin

Smithsonian Institution, Oracle History Interview with Lawrence Ellison

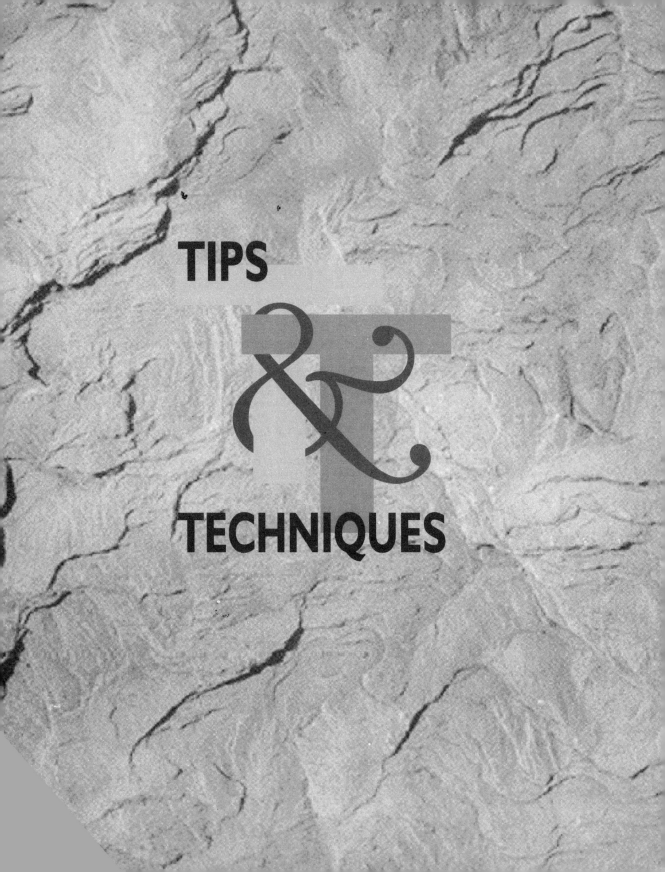

# TIPS & TECHNIQUES

# CHAPTER

# 1

# Over a Decade of Tuning Experience*

*Read only this chapter for the 90 percent quick impact answer to tuning

TIPS
&
COVERED

Oracle is a symphony and you are the conductor, with an opportunity to a create world class performance. As with an orchestra, there are many different sections that must be coordinated with perfection if you are to succeed. Each chapter in this book represents a section of the orchestra that must be tuned. A single query (a single note) or a poorly configured init.ora (the violin section) can be the cymbals (the ad hoc query user) that will crash at an inopportune time to bring your system to its knees. The key to tuning often comes down to how effectively you can tune the database memory and single problem queries. Although your queries (and your symphony) will be more complicated and different than those covered in this chapter, the same techniques can be applied to all queries. Lastly, since people are always saying that I cover so much material in a presentation, and that I go at a "lightning speed" pace; please read this at "Evelyn Wood" speed (four times your normal speed unless you *are* Evelyn Wood) for the "presentation effect."

This chapter is for people like me that never have the time to read an entire book. Now that I've written one, I know the incredible value that reading an entire book can bring. If you read and understand this entire book, I guarantee that it will change your life. When applied, it will give you incredible joy in life, as reports take from hours to seconds. You'll experience people who will hand the report back to you because they believe that something is wrong (the reduction of time for running the report will be that phenomenal). I have been greatly blessed with many tips, and went through incredible pain with only one purpose—to make a difference in your life. Don't miss this opportunity—read the entire book! Create a world class performance!

This chapter offers the following tips and techniques:

- Where the performance problems are in a typical system
- Five quick goals to instantly improve performance
- Setting DB_BLOCK_BUFFERS, SHARED_POOL_SIZE, and SORT_AREA_SIZE
- Getting data cached into memory
- Pinning packages into the Shared Pool
- Using the V$SQLAREA view to find problem queries
- What you need to know to tune your system

* Read only this chapter for the 90 percent quick impact answer to tuning

- Using AUTOTRACE and set timing on
- Using TRACE and EXPLAIN PLAN
- Cost-based optimization and ANALYZE command
- The 95/5 rule
- Using hints
- Unintentional index suppression
- Comparing the wrong data types
- Function-based indexes in Oracle8i
- Using the OR and nested queries
- The driving table and join methods
- Using Parallel Query Option
- Using partitioned tables
- The TPI, Profiles, Oracle Expert, and using mathematical techniques

Throughout this book we have repeated essential information for your benefit.

# Where Are the Performance Problems in a Typical System?

The key to tuning is to know *where* to look for performance problems. Every system is different, so don't take the statistics presented in Figure 1-1 as 100 percent true for *your* system. It is, however, helpful to know where performance problems usually exist.

## What Should You Do?

Sixty percent of the performance problems are attributable to application/program tuning—tune the individual SQL queries to fix this problem (proof that it's usually the developer's fault). Train your developers to eliminate this problem (buy them this book).

Twenty percent of the performance problems are attributable to database design and indexing—look for bad/missing indexes to fix this problem area (proof that it's sometimes the designer's fault).

Performance Problems in a System

**Five Goals to Improve Performance**

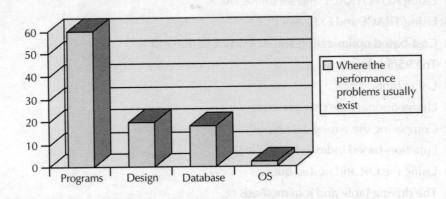

**FIGURE 1-1.** *The typical location of performance problems*

Eighteen percent of the performance problems are attributable to database tuning—tune the Oracle SGA (System Global Area) to fix this problem (proof that it's occasionally the DBA's fault).

Two percent of the performance problems are attributable to operating system tuning—bring in the "OS expert" for a day to fix this area (proof that it's rarely the operations person's fault).

# Five Quick Goals to Instantly Improve Performance

- Goal 1: Allocate enough memory to Oracle
- Goal 2: Get data cached in memory
- Goal 3: Find the problem queries
- Goal 4: Tune the problem queries
- Goal 5: Read the rest of the book for an in-depth tuning process (you'll do this later)

## Goal 1: Have Enough Memory Allocated to Oracle

This section will focus on memory allocation for the Oracle database. The topic is briefly covered in this chapter; for detailed information on setting init.ora parameters, read Chapter 4 and Appendix A.

## How to Look at Your init.ora Parameters Settings

The following four init.ora parameters are the most crucial for a well-running system (Chapter 4 and Appendix A show my top 25 init.ora parameters, as well as my top 13 undocumented init.ora parameters):

- DB_BLOCK_BUFFERS
- SHARED_POOL_SIZE
- SORT_AREA_SIZE
- DB_BLOCK_SIZE

To find your init.ora parameter settings, run the following query:

```
select      name, value
from        v$parameter
where       name in ('db_block_buffers', 'db_block_size',
            'shared_pool_size', 'sort_area_size');


NAME                    VALUE
db_block_buffers        4000
db_block_size           4096
shared_pool_size        7,000,000
sort_area_size          262,144
```

Note that in these values, DB_BLOCK_BUFFERS is measured in blocks and must be multiplied by the DB_BLOCK_SIZE to get the memory allocated to Oracle for data. The SHARED_POOL_SIZE is measured in bytes and is the memory allocated to Oracle for Oracle's data dictionary, stored procedures, and statement information. The SORT_AREA_SIZE is measured in bytes, and is a per-user value that is *not* part of the Oracle SGA. Also note that Chapter 14 and Appendix B focus on queries to the V$ views.

**TIP**

*Tuning the memory allocated to Oracle means setting the init.ora parameters correctly. The crucial parameters are DB_BLOCK_BUFFERS, DB_BLOCK_SIZE, SHARED_POOL_SIZE, and SORT_AREA_SIZE. Set one of these four parameters too low or too high and your system will run poorly! You can also run UTLBSTAT to generate overall system statistics that will help you size your init.ora parameters. UTLBSTAT/UTLESTAT is covered in Chapter 16.*

## Enterprise Manager Output

You can also view the settings for the init.ora parameters through the Instance Manager section of Enterprise Manager, Server Manager, or another GUI front-end tool provided by Oracle. In Figure 1-2, you can view the Server Manager output. See Chapter 5 for detailed information regarding the Enterprise Manager. Figure 1-2 illustrates a section of the Instance Manager detailing the init.ora parameters. It shows the current settings for the parameter, as well as if the parameter can be modified (dynamic=Yes) without shutting down the database. The Oracle init.ora parameters are covered in detail in Chapter 4 and Appendix A.

**THE MEMORY PARAMETER: DB_BLOCK_BUFFERS**  The most important parameter to look at is the init.ora parameter DB_BLOCK_BUFFERS. This is the area of the SGA that is used for the storage and processing of data in memory. As users request information, the information is put into memory. If the DB_BLOCK_BUFFERS parameter is set too low, then the Least Recently Used (LRU) data will be flushed from memory. If the data flushed is recalled with a query, it must be reread from a disk

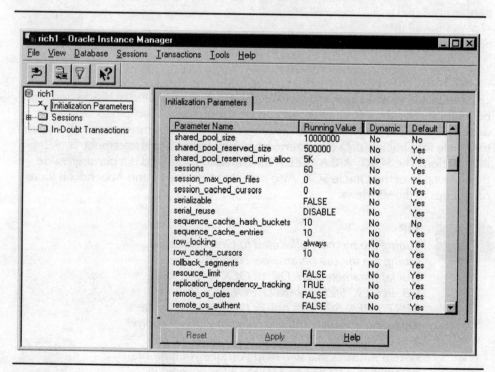

**FIGURE 1-2.**  *Instance Manager—init.ora parameters*

(causing I/O and CPU resources to be used). If DB_BLOCK_BUFFERS is too low, users will not have enough memory to operate efficiently. If DB_BLOCK_BUFFERS is too high, your system may become too swapped and may come to a halt. The default value for the DB_BLOCK_BUFFERS parameter varies for different hardware platforms, but it is generally lower than necessary for production applications.

```
Memory Allocated for Data in Bytes = db_block_buffers x db_block_size
```

**V8 TIP**

*The allowable DB_BLOCK_SIZE has increased in Oracle8 to 32K. Remember that changing the block size can only be accomplished by rebuilding the database.*

### Determine If the Data Block Buffers Parameter Is Set High Enough

Common logic would make the DB_BLOCK_BUFFERS parameter 25 percent of the size allocated to your main memory. A large number of users (300+) or a small amount of available memory may force you to make this 15-20 percent of physical memory. A small number of users (less than 100) or a large amount of physical memory may allow you to make this 30-50 percent of physical memory.

Larger systems may choose to set their DB_BLOCK_BUFFERS much higher. You can run the following script to determine if the data block buffers setting is set high enough. The following query will tell you how much of the data selected by users is hit in memory (the memory or buffer hit ratio):

```
select     (1 - (sum(decode(name, 'physical reads',value,0)) /
           (sum(decode(name, 'db block gets',value,0)) +
           sum(decode(name, 'consistent gets',value,0)))))
           * 100 "Hit Ratio"
from       v$sysstat;

Hit Ratio
99.08%
```

**TIP**

*The buffer hit ratio should be 95 percent or higher. This ratio can be found by querying the V$SYSSTAT view. However, increasing the buffer hit ratio from 95 to 99 percent can yield performance gains of over 400 percent. Oracle recommends a buffer hit ratio greater than 90 percent. See Chapter 14 and Appendix B for more V$ tips.*

**Five Goals to Improve Performance**

Setting the init.ora parameter DB_BLOCK_BUFFERS too low is the leading cause of inadequate buffer hit ratios (Chapter 4 looks at mythically raising buffer blocks). The inadequate results may also be caused by insufficient indexing, contributing to full table scans. Consider Figure 1-3, which illustrates the effect to response times of a query when DB_BLOCK_BUFFERS is set too low. When conducting full table scans, increase the amount of data read into memory in a single I/O by increasing DB_BLOCK_SIZE to 8K or 16K (or 32K in Oracle8), or by increasing the DB_FILE_MULTIBLOCK_READ_COUNT to 16 or 32. The database must be rebuilt if you want to increase the DB_BLOCK_SIZE.

Environments that run a lot of single queries to retrieve data could use a smaller block size, but "hot spots" in those systems will still benefit from using a larger block size. Sites that need to read large amounts of data in a single I/O read should increase the DB_FILE_MULTIBLOCK_READ_COUNT. Setting the DB_FILE_MULTIBLOCK_READ_COUNT higher is especially important for data warehouses that retrieve a large amount of records.

**TIP**
*The database must be rebuilt if you increase the DB_BLOCK_SIZE. Increasing the DB_FILE_MULTIBLOCK_READ_COUNT will allow more block reads in a single I/O, giving a benefit similar to a larger block size.*

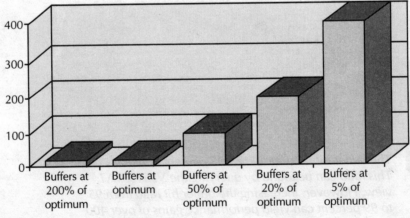

Response time in minutes

Buffers at 200% of optimum · Buffers at optimum · Buffers at 50% of optimum · Buffers at 20% of optimum · Buffers at 5% of optimum

**FIGURE 1-3.** *Response time for a memory-intensive report with given SGA (buffer) settings*

Five Goals to Improve Performance

**TIP**

*Retrieving information from memory is over 10,000 times (depending on the memory you have) faster than retrieving it from disk; consequently, ensure that the SGA is large enough to accommodate this benefit.*

## Using the Buffer Pools in Oracle8

DB_BLOCK_BUFFERS times the DB_BLOCK_SIZE refers to the total size, measured in bytes, of the main buffer cache (or memory for data) in the SGA. In Oracle8, two new buffer pools were introduced: BUFFER_POOL_KEEP and BUFFER_POOL_RECYCLE. These additional two pools serve the same purpose as the main buffer cache (used to store data in memory), with the exception that the algorithm to maintain the pool is different for all three available pools. For further detailed information regarding this Oracle8 feature, see Chapter 13.

**V8 TIP**

*The additional buffer pools (BUFFER_POOL_KEEP and BUFFER_POOL_RECYCLE) available in Oracle8 are initially set to zero. The BUFFER_POOL_KEEP and BUFFER_POOL_RECYCLE are a subset of the DB_BLOCK_BUFFERS. When you set the BUFFER_POOL_KEEP and BUFFER_POOL_RECYCLE parameters, you are taking blocks of memory from the DB_BLOCK_BUFFERS and allocating to the other two pools. See Chapter 13 for additional details on this topic.*

## Hit Ratio Distortion

Although the equations for finding hit ratio problems seem easy, sometimes the results are not accurate. In the following examples, I have shown a case where misinformation has been returned.

The following example illustrates the temporary segment distortion for a single query (false low/bad hit ratio):

```
Tries = 1
Physical = 100

% hit ratio      =      (1   -      Physical/Tries) x 100
% hit ratio      =      (1 - 100/1) x 100%
% hit ratio      =      -9900%
```

There are many other false hit ratio distortions; SQL*Forms can cause a false high hit ratio, rollback segments can cause a false high hit ratio impact, and indexes can have hit ratios as high as 86 percent when none of the blocks were cached prior to the query executing. See Chapter 3 for detailed information on disk I/O.

**THE MEMORY PARAMETER: SHARED_POOL_SIZE**   The SHARED_POOL_SIZE is the memory allocated for the library and data dictionary cache. With a greater amount of procedures, packages, and triggers utilized with Oracle, the SHARED_POOL_SIZE makes up a much greater portion of the Oracle SGA. If the SHARED_POOL_SIZE (memory allocated for Oracle internals and statements) is set too low, then you will not receive the full advantage of your DB_BLOCK_BUFFERS (memory allocated for data). The Shared Pool is divided into two areas, the dictionary cache and library cache, and both should be checked for an effective hit ratio.

### Determine the Dictionary Cache Hit Ratio

The dictionary hit ratio displays the percentage of memory reads for the data dictionary and other objects. The data dictionary cache is very important because that is where the data dictionary components are buffered. Oracle references the data dictionary several times when a SQL statement is processed. Therefore, the more information (database and application schema and structure) stored in memory, the less information to be retrieved from disk.

The data dictionary cache operates the same way as the DB_BLOCK_BUFFERS when caching information. It would be great if the entire Oracle data dictionary could be cached in memory. Unfortunately, this is not usually feasible. Instead, executed SQL statements are cached in the shared SQL area.

The dictionary cache is the cache that is allocated to Oracle for calls to the data dictionary and calls that require a validation check to the Oracle data dictionary. To check the dictionary hit ratio, execute the following query below to examine the V$ROWCACHE view. A hit ratio below 95 percent usually indicates that the init.ora parameter SHARED_POOL_SIZE is set too low.

**Query for dictionary hit ratio:**

```
select     (1-(sum(getmisses)/sum(gets))) * 100 "Hit Ratio"
from       v$rowcache;


Hit Ratio
95.40%
```

This would be an ideal hit ratio (95 percent) and probably not require further tuning to the SHARED_POOL_SIZE, unless there was a problem with the library cache hit ratio (covered in the following section).

**TIP**

*Measure hit ratios for the dictionary cache section of the Shared Pool with the V$ROWCACHE view. A hit ratio of over 95 percent should be achieved. Increasing the init.ora parameter SHARED_POOL_SIZE will usually increase your dictionary hit ratio. However, when the database is initially started, hit ratios will be around 85 percent.*

### Determine the Library Cache Hit Ratio

The library hit ratio reveals the percentage of memory reads for actual statements and PL/SQL objects by executing the following query. For optimal performance, keep the library cache reload ratio [sum(reloads)/sum(pins)] at zero and the library cache ratio above 95 percent. If the reload ratio is not zero, there are statements that are being "aged out" that will be needed later and brought back into memory. If the reload ratio is zero (0), items in the library cache will never be "aged out" or invalidated. If the reload ratio is above 1 percent, the SHARED_POOL_SIZE parameter should be increased. Likewise, if the library cache hit ratio comes in below 95 percent, the SHARED_POOL_SIZE parameter may need to be increased. Chapter 4 looks at the reloads in detail.

```
select      Sum(Pins) / (Sum(Pins) + Sum(Reloads)) * 100  "Hit Ratio"
from        v$librarycache;

Hit Ratio
99.40%
```

If the hit ratio is less than 95 percent or the reload ratio is high (greater than 5 percent), increase the SHARED_POOL_SIZE init.ora parameter.

**TIP**

*Measure hit ratios for the library cache section of the Shared Pool with V$LIBRARYCACHE. A hit ratio of over 95 percent should be achieved. Increasing the init.ora parameter SHARED_POOL_SIZE will usually increase your library cache hit ratio. However, when the database is initially started, hit ratios will be around 85 percent, so make sure that you don't measure the hit ratio until the database has been running for a while.*

**PERFORMANCE MANAGER—LIBRARY CACHE HIT RATIO**   The buffer cache hit ratio, dictionary cache hit ratio, and the library cache hit ratio can also be

**Five Goals to Improve Performance**

viewed using the Performance Manager section of Oracle's Enterprise Manager (see Chapter 5 for detailed information). However, the Performance Manager not only displays the hit ratio for the library cache (memory allocated for user statements such as SQL and PL/SQL), but it also graphically illustrates the output. In Figure 1-4, the hit ratio displayed is ideal (99.66 percent). If this hit ratio was below 95 percent, we would investigate the SHARED_POOL_SIZE init.ora setting, which may be too low, or we would pin some of the often-used PL/SQL into memory.

A detailed output of the individual parameters that make up the library cache is displayed in Figure 1-5. See Chapter 5 for a detailed look at the Performance Manager and Chapter 14, which covers this access to the V$ view for information related to this area.

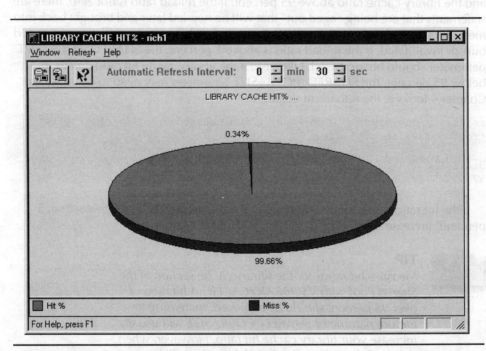

**FIGURE 1-4.**   *Library cache hit ratio*

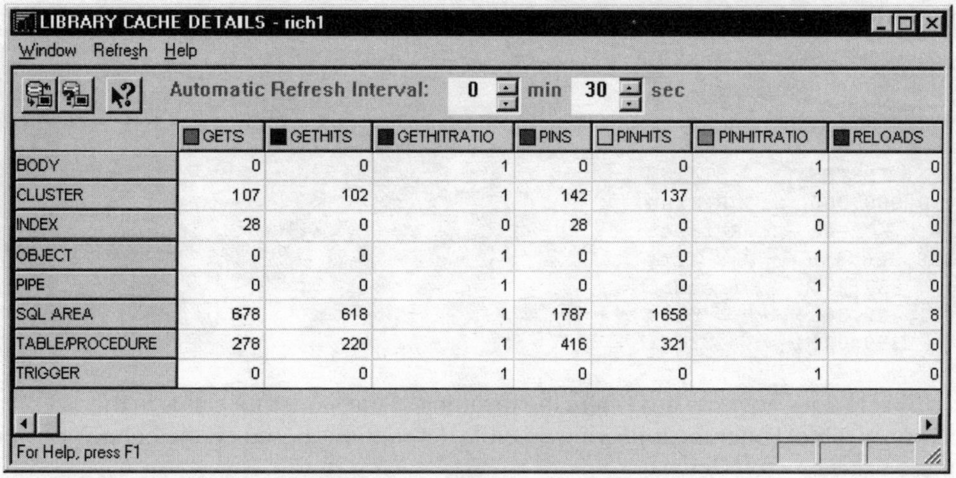

```
LIBRARY CACHE DETAILS - rich1                                    _ □ ×
Window  Refresh  Help
```

| | GETS | GETHITS | GETHITRATIO | PINS | PINHITS | PINHITRATIO | RELOADS |
|---|---|---|---|---|---|---|---|
| BODY | 0 | 0 | 1 | 0 | 0 | 1 | 0 |
| CLUSTER | 107 | 102 | 1 | 142 | 137 | 1 | 0 |
| INDEX | 28 | 0 | 0 | 28 | 0 | 0 | 0 |
| OBJECT | 0 | 0 | 1 | 0 | 0 | 1 | 0 |
| PIPE | 0 | 0 | 1 | 0 | 0 | 1 | 0 |
| SQL AREA | 678 | 618 | 1 | 1787 | 1658 | 1 | 8 |
| TABLE/PROCEDURE | 278 | 220 | 1 | 416 | 321 | 1 | 0 |
| TRIGGER | 0 | 0 | 1 | 0 | 0 | 1 | 0 |

Automatic Refresh Interval:  0  min  30  sec

For Help, press F1

**FIGURE 1-5.**   *Library cache hit ratio detail*

The following query will determine how much memory is left for
SHARED_POOL_SIZE:

```
col value for 999,999,999,999 heading "Shared Pool Size"
col bytes for 999,999,999,999 heading "Free Bytes"
select    to_number(v$parameter.value) value, v$sgastat.bytes,
          v$sgastat.bytes/v$parameter.value)*100 "Percent Free"
from      v$sgastat, v$parameter
where     v$sgastat.name = 'free memory'
and       v$ parameter .name = 'shared_pool_size;

Shared Pool Size    Free Bytes      Percent Free
100,000,000         82,278,960        82.27896
```

If there is an abundance of free memory (greater than 2MB), there is no need to
increase the SHARED_POOL_SIZE parameter. I have never seen this parameter go
to zero (Oracle saves a portion for emergency operations), but I have seen it go to
2GB when the Shared Pool was too near to zero (go figure that one?). The next
section breaks the Shared Pool into smaller allocations by viewing information from
the x$ tables.

**Five Goals to Improve Performance**

**Shared Pool detail breakdown of 1,000MB upon startup (see Chapter 15 for further information):**

```
select      sum(ksmchsiz) Bytes, ksmchcls Status
from        x$ksmsp
group by    ksmchcls;

      BYTES        STATUS
 50,000,000        R-free
         40        R-freea
888,326,956          free
    837,924       freeabl
 61,702,380          perm
    359,008          recr
```

Oracle does not state anywhere the meaning of the values for status in the x$ksmsp table. I offer the following possible descriptions based on the behavior of these values:

| Status | Possible Meaning |
| --- | --- |
| R-free | This *is* SHARED_POOL_RESERVED_SIZE (default 5 percent of SP). |
| R-freea | This is probably reserved memory that has been used but free-able. |
| free | This *is* the amount of contiguous free memory available. |
| freeabl | This is probably memory that has been used but is freeable. |
| perm | This *is* free memory not yet moved to the free area for use. |
| recr | I am not sure what this is. Possibly reserved memory for Oracle. |

**V8 TIP**

*The V$SGASTAT view has an additional column named pool.* This column shows a more detailed Shared Pool breakdown.

### The SHARED_POOL_SIZE Is Overfull and Causing Errors

In the event the SHARED_POOL_SIZE was set too small and is overfull and an ORA-4031 is encountered, there is a way to flush everything out and refresh the Shared Pool. Using the following statement, you can survive this problem. However, you need to take a look at increasing the SHARED_POOL_SIZE and physical memory (if necessary for an increased SHARED_POOL_SIZE).

```
SQL> ALTER SYSTEM FLUSH SHARED_POOL;
```

**TIP**
*Don't flush the Shared Pool unless you are receiving errors. Flushing the Shared Pool pushes everything out of memory, which will cause degradation to all users —who must now reread everything back into memory. A low amount of free memory is not necessarily the precursor to an error.*

**TIP**
*An ORA-4031 is usually caused when the Shared Pool gets fragmented into smaller pieces over the course of a day and a request for a large piece of memory is issued and consequently cannot be filled.*

**THE MEMORY PARAMETER: SORT_AREA_SIZE** The init.ora parameter SORT_AREA_SIZE will allocate memory for sorting. The number of bytes that you allocate to this parameter will determine the amount of memory that *each* user will receive for sorting. This area is the space allocated in main memory outside of the Oracle SGA. It is a per-user allocation and the memory is returned back to the OS when the user's sort is complete. If the sort cannot be performed in memory, temporary segments are allocated on disk to hold intermediate runs. Increasing the value of SORT_AREA_SIZE will reduce the total number of disk sorts, thus reducing disk I/O. Setting this too high can cause swapping; leaving little memory for other processes.

**Statements that will generate temporary segments include the following:**

- CREATE INDEX
- SELECT .... ORDER BY
- DISTINCT
- GROUP BY
- UNION
- unindexed joins
- some correlated subqueries

**TIP**
*Since temporary segments were created to handle the sorts that cannot be handled in memory, the initial extent default for temporary segments should be at least as large as the value of SORT_AREA_SIZE. This will minimize extension of the segment.*

**Five Goals to Improve Performance**

Running ESTAT/BSTAT utilities (see Chapter 16) will reveal to you the following statistics on where user sorts are being performed:

- **sorts (disk)** The number of sorts that were unable to be performed in memory required the creation of a temp segment in the temporary tablespace. This statistic divided by the sorts (memory) should not be above 5 percent. If so, you should increase the SORT_AREA_SIZE parameter in the init.ora.

- **sorts (memory)** The number of sorts that were performed in memory.

- **sorts (rows)** The total number of rows that were sorted.

You can receive specific sorting statistics (memory, disk, and rows) by running the following query, or you can also go to the UTLESTAT output file (report.txt) to receive additional related statistics (see Chapter 16 for more information on UTLBSTAT).

**Query to get memory and disk sorts:**

```
select      a.value "Disk Sorts", b.value "Memory Sorts",
            round(100*b.value)/decode((a.value+b.value),
            0,1,(a.value+b.value)),2) "Pct Memory Sorts"
from        v$sysstat a, v$sysstat b
where       a.name = 'sorts (disk)'
and         b.name = 'sorts (memory)';


Disk Sorts   Memory Sorts    Pct Memory Sorts
        16         66977               99.98
```

**TIP**

*The SORT_AREA_SIZE parameter of the init.ora is measured in bytes and is on a per-user process basis, only allocated when a specific user needs it. Be careful or you will run out of operating system memory if it is set too high!*

**TIP**

*The SORT_AREA_RETAINED_SIZE should be set smaller or equal to the value of the SORT_AREA_SIZE. The SORT_AREA_RETAINED_SIZE is the size that the SORT_AREA_SIZE will be reduced to when the sort is complete. See Chapter 4 for additional details.*

**Five Goals to Improve Performance**

**Lookout! The SORT_AREA_SIZE Can Also Be Set by Individual Users**

Many parameters can be set within an individual session. Since a single user can allocate his or her own memory, the entire system performance can be ruined by a renegade user. The following statement shows how one user can potentially hoard all of the memory on the system and ruin the performance for everyone else:

```
Alter session set sort_area_size=100000000;

Session altered.
```

The problem in the preceding query is the developer has granted the session the capability of using 100MB of memory for a sorting in this session.

**TIP**
*Changing init.ora parameters with an ALTER SESSION is a powerful feature for both developers and DBAs. Consequently, a user with the ALTER SESSION privilege is capable of irresponsibly allocating 100MB+ for the SORT_AREA_SIZE for a given session, if it is not restricted. See Chapter 13 for parameters that can be modified using this method.*

# Goal 2: Get Data Cached into Memory

Once you have enough memory allocated to Oracle, the focus must shift to ensuring that the most important information is getting into memory and staying there. We will look at using x$bh and using the CACHE parameter of ALTER TABLE... to achieve this goal.

The goal would be to have the following scenario:

| | |
|---|---|
| At 5:00 P.M. | Select from all lookup tables that users will use |
| At 5:15 P.M. | Run all expected ad hoc queries with full scan of index |
| At 5:30 P.M. | Run full table scans of frequently scanned tables |
| At 6:00 P.M. | Check the x$bh table to ensure enough memory is still free |
| At 6 P.M.–5 P.M. | The system runs like a dream |
| At 5:00 P.M. | Users throw you a party!!!! (Yeah, sure they will...) |

To achieve this goal, not only must you have a good hit ratio, but you must also have memory available for any unanticipated ad hoc queries. It is a good idea to ensure that there is enough memory allocated for data after the system has been running most of the day. To find out how much memory is available for data at any given time, run the following query of the x$bh table (Note: You must be the SYS user to run this query). See Chapter 15 and Appendix C for detailed information about the x$ tables and the myths associated with deleting data from these tables.

```
select     state, count(*)
from       x$bh
group by   state;


STATE      COUNT(*)
0               371
1               429


In the above result:
Total DB_BLOCK_BUFFERS = 800 (371+429)
Total buffers that have been used = 429
Total buffers that have NOT been used = 371
```

**A more accurate query (see Chapter 15 for more information):**

```
select     decode(state,0, 'FREE',
           1,decode(lrba_seq,0,'AVAILABLE','BEING USED'),
           3, 'BEING USED', state) "BLOCK STATUS",
           count(*)
from       x$bh
group by   decode(state,0,'FREE',1,decode(lrba_seq,0,'AVAILABLE',
           'BEING USED'),3, 'BEING USED', state);


BLOCK STATUS        COUNT(*)
AVAILABLE               779
BEING USED              154
FREE                    167
```

**TIP**

*If free buffers are not available (none with state=0) within the first 30 minutes of business hours, you probably need to set DB_BLOCK_BUFFERS higher.*

**V8 TIP**

*In Oracle8, the results are adjusted more frequently; as a result, the query is more accurate.*

### Using the CACHE Parameter of ALTER TABLE...)

If you find that "key" tables or data are being pushed out of memory, you may need to "pin" them into memory using the CACHE parameter. When you use this parameter, full table scan results will be placed on the Most Recently Used (MRU) list instead of the Least Recently Used (LRU) list. This keeps them in memory for future use. The following examples investigate the syntax and uses of this command.

### Create a Table with CACHE

This example illustrates how to create a table that will be cached as soon as the first person accesses the data. Note that NOCACHE is the default setting when a table is created.

```
CREATE TABLE TEST_TAB (COL1 NUMBER)
TABLESPACE USERS
CACHE;
```

### Alter a Table to Be CACHEd

This example shows how to alter a table to be cached as soon as the first person accesses the data. This query is used for tables that are created without the CACHE setting and are later discovered to need the CACHE setting.

```
ALTER TABLE TEST_TAB
CACHE;
```

### Using the CACHE Hint

When you would like to cache a table, but only until the next time that the database is shut down, you can use the CACHE hint. This hint will cache the table once the query is executed and will remain in effect until the database has shut down.

```
select    /*+ CACHE(cust) */ ename, job
from      cust
where     table_name = 'EMP';
```

### The NOCACHE Hint

If a table has been created or altered to CACHE, but you would like to run a query accessing the table without the table becoming cached, use the NOCACHE hint. This will allow access to the table without caching the data, even if the table is set to CACHE in the data dictionary.

```
select    /*+ FULL(cust)  NOCACHE(cust) */  ename, job
from      cust
where     table_name = 'EMP';
```

**Five Goals to Improve Performance**

### You May Also Pin (Cache) PL/SQL Object Statements into Memory

In the event that you cannot maintain a sufficient SHARED_POOL_SIZE, it may be imperative to keep the most important objects cached (pinned) in memory. The following example illustrates how to pin PL/SQL object statements in memory using the DBMS_SHARED_POOL.KEEP procedure. For additional PL/SQL tips, see Chapter 10.

```
begin
dbms_shared_pool.keep('PROCESS_DATE','P');
end;
```

**TIP**

*Pin PL/SQL objects into memory immediately upon starting the database to avoid insufficient memory errors later in the day. To accomplish this, use the DBMS_SHARED_POOL.KEEP procedure for PL/SQL object statements. Ensure that the STANDARD procedure is pinned soon after startup since it is so large.*

### You May Also Pin All Packages

To pin all packages in the system, execute the following (from Oracle's Metalink):

```
declare
own varchar2(100);
nam varchar2(100);
cursor pkgs is
    select    owner, object_name
    from      dba_objects
    where     object_type = 'PACKAGE';
begin
    open pkgs;
    loop
        fetch pkgs into own, nam;
        exit when pkgs%notfound;
        dbms_shared_pool.keep(own || '.' || nam, 'P');
    end loop;
end;
```

Common "problem packages" that are shipped with Oracle (and should be kept) include STANDARD, DBMS_STANDARD, and DIUTIL.

**TIP**
*Use the DBMS_SHARED_POOL.KEEP procedure to pin objects into the Shared Pool. You can also use the PL/SQL procedure listed in this section to pin all packages into memory when the database is started (if memory/Shared Pool permits). This will help you to avoid errors involving loading packages when there isn't enough contiguous memory. See Chapter 10 for additional PL/SQL and pinning tips.*

**AVOID I/O DISK CONTENTION**   If data must be retrieved from the physical disk (if not already in memory), you must also take steps to reduce disk contention when retrieving the data. Disk contention occurs when multiple processes try to access the same disk simultaneously. Disk contention can be reduced, thereby increasing performance, by distributing the disk I/O more evenly over the available disks. Decreasing disk I/O can also reduce disk contention. To monitor disk contention and identify imbalances, use the FILE I/O Monitor in Enterprise Manager.

Use the FILE I/O Monitor within Enterprise Manager to determine the I/O that is taking place on each database file. If the reads and writes are not distributed evenly between disks, the tablespaces may need to be restructured for better performance. Figure 1-6 depicts a database that isn't distributed correctly—the users are hitting Disk1 more. This is happening because the SYSTEM Tablespace, which contains the TEMP directory, is stored there. An optimally balanced I/O distribution is shown in Figure 1-6 for comparison with the actual distribution.

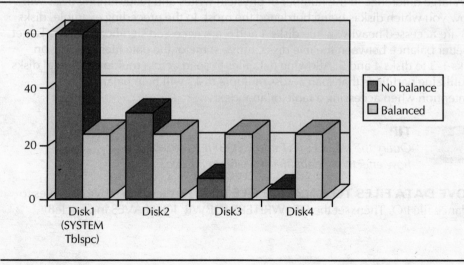

**FIGURE 1-6.**   *File I/O percentage of hits across all system disks (simple view)*

You can also determine file I/O problems by running a query:

```
col PHYRDS   format 999,999,999
col PHYWRTS  format 999,999,999
ttitle  "Disk Balancing Report"
col READTIM  format 999,999,999
col WRITETIM   format 999,999,999
col name format a40
spool fio1.out

select    name, phyrds, phywrts, readtim, writetim
from      v$filestat a, v$dbfile b
where     a.file# = b.file#
order by  readtim desc
/
spool off

Fri Mar 24                                              page 1
                    Disk Balancing Report

NAME                   Phyrds       Phywrts     ReadTim     WriteTim
/d01/psindex_1.dbf     48,310       51,798      200,564     903,199
/d02/psindex_02.dbf    34,520       40,224      117,925     611,121
/d03/psdata_01.dbf     35,189       36,904      97,474      401,290
/d04/rbs01.dbf         1,320        11,725      1,214       39,892
/d05/system01.dbf      1,454        10          10          956
```

A large difference in the number of physical writes and reads among disks will show you which disk is being burdened the most. In the preceding example, disks 1-3 are accessed heavily, while disks 4 and 5 are accessed significantly less. To get a better balance between the five disks, move some of the data files residing on disks 1-3 to disks 4 and 5. Allowing data files to span across multiple physical disks or utilizing partitions that span across multiple disks will help balance disk contention when accessing a table or an index.

**TIP**
*Query the V$FILESTAT and V$DBFILE views to see how effectively data files have been balanced.*

**MOVE DATA FILES TO BALANCE FILE I/O**   The key is to move data files to balance file I/O. Then, set the DB_WRITERS (DBWR_IO_SLAVES in Oracle8) parameter in the init.ora parameter to the number of database files or disks for maximum efficiency in writing data. See Chapter 4 and Appendix A for additional information on DB_WRITERS and DBWR_IO_SLAVES. See Chapter 3 for instruction on how to physically move a data file that is causing file contention and for other files that need to be addressed involving disk contention.

## Goal 3: Find the Problem Queries

*The query to V$SQLAREA is the most important tuning query in Oracle!* A single index or a single query can bring an entire system to a near standstill. By using V$SQLAREA, you can find the problem queries on your system. The following examples illustrate how to find the problem queries.

### Finding the Largest Amount of Physical Reads by Any Query

This query below is searching for queries where the disk reads are greater than 10,000. If your system is much larger, you may need to set this to a higher number.

```
select      disk_reads, sql_text
from        v$sqlarea
where       disk_reads > 10000
order by    disk_reads desc;

DISK READS       SQL TEXT
   12987         select     order#,columns,types
                 from       orders
                 where      substr(orderid,1,2)=:1
   11131         select     custid, city
                 from       customer
                 where      city = 'CHICAGO'
```

This output suggests that there are two problem queries causing heavy disk reads. The first has the index on orderid suppressed by the SUBSTR function. The second shows that there is a missing index on city. Chapter 17 provides a PL/SQL procedure that retrieves the top 25 memory and disk reads from the V$SQLAREA view in a formatted manner. Chapter 8 looks at query tuning in detail and leveraging the results that you retrieve from the V$SQLAREA view.

**TIP**
*To view the SQL_TEXT that is longer than the 2,000 characters in the V$SQLAREA view, join the V$SQLTEXT view to the V$SQLAREA view.*

### Finding the Largest Amount of Logical (Memory) Reads by Query

In this next query to the V$SQLAREA view, search for queries where the memory reads are greater than 200,000 reads (overindexed query potentials). If your system is much larger, you may need to set this to a higher number.

```
select      buffer_gets, sql_text
from        v$sqlarea
where       buffer_gets > 200000
order by    buffer_gets desc;

BUFFER GETS     SQL TEXT
   300219       select      order#,cust_no,
               from        orders
               where       division = '1'
```

**TIP**

*The preceding output above suggests that there is one problem query causing heavy memory reads. The index on division appears to have a cardinality of one (there is only one division), and should be suppressed for this statement to improve the performance.*

**TIP**

*Accessing the V$SQLAREA view will point you to the worst queries on your system. THE QUERY TO THE V$SQLAREA VIEW IS THE MOST IMPORTANT QUERY IN TUNING ORACLE!*

**V8 TIP**

*In Oracle8, you use the Oracle Analyzer (the name as of the writing of this book, and always subject to change) to find problem queries and alternative SQL paths. In Oracle8, partitioned tables are also displayed in the V$SQLAREA view.*

### You May Need to Join to the V$SQLTEXT View

You may have to join the V$SQLTEXT view with V$SQLAREA to get the full text since the V$SQLAREA view only shows a portion of the sql_text column. See Chapter 4 for a detailed look and analysis of the next example:

```
break on   User_Name on Disk_Reads on Buffer_Gets on Rows_Processed
select     A.User_Name, B.Disk_Reads, B.Buffer_Gets,
           B.Rows_Processed, C.SQL_Text
from       V$Open_Cursor A, V$SQLArea B, V$SQLText C
where      A.User_Name = Upper('&&User')
  and      A.Address = C.Address
  and      A.Address = B.Address
order by   A.User_Name, A.Address, C.Piece;
```

| User Name | Disk Reads | Buffer Gets | Rows Processed | SQL text | |
|-----------|-----------|-------------|----------------|----------|---|
| Angelina | 2 | 2300 | 210 | select | itemno, custno |
| | | | | from | items |
| | | | | where | custno = 'A101' |
| Bbrown | 3 | 23213 | 7015 | select | itemno, custno |
| | | | | from | items |
| | | | | where | state = 'IL' |
| Jtrezzo | 0 | 200 | 2 | select | itemno, custno |
| | | | | from | items |
| | | | | where | orderno = 131313 |
| Rniemiec | 32000 | 45541 | 7100 | select | itemno, custno |
| | | | | from | items |
| | | | | where | nvl(orderno,0) = 131313 |
| | | | | or | nvl(orderno,0) = 777777 |

# Goal 4: Tune the Problem Queries

Developers often ask what the difference is between a DBA and a terrorist. The answer is that you can negotiate with a terrorist. The reason why DBAs seem so unreasonable lies in the fact that they are exhausted from tuning developers' poorly written and untuned queries.

The following list shows the basic items to be addressed when tuning individual problem queries:

- What you need to know to tune your system
- Using AUTOTRACE and SET TIMING ON
- Using TRACE and EXPLAIN PLAN
- Cost-based optimization and analyze
- The 95/5 rule
- Using hints
- Index use and abuse
- The driving table
- Using Parallel Query Option

### What You Need to Know Before You Tune Your System

The first thing you need to know is the data. The volume of data and the distribution of data will affect how you tune individual queries. You also need to have a "shopping cart" full of possible tuning methods. Multiple approaches must be made to cover all types of queries. A single method of tuning or a single tuning product is *not* enough. You also need to know where the system is slow. Many DBAs and developers spend endless hours attempting to find the problem queries instead of asking the everyday users of the system. Users will almost always be happy to volunteer this information. You also need to network with other developers that work on similar systems. Sharing information at user groups is a great way to network. Note that Chapter 2 focuses entirely on beginner tuning topics.

When setting timing on to see whether you are improving the performance of a query, you must have a benchmark or way to time the query. While a stopwatch can be used, the SET TIMING feature in SQLPLUS is an excellent way to time queries. Unfortunately, the users may compromise the accuracy of the timing, but those of us who tune, usually do it at 2 A.M. Use the following SQL statements for the SET TIMING feature.

```
SQL> SET TIMING ON
SQL>    select      count(name)
        from        emp7
        where       name = 'branches';


COUNT(NAME)
100

Elapsed: 00:00:00.84   (HOURS:MINUTES:SECONDS)
```

## Setting AUTOTRACE On

A better way for measuring the performance of queries (in SQL*Plus 3.3 and later releases) is to use the AUTOTRACE command. Use the following SQL statements for the AUTOTRACE feature:

```
SQL> SET AUTOTRACE ON
SQL>   select    count(name)
       from      emp7
       where     name = 'branches';

COUNT(NAME)
100


Execution Plan
    0       SELECT     STATEMENT Optimizer=CHOOSE
    1       0          SORT (AGGREGATE)
    2       1          INDEX (RANGE SCAN) OF 'EMP7_I1' (NON-UNIQUE)


Statistics
0       recursive calls
0       db block gets
1       consistent gets
1       physical reads
0       redo size
223     bytes sent via SQL*Net to client
274     bytes recd via SQL*Net from client
2       SQL*Net roundtrips to/from client
1       sorts (memory)
0       sorts (disk)
1       rows processed
```

## The Oracle TRACE Utility (See Chapter 6 for more information)

In order to tune queries, you must be able to find problem queries and analyze those potential problems. The Oracle TRACE utility is used to measure timing statistics for a given query or batch process (with multiple queries), or an entire system. It is a fast method of finding where potential bottlenecks on the system reside. It also has an option to run an EXPLAIN PLAN to generate the optimizer's path for executing a query. This section will focus briefly on how to use this powerful tool. Chapter 6 is completely devoted to TRACE and EXPLAIN PLAN.

- TRACE generates statistics about an Oracle query that has been executed.
- TRACE helps the developer analyze every section of a query.

Five Goals to Improve Performance

**SIMPLE STEPS FOR TRACE WITH A SIMPLE QUERY** The following outlines a few elementary steps to utilize the TRACE function:

**1a.** Set the following init.ora parameters:

```
TIMED_STATISTICS = TRUE
MAX_DUMP_FILE_SIZE = 2000000 (Not 2M)
USER_DUMP_DEST = /oracle/rich_trc
```

**2a.** Enable TRACE for a SQL+ session:

```
SQL> ALTER SESSION SET SQL_TRACE TRUE;
```

**3a..** Run the query to be TRACEd:

```
select    table_name, owner,
          initial_extent, uniqueness
from      ind2
where     owner || '' = 'SCOTT' ; (Note: Index on "OWNER" suppressed)
```

**4a.** Disable TRACE for the same SQL+ session:

```
SQL>ALTER SESSION SET SQL_TRACE FALSE;
```

**5a.** You can *also* enable TRACE for all sessions (*not suggested*):

```
SQL_TRACE = TRUE   (In the INIT.ORA)
```

After running TRACE, your output file may be something like: 5_19554.trc.

**6a.** Run TKPROF to put the TRACE file into "readable" format:

```
tkprof 5_19554.trc rich2.prf explain=system/manager
```

The TKPROF utility translates the TRACE file generated by the SQL TRACE facility to a readable format. You can run TKPROF against a TRACE file that you have previously created. You may also run the utility while the program, creating the TRACE file, is still running. Options for TKPROF are listed here.

**7a.** The output of the file rich2.prf (with the index suppressed):

```
select    table_name, owner,
          initial_extent, uniqueness
from      ind2
where     owner || '' = 'SCOTT';
```

| | count | cpu | elap | disk | query | current | rows |
|---|---|---|---|---|---|---|---|
| Parse: | 1 | 1 | 2 | 0 | 0 | 0 | |
| Execute: | 1 | 0 | 0 | 0 | 0 | 2 | 0 |
| Fetch: | 2 | 69 | 113 | 142 | 430 | 0 | 36 |

Execution plan: *(No Index Used)*
TABLE ACCESS (FULL) OF 'IND2'

**7b.** Rerun the query to be TRACEd, now using the index:

```
select      table_name, owner,
            initial_extent, uniqueness
from        ind2
where       owner = 'SCOTT' ;  (The index on "OWNER" is not
suppressed)
```

The output of the file rich2.prf:

```
select      table_name, owner,
            initial_extent, uniqueness
from        ind2
where       owner = 'SCOTT' ;
```

| | count | cpu | elap | disk | query | current | rows |
|---|---|---|---|---|---|---|---|
| Parse: | 2 | 0 | 0 | 0 | 0 | 0 | |
| Execute: | 2 | 0 | 0 | 0 | 0 | 0 | 0 |
| Fetch: | 4 | 6 | 6 | 0 | 148 | 0 | 72 |

Execution plan: *(Index Used)*
TABLE ACCESS (BY ROWID) OF 'IND2'
  INDEX (RANGE SCAN) OF 'IND2_1' (NON-UNIQUE)

**TIP**
*A TRACEd query with a large number of physical reads usually indicates a missing index. The disk column indicates the physical reads (usually where an index is not used) and the query added to the current columns indicates the memory reads (usually reads where an index is being used).*

## Using EXPLAIN PLAN (See Chapter 6 for more information)

The EXPLAIN PLAN command allows a developer to view the query execution plan that the Oracle optimizer will use to execute an SQL statement. This command is very helpful in improving performance of SQL statements. It does not actually execute the SQL statement; it only outlines the plan to use and inserts this execution plan in an Oracle table.

**WHY USE EXPLAIN PLAN WITHOUT TRACE?**   The statement is *not* executed. It only shows what will happen if the statement is executed.

**WHEN TO USE EXPLAIN PLAN WITHOUT TRACE**   When the query will take exceptionally long to run.

### How Do I Use EXPLAIN PLAN by Itself?

1. Find the script; it is usually in $ORACLE_HOME/rdbms/admin.

   "utlxplan.sql"

2. Execute the script utlxplan.sql in SQL+:

   ```
   SQL>@utlxplan    (In V7)
   ```

   *(This creates the PLAN_TABLE for the user executing the script)*

3a. Run EXPLAIN PLAN for the query to be optimized:

   ```
   explain plan for
   select     customer_number
   from       customer
   where      customer_number = 111;


   Explained.
   ```

3b. Run EXPLAIN PLAN for the query to be optimized (using a tag for the statement):

   ```
   explain plan
   SET STATEMENT_ID = 'CUSTOMER' FOR
   select     customer_number
   from       customer
   where      customer_number = 111;
   ```

**4.** Select the output from the plan_table:

```
select    operation, options, object_name, id, parent_id, position
from      plan_table
where     statement_id = 'CUSTOMER';
```

| Operation | Options | Object Name | ID | Parent |
|-----------|---------|-------------|----|--------|
| Select Statement | | | 0 | |
| Table Access | By Rowid | Customer | 1 | |
| Index | Range Scan | CUST_IDX | 2 | 1 |

**TIP**
*Use EXPLAIN PLAN instead of TRACE so that you don't
have to wait for the query to run. The EXPLAIN PLAN
will reveal the path of a query without actually running
the query. Use TRACE only for multiquery batch jobs
to find out which of the many queries in the batch job
are slow.*

## EXPLAIN PLAN—READ IT TOP TO BOTTOM OR BOTTOM TO TOP?

It depends—how you write the query determines how it retrieves the information
from the plan_table table. That is probably why many people differ on which way to
read the result (all of them may be correct). Next is an example with the order of
execution based on the query that retrieves the information:

```
Delete From Plan_Table;
explain plan
  set     Statement_Id = 'SQL1' For
select    To_Char(SysDate, 'MM/DD/YY HH:MM AM'),
          To_Char((Trunc((SysDate -4 -1), 'day') +1), 'DD-MON-YY'),
from      bk, ee
where     bk_shift_date >= To_Char((Trunc(( SysDate - 4 - 1),
          'day') + 1), 'dd-mon-yy')
and       bk_shift_date <= To_Char((SysDate - 4), 'dd-mon-yy')
and       bk_empno = ee_empno(+)
and       SubStr(ee_hierarchy_code, 1, 3) in
                ('PNA', 'PNB', 'PNC', 'PND', 'PNE', 'PNF')
order by ee_job_group, bk_empno, bk_shift_date
/
```

```
select    LPad(' ', 2*(Level-1)) || Level || '.' || Nvl(Position,0)||
          ' ' || Operation || ' ' || Options || ' ' || Object_Name || ' '
||
          Object_Type || ' ' || Decode(id, 0, Statement_Id ||' Cost = '
||
          Position) || Other || ' ' || Object_Node
          "Query Plan"
from      plan_table
start     with id = 0 And statement_id = 'SQL1'
connect by prior id = parent_id
and       statement_id = 'SQL1'

/

Query Plan
1.0 SELECT STATEMENT     SQL1  Cost =
    2.1 SORT ORDER BY
        3.1 FILTER
            4.1 NESTED LOOPS OUTER
                5.1 TABLE ACCESS BY ROWID BK
                    6.1 INDEX RANGE SCAN I_BK_06 NON-UNIQUE
                5.2 TABLE ACCESS BY ROWID EE
                    6.1 INDEX UNIQUE SCAN I_EE_01 UNIQUE
```

### Reading the EXPLAIN PLAN

Using the preceding EXPLAIN PLAN, it will explain the steps. Each step has been identified by the number on the left-hand-side. I have illustrated below the order in which they were executed.

| Step | Action |
| --- | --- |
| 6.1 | This is the index range scan of I_BK_06. This is the first step. This index is on the bk_shift_dt column. This step performs a scan of this index to produce a list of row numbers that fall between the two dates. |
| 5.1 | Retrieve the rows from the bk table. |
| 6.1 | Scan of the I_EE_01 index. This index is on the ee_empno column. Using the bk_empno retrieved from the previous step, this index is scanned to retrieve the ROWIDs to produce a list of the ee_empnos that match the bk_empnos. |
| 5.2 | Retrieve the rows from the ee table. |
| 4.1 | NESTED LOOP. The two lists are joined, producing one list. |
| 3.1 | FILTER. The rest of the conditions of the WHERE clause are applied. |
| 2.1 | SORT ORDER BY. The remaining rows are sorted according to the ORDER BY clause. |
| 1.0 | This tells what type of statement it is. |

**TIP**

*Whether the EXPLAIN PLAN is read from top to bottom or from the bottom to the top is dependent entirely on the query used to select information from the plan_table table. Both methods of reading the query may be correct, given the query selecting the information is correctly structured.*

## Yet Another EXPLAIN PLAN Output Method: Building the Tree Structure

While many people will find that the EXPLAIN PLAN methods in previous sections are sufficient, still others require a more theoretical approach that ties to the parent/child relationships of a query and the corresponding tree structure. For some people, the following query makes using EXPLAIN PLAN easier to visualize, and it is included for that audience. See Chapter 6 for detailed information regarding this approach. A synopsis is included here:

```
explain plan
  set statement_id = 'SQL2' For
select    cust_no ,cust_address ,cust_last_name,
          cust_first_name ,cust_mid_init
from      customer
where     cust_phone = '3035551234';
```

1. The query used for this approach:

```
select    LPAD(' ',2*(LEVEL-1))||operation  "OPERATION",
          options "OPTIONS",
          DECODE(TO_CHAR(id),'0','COST =' ||
          NVL(TO_CHAR(position),'n/a'), object_name) "OBJECT NAME",
          id ||'-'|| NVL(parent_id, 0)||'-'|| NVL(position, 0) "ORDER",
          SUBSTR(optimizer,1,6) "OPT"
from      plan_table
start     with id = 0
and       statement_id = 'SQL2'
connect by prior id = parent_id
and       statement_id = 'SQL2';
```

2. The output for this approach:

| OPERATION | OPTIONS | OBJECT NAME | ORDER | OPT |
|---|---|---|---|---|
| SELECT STATEMENT | | COST = n/a | 0-0-0 | RULE |
| TABLE ACCESS | BY ROWID | CUSTOMER | 1-0-1 | |
| INDEX | RANGE SCAN | IX_CUST_PHONE | 2-1-1 | |

**Five Goals to Improve Performance**

### EXPLAIN PLAN When Using Partitions

Table partitions yield different outputs for the EXPLAIN PLAN (as shown in the example following). In this example, we access a partitioned table that is segmented into three parts. This example is covered in detail in Chapter 6; this section shows only the EXPLAIN PLAN for a partitioned table. For more detailed information on partitioning tables, refer to Chapter 13.

```
select    operation, options, id, position , object_name,
          partition_start, partition_stop
from      plan_table;
```

| OPERATION | OPTIONS | ID | OBJECT NAME | PARTITION START | PART STOP |
|---|---|---|---|---|---|
| SELECT STATEMENT | | | | | |
| PARTITION | CONCATENATED | 1 | | NUMBER(1) | NUMBER(3) |
| TABLE ACCESS | FULL | 2 | DEPT1 | NUMBER(1) | NUMBER(3) |

This example above shows that a full table scan is performed on the dept1 table. All three partitions are scanned. The starting partition is 1 and the ending partition is 3.

**TIP**

*Partitions can also be viewed by the EXPLAIN PLAN by accessing the columns partition_stop and partition_stop in the plan_table table.*

## SQL Analyze—Comparing Different Plans

Oracle's Enterprise Manager can also be used to generate and compare EXPLAIN PLANs. Chapter 5 looks at the Enterprise Manager utility in detail. As shown in Figure 1-7, a user creates a different plan for the S4 statement using the FIRST_ROWS optimizer mode, then uses the SQL Analyze Comparison feature to split the screen to examine and walk each plan through side by side. The comparison for this query reveals whether using ALL_ROWS or FIRST_ROWS will be a better solution when the query is executed.

**TIP**

*The SQL Analyze Comparison feature allows a side-by-side comparison of SQL statements to help you find the best execution path. By using these "what if" scenarios, you can find the best solution before actually executing the query.*

Five Goals to Improve Performance

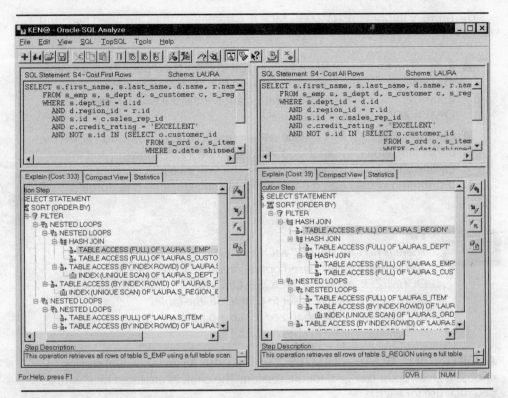

**FIGURE 1-7.**   *Performance Pack SQL Analyze*

## The Cost-Based Optimization and Analysis

In order to effectively tune queries, we must understand how Oracle internally processes the query. Once we understand Oracle's method for processing the query, we can investigate potential alternatives. Oracle has two choices for optimization: cost-based optimization and rule-based optimization. Cost-based optimization takes into account the distribution of the data and makes choices based on that distribution. To enable cost-based optimization, you must set the OPTIMIZER_MODE init.ora parameter to CHOOSE and also ANALYZE the tables that are to use cost-based optimization. Rule-based optimization is the older method that Oracle first employed in version 5 of the database. It was based on preset paths for optimizing queries based on the indexes that were available. The distribution of data was not taken into account by the rule-based optimizer.

The primary init.ora OPTIMIZER_MODE parameter values are listed here and include a brief explanation:

- **Rule**   The Oracle database will default to rule-based optimization unless the underlying tables are analyzed with the ANALYZE command. The optimizer will use rule-based optimization if the init.ora parameter OPTIMIZER_MODE is set to rule.

- **Choose**   The Oracle database will use cost-based optimization when the underlying tables are analyzed with the ANALYZE command and the OPTIMIZER_MODE is set to choose. This will take into account the distribution of data based on the level of analyzing that is performed.

**TIP**
*There is no OPTIMIZER_MODE=COST setting. The setting for cost-based optimization is OPTIMIZER_MODE=CHOOSE. Once the OPTIMIZER_MODE is set to CHOOSE, the tables will still need to be analyzed for cost-based optimization to be in effect.*

**A. OPTIMIZER_GOAL—VALUES**   You can also set an individual session to choose a given optimizer goal for the session. The choices are listed here with a potential use for each.

- **Rule**   Don't have time to tune all of this code that came from version 6 rule-based. Keep it rule-based.
- **ALL_ROWS**   Get all rows fast (long-running reports retrieving most rows).
- **FIRST_ROW**   Get the first row fast (forms single-row query applications).
- **Choose**   Fix problem areas, but primarily let the Optimizer choose the path.

To change the OPTIMIZER_MODE for a given session, issue the command listed here.

```
Alter Session set Optimizer_Goal = <mode>;
```

**THE ANALYZE COMMAND**   The Oracle ANALYZE command is used by Oracle to compile details about the data distribution of both tables and indixes. When the init.ora parameter OPTIMIZER_MODE is set to choose for cost-based optimization, the query will still use rule-based optimization unless the individual tables in the query have been analyzed. A table can be ANALYZEd partially or fully, as in the following queries. A table can also be de-ANALYZEd, by using the delete statistics.

### ANALYZE Examples

The following query analyzes a table sampling 5000 rows in the table. If the table has equal distribution of values, then this is sufficient. If the table is unequally balanced, this will lead to potentially poor performance.

```
SQL> ANALYZE TABLE CUSTOMER
ESTIMATE STATISTICS sample 5000 rows;
```

The following query analyzes a table and looks at every single row in the table. This is absolutely the best method for analyzing a table, but may be too slow for very large databases (VLDBs).

```
SQL> ANALYZE TABLE CUSTOMER
COMPUTE  STATISTICS;
```

The following query analyzes a table sampling 25 percent of the rows in the table. If the table has equal distribution of values, then this is sufficient. If the table is unequally balanced, this could lead to potentially poor performance.

```
SQL> ANALYZE TABLE CUSTOMER
ESTIMATE STATISTICS sample 25 percent;
```

The following query analyzes a table and deletes the statistics on the table. For systems that have converted from rule-based to cost-based and have found their system is running slower, it may be necessary to take out the statistics. However, even after the tables in a system have been analyzed, rule-based optimization can be set in the init.ora rather than deleting the statistics (as discussed in the previous section).

```
SQL> ANALYZE TABLE CUSTOMER
DELETE STATISTICS;
```

Use the following statement to ANALYZE all of the tables and indices in an entire schema:

```
execute dbms_utility.analyze_schema('SCOTT','COMPUTE');
```

## The 95/5 Rule (The version 7 Rule)

When the optimizer finds a query to retrieve less than 4-7 percent of the rows, the optimizer will choose to drive the query with an index if one exists. Looking at

Figure 1-8, we can see that Oracle's direction for the optimization of queries continues to be skewed toward queries that retrieve smaller and smaller amounts of data. This trend shows a direction toward faster online transaction processing (OLTP) systems. However, larger queries involving full table scans are much faster than in previous versions of Oracle, as Oracle has also increased the maximum size for the SGA over the subsequent releases (the max SGA for version 5 was 2M).

Consider the following example; the statement WHERE TABLE_NAME='EMP' retrieves 1 percent of the rows from the cust table. Based on this figure, it is a prime query to use the index on the table_name column. Note the performance degradation when we force the table into a full table scan in the second query.

Given that:

- There is an index on table_name
- table_name = 'EMP' *(retrieves 1 percent)*

The optimizer uses the table_name index since the distinct key ratio is 1.5 percent.

```
The optimizer uses the INDEX:
select    blocks
from      cust
where     table_name = 'EMP';

Execution Time - 1.1 seconds
```

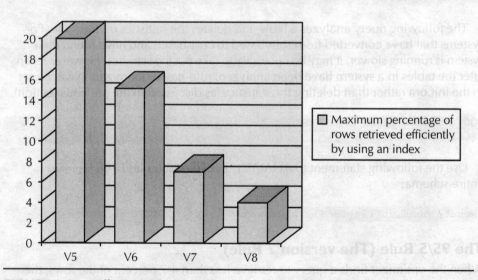

**FIGURE 1-8.** *Efficient index use relative to percentage of rows retrieved*

We force full table scan; *bad choice:*

```
select    /*+ FULL(cust) */ blocks
from      cust
where     table_name = 'EMP';

Execution Time - 75.1 seconds
```

By forcing a full table scan, we have significantly reduced the performance of the query.

When the optimizer (cost-based) finds a query to retrieve less than 4-7 percent (based on the average distribution) of the rows in a table, the optimizer will choose to drive the query with an index if one exists. Figure 1-9 shows how Oracle has evolved through the past years. While Oracle7 shows the best performance at all levels, the developer must know when to override the optimizer (see Chapters 8 and 9 for information about individual query tuning and Chapter 4 for more information concerning the optimizer. Chapter 9 shows how you can build these graphs for your own queries.)

**TIP**

*When a query retrieves less than 4-5 percent of the rows from a table, we generally want to use an index (the 95/5 Rule). When a query retrieves more than 7 percent of the rows from a table, we generally (but not always) want to force a full table scan by either eliminating or suppressing an index (the optimizer will often do this for us with cost-based optimization).*

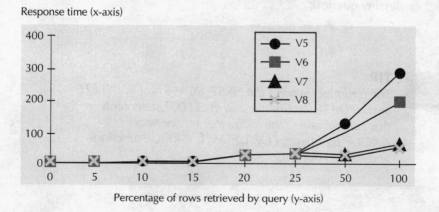

Response time (x-axis)

Percentage of rows retrieved by query (y-axis)

**FIGURE I-9.**   *Optimum percentage of rows for index for a given version of Oracle*

Five Goals to Improve Performance

## Using Hints for Optimization

The Oracle optimizer is not perfect. However, there are hints that can be used to change how the optimizer behaves. Eventually, you will find a query that requires specific tuning attention. When the query is found, you must take advantage of the hints that Oracle offers for tuning individual queries. The syntax for the main hints is listed next. Keep in mind, the syntax *must* be correct or the hint will be ignored and no error message will be issued. Also, remember that hints only apply to the statement they are in. Nested statements are treated as totally different statements, requiring their own hints. I will cover the most effective hints (many more are available and covered in Chapter 7) for query tuning.

- **Full**   Force a full table scan:

```
select   /*+ FULL(table_name) */ column1, column2 ...
```

- **Index**   Force an indexed search:

```
select   /*+ INDEX(table_name index_name1 index_name2...) */
```

- **Ordered**   Force the driving table as in a FROM clause:

```
select    /*+ ORDERED */ column1, column2 ...
from      table1, table2
```

- **ALL_ROWS**   Explicitly chooses the cost-based approach with a *goal of best throughput* (usually forces a full table scan for medium to high cardinality queries):

```
select   /*+ ALL_ROWS */ ...
```

- **FIRST ROWS**   Explicitly chooses the cost-based approach with a *goal of best response time* (usually forces an index search for low to medium cardinality queries):

```
select   /*+ FIRST_ROWS */ ...
```

**TIP**
*The optimizer ignores the FIRST_ROWS hint in DELETE and UPDATE statements, and in SELECT statements that contain any of the following: set operators, GROUP BY clause, FOR UPDATE, GROUP functions and distinct operators.*

■ **USE_NL**   This forces the use of NESTED LOOPS. The table listed in the hint will be used as the inner table (nondriving table) of the NESTED LOOP. This means that if there are only two tables to be joined, the table *not* listed in this hint will be the driving table. See Chapter 7 for an overview of all join method hints and Chapter 9 for detailed information regarding joins.

```
select   /*+ Use_NL(table table) */
```

**TIP**
*When using an alias for a table in a query, the hint must reference the alias (not the table) or the hint will be ignored. Currently (as of the writing of this book), there is a 255-character limit to hints.*

**HINT EXAMPLES**   This query is correctly using an index by the cost-based optimizer:

```
The optimizer uses the INDEX:
select    blocks
from      cust
where     table_name = 'EMP';

Execution Time - 1.1 seconds
```

We use the FULL hint to force a full table scan on the cust table. Note that we have now degraded performance (hints are not always a good thing). Also note that in Oracle8i, we can use the NO_INDEX hint to turn off specific indexes instead of using the FULL hint, which disallows all indexes (see Chapter 13 for detailed information on hints).

A full table scan has been forced; *bad choice*:

```
select    /*+ FULL(cust) */ blocks
from      cust
where     table_name = 'EMP';

Execution Time - 75.1 seconds
```

If we specify an incorrect syntax for a hint, we do not receive an error. The query behaves as if we had not added a hint at all. In the next query, we have incorrectly specified the FULL hint by forgetting the "+" sign (luckily in this case, since a correctly specified FULL hint would have slowed down this query, as shown in the previous example). The hint syntax should be /*+ FULL(cust) */.

The hint syntax is incorrect (the hint is ignored):

```
select     /*  FULL(cust) */ blocks
from       cust
where      table_name = 'EMP';


Execution Time - 1.1 seconds
```

**TIP**
*If the syntax for a hint is incorrect, the hint will be
ignored and an error message will not occur.*

### Where Are the Indexes on These Tables?

To get the specific columns that are indexed for a given table, access the
DBA_IND_COLUMNS view. This query is displayed next. Also, note that you
can retrieve the columns that are indexed for your schema only, by accessing
USER_IND_COLUMNS. See Chapter 2 for an in-depth look at beginning tuning
topics such as finding indexes and understanding how indexes work.

```
select     table_name, index_name, column_name, column_position
from       dba_ind_columns
order by   table_name, index_name, column_position;
```

| TABLE NAME | INDEX NAME | COLUMN NAME | COLUMN POSITION |
|------------|------------|-------------|-----------------|
| EMP | EMP_IDX1 | EMPID | 1 |
| EMP | EMP_IDX1 | ENAME | 2 |
| EMP | EMP_IDX1 | DEPTNO | 3 |
| EMP | EMP_IDX2 | SALARY | 1 |

This emp table has two indexes. The first index, emp_idx1, is a concatenated
index that indexes the empid, ename, and deptno columns. The second index,
emp_idx2, is only indexing the salary column.

**TIP**
*Query DBA_INDEXES and DBA_IND_COLUMNS to
retrieve a list of the indexes on a given table. Use
USER_INDEXES and USER_IND_COLUMNS to retrieve
information for your schema only.*

### The Fast Full Scan Hint (Oracle8 only)

If we could index both the columns in the SELECT and the WHERE clauses of a query, it could use a fast full scan of the index. The INDEX_FFS hint forces a fast full scan of such an index. This hint will access only the index and not the corresponding table. Consider the following query using the INDEX_FFS hint:

```
select     /*+ index_ffs(employees emp_idx1) */ emp_name
from       employees
where      dept_no = 10;

Elapsed time: Less than 1 second (only the index is accessed)

OPERATION             OPTIONS         OBJECT NAME
SELECT STATEMENT
INDEX                 RANGE SCAN      EMP_IDX1
```

The query is now guaranteed to only access the index.

**V8 TIP**
*The INDEX_FFS (available in Oracle8) will process only the index and will not access the table. All columns that are used and retrieved by the query must be contained in the index. This is a better way to guarantee that the index will be used as the versions of Oracle change. Chapters 7 and 8 contain more information concerning the INDEX_FFS hint.*

**UNINTENTIONAL INDEX SUPPRESSION**   You must be careful when writing queries or you may unintentionally suppress (turn off) an index that you may have intended using. Any function that modifies the column name in a WHERE clause will suppress the corresponding index. In Oracle8i, there are function-based indexes, allowing indexes to be built on functions like UPPER, SUBSTR, and DECODE (see Chapter 13 for additional information). Many common functions that are used to suppress a standard index are listed here:

- NOT / IS NULL / != or < >
- Comparing a number field to a character field
- Any modification to the indexed column name
- (TO_CHAR, TO_DATE, +0, ☐ II ", ☐SUBSTR, DECODE...)

The following is a suppression example. Despite the intended hint to use the index, the SUBSTR function will suppress the index on the cust_no column here:

```
select     /*+ index(customer custidx) */  cust_no, zip_code
from       customer
where      SUBSTR(CUST_NO,1,4) = '2502';

Execution Time - 280 seconds
```

The SUBSTR function was rewritten with a LIKE instead and part of the index is used, and the performance is substantially increased:

```
select     cust_no, zip_code
from       customer
where      cust_no like '2502%';

Execution Time - 3 seconds
```

**TIP**

*Prior to Oracle 8.1, if a column is modified in the WHERE clause, the index on the column will not be used (it will be internally suppressed).*

**COMPARING WRONG DATA TYPES**   If you compare the wrong data types, your index may be suppressed internally. Oracle rewrites the query internally (usually suppressing the index) so that the data types match. This type of internal index suppression is a real problem and is difficult to hunt down. The following WHERE clauses show when mismatches cause problems.
Comparing characters to numbers:

```
where    char_data = 123
```

This might be rewritten internally (potentially suppressing an index) to be:

```
where    To_Number(char_data) = 123
```

Comparing numbers to characters:

```
where    num_data = '123'
```

This might be rewritten internally (potentially suppressing an index) to be:

```
where    To_Char(num_data) = '123'
```

**TIP**

*Comparing mismatched data types could cause an
internal index suppression that is difficult to track
down. Oracle will often place a function on the
column that fixes the mismatch, but suppresses
the index.*

### Function-Based Indexes (Oracle8i)

One of the largest problems with indexes is that they are often suppressed by
developers. Developers using the UPPER function can suppress an index on a
column for a given query. In Oracle 8.1, there is a way to combat this problem.
Function-based indexes allow you to create an index based on a function or
expression. The value of the function or expression is specified by the person
creating the index and is stored in the index. Function-based indexes can involve
multiple columns or arithmetic expressions, or may be a PL/SQL function or C
callout. The following example shows an example of a function-based index:

```
CREATE INDEX emp_idx ON emp (UPPER(ename));
```

An index has been created on the ename column when the UPPER function is
used on this column:

```
select     ename, job, deptno
from       emp
where      upper(ename) = 'ELLISON';
```

The function-based index (emp_idx) can be used for the preceding query. For
large tables where the condition retrieves a small number of records, the query
yields substantial performance gains over a full table scan.

**V8i TIP**

*Function-based indexes can lead to dramatic
performance gains when used to create indexes
on functions often used on selective columns. See
Chapter 13 for additional Oracle 8.1 performance
enhancements.*

**USING OR CAN BE HAZARDOUS TO A QUERY**   Correctly indexing on
statements having an OR clause and multiple WHERE conditions can be difficult.
While in previous versions it was essential to index at least one column in each
clause ORed together, the merging of indexes in Oracle8 becomes potentially

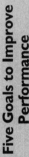

Five Goals to Improve
Performance

hazardous to the performance. The solution is often to suppress all indexes except the most limiting (retrieves the least amount of rows) for each table in the query. Consider the following examples:

Given indexes on empno, ename, and deptno:

```
select      ename,deptno,city,division
from        emp1
where       empno = 1
or          ename = 'LONEY'
or          deptno = 10;

Execution Time: 4400 Seconds

Execution Plan
    TABLE ACCESS EMP1 FULL

The Solution
select      /*+ INDEX(emp emp11) */
            ename,  deptno, city, division
from        emp1
where       empno = 1
or          ename = 'LONEY'
OR          deptno = 10;

Execution Time: 280 Seconds

Execution Plan
    TABLE ACCESS   EMP1   ROWID
    TABLE ACCESS   EMP11 INDEX RS
```

**TIP**
*Performance tuning involving the OR continues to change from version to version of Oracle. Currently, forcing the use of the most restrictive index only usually leads to best performance. However, Oracle tends to be cyclical in nature and indexing all clauses of the OR conditions should also be tested when using the OR.*

**DEALING WITH INEQUALITIES**    The cost-based optimizer tends to have problems with inequalities. Since Oracle records the high and low value for a column and assumes a linear distribution of data, problems occur when an inequality is used on a table with a nonlinear distribution of data. This can be solved by overriding the optimizer (discussed next) or by using histograms (discussed in Chapter 2).

This is given regarding the following query:

- The order_line table has 10,000 rows between 1 and 10,000
- There are 5,000 records (half the table) with an item number > 9990
- There is an index on item_no

The optimizer chooses to use the index, since it believes there are only 10 rows to be retrieved:

```
select    size, item_no
from      order_line
where     item_no > 9990;

Execution Time: 530 Seconds
```

Half of the data from the table will be retrieved by the preceding query. If we suppress the index on the item_no column, we can substantially increase performance. The reason why we want to suppress the index (and override the optimizer) is because the query retrieves 50 percent of the table (which is much more than the 5 percent or less rule for using the index)!

```
select    /*+ FULL(order_line) */  size, item_no
from      order_line
where     item_no > 9990;

Execution Time: 5 Seconds
```

**TIP**
*Strongly consider using hints to override the optimizer when using the "<" and ">" when the distribution of data is not linear between the high and low values of a column. Histograms may also be employed.*

**NESTED SUBQUERIES**   Using nested subqueries instead of joining tables in a single query can lead to dramatic performance gains (at times over 1,000 percent). Only certain queries will meet the criteria for making this modification. When you find the right one, this trick will take performance improvement to an exponentially superior height. The conditions for changing a query to a nested subquery occur when:

- Tables are being joined to return the rows from *only* one table.
- Conditions from each table will lead to a reasonable percentage of the rows to be retrieved (more than 10 percent).

**The original query:**

```
select    A.col1, A.col2
from      table1 A, table2 B
where     A.col3 = var
and       A.col4 = B.col1
and       B.col2 = var;
```

**The new query:**

```
select    A.col1, A.col2
from      table1 A
where     A.col3 = var
and       Exists
(Select 'x'
 from      table B
 where     A.col4 = B.col1
 and       B.col2 = var);
```

**A real-life example:**

```
select    ordno, custno
from      order_line ol, order
where     order.ordno = ol.ordno
and       order.custno = 5
and       ol.price = 200;

Execution Time: 240 Minutes
```

**The solution:**

```
select    ordno, custno
from      order
where     custno = 5
and       exists
(select    'x'
 from      order_line ol
 where     order.ordno = ol.ordno
 and       ol.price = 200);

Execution Time: 9 Seconds
```

**THE DRIVING TABLE**    In Oracle, the cost-based approach uses various factors in determining which table should be the driving table (the table that drives the query) in a multitable join query. The best thing to remember is that you have control over which table will drive a query through the effective use of the

ORDERED hint. The order of table access can always be forced through the use of the ORDERED hint. The key is to use the ORDERED hint and vary the order of the tables to get the correct order from a performance standpoint. See Chapter 9 for a *very* detailed look at the driving table and the ORDERED hint.

```
select     tabA.col_1, tabB.col2
from       tabA, tabB
where      tabB.col2 = 'ANL';

select     /*+ ORDERED */
           tabA.col_1, tabB.col2
from       tabA, tabB
where      tabB.col2 = 'ANL';
```

In a nested loops join method, tabA will be the driving table in this query.

**JOIN METHODS**   Since the days of Oracle6, the optimizer has used three different ways to join row sources together. These are the NESTED LOOPS join, the SORT-MERGE join, and the CLUSTER join. With Oracle 7.3 the HASH join was introduced, and in Oracle 8.1 the INDEX join was introduced, making for a total of five primary join methods. Each has a unique set of features and limitations. Chapter 9 reviews the complex nature of table joins in detail.

## NESTED LOOPS Joins

In a NESTED LOOPS join, Oracle reads the first row from the first row source and then checks the second row source for matches. All matches are then placed in the result set and Oracle goes on to the next row from the first row source. This continues until all rows in the first row source have been processed. The first row source is often called the *outer* table or *driving* table, while the second row source is called the *inner* table. This is one of the fastest methods of receiving the first records back from a join.

NESTED LOOPS joins are ideal when the driving row source (the records that you're looking for) is small and the joined columns of the inner row source are uniquely indexed or have a highly selective nonunique index. NESTED LOOPS joins have an advantage over other join methods in that they can quickly retrieve the first few rows of the result set without having to wait for the entire result set to be determined.

## SORT-MERGE Joins

In a SORT-MERGE join, Oracle sorts the first row source by its join columns, sorts the second row source by its join columns, and then "merges" the sorted row sources together. As matches are found, they are put into the result set.

SORT-MERGE joins can be effective when the lack of data selectivity or useful indexes render a NESTED LOOPS join inefficient, or when both of the row sources are quite large (greater than 5 percent of the records). However, SORT-MERGE joins can only be used for equijoins (WHERE D.deptno = E.deptno, as opposed to WHERE D.deptno >= E.deptno). Also, SORT-MERGE joins require temporary segments for sorting (if SORT_AREA_SIZE is set too small). This can lead to extra memory utilization and/or extra disk I/O in the temporary tablespace.

## CLUSTER Joins

A CLUSTER join is a special case of the NESTED LOOPS join. If the two row sources being joined are actually tables that are part of a cluster, and if the join is an equijoin between the cluster keys of the two tables, then Oracle can use a CLUSTER join. In this case, Oracle reads each row from the first row source and finds all matches in the second row source by using the CLUSTER index.

CLUSTER joins are extremely efficient, since the joining rows in the two row sources will actually be located in the same physical data block. However, clusters carry certain caveats of their own, and you can't have a CLUSTER join without a cluster. Therefore, CLUSTER joins are not very commonly used.

## HASH Joins (Oracle 7.3+)

In a HASH join, Oracle reads all of the join column values from the second row source, builds a hash table (in memory if HASH_AREA_SIZE is large enough), and then probes the hash table for each of the join column values from the first row source. This is identical to a NESTED LOOPS join, except that first Oracle builds a hash table to facilitate the operation. When using an ORDERED hint, the first table in the FROM clause is the driving table, but only after the second table is loaded in the HASH table. The first table then accesses the hash table for matches. If enough memory is available (HASH_AREA_SIZE for the hash table and DB_BLOCK_BUFFERS for the other table), then the join will be completely processed in memory.

HASH joins can be effective when the lack of a useful index renders NESTED LOOPS joins inefficient. The HASH join might be faster than a SORT-MERGE join in this case because only one row source needs to be sorted, and could possibly be faster than a NESTED LOOPS join because probing a hash table in memory can be faster than traversing a B-tree index.

## INDEX Joins (Oracle8i)

In versions prior to Oracle8i, you would have to access the table unless the index contained all of the information required. In Oracle8i, if a set of indexes exists that collectively contain all of the information required by the query, then the optimizer can choose to generate a sequence of HASH joins between the indexes. Each of the indexes is accessed using a range scan or fast full scan, depending on the conditions available in the WHERE clause. This method is extremely efficient when a table has a large number of columns and you only want to access a limited number of those columns. The more limiting the conditions in the WHERE clause, the faster the execution. In Oracle8i, the optimizer will evaluate this as an option when looking for the optimal path of execution.

You must create indexes on the appropriate columns (those that will satisfy the entire query) to ensure that the optimizer has enabled the INDEX join as an available choice. This usually involves adding indexes on columns that may not be indexed or on columns that previously were not indexed together. Please consult the latest Oracle8i documentation for the latest information on this feature. Oracle8i was not in production at the time of the writing of this chapter.

**TIP**
*To change the way Oracle joins multiple tables, use the USE_MERGE, USE_NL, and USE_HASE hints. See Chapter 9 for detailed information on this complex topic.*

## Sometimes the optimizer "goes to lunch":

- I converted something from rule-based to cost-based and the EXPLAIN PLAN went from 7 lines to 186 lines.

- Then I simply added the ORDERED hint in the query; the result was seven lines and it was light years faster (from 4 hours to 35 seconds).

## Other hints on the driving table:

- The table that returns the fewest number of rows the fastest should be the driving table.

- If there are three or more tables, the driving table should be the intersection table.

**TIP**
*By using the ORDERED hint and varying the order of the tables in the FROM clause of the query, you can effectively change which table drives a query and dramatically increase performance.*

**PARALLEL QUERY OPTION**    Oracle's Parallel Query Option has opened a new avenue for performance enhancements. DBAs can now spread a CPU-intensive report across many processors, taking full advantage of the speed of the box. You can also use the PARALLEL=TRUE with DIRECT=TRUE with SQL*Loader. On the downside, you can also take down a 10-processor box with a single query if you force the use of 10+ processes. The query listed next should give you the general syntax and uses for the PARALLEL hint. Figure 1-10 shows how the query is processed, detailing the processor requirements. Chapter 11 focuses entirely on parallel operations.

```
select    /*+ FULL(cust)  PARALLEL(cust, 4) */
          ename, job
from      cust
where     table_name = 'EMP';

Operation    Processors   Minutes
Index             1         38.4
                 20          3.0
 Scan             1         46.4
                 20          3.1
```

**Version 8 Parallel Query changes:**

■ PARALLEL hints may now be used on indexed searches, partitioned tables, and indexes.

■ PARALLEL hints may be used in a DML statement.

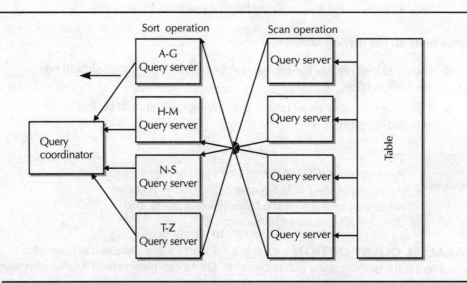

**FIGURE 1-10.** *Using parallel operations could use nine processes for a parallel degree of 4*

**V8 TIP**
*PARALLEL hints can now be used with DML statements and also at a partition level.*

### The NOPARALLEL Hint

If a table is created with a parallel degree set, the table will use that degree for all full table scan queries. However, you may also "turn off" the use of parallel operations in a given query on a table that has been specified to use parallel operations using the NOPARALLEL hint. The NOPARALLEL hint is basically a query with a degree of 1.

```
select    /*+ NOPARALLEL (table) */...
```

```
select    /*+ NOPARALLEL (oli) */ invoice_number, invoice_date
from      order_line_items oli
order by  invoice_date;
```

The NOPARALLEL hint is basically a query with a degree of 1.

**TIP**
*The use of the NOPARALLEL hint will disable parallel operations in a statement that would otherwise utilize parallel processing due to a parallel object definition.*

**ORACLE8 PARTITIONS**   Parallel features allowed us to break a query into multiple pieces so that multiple processes could work on the same query. Partitioning allows us to break large tables into multiple pieces (like minitables). The performance improvements for data warehouses and large table operations using table partitions is staggering!

Tables can now be split into thousands of pieces. Some of the benefits of partitions are listed here:

- Only a subset of the data is queried.
- All of the data *could* be queried.
- Partitions usually provide enhanced performance when accessing large tables.
- Partitioned views were the precursor to partitioned tables.
- Data warehouses can be tuned greatly!
- Table reorganizations can be done on a partition level.

Total Performance Index (TPI)

### Creating a Partitioned Table

The following statement creates a table called emp with columns empno, deptno, and ename. The table has been partitioned into three pieces (p1, p2, and p3) and is segmented based on the value of deptno. For deptnos less than 11, the data is placed in partition p1. For deptnos greater than or equal to 11 but less than 21, the data is placed in partition p2. For all other deptnos greater than or equal to 21, the data is placed in partition p3. Chapter 13 takes a closer look at partitioned tables and indexes.

```
Create table emp (empno number(10) unique,
                  deptno number(5) not null,
                  ename varchar2(30))
partition by range (deptno)
(partition p1 values less than (11) tablespace emp1,
 partition p2 values less than (21) tablespace emp2,
 partition p3 values less than (maxvalue) tablespace emp3);
```

**V8i TIP**
*For large tables, use partitioned tables, and witness potentially staggering performance gains. See Chapter 13 for detailed information.*

# Total Performance Index (TPI)

TUSC invented the Total Performance Index (TPI) to help Oracle DBAs measure their system to other systems, using a quick and simple scoring method. Many systems differ in categories based on their business case, but this system tells you how close or far your system is from others in the industry. There are four performance categories: memory, disk, knowledge (education), and overall system. Chapter 17 will show how you can measure your TPI using several simple queries and detailed information on a particular category. To help identify how your system is progressing, use your TPI to project future growth in the number of users or changes in hardware and software.

# Last Resort—Limit Users by Using Profiles

I created a profile called limited1 and then dragged and dropped the user, SCOTT, into this profile using the Security section of the Enterprise Manager (see Chapter 5 for a detailed look). Figure 1-11 illustrates that the user can be limited by CPU per session, CPU per call, connect time, idle time, concurrent sessions (very helpful for users that like to log on multiple times at different workstations), reads per session (helpful for ad hoc query users), private SGA, and composite limit (a composite of all units in all sections). The query generated (as shown next) to create the profile that is displayed in Figure 1-11 can also be viewed by pressing the View SQL button in the Enterprise Manager (which changes to the Hide SQL button when the SQL is visible).

```
CREATE PROFILE Limited1 LIMIT CPU_PER_SESSION 360 CPU_PER_CALL 60
CONNECT_TIME 60 IDLE_TIME 15 SESSIONS_PER_USER 1
LOGICAL_READS_PER_SESSION 5000 LOGICAL_READS_PER_CALL 5000
PRIVATE_SGA 256 K COMPOSITE_LIMIT 1000000;
```

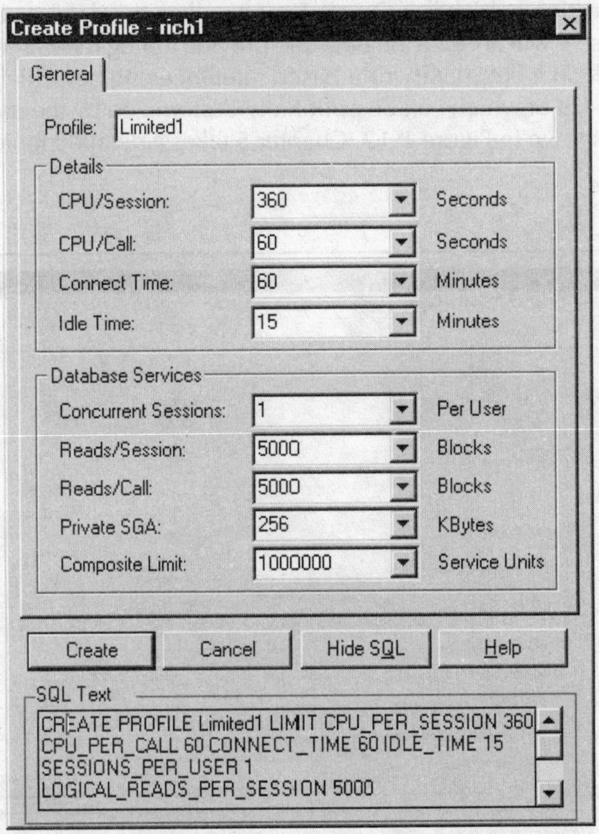

**Limit Users by Using Profiles**

**FIGURE 1-11.** *Security Manager—adding a new profile*

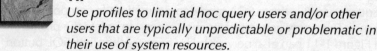

**TIP**
*Use profiles to limit ad hoc query users and/or other users that are typically unpredictable or problematic in their use of system resources.*

# Tuning Everything—Oracle Expert

Within Oracle's Enterprise Manager is a utility called the Oracle Expert (version 1.6 is used in the example covered here), which focuses on tuning from a more global perspective. Oracle Expert automates overall database tuning in three areas: The top 25 instance parameters, indexes (add, drop, modify, rebuild) and structures (sizing, placement, OFA compliance). The DBA selects the scope for the tuning session, then sets up the data collection (which has Oracle Expert collect the data) and starts the Oracle Expert utility so it will analyze the data and provide tuning recommendations. Oracle Expert is built on a proprietary rule-based inference engine, which has over 1,000 tuning rules—1/3 of which can be optionally customized by the user. A screen shot of this utility is shown in Figure 1-12. Chapter 5 takes a detailed look at the utility.

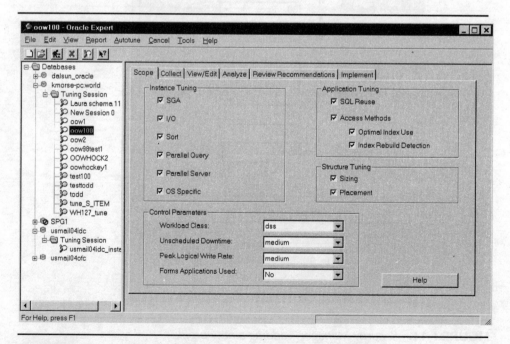

**FIGURE 1-12.** *Performance Pack Oracle Expert tuning session*

**TIP**
*Oracle Expert looks at the entire database system for areas requiring improvement.*

# Tuning Using Simple Mathematical Techniques

This section (which is covered in detail in Chapter 9) discusses some simple but effective mathematical techniques you can use to significantly improve the performance of some Oracle SQL-based systems. These techniques can leverage the effectiveness of Oracle performance diagnostic tools and uncover hidden performance problems that can be overlooked by other methods. It also makes it easier to make performance predictions at higher loads. This section was provided by Joe A. Holmes. I am extremely grateful for his contribution, as I believe it ties all of tuning together.

The methodology, called Simple Mathematical Techniques, involves isolating and testing the SQL process in question under ideal conditions, graphing the results of rows processed versus time, deriving equations using simple methods (without regression), predicting performance, and interpreting and applying performance patterns directly to tuning SQL code.

## Simple Quadratic Equation Determination

The following is a simple three-point method for determining a quadratic best performance equation:

$$y = a0 + a1x + a2x2$$

This equation can be calculated for any query, and using the techniques detailed in Chapter 9, you can retrieve one of several possible graphs for a given query. Consider some of the graphs in Figure 1-13 and the problems that are detailed in the following table:

| Pattern in Figure 1-13 | Possible Problem | Possible Solution |
| --- | --- | --- |
| A | Missing index on a query SELECTing values | Create an index. Fix a suppressed index. |
| A | Overindexed table suffering during an INSERT | Delete some of the indexes or index fewer columns (or smaller columns) for the current indexes. |
| B | No problem | Don't touch it! |
| C | Missing index on a query SELECTing values | Create an index. Fix a suppressed index. |

*(side margin)* Tuning Everything—Oracle Expert

| Pattern in Figure 1-13 | Possible Problem | Possible Solution |
|---|---|---|
| C | Overindexed table suffering during an INSERT | Delete some of the indexes or index fewer columns (or smaller columns) for the current indexes. |
| D | Doing a FULL table scan or using the ALL_ROWS hint when you shouldn't be | Try to do an indexed search. Try using the FIRST_ROWS hint to force the use of indexes. |
| E | The query was fine until some other limitation (such as disk I/O or memory) was encountered | You need to find which ceiling you hit to cause this problem. Increasing the SGA may solve the problem, but this could be many things. |

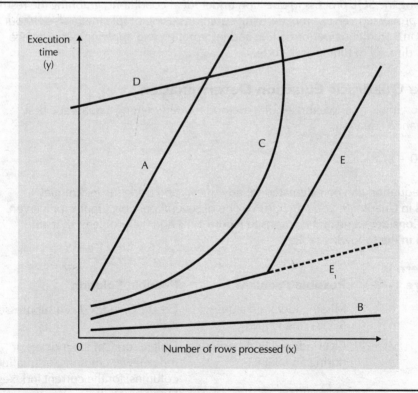

**FIGURE 1-13.** *The number of rows processed in a relative execution time*

### Pattern Interpretation

Graphical performance patterns provide clues to underlying SQL problems and solutions. Our ultimate goal in using these methods is to convert a steep linear or quadratic best performance line to one that is both shallow and linear by optimizing the SQL process. This may involve experiments with indexes, temp tables, optimizer hint commands, or other methods of Oracle SQL performance tuning.

With pattern interpretation, it is important to do your own application-specific SQL experiments to develop an expertise at using these methods. The following are more specific interpretations based on my personal experience that provide a basic idea of how to apply what is observed directly to tuning SQL code. Provided the scale is correct, pattern interpretation will often provide a more accurate picture of what is actually happening to a process, and may support or even contradict what a diagnostic tool may tell you.

An upward sloping (concave) quadratic curve almost always indicates a problem with the process because, as more rows are added, the time to process each additional row increases. If the sloping is very small, the equation may be more linear. However, a very slight bowing may be an indicator of something more insidious under much higher volumes.

In rare cases a quadratic curve might appear downward sloping (convex), indicating a process where as more rows are added, the time to process each additional one decreases (i.e., economies of scale). This is desirable, and may occur at a threshold where a full table scan is more efficient than using an index.

> **TIP**
> *If you want an Oracle symphony as great as Beethoven's, you must learn and know how to apply mathematical techniques to your tuning efforts. You don't have to learn everything that you learned in college calculus; simply apply the simple equations in this chapter to tie everything in this book together. Thank you Joe Holmes for doing the math for us (detailed with examples in Chapter 9)!*

## Niemiec's Seven Rules of Tuning

**Rule 1:** The level of tuning achieved can be directly attributable to the number of straight hours that you can work and how much junk food is available.

**Rule 2:** The level of tuning achieved is tremendously increased if user input is solicited and those users are *not* of the type that try to be politically correct (i.e., you need users that are not afraid to say that this report runs horribly!).

**Rule 3:** The level of tuning achieved can be directly attributable to the security access to the system that the tuning professional has.

**Rule 4**: The level of tuning achieved is severely hampered by the level of theoretical knowledge required by the tuning professional.

**Rule 5**: The level of tuning achieved is severely hampered by the amount of time that a manager is present.

**Rule 6**: The level of tuning achieved is directly related to the number of keyboards, terminals, monitors, and PCs that are within the reach of the tuning professional.

**Rule 7**: The usual attributes of a good tuning professional (outside of actual performance) can usually be spotted by the person who: calculates the shortest line at McDonalds; calculates the most efficient method for getting each task done yet still leaves at 1 A.M.; has coupons for every pizza place that stays open 24 hours at his or her desk; tends to use twice as much coffee grounds when making the coffee or uses caffeine-enhanced water when making the coffee; asks if you would like to go to lunch when it is time for dinner; answers e-mail with a single or half sentence (never a paragraph); has an occasional triple-digit weekly hours report; has no time to be political; and, finally, when they have one hour left to go with a problem, you can guarantee that you better multiply by at least four.

## Tips Review

- Tuning the memory allocated to Oracle means setting the init.ora parameters correctly. The crucial parameters are DB_BLOCK_BUFFERS, SHARED_POOL_SIZE, and SORT_AREA_SIZE. Set any of these three parameters too low or too high, and your system will run poorly!

- The allowable DB_BLOCK_SIZE has increased in Oracle8 to 32K. Remember that changing the block size can only be accomplished by rebuilding the database.

- The buffer hit ratio should be 95 percent or higher. This ratio can be found by querying the V$SYSSTAT view. However, increasing the buffer hit ratio from 95 percent to 99 percent can yield performance gains of over 400 percent.

- Increasing the DB_FILE_MULTIBLOCK_READ_COUNT will allow more block reads in a single I/O, giving a benefit similar to a larger block size.

- Retrieving information from memory is over 10,000 times (depending on the memory you have) faster than retrieving it from disk, so make sure that the SGA is large enough.

■ The additional buffer pools (BUFFER_POOL_KEEP and BUFFER_POOL_RECYCLE) available in Oracle8 are initially set to zero. The BUFFER_POOL_KEEP and BUFFER_POOL_RECYCLE are a subset of the DB_BLOCK_BUFFERS. When you set the BUFFER_POOL_KEEP and BUFFER_POOL_RECYCLE parameters, you are taking blocks of memory from the DB_BLOCK_BUFFERS and allocating to the other two pools. See Chapter 13 for additional details on this topic.

■ Measure hit ratios for the dictionary cache section of the Shared Pool with V$ROWCACHE. A hit ratio of over 95 percent should be achieved. Increasing the init.ora parameter SHARED_POOL_SIZE will usually increase your dictionary hit ratio. However, when the database is initially started, hit ratios will be around 85 percent.

■ Measure hit ratios for the library cache section of the Shared Pool with V$LIBRARYCACHE. A hit ratio of over 95 percent should be achieved. Increasing the init.ora parameter SHARED_POOL_SIZE will usually increase your library cache hit ratio. However, when the database is initially started, hit ratios will be around 85 percent.

■ Don't flush the Shared Pool unless you are getting errors. Flushing the Shared Pool pushes everything out of memory, which will cause degradation to all users—who then must reread everything back in. A low amount of free memory is not necessarily the precursor to an error.

■ An ORA-4031 is usually caused when the Shared Pool gets fragmented into smaller pieces over the course of a day and a request for a large piece of memory is issued that cannot be filled.

■ The SORT_AREA_SIZE parameter of the init.ora is specified in bytes and is on a per-user process basis, and only allocated when a specific user needs it. Be careful or you will run out of operating system memory if it is set too high!

■ The SORT_AREA_RETAINED_SIZE should be set as large as the value of the SORT_AREA_SIZE. The SORT_AREA_RETAINED_SIZE is the size that the SORT_AREA_SIZE will be reduced to when the sort is complete.

■ Changing init.ora parameters with an ALTER SESSION is a powerful feature for both developers and DBAs. Consequently, a user with the ALTER SESSION privilege is capable of irresponsibly allocating 100M+ for the SORT_AREA_SIZE for a given session if not restricted.

■ If free buffers are not available (none with state=0) within the first 30 minutes of business hours, you probably need to set DB_BLOCK_BUFFERS higher.

**Tips Review**

- Pin PL/SQL objects into memory immediately upon starting the database to avoid insufficient memory errors later in the day. To accomplish this, use the DBMS_SHARED_POOL.KEEP procedure for PL/SQL object statements. Ensure that the STANDARD procedure is pinned soon after startup since it is so large.

- Query v$filestat and v$dbfile to see how effectively data files have been balanced.

- To view the sql_text that is longer than the 2,000 characters in the V$SQLAREA view, join the V$SQLTEXT view to the V$SQLAREA view. Accessing the V$SQLAREA view will point you to the worst queries on your system. THE QUERY TO V$SQLAREA IS THE MOST IMPORTANT QUERY IN TUNING ORACLE! In Oracle8, partitioned tables are also displayed in the V$SQLAREA.

- A TRACEd query with a large number of physical reads usually indicates a missing index. The "disk" column indicates the physical reads (usually where an index is not used) and the "query" added to the "current" columns indicates the memory reads (usually reads where an index is being used).

- Use EXPLAIN PLAN instead of TRACE so that you don't have to wait for the query to run. EXPLAIN PLAN will show the path of a query without actually running the query. Use TRACE only for multiquery batch jobs to find out which of the many queries in the batch job are slow.

- The SQL Analyze Comparison feature allows a side-by-side comparison of SQL statements to help you find the best execution path. By using these "what if" scenarios, you can find the best solution before actually executing the query.

- There is no OPTIMIZER_MODE=COST setting. The setting for cost-based optimization is OPTIMIZER_MODE=CHOOSE. Once the OPTIMIZER_MODE is set to CHOOSE, the tables still need to be analyzed for cost-based optimization to be in effect.

- When a query retrieves less than 4-5 percent of the rows from a table, we generally want to use an index (the 95/5 Rule).

- When using an alias for a table in the statement, the alias (*not* the table) needs to appear in the hint or the hint will be ignored.

- If the syntax for a hint is incorrect, the hint will be ignored and an error message will not be given.

- Query DBA_INDEXES and DBA_IND_COLUMNS to retrieve a list of the indexes on a given table. Use USER_INDEXES and USER_IND_COLUMNS to retrieve information for only your schema.

- The INDEX_FFS (available in Oracle8) will process only the index and will not access the table. All columns that are used and retrieved by the query must be contained in the index.

- Prior to Oracle8i, if a column is modified in any way in the WHERE clause, the index on the column will not be used (it will be internally suppressed).

- Comparing mismatched data types could cause an internal index suppression that is difficult to track down. Oracle will often place a function on the column that fixes the mismatch but suppresses the index.

- In Oracle8i, function-based indexes can lead to dramatic performance gains when used to create indexes on functions often used on selective columns. See Chapter 13 for additional Oracle8i performance enhancements.

- Strongly consider using hints to override the optimizer when using the "<" and ">" when the distribution of data is not linear between the high and low values of a column. Histograms may also be employed.

- To change the method that Oracle uses to join multiple tables, use the USE_MERGE, USE_NL, and USE_HASE hints. See Chapter 9 for detailed information on this very complex topic.

- In Oracle8, PARALLEL hints can now be used with DMLs and also at a partition level.

- For large tables, use partitioned tables, and witness potentially staggering performance gains.

- Use profiles to limit ad hoc query users and/or other users that are typically unpredictable or problematic in their use of system resources.

- Keep plenty of junk food and an open schedule when you are ready to seriously tune a system. And read the entire book to create an Oracle symphony that is a world-class performance.

# References

*Performance Tuning; Now YOU are the Expert*, Rich Niemiec, TUSC, 1990-1999

Get the most for your Money: Utilize the V$ Tables, Joseph C. Trezzo, TUSC

*Tuning an Oracle Database*, Sue Jang, Oracle Corporation

Index Suppression, Joe Trezzo, TUSC, 1989

Database Administration, Version 7 Conversion Courses, TUSC, 1991-1994

Version 6 & 7 DBA, Migration and Performance Tuning Guides, Oracle Corporation

What is a Client/Server and Implementing it, Mir W. Ali, First National Bank of Chicago

*Version 7 SQL Language Manual*, Oracle Corporation

TUSC, "Downsizing...Where to start Article," Richard J. Niemiec

TUSC, "Database Planning and Sizing," Richard J. Niemiec

TUSC, "Backup and Recover Planning," Richard J. Niemiec

TUSC, "Oracle Installation, Migration and Tuning," Richard J. Niemiec

*IOUG Proceedings*, Multiple Downsizing and Distributed Database Articles

*MOUG Magazine*, Multiple Database Articles

*Application Developer's Guide*, Oracle Corporation

*IOUG Proceedings*, Walter Lindsay, EcoSystems Software, 1993

*IOUG Proceedings*, Gita Kulandaiswamy, Oracle Corporation, 1993

*Oracle7 Internals*, Oracle Corp., Craig A. Shallahamer

Oracle 7.1, *Summary of New Features*, Oracle Corp., Gary Dodge

Oracle7 release 7.1, *Feature Overview*, Oracle Corp.

"Oracle 7.1 Release Features Parallel Everything," *Integrator,* Summer 1994

*Oracle8 Tuning Guide*, Oracle Corp.

*Oracle8 System Admin Guide*, Oracle Corp.

"Tuning Oracle for Batch and On-Line Processing," Eyal Aronoff, *Select Magazine*

Special thanks to Brad Brown, Joe Trezzo, Burk Sherva, Jake Van der Vort, Dave Kaufman, Greg Pucka, Curt Loomis, and Mike Henderson for contributions to this chapter.

Please report errors to TUSC. Neither TUSC nor the author warrant that this document is error-free.

References

# TIPS
# &
# TECHNIQUES

# CHAPTER
## 2

Basic Index Principles
(Beginner Developer
and Beginner DBA)

T8his chapter is neither for the experts nor for those looking for fast answers. This is a chapter (maybe the only one) that looks at basic indexing theory. The toughest part of being a beginner is finding information that will fill in the most basic gaps and visualization of Oracle's indexing capabilities. This chapter looks to serve that purpose. While there is a considerable amount of material published at the intermediate and advanced level, the beginner's information is usually scarce, yet highly desirable. Oracle offers a variety of indexing options. Knowing which option to use in a given situation can be crucial to an application's performance. A wrong choice may cause performance to come to a grinding halt or cause processes to be terminated because of deadlock situations. Making the correct choice can make you an instant hero, by taking processes that previously took hours or even days to run and providing the resources to finish these processes in minutes. This chapter will discuss each of the indexing options and point out the benefits and limitations of each. Tips covered in this chapter include the following:

- Basic index concepts
- Finding which tables are indexed and which have concatenated indexes
- How concatenated indexes are used
- Oracle ROWID structure in versions 7 and 8
- Functions causing index suppression
- How to avoid comparing unmatched data types causing index suppression
- Cluster factors as an index strategy
- Using the INDEX_STATS view
- The binary height of an index
- About histograms
- Fast full scans
- Explanation of B-tree indexes
- When to use bitmap indexes
- When to use HASHing
- When to use the index-ordered table
- Local and global partitioned indexes

# Basic Index Concepts

When accessing data from tables, Oracle has two options: to read every row in the table (also referred to as a full table scan), or to access rows by searching an index ROWID. When accessing less than 5 percent of the rows of a table, you would want to use an index. If an index doesn't exist, you generally want to create one. Indexes will generally increase performance for SELECT, UPDATE, and DELETE statements (when few rows are accessed) and decrease performance for INSERT statements (since inserts to both the table and index must be performed). However, a DELETE statement deleting half of a table will also need to delete half of the rows for the index (very costly for this specific situation).

To get a listing of all of the indexes on a table, query the DBA_INDEXES view as shown in the following query. Also, note that you can retrieve the indexes for your schema only by accessing USER_INDEXES. The output from this query illustrates the indexes on the emp table.

```
select      table_name, index_name
from        dba_indexes
where       table_name = 'EMP';

table name         index name
emp                emp_idx1
emp                emp_idx2
```

To get the specific columns that are indexed for a given table, access the DBA_IND_COLUMNS view. This query is displayed next. Also note that you can retrieve the columns that are indexed for only your schema by accessing USER_IND_COLUMNS.

```
select      table_name, index_name, column_name, column_position
from        dba_ind_columns
order       by table_name, index_name, column_position;

table name         index name      column name      column position
emp                emp_idx1        empid            1
emp                emp_idx1        ename            2
emp                emp_idx1        deptno           3
emp                emp_idx2        salary           1
```

This emp table has two indexes. The first, emp_idx1, is a concatenated index that indexes the empid, ename, and deptno columns. The second, emp_idx2, is indexing the salary column only.

**TIP**
*Query DBA_INDEXES and DBA_IND_COLUMNS to retrieve a list of the indexes on a given table. Use USER_INDEXES and USER_IND_COLUMNS to retrieve information for only your schema.*

# Concatenated Indexes

When a single index has multiple columns that are indexed, it is called a concatenated or composite index. An index may only use the trailing column(s) of a concatenated index if it also uses the leading column(s). Consider the next example where the emp table has a concatenated index on empid, ename, and deptno. Note that empid is the first part, ename is the second part, and deptno is the third part. You cannot use ename without using empid, and you cannot use deptno without using both empid and ename.

```
create index emp_idx1 on emp(empid, ename, deptno);
select     job, empid
from       emp
where      ename = 'RICH';
```

The index *is not used* since empid is not used in the WHERE clause.

```
select     job, empid
from       emp
where      deptno = 30;
```

The index *is not used* since empid is not used in the WHERE clause.

```
select     job, empid
from       emp
where      empid = 7777;
```

A *part* of the index *is used*. The leading part, empid, is in the WHERE clause.

```
select     job, empid
from       emp
where      empid = 7777
and        ename = 'RICH';
```

A *part* of the index *is used*. The leading two parts are in the WHERE clause.

```
select     job, empid
from       emp
```

```
where        empid = 7777
and          ename = 'RICH'
and          deptno = 30;
```

The *full* index *is used*. All parts of the index are used in the WHERE clause.

**TIP**
*A concatenated index will only be used if the leading column(s) of the index is being used.*

# The Oracle ROWID Structure in Versions 7 and 8

Indexes provide Oracle with the ability to access a single row of data by supplying the ROWID of the individual row. The ROWID is a road map directly to the location of the individual row. The following illustration is an explanation of the ROWID structure in Oracle7 and Oracle8:

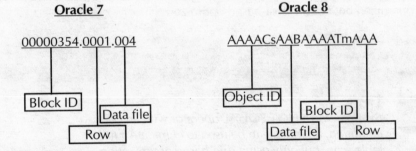

**TIP**
*Be careful when hard-coding Oracle's ROWID into specific code. The ROWID structure changed from Oracle7 to Oracle8, and may change again in future releases. I recommend against ever hard-coding a ROWID.*

Although performance varies depending on the applications and the data, the hardware recommendation states if the statement will affect 5 percent or less of the data, indexes will provide better performance. With some of the new options available in Oracle8—like partitioning, parallel DML, improvements in parallel query, and larger I/O using DB_FILE_MULTIBLOCK_READ_COUNT—the balance point between full table scans and index lookups is changing.

Oracle ROWID Structure

# Suppressing Indexes

Inadvertently suppressing indexes is one of the most common mistakes of an inexperienced developer. There are many traps within SQL that will cause indexes not to be used. Some of the most common problems will be discussed in the following sections.

## Using the NOT EQUAL Operators '< >', '!='

Indexes can only be used to find data that exists within a table. Whenever the NOT EQUAL operators are used in the WHERE clause, indexes on the columns being referenced cannot be used.

The following statement would cause a full table scan (which is usually desired since most records would *usually* be retrieved) to be performed even with the index on the cust_rating column:

```
select      cust_id, cust_name
from        customers
where       cust_rating <> 'aa';
```

Changing the statement to the following would now use an index with the rule-based optimizer, but not the cost-based optimizer:

```
select      cust_id, cust_name
from        customers
where       cust_rating < 'aa' or cust_rating > 'aa';
```

**TIP**
*By replacing a NOT EQUAL operator with an OR condition, an index can be used to eliminate a full table scan, but only using rule-based optimization. Ensure that the result set retrieved is still less than 5 percent of the records for optimal performance. Future revisions may allow the use of the index in these circumstances.*

## Using 'IS NULL' or 'IS NOT NULL'

By using 'IS NULL' or 'IS NOT NULL', index usage will also be suppressed since the value of NULL is undefined. There is not a value in the database that will equal a NULL value; not even NULL equals a NULL. The debate over NULL values in the databases has gone on for many years. There are those who are strongly opposed to their use, and those who believe in the need to allow NULL values. The NULL values pose several difficulties for SQL statements. Indexed columns that have rows containing a NULL value will not have an entry in the index. If the index is a concatenation of several columns, there will be an entry in the index but no value is used. Version 7.3 of Oracle made a change concerning NULL—the '' is no longer considered a NULL; it is now considered an empty string.

The following statement would cause a full table scan to be performed, even though the deptno column is indexed:

```
select      empl_id, first_name, last_name
from        employee
where       deptno is null;
```

To disallow NULL values for all three of the columns, use NOT NULL when creating the table, as described here:

```
create table employee
(empl_id number(8) not null, first_name varchar2(20) not null,
 last_name varchar2(20) not null, deptno number(4) not null);
```

Note that an error will be returned if the insert of a NULL value is attempted.

**TIP**
*Creating a table specifying NOT NULL for a column
will cause NULL values to be disallowed and eliminate
the performance problems associated with using
NULL values.*

The following table creation statement provides a default value for the deptno column. When the column is not specified, the default value will be used.

```
create table employee
(empl_id number(8) not null, first_name varchar2(20) not null,
 last_name varchar2(20) not null, deptno number(4) default 10));

insert into employee(empl_id, first_name, last_name)
values (8100, 'REGINA', 'NIEMIEC');

1 row created.
```

```
select      *
from        employee;
```

| empl id | first name | last name | deptno |
|---------|-----------|-----------|--------|
| 8100    | REGINA    | NIEMIEC   | 10     |

**Suppressing Indexes**

```
insert into employee
values (8200, 'RICH', 'NIEMIEC', NULL);

1 row created.
```

```
select      *
from        employee;

empl_id     first_name    last_name     deptno
8100        REGINA        NIEMIEC       10
8100        RICH          NIEMIEC
```

**TIP**

*NULL values often cause indexes to be suppressed. Creating a table and specifying DEFAULT for an unspecified column and help avoid a potential performance issue.*

## Using Functions

By using functions on indexed columns in the WHERE clause of a SQL statement, it will cause the optimizers to bypass indexes. Some of the most common functions are TRUNC, SUBSTR, TO_DATE, TO_CHAR, and INSTR. All of these functions will cause the value of the column to be altered. Therefore, the indexes and the columns being referenced will not be used.

The following statement would cause a full table scan to be performed, even though there is an index on the hire_date column:

```
select      empl_id, first_name, last_name
from        employee
where       trunc(hire_date) = '05-JUL-1998';
```

Changing the statement to the following would allow for an index lookup:

```
select      empl_id, first_name, last_name
from        employee
where       hire_date between '05-JUL-1998',
            and '05-JUL-1998' + .99999;
```

**TIP**

*By altering the values being compared to the column, and not the columns themselves, the indexes become available. This is used to eliminate full table scans.*

**V8 TIP**
*Functional indexes are now available; see Chapter 13*
*for additional information.*

## Comparing Mismatched Data Types

One ot the more difficult performance issues to find is when there is a comparison of the wrong data types. Oracle does not complain about the types being incompatible—quite the opposite. Oracle implicitly converts the data in the VARCHAR2 column to match the numeric data type that it is being compared to. nsider the following example where account_number is a VARCHAR2.

The following statement would cause a full table scan to be performed:

```
select     bank_name, address, city, state, zip
from       banks
where      account_number = 990354;
```

Oracle internally changes the WHERE clause to be *to_number(account_number)=990354*, which suppresses the index. An EXPLAIN PLAN of this query only shows that the table was accessed using a "FULL SCAN" (usually to the bewilderment of the coder). To some DBAs and developers, this would appear to be a rare situation, but in many systems numeric values are zero-padded and specified as VARCHAR2. The previous statement should be rewritten as follows to use the index on the account number by correctly using the single quote marks for the field:

```
select     bank_name, address, city, state, zip
from       banks
where      account_number = '000990354';
```

**TIP**
*Comparing mismatched data types can cause Oracle to internally suppress an index. Even an EXPLAIN PLAN on the query will not lead you to why a full table scan is being performed. Only the knowledge of your data types can help you solve this problem. In many instances, Oracle does not allow mismatched data types.*

## Selectivity

Oracle offers several methods to determine the value of using an index, which depends upon both the query and the data. One of the first ways is to determine the number of unique or distinct keys in the index. This can be accomplished by analyzing the table or the index. Using the 'USER_INDEXES' view, there is a column called distinct_keys. Comparing the number of distinct keys to the number of rows in the table, you can determine the selectivity of the index. The greater the selectivity, the better the index would be for returning small amounts of data.

**TIP**
*The selectivity of an index is what helps the cost-based optimizer determine an execution path. The more selective, the fewer the number of rows that will be returned. You can improve the selectivity by creating concatenated/composite indexes, but if the additional columns added to the index do not improve the selectivity greatly, then the cost of the additional columns may outweigh the gain.*

## The Clustering Factor

The clustering_factor column is located in the USER_INDEXES view. This column gives an indication as to how organized the data is compared to the indexed columns. If the value of the clustering_factor column is close to the number of leaf blocks in the index, the data is well ordered in the table. If the value is close to the number of rows in the table, the data in the table is not well ordered.

For example, say the customer_id for the customers table was generated from a sequence generator and the customer_id was the primary key on the table. The index on customer_id would have a very low clustering factor. As the customers are added to the database, they are stored sequentially in the table the same way the sequence numbers are issued from the sequence generator. However, an index on the customer_name column would have a very high clustering factor because the arrangement of the customer names is random throughout the table.

The clustering factor can have an impact on SQL statements that perform range scans. With a low clustering factor, the number of blocks needed to satisfy the query is reduced. This increases the possibility that the data blocks would already be in memory. A high clustering factor increases the number of data blocks required to satisfy the query.

**TIP**
*The clustering of data within the table can be used to improve the performance of statements that perform range scan type operations. By determining how the column is being used in the statements, indexing these column(s) may be a great benefit.*

## The Binary Height

The binary height of an index plays a major role in the amount of I/O that needs to be performed to return the ROWID to the user process. Each level in the binary height adds an extra block that needs to be read, and because the blocks are not being read sequentially, they each require a separate I/O operation. In the following example, an index with a binary height of three returning one row to the user would require four blocks to be read, three from the index and one from the table. As the binary height of an index increases, so will the amount of I/O required retrieving the data.

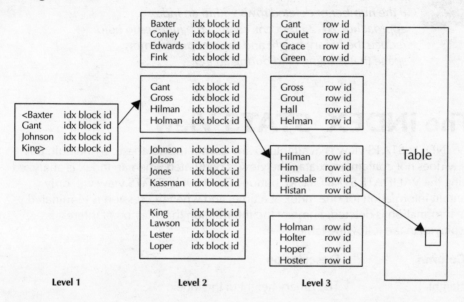

| Level 1 | Level 2 | Level 3 |

Retrieving blevel from the DBA_INDEXES view is done using the following code:

```
analyze index emp_idx1 compute statistics;

Index analyzed.

select      blevel, index_name
from        dba_indexes
where       index_name = 'EMP_IDX1';

blevel      index name
1           emp_idx1
```

**TIP**
*Analyzing the index or the table will provide the binary height of the index. Use the blevel column in the USER_INDEXES view to check the binary height of the indexes.*

The Binary Height

The binary height increases mainly due to the size of the table and the fact that the range of values in the indexed columns is very narrow. Having a large number of deleted rows in the index can also cause the height to increase. Rebuilding the index may help to decrease the height.

**TIP**
*If the number of deleted rows within an index approaches 20–25 percent, rebuild the indexes to help reduce the binary height and the amount of empty space that is being read during an I/O.*

# The INDEX_STATS View

The INDEX_STATS view is available to any user in the database. By default, this view does not contain any data. The view is populated when an index is analyzed using the VALIDATE STRUCTURE option. The INDEX_STATS view will only contain information for one index at a time, and when the session is terminated, the information is deleted. Some of the information that may be of interest is displayed in the following table:

| Column | Description |
| --- | --- |
| Height | The binary height of the index. |
| Blocks | The number of database blocks that have been allocated to the index. |
| if_rows | The number of values in the index. If the column(s) is/are NOT NULL, this will be the number of rows in the table. |
| br_rows | The number of branch rows in the index. Branch rows contain a block ID that points to the leaf blocks. |
| del_if_rows | The number of deleted entries in the index. When rows are deleted within an index, the space is not reused unless a key with the same value is inserted into the table again. |
| distinct_keys | The number of distinct values within the index. |
| most_repeated_key | The number of times the most repeated key is repeated in the index. Provides information on how skewed the data may be. |

| Column | Description |
|---|---|
| btree_space | The amount of space within the index that has been allocated to the binary tree. |
| used_space | The amount of space within the binary tree that has been used by entries in the index. |
| rows_per_key | The average number of rows per key. |
| blk_gets_per_access | The expected number of blocks that will need to be accessed from the index and the table per row. |

Queries to populate and check the INDEX_STATS view:

```
analyze index emp_idx1 validate structure;
select    name, height, blocks, distinct_keys
from      index_stats
where     name = 'EMP_IDX1';

NAME        HEIGHT      BLOCKS      DISTINCT KEYS
emp_idx1    2           5           302
```

**TIP**
*Using the information provided by the INDEX_STATS view from the VALIDATE STRUCTURE option of the ANALYZE command, it is possible to determine where the data is skewed, the expected number of blocks that will need to be read per row, and the selectivity of the index.*

# Using Histograms (Oracle 7.3+)

The use of histograms is not limited to indexes. Any column of a table can have a histogram built on it. Building the histograms on the indexed columns assists Oracle to determine the usefulness of an index in particular situations due to the data being skewed.

The main reason for producing histograms is if the data in a table is heavily skewed, meaning that one or two values make up a large percentage of a table. The creation of a histogram will let the cost-based optimizer know when using the index is appropriate, or when 80 percent of the table is going to be returned due to the value in the WHERE clause.

When creating histograms, a size is specified. This size relates to the number of buckets for the histogram. Each bucket will contain information about the value of the column(s) and the number of rows. For example, say there is a table containing information about orders, and each order has a company code associated with it. If one company is responsible for 80 percent of the orders, the histogram may appear as follows:

```
analyze table company compute statistics for columns
    company_code size 10;

Table analyzed.
```

This query will create a 10-bucket histogram on the company table. The values for the company_code column will be divided into the 10 buckets as displayed next. This example shows a large number (80 percent) of the company_code = 1430.

Width Balanced

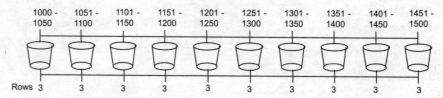

Create a histogram on the company_code field with a size of 10. This would create 10 buckets to hold the values of the company_code column. Each bucket would contain 10 percent of the rows in the table. In the example below, 80 percent of the buckets contain the value 1430. This disparity in distribution would cause the cost-based optimizer to select a different execution plan based on the values used in the WHERE clause.

Height Balanced

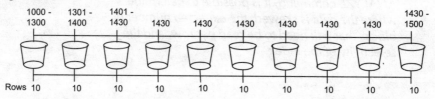

Oracle's histograms are height-balanced as opposed to width-balanced. Consequently, all of the buckets in the histogram contain the same number of rows. The starting and ending points for a bucket are determined by the number of rows containing those values. The width-balanced histogram would specify the range values for each bucket and then count the number of rows within that range, not an ideal option. Note that in the previous example, if the table contained 100 rows and the value of the company_code columns contained the values from 1000–1500, the histograms would appear as follows:

Height Balanced

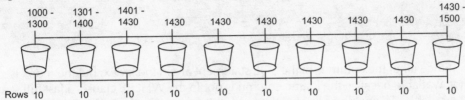

| 1000 - 1300 | 1301 - 1400 | 1401 - 1430 | 1430 | 1430 | 1430 | 1430 | 1430 | 1430 | 1430 - 1500 |
|---|---|---|---|---|---|---|---|---|---|
| Rows 10 | 10 | 10 | 10 | 10 | 10 | 10 | 10 | 10 | 10 |

Width Balanced

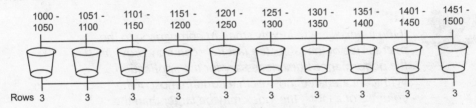

| 1000 - 1050 | 1051 - 1100 | 1101 - 1150 | 1151 - 1200 | 1201 - 1250 | 1251 - 1300 | 1301 - 1350 | 1351 - 1400 | 1401 - 1450 | 1451 - 1500 |
|---|---|---|---|---|---|---|---|---|---|
| Rows 3 | 3 | 3 | 3 | 3 | 3 | 3 | 3 | 3 | 3 |

Note that Oracle uses only height-balanced histograms.

**TIP**
*If the data in a table is skewed, histograms will provide the cost-based optimizer a balanced picture of the distribution (by balancing it into buckets). Using the histograms on columns that are not skewed will not provide an increase in performance.*

# Fast Full Scans

Fast full scans are an option that became available with the release of version 7.3. This option allows Oracle to perform a full table scan operation on an index. The fast full scan reads all of the leaf blocks in a B-tree index. The index is being read sequentially, so multiple blocks can be read at once. The DB_FILE_MULTIBLOCK_READ_COUNT parameter in the initialization file controls the number of blocks that can be read simultaneously.

Fast Full Scans

For the fast full scan to be available, all of the columns in the query for the table must be in the index with the leading edge of the index not part of the WHERE condition. In the following example, an employee table is being used:

```
Create Index Emp_N_2 On Employee (fname, Lname, hire_date);
select      fname, lname
from        employee
where       hire_date > to_date('01-AUG-1998', 'DD-MON-YYYY');
```

Since all of the columns in the SQL statement are in the index, but the index is not available because the fname column is not in the WHERE clause, a fast full scan is available. To enable or disable the fast full scan, modify the V733_PLANS_ ENABLED (obsolete in Oracle8) parameter in the database initialization file.

**TIP**
*If the indexes are relatively small in comparison to the overall size of the table, the fast full scan may provide the performance burst necessary for the application. With concatenated indexes that contain most of the columns of a table, the index may be larger than the actual table and the fast full scan could cause a degradation in performance.*

## Types of Indexes
The following is a list of indexes discussed in this section:

- B-tree
- Bitmap
- HASH
- Index-ordered table
- Local and global partitioned

# B-tree Indexes
B-tree indexes are the general-purpose indexes in Oracle. They are the default index types created when creating indexes. B-tree indexes can be single-column (simple) indexes or composite/concatenated (multi-column) indexes. In Oracle7, the

maximum number of columns in a composite index is 16; in Oracle8, the number of columns increases to 32.

In the following example, a B-tree index is located on the last_name column of the employee table. This index has a binary height of three; consequently, Oracle must go through two branch blocks to get to the leaf block containing the ROWID. Within each branch block, there are branch rows containing the block ID of the next block ID within the chain.

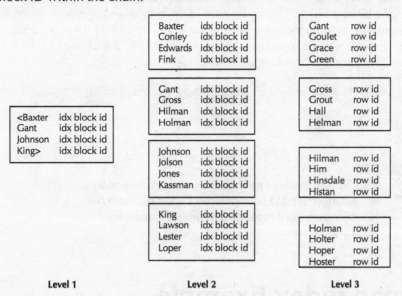

| | Level 1 | | Level 2 | | Level 3 |

The leaf block contains the index values, the ROWID, and the block ID for the branch block. Oracle then has the ability to transverse the binary tree in both directions. B-tree indexes contain the ROWIDs for every row in the table that has a value in the indexed column. Oracle does not index rows that contain NULL values in the indexed column. If the index is a concatenation of multiple columns and one of the columns contains a NULL value, the row will be in the index column containing the NULL value and will be left empty.

**TIP**
*The values of the indexed columns are stored in an index. For this reason, you can build concatenated/ composite indexes that can be used to satisfy a query without accessing the table. This eliminates the need to go to the table to retrieve the data, reducing I/O.*

B-tree Indexes

# Bitmap Indexes (Oracle 7.3+)

Bitmap indexes were introduced with the release of version 7.3. This type of index is ideal for decision support systems (DSS) and data warehouses. They provide fast access of very large tables using low to medium cardinality (number of distinct values) columns. An example would be a column called sex with two possible values: male and female. The cardinality would be only 2 and it would be a prime column for a bitmap index. The real power of the bitmap index is seen when a table contains multiple bitmap indexes. Then, Oracle has the ability to merge the result sets from each of the bitmap indexes to quickly eliminate the unwanted data.

Here is an example of creating a bitmap index:

```
create bitmap index dept_idx2_bm on dept (deptno);

Index created.
```

**TIP**
*Use bitmap indexes for columns with a low cardinality.
An example would be a column called sex with two
possible values of male or female (the cardinality
is only 2).*

# Bitmap Index Example

Consider a sample table call participant that contains surveys from individuals. The columns age_code, income_level, education_level, and marital_status have a separate bitmap index built on them. The balance of the data in each histogram and the EXPLAIN PLAN output for a query accessing each of the bitmap indexes are displayed in the following illustration. The EXPLAIN PLAN output shows how the multiple bitmap indexes have been merged creating a significant performance gain.

| AGE_CODE | | INCOME_LEVEL | | EDUCATION_LEVEL | | MARITAL_STATUS | |
|---|---|---|---|---|---|---|---|
| 18 - 22 | A | 10,000 - 14,000 | AA | HIGH SCHOOL | HS | SINGLE | S |
| 23 - 27 | B | 14,001 - 18,000 | BB | BACHELOR | BS | MARRIED | M |
| 28 - 32 | C | 18,001 - 22,000 | CC | MASTERS | MS | DIVORCED | D |
| 33 - 37 | D | 22,001 - 26,000 | DD | DOCTORATE | PhD | WIDOWED | W |
| ... | | ... | | ... | | ... | |

```
Select ...
From Participant
Where Age_Code = 'B'
  And Income_Level = 'DD'
  And Education_Level = 'HS'
  And Marital_Status = 'M';

SELECT STATEMENT Optimizer=CHOOSE
  SORT (AGGREGATE)
    BITMAP CONVERSION (ROWID)
      BITMAP AND
        BITMAP INDEX (SINGLE VALUE) OF 'PART_INCOME_LEVEL'
        BITMAP INDEX (SINGLE VALUE) OF 'PART_AGE_CODE'
        BITMAP INDEX (SINGLE VALUE) OF 'PART_EDUCATION_LEVEL'
        BITMAP INDEX (SINGLE VALUE) OF 'PART_MARITAL_STATUS'
```

**TIP**

*Merging multiple bitmap indexes can lead to significant performance improvement when combined in a single query. Bitmap indexes also work better with fixed- ength data types than they do with variable-length data types. Large block sizes improve the storage and read performance of bitmap indexes.*

Here is a query to display bitmap indexes:

```
select      index_name, index_type
from        user_indexes;

index name          index type
ord_itm_item        bitmap
ord_itm_ord_id      normal
ord_itm_pk          normal
```

Bitmap Index Example

**TIP**
*To query a list of your bitmap indexes, query the index_type column (type of bitmap) in the USER_INDEXES view.*

Bitmap indexes are not recommended for online transaction processing (OLTP) applications. B-tree indexes contain a ROWID with the indexed value, so Oracle has the ability to lock the index at the row level. Bitmap indexes are stored as compressed indexed value, which can contain a range of ROWIDs, so Oracle has to lock the entire range of the ROWIDs for a given value. This type of locking has the potential to cause deadlock situations with certain types of DML statements. SELECT statements are not affected by this locking problem.

Bitmap indexes have several restrictions:

- Bitmap indexes are not considered by the rule-based optimizer.

- Performing an ALTER TABLE statement and modifying a column that has a bitmap index built on it invalidates the index.

- Bitmap indexes do not contain any of the data from the column, and cannot be used for any type of integrity checking.

- Bitmap indexes cannot be declared as unique.

- Bitmap indexes have a maximum length of 30 characters.

**TIP**
*Don't use bitmap indexes in heavy OLTP environments and you need to know the restrictions associated with bitmap indexes.*

# HASH Indexes

Using HASH indexes requires the use of HASH clusters. When a cluster or HASH cluster is created, a cluster key is defined. This key tells Oracle how to store the tables in the cluster. When data is stored, all the rows relating to the cluster key are stored in the same database blocks. With the data being stored in the same database blocks, using the HASH index Oracle can access the data by performing one HASH function and one I/O—as opposed to accessing the data by using a B-tree index with a binary height of four, where there would potentially need to be four I/Os performed to retrieve the data. The following diagram gives an example:

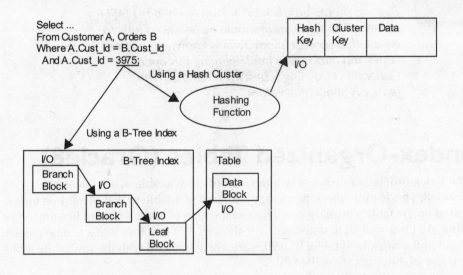

```
Select ...
From Customer A, Orders B
Where A.Cust_Id = B.Cust_Id
  And A.Cust_Id = 3975;
```

HASH indexes can potentially be the fastest way to access data in the database, but they do come with their drawbacks. The number of distinct values for the cluster key needs to be known before the HASH cluster can be created. This value needs to be specified at the time of creation. Underestimating the number of distinct values can cause collisions (two cluster key values with the same HASH value) within the cluster. These collisions are very costly. Collisions cause overflow buffers to be used to store the additional rows, thus causing additional I/O. If the number of distinct HASH values has been underestimated, the cluster will need to be re-created to alter the value. An ALTER CLUSTER command cannot change the number of HASHKEYS.

HASH clusters have a tendency to waste space. If it is not possible to determine how much space is required to hold all of the rows for a given cluster key, space may be wasted. If it is not possible to allocate additional space within the cluster for future growth, then HASH clusters may not be the best option.

If the application often performs full table scans on the clustered table(s), HASH clusters may not be the appropriate option. Because of the amount of empty space within the cluster to allow for future growth, full table scans can be very resource-intensive.

HASH Indexes

**TIP**

*Caution should be taken before implementing HASH clusters. The application should be reviewed fully to ensure that enough information is known about the tables and data before implementing this option. Generally, HASHing is best for static data with primarily sequential values.*

# Index-Organized Tables (Oracle8)

The index-ordered table is a new indexing option available in the release of Oracle8. This feature alters the storage structure of a table to that of a B-tree index, sorted on the table's primary key. This unique type of table is treated like any other table. All DML and DDL statements are allowed, but no other index can be created on an index-organized table. ROWIDs are not associated with the row of the table because of the structure of the table.

Index-organized tables provide faster key-based access to the data for statements involving exact match and range searches. UPDATE and DELETE statements are also improved because only the single structure needs to be modified. The amount of storage required is reduced because values of the key columns are not duplicated in the table and then again in an index.

**TIP**

*Consider using index-organized tables for tables that are always accessed using exact matches or range scans on the primary key.*

**V8I TIP**

*You can create secondary indexes on index-organized tables in Oracle8i.*

# Partitioned Indexes (Oracle8 Only)

A partitioned index is simply an index broken into multiple pieces. By breaking an index into multiple pieces, you are accessing much smaller pieces (faster), and you may separate the pieces onto different disk drives (eliminating I/O issues).

Partitioned indexes were introduced in the release of Oracle8. Both B-tree and bitmap indexes can be partitioned. HASH indexes cannot be partitioned. Partitioning can work several different ways. The tables can be partitioned and the indexes are not partitioned; the table is not partitioned, but the index is; or both the table and index are partitioned. Either way, the cost-based optimizer must be used. Partitioning adds many possibilities to help improve performance and increase maintainability.

There are two types of partitioned indexes: local and global. Each type has two subsets, prefixed and non-prefixed. A table can have a number of combinations of the different types of indexes built on its columns. If bitmap indexes are used, they must be local indexes. The main reason to partition the indexes is to reduce the size of the index that needs to be read and the ability to place the partitions in separate tablespaces to help improve reliability and availability.

Oracle8 also supports parallel query and parallel DML when using partitioned tables and indexes (see Chapter 11 for more information). This will add the extra benefit of multiple processes helping to process the statement faster. The maximum degree of parallelism is limited to the number of partitions.

# Local (Commonly Used Indexes)

Local indexes are indexes that are partitioned using the same partition key and same range boundaries as the table. Each partition of a local index will only contain keys and ROWIDs from its corresponding table partition. Local indexes can be B-tree or bitmap indexes. If they are B-tree indexes, they can be unique or non-unique.

This type of index supports partition independence, meaning that individual partitions can be added, truncated, dropped, split, taken offline, etc., without dropping or rebuilding the indexes. Oracle maintains the local indexes automatically. Local index partitions can also be rebuilt individually while the rest of the partition goes unaffected.

## Prefixed

Prefixed indexes are indexes that contain keys from the partitioning key as the leading edge of the index. For example, let's take the participant table again. If the table was created and range-partitioned using the survey_id and survey_date columns and a local prefix index is created on the survey_id column. The partitions of the index are equipartitioned, meaning that the partitions of the index are created with the same range boundaries as those of the table, as shown here:

Partitioned Indexes
(Oracle8 Only)

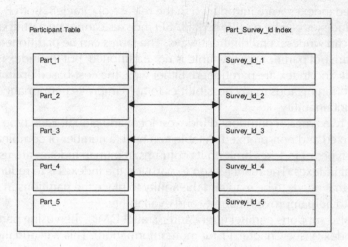

 **TIP**
*Local prefixed indexes allow Oracle to quickly prune
unneeded partitions. This means that the partitions that
do not contain any of the values appearing in the
WHERE clause will not need to be accessed, thus
improving the performance of the statement.*

## Non-Prefixed

Non-prefixed indexes are indexes that do not have the leading column of the
partitioning key as the leading column of the index. Using the same participant table
with the same partitioning key (survey_id and survey_date), an index on the
survey_date would be a local non-prefixed index. A local non-prefixed index could
be created on any column in the table, but each partition of the index will only
contain the keys for the corresponding partition of the table, as shown here:

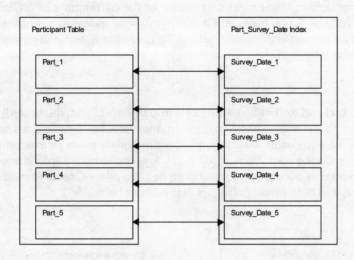

For a non-prefixed index to be unique, it must contain a subset of the partitioning key. In this example, we would need a combination of columns, including the survey_date and/or the survey_id columns (as long as the survey_id column was not the leading edge of the index, it would be a prefixed index).

**TIP**
*For a non-prefixed index to be unique, it must contain a subset of the partitioning key.*

# Global

Global partitioned indexes contain keys from multiple table partitions in a single index partition. The partitioning key of a global partitioned index is different or specifies a different range of values. The creator of the global partitioned index is

**Partitioned Indexes (Oracle8 Only)**

responsible for defining the ranges and values for the partitioning key. Global indexes can only be B-tree indexes. Global partitioned indexes are not maintained by Oracle. If a partition is truncated, added, split, dropped, etc., the indexes will need to be rebuilt.

### Prefixed

Normally, global prefixed indexes are not equipartitioned with the underlying table. Nothing prevents the index from being equipartitioned, but Oracle does not take advantage of the equipartitioning when generating query plans or executing partition maintenance operations. If the index is going to be equipartitioned, it should be created as a local index, as shown next, to allow Oracle to maintain the index and use it to help prune partitions that will not be needed.

Partitioned Indexes (Oracle8 Only)

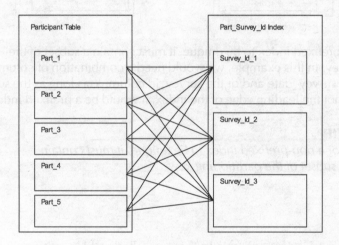

**TIP**
*If a global index is going to be equipartitioned, it should be created as a local index to allow Oracle to maintain the index and use it to help prune partitions that will not be needed.*

### Non-Prefixed

Non-prefixed global indexes are not supported by Oracle.

# Fast Index Rebuilding

The REBUILD option of the ALTER INDEX statement is executed to quickly rebuild an index using the existing index instead of the table:

```
alter index cust_idx1 rebuild parallel
tablespace cust_tblspc1
storage (pctincrease 0);

Index altered.
```

Modifications to the STORAGE clause can be made at this time and the parallel option may also be used.

**TIP**
*Use the REBUILD option of the ALTER INDEX statement for quickly rebuilding an index using the existing index instead of the table. You must have enough space to store both indexes during this operation.*

# Tips Review

- Query dba_indexes and dba_ind_columns to retrieve a list of the indexes on a given table. A concatenated index will only be used if the leading edge of the index is being used.

- Be careful when hard-coding Oracle's ROWID into specific code. The ROWID structure changed from Oracle7 to Oracle8.

- By replacing a NOT EQUAL operator with an OR condition, an index can be used to eliminate a full table scan.

- Using the default values clause for a column of a table will cause NULL values to be disallowed and eliminate the performance problems associated with using NULL values.

- By altering the values being compared to the column and not the columns themselves, the indexes become available. This is used to eliminate full table scans.

- Comparing mismatched data types can cause Oracle to internally suppress an index. Even an EXPLAIN PLAN on the query will not lead you to why a full table scan is being performed.

Tips Review

■ The selectivity of an index is what helps the cost-based optimizer determine an execution path. The more selective, the fewer number of rows that will be returned. Improve the selectivity by creating concatenated/composite indexes.

■ The clustering of data within the table can be used to improve the performance of statements that perform range scan type operations. By determining how the column is being used in the statements, indexing these column(s) may be a great benefit.

■ Analyzing the index or the table will provide the binary height of the index. Use the blevel column in the USER_INDEXES view to check the binary height of the indexes.

■ If the number of deleted rows within an index approaches 20–25 percent, rebuild the indexes to help reduce the binary height and the amount of empty space that is being read during an I/O.

■ Using the information provided by the INDEX_STATS view from the VALIDATE STRUCTURE option of the ANALYZE command, it is possible to determine where the data is skewed, the expected number of blocks that will need to be read per row, and the selectivity of the index.

■ If the data in a table is skewed, histograms will provide the cost-based optimizer a picture of the distribution. Using the histograms on columns that are not skewed will not provide an increase in performance, but will probably degrade it.

■ If the indexes are relatively small in comparison to the overall size of the table, then the fast full scan may provide the performance burst necessary for the application. With concatenated indexes that contain most of the columns of a table, the index may be larger than the actual table and the fast full scan could cause a degradation on performance.

■ The values of the indexed columns are stored in an index. For this reason, you can build concatenated (composite) indexes that can be used to satisfy a query without accessing the table. This eliminates the need to go to the table to retrieve the data, reducing I/O.

■ Use bitmap indexes for columns with a low cardinality. An example is a column called sex with two possible values of male or female (the cardinality is only 2).

■ To query a list of your bitmap indexes, query the USER_INDEXES view for the uniqueness column in Oracle7 or the index_type column in Oracle8.

- Don't use bitmap indexes in heavy OLTP environments and you need to know the restrictions associated with bitmap indexes.

- Caution should be taken before implementing HASH clusters. The application should be reviewed carefully to ensure that enough information is known about the tables and data before implementing this option. Generally speaking, HASHing is best for static data with primarily sequential values.

- Consider using index-organized tables for tables that are always accessed using exact matches or range scans on the primary key.

- Local prefixed indexes allow Oracle to quickly prune unneeded partitions. The partitions that do not contain any of the values appearing in the WHERE clause will not need to be accessed, thus improving the performance of the statement.

- For a non-prefixed index to be unique, it must contain a subset of the partitioning key.

- If a global index is going to be equipartitioned, it should be created as a local index to allow Oracle to maintain the index and use it to help prune partitions that will not be needed.

- Use the REBUILD option of the ALTER INDEX statement for quickly rebuilding an index using the existing index instead of the table.

# References

*Oracle Indexing*; Greg Pucka, TUSC

*Oracle7 Server Tuning*; Oracle Corporation

*Oracle8 Server Tuning*; Oracle Corporation

*Server Concepts*; Oracle Corporation

*Server Reference*; Oracle Corporation

*Oracle8 DBA Handbook*; Kevin Loney, Oracle Press

*Tuning Tips: You will be Toast!*; Rich Niemiec

Greg Pucka contributed the major portion of this chapter.

**Tips Review**

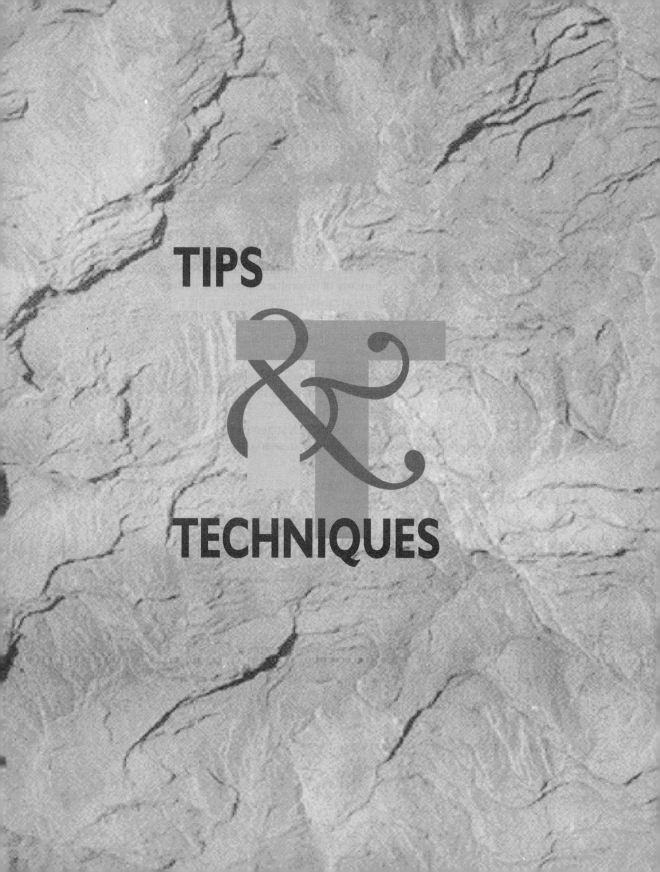

TIPS

&

TECHNIQUES

# CHAPTER 3

## Disk I/O and Fragmentation (DBA)

U nbalanced disk I/O and fragmentation can hamper performance. This chapter investigates correctly locating some of the physical data files related to the Oracle database. The init.ora parameters that relate to disk I/O are covered in Chapter 4 and also in Appendix A. This chapter will focus entirely on the physical files that make up the Oracle database and those tips that can help you use your hardware most effectively. The chapter concludes with a checklist to help you plan your next system, or system upgrade, by posing questions designed to address common database administration issues.

To keep your system running at its peak, this chapter offers the following tips and techniques:

- Distributing "key" data files across hardware disk to minimize contention
- Moving data files to balance file I/O
- Viewing file and tablespace information using Enterprise Manager
- Avoiding disk contention by using partitions
- Finding and fixing fragmentation and chaining
- Increasing the log file size and LOG_CHECKPOINT_INTERVAL for speed
- Creating enough rollback segments and spreading them across multiple disks
- Isolating large transactions to use their own rollback segments
- Do not sort in the SYSTEM tablespace
- Having multiple control files on different disks and controllers
- Using disk arrays and raw devices to improve performance
- Issues to consider in the planning stages of your system

# Distributing "Key" Data Files Across Available Hardware Disks

To operate the Oracle database efficiently, special care must be taken to distribute "key" data files across available hardware disks. For example, heavily accessed tables must be located on separate disks (and preferably separate controllers) from the corresponding index. In addition, online redo logs and archive logs should be stored separately from data files for recovery purposes.

The files that are of major concern are

- The SYSTEM tablespace
- The TEMPORARY tablespace
- The ROLLBACK SEGMENTS tablespace
- The online redo log files
- The operating system disk
- Key Oracle files located in the ORACLE_HOME directory
- Data files for heavily accessed tables
- Data files for heavily accessed indexes
- The operating system

The following example illustrates file distribution across 11 disks:

```
Disk0: Operating System
Disk1: Temporary Tablespace, Control File 1
Disk2: Rollback Segments, Control File 2
Disk3: Redo Logs, Archive Logs
Disk4:    System Tablespace
Disk5: Data1, Control File 3
Disk6: Index3, Control File 4
Disk7: Data2
Disk8: Index2
Disk9:   Data3
Disk10: Index1
```

## Storing Data and Index Files in Separate Locations

Tables that are joined (simultaneously accessed during a query) often should have their data and index separated. The following example shows a table join and one possible solution for managing the data:

```
select  COL1, COL2 ....
from    CUST_HEADER, CUST_DETAIL
where   ...;
```

**Data management solution:**

```
Disk1:  CUST_HEADER Table
Disk5:  CUST_HEADER Index
Disk8:  CUST_DETAIL Table
Disk12: CUST_DETAIL Index
```

The preceding solution allows the table join to be done while accessing four different disks and controllers. Separate data and index files onto different physical disks and controllers; consequently, when tables and indexes are accessed at the same time, they will not be accessing the same physical disk. This could be expanded to involve a larger number of disks. We will see later in the chapter that table and index partitioning will help us to accomplish this with ease.

**TIP**
*Separate key Oracle data files to ensure that disk contention is not a bottleneck. By separating tables and indexes of often-joined tables, you can ensure that even the worst of table joins do not result in disk contention.*

**Remember:**

- Distribute key data files (SYSTEM tablespace, TEMPORARY tablespace, rollback segments, online redo logs files, operating system disk, key Oracle files located in the ORACLE_HOME directory, data files for heavily accessed tables, and data files for heavily accessed indexes) across available hardware disks.

- Store data and index files in separate locations.

- For frequently joined tables, separate all data and index tablespaces so that none of the information from either table is located on the same disk.

- Store multiple copies of your control files on different disks and controllers.

## Avoiding I/O Disk Contention

Disk contention occurs when multiple processes try to access the same disk simultaneously. Disk contention can be reduced, thereby increasing performance, by distributing the disk I/O more evenly over available disks. Disk contention can also be reduced by decreasing disk I/O. To monitor disk contention, use the FILEIO Monitor to:

- Show how the actual database files are being "hit" by the users
- Move tables and indexes to spread "hits" equally across all disks

Use the FILEIO Monitor within Enterprise Manager to determine the I/O that is taking place on each database file. If the reads and writes are not distributed evenly between files, the tablespaces may need to be restructured for better performance. Figure 3-1 depicts a database that isn't distributed correctly because Disk1 is getting more hits by users. This is happening because the SYSTEM tablespace, which contains the TEMP directory, is stored in disk 1. An optimally balanced I/O distribution is also shown in Figure 3-1 for comparison with the actual distribution.

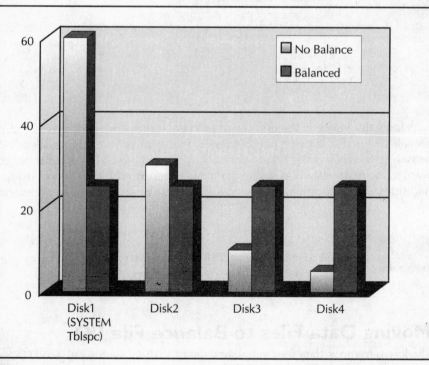

**FIGURE 3-1.**   *File I/O percentage of hits across all system disks (simple view)*

You can also determine file I/O problems by running a query:

```
col PHYRDS    format 999,999,999
col PHYWRTS   format 999,999,999
ttitle  "Disk Balancing Report"
col READTIM    format 999,999,999
col WRITETIM    format 999,999,999
col name format a40
spool fio1.out

select    name, phyrds, phywrts, readtim, writetim
from     `v$filestat a, v$dbfile b
where     a.file# = b.file#
order by readtim desc
/
spool off
```

**Query output:**

```
                    Disk Balancing Report

NAME                        Phyrds      Phywrts     ReadTim      WriteTim
/d01/psindex_1.dbf          48,310      51,798      200,564      903,199
/d02/psindex_02.dbf         34,520      40,224      117,925      611,121
/d03/psdata_01.dbf          35,189      36,904       97,474      401,290
/d04/rbs01.dbf               1,320      11,725        1,214       39,892
/d05/system01.dbf            1,454          10           10          956
```

A large difference in the number of physical writes and reads between disks reveals which disk is being overburdened. In the previous example, disks 1-3 are heavily used while disks 4-5 are only lightly used. To get a better balance, you'll want to move the data files. Splitting data files across multiple disks or using partitions would also help move access to a table or an index to an additional disk.

**TIP**
*Query V$FILESTAT and V$DBFILE views to see how effectively data files have been balanced.*

# Moving Data Files to Balance File I/O

The key is to move data files to balance file I/O. Then, set the DB_WRITERS (DBWR_IO_SLAVES in Oracle8) parameter in the init.ora parameter to the number of database files or disks for maximum efficiency in writing data. (See Chapter 4 and

Appendix A for additional information on DB_WRITERS and DBWR_IO_SLAVES.)
To physically move a data file that is causing file contention, use the following steps:

1. Take the tablespace corresponding to the data file offline:

```
$svrmgrl
SVRMGRL> connect internal
SVRMGRL> ALTER TABLESPACE ORDERS OFFLINE;
SVRMGRL> exit
```

2. Copy the data file to the new location on disk:

```
$cp  /disk1/orders1.dbf  /disk2/orders1.dbf  (UNIX copy command)
```

3. Rename the data file to the *new* data file location for the tablespace:

```
ALTER TABLESPACE ORDERS
RENAME '/disk1/orders1.dbf' to '/disk2/orders1.dbf';
```

4. Bring the tablespace back online:

```
$svrmgrl
SVRMGRL> connect internal
SVRMGRL> ALTER TABLESPACE ORDERS ONLINE;
SVRMGRL> exit
```

5. Delete the old data file (when you are sure the moved data file can be
accessed):

```
$rm /disk1/orders1.dbf  (UNIX delete command)
```

**TIP**
*Solve disk contention problems by moving data files to
disks that are not as heavily accessed.*

## Remember:

- Use the FILEIO Monitor in Enterprise Manager to determine the I/O that is
taking place on each database file (data dictionary).

- Restructure the tablespace if reads and writes are not distributed evenly
between files.

# Viewing File/Tablespace Information Using Enterprise Manger

You can also view tablespace and data file information by utilizing Oracle's
Enterprise Manager. Chapter 5 covers this tool in depth, but there are a few utilities
that are worth an additional mention here.

**Distributing Data Files**

## Performance Manager—Database Instance Information

Figure 3-2 reveals how we can display I/O information related to a given instance in the Enterprise Manager utility provided by Oracle Corporation. The I/O-specific areas are located in the Performance Manager section of the tool. There are a variety of options within the tool, yet in this section we will focus on those related to data files and tablespaces.

You can access specific file I/O information or even system I/O, which includes information about memory access, block writes and physical reads. While Chapter 4 addresses issues related to init.ora parameters and memory, we must remember that if we allocate memory properly, physical disk I/O will be reduced. Tuning queries and using indexes will also decrease physical disk reads. The lesson to learn is that major file I/O cannot always be directly attributed to disk balancing or object balancing. There are many factors to consider. Figure 3-3 shows an example of the System I/O screen from the Performance Manager. This can serve as a helpful benchmark of the health of the system.

Sections of the Performance Manager are also available that pertain to preventative maintenance. In Figure 3-4, we can see the free space that is available in each of our tablespaces. By adding data files (or allowing them to autoextend), we can eliminate potential errors that users may encounter from inadequate space needed for expansion of objects.

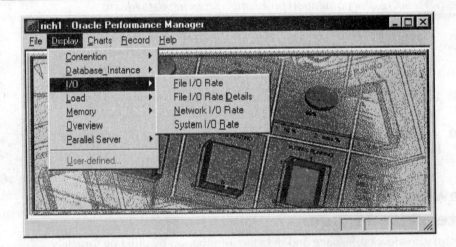

**FIGURE 3-2.** *Accessing I/O information about an Oracle instance*

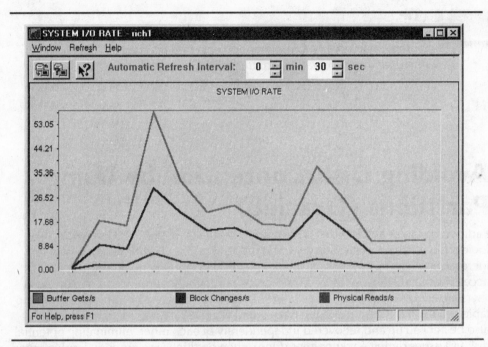

**FIGURE 3-3.** *The System I/O screen in the Performance Manager*

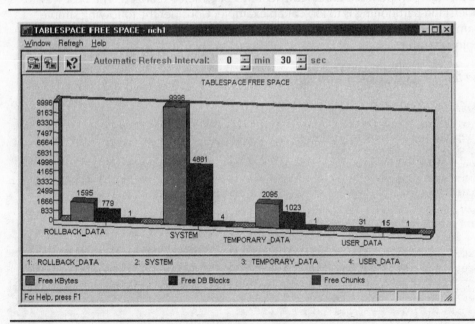

**FIGURE 3-4.** *Tablespace free space*

Distributing Data Files

**TIP**
*The Performance Manager can quickly display information about tablespaces and data files that can be used for preventative maintenance. These utilities can also give us a general view of comparative overall system "health" if accessed on a regular basis. See Chapter 5 for additional information.*

# Avoiding Disk Contention by Using Partitions (Oracle8)

Partitioning tables and indexes is covered in detail in Chapter 13. Here, we will look at it briefly as a method of avoiding disk contention. Partitioning is a way to increase efficiency by accessing smaller pieces of a table or index instead of accessing the full table or index. This can be particularly useful when one or more users are accessing multiple parts of the same table. If these partitions (pieces) of the table reside on different disks, the throughput is greatly increased. Partitions can also be backed up and recovered independently of each other, eliminating potential disk I/O issues during backup times. Only when partitions are properly implemented are the best performance-enhancing features of Oracle8 realized. The best way to understand partitioning is to look at an example. Consider the following simple example where we partition the dept table into three partitions (pieces) using the deptno column.

**The table dept is created with three partitions:**

```
create table dept
 (deptno       number(2),
  dept_name    varchar2(30))
  partition    by range(deptno)
 (partition d1 values      less than (10) tablespace dept1,
  partition d2 values      less than (20) tablespace dept2,
  partition d3 values      less than (maxvalue) tablespace dept3);
```

**Data is entered into all three partitions of the table:**

```
insert into dept values (1,  'ADMIN');
insert into dept values (7,  'MGMT');
insert into dept values (10, 'MANUF');
insert into dept values (15, 'ACCT');
insert into dept values (22, 'SALES');
```

**The dept table still looks like a single table when we select from it:**

```
select    *
from      dept;

DEPTNO    DEPT_NAME
1         ADMIN
7         MGMT
10        MANUF
15        ACCT
22        SALES
```

We selected all records from all of the partitions in this example. In the next three examples, we select individually from each partition.

**We select from a single partition and access only a *single* partition:**

```
select    *
from      dept partition (d1);

DEPTNO    DEPT_NAME
1         ADMIN
7         MGMT

select    *
from      dept partition (d2);

DEPTNO    DEPT_NAME
10        MANUF
15        ACCT

select    *
from      dept partition (d3);

DEPTNO    DEPT_NAME
22        SALES
```

In the preceding example, we built three distinct partitions on the dept table. The key to getting better throughput is to ensure that each partition is placed on a different physical disk; that all three partitions can be accessed simultaneously. The tablespaces dept1, dept2, and dept3 must have physical files that are located on different physical disks. Remember, the tablespace is the logical holder of information where the data file is the physical disk. You can have one tablespace that includes multiple data files, but a data file can only relate to a single tablespace. The key to partitioning to improve disk I/O is to ensure that the partitions that will be accessed simultaneously are located on different physical disks. Partitioning indexes and using the parallel option along with partitions make this option even more powerful. Chapter 13 looks at many more examples and options with partitions and Chapter 11 and Chapter 13 look at the parallel option.

 **TIP**
*To minimize disk I/O on a single large table, break the table into multiple partitions that reside on different physical disks.*

## Getting More Information About Partitions

We can retrieve the information regarding partitions by accessing user_tables, dba_part_tables and user_segments. Example queries to these three tables are displayed next with corresponding output for the examples in the previous section.

```
select   table_name, partitioned
from     dba_tables
where    table_name in ('DEPT','EMP');


TABLE NAME        PAR
DEPT              YES
EMP               NO
```

In this example, the par column indicates whether a table is partitioned.

```
select   owner, table_name, partition_count
from     dba_part_tables
where    table_name = 'DEPT';

OWNER       TABLE NAME        PARTITION COUNT
KEVIN       DEPT              3
```

In the preceding and following examples, the number of partitions on the dept table is 3.

```
select   segment_name, partition_name, segment_type, tablespace_name
from     user_segments;

SEGMENT NAME   PARTITION NAME    SEGMENT TYPE      TABLESPACE NAME
EMP                              TABLE             USER_DATA
```

```
DEPT          D1                    TABLE PARTITION    DEPT1
DEPT          D2                    TABLE PARTITION    DEPT2
DEPT          D3                    TABLE PARTITION    DEPT3
```

**TIP**
*Tables can be easily partitioned for individual pieces to be accessed and/or manipulated; you can still access the entire table of a partitioned index. Accessing the tables dba_tables, dba_part_table, and dba_segments provides additional information concerning tables that have been partitioned. See Chapter 13 for additional information on table and index partitioning.*

# Avoiding and Fixing Fragmentation

Fragmentation can appreciably hurt the performance of a database. Generally speaking, fragmentation decreases performance by 10–20 percent on average while chaining hampers performance by 10–50 percent on average.

To avoid and/or fix fragmentation you can do the following:

- Use the correct table size
- Create a new tablespace and move the data to it
- Export, compress, and then reimport the table
- Increase the size of the next extent
- Avoid chaining by setting percents correctly
- Rebuild the database to resolve fragmentation

To repair fragmentation, you'll need to find the fragmented tables/indexes. It's recommended that you regularly monitor your database to find tables/indexes fragmented into more than five pieces (or extents). The following query can help you find the fragments:

```
select    segment_name, segment_type, extents, bytes
from      dba_segments
where     extents > 5;
```

| SEGMENT NAME | SEGMENT TYPE | EXTENTS | BYTES |
|---|---|---|---|
| ORDER | TABLE | 22 | 22000000 |
| ORDER_IDX1 | INDEX | 12 | 12000000 |
| CUSTOMER | TABLE | 7 | 7000000 |

**Fixing Fragmentation**

**TIP**
*Query dba_segments on a regular basis to ensure that objects are not becoming fragmented. Catching problems early is the key to avoiding performance issues later. Correctly sizing storage parameters for objects is the key to avoiding fragmentation.*

## Using the Correct Table Size

Fragmentation occurs because tables extend into multiple extents, records are updated and the blocks, which contain the data, don't have enough room to store the changes, or the "Oracle-created" data dictionary tables are expanded. (This occurs with every added table, index, user, constraint, etc., or when any other database object is added.) The key to eliminating fragmentation is rebuilding the table or specifying the correct size in the first place. Using the preceding output as a base, the order table should have been created using an initial extent of at least 22M. (The size it has currently grown to.) If the order table continues to grow, 22M will not be sufficient in the future. If the order table will grow 2M per month and store 24 months of data, then the initial extent should be sized at 2M $\square$ 24 months = 48M. Taking the time to estimate future growth can help prevent fragmentation. But keep in mind user recommendations may be inaccurate.

## Create a New Tablespace and Move the Data to It

If you have enough room, you can resolve table fragmentation by creating a new tablespace and moving the data to the new location. In the example, the customer table is fragmented into seven extents of 1M each, which can be found by querying the dba_extents:

```
select   SEGMENT_NAME, BYTES
from     DBA_EXTENTS
where    SEGMENT_NAME = CUSTOMER;

SEGMENT_NAME          BYTES
CUSTOMER              1000000
CUSTOMER              1000000
CUSTOMER              1000000
CUSTOMER              1000000
CUSTOMER              1000000
CUSTOMER              1000000
CUSTOMER              1000000
```

First, create a new customer table called customer1:

```
CREATE TABLE CUSTOMER1
TABLESPACE NEW
STORAGE (INITIAL 10M NEXT 5M PCTINCREASE 0)
AS SELECT * FROM CUSTOMER;
```

After ensuring that the customer1 table was created, then drop the original:

```
DROP TABLE CUSTOMER;
```

You can now rename your new table and build its corresponding indexes:

```
RENAME CUSTOMER1 TO CUSTOMER;
```

The new customer table now occupies only one extent that is 10M in size. If the customer table is growing even faster, you will want to make the initial extent even larger to accommodate this growth. While you will still have to rebuild the indexes on the customer table (one of the drawbacks to this method), it does ensure that the table is never physically gone from the database until the new table is created. You can also use the COPY command to avoid the rollback segment requirements. You can also use the UNRECOVERABLE option (as of version 7.2) or the NOLOGGING option (as of version 8) to avoid rollback issues. An example of using the NOLOGGING feature is displayed in the two examples listed next. See Chapter 13 for detailed information concerning using NOLOGGING.

**An example of creating a table with NOLOGGING:**

```
Create table orders_temp
As select * from orders
nologging;

Table created.
```

**An example of creating an index with NOLOGGING:**

```
Create index ot_idx1 on orders_temp (order_no) nologging;

Index created.
```

**TIP**
*Use the UNRECOVERABLE (version 7.2) and NOLOGGING (version 8) options when rebuilding a problem table. Examples using NOLOGGING are covered in Chapter 13.*

**Fixing Fragmentation**

## Exporting, Compressing, and then Reimporting the Table

You can also resolve table fragmentation by exporting, compressing, and then reimporting the table. Don't forget to include your indexes, grants, and constraints (set their import parameters to Y when you import) and make sure you create a large enough rollback segment for the import. You can minimize the rollback area needed by setting COMMIT=Y (to commit during the table import) and you can set the buffer setting higher to increase the speed of the import. The following procedure handles the operation:

```
Export the CUSTOMER Table (Compress=Y)
Drop the CUSTOMER Table
Import the CUSTOMER Table
```

Using the option COMPRESS=Y when you export automatically builds an initial extent equal to all of the current extents that the table is occupying. This method is faster than the method in the previous section, but could be a problem if something were to happen to the export file before you have a chance to do the import. Although this will put all of the data into the initial extent, it will not necessarily create the next extent at an appropriate size. Precreating the table with an initial extent large enough for growth is also recommended (must use IGNORE=Y). The next section shows how to dynamically change this table storage parameter.

## Increasing the Size of the Next Extent

When you do not have the time or space to rebuild a table, try altering the table's storage by increasing the size of the *next extent* to prevent further fragmentation. For example, let's say an order table was built two weeks ago with the following space definition:

| Initial Extent | 2M |
| --- | --- |
| Next Extent | 1M |
| Pctincrease | 0 |

The order table currently has four extents (2M, 1M, 1M, and 1M) totaling 5M. But, the order entry personnel are putting in more orders than expected and you can see that the order table will grow to be 40M by the end of the year. You would like to keep one year of orders in the system. To solve this, make the next extent 35M so the total table storage is 40M in only five extents using the following code:

```
ALTER TABLE ORDER
STORAGE (NEXT 35M);
```

**TIP**
*If you can't fix a problem object's fragmentation problem immediately, alter the next extent to ensure that it doesn't become a worse problem.*

# To Avoid Chaining, Set Percents Correctly

Chaining can occur when there is not enough room in the data blocks to store changes. A chained record is one that exists in multiple blocks instead of a single block. Accessing multiple blocks for the same record can be costly in terms of performance. To see if you have chaining problems, run the utlchain.sql script that Oracle provides to create the chained_rows table. The utlchain.sql file is a file that comes with Oracle and is in the /rdbms/admin subdirectory of your ORACLE_HOME. You should check for chaining on a weekly basis and fix problems immediately. To generate the level of chaining in a table (customer in this example) run the following query:

```
ANALYZE TABLE CUSTOMER
LIST CHAINED ROWS;
```

Then, run the following query accessing the chained_rows table to check the customer table for chaining:

```
select  HEAD_ROWID
from    CHAINED_ROWS
where   TABLE_NAME = 'CUSTOMER';
```

If no rows are returned, then you do not have a chaining problem. If there is a chaining problem, then the query will return the head_rowid for all chained rows. You can also select "count(*)" to find the number of chained rows.

To avoid chaining, set PCTFREE (amount of space reserved in a block for updates) correctly. This parameter is set when the table is created. The default value is set to 10 (10 percent free for updates) but this needs to be much higher in a table where there is a large frequency of update activity.

**TIP**
*Find chaining problems by accessing the chained_rows table. Avoid chaining problems by correctly setting PCT FREE.*

# Rebuilding the Database to Resolve Fragmentation

Each time you create or alter an object in the Oracle database, several internal tables are also updated and/or inserted into Oracle's internal data dictionary. As a result, your data dictionary is also at risk for fragmentation if you have a large number of objects and records associated with those objects. You can resolve data dictionary fragmentation by rebuilding the database. However, be aware that this is a very large step to take and can be very time-consuming (e.g., take up an entire weekend). Therefore, it should be planned in advance. To rebuild the database, complete the following steps in the order presented:

1. Complete a full-database export.

2. Complete a full-image backup, which includes the following:

   ■ The database files

   ■  The control files

   ■ The online redo log files

   ■ The init.ora(s)

3. Run a rebuild on the database by using the CREATE DATABASE command.

4. Make sure you have a large enough rollback segment and large enough temporary tablespace to handle importing the database and the creation of indexes.

5. Import the entire database.

Refer to the *DBA Administrators Guide* for a more detailed approach.

## Oracle Tuning Pack 2.0—Tablespace Viewer

The Tablespace Viewer (which is part of Tablespace Manager) is new in the 2.0 version of the product. The Tablespace Viewer provides a graphical view of all tablespaces, data files, segments, total data blocks, free data blocks, and percentage of free blocks available in the tablespace's current storage allocation. The tool provides the option of displaying all segments for a tablespace or all segments for a data file. The Tablespace Viewer can be used to provide information for each segment, including average free space per block, chained rows, and other information that can be helpful in improving disk performance. Figure 3-5 shows an example of the Tablespace Viewer.

When a reorganization is necessary, the DBA can use a new feature called the Oracle Tablespace Manager Reorganization Wizard to automatically fix problematic objects. The wizard uses Oracle's export and import (checking for sufficient space prior to executing) for the fragmented or problematic objects. The DBA can select a single segment, multiple segments, or the entire tablespace for defragmentation, including tables, indexes, and clusters. Segments can also be moved between tablespaces using the Tablespace Manager.

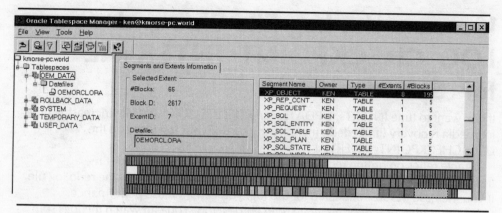

**FIGURE 3-5.** *Oracle Tuning Pack 2.0—Tablespace Viewer*

# Remember:

- Build the correct table and index sizes to avoid table and index fragmentation.
- Create a new tablespace when necessary to move objects to another disk.
- Defragment your data by exporting, compressing, and then reimporting the table.
- When time is a factor, increase the size of the next extent to avoid fragmentation.
- Avoid chaining by setting PCTFREE correctly.
- Resolve data dictionary fragmentation by rebuilding the database.
- Oracle Enterprise Manager utilities can help you fix fragmentation problems easier.

# Increase the Log File Size and LOG_CHECKPOINT_INTERVAL for Speed

If you want to tune INSERTs, UPDATEs, and DELETEs (DMLs) while increasing time for media recovery (if needed), increase the size of your log files and the LOG_CHECKPOINT_INTERVAL.

Oracle relies on online redo log files to record transactions. Each time a transaction takes place in the database, an entry is added to the online redo log file. If you increase the size allocated for the log, you can increase performance. Uncommitted transactions generate redo entries, too. You can watch the logs spin during a large batch transaction. But keep the following characteristics in mind when you make modifications:

- A log file must be online and available while the database is up or the database will halt.

- Online redo log files are recycled and offline redo log files are created automatically (if archiving is activated).

- Offline logs are the ones that have been closed for archiving or backup.

- Minimum is two online redo log files. Online redo log file multiplexing (additional copies) is recommended in the event that an online redo log file is lost.

- Log files are controlled by the following init.ora parameters:
  ```
  LOG_FILES
  LOG_ALLOCATION
  LOG_CHECKPOINT_INTERVAL
  LOG_ARCHIVE_START
  LOG_ARCHIVE_DEST
  ```

- The number of initial log files and their size is determined when the database is created.

- Archive logging can be turned on and off by the ALTER DATABASE command.

- Checkpoints are points when committed transactions in redo logs get written to the database.

## Determining If Redo Log File Size Is a Problem

Two potential problems are possible and should be addressed regarding the redo log file size. The first concerns batch jobs that do not have enough total redo space to complete or are so fast that the online redo logs wraps (all redo logs are used but not yet archived) before they have a chance to be archived to the offline redo logs. By listing the online redo logs with their last update date and time at the operating system level, you can determine how often they are switching. You can also query V$LOG_HISTORY view for the last 100 log switches. If you increase the size of the online redo logs, it may provide the space for large batch jobs doing large INSERT, UPDATE, and DELETE transactions. A better solution may be to increase the number of online redo logs so that the additional space is provided while also having a frequent log switch (smaller but more online redo logs), which gives a shorter time between offline redo logs that may be required for recovery.

The second concern is for very long-running jobs that are spending a large amount of time switching online redo logs. Long-running jobs are often much faster when the entire job fits into a single online redo log. For the online transaction processing (OLTP) type of environment, smaller online redo logs are usually better. My rule of thumb for online redo logs is to switch every half hour (not counting the long-running batch jobs that shorten this time). By monitoring the date and time of the online redo logs at the operating system level (or querying V$LOG_HISTORY view), you can make a determination to increase the size or number of online redo logs to reach an optimum switching interval.

## Determining the Size of Your Log Files and Checkpoint Interval

You can determine the size of your online redo log files by checking the size at the operating system level or querying the V$LOG and V$LOGFILE views. Then, you can add additional logs by using the ALTER DATABASE ADD LOGFILE... command to create larger logs and drop the smaller ones. Keep in mind that the checkpoint interval will force a checkpoint based on the number of blocks specified for the CHECKPOINT_INTERVAL in the init.ora file. So, if you increase the size of your online redo logs, make sure that you also increase your checkpoint interval. Displaying information about redo logs is shown in the query listed here:

```
select   a.member, b.*
from     v$logfile a, v$log b
where    a.group# = b.group#;
```

| MEMBER | GRP# | THRD# | BYTES | MEMBERS | STATUS |
|--------|------|-------|-------|---------|--------|
| /disk1/log1a.ora | 1 | 1 | 2048000 | 2 | INACTIVE |
| /disk1/log2a.ora | 2 | 1 | 2048000 | 2 | CURRENT |
| /disk2/log1b.ora | 1 | 1 | 2048000 | 2 | INACTIVE |
| /disk2/log2b.ora | 2 | 1 | 2048000 | 2 | CURRENT |

The query output shows two groups of log files (one primary group and one multiplexed group). Each group has two log files in it. The data in /disk1/log1a.ora and /disk2/log1b.ora is exactly the same (multiplexing log files is for availability and recoverability purposes).

## Other Helpful Redo Log Commands

To multiplex online redo log files (create a mirrored copy) use the command here:

```
alter database add logfile member '/disk2/log1b.ora' to group 1;
alter database add logfile member '/disk2/log2b.ora' to group 2;
```

To drop an online redo log member, use this command:

```
alter database drop logfile member '/disk2/log2b.ora';
```

To add a new online redo log group, use this command:

```
alter database add logfile member '/disk1/log3a.ora' size 10M;
```

To drop an entire online redo log group (all copies), use this command:

```
alter database drop logfile group 1;
```

To switch log files, use this command:

```
alter system switch logfile;
```

**TIP**
*Add larger log files and drop the smaller log files to increase the speed of large INSERT, UPDATE, and DELETE statements.*

## Remember:

- Increase the size of your log files to increase the rate at which large INSERTs, DELETEs, and UPDATEs (DMLs) are processed.

- Increase the number of online redo logs if the checkpoints are occurring less than every half hour during normal business conditions (excluding infrequent large batch jobs).

- Increase the LOG_CHECKPOINT_INTERVAL to keep pace with the size of your redo logs. The LOG_CHECKPOINT_INTERVAL is the first determining factor as to when the online redo logs are switched.

■ The init.ora parameter LOG_CHECKPOINT_INTERVAL is measured in blocks, not bytes. If you accidentally put in the number of bytes that you want, then your interval will be *too* high since the interval is measured in blocks.

### Additional init.ora Parameters in Oracle8 (See Appendix A for More Detail)

■ **LOG_ARCHIVE_DUPLEX_DEST**   Directory location with archive prefix (arch). This is a location to write an additional copy of archive logs (as redo logs are filled and are archived in ARCHIVELOG mode only). If you have the space, this is a nice safety net to save you if archiving errors occur.

■ **LOG_ARCHIVE_MIN_SUCCEED_DEST**   You set this to either 1 or 2. This is the minimum number of successful archives written for a redo log. You can set this to either 1 or 2. If you set this to 2, you basically defeat the benefit of having multiple archive logs being written.

■ **DBWR_IO_SLAVES**   This replaces the Oracle7 init.ora DB_WRITERS and is the number of writers to write data from the SGA to disk. It simulates asynch I/O for systems that do not have it. It also works for systems that *do* have asynch I/O.

# Increasing Chances of Recovery— Committing After Each Batch

To increase your chances of recovering large batch processes, COMMIT after each batch process. While this will slow processing, it will save time if a recovery is necessary. A large batch process really depends on how large your system is, but a job that takes several hours should be broken into smaller jobs that can have frequent COMMITs so that the entire job does not need to be rerun in its entirety.

# Creating Enough Rollback Segments

Rollback segments hold the data snapshot (before image) during an update. If the transaction is rolled back, then the data snapshot is applied. When setting up your database, reserve multiple tablespaces for rollback segments so that users do not

**Improving Recovery**

contend with each other in the same tablespace (which usually means the same physical disk):

```
Tablespace1/disk1: rbseg1
Tablespace2/disk2: rbseg2
Tablespace3/disk3: rbseg3
Tablespace4/disk4: rbseg4
Tablespace1/disk1: rbseg5
Tablespace2/disk2: rbseg6
Tablespace3/disk3: rbseg7
Tablespace4/disk4: rbseg8
```

## Avoiding Contention Among Rollback Segments

As a rule of thumb, you do not have more than one user using a rollback segment at a given time. Although Oracle's recommendation for the number of rollback segments is based on four concurrent transactions per rollback segment (see Table 3-1), you should base the number of rollback segments on the needs of your system.

## Monitoring Rollback Segment Waits and Contention

You can use Oracle's Enterprise Manager utility to check rollback fragmentation and use. The V$ views are a good tool for monitoring rollback segment waits and contention. SQL statements like the following one can also be used to display rollback information:

```
select  a.name, b.extents, b.rssize, b.xacts, b.waits, b.gets,
        optsize, status
from    v$rollname a, v$rollstat b
where   a.usn = b.usn;
```

| NAME | EXTENTS | RSSIZE | XACTS | WAITS | GETS | OPTSIZE | STATUS |
|------|---------|--------|-------|-------|------|---------|--------|
| SYSTEM | 4 | 540672 | 1 | 0 | 51 | | ONLINE |
| RB1 | 2 | 10240000 | 0 | 0 | 427 | 10240000 | ONLINE |
| RB2 | 2 | 10240000 | 1 | 0 | 425 | 10240000 | ONLINE |
| RB3 | 2 | 10240000 | 1 | 0 | 422 | 10240000 | ONLINE |
| RB4 | 2 | 10240000 | 0 | 0 | 421 | 10240000 | ONLINE |

Examine the results, to determine if you need to add rollback segments. If the xacts (active transactions) are regularly above 1 for any of the rollback segments, increase the number of rollback segments to eliminate potential

| Number of Concurrent Transactions | Number of Rollback Segments |
| --- | --- |
| Less than 16 | 4 |
| 16–32 | 8 |
| >32 | n/4 but not more than 50 |

**TABLE 3-1.**   *Built-in packages available in the Oracle Developer Forms module from Forms version 5.0.5.4.0*

contention. If the wait is greater than 0, then increase the number of rollback segments to eliminate contention.

## Increasing Rollback Segments

If demand is high, you can increase the number of rollback segments by adding a rollback segment named rb9 into the rollback2 tablespace, as shown here:

```
Create rollback segment rb9
tablespace rollback2
storage (initial 1M next 2M);
```

**TIP**
*Try to keep the number of users per rollback segment to one. This can be accomplished by monitoring the number of users per rollback segment and adding rollback segments if needed. This will keep waits and contention to a minimum.*

## Killing Problem Sessions

If the demand is at a temporary peak, you can stop a problem session by using the system KILL command. First, you must find the user who's running the job that is draining system resources. The following commands will help you find and KILL the problematic users:

```
select  sid, serial#
from    v$session
where   username = 'BADUSER'
```

**Query output:**

```
SID     SERIAL#
5       33
```

The following command is used to KILL the session:

```
alter system kill session '5,33';
```

You can also use the following code to determine which rollback segment is processing each transaction, along with the corresponding user and SQL statement. The output has been slightly modified for readability:

```
select   a.name, b.xacts, c.sid, c.serial#, c.username, d.sql_text
from     v$rollname a, v$rollstat b, v$session c, v$sqltext d,
         v$transaction e
where    a.usn = b.usn
and      b.usn = e.xidusn
and      c.taddr = e.addr
and      c.sql_address = d.address
and      c.sql_hash_value = d.hash_value
order by a.name, c.sid, d.piece;


name    xacts   sid   serial#   username   sql text
RB1     1       5     33        USER1      delete from test1;
RB2     1       7     41        USER9      update orders
                                             set items = 5
                                             where orderno = 555;
```

This output reveals which users are currently using rollback segments. This query will also show how many users are utilizing or waiting for the same rollback segment.

## Isolating Large Transactions to Their Own Rollback Segments

When creating your rollback segments, keep in mind that batch processes require one large rollback segment. Use the "set transaction use rollback segment rollbig" commands for large transactions. An example is displayed next. Also, note that you must precede the "set transaction" with a COMMIT even if it is the first command for your session.

```
commit;

set transaction use rollback segment rb_big;
delete from big_table;

commit;
```

Improving Recovery

**TIP**
*Failure to use the "set transaction use rollback segment rollbig" command for a given UPDATE, INSERT, DELETE, or batch program could cause the rollback segments to become fragmented and potentially too large for the corresponding tablespace. The "set transaction…" command must be reissued after a COMMIT or rollback process.*

A rollback segment is dynamically extended as needed by a transaction up to the total available space in the tablespace (transactions cannot span rollback segments) in which it resides. The OPTIMAL storage option for a rollback segment will dynamically shrink extended rollback segments to a specified size. While large transactions should be preceded with the "set transaction…" command, it is still a good idea to set the OPTIMAL option so that rollback segments are not accidentally extended and not returned to their original size. Use the following statement to alter a rollback segment to OPTIMAL:

```
alter rollback segment rb1
storage (optimal 15M);
```

Note that you may also use the OPTIMAL storage setting at rollback creation time.

You can also force a rollback segment to shrink to its OPTIMAL setting or a specified size using these commands below:

```
alter rollback segment rb1 shrink;
```

```
alter rollback segment rb1 shrink to 15M;
```

**TIP**
*Do not depend on the OPTIMAL setting to constantly shrink rollback segments as this is a costly process in terms of performance. The OPTIMAL setting should be activated infrequently. Also, note that you cannot shrink a rollback segment to less than the combined value of its first two extents.*

## Remember:

- Create enough rollback segments.
- Reserve multiple tablespaces for rollback segments.
- Try to keep the number of users per rollback segment to one. This can be accomplished by monitoring the number of users per rollback segment. This will keep waits and contention to a minimum.

Improving Recovery

- Avoid contention and waits on rollback segments.
- Isolate large transactions to their own rollback segment.

# Don't Sort in the SYSTEM Tablespace

Having the init.ora parameter SORT_AREA_SIZE set too small to accommodate sorts in memory is the leading cause of fragmentation in the SYSTEM tablespace. The fragmentation occurs because the temporary tablespace is used for disk sorting instead of the SORT_AREA. When setting up your system, be aware that the temporary tablespace adheres to the following characteristics:

- It defaults to SYSTEM tablespace unless specified with ALTER USER.
- It is created when memory is not large enough to process the entire data set.
- It uses the following statements to generate temporary segments:
  ```
  Create Index
  select.... Order By
  select.... Distinct
  select.... Group By
  select.... Union
  select.... Intersect
  select.... Minus
  Unindexed Joins
  Some Correlated Subqueries
  ```

To lower your chances of fragmentation, use the init.ora parameter (see Chapter 4 for more information on tuning the init.ora) SORT_AREA_SIZE to eliminate disk sorts and create a separate tablespace for temporary use. Then, direct users to that tablespace using the following statement:

```
SQL> ALTER USER username TEMPORARY TABLESPACE temp1;
```

**TIP**
*Ensure the init.ora parameter SORT_AREA_SIZE is large enough to accommodate sorts in memory; otherwise, the sort will take place on disk. In the event that large sorts must be performed on disk, create a separate tablespace for temporary use so that the SYSTEM tablespace is not used.*

# Having Multiple Control Files on Different Disks and Controllers

Control files store information regarding startup, shutdown, and archiving. Your system is useless without at least one good control file and you should store three copies of the control files on separate disks and controllers (if possible). To view current control files, run the following query:

```
select   name, value
from     v$parameter
where    name = 'control_files';


NAME                   VALUE
control_files          /disk1/ora8/ctl1.ora,  /disk2/ora8/ctl2.ora,
                       /disk3/ora8/ctl3.ora
```

# Using Disk Arrays to Improve Performance

A disk array is created by grouping several disks in such a way that the individual disks act as one logical disk. If a disk fails and all the data on the disk is destroyed, the system is striped so the data exists in more than one place. The system never goes down due to the failure of a single disk. Users continue to operate as if nothing has happened when there is a disk failure. The system alerts the system administrator that a specific disk has failed. The administrator pulls out the disk (some even have handles on them) and slides in a new disk. The operating system automatically writes the missing information on the new disk. The system goes on without missing a beat.

## What Are Some of the RAID Levels Available?

Many hardware companies now offer disk arrays with their operating system to improve performance. While the RAID levels available for use vary from system to system, the following list describes some of the more common options:

- **RAID0**   Automatic disk striping. This means that the distribution of Oracle is automatically spread across multiple disks. The tablespace's corresponding data file pieces can be spread across and accessed from 10 disks at the same time instead of one (a large savings in disk I/O).

**Using Disk Arrays**

- **RAID1** Automatic disk mirroring is available on most systems today. It's usually used for the operating system itself, but can be used with Oracle for higher availability.
- **RAID3** Heavy scientific applications can take advantage of this array that is usually used on query-only systems.
- **RAID5** This level carries the parity on an extra disk, which allows for media recovery. Heavy read applications get the maximum advantage from this disk array distribution.

I have seen numerous DBAs installing systems with a RAID5 disk array. While RAID5 is a good choice for inexpensive redundancy, it is usually a poor choice for performance. When a write request is made to a RAID5 array, a stripe of data must first be read from the array (usually 64–256K), the new data is added to the stripe, a new parity block is calculated, and the data is written to disk. This process, regardless of the size of the write request, can limit throughput. I only recommend RAID5 for mostly read or read-only file systems. I prefer to see RAID1+0 (striping with mirroring). RAID1+0 is faster because it does not have the same parity computation overhead as RAID5 and most RAID controllers will read from both sides of the mirror at the same time, effectively doubling your read throughput. Of course, with drive manufactures pushing 46GB hard drives these days, spreading out I/O is increasingly difficult.

## How Does This Impact Setup and Maintenance?

Using disk arrays makes Oracle data file setup and maintenance *much* easier for the novice DBA since manually balancing disks is not necessary. While the automatic striping means that placement of database files is less crucial and more I/O efficient, it's still recommended that you manually balance disk I/O. Using multiple arrays is one way to gain the advantages of arrays while still retaining the control achieved by balancing, because you can balance between the arrays.

## Is the Disk Array Made for a 24-Hour Shop?

Absolutely! The disk array means that media recovery relying or based on backups is less likely (higher availability). The operating system can take care of the recovery on its own, most of the time, if a single disk goes bad. Usually, the operator needs only to replace the bad disk and the information that is redundant in the array is automatically copied to disk. This affords the system less duplication in backup and recovery schemes.

## What Is the Cost?

To support disk arrays, you need more (much more) disk storage along with faster and/or more processors. While this can make the price of your initial system go up, the benefits are usually well worth it. For these reasons, before making the decision to use disk arrays, think about how valuable it is to keep your system "up and running."

### Remember:

■ Use disk arrays to improve performance and protect your data against disk failure.

■ Select the RAID level based on the availability your corporation needs to support compared to the costs of the additional hardware.

# Using Raw Devices to Improve I/O for Write-Intensive Data

A raw device is an unmounted disk slice that Oracle can read and write without the overhead of UNIX I/O buffering. While raw devices may improve performance, the jury's still out on their real value. Most claims of substantial performance improvements resulting from using raw devices come from hardware sales representatives. It's hard to find examples of raw devices in use. (Oracle Corporation uses raw devices extensively in TPC benchmarks to increase the number of transactions per second.) However, there is so little documented evidence regarding performance gains achieved with raw devices, it is recommended that you only use raw devices when you see a substantial increase in performance. Only use them when there are no other options available *and* the environment has been thoroughly tested. In my tests, raw devices have increased performance from 5–10 percent with an unacceptable cost in user maintenance. However, for large data warehouses, raw devices can provide excellent performance and should definitely be explored.

## Reasons for Using Raw Devices

There are several reasons you may choose to use raw devices (especially for a data warehouse):

■ If you plan to use Oracle's Parallel Server on a UNIX cluster with multiple nodes on the same database in a shared disk subsystem, raw devices are the only choice.

Using Raw Devices

- If asynchronous I/O is available on your platform.
- If I/O is the problem on your system *and* the CPU sits relatively idle.
- If you have variable disk partitioning (able to "slice" the disk easily), then raw devices become a choice for write-intensive, sequentially accessed data and redo log files not included in backup procedures.

## Drawbacks

While there are a number of advantages to using raw devices, there are some drawbacks:

- Administration of raw devices is more costly. Many common operating system backup utilities provided by the hardware vendor cannot be used with raw devices.
- If I/O is not the bottleneck, raw devices will probably not help much.
- If variable disk partitioning is not available, you will often allocate far more space than is needed for a given file, causing space to be wasted (very common).
- If raw devices are used in a production environment, Oracle recommends that backup and recovery be thoroughly tested before employing the raw devices.

### Remember:
Use raw devices if:

- They give you a substantial increase in performance (based on testing).
- You plan to use Oracle's Parallel Server on a UNIX cluster with multiple nodes on the same database in a shared disk subsystem.
- Asynchronous I/O is available on your platform.
- I/O is the problem on your system and the CPU sits relatively idle.
- You have variable disk partitioning.

Don't use raw devices if:

- I/O is not the bottleneck.
- Variable disk partitioning is not available.

Finally, if you use raw devices in a production environment, make sure you thoroughly test your backup and recovery system before employing the raw devices.

# Other Disk I/O Precautions and Tips

- Heavy batch processing may need much larger rollback, redo, and temp tablespace sizes.
- Heavy DML (INSERT, UPDATE, and DELETE) processing may need much larger rollback, redo, and temporary tablespace sizes.
- Heavy user access to large tables will require more CPU and memory, and larger temporary tablespace sizes.
- Poorly tuned systems will require more CPU and memory, and larger temporary tablespace sizes.
- A greater number of well-balanced disks and controllers will always increase performance (by reducing I/O contention).
- An increase in the disk capacity can speed backup and recovery time by keeping a copy of the backup on disk instead of tape.

# Issues to Consider in the Planning Stages

If you're planning a new system or an upgrade, here are some things you'll want to consider:

- What is the maximum possible disk capacity for the hardware?
- What disk sizes are available?
- What will be the initial size of the database?
- What will be the future size of the database?
- Will there be a RAID (striping) level for database files or OS?
- What recovery methods will be employed?
- What archiving methods will be used to store historical information?
- How often will report output be kept on the system?
- What development space will be needed?

**Disk Tips**

- What software will be installed and how much space will it need to function efficiently?

- What system utilities will be installed and how much space will they need to function efficiently?

- What type of mail system is going to be installed?

- What kind of data transfer methods are going to be employed?

### TIP
*When you are in the system planning stage, ensure that you find out all of the information related to the current and future use of the system. Don't just think about the Oracle database needs—investigate the other software and applications that will have performance implications on your Oracle database.*

## Tips Review

- Separate key Oracle data files to ensure that disk contention is not a bottleneck. By separating tables and indexes of often-joined tables, you can ensure that even the worst of table joins do not result in disk contention.

- Query V$FILESTAT and V$DBFILE views to see how effectively data files have been balanced.

- Solve disk contention problems by moving data files to disks that are not as heavily accessed.

- The Performance Manager can be used to quickly display information about tablespaces and data files that can be used for preventative maintenance. These utilities can also give us a general view of comparative overall system "health" if accessed on a regular basis. See Chapter 5 for additional information.

- To minimize disk I/O on a single large table, break the table into multiple partitions that reside on different physical disks.

- Accessing the tables dba_tables, dba_part_table, and dba_segments provides additional information concerning tables that have been partitioned.

■ Query dba_segments on a regular basis to ensure that objects are not becoming fragmented. Catching problems early is the key to avoiding performance issues later. Correctly sizing storage parameters for objects is the key to avoiding fragmentation.

■ Use the UNRECOVERABLE (version 7.2) and NOLOGGING (version 8) options when rebuilding a problem table. Examples using NOLOGGING are covered in Chapter 13.

■ If you can't fix an object's fragmentation problem immediately, alter the next extent to ensure that it doesn't become a worse problem.

■ Find chaining problems by accessing the chained_rows table. Avoid chaining problems by correctly setting PCT_FREE.

■ Add larger log files and drop the smaller log files to increase the speed of large INSERT, UPDATE, and DELETE statements.

■ Try to keep the number of users per rollback segment to one. This can be accomplished by monitoring the number of users per rollback segment and adding rollback segments if needed. This will keep waits and contention to a minimum.

■ Failure to use the "set transaction use rollback segment rollbig" command for a given UPDATE, INSERT, DELETE, or batch program could cause the rollback segments to become fragmented and potentially too large for the corresponding tablespace.

■ Ensure the init.ora parameter SORT_AREA_SIZE is large enough to accommodate sorts in memory; otherwise, the sort will take place on disk. In the event that large sorts must be performed on disk, create a separate tablespace for temporary use so that the SYSTEM tablespace is not used.

■ When you are in the system planning stage, ensure that you find out all of the information related to the current and future use of the system. Don't just think about the Oracle database needs, investigate the other software and applications that will have performance implications on your Oracle database.

**Tips Review**

# References

*TUSC DBA Guide*, 1995-1997
*DBA Reference Guide*, Oracle Corporation

# TIPS

# TECHNIQUES

# CHAPTER
# 4

## Tuning the init.ora
## (DBA Related)

The init.ora file determines many Oracle operating system environment attributes, such as memory allocated for data, resources allocated for I/O, and other crucial performance-related parameters. The key to an optimized Oracle database is often the architecture of the system and the parameters that set the environment for the database. Setting four key init.ora parameters (DB_BLOCK_ BUFFERS, DB_BLOCK_SIZE, SHARED_POOL_SIZE, and SORT_AREA_SIZE) can be the difference between subsecond queries and queries that take several minutes. This chapter will investigate the crucial init.ora parameters, but also look at the top 25 init.ora parameters. The chapter concludes with a look at a real-life system that yielded a 69 percent gain in performance using the very tips and techniques discussed in this chapter. Appendix A lists all documented and undocumanted init.ora parameters.

This chapter contains the following tips and techniques designed to achieve the greatest performance gain with the least effort by focusing on the parameters that yield the biggest impact:

- The crucial init.ora tuning parameters in Oracle
- Modifying the init.ora file without a restart
- Viewing the init.ora parameters via the Instance Manager
- Tuning DB_BLOCK_BUFFERS and monitoring hit ratios
- Finding the worst queries on your system
- Using the x$bh table to monitor buffer use
- Caching data into memory
- Tuning the SHARED_POOL_SIZE
- Checking library cache and dictionary cache
- Querying the x$ksmsp table to get another picture of SHARED_POOL_SIZE
- Setting the SHARED_POOL_RESERVED_SIZE
- Using buffer pools in Oracle8
- Tuning the SORT_AREA_SIZE and SORT_AREA_RETAINED_SIZE
- User, session, and system memory use
- Cost- versus rule-based optimization
- Checking latches, MTS options, and open cursors
- The top 25 init.ora parameters to consider (as I see it)

- Changed init.ora parameters in Oracle8
- Undocumented init.ora parameters (more in Appendix A)
- Test case of tuning scenarios
- Typical server setups with different size databases

# What Are the Crucial init.ora Tuning Parameters?

While tuning specific queries alone can lead to performance gains, the system will still be slow if the parameters for the initialization file are not set correctly because the initialization file plays such an integral role in the overall performance of an Oracle database. While you can spend time setting all the init.ora parameters, there are just four main parameters that need to be set correctly to realize significant performance gains:

- DB_BLOCK_BUFFERS
- DB_BLOCK_SIZE
- SHARED_POOL_SIZE
- SORT_AREA_SIZE

**TIP**
*The key init.ora parameters in Oracle are DB_BLOCK_BUFFERS, DB_BLOCK_SIZE, SHARED_POOL_SIZE, and SORT_AREA_SIZE.*

The following query can be used to find the current settings of the key init.ora parameters on your database:

```
select    name, value
from      v$parameter
where     name in ('db_block_buffers', 'db_block_size',
          'shared_pool_size', 'sort_area_size');


NAME                                          VALUE
db_block_buffers                              4000
db_block_size                                 4096
shared_pool_size                              7000000
sort_area_size                                262144
```

# Changing the init.ora without a Restart

One of the new features of Oracle8 is an increase in the number of init.ora parameters that can be dynamically changed in a session (without shutting down the database). In earlier versions of Oracle, most of the init.ora parameters required a shutdown and restart of the database. In Oracle8, however, some very important parameters can be modified spontaneously without a restart. Be careful, though, because these parameters can be a place of concern as much as a benefit. Even knowledgeable developers can set individual parameters that positively affect their session at the expense of others on the system. The following query illustrates a list of init.ora parameters that can be set without shutting down and restarting the database.

**There are two key fields in the V$PARAMETER view:**

- *ISSES_MODIFIABLE* - Indicates if a user with the ALTER SESSION privilege can modify this init.ora parameter for their session.

- *ISSYS_MODIFIABLE* - Indicates if someone with ALTER SYSTEM privilege can modify this particular parameter.

The following query will display the init.ora parameters that can be modified with an ALTER SYSTEM or ALTER SESSION command:

```
select    name, value, isdefault, isses_modifiable, issys_modifiable
from      v$parameter
where     issys_modifiable <> 'FALSE'
or        isses_modifiable <> 'FALSE'
order by  name;
```

The result of the query is all of the init.ora parameters that may be modified (a complete listing is displayed in Chapter 13):

| NAME | VALUE | ISDEFAULT | ISSES | ISSYS |
|------|-------|-----------|-------|-------|
| ALLOW_PARTIAL_SN_RESULTS | FALSE | TRUE | TRUE | DEFERRED |
| AQ_TM_PROCESSES | 0 | TRUE | FALSE | IMMEDIATE |
| B_TREE_BITMAP_PLANS | FALSE | TRUE | TRUE | FALSE |
| BACKUP_DISK_IO_SLAVES | 0 | TRUE | FALSE | DEFERRED |
| BACKUP_TAPE_IO_SLAVES | FALSE | TRUE | FALSE | DEFERRED |

**TIP**
*Changing init.ora parameters spontaneously is a powerful feature for both developers and DBAs. Consequently, a user with the ALTER SESSION privilege is capable of irresponsibly allocating 100M+ for the SORT_AREA_SIZE for a given session, if it is not restricted.*

# Viewing the init.ora Parameters with Enterprise Manager

You can also use the Instance Manager of Enterprise Manager to view these settings under the Instance option. The section of the Instance Manager displayed in Figure 4-1 shows the init.ora parameters. It shows the current settings for the parameters as well as if the parameters can be modified (dynamic = Yes) without shutting down the database. The Oracle Enterprise Manager and the Instance Manager are covered in detail in Chapter 5.

# Increasing Performance by Tuning the DB_BLOCK_BUFFERS

When tuning your system, DB_BLOCK_BUFFERS is the first parameter to look at in the init.ora because it's the most crucial parameter in Oracle. If the DB_BLOCK_BUFFERS is too low, users won't have enough memory to operate efficiently and it may cause the system to run poorly, no matter what else you do to it. If DB_BLOCK_BUFFERS is too high, your system may begin to swap and may come to a halt.

DB_BLOCK_BUFFERS makes up the area of the SGA that is used for storing and processing data in memory. As users request information, data is put into memory. If the DB_BLOCK_BUFFERS parameter is set too low, then the least recently used data will be flushed from memory. If the flushed data is recalled with a query, it must be reread from disk (causing I/O and CPU resources to be used).

Retrieving data from memory is over 10,000 times faster than retrieving it from disk. Therefore, the higher the percentage of time records are found in memory (without being retrieved from disk), the faster the overall system performance. Having enough memory allocated to store data in memory depends on whether enough memory is allocated to the DB_BLOCK_BUFFERS.

Tuning the DB_BLOCK_BUFFERS

*Setting DB_BLOCK_SIZE*

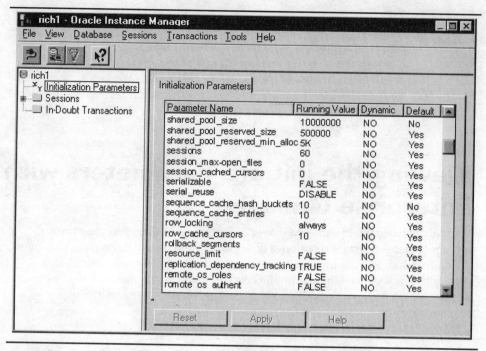

**FIGURE 4-1.** *Instance Manager—init.ora parameters*

**TIP**
*Retrieving information from memory is over 10,000 times faster than retrieving it from disk, so make sure that the SGA is large enough.*

# Setting DB_BLOCK_SIZE to Reflect the Size of Your Data Reads

The DB_BLOCK_SIZE is the size of the holding area within Oracle for the data. The larger the DB_BLOCK_SIZE, the faster you will retrieve large amounts of data. However, a small DB_BLOCK_SIZE actually lets you retrieve single records faster and saves space in memory.

To determine the actual memory required, the DB_BLOCK_BUFFERS must be multiplied by the init.ora parameter DB_BLOCK_SIZE, since the DB_BLOCK_

BUFFERS parameter is specified in the number of blocks rather than in the actual memory allocated:

```
(Memory Allocated = db_block_buffers x db_block_size.)
```

The default value for the DB_BLOCK_BUFFERS parameter varies per hardware platform, but it is generally lower than necessary for production applications.

When conducting full table scans, which are limited to the maximum I/O of the box (usually 64K), you can up the amount of data read into memory in a single I/O by increasing DB_BLOCK_SIZE to 8K or 16K, or by increasing the DB_FILE_MULTIBLOCK_READ_COUNT to 16 or 32. The database must be rebuilt if you want to increase the DB_BLOCK_SIZE.

Environments that run a lot of single queries to retrieve data could use a smaller block size, but "hot spots" in those systems will still benefit from using a larger block size. Sites that need to read large amounts of data in a single I/O read should increase the DB_FILE_MULTIBLOCK_READ_COUNT. Setting the DB_FILE_MULTIBLOCK_READ_COUNT higher is especially important for data warehouses that retrieve lots of records.

**TIP**

*The database must be rebuilt if you increase the DB_BLOCK_SIZE. Increasing the DB_FILE_MULTIBLOCK_READ_COUNT will allow more block reads in a single I/O, giving a benefit similar to a larger block size without a rebuild.*

**V8 TIP**

*The allowable DB_BLOCK_SIZE has increased in Oracle8 to be 32K. It was only 16K in the latest versions of Oracle7.*

# Setting DB_BLOCK_BUFFERS to 25 Percent of the Size Allocated to Main Memory

The general rule of thumb is to make the DB_BLOCK_BUFFERS parameter 25 percent of the size allocated to your main memory. A large number of users (300+) or a small amount of available memory may force you to make this 15-20 percent of physical memory. A small number of users (less than 100) or a large amount of physical memory may allow you to make this 30-50 percent of physical memory.

Larger systems may choose to set their DB_BLOCK_BUFFERS to 125000, which equates to 500M when the DB_BLOCK_SIZE is 4096 (4K). You can run the following script to determine if the data block buffers are set high enough:

```
select     name, value
from       v$sysstat
where      name in ('db block gets', 'consistent gets','physical
reads');


NAME                    VALUE
db block gets           3740673
consistent gets         19708538
physical reads           712833
```

In this output, 'db block gets' and 'consistent gets' are memory reads. 'Physical reads' are disk reads. The physical (disk) reads should be kept to below 5 percent of the total reads. A more detailed query that calculates the hit ratio to use is as follows:

```
column phys        format 999,999,999    heading 'Physical Reads'
column gets        format 999,999,999    heading ' DB Block Gets'
column con_gets    format 999,999,999    heading 'Consistent Gets'
column hitratio    format 9.999          heading ' Hit Ratio '
 select    sum(decode(name,'physical reads',value,0))phys,
           sum(decode(name,'db block gets',value,0)) gets,
           sum(decode(name,'consistent gets', value,0)) con_gets,
           (1 - (sum(decode(name,'physical reads',value,0)) /
           (sum(decode(name,'db block gets',value,0)) +
           sum(decode(name,'consistent gets',value,0))))) hitratio
from       v$sysstat;


Physical Reads     DB Block Gets     Consistent Gets     Hit Ratio
712,833            3,740,673         19,708,538          .970
```

**TIP**
*Check the V$SYSSTAT view and ensure that the buffer hit ratio is 95 percent for fastest performance. You may need to increase DB_BLOCK_BUFFERS if your buffer hit ratio is not above 95 percent. A hit ratio below 95 percent indicates that a large amount (> 5 percent) of the data requested by users is not getting cached in memory.*

# Getting the Hit Ratio Using Enterprise Manager

The buffer cache hit ratio can be calculated by accessing the V$SYSSTAT view as seen in the last section. However, the Performance Manager (within Enterprise

Manager) not only displays the hit ratio for the database buffers (memory allocated
for user's data), but it also graphically shows the output. Information can be stored in
a repository to trend your database as well. In Figure 4-2, the hit ratio displayed
is very low (86.92 percent) and should be closer to 95 percent. The Performance
Manager is covered in detail in Chapter 5.

## Keeping the Hit Ratio for the Data Cache Above 95 Percent

The hit ratio for the data cache should be above 95 percent. If your hit ratio is
below 95 percent, you may need to increase the number of DB_BLOCK_BUFFERS.
In some instances, you can increase performance substantially by increasing the hit
ratio from 95 to 98 percent—especially if the last 5 percent of the hits going to disk
are the main lag on the system.

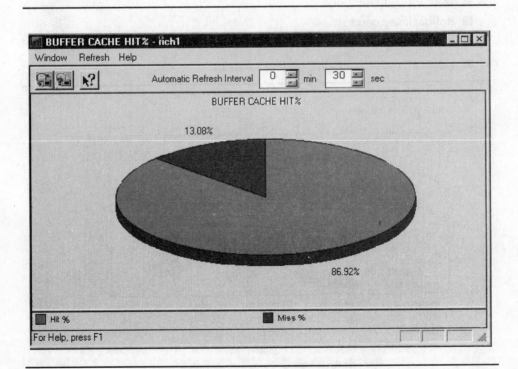

**FIGURE 4-2.**    *Use Oracle's Performance Manager to view hit ratios*

In Figure 4-3, notice how much of a performance problem is caused by setting DB_BLOCK_BUFFERS too low. Setting the DB_BLOCK_BUFFERS at optimal (instead of setting it too low) results in a tremendous performance gain. Also note that setting it too high (200 percent of optimal) does not result in any additional gains in performance.

## Monitoring the V$SQLAREA View to Find Bad Queries

Although hit ratios below 95 percent are usually a sign that your DB_BLOCK_ BUFFERS is set too low or that you have poor indexing, distortion of the hit ratio numbers is possible and needs to be taken into account while tuning. Hit ratio distortion and non-DB_BLOCK_BUFFER issues include the following:

- Recursive calls
- Missing or suppressed indexes
- Data sitting in memory
- Rollback segments
- Multiple logical reads
- Physical reads causing the system to use CPU

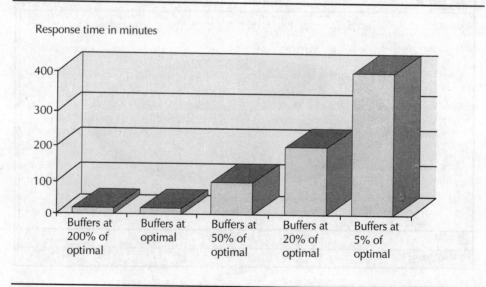

**FIGURE 4-3.** *Response time—memory-intensive report with given SGA (buffer) settings*

To avoid being misled, locate bad queries by monitoring the V$SQLAREA view. Once you isolate the queries that are causing performance hits, tune the queries or modify how the information is stored to solve the problem. Using Oracle's SQL Analyze, a DBA can generate the TopSQL for their system. The TopSQL screen (Figure 4-4) displays a list of the worst SQL statements in the current cache based on disk reads per execution. The DBA can then "drag" the problem SQL from TopSQL into a tuning session to begin the process of analyzing and tuning the problem SQL. Chapter 5 discusses the benefits of Oracle's Enterprise Manager product in detail.

**V8 TIP**

*In Oracle8, use the TopSQL monitor of Oracle's SQL Analyze to find problem queries.*

**Finding Bad Queries**

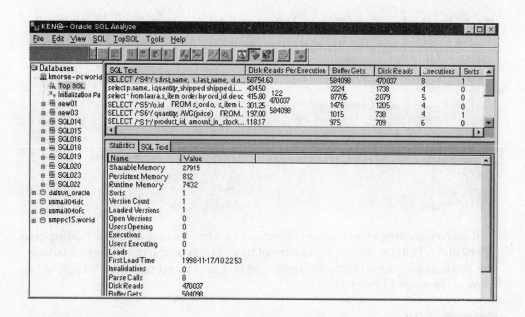

**FIGURE 4-4.** *Use Oracle's TopSQL of SQL Analyze to find problem queries*

## Hit Ratios Are Not Accurate: Recursive Calls Aren't Counted as Tries

Due to the large number of recursive calls performed in some sorting applications, temporary segments often "throw off" the hit ratio with inaccurate results. The recursive calls are not counted as logical reads, yet the physical reads are counted. Therefore, you can get *100 physical reads* with only *one recorded logical read* due to uncounted recursive calls. The result can be a large negative hit ratio figured into your overall hit ratio, making your system seem worse than it really is:

```
Tries(Logical Reads) = 1     Physical = 100
% hit ratio     =     (1   -         Physical/Tries) x 100
% hit ratio     =     (1 - 100/1) x 100%
% hit ratio     =     -9900%
```

If you are looking at this in the Enterprise Manager, your system could be experiencing hit ratio distortion. This usually just lasts for a cycle or two at the most, and then you're able to get an accurate reading.

## Bad Hit Ratios Can Occur When an Index Is Suppressed

Consider the following query where the customer table is indexed on the unique custno column. It is *not* optimal to have this index suppressed by using the NVL because it results in a poor hit ratio.

```
select     custno, name
from       customer
where      nvl(custno,0)  = 5789;

Tries (Logical Reads) = 105       Physical = 100
% hit ratio     =     (1    -       Physical/Tries) x 100
% hit ratio     =     (1 - 100/105) x 100%
% hit ratio     =     4.8%   (A very low/bad hit ratio)
```

If you are looking at this in the Enterprise Manager, there is an index missing on a query that is being executed at the current time. Focus on the query that is causing this problem and fix the query. The query can be found by accessing the V$SQLAREA view as shown in Chapter 5.

**TIP**
*A low hit ratio for a query is an indication of a missing or suppressed index.*

## Get Good Hit Ratios with Well-Indexed Queries

Consider the following query where the customer table is indexed on the unique custno column. In this situation, it is optimal to utilize the custno index because it results in an excellent hit ratio.

```
select     custno, name
from       customer
where      custno = 5789;

Tries (Logical Reads) = 105       Physical = 1
% hit ratio    =    (1    -       Physical/Tries) x 100
% hit ratio    =    (1 - 1/105) x 100%
% hit ratio    =    99%  (A very high/good hit ratio)
```

If you see a high hit ratio like this one for a query in the Enterprise Manager, there is usually an index on the query that is being executed.

## Bad Queries Executing a Second Time Can Result in Good Hit Ratios

When a full table scan is completed for the second time and the data is still in memory, you may see a good hit ratio even though the system is trying to run a bad query.

```
Tries (Logical Reads) = 105       Physical = 1
% hit ratio    =    (1    -       Physical/Tries) x 100
% hit ratio    =    (1 - 1/105) x 100%
% hit ratio    =    99%  (A very high/good hit ratio)
```

If you are looking at this in the Enterprise Manager, it appears that there is an index on the query being executed when in fact the data is in memory from the last time it was executed. The result is that you are "hogging up" a lot of memory even though it appears that an indexed search is being done.

**TIP**
*Bad (slow) queries will appear in V$SQLAREA view with poor hit ratios the first time they are executed. Make sure you tune them at that time. The second time that they execute they may not show a poor hit ratio.*

## Other Hit Ratio Distortions

There are other situations that can lead to hit ration distortions. A brief description of a selection of situations is given here.

■ **Oracle Forms distortion**  Systems that use Oracle Forms (screens) on a large basis do a lot of reuse of information on a regular basis. This reuse by some of the users of the system will drive up the hit ratio. Other users on the system may not be experiencing hit ratios that are as good as the Forms users, yet the overall system hit ratio may look very good. The DBA must take into consideration that the Forms users can be helping the hit ratio to an artificially high level.

**TIP**
*Oracle Forms applications usually have an unusually high hit ratio. If your site uses a lot of Oracle Forms, shoot for a higher hit ratio since the hit ratio will be artificially high.*

■ **Rollback segment distortion**  Since the header block of the rollback segment is usually cached, the activity to the rollback segment gives a falsely high hit ratio impact when truly there is no significant impact on the hit ratio.

**TIP**
*Sites that use rollbacks to a greater extent by most users of the system should shoot for a higher hit ratio since the hit ratio could be artificially high from rollback use.*

■ **Index distortion**  An index range scan results in multiple logical reads on a very small number of blocks. Hit ratios as high as 86 percent can be recorded when none of the blocks are cached prior to the query executing. Make sure you monitor the hit ratio of individual poorly tuned queries in addition to monitoring the big picture (overall hit ratio).

■ **I/O distortion**  Physical reads that appear to be causing heavy disk I/O may be actually causing you to be CPU bound. In tests, the same amount of CPU was used for 89 logical reads as it was to process 11 physical reads. The result is that the physical reads are CPU costly because of *buffer management*. Fix the queries causing the disk I/O problems and you will usually free up a large amount of CPU as well. Performance degradation can be exponentially downward-spiraling, but the good news is that when you begin to fix your system, it is often an exponentially upward-spiraling event. It's probably the main reason why people live to tune—it can be exhilarating.

# Tuning Queries to Avoid Performance Hits

To effectively tune the init.ora parameters, you must not do it blindly with respect to the queries that are running on the system. If there are poorly written statements on your system, you will inaccurately set the init.ora parameters to accommodate query problems. Correctly setting the init.ora parameters also includes a review of the worst statements that may otherwise push you to grossly set parameters incorrectly. The key is to find and fix the *major* problem queries and then get the init.ora parameters set correctly for the current state of the system and future growth.

A poorly written query that uses up buffer space can bring an entire system to a near standstill. To locate the queries that need to be tuned, use the V$SQLAREA view to find queries that:

■ Cause heavy disk reads

■ Cause heavy memory reads

■ Cause large tables to be cached in memory with a full table scan

Increase Performance by Finding and Tuning Heavy Disk Read Queries
One of the most effective ways to increase performance is to locate and tune heavy disk read queries. Use the following query to search for problem queries with disk reads greater than 10,000:

```
select    disk_reads, sql_text
from      v$sqlarea
where     disk_reads > 10000
order     by disk_reads desc;


DISK READS     SQL TEXT
    12987      select order#,columns,types from orders
               where substr(orderid,1,2)=:1
    11131      select custid, city from customer
               where city = 'CHICAGO'
```

The first record just shown is a query that has the index on orderid suppressed by the function SUBSTR, which forces a slow disk read (the only kind of disk read is a *slow* disk read). The second record shows a query that has many disk reads due to a column (city) that is not indexed. Although most people would say that you need to query DBA_INDEXES to know that city wasn't indexed, I disagree. The large amount of physical reads tells you that there is no index on city. As your tuning skills increase, you will begin to intuitively know more about a system looking in the V$SQLAREA view rather than looking in the DBA views.

The first query can be fixed by changing the SUBSTR to a LIKE, and the second query can be fixed by indexing the city column. (See Chapters 8 and 9 for more information on query tuning.)

**TIP**

*If your system is much larger, you may need to set the disk reads value to a higher number in the WHERE clause of your query to the V$SQLAREA view.*

**TIP**

*To see how many times a query is executed, add the column executions to the previous query. Keep in mind that statements that take two to three seconds to execute but are executed 25,000 times could also be part of the performance problem.*

**TIP**

*To view the SQL_TEXT that is longer than the 2,000 characters in the V$SQLAREA view, join the V$SQLTEXT view to the V$SQLAREA view.*

## Search the V$SQLAREA View to Find Memory Killing Queries

Queries that use an inordinately high amount of buffer space can "hog up" all of the memory that you have allocated to DB_BLOCK_BUFFERS. This may not leave enough memory for everyone else to run their queries in the SGA. A very exhaustive piece of PL/SQL code for finding the top 25 and top 10 queries is included in Chapter 17. The queries to the V$SQLAREA view in this chapter are for quick checking and tuning.

**TIP**

*Find the memory killing queries by searching the V$SQLAREA view for the queries that use the largest number of buffers. This will often show a query that has an index on a column that should not be indexed. Use BUFFER_GETS divided by executions to get the number of BUFFER_GETS each time the query is executed.*

**Avoiding Performance Hits**

**Example—Finding the largest number of memory reads by query:**

```
select     buffer_gets, sql_text
from       v$sqlarea
where      buffer_gets > 200000
order by  buffer_gets desc;

BUFFER GETS     SQL TEXT
    300219      select order#,cust_no,
                from orders where division = '1'
```

The record shown here is a query that has an index on the division column when there is only one division (division = 1) in the entire table. This is not a very unique column (understatement) and should not be indexed. The cost of reading in the entire table and index is hogging up memory on the system. The column should not be indexed. (See Chapters 8 and 9 for more information on query tuning.)

## Using the V$SQLAREA and V$SESSION Views to Find Users That Are Killing Performance

You can find a user that is killing the performance of your system if you know the username of the offending party. Since users don't usually volunteer this information (usually the offending party will CTRL/ALT/DEL if he or she knows you're coming), you can also use the following query to find the user and what the user is executing (the output has been modified for readability):

```
select     s.sid, s.username, s.status, disk_reads,
           buffer_gets, executions, loads, sql_text
from       v$sqlarea q, v$session s
where      q.address = s.sql_address
and        s.username = UPPER('&1')
order by sid;

SID USERNAME  STATUS  DISK READS  BUFFER GETS   EXECUTIONS LOADS
SQL TEXT
12   C09962   ACTIVE      1934         98            2         4
Select crew_no, name, description from CREWS where substr(crew_no,4,1) = 'A'
```

Check the SQL_TEXT at the bottom of the output. In this example, it is the query that is causing the problem. According to the output, the index on crew_no has been suppressed, causing a large number of disk reads that are causing a slowdown in the system. This query could be combined with the conditions of the previous two queries to find the worst query and user on the system. Never forget that some queries that use a lot of resources cannot be tuned because they must access a large amount of information to serve a business need. Don't blame the user for writing a query that uses a large amount of information. Instead, try looking at the way the information is stored to solve the problem, or offer to run the query in a nightly batch process.

**Avoiding Performance Hits**

**TIP**
*You may have to join in the V$SQLTEXT view to get the full text since the V$SQLAREA view only shows a portion of the SQL_TEXT.*

```
Break on  User_Name On Disk_Reads on Buffer_Gets on Rows_Processed
select    A.User_Name, B.Disk_Reads, B.Buffer_Gets,
          B.Rows_Processed, C.SQL_Text
from      V$Open_Cursor A, V$SQLArea B, V$SQLText C
where     A.User_Name = Upper('&&User')
  and     A.Address = C.Address
  and     A.Address = B.Address
order by A.User_Name, A.Address, C.Piece;
```

```
User Name       Disk Reads   Buffer Gets    Rows Processed
SQL text
Angelina        2            2300           210
select itemno, custno from items where custno = 'A101'
Bbrown          3            23213          7015
select itemno, custno from items where state = 'IL'
Jtrezzo         0            200            2
select itemno, custno from items where orderno = 131313
Rniemiec        32000        45541          7100
select itemno, custno from items where nvl(orderno,0) = 131313
 or nvl(orderno,0) = 777777
```

In this output, the data is formatted slightly different (for readability) than that which you would receive using this query. Based on the output, the DBA might consider disabling rniemiec's account until he learns how to write a query without suppressing indexes (perhaps bbrown and jtrezzo can help him). But, rniemiec's problem could also be that he is running an application that was not written by him (perhaps written by bbrown or jtrezzo), so don't disable him until you know the facts on who wrote the problem query that is causing the problem. In the example, rniemiec is probably at the mercy of the developer and the DBA and is just an honest, hardworking data entry person.

## Partitions and Large Tables Used in Queries to Increase Performance

Queries that must use large tables to access all of the information in a table are prime candidates to be partitioned and striped. This is a new feature in Oracle8 and is one of the best performance features ever introduced by Oracle Corporation. By partitioning a table into multiple pieces (Oracle8 partitioning), you are accessing only a small piece of the table (fast) instead of accessing the entire table (slower). However, having multiple partitions can also cost you in terms of performance for inserts. See information on this subject in Chapter 3 under partitioning.

## Use the x$bh table to Monitor Buffer Use

Querying the x$bh table will show you how many DB_BLOCK_BUFFERS are currently in use. The query may only be done as user SYS, so be careful. Never do an INSERT, UPDATE, or DELETE while connected as the SYS user, or be prepared to explore the world of backup and recovery.

**Example—Using x$bh to see how fast the SGA gets filled:**

```
select          state, count(*)
from            x$bh
group by        state;

STATE           COUNT(*)
    0           371
    1           429
```

Note that there are states other than 1 (used) and 0 (unused), but they are usually insignificant.

In the preceding results:

```
Total DB_BLOCK_BUFFERS = 800 (371+429)
Total buffers that have NOT been used = 371
Total buffers that have been used = 429
```

**TIP**
*If there are no free buffers (none with state 0) within the first 30 minutes of business hours, you probably need to set DB_BLOCK_BUFFERS higher.*

A way to get an even more detailed look at memory use is explained in Chapter 15, "The x$ Tables." To accomplish this, take the number of blocks with state = 3, and call these the currently used blocks of memory. Then we have to map that memory back to physical objects. The new query takes the records that were at a state = 1, but also with a LRBA_SEQ<>0, and places them with the records that were set to a state = 3 or *being used* for a more accurate picture.

**Example—Using the x$bh table in a more precise manner:**

```
select      decode(state,0, 'FREE',
            1,decode(lrba_seq,0,'AVAILABLE','BEING USED'),
            3, 'BEING USED', state) "BLOCK STATUS",
            count(*)
from        x$bh
group by    decode(state,0,'FREE',1,decode(lrba_seq,0,'AVAILABLE',
            'BEING USED'),3, 'BEING USED', state);


BLOCK STATUS         COUNT(*)
AVAILABLE            779
BEING USED           154
FREE                 167
```

See Chapter 15 for detailed information on arriving at this query to the x$bh table.

### Building the Utopian System

Now that you know that you want every query to be in memory before the user executes it, you can follow the steps here to build the utopian system:

1. **At 5:00 A.M.:** Select from all "lookup" Tables. Use all query values *(SELECT ...WHERE...).*

2. **At 5:15 A.M.:** Run all "ad hoc" queries and force the index with full scan of index. *(Use the INDEX hint.)*

3. **At 5:30 A.M.:** Run full table scans of tables frequently accessed. *(Use the INDEX and FULL hints.)*

4. **At 6:00 A.M.:** Check the x$bh table to ensure enough memory is still free.

5. **At 5:00 P.M.: Users throw you a party (not in this lifetime)!**

# Using the CACHE Parameter to Pin Data into Memory

Once you have enough memory allocated to Oracle, the focus must shift to ensuring that the most important information is getting into memory and staying there. If you find that key tables are being pushed out of memory, you may need to "pin" them into memory using the CACHE parameter. When you use this parameter, full table scans result in being placed on the *most recently used* list instead of the *least recently used* list. This keeps them in memory for future use. The following examples investigate the syntax and uses of this command.

**Example—Create a table with the CACHE option:**
This statement creates a table that is cached in memory after the data is accessed the first time:

```
CREATE TABLE test_tab (col1 number)
TABLESPACE users
CACHE;
```

Note that NOCACHE is the default!

**Example—Alter a table to the CACHE option:**
This statement alters a table to stay cached once it is accessed:

```
ALTER TABLE test_tab
CACHE;
```

**Example—The CACHE hint:**
This statement caches a table that is accessed:

```
select    /*+ CACHE(cust) */ ename, job
from      cust
where     table_name = 'EMP';
```

**Example—The NOCACHE hint:**
This statement will *not* cache a table that is accessed even if the table was created or altered to be cached (as in the first two examples):

```
select    /*+ FULL(cust)  NOCACHE(cust) */  ename, job
from      cust
where     table_name = 'EMP';
```

**TIP**
*Cache tables are frequently used into memory so that they are not flushed out of memory by infrequently used tables.*

## Additional Methods to Determine the Number of Buffers to Use
The queries in this section are included because there are folks who like to use them, but they should only be used as a last resort, because at times the hit ratio

doesn't always increase by the amount that the query says it will. One bad query may make these results inaccurate. It's best to use the longer approach presented earlier in the chapter first.

## Mythically Raise the DB_BLOCK_BUFFERS by 1,000 to Estimate the Hit Ratio

To get an idea of your hit ratio with a mythical increase in DB_BLOCK_BUFFERS, you can use the following method. Set DB_BLOCK_LRU_STATISTICS = "number of buffers you will mythically increase by" in the init.ora, shut down and start up the database, and then run the query to the x$kcbrbh table.

Let's say that I get the following results for my current hit ratio by querying the V$SYSSTAT view (this is my starting point before I do any raising or lowering):

```
NAME                   VALUE
db block gets          10000
consistent gets        90000
physical reads         20000

hit ratio        =     1    -       Physical/Logical Reads  x 100%
                 =     1    -       (20000)/(10000+90000) x 100%
                 =          80%
```

The following statement shows how many more memory (logical) hits would occur if I added 1,000 more buffers to DB_BLOCK_BUFFERS:

```
select    sum(count) Hits
from      sys.x$kcbrbh
where     indx < 1000;

Hits: = 10000
```

There would be 10,000 more memory (logical) hits instead of disk (physical) hits. Now I can calculate a new hit ratio that I would estimate to have by adding 1,000 buffers (using my original starting point and moving 10,000 reads from the physical to the logical bucket).

```
NAME                   VALUE
db block gets          10000
consistent gets        90000 + 10000 (new logical reads added) = 100,000
physical reads         20000 - 10000 (new physical reads lost) = 10,000

hit ratio        =     1    -       Physical/Logical Reads  x 100%
                 =     1    -       (10000)/(10000+100000) x 100%
                 =          91% (new hit ratio estimate by adding 1000 buffers)
```

By adding 1,000 buffers in this scenario, my hit ratio would go from 80 percent to 91 percent ... theoretically, of course.

## Mythically Lower the DB_BLOCK_BUFFERS by 1,000 to Estimate the Hit Ratio

You may find you are not using all of the buffers that you have allocated. And, decreasing the buffer could give the memory back to the operating system for other processes, but you're not sure what the new hit ratio would be. You can use the following method to mythically decrease the DB_BLOCK_BUFFERS to see how it will impact your system's performance. To decrease the hit ratio, Set DB_BLOCK_LRU_STATISTICS = TRUE in the init.ora, shut down and start up the database and then run the query to the x$kcbrbh table.

Let's say that I get the following results for my current hit ratio by querying the V$SYSSTAT view with a starting number of buffers of 8,000 (this is my starting point before I do any raising or lowering):

```
NAME                    VALUE
db block gets           10000
consistent gets         90000
physical reads          20000


hit ratio       =       1    -          Physical/Logical Reads   x 100%
                =       1    -          (20000)/(10000+90000) x 100%
                =          80%
```

The following statement shows how many fewer memory (logical) hits would occur if I lowered my DB_BLOCK_BUFFERS from 8,000 to 7,000:

```
select      sum(count) Hits
from        sys.x$kcbcbh
where       indx >= 7000;


Hits: = 5000


NAME                    VALUE
db block gets           10000
consistent gets         90000 - 5000 = 85,000 (new amount of logical reads lost)
physical reads          20000 + 5000 = 25,000 (new amount of physical reads added)
hit ratio = 1     -     Physical/Logical Reads   x 100%
          = 1     -     (25000)/(10000+85000) x 100%
          =             74%
```

By lowering DB_BLOCK_BUFFERS by 1,000 buffers in this scenario (from 8,000 to 7,000) my hit ratio would go from 80 percent to 74 percent ... theoretically, of course.

**TIP**
*While using x$kcbrbh and x$kcbcbh tables may give
you a rough idea for your SGA size, it will not give you
the exact answer. Only day-to-day production use with
monitoring will achieve the optimum SGA size. I
personally do not recommend this approach for
estimating,* but I am including it as others have found
it useful.

## Remember:

- Setting DB_BLOCK_BUFFERS correctly is crucial to your system performance.
- DB_BLOCK_BUFFERS is the memory allocated for data.
- A missing index is found by looking for a hit ratio of 0.95 or less.
- A highly intensive process (the one killing the system) can be found with the Enterprise Manager or by querying the V$SQLAREA view.
- Hit ratios can be distorted.
- Hit ratios below 95 percent usually indicate undersized DB_BLOCK_BUFFERS, but could also mean missing or poorly used indexes.

## Tuning the SHARED_POOL_SIZE for Optimal Performance

Now that we have the memory available for the data set correctly (DB_BLOCK_BUFFERS), we need to ensure that the query gets executed. If the query never makes it into memory, it can never request the data be put in memory; that's where the SHARED_POOL_SIZE comes in. SHARED_POOL_SIZE specifies the memory allocated in the SGA for data dictionary caching and shared SQL statements.

The data dictionary cache is very important because that's where the data dictionary components are buffered. Oracle references the data dictionary several times when an SQL statement is processed. Therefore, the more information (database and application schema and structure) that's stored in memory, the less information that'll have to be retrieved from disk.

The data dictionary cache operates the same as the DB_BLOCK_BUFFERS when caching information. For the best performance, it would be great if the entire Oracle data dictionary could be cached in memory. Unfortunately, this usually is not feasible. Instead, executed SQL statements are cached in the shared SQL area.

## Using Stored Procedures for Optimal Use of the Shared SQL Area

Each time a SQL statement is executed, the statement is searched for in the shared SQL area and, if found, used for execution. This saves parsing time and improves overall performance. Therefore, to ensure optimal use of the shared SQL area, use stored procedures as much as possible. However, keep in mind the only time the SQL statement being executed can use a statement already in the shared SQL area is if the statements are identical (meaning they have the same content exactly, the same case, the same number of spaces, etc.). If the statements are not identical, the new statement will be parsed, executed, and placed in the shared SQL area.

In the following example, the statements are identical in execution, but the word *from* causes Oracle to treat the two statements as if they were different, thus *not* reusing the original cursor that was located in the shared SQL area:

```
SQL>     select name, customer from customer_information;
SQL>     select name, customer FROM customer_information;
```

**TIP**
*PL/SQL must be written exactly the same to be reused. Case differences and any other differences will cause a reparse of the statement.*

## Setting the SHARED_POOL_SIZE High Enough to Fully Use the DB_BLOCK_BUFFERS

If the SHARED_POOL_SIZE is set too low, then you will not get the full advantage of your DB_BLOCK_BUFFERS. The queries that can be performed against the Oracle V$ views to determine the data dictionary cache hit ratio and the shared SQL statement usage are listed next. These will help you determine if increasing the SHARED_POOL_SIZE will improve performance.

The SHARED_POOL_SIZE parameter is specified in bytes. The default value for the SHARED_POOL_SIZE parameter varies per system, but it is generally lower than necessary for large production applications.

## Keeping the Data Dictionary Cache Hit Ratio at or Above 85 Percent

The data dictionary cache is a key area to tune because the dictionary is accessed so frequently, especially by the internals of Oracle. At startup, the data dictionary cache contains no data. But as more data is read into cache, the likelihood of cache misses decreases. For this reason, monitoring the data dictionary cache should be done only after the system has been up for a while and stabilized. If the dictionary cache hit ratio is below 95 percent, then you'll probably need to increase the size of the SHARED_POOL_SIZE parameter in the init.ora. However, keep in mind that this area is also the holder of the library cache.

Note that the dc (Version 6) SGA storage is now a part of the Shared Pool along with the library cache. There are no more "dc_" parameters in the init.ora.

Use the following query against the Oracle V$ view to determine the data dictionary cache hit ratio:

```
select     ((1 - (Sum(GetMisses) / (Sum(Gets)
           + Sum(GetMisses)))) * 100) "Hit Rate"
from       V$RowCache
where      Gets + GetMisses <> 0;

Hit Rate
91.747126
```

**TIP**

*Measure hit ratios for the row cache of the Shared Pool with the V$ROWCACHE view. A hit ratio of over 95 percent should be achieved. However, when the database is initially started, hit ratios will be around 85 percent.*

## Using Individual Row Cache Parameters to Diagnose Shared Pool Use

To diagnose a problem or overuse of the Shared Pool, use a modified query on the same table to see how each individual parameter makes up the row cache. This query looks at the row cache in detail and places an '*' by those values that have a miss ratio greater than 10 percent.

```
column parameter        format a20          heading 'Data Dictionary Area'
column gets             format 999,999,999  heading 'Total|Requests'
column getmisses        format 999,999,999  heading 'Misses'
column modifications    format 999,999      heading 'Mods'
column flushes          format 999,999      heading 'Flushes'
column getmiss_ratio    format 9.99         heading 'Miss|Ratio'
ttitle 'Shared Pool Row Cache Usage'

select  parameter, gets, getmisses, modifications, flushes,
        (getmisses / decode(gets,0,1,gets)) getmiss_ratio,
        decode(trunc((getmisses / decode(gets,0,1,gets)),1),.0,' ','*') " "
from    v$rowcache
where   Gets + GetMisses <> 0;
order by gets desc;
```

```
Sun Mar 19                      page 1
                         Shared Pool Row Cache Usage
                    Total                                      Miss
Data Dictionary Area Requests    Misses     Mods    Flushes    Ratio
DC_TABLES            249,119     134        34                 .00
DC_COLUMNS           9,695       1,792      197                .18  *
DC_FREE_EXTENTS      2,218       95         51      34         .04
DC_CONSTRAINT_DEFS   1,321       584                           .44  *
DC_INDEXES           1,176       186        21                 .16  *
DC_OBJECTS           934         154        43                 .16  *
DC_TABLE_GRANTS      261         83                            .32  *
DC_ROLLBACK_SEGMENTS 456         7          13      12         .02
...
```

This query places an '*' for any query that has misses greater than 10 percent. It does this by using the TRUNC to limit the miss ratio to the tenths digit, and then analyzes that digit for any value greater than 0 (which would indicate a hit ratio of 10 percent or higher). So, a .1 or higher would return an *. Explanations of each of the parameters are listed in the following section.

### The V$ROWCACHE view—Interpreting its contents:

- **parameter**   Identifies the specific data dictionary cache item (i.e., dc_ parameter).
- **count**   Shows the total number of entries in the cache.
- **usage**   Shows the number of cache entries that contain valid data.
- **fixed**   Shows the number of fixed entries in the cache.
- **gets**   Shows the total number of requests for information.
- **getmisses**   Shows the number of data requests resulting in cache misses.
- **scans**   Shows the number of scan requests.
- **scanmisses**   Shows the number of times a scan failed to find the data in the cache.
- **scancompletes** (for subordinate cache type only)   Shows the number of times the list was scanned completely.
- **modifications**   Shows the number of INSERTs, UPDATEs, and DELETEs.
- **flushes**   Shows the number of times flushed to disk.

**Tuning for Optimal Performance**

## Keeping the Library Cache Reload Ratio at 0 and the Hit Ratio Above 95 Percent

For optimal performance, you'll want to keep the library cache reload ratio [sum(reloads)/sum(pins)] at zero and the library cache ratio above 95 percent. If the reload ratio is not zero, then there are statements that are being "aged out" that are later needed and brought back into memory. If the reload ratio is zero (0), that means items in the library cache were never aged or invalidated. If the reload ratio is above 1 percent, the SHARED_POOL_SIZE parameter should probably be increased. Likewise, if the library cache hit ratio comes in below 95 percent, then the SHARED_POOL_SIZE parameter may need to be increased.

There are a couple of ways to monitor the library cache. The first method is to execute the UTLBSTAT/UTLESTAT report (ESTAT/BSTAT are covered in detail in Chapter 16). The second is to use the V$LIBRARYCACHE view. The following query uses the V$LIBRARYCACHE view to examine the reload ratio in the library cache:

```
select      Sum(Pins) "Hits",
            Sum(Reloads) "Misses",
            ((Sum(Reloads) / Sum(Pins)) * 100)"Reload %"
from        V$LibraryCache;

Hits        Misses    Reload %
1969            50    0.253936
```

The next query uses the V$LIBRARYCACHE view statement to examine the library cache's hit ratio in detail:

```
select      Sum(Pins) "Hits",
            Sum(Reloads) "Misses",
            Sum(Pins) / (Sum(Pins) + Sum(Reloads)) "Hit Ratio"
from        V$LibraryCache;

HITS        MISSES    HIT RATIO
1989             5    .99749248
```

The hit ratio is excellent (over 99 percent) and would not require any increase in the SHARED_POOL_SIZE parameter.

## Using Individual Library Cache Parameters to Diagnose Shared Pool Use

Using a modified query on the same table, we can see how each individual parameter makes up the library cache. This may help diagnose a problem or overuse of the Shared Pool.

```
set numwidth 3
set space 2
set newpage 0
set pagesize 58
set linesize 80
set tab off
set echo off
ttitle 'Shared Pool Library Cache Usage'
column namespace    format a20              heading ' '
column pins         format 999,999,999      heading 'Executions'
column pinhits      format 999,999,999      heading 'Hits'
column pinhitratio  format 9.99             heading 'Hit|Ratio'
column reloads      format 999,999          heading 'Reloads'
column reloadratio  format .9999            heading 'Reload|Ratio'
spool cache_lib.lis
select   namespace, pins, pinhits, pinhitratio, reloads, reloads
         /decode(pins,0,1,pins) reloadratio
from     v$librarycache;
```

```
Sun Mar 19                                             page     1
                     Shared Pool Library Cache Usage
                                        Hit                 Reload
Entity        Executions    Hits        Ratio    Reloads    Ratio
SQL AREA      1,276,366     1,275,672   1.00     2          .0000
TABLE/PROC    539,431       539,187     1.00     5          .0000
BODY                                    1.00                .0000
TRIGGER                                 1.00                .0000
INDEX         21                         .00                .0000
CLUSTER       15            5            .33                .0000
OBJECT                                  1.00                .0000
PIPE                                    1.00                .0000

8 rows selected
```

Use the following list to help interpret the contents of the V$LIBRARYCACHE view:

■ **namespace**   Values SQL AREA, TABLE/PROCEDURE, BODY, and TRIGGER are the key types.

■ **gets**   Shows the number of times a handle was requested for an item in library cache.

**Tuning for Optimal Performance**

- **gethits**   Shows the number of times a requested handle was already in cache.
- **gethitratio**   Is (gethits/gets).
- **pins**   Shows the number of times an item, in library cache, was executed.
- **pinhits**   Shows the number of times an item was executed where that item was already in cache.
- **pinhitratio**   Is (pinhits/pins).
- **reloads**   Shows the number of times an item had to be reloaded into cache because it aged out or was invalidated.

## Keep the Pin Hit Ratio for Library Cache Items Close to 1

The pin hit ratio for all library cache items "sum(pinhits)/sum(pins)" should be close to one (1). A pin hit ratio of one (1) means that every time the system executed something in library cache, it was already allocated and valid in cache. While there will always be some misses due to the first time a request is made, misses can also be reduced by writing identical SQL statements.

## Keep the Miss Ratio Less Than 15 percent

The miss ratio for data dictionary cache "sum(getmisses)/sum(gets)" should be less than 10-15 percent. A miss ratio of zero (0) means that every time the system went into the data dictionary cache, it found what it was looking for and did not have to retrieve the information from disk. If the miss ratio "sum(getmisses)/sum(gets)" is greater than 10-15 percent, then the init.ora SHARED_POOL_SIZE parameter should be increased.

**TIP**
*Measure hit ratios for the library cache of the Shared Pool with the V$LIBRARYCACHE view. A hit ratio of over 95 percent should be achieved. However, when the database is initially started, hit ratios will be around 85 percent.*

## Available Memory on a Regular Basis May Mean the SHARED_POOL_SIZE Is Set Correctly

The main question that people usually want answered is, "Is there any memory left in the Shared Pool?" To find out how fast memory in the Shared Pool is being depleted (made noncontiguous) and also what percent is unused (and still contiguous), run the following query after starting the database and running production queries for a short period of time (after the first hour of the day):

```
col value for 999,999,999,999 heading "Shared Pool Size"
col bytes for 999,999,999,999 heading "Free Bytes"
select   to_number(v$parameter.value) value, v$sgastat.bytes,
         (v$sgastat.bytes/v$parameter.value)*100 "Percent Free"
from     v$sgastat, v$parameter
where    v$sgastat.name = 'free memory'
and      v$ parameter .name = 'shared_pool_size;

Shared Pool Size     Free Bytes     Percent Free
    100,000,000     82,278,960      82.27896
```

If there is plenty of contiguous free memory (greater than 2M) after running most queries in your production system (you'll have to determine how long this takes), then there is no need to increase the SHARED_POOL_SIZE parameter. I have never seen this parameter go all of the way to zero (Oracle saves a portion for emergency operations via the SHARED_POOL_RESERVED_SIZE parameter). I have seen it go to 2GB (with a Shared Pool of only 100M) when the Shared Pool started approaching zero (an indicator that the SHARED_POOL_RESERVED_SIZE is set too low).

**TIP**
*The V$SGASTAT view will show you how fast the memory in the Shared Pool is being depleted. Remember that it is only a rough estimate. It shows you any memory that has never been used combined with any piece of memory that has been reused. Free memory will go up and down as the day goes on based on how the pieces are fragmented.*

**V8 TIP**
*The V$SGASTAT view is refreshed much better in Oracle8 than in Oracle7 and is an excellent source for monitoring the Shared Pool.*

## Use the x$ksmsp Table to Get a Detailed Look at the Shared Pool

The x$ksmsp table is a method of looking at the total breakdown for the Shared Pool. This table will show the amount of memory that is free, freeable, and memory that is retained for large statements that won't fit into the current Shared Pool.

Consider the next query for a more accurate picture of the Shared Pool. Refer to Chapter 15 for an in-depth look at this query and how it is adjusted as Oracle is started and as the system begins to need Shared Pool memory.

```
select     sum(ksmchsiz) Bytes, ksmchcls Status
from       x$ksmsp
group by ksmchcls;

BYTES             STATUS
 50,000,000       R-free
         40       R-freea
888,326,956       free
    837,924       freeabl
 61,702,380       perm
    359,008       recr
```

Oracle does not state anywhere what the values for status in the x$ksmsp table mean. I offer the following possible descriptions based on the behavior of these values as researched in Chapter 15. In Chapter 5, I also show how to graph these results in Enterprise Manager.

| Status | Possible Meaning |
| --- | --- |
| R-free | This is SHARED_POOL_RESERVED_SIZE (default 5 percent of SP). |
| R-freea | This is probably reserved memory that has been used but is freeable. |
| free | This is the amount of contiguous free memory available. |
| freeabl | This is probably memory that has been used but is freeable. |
| perm | This is free memory not yet moved to the free area for use. |
| recr | I am not sure what this is—possibly reserved memory for Oracle. |

**TIP**
*The general rule of thumb is to make the SHARED_POOL_SIZE parameter 50-150 percent of the size of your DB_BLOCK_BUFFERS. In a system that makes use of a large amount of stored procedures but has limited physical memory, this parameter could make up as much as 150 percent the size of DB_BLOCK_BUFFERS. In a system that uses no stored procedures but has a large amount of physical memory to allocate to DB_BLOCK_BUFFERS, this parameter may be 10-20 percent of the size of DB_BLOCK_BUFFERS. I have worked on larger systems where the SHARED_POOL_SIZE was set as high as 500M.*

## The SHARED_POOL_RESERVED_SIZE

This is a holding area of bytes in the Shared Pool for large requests that the Shared Pool doesn't have enough contiguous blocks to meet. This is only used if the request is *larger* than the SHARED_POOL_MIN_ALLOCATION. When this parameter is set below 1M, I have seen strange Oracle errors and behavior. If you make this 10 percent, then *do not* change the SHARED_POOL_MIN_ALLOCATION. Generally, this is set to 10 percent of the SHARED_POOL_SIZE but not less than 1M. If you begin to get errors regarding the SHARED_POOL_SIZE, then this parameter should probably be set. By pinning packages and procedures in memory (see Chapter 10), you can usually avoid most errors that cause people to use this parameter. Chapter 10 also has a volume of PL/SQL procedures for checking what is in the Shared Pool at a given time, as well as a procedure to pin all objects into memory.

### Remember:

- If the dictionary cache hit ratio is low (below 95 percent), then consider increasing SHARED_POOL_SIZE.
- If the reload ratio is high (> 1 percent), then consider increasing SHARED_POOL_SIZE.
- If the row cache hit ratio is low (below 95 percent), then consider increasing SHARED_POOL_SIZE.

# Using the Buffer Pools in Oracle8

There are new "pools" introduced in Oracle8 for the allocation of memory. They relate to the DB_BLOCK_BUFFERS and SHARED_POOL_SIZE. Each of these parameters, which were all inclusive of the memory they allocate, now have additional options for memory allocation within each memory pool. I will cover each of the two separately.

## Pools Related to DB_BLOCK_BUFFERS and Allocating Memory for Data

In this section, we will focus on the Oracle8 pools that are used to store the actual data in memory. The init.ora parameters DB_BLOCK_BUFFERS, DB_BLOCK_SIZE, BUFFER_POOL_KEEP, and BUFFER_POOL_RECYCLE will be the determining factors for memory used to store data.

DB_BLOCK_BUFFERS times the DB_BLOCK_SIZE refers to the total size in bytes of the main buffer cache (or memory for data) in the SGA. In Oracle8, two additional buffer pools are introduced: BUFFER_POOL_KEEP and BUFFER_POOL_RECYCLE. These additional two pools serve the same purpose as the main buffer cache (DB_BLOCK_BUFFERS), with the exception that the algorithm to maintain the pool is different for all three available pools.

The *main buffer cache* (defined by DB_BLOCK_BUFFERS) maintains the LRU (Least Recently Used) list and flushes the oldest buffers in the list. The number of blocks specified in DB_BLOCK_BUFFERS make up all three pools. The main buffer cache is the amount of buffers that are left over from DB_BLOCK_BUFFERS after specifying the BUFFER_POOL_KEEP and the BUFFER_POOL_RECYCLE.

The *Keep Pool* (defined by BUFFER_POOL_KEEP) is never flushed, and is intended for buffers that need to be "pinned" indefinitely (buffers that are very important and need to stay in memory). Use the Keep Pool for small tables that are frequently accessed and need to be in memory at all times.

The *Recycled Pool* (defined by BUFFER_POOL_RECYCLE) is instantly flushed in order to reduce contention and waits in the pool by leaving the LRU list empty at all times. Data that would rarely be on the list in a normal mode would search the list with no success. This overhead can be avoided with this pool. Use the Recycle Pool for large, less important data that is usually accessed only once in a long while.

The following examples give a quick look on how information is allocated to the various buffer pools. Remember, if no pool is specified, then the buffers in the main pool (DB_BLOCK_BUFFERS minus other pool allocations) are used.

**Create a table that will be stored in the Keep Pool upon being accessed:**

```
Create table state_list (state_abbrev varchar2(2), state_desc varchar2(25))
Storage (buffer_pool keep);
```

**Alter the table to the Recycle Pool:**

```
Alter table state_list storage (buffer_pool recycle);
```

**Alter the table back to the Keep Pool:**

```
Alter table state_list storage (buffer_pool keep);
```

**Find the disk and memory reads in the Keep Pool:**

```
select    physical_reads "Disk Reads", block_gets +
          consistent_gets "Memory Reads"
from      v$buffer_pool
where     name = 'KEEP';
```

Use the following example to query the V$PARAMETER view and list the various buffer pool settings.

## Pools Related to SHARED_POOL_SIZE and Allocating Memory for Statements

In this section, we will focus on the Oracle8 pools that are used to store the actual statements in memory. Unlike the pools related to the data, the LARGE_POOL_SIZE is allocated outside the memory allocated for SHARED_POOL_SIZE.

The LARGE_POOL_SIZE is a pool of memory used for the same opearation as the SHARED_POOL_SIZE is used to store. Oracle defines this as the size set aside *within* the SHARED_POOL_SIZE for large allocations in the Shared Pool. I have found in testing that this memory (at the writing of this book) was allocated outside the SHARED_POOL_SIZE and taken from physical memory. You'll have to do your own testing to ensure where the allocations are coming from in your system and version of Oracle. The minimum setting is 300K, but the setting must also be as big as the LARGE_POOL_MIN_ALLOC, which is the minimum size of Shared Pool memory requested that will force an allocation in the LARGE_POOL_SIZE memory.

**You can view your pool settings by querying the V$PARAMETER view:**

```
select    name, value, isdefault, isses_modifiable, issys_modifiable
from      v$parameter
where     name like '%pool%';


NAME                               VALUE      ISDEFAULT   ISSES     ISSYS
SHARED_POOL_SIZE                   10000000   FALSE       FALSE     FALSE
SHARED_POOL_RESERVED_SIZE          500000     TRUE        FALSE     FALSE
SHARED_POOL_RESERVED_MIN_ALLOC     5K         TRUE        FALSE     FALSE
LARGE_POOL_SIZE                    0          TRUE        FALSE     FALSE
LARGE_POOL_MIN_ALLOC               16K        TRUE        FALSE     FALSE
BUFFER_POOL_KEEP                              TRUE        FALSE     FALSE
BUFFER_POOL_RECYCLE                           TRUE        FALSE     FALSE
PARALLEL_MIN_MESSAGE_POOL          48330      TRUE        FALSE     FALSE

8 rows selected.
```

**V8 TIP**
*The additional buffer pools (memory for data) available in Oracle8 are initially set to zero. By setting values for the BUFFER_POOL_KEEP and BUFFER_POOL_ RECYCLE, we eliminate from the blocks set by DB_BLOCK_BUFFERS that are allocated for the main memory for data and give them to the other two pools.*

# Tuning the SORT_AREA_SIZE for Optimal Use of Memory

The SORT_AREA_SIZE specifies the amount of memory that Oracle allocates per user process for sorting data. This memory allocated is outside of the SGA and is only used when sorting. The memory is given back to the operating system when sorting is complete. When sorting cannot be sufficiently handled by the size of the SORT_AREA_SIZE, the user's process is sorted on disk (can be very slow for a large query) in the temporary tablespace specified for that user. The temporary tablespace should be monitored for activity to determine if an increase in the

SORT_AREA_SIZE can have a positive effect on overall performance by sorting in memory instead of disk sorts in the temporary tablespace.

Note that the temporary tablespace is utilized for the temporary tables created internally for sorting operations when SORT_AREA_SIZE is insufficient.

**TIP**

*The SORT_AREA_SIZE parameter of the init.ora is specified in bytes and is on a per user process basis and is only allocated when a specific user needs it. Be careful or you will run out of operating system memory if this is set too high!*

In deciding whether to modify the value, there are many issues to take into consideration that center around the amount of the total physical memory, the size of the Oracle database and application, the number of users, and the types of processing being performed on the system on both a daily and nightly basis. Total physical memory is the key component when raising these parameters. The intent is to use as much memory for Oracle without sacrificing performance on the operating system end. There must be no swapping of processes to disk—this could substantially degrade overall system performance.

**TIP**

*Since temporary segments are created to handle sorts that cannot be handled in memory, the initial extent default for temporary segments should be at least as large as the value of SORT_AREA_SIZE. This will minimize extension of the segment.*

## Sort in Memory—Not on Disk

You do *not* want to sort on disk (temporary segments), so set the SORT_AREA_SIZE init.ora parameter high enough to sort in memory. Next is a list of statements that cause sorting operations to occur in memory:

```
    .    create index
    .    select .... order by
    .    select .... distinct
    .    select .... group by
    .    select .... union
    .    select .... intersect
    .    select .... minus
    .    unindexed joins
    .    some correlated subqueries
```

## Remember:

- SORT_AREA_SIZE is used to determine the space allocated in main memory for each process to perform sorts.
- If the sort cannot be performed in memory, temporary segments are allocated on disk to hold intermediate runs (slow).
- Increasing the value of SORT_AREA_SIZE will reduce the total number of disk sorts, thus reducing disk I/O.
- Setting SORT_AREA_SIZE too high can cause swapping if too little memory is left over for other processes.

**TIP**

*The SORT_AREA_RETAINED_SIZE should be set as large as the value of the SORT_AREA_SIZE. The SORT_AREA_RETAINED_SIZE is the size that the SORT_AREA_SIZE will be reduced to when the sort is complete. It also ensures that memory is held for the entire duration of the sort and allows multiple memory sort areas in the event of concurrent sorts within the same query. But, be careful—this also requires more physical memory for not only the duration of the sort but after the sort is complete. The memory allocated to SORT_AREA_RETAINED_SIZE is only released when the session is exited. The memory allocated to SORT_AREA_SIZE is released (provided that the retained size is specified) when the last row is fetched from the sort space.*

Although, it is always better to sort in memory using an appropriate SORT_AREA_ SIZE, if you must sort to disk, you can ensure that a user is sorting in a temporary tablespace rather than in the SYSTEM tablespace by using the following statements:

```
ALTER USER username TEMPORARY TABLESPACE tempspc;

ALTER USER BROECH TEMPORARY TABLESPACE TEMP1;
```

**TIP**

*If you can't set a high enough SORT_AREA_SIZE for sorting, make sure that users are not sorting in the SYSTEM tablespace. Also, if you must sort on disk, set up multiple temporary tablespaces for sorting on various disks so that users are sorting in different areas from each other. This improves I/O.*

**TIP**
*In a high-volume, high-user OLTP environment, the SORT_AREA_SIZE parameter is usually set between 64K and 256K. For large nightly batch processes and database re-creations (for the creation of indexes), this parameter is often set as high as 20-50M.*

## Modifying the Size of Your SGA to Avoid Paging and Swapping

Before you increase the size of your SGA, you must understand the effects on the physical memory of your system. If you increase parameters that use more memory than what is available on your system, then serious degradation in performance may occur. When your system processes jobs, if it doesn't have enough memory, it will start paging or swapping to complete the active task.

When *paging* occurs, information that is *not currently* being used is moved from memory to disk. This allows memory to be used by a process that *currently* needs it. If paging happens a lot, the system will experience decreases in performance, causing processes to take longer to run.

When *swapping* occurs, an *active* process is moved from memory to disk temporarily so another *active* process that also desires memory can run. Swapping is based on system cycle time. If swapping happens a lot, your system is dead. Depending on the amount of memory available, an SGA that is too large can cause swapping. Figure 4-5 gives a rough idea of how people in the industry size the SGA

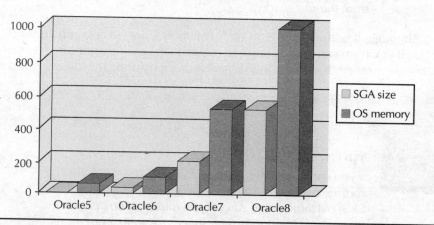

**FIGURE 4-5.** *General SGA sizing (given that system memory is available)*

as it relates to total physical memory. It gives you a feel for where Oracle is heading (the entire database in memory) while also giving you a rough view as to whether your settings are "way out of the ballpark" compared to others.

**TIP**

*Get to know your operating system commands for swapping and paging to monitor system memory. If your system is swapping often, your SGA may be too large, but there is always a possibility that the queries performed are poorly written—as covered in Chapters 8 and 9.*

**V9 TIP**

*Perhaps in version 9 of Oracle, the SGA will be 400GB and physical memory will be 800GB, given the growth rate displayed in Figure 4-5. The goal continues to be to get the entire database into memory. For now (in V7 & V8), we must hope to get everything used frequently into memory.*

# Using SHOWUSER, SHOWOTHER, and USERSQL to Find System Drains

One of the needs that seems to come up regularly is having a quick way to find the programs that are burying the system. The key is to identify and tune problem queries so that other users are not adversely affected by another user on the system. Keeping the system running at top speed not only takes consistent database maintenance but immediate action when a program begins to slow your system down. The queries listed here will help you quickly identify the users and programs that are causing the slowdown:

| Query | Description |
|---|---|
| SHOWUSER | This query identifies all users and programs that are being executed. |
| SHOWOTHER | This query identifies processes that will not show up in SHOWUSER. |
| USERSQL | Identifies a query for a particular user (usually a query that needs tuning). |

Finding System Drains

Make your life easier by using these programs in the three-step process outlined next to figure out who is hitting your database and with what commands:

## Step 1: Locate the Users and Programs Being Executed

The SHOWUSER query finds all of the users and the programs that they are currently executing. It retrieves information about the user that allows you to identify both the person and the query that is being executed:

```
rem This is the showuser.sql query.  It does a display of oracle processes
spool  showuser.out
select    substr(a.username,1,10) USERNAME,
          substr(a.osuser,1,8) OSUSER,
          substr(b.spid,1,6) SRVPID,
          substr(to_char(a.sid),1,3) ID,
          substr(a.machine,1,8) HOST,
          substr(a.program,1,25) PROGRAM
from      v$process b, v$session a
where     a.paddr = b.addr
order by  a.username;
spool off
```

| USERNAME | OSUSER | SRVPID | ID | PROGRAM | |
|---|---|---|---|---|---|
| C09962 | OraUser | 25005 | 12 | 2791 | O:\IS\ORA456\BIN\F45DES.EXE |
| C11250 | OraUser | 23228 | 11 | 2855 | O:\IS\ORA456\BIN\F45DES.EXE |
| C11250 | OraUser | 26847 | 17 | 17223 | C:\WINNT35\SYSTEM32\OLE2.EXE |
| C11250 | OraUser | 27384 | 6 | 17295 | O:\IS\ORA456\BIN\F45RUN.EXE |
| C11285 | OraUser | 8770 | 16 | 9455 | O:\IS\ORA456\BIN\R25DES.EXE |
| OPS$ORACLE | oracle | 1705 | 14 | 1702 | sqlplus@hp014 (TNS interf |
| WMSOBJTEST | OraUser | 15978 | 21 | 3463 | O:\IS\ORA456\BIN\F45RUN.E |
| WMSOBJTEST | OraUser | 16386 | 9 | 2463 | O:\IS\ORA456\BIN\F45RUN.E |
| oracle | oracle | 1688 | 1 | 1688 | oracle@hp014 (PMON) |
| oracle | oracle | 1689 | 2 | 1689 | oracle@hp014 (DBWR) |
| oracle | oracle | 1696 | 3 | 1696 | oracle@hp014 (LGWR) |
| oracle | oracle | 1697 | 4 | 1697 | oracle@hp014 (SMON) |
| oracle | oracle | 1698 | 5 | 1698 | oracle@hp014 (RECO) |

## Step 2: Locate Sessionless Processes

Since there could also be processes running that have no associated sessions, you'll want to run the SHOWOTHER.sql query after the SHOWUSER.sql query. The SHOWOTHER.sql query finds all of the users and the current programs they are executing not picked up by the SHOWUSER.sql query. It retrieves information about the user that allows you to identify both the person and the query that is being executed. While this query can be combined with the previous query to show a complete list at one time, it is usually worthwhile to view the queries separately so the different type of processes can be identified.

```
rem  This is the showother.sql query and shows all processes with
     no session
spool  showuser.out

select    substr(spid,1,6) SRVPID ,
          username, program
from      v$process
where     BACKGROUND <> 1
and       ADDR not in
          (select    paddr
           from      v$session);
spool  off
```

## Step 3: Locate the Problem Query or Program

Once you've found the userid that you are interested in, use the USERSQL.sql query to find out exactly what the problem user is executing.

**NOTE**

*For this example we will assume that username 'co9962' is the problem user found in Step 1 that we need to check on. Also, note that the output is modified slightly for readability.*

```
select    s.sid, s.username, s.status, disk_reads, buffer_gets,
          executions, loads, sql_text
from      v$sqlarea q, v$session s
where     q.address = s.sql_address
and       s.username = 'CO9962'
order by  sid;
```

| SID | USERNAME | STATUS | DISK READS | BUFFER GETS | EXECUTIONS | LOADS SQL TEXT |
|-----|----------|--------|------------|-------------|------------|----------------|
| 12  | C09962   | ACTIVE | 1934       | 98          | 2          | 4              |

```
select crew_no, name, description from CREWS where substr(crew_no,4,1) = 'A'
```

Check the SQL_TEXT. This could be a query that is causing the problem. The query shows us that the index on crew_no has been suppressed by the SUBSTR function. This in turn can have a negative impact. Also note that you may have to join in the V$SQLTEXT view to get the full text since the V$SQLAREA view only shows a portion of the SQL_TEXT.

Finding System Drains

**TIP**
*Use the V$PROCESS and V$SESSION views to find
problem users. Use the V$SQLAREA and V$SQLTEXT
views to find the problem query that the user is
executing.*

## Other Queries for Pinpointing Performance Problems

If you know the V$ tables, you will understand the heart of your Oracle system! The
V$ queries contained in this section are helpful in pinpointing performance problems.
They include queries that show memory, sessions, queries, logistics, and waits
encountered by users. While only the queries and a brief description are listed here,
Chapter 14 is exclusively dedicated to the V$ views.

**Determine the memory usage per session:**

```
select    a.sid, a.username, b.value
from      v$session a, v$sesstat b, v$statname c
where     a.sid = b.sid
and       b.statistic# = c.statistic#
and       c.name = 'session memory';
```

**Display the entire SQL statement being executed by a session:**

```
select    a.sid, a.username, b.sql_text
from      v$session a, v$sqltext b
where     a.sql_address = b.address
and       a.sql_hash_value = b.hash_value
order by  a.sid, a.username, b.piece;
```

**Display the current cursor being executed by a session:**

```
select    a.sid, a.username, b.sql_text
from      v$session a, v$open_cursor b
where     a.saddr = b.saddr;
```

**Determine the number of sessions for each user:**

```
select    username, count(*)
from      v$session
group by  username;
```

**Display detail information about a session (include the operating system username, process, and terminal):**

```
select    sid, username, program, osuser, process, machine,
          terminal, type
from      v$session;
```

**Display detailed statistics per session to determine a session's resource usage:**

```
select    a.sid, a.username, b.name, c.value
from      v$session a, v$statname b, v$sesstat c
where     a.sid = c.sid
and       b.statistic# = c.statistic#
and       a.username = upper('&username')
order by  a.sid, a.username, b.name;
```

**Identify SQL activity being executed by a session:**

```
select    a.sid, a.user_name, s.sql_text
from      v$session a, v$sqltext s
where     a.sql_address = s.address
and       a.sql_hash_value = s.hash_value
order by  a.user_name, a.sid, s.pieces;
```

**The V$WAITSTAT view—determining waits:**

```
select    Class, Count, Time
from      V$WaitStat;
```

**The V$SESSION_WAIT view—determining waits:**

```
select    SID, Event, Wait_Time, State
from      V$Session_Wait;
```

**The V$SYSTEM_EVENT view—querying events:**

```
select    Event, Total_Waits, Time_Waited, Average_Wait
from      V$System_Event;
```

**TIP**
*Many of the V$ TIMING FIELDS views, within the V$ views, are dependent on the TIMED_STATISTICS init.ora parameter being set to TRUE; otherwise, there are no timing statistics in these fields.*

Pinpointing Performance Problems

## Using the V$SYSSTAT View to View System Memory Use

Using the V$SYSSTAT view, only a partial listing below, we can view Oracle's system-wide memory use in a single snapshot. The important values accessed via these queries are highlighted in this section. The V$SYSSTAT view, as you can see here, gives us a tremendous amount of system information that can be used to monitor performance:

```
select        name , value
from          v$sysstat;


Name                                Value
cumulative logons                      40
cumulative opened cursors           3,164
recursive calls                    73,028
recursive cpu usage                   649
session logical reads          23,197,189
CPU used by this session          340,984
session connect time            1.039E+09
session memory                    601,456
max session memory             49,783,888
session max pga memory         96,085,728
enqueue timeouts                        0
enqueue waits                          27
db block gets                   3,649,199
consistent gets                19,750,615
physical reads                    748,799
physical writes                   283,095
DBWR timeouts                         539
DBWR checkpoints                      172
redo size                     343,424,304
parse time cpu                      6,323
parse time elapsed                 10,620
parse count                       132,626
execute count                     765,334
sorts (memory)                        789
sorts (disk)                            0
```

When viewing data from the V$SYSSTAT view, be sure to check the critical areas listed here:

■ The buffer hit ratio for buffer cache "logical reads/(physical + logical reads)" should be greater than 95 percent. A buffer hit ratio of 100 percent means that all data from data tables, indexes, rollback segments, clusters, and sequences was read from buffer cache. No physical reads were necessary.

- The value for "physical reads" is the total number of requests for data resulting in a physical access to a data file on disk.

- Buffer contention can be identified from the "buffer busy waits" statistics in the UTLBSTAT statistics report or by viewing data from the V$WAITSTAT view. Contention for rollback segments can be determined by looking at contention for buffers that contain rollback segment blocks.

**TIP**
*The V$SYSSTAT view will show overall performance since the database was last started. This usually will be a good benchmark for how well your tuning efforts are doing. Db block gets and consistent gets are the memory reads in your SGA. Physical reads are the disk reads. As you continue to tune each week, the memory reads should go up and the physical reads should go down.*

- The DBWR (Database Writer) checkpoints are the number of times DBWR was notified to do a checkpoint. Frequent checkpoints reduce recovery time in the event of instance failure, but also cause the DBWR to be invoked more often during batch jobs or queries that process a large number of UPDATEs, INSERTs, or DELETEs. The minimum number of checkpoints can be achieved by setting the init.ora parameter LOG_CHECKPOINT_INTERVAL to a value larger than the size of the largest redo log file and the LOG_CHECKPOINT_TIMEOUT parameter to 0.

- The Free Buffer Requested is the total number of free buffers that were requested by a user.

## Use UTLBSTAT and UTLESTAT to Monitor Memory and Performance

The scripts UTLBSTAT.sql and UTLESTAT.sql are tools to monitor system memory and performance. The UTLBSTAT.sql script creates statistical tables and collects beginning statistics. The UTLESTAT.sql script collects ending statistics and generates a variety of reports. The following conditions must be met to run the scripts:

- The database must first be started up with the TIMED_STATISTICS init.ora parameter set to TRUE.

- Once the buffers and cache have stabilized, the UTLBSTAT script can be run to create statistical tables and to collect beginning statistics.

- Run the application(s) through their paces with a full complement of users.

**Viewing System Memory Use**

■ The UTLBSTAT script can be run to collect ending statistics and generates a variety of reports (as described in Chapter 16).

■ Utilize ESTAT/BSTAT whenever you need statistics for a specific time period (e.g., between 1-3 P.M.). These reports show the difference between the data at the beginning of the time period and the data at the end of the time period.

**NOTE**
*For a more detailed description, see Chapter 16, which is entirely devoted to this subject.*

# The OPTIMIZER_MODE: Cost- Versus Rule-Based Optimization

The cost-based optimizer was built to make your tuning life easier by choosing better paths for your poorly written queries. Rule-based optimization was built on a set of rules on how Oracle processes statements. It is recommended that cost-based optimization be used at all times, because rule-based optimization is expected to eventually go away and won't be available for use. Rule-based optimization is still available in Oracle8, but now is the time to convert problem queries, created using rule-based optimization, to cost-based optimization, and to tune those queries for cost-based optimization. In Oracle8i, some actions run cost-based optimization only.

## How Optimization Looks at the Data

Rule-based optimization is *Oracle-centric* while cost-based optimization is *data-centric*. The optimizer mode under which the database operates is set via the init.ora parameter OPTIMIZER_MODE. The possible optimizer modes are as follows:

■ **CHOOSE**   Uses cost-based optimization for all analyzed tables. This is a good mode for well-built and well-tuned systems (for advanced users).

■ **RULE**   Always uses rule-based optimization. This is good for systems migrating from V5/V6 that have not been tuned for cost-based optimization.

■ **FIRST_ROWS**   Gets the first row faster (generally forces index use). This is good for untuned systems that process lots of single transactions (for beginners).

■ **ALL_ROWS**   Gets all rows faster (generally forces index suppression). This is good for untuned, high-volume batch systems (usually not used).

The default optimizer mode for V7 and V8 is CHOOSE, but the optimizer will use rule-based optimization until the tables are ANALYZEd (statistics are gathered for cost-based) even when the optimizer is set to CHOOSE.

**TIP**
*Although an OPTIMIZER_MODE = CHOOSE will use cost-based optimization (when tables are analyzed), there is no OPTIMIZER_MODE called COST. This is a common misconception.*

**TIP**
*If you are not sure what optimizer mode to use, then use CHOOSE and analyze all tables. By doing this, you will be using cost-based optimization. The cost-based optimizer is where the future of Oracle will be focused.*

## The 95/5 Rule (TUSC Tuning Rule)

When the "optimizer" (cost-based) finds a query to retrieve less than 5-6 percent (based on the average distribution) of the rows in a table, the optimizer will choose to drive the query with an index if one exists. Figures 4-6 and 4-7 show how Oracle has evolved through the past years. While Oracle7 shows the best performance at all levels, the developer must know when to override the optimizer (see Chapters 8 and 9 for information about individual query tuning).

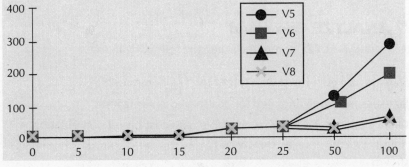

**FIGURE 4-6.** *Optimum percentage of rows for index for a given version of Oracle*

The OPTIMIZER_MODE

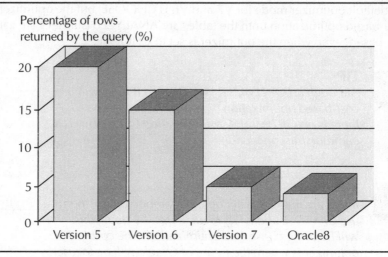

Percentage of rows
returned by the query (%)

**FIGURE 4-7.** *Determining when to use an index depends on the version of Oracle*

## Cost-Based Optimization

When using cost-based optimization, keep in mind the following,

- The ANALYZE command must be used to "turn on" cost-based for a table (this is in addition to having the OPTIMIZER_MODE = CHOOSE).

- DBAs must ensure that tables are re-ANALYZEd as the distribution of data changes or performance may suffer.

- In the init.ora, set OPTIMIZER_MODE = RULE to practice tuning your system and evaluate statistics.

## The V7 ANALYZE Command

When using the ANALYZE command, keep the following in mind:

- Statistics are generated with the ANALYZE command.

- Statistics must be generated for cost-based optimization.

- Once a table is ANALYZEd, the table uses cost-based optimization.

- A table can also be de-ANALYZEd using the delete statistics command shown next.

The following code analyzes a small sample of the table and generates statistics based on that sample:

```
SQL> ANALYZE TABLE CUSTOMER
     ESTIMATE STATISTICS;
```

The following example analyzes the entire table and generates statistics:

```
SQL> ANALYZE TABLE CUSTOMER
     COMPUTE STATISTICS;
```

The following example removes the statistics and moves queries back to rule-based optimization:

```
SQL> ANALYZE TABLE CUSTOMER
          DELETE STATISTICS;
```

The following example finds records that have been placed in multiple blocks (*chaining*). Chaining records causes poor performance.

```
SQL> ANALYZE TABLE CUSTOMER
     LIST CHAINED ROWS;
```

**TIP**

*Oracle will only use cost-based optimization if at least one of the tables in the query is analyzed. Otherwise, it uses rule-based. If multiple tables are joined in a query, either all tables should be analyzed (cost) or all tables should not be analyzed (rule). If one or more of the tables are analyzed, yet others are not, then cost-based optimization is performed without statistics on the nonanalyzed tables. This usually results in a slow query.*

**TIP**

*If both the WHERE and the SELECT are indexed, then only the index has to be accessed without any subsequent table access. In fact, indexing columns that are in the WHERE and the SELECT clauses can reduce response time by a factor of 100 when compared to just indexing the WHERE clause. There is also an INDEX_FFS (fast full scan) hint (see Chapter 7) that forces this behavior for a query.*

# Creating Enough Latches, Dispatchers, and Open Cursors

For a small number of DBAs, a shortage of latches, dispatchers, and open cursors prevents their applications from running. This section takes a look at how latches, dispatchers, and open cursors can bring an application to a standstill.

## To Avoid Contention, Modify the LOG_SIMULTANEOUS_COPIES Parameter

Latches are like locks on memory. They are used to protect shared data structures in the SGA. If you have enough latches, then you will never know that latches exist. If you don't have enough latches, you will be very aware of latches and you will need to increase the parameter associated with latches. The goal is to know it before it stops your system. The key to achieving this goal is to examine your latch data by using the following query:

```
select     Name "Latch",
           Sum(Gets) "WTW Gets",
           Sum(Misses) "WTW Misses",
           Sum(Immediate_Gets) "IMM Gets",
           Sum(Immediate_Misses) "IMM Misses"
from       V$Latch
where      Name Like 'redo%'
group by   Name;
```

| NAME | WTW GETS | WTW MISSES | IMM GETS | IMM MISSES |
|---|---|---|---|---|
| redo allocation | 359 | 0 | 0 | 0 |
| redo copy | 0 | 0 | 0 | 0 |

If the number of immediate misses (IMM Misses in this query) is more than 1 percent of the immediate gets, or the misses are more than 1 percent of the gets, you may have a contention problem. If this is the redo allocation latch, setting the LOG_SIMULTANEOUS_COPIES to two per CPU should take care of any problems. If it is the redo copy latch, then decreasing the LOG_SIMULTANEOUS_COPIES parameter should solve your problems.

Other key latches that impact performance include the following:

- **cache buffers chain**   This latch indicates user processes are waiting to scan SGA for block access (to tune, adjust init.ora parameter DB_BLOCK_BUFFERS).

- **cache buffers LRU chain**   This latch indicates user processes are waiting to scan the LRU (Least Recently Used) chain that contains all the used blocks in the database buffers (to tune, adjust init.ora parameter DB_BLOCK_BUFFERS or DB_BLOCK_WRITE_BATCH).

- **enqueues**   This latch is used for enqueues to tune. Adjust the init.ora parameter ENQUEUE_RESOURCES to be greater than 10.

- **redo allocation**   This latch controls the allocation of space in the redo buffer. To reduce contention for this latch, reduce the value of the init.ora parameter LOG_SMALL_ENTRY_MAX_SIZE on a multi-CPU system to force the use of a redo copy latch.

- **row cache objects**   This latch indicates waits for user processes attempting to access the cached data dictionary values. To reduce contention on this latch, tune the data dictionary init.ora parameter SORT_AREA_SIZE.

The primary columns of interest in the V$LATCH view are as follows:

- **gets**   Shows the total number of successful "willing to wait" requests for a latch.

- **misses**   Shows the number of times an initial "willing to wait" request was unsuccessful.

- **sleeps**   Shows the number of times a process waited and requested a latch after an initial "willing to wait" request.

- **IMMEDIATE_GETS**   Shows the number of successful "immediate" requests for a latch.

- **IMMEDIATE_MISSES**   Shows the number of unsuccessful "immediate" requests for a latch.

## Decrease Wait Times on Multithreaded Servers by Adding Dispatchers

When using the multithreaded servers, some of the things you need to watch for are high busy rates for the existing dispatcher processes and increases in wait times for response queues of existing dispatcher processes. If the wait time increases, as the application runs under normal use, you may wish to add more dispatcher processes, especially if the processes are busy more than 50 percent of the time.

Use the following statement to determine busy rate:

```
select    Network,
          ((Sum(Busy) / (Sum(Busy) + Sum(Idle))) * 100) "% Busy Rate"
from      V$Dispatcher
group by Network;
```

Creating Latches, Dispatchers, and Open Cursors

```
NETWORK        % Busy Rate
TCP1              0.
TCP2              0
```

Use the following statement to check for responses to user processes that are waiting in a queue to be sent to the user:

```
select     Network Protocol,
           Decode (Sum(Totalq), 0, 'No Responses',
           Sum(Wait) / Sum(TotalQ) || 'hundredths of a second')
           "Average Wait Time Per Response"
from       V$Queue Q, V$Dispatcher D
where      Q.Type = 'DISPATCHER'
and        Q.Paddr = D.Paddr
group by   Network;

PROTOCOL          Average Wait Time Per Response
TCP1              0 hundredths of a second
TCP2              1 hundredths of a second
```

Use the following statement to check the requests from user processes that are waiting in a queue to be sent to the user:

```
select     Decode (Sum(Totalq), 0, 'Number of Requests',
           Sum(Wait) / Sum(TotalQ) || 'hundredths of a second')
           "Average Wait Time Per Request"
from       V$Queue
where      Type = 'COMMON';

AVERAGE WAIT TIME PER REQUEST
12 hundredths of a second
```

## Open Cursors

If you don't have enough open cursors, you will receive errors to that effect. The key is to stay ahead of your system by increasing this init.ora parameter before you run out of open cursors. My recommendation is to use the operating system maximum as the setting for open cursors.

# The Top 25 init.ora Parameters

These are what I consider to be the 25 most important init.ora parameters (detail is listed in Appendix A):

1. NLS_DATE_FORMAT - "DD_MON_RR", "DD_MON_YYYY", or "FXDD_MON_YYYY" depending on your system; used for Y2K effort

2. DB_BLOCK_BUFFERS - Memory allocated for the data

3. SHARED_POOL_SIZE - Memory allocated for data dictionary and SQL and PL/SQL

4. OPTIMIZER_MODE - CHOOSE, RULE, FIRST_ROWS or ALL_ROWS

5. SORT_AREA_SIZE - Memory used for sorting and merging tables

6. SORT_AREA_RETAINED_SIZE - Memory held after the sort for a session

7. LOG_CHECKPOINT_INTERVAL - How often committed transactions are archived

8. OPEN_CURSORS - Holds user statements to be processed (private area)

9. SHARED_POOL_RESERVED_SIZE - Memory held for future big PL/SQL or ORA-error

10. DB_BLOCK_SIZE - Size of the blocks (DB_BLOCK_SIZE □ DB_BLOCK_BUFFERS=bytes for data)

11. DBWR_IO_SLAVES - In Oracle7 DB_WRITERS; more writers from memory to disk

12. DB_FILE_MULTIBLOCK_READ_COUNT - For a DWHSE; you can read more blocks per I/O

13. SORT_DIRECT_WRITES - Writes to temporary segments; bypass the buffer cache

14. LOG_BUFFER - Buffer for uncommitted transactions in memory

15. BUFFER_POOL_KEEP - How many buffers to have for pinned objects?

16. BUFFER_POOL_RECYCLE - How many buffers to have for new stuff?

17. LOG_ARCHIVE_DUPLEX_DEST - Write archives to multiple places

18. LOG_ARCHIVE_MIN_SUCCEED_DEST - Minimum number of archive copies that must succeed

19. LOCK_SGA - Keeps SGA from being pushed out of memory (not all platforms)

20. PRE_PAGE_SGA - Causes all of the SGA pages to be touched and brought into memory

21. LOCK_SGA_AREAS - Can lock only selective portions of the SGA (not all platforms)

22. DBWR_IO_SLAVES - Number of writers from SGA to disk for simulated asynch I/O

23. LARGE_POOL_SIZE - Total blocks in the large pool allocation for large PL/SQL

24. LARGE_POOL_MIN_ALLOC - Minimum bytes for large PL/SQL to allocate in shared pool

25. LOG_SIMULTANEOUS_COPIES - Maximum redo buffer copy latches for simultaneous writes

**TIP**

*Setting certain init.ora parameters correctly could be the difference between a report taking two seconds and two hours. Try changes out on a test system thoroughly before* implementing those changes in a production environment!

# Changes to the init.ora Parameters in Oracle8

The following parameters in the init.ora initialization file have been changed:

- SNAPSHOT_REFRESH_INTERVAL becomes JOB_QUEUE_INTERVAL
- SNAPSHOT_REFRESH_PROCESS becomes JOB_QUEUE_PROCESS
- DB_WRITERS becomes DBWR_IO_SLAVES

**V8 TIP**

*Previously undocumented _DISABLE_LOGGING is available and documented in Oracle8 and does not cause corruption.*

**V9 TIP**

*Many of the undocumented init.ora parameters form the basis for the next version of Oracle (your window to the next version). You only want to use these in extreme circumstances or a test environment.*

# Undocumented init.ora Parameters

Querying the table x$ksppi shows you documented as well as undocumented init.ora parameters. The query may only be done as user SYS, so be careful. See Chapter 15 for a complete look at the x$ tables. My top 13 undocumented init.ora parameters are listed in Appendix A. Appendix C gives a complete listing as of the writing of this book of the x$ tables.

```
select      ksppinm, ksppivl,ksppidf
from        x$ksppi;
```

The following is a brief description of the columns in the x$ksppi table:

KSPPINM = Parameter name
KSPPIVL = Current value for the parameter
KSPPIDF = Default value for the parameter

A partial output listing of the init.ora parameters is shown here:

```
KSPPINM                   KSPPIVL        KSPPIDF
_DEBUG_SGA                FALSE          TRUE
_TRACE_EVENTS                            TRUE
DB_BLOCK_BUFFERS          40000          FALSE
DB_BLOCK_SIZE             2048           FALSE
...
```

**TIP**
*Using _DISABLE_LOGGING can cause data corruption in version 7, so be careful with any undocumented init.ora parameters! They should only be used as a last resort, and only after testing them on your "crash and burn" test box.*

**TIP**
*Use _CORRUPTED_ROLLBACK_SEGMENTS to get a database up that has corrupted rollback segments. Once up, drop and re-create the problem rollback segments. Use _ALLOW_RESETLOGS_CORRUPTION for the databases that were backed up (image copy) while the database was up.*

# A Test Case That Yielded a 69 Percent Gain in Performance

On this critical batch process application, the Oracle tuning amounted to a gain of 48 percent overall. Since the application was a "canned package," *no changes* were

Test Case

made to the application. The application included a large amount of queries, UPDATEs, and INSERTs. The following table illustrates the improvements that were achieved with this system.

|  | Original Times | Hardware Tuning | Oracle Tuning | Improved % |
|---|---|---|---|---|
| **Batch1** | 59 min | 54 min | 26 min | 65 |
| **Batch2** | 76 min | 41 min | 20 min | 65 |
| **Batch3** | 105 min | 65 min | 31 min | 70 |
| **Batch4** | 81 min | 50 min | 28 min | 65 |
| **Batch5** | 53 min | 36 min | 19 min | 64 |
| **Batch6** | 101 min | 57 min | 33 min | 67 |
| **Net Time** | 206 min | 122 min | 64 min | 69 |

## About the Test

The initial gain in the performance on the hardware was attributable to memory allocations and settings that allowed Oracle to use more operating system memory.

The gain in tuning performance came primarily from modifying the init.ora (SGA) parameters (accounting for 26 percent of the gain). In a later test, which included distributing the data and additional init.ora changes by modifying the block size, an additional 22 percent gain in performance was achieved.

### TIP
*When making tuning decisions, instead of looking at overall file I/O, focus on instantaneous file I/O based on the application since overall file I/O can balance itself out over time.*

## Balance Load I/O

One of the more significant changes made had to do with load balancing the I/O. There were significant bottlenecks with throughput since the data was not appropriately balanced between the physical disks. The key to balancing the load I/O is to scan through the application to find out where to place both the tables and the indexes. Balancing the redo logs across several disks improved the performance of "multithreaded" (simultaneous) jobs. Some of the changes I made on the instance reduced the physical reads, but I/O still remained an issue.

Note that additional disks and controllers could lead to even more significant improvements.

The database structural changes made included increasing the size of the temp tablespace and the size of the rollback segments. Increasing rollback segments ensured that there were no extents added during the production processing.

**TIP**
*Each extent added to a database object requires disk-intensive writes to allocate the extent within the tablespace file. The Temp tablespace storage allocation was increased so that sorting operations would not result in costly temp table extensions.*

## Init.ora Sizing for a 2.5G Database with 256M of Memory

The following estimates are provided to help you determine the optimal size for the init.ora parameters. The settings for your parameter depend on your unique system.

| Parameter | Typical | Suggested |
|---|---|---|
| DB_BLOCK_SIZE | 2,048 | 8,192 |
| DB_BLOCK_BUFFERS | 3,200 | 5,000 |
| SHARED_POOL_SIZE | 9,000,000 | 20,000,000 |
| LOG_CHECKPOINT_INTERVAL | 10,000 | 0 |
| DML_LOCKS | 200 | 1,000 |
| PROCESSES | 100 | 200 |
| LOG_BUFFER | 65,536 | 327,680 |
| ROW_CACHE_CURSORS | 100 | 200 |
| OPEN_CURSORS | 200 | 600 |
| SORT_AREA_SIZE | 102,400 | 2,000,000 |
| MAX_DUMP_FILE_SIZE | 10,240 | 10,240 |
| DB_FILES | OS dependent | 121 |
| DB_WRITERS In Oracle8, this is DBWR_IO_SLAVES) | — | 4 |
| CHECKPOINT_PROCESS | — | TRUE |
| OPTIMIZER_MODE | CHOOSE | CHOOSE |
| TIMED_STATISTICS | FALSE | TRUE |
| Estimated SGA Size | 15M | 62M |

Test Case

## Init.ora Sizing for a 20GB Database with 512M of Memory

The following table illustrates which init.ora parameters were altered for this system:

| Parameter | Typical | Suggested |
|---|---|---|
| DB_BLOCK_SIZE | 2,048 | 8,192 |
| DB_BLOCK_BUFFERS | 3,200 | 12,500 |
| SHARED_POOL_SIZE | 9,000,000 | 50,000,000 |
| LOG_CHECKPOINT_INTERVAL | 10,000 | 0 |
| DML_LOCKS | 200 | 1,000 |
| PROCESSES | 100 | 250 |
| LOG_BUFFER | 65,536 | 655,360 |
| ROW_CACHE_CURSORS | 100 | 200 |
| OPEN_CURSORS | 200 | 600 |
| SORT_AREA_SIZE | 102,400 | 5,000,000 |
| MAX_DUMP_FILE_SIZE | 10,240 | 10,240 |
| DB_FILES | OS dependent | 121 |
| DB_WRITERS DBWR_IO_SLAVES in Oracle8) | — | 10 |
| CHECKPOINT_PROCESS | — | TRUE |
| OPTIMIZER_MODE | CHOOSE | Depends |
| TIMED_STATISTICS | FALSE | TRUE |
| Estimated SGA Size | 15M | 152M |

Note that you *must* have enough memory to bump your SGA this high (> 256M)!

## Decrease Physical Reads by Increasing the SGA

Increasing the System Global Area (SGA) by upping the DB_BLOCK_BUFFERS to 15,000 and the SHARED_POOL_SIZE to 40M reduced the number physical reads (otherwise known as fetches from disk) by 740,000. This is because DB_BLOCK_BUFFERS is the amount of memory dedicated in the SGA for reading in database records. The more records that can be retrieved from volatile memory, the faster the database operation can be performed. The SHARED_POOL_SIZE is that area of the SGA used for caching the data dictionary, data structures, small tables, preparsed procedures, and triggers, as well as recently executed SQL statements. The database references the information in this area frequently, and if it is not large enough, the system is forced to fetch the dictionary information from disk or not hold SQL statements long enough for re-execution without reparsing.

## Increase Redo Logs and Checkpoint Intervals to Reduce Writes to Disk

The LOG_CHECKPOINT_INTERVAL was set fairly high at 65,535. When the log buffers fill to this amount, a forced write to disk occurs. The problem with forcing the database to checkpoint in this method is that the database writes to the redo logs more often than it may need to. A more efficient method is to have the database write to the redo logs only when all the log buffers are filled or when a COMMIT is performed. This happens when the value of the LOG_CHECKPOINT_INTERVAL is set to zero which reduces the writes to disk.

## Reduce Wait Time by Increasing DML Locks

DML_LOCKS were increased from 400 to 1,000. This reduced the wait time the database experienced when it used all the available locks it had to allocate. When this happens, the database must wait until a lock becomes free to issue another lock. A high number of locks does not require very much additional memory, and it can have a significant impact on performance if the database is locking a significant number of records.

## Read More Data Per Fetch by Increasing Block Size

DB_BLOCK_SIZE was increased from 2K to 8K. This change allowed the database to fetch the data in bigger chunks. In this instance, the database was able to read four times as much data with each fetch from disk. This also can be achieved by setting DB_FILE_MULTIBLOCK_READ_COUNT.

## Increase rocesses to Avoid User Contention

Processes were increased from 100 to 200 to allow us to increase the sum of the background processes without running the risk of the database rejecting a cursor because too many processes already existed.

## Decrease the Number of Physical Reads by Increasing the Size of the Log Buffer

The LOG_BUFFER size was increased from 65K to 655K. As we increased the checkpoint interval to force the database to wait until the buffers were full, we also increased the number of buffers. This pushed off the writes to the redo log files even longer. Although this made the physical write to disk somewhat longer, the number of times it actually was forced to write to disk went down significantly.

### Decrease the Number of Recursive Calls by Increasing Row Cache Cursors

The ROW_CACHE_CURSORS were increased because the database used these for tracking the recursive calls to the data dictionary. Increasing this number also reduced the number of RDBMS recursive calls.

### To Reduce Waits, Increase Open Cursors

The OPEN_CURSORS were set to 600 from 200. This, like increasing locks, reduces waits the RDBMS experiences. This typically happens when all of the available cursors have been allocated and the database must wait until one cursor has closed before opening a new one.

### If Space Allows, Increase the Sort Area Size to Ensure that Sorts Run in Memory

SORT_AREA_SIZE was increased from 1M to 10M. Since this system had a large amount of available physical memory, we were able to set the SORT_AREA_SIZE at a higher level to run sorts in memory instead of on disk. The memory for SORT_AREA_SIZE is taken from outside of the SGA, and it generally is opened up for each process that requires sort space. SORT_AREA_RETAINED_SIZE was set to 10M also since we wanted the batch to continue to hold the memory for future sorts.

**TIP**
*In a system where many users are constantly doing sorts, the SORT_AREA_SIZE parameter should not be set this high or swapping (bad news for performance) may occur.*

### To Support Multithreaded Writes, Add DB Writers

DB_WRITERS was set to 2. This allowed multithreaded writes to the database files. Note that in Oracle8 this parameter has changed to DBWR_IO_SLAVES.

### Dedicate a Background Process to Handle Log Buffers

The checkpoint process was set to TRUE. This allowed the O/S to dedicate a specific background process to moving the log buffers upon checkpoint to redo log files. This also allowed the log writer process to just focus on managing the log buffers.

Given the previous changes, the following changes occurred in our test system:

| Statistic | Old | New |
|---|---|---|
| Physical_Reads | 1,408,662 | 748,799 |
| Shared Pool Hit Ratio | 93.8 percent | 97.0 percent |
| SQL Area Reload | 9 | 2 |
| Recursive Calls | 86,743 | 73,028 |
| Max Session Memory | 22,646,008 | 49,783,888 |
| Change Write Time | 17,242 | 12,058 |
| Redo Write Time | 91,753 | 54,579 |
| Redo Log Space Requests | 132 | 1 |
| Redo Log Space Wait Time | 6969 | 70 |

Note that these statistics were generated from V$SYSSTAT, V$ROWCACHE, and V$LIBRARYCACHE views. It took nine runs to achieve the optimal performance.

# The Typical Server

The key to understanding Oracle is to understand its dynamic nature. Oracle continues to have many attributes of previous versions while also attacking the future of distributed database and object-oriented programming stored within the database. Experience from earlier versions of Oracle always benefits the DBA in future versions of Oracle. Some of the future changes that should be considered as you build your system are listed here:

■ Oracle can be completely distributed and maintained at a single point (many databases and locations with one DBA managing the system looks like the corporate future).

■ Database maintenance is becoming completely visual (all point-and-click maintenance as in the Enterprise Manager). The V$ views are still your best access.

■ Network throughput continues to be an issue that looks to be solved by technology (next two years).

■ Internet and intranet access is pushing client/server back to browser/host types of setups with big security risks that are often overcome by the use of multiple databases.

- CPUs will continue to get faster, eliminating CPU as an issue. (I/O and correct design will continue to be the issues.)
- Object-oriented development will be crucial to rapid system development.
- Current database design theory is being rewritten to focus more on denormalization.
- Graphics are causing the sizes of databases to become increasingly larger than they were in the past.

## Model of a Typical Server

This section contains rough estimates designed as setup guidelines. However, it is important to emphasize that these are only guidelines and that the reality is that every system is different and must be tuned based on the system's demands.

| Database Size | Up to 5GB | 10–25GB | 50–100GB | 150–1,000GB |
|---|---|---|---|---|
| Number of users | 50-100 | 100 | 200 | 350 |
| Number of CPUs | 2–4 | 4–8 | 8 | 8–16 |
| System memory | 250M+ | 512M | 1GB | 2GB |
| SGA size | 115M | 260M | 500M | 1GB |
| Number of buffers | 80M | 180M | 350M | 750M |
| Shared Pool | 35M | 80M | 150M | 250M |
| Total disk capacity | Up to 15GB | 20–50GB | 100–150GB | 200–400GB |
| Percentage of query | 75 percent | 75 percent | 75 percent | 75 percent |
| Percentage of DML | 25 percent | 25 percent | 25 percent | 25 percent |
| Percent batch | 20 percent | 20 percent | 20 percent | 20 percent |
| Percent online | 80 percent | 80 percent | 80 percent | 80 percent |
| Number of redo logs multiplexed? | 4–8 Yes | 4–8 Yes | 6–10 Yes | 6–12 Yes |
| Number of control files | 4 | 4 | 4 | 4 |
| Number of temporary tablespaces | 1–4 | 1–4 | 1–4 | 2–5 |

Typical Server Model

| Database Size | Up to 5GB | 10–25GB | 50–100GB | 150–1,000GB |
|---|---|---|---|---|
| Number of rollback segments (depends on DMLs) | 4–8 | 4–10 | 8–20 | 10–25 |
| Rollback segment size-initial+next extent | 2M + 10M | 2M + 10M | 5M + 20M | 20M + 20M to 20M + 100M |
| Archiving used? | Yes | Yes | Yes | Yes |
| Image backup frequency | Nightly | Nightly | Nightly | Nightly |
| Export backup frequency | Weekly or nightly | Weekly or nightly | Weekly or nightly | Weekly or nightly |
| Buffer hit ratio | 95 percent + | 95 percent + | 95 percent + | 97 percent + |
| Dictionary hit ratio | 90 percent + | 90 percent + | 95 percent + | 95 percent + |
| Library hit ratio | 90 percent + | 90 percent + | 95 percent + | 95 percent + |
| Other system software (other than Oracle) | Minimum | Minimum | Minimum | Minimum |
| Use raw devices? | No | No | No | No |
| Use parallel query? | Depends on queries | Depends on queries | Depends on queries | Probably in many queries |

The following variables can cause diversion from the typical server:

- Heavy batch processing may need much larger tollback, redo, and temp tablespace sizes.

- Heavy DML processing may need much larger rollback, redo, and temp tablespace sizes.

- Heavy user access to large tables requires more CPU and memory, and larger temp tablespace sizes.

- Poorly tuned systems require more CPU and memory, and larger temp tablespace sizes.

- A greater number of disks and controllers always increases performance by reducing I/O.

Typical Server Model

■ An increase in the disk capacity can speed backup and recovery time by going to disk and not tape.

# Tips Review

■ The key init.ora parameters in Oracle are DB_BLOCK_BUFFERS, DB_BLOCK_SIZE, SHARED_POOL_SIZE, and SORT_AREA_SIZE.

■ Changing init.ora parameters spontaneously is a powerful feature for both developers and DBAs. Consequently, a user with the ALTER SESSION privilege is capable of irresponsibly allocating 100M+ for the SORT_AREA_SIZE for a given session if it is not restricted.

■ Retrieving information from memory is over 10,000 times faster than retrieving it from disk, so make sure that the SGA is large enough.

■ The database must be rebuilt if you increase the DB_BLOCK_SIZE. Increasing the DB_FILE_MULTIBLOCK_READ_COUNT will allow more block reads in a single I/O, giving a benefit similar to a larger block size.

■ The allowable DB_BLOCK_SIZE has increased in Oracle8 to be 32K. It was only 16K in the latest versions of Oracle7.

■ Check the V$SYSSTAT view and ensure that the buffer hit ratio is 95 percent for fastest performance. You may need to increase DB_BLOCK_BUFFERS if your buffer hit ratio is not above 95 percent. A hit ratio below 95 percent indicates that a large amount (> 5 percent) of the data requested by users is not getting cached in memory.

■ In Oracle8, use the TopSQL monitor of Oracle's SQL Analyze to find problem queries.

■ Bad (slow) queries show in the V$SQLAREA view with poor hit ratios the first time they are executed. Make sure you tune them at that time. The second time that they execute may not show a poor hit ratio.

■ Oracle Forms applications usually have an unusually high hit ratio. If your site uses a lot of Oracle Forms, shoot for a higher hit ratio since the hit ratio will be artificially high.

■ Sites that use rollbacks to a greater extent by most users of the system should shoot for a higher hit ratio since the hit ratio could be artificially high from rollback use.

■ Find the memory killing queries by searching the V$SQLAREA view for the queries that use the largest number of buffers. This will often show a query that has an index on a column that should not be indexed. Use BUFFER_GETS divided by executions to get the number of BUFFER_GETS each time the query is executed.

- You may have to join in the V$SQLTEXT view to get the full text since the V$SQLAREA view only shows a portion of the SQL_TEXT.

- Cache frequently used tables into memory so that they are not flushed out of memory by infrequently used tables.

- PL/SQL must be written *exactly* the same to be reused. Case differences and any other differences will cause a re-parse of the statement.

- Measure hit ratios for the row cache and library cache of the shared pool with queries to the V$ROWCACHE and V$LIBRARYCACHE views. A hit ratio of over 95 percent should be achieved. However, when the database is initially started, hit ratios will be around 85 percent.

- The V$SGASTAT view will show you how fast the memory in the shared pool is being depleted. Remember that it is only a rough estimate. It shows you any memory that has never been used combined with any piece of memory that has been reused. Free memory will go up and down as the day goes on based on how the pieces are fragmented. A query to x$ksmsp can give the full breakdown for memory allocated in the Shared Pool.

- The general rule of thumb is to make the SHARED_POOL_SIZE parameter 50-150 percent of the size of your DB_BLOCK_BUFFERS. In a system that makes use of a large number of stored procedures but has limited physical memory, this parameter could make up as much as 150 percent the size of DB_BLOCK_BUFFERS.

- The SORT_AREA_RETAINED_SIZE should be set as large as the value of the SORT_AREA_SIZE. The SORT_AREA_RETAINED_SIZE is the size that the SORT_AREA_SIZE will be reduced to when the sort is complete. It also ensures that memory is held for the entire duration of the sort and also allows multiple memory sort areas in the event of concurrent sorts within the same query. But be careful—this also requires more physical memory for not only the duration of the sort but after the sort is complete. The memory allocated to SORT_AREA_RETAINED_SIZE is only released when the session is exited. The memory allocated to SORT_AREA_SIZE is released (provided that the retained size is specified) when the last row is fetched from the sort space.

- The additional buffer pools (memory for data) available in Oracle8 are initially set to zero. By setting values for the BUFFER_POOL_KEEP and ·

Tips Review

BUFFER_POOL_RECYCLE, we eliminate from the blocks set by DB_BLOCK_BUFFERS that are allocated for the main memory for data and give them to the other two pools.

■ Get to know your operating system commands for swapping and paging to monitor system memory (Chapter 18 focuses on this for UNIX). If your system is swapping often, your SGA may be too large, but there is always a possibility that the queries performed are poorly written (as covered in Chapters 8 and 9).

■ Use V$PROCESS and V$SESSION views to find problem users. Use V$SQLAREA and V$SQLTEXT views to find the problem query that the user is executing.

■ Although an OPTIMIZER_MODE = CHOOSE will use cost-based optimization (when tables are analyzed), there is no OPTIMIZER_MODE called COST. This is a common misconception.

■ If you are not sure what optimizer mode to use, then use CHOOSE and analyze all tables. By doing this, you will be using cost-based optimization. The cost-based optimizer is where the future of Oracle will be focused.

■ Oracle will only use cost-based optimization if at least one of the tables in the query is analyzed. Otherwise, it uses rule-based. If multiple tables are joined in a query, either all tables should be analyzed (cost) or all tables should *not* be analyzed (rule). If one or more of the tables are analyzed, yet others are not, then cost-based optimization is performed without statistics on the nonanalyzed tables. This usually results in a slow query.

■ Use _CORRUPTED_ROLLBACK_SEGMENTS to get a database up that has corrupted rollback segments. Once up, drop and re-create the problem rollback segments. Use _ALLOW_RESETLOGS_CORRUPTION for the databases that were backed up (image copy) while the database was up.

■ In a system where many users are constantly doing sorts, the SORT_AREA_SIZE parameter *should not* be set this high or swapping (bad news for performance) may occur.

# References

*DBA Tuning; Now YOU are the Expert,* Rich Niemiec; TUSC

*Performance Tuning Guide,* Oracle Corporation

# TIPS

# &

# TECHNIQUES

# CHAPTER
# 5

# Enterprise Manager
# and Tuning Pack
# (DBA and Developer)

The goal of this chapter is to provide a quick tour of Oracle's Enterprise Manager (OEM). The tour will not explore the entire product, or teach you how to use all of the features (it would take an entire book). Rather, the tour will expose you to some of the tools and tuning features that may be helpful in your tuning endeavors. Oracle Enterprise Manager is an excellent tuning tool for all levels of DBAs.

One way to ensure great performance is to monitor your system for potential performance issues before those issues become major problems. One of the vehicles that provides a GUI interface to tuning is the Oracle Enterprise Manager and related performance tuning add-on products. Oracle Enterprise Manager continues to change over time, but the overall information has generally remained the same, and it becomes easier to implement with the addition of provided implementation scripts. While the overall Oracle Enterprise Manager tool is most suited for work by the DBA, the SQL Analyze utility is suited for both the developer and the DBA who performs query tuning.

Oracle's Enterprise Manager standard applications include the Instance Manager, Schema Manager, Security Manager, Storage Manager, SQL Worksheet, Backup Manager, Data Manager and Oracle Software Manager. The Oracle Tuning Pack version 1.6 includes Oracle Expert, SQL Analyze and the Tablespace Manager. The Oracle Diagnostics Pack 1.6 includes the Performance Manager, TopSessions, Lock Manager, Capacity Planning, Oracle Trace, and the Advanced Events. Version 2.0 of the Tuning Pack will also add an Index Tuning Wizard and an Auto-Analyze tool that automatically keeps your Oracle8i statistics up-to-date. The screen shots in this chapter use version 1.2.2 (except where specified to be 1.5.5, 1.6 or 2.0). Tips covered in this chapter include the following:

- Using Oracle's Schema Manager within Enterprise Manager
- Using the Storage Manager within Enterprise Manager to view disk reads/writes
- Using the Performance Manager to graphically look at strategic tuning areas
- Graphical view of buffer cache, library cache, row cache, and memory sort hit ratios
- The Performance Manager Overview Screen to view overall system performance
- Creating your own custom charts in the Performance Manager
- Using SQL Analyze's TopSQL to get the worst performing queries on your system
- Using SQL Analyze to quickly view the EXPLAIN PLAN tree of a query

- Using SQL Analyze for a side-by-side comparison of SQL
- Using the Tuning Wizard within SQL Analyze
- Using Oracle Expert to generate a tuning report of suggested changes
- New in Tuning Pack 1.6: the Tablespace Manager
- Using Oracle Expert to generate an implementation file for your tuning session to fix problem performance areas

# The Instance Manager

The Instance Manager can be used to look at information about individual sessions or the system-wide init.ora parameters. The Instance Manager screen has a window that will have nodes for all databases. Icons at the top of this screen include options to connect to another database that is available, and an option to refresh the current database, as shown next. A pull-down menu choice under Sessions includes the option to restrict or allows all sessions, usually used in conjunction with starting/stopping the database. The option to restrict can be particularly helpful for database maintenance where it is important to disallow users from logging in to the database.

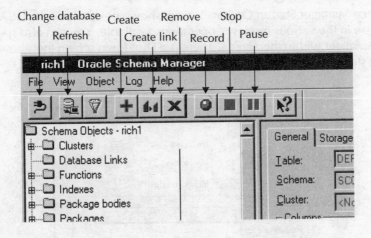

**TIP**

*Most of the Toolbar buttons are the same in each of the Enterprise Manager products. Get to know them for fast access to different areas within a tool.*

The Instance Manager

## Instance Manager—Status Screen

The Instance Manager Status screen shows the output from the V$SGA view. It shows the general memory allocations to Oracle, the version of Oracle being used, and the options that you have installed.

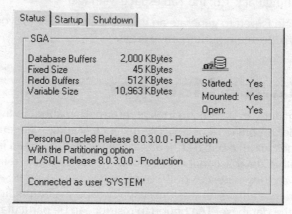

## Instance Manager—Startup Options

The Instance Manager Startup Options screen, shown next, allows the DBA to start the database in the various modes of operations available. You can also specify an init.ora parameter within this screen. There is a Shutdown screen (not shown) that shows the standard shutdown options (Normal, Immediate, Abort).

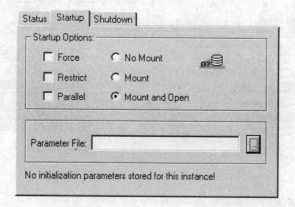

## Instance Manager—init.ora Parameters

This section of the Instance Manager shows the init.ora parameters. It identifies the current setting for the parameters, as well as if the parameter can be modified

(Dynamic=Yes) without shutting down the database. The Oracle init.ora parameters are covered in detail in Chapter 4 and Appendix A.

Initialization Parameters

| Parameter Name | Running Value | Dynamic | Default |
|---|---|---|---|
| shared_pool_size | 10000000 | No | No |
| shared_pool_reserved_size | 500000 | No | Yes |
| shared_pool_reserved_min_alloc | 5K | No | Yes |
| sessions | 60 | No | Yes |
| session_max_open_files | 0 | No | Yes |
| session_cached_cursors | 0 | No | Yes |
| serializable | FALSE | No | Yes |
| serial_reuse | DISABLE | No | Yes |
| sequence_cache_hash_buckets | 10 | No | No |
| sequence_cache_entries | 10 | No | Yes |
| row_locking | always | No | Yes |
| row_cache_cursors | 10 | No | Yes |
| rollback_segments | | No | Yes |
| resource_limit | FALSE | No | Yes |
| replication_dependency_tracking | TRUE | No | Yes |
| remote_os_roles | FALSE | No | Yes |
| remote_os_authent | FALSE | No | Yes |

# Instance Manager—View a Single Session

You can view all information related to a given user by looking at the sessions screen, shown next. This screen can be particularly helpful in identifying an actual user known to be problematic. The Session ID and Serial # are displayed, enabling the user to be killed. An actual kill user screen will be displayed later in the chapter. A section called In-Doubt Transactions (not shown) within the Instance Manager is where a forced commit or forced rollback may be issued for a given session. While a single session is shown here, you can select the Sessions folder to view all sessions in a single screen. All session IDs, usernames, terminals, and programs running are displayed in the screen.

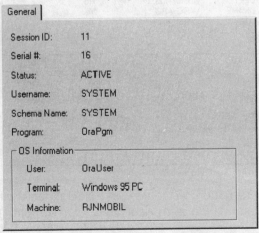

General

| | |
|---|---|
| Session ID: | 11 |
| Serial #: | 16 |
| Status: | ACTIVE |
| Username: | SYSTEM |
| Schema Name: | SYSTEM |
| Program: | OraPgm |

OS Information

| | |
|---|---|
| User: | OraUser |
| Terminal: | Windows 95 PC |
| Machine: | RJNMOBIL |

The Instance Manager

# The Schema Manager

The Instance Manager shows the information for a given instance, but the Schema Manager is one level deeper, showing an individual schema (within a given instance) and the objects that are associated with that schema. While this section will not endeavor to show every screen that is possible within the Schema Manager, the choices available from the navigator are clusters, database links, functions, indexes, package bodies, packages, procedures, refresh groups (for snapshots), snapshots, synonyms, tables, triggers, and views. There are multiple screens associated with each of the choices.

## Schema Manager—View Specific Tables

In the following illustration, we have drilled down into the table section for the SCOTT schema to view the dept table. All of the columns for the given table are displayed. The Storage tab will show all storage information for the table (INITIAL EXTENT, NEXT EXTENT, PCTINCREASE, MINEXTENTS, MAXEXTENTS, PCTFREE, and PCTUSED). The Constraints tab will show any constraints and options for adding or removing constraints. The Status tab shows the current status for all constraints and allows for enabling or disabling constraints. Note that the number of rows and average row length are displayed under the General tab—it will only show up if the table has been analyzed.

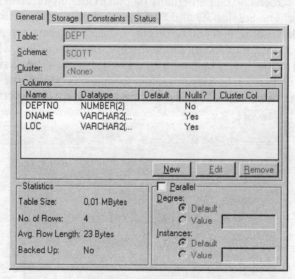

Using the Create Like button, we could create a dept2 table with the same column and storage information as the dept table. To accomplish this, press the

Record button prior to pressing the Create Like button and then press the Stop button—we would then create a file like the one shone here:

```
REM
CREATE TABLE "SYSTEM".dept2 (DEPTNO NUMBER(2) NOT NULL, DNAME VARCHAR2(14)
NULL, LOC VARCHAR2(13) NULL)  TABLESPACE USER_DATA PCTFREE 10 PCTUSED 40
INITRANS 1 MAXTRANS 255 STORAGE ( INITIAL 10K NEXT 10K MINEXTENTS 1
MAXEXTENTS 121 PCTINCREASE 50);
EXIT;
```

# Schema Manager—View Specific Indexes

In the illustration shown next, we have drilled down one level deeper into the dept table, viewing the indexes that are on the table. We find that there is a primary key called PK_DEPT on this table. We can view the general information about the index (a primary key constraint in this example), such as the columns that are indexed. We can look at the storage information as we would the table definition by clicking on the Storage tab.

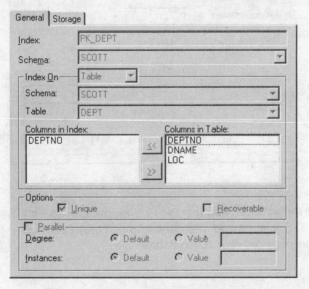

**TIP**

*The Schema Manager within the Enterprise Manager is a very quick way to look at tables and indexes when you are tuning your system.*

The Schema Manager

## Schema Manager—View SYS Information

The more advanced DBAs may want to investigate Oracle's setup of the underlying tables that make up the database. In the example shown next, the source$ table was created with MAXEXTENTS set to unlimited (actually 2,147,483,645 extents). Depending on the size of certain objects within your database, the database may need to be configured so certain internal tables are not fragmented. Be careful—modifying certain internal tables in sql.bsq causes database corruption and can render your database useless! In general, you *cannot* modify the PCTUSED, PCTFREE, INITRANS or MAXTRANS. In general, you *cannot* add a storage clause or change the tablespace_name. Some tables *cannot* be modified at all! Check with Oracle for modifications that you *can* make.

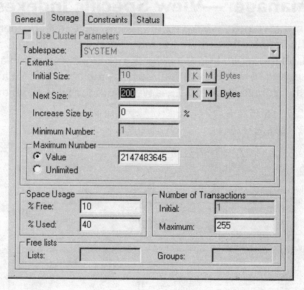

**TIP**

*Use the Schema Manager to view information about the SYS schema and internal tables that may be set up improperly for your size database.*

## Schema Manager—Viewing Packages, Procedures, and Triggers

A new source of performance bottlenecks arrived with the advent of functions, packages, procedures, and triggers. At times, it is difficult to find the source code for a function, package, procedure, or trigger; with the Enterprise Manager, the process is simplified by using the Schema Manager to select the code that is in question. You can cut and paste into SQL*Plus or use the Tuning Pack (covered later in this chapter) to tune the query that is causing problems. The Schema Manager (see the following illustration) is a quick way to find the code that may need to be tuned within packages, procedures, and triggers.

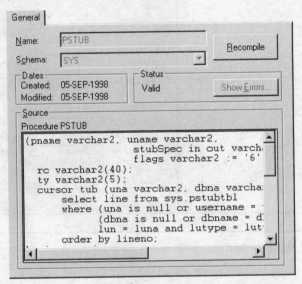

**TIP**

*Use the Schema Manager to quickly find code to tune that is related to packages, procedures, and triggers for a given schema.*

# The Security Manager

The Security Manager is a quick way to look at security and limitations placed on individual users. The Users folder shows a list of all Oracle users. It includes tabs that allow displaying and changing of a user's password, tablespace quotas, system privileges, and roles that are assigned to the user. The Roles folder displays all roles that are available in the database. If you often grant connect, resource, or DBA roles to a user, this can be a helpful screen to view or modify privileges. The Profiles folder, shown in Figure 5-1, is the last folder in the Security Manager. It is the most

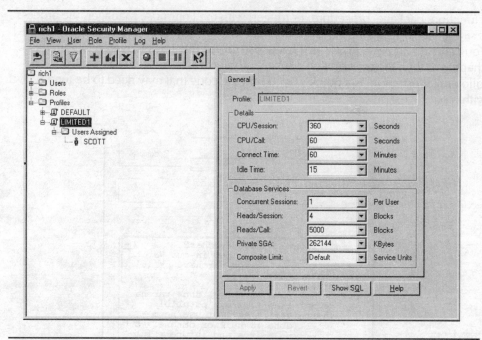

**FIGURE 5-1.** *Security Manager—Profiles*

helpful option for performance tuning. By assigning profiles to individual users, we can limit the user's ability to consume your entire system. The next section will examine some of the choices that are available.

## Security Manager—Creating a Profile

In Figure 5-1, I created the limited1 profile, then dragged and dropped the user SCOTT into this profile. As shown next, the user can be limited by CPU per session, CPU per call, connect time, idle time, concurrent sessions, reads per session (helpful for ad hoc query users), private SGA, and composite limit. The query used to create the profile, displayed in the illustration, can be viewed by pressing the View SQL button (which changes to the Hide SQL button when the SQL is visible).

```
CREATE PROFILE Limited1 LIMIT CPU_PER_SESSION 360 CPU_PER_CALL 60 CONNECT_TIME 60
IDLE_TIME 15 SESSIONS_PER_USER 1 LOGICAL_READS_PER_SESSION 5000 LOGICAL_READS_PER_CALL
5000 PRIVATE_SGA 256 K COMPOSITE_LIMIT 1000000;
```

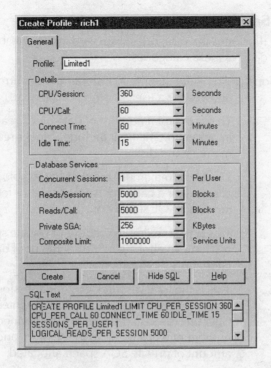

**TIP**
*Use profiles to limit ad hoc query users and/or other users that are typically unpredictable or problematic in their use of system resources.*

## The Details Section

The following table illustrates the categories displayed in the Details section and defines each of these categories:

| | |
|---|---|
| CPU/Session | This is the total amount of CPU time allowed in a session. The limit is expressed in seconds. |
| CPU/Call | This is the maximum amount of CPU time allowed for a call (a parse, execute, or fetch). The limit is expressed in seconds. |
| Connect Time | This is the maximum elapsed time allowed for a session. The limit is expressed in minutes. |
| Idle Time | This is the maximum idle time allowed in a session. Idle time is a continuous period of inactive time during a session. Long-running queries and other operations are not subject to this limit. The limit is expressed in minutes. |

## The Database Services Section

The following table illustrates the categories displayed in the Database Services section and defines each of these categories:

| | |
|---|---|
| Concurrent Sessions | This is the maximum number of concurrent sessions allowed for a user. |
| Reads/Session | This is the total number of data block reads allowed in a session. The limit includes blocks read from memory and disk. |
| Reads/Call | This is the maximum number of data block reads allowed for a call (a parse, execute, or fetch) to process a SQL statement. |
| Private SGA | This is the maximum amount of private space a session can allocate in the shared pool of the System Global Area (SGA). |
| Composite Limit | This is the total resource cost for a session. The resource cost for a session is the weighted sum of the CPU time used in the session, the connect time, the number of reads made in the session, and the amount of private SGA space allocated. |

## The Drop-Down List

You can enter a value in a field or choose from the drop-down list adjacent to the field. Click on the down arrow to display the list.

| | |
|---|---|
| Default | Use the limit specified for this resource in the DEFAULT profile. |
| Unlimited | The user's access to this resource is unlimited. |
| Values | Select one of the existing values. The default values vary by field. If you have entered a value in the field, that value appears in the drop-down list. |

# The Storage Manager

The Storage Manager, shown in Figure 5-2, is an excellent tool for viewing and modifying tablespaces, data files, and rollback segments. This is also an extremely

**The Security Manager**

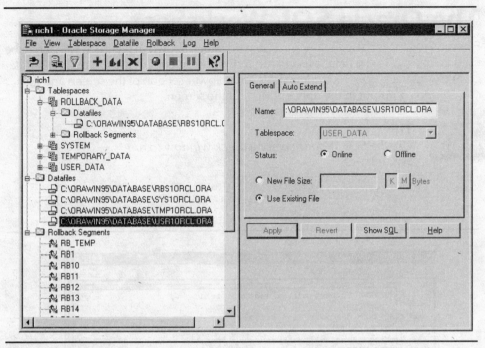

**FIGURE 5-2.**   *Storage Manager*

dangerous area to make changes. The changes that you make (such as taking a tablespace or data file offline) can seriously impact users. This is not an area to "play around in" when connected to a production database.

The Storage Manager is an excellent area to quickly view the location of data files and rollback segments for potential disk balancing. It is an effective way to view the storage parameters for tablespaces and rollback segments. You can click on a data file in the Object Navigator, and choose the Auto Extend tab to allow a data file to grow dynamically as space is needed. Remember that multiple data files can be part of a single tablespace, but a data file cannot span multiple tablespaces.

**TIP**
*Use the Storage Manager to quickly find where database files and tablespaces are located, so you can strategically balance disk reads and writes.*

# The Oracle SQL Worksheet

Enterprise Manager also includes a SQL worksheet, shown in Figure 5-3, that can be used to connect to the database and run individual queries. It is a GUI SQLDBA-like connection that shows your commands in the lower section of the screen and the corresponding output in the upper portion of the screen.

**TIP**
*Use the SQL Worksheet for a quick window to run SQL queries.*

**FIGURE 5-3.** *SQL Worksheet screen*

# The Performance Manager

Enterprise Manager also has a subutility Performance Manager that can be used to monitor some of the crucial performance-related areas within the database. Many of the queries that are used to retrieve the information displayed in this section are queries to the V$ view that Oracle has built. For Enterprise Manager 1.5.5 and higher, the Performance Manager is provided with the optional Oracle Diagnostics Pack. Using the drop-down menus, access the various areas of the Performance Manager.

**TIP**

*The Performance Manager includes many of the best performance queries to the V$ view. It shows a graphical look at the output to many of these strategic areas. It is the fastest way to get a snapshot of your performance problems and areas for potential performance improvements.*

## Performance Manager—Buffer Cache Hit Ratio

The buffer cache hit ratio can be calculated by accessing the V$SYSSTAT view, as seen in Chapter 14. However, the Performance Manager not only displays the hit ratio for the database buffers (memory allocated for user's data), but it also graphically shows the output. Information can be stored in the repository (beyond the scope of this chapter) to trend your database as well over time. In Figure 5-4, the hit ratio displayed is very low (86.92 percent) and should be closer to 95 percent. The possible culprit in this case may be that a DB_BLOCK_BUFFERS init.ora setting is too low or a poorly written query is executing an inordinate amount of physical reads. A query of the V$SQLAREA view will show the queries that are causing the poor hit ratio. See Chapter 14, detailing this access to the V$ view, for further information.

**TIP**

*Use the buffer cache hit ratio to instantly view the ratio of memory reads to disk reads for your system. If the ratio is below 95 percent, it may be necessary to tune the DB_BLOCK_BUFFERS in the init.ora or find queries that are causing a large number of disk reads.*

## Performance Manager—Library Cache Hit Ratio

The library cache hit ratio can be calculated by accessing the V$LIBRARYCACHE view, as seen in Chapter 14. However, the Performance Manager not only displays

The Performance Manager

The Performance Manager

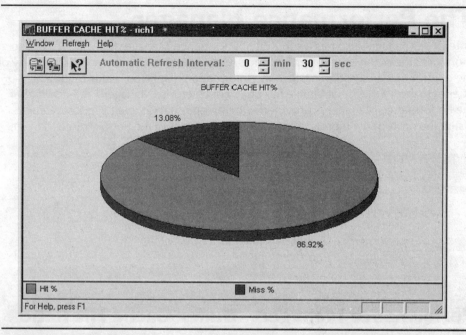

**FIGURE 5-4.** *Buffer cache hit ratio*

the hit ratio for the library cache (memory allocated for user statements such as SQL and PL/SQL), but it also graphically shows the output. In Figure 5-5a, the hit ratio displayed is great (99.66 percent). If the hit ratio is below 95 percent, investigate the SHARED_POOL_SIZE init.ora setting to determine if the setting could be too low, or pin some of the often-used PL/SQL into memory. A detailed output of the individual parameters that make up the library cache is displayed in Figure 5-5b. See Chapter 14, detailing the access to the V$ view, for further information.

## Performance Manager—Data Dictionary Cache Hit Ratio

The data dictionary cache hit ratio can be calculated by accessing the V$ROWCACHE view as seen in Chapter 14. However, the Performance Manager not only displays the hit ratio for the data dictionary cache (memory allocated for accessing to Oracle's underlying tables), but it also graphically shows the output. In Figure 5-6, the hit ratio displayed could probably use improving (90.85 percent). This hit ratio should typically be 95 percent or higher. Investigate increasing the SHARED_POOL_SIZE init.ora when this hit ratio is too low. See Chapter 14, detailing the access to the V$ view, for further information.

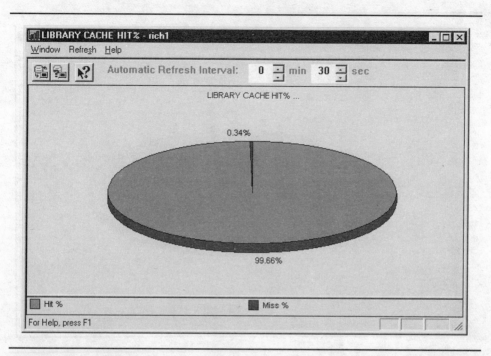

**FIGURE 5-5a.** *Library cache hit ratio*

| | GETS | GETHITS | GETHITRATIO | PINS | PINHITS | PINHITRATIO | RELOADS |
|---|---|---|---|---|---|---|---|
| BODY | 0 | 0 | 1 | 0 | 0 | 1 | 0 |
| CLUSTER | 107 | 102 | 1 | 142 | 137 | 1 | 0 |
| INDEX | 28 | 0 | 0 | 28 | 0 | 0 | 0 |
| OBJECT | 0 | 0 | 1 | 0 | 0 | 1 | 0 |
| PIPE | 0 | 0 | 1 | 0 | 0 | 1 | 0 |
| SQL AREA | 678 | 618 | 1 | 1787 | 1658 | 1 | 8 |
| TABLE/PROCEDURE | 278 | 220 | 1 | 416 | 321 | 1 | 0 |
| TRIGGER | 0 | 0 | 1 | 0 | 0 | 1 | 0 |

**FIGURE 5-5b.** *Library cache hit ratio detail*

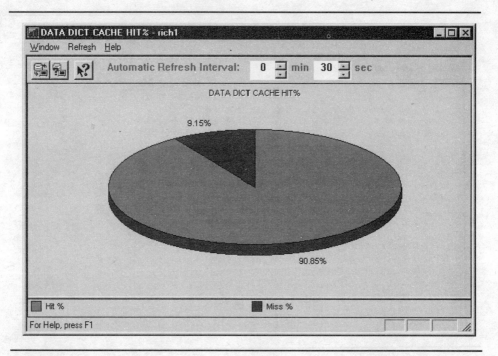

**FIGURE 5-6.** *Data dictionary cache hit ratio*

 **TIP**
*Use the library cache and row cache hit ratios for an instant view of the hit ratios related to the SHARED_POOL_SIZE init.ora parameter. Hit ratios that are below 95 percent indicate either a need to increase the SHARED_POOL_SIZE or other problems. See Chapter 14 for more information.*

## Performance Manager—SQL Area

The next illustration shows the Performance Manager output for a query to the SQL area (V$SQLAREA). This shows all of the memory that is being used for individual statements. Individual statements that identify themselves as "memory hogs" can be identified here and tuned for better performance.

*The Performance Manager*

| | SQL Text | Version Count | Sharable Memory | Mem/User Persistent |
|---|---|---|---|---|
| 1 | ALTER DATABASE MOUN` | 1 | 875 | 0 |
| 2 | BEGIN sys.dbms_ijob.remo | 1 | 25188 | 420 |
| 3 | alter database open | 1 | 864 | 0 |
| 4 | alter session set nls_langu | 1 | 1093 | 0 |
| 5 | alter session set nls_langu | 1 | 3977 | 408 |
| 6 | select (1 - (sum(decode(a. | 1 | 15691 | 532 |
| 7 | select * from v$librarycach | 1 | 23596 | 1156 |
| 8 | select /*+ index(idl_char$ i_ | 1 | 8644 | 636 |
| 9 | select /*+ index(idl_sb4$ i_ | 1 | 7235 | 512 |
| 10 | select /*+ index(idl_sb4$ i_ | 1 | 8553 | 636 |
| 11 | select /*+ index(idl_ub1$ i_ | 1 | 8509 | 636 |
| 12 | select /*+ index(idl_ub2$ i_ | 1 | 8641 | 636 |
| 13 | select TOTAL from SYS.ID | 1 | 4883 | 468 |
| 14 | select audit$,options from | 1 | 6200 | 544 |
| 15 | select blevel, leafcnt, distk | 1 | 981 | 0 |
| 16 | select charsetid, charsetfc | 1 | 915 | 0 |

For Help, press F1

# Performance Manager—Memory Sort Hit Ratio

The memory sort hit ratio can be viewed by accessing the V$SYSSTAT view as seen in Chapter 16 or by accessing the screen within Performance Manager. This screen shows details of the sorts performed in memory versus performing the sort in temporary segments (on disk) in a graphical manner. In Figure 5-7, the memory hit ratio displayed is very high (99 percent). If this hit ratio is below 99 percent, you may want to increase the SORT_AREA_SIZE init.ora parameter, but be careful as this is a per-session parameter. See Chapter 4 and Appendix A for further information.

**TIP**
*If the memory sort hit ratio is below 99 percent, it may indicate a need for an increase to the SORT_AREA_SIZE init.ora parameter. Be careful, though; increasing the SORT_AREA_SIZE can cause problems if it is set too high. See Chapter 4 and Appendix A for detailed information.*

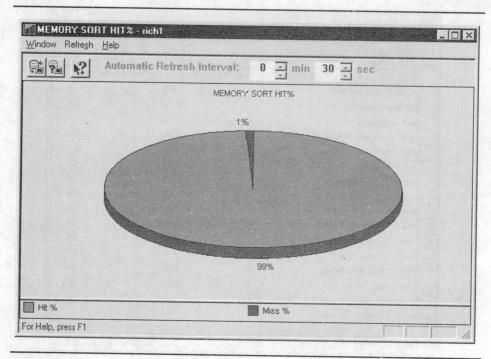

**FIGURE 5-7.** *Memory sort hit ratio*

# Performance Manager—Overview Screen

This screen is the best of all worlds. It illustrates a large portion of performance-related screens in a single screen. It is a snapshot of how the database "heart" is beating. The top section shows all of the hit ratios previously discussed in this chapter. The middle section shows user-related information. The bottom section displays the file I/O rate (physical reads and writes), the system I/O rate (memory reads and writes), and user throughput. In Figure 5-8, the data dictionary hit ratio appears to be the only cause for concern. After the database has been running for a while, we refresh the Overview screen and the data dictionary hit ratio levels off (see Figure 5-9).

In Figure 5-9, the system has been running for a while and the data cache hit ratio is not a problem, and other issues level off. The physical writes are reasonably

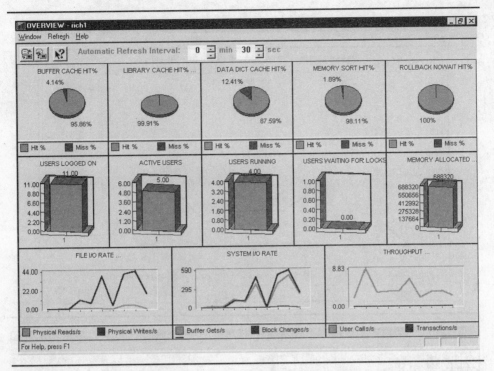

**FIGURE 5-8.** *The performance Manager Overview screen*

heavy compared to the reads, and could cause a bottleneck of contention if the data files are not well balanced.

**TIP**
*The Performance Manager Overview screen is probably the most helpful screen within Enterprise Manager. It is a simple way to see the overall performance of your system in a single screen.*

# Performance Manager—System I/O Rate

The following illustration shows the buffer to physical read graphical system I/O output.

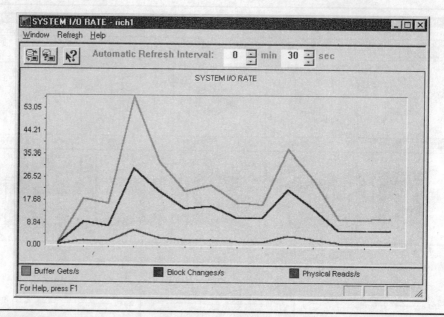

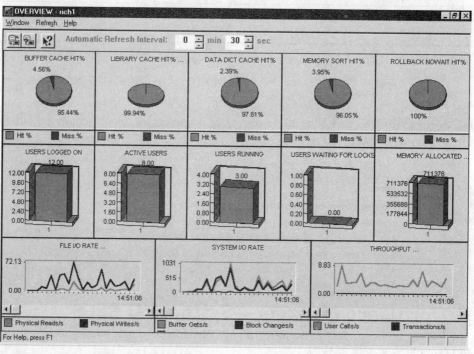

**FIGURE 5-9.** *The Overview screen*

This can be a very useful screen if you have a system that usually runs well and then receives a large spike in physical and/or buffer reads. If an uncharacteristic spike occurs, you can use the Process screen, shown next, to find the user and the Table screen to find table accesses that are potentially missing indexes. You could also query the V$SQLAREA view for the username to find the query that is being executed.

| | TABLE ACCESS - rich1 | | |
|---|---|---|---|
| Window | Refresh | Help | |

Automatic Refresh Interval: **0**

| | Session ID | Owner | Object |
|---|---|---|---|
| 24 | 18.00 | SYS | V_$SQLAREA |
| 25 | 18.00 | SYS | X$KGLCURSOF |
| 26 | 18.00 | SYSTEM | V$SQLAREA |
| 27 | 20.00 | SYS | DBMS_OUTPUT |
| 28 | 20.00 | SYS | DBMS_STAND, |
| 29 | 20.00 | SYS | GV$SQLAREA |
| 30 | 20.00 | SYS | STANDARD |
| 31 | 20.00 | SYS | V$SQLAREA |
| 32 | 20.00 | SYS | X$KGLCURSOF |
| 33 | 23.00 | SCOTT | EMP |

For Help, press F1

# Performance Manager—Database Instance Information

From the main menu, choose Display | Database_Instance to access information related to a given instance. In Figure 5-10, we access the Tablespace Free Space portion. Sections of the Performance Manager are also available that pertain to preventative maintenance. In the figure, we can see the free space that is available in each of our tablespaces. By adding data files (or allowing them to autoextend), we can eliminate potential errors that users may get from inadequate space needed for expansion of objects.

**TIP**

*The Performance Manager can also be accessed to display information that can be deployed for preventative maintenance. The Tablespace Free Space screen is one example of a preventative maintenance screen that is available.*

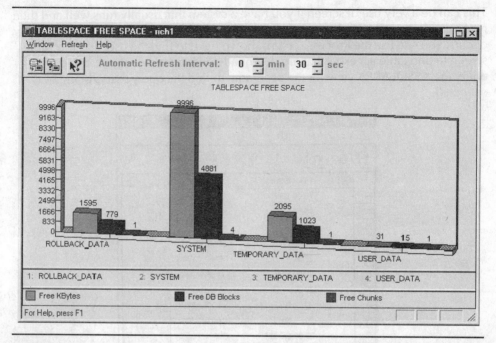

**FIGURE 5-10.** *Tablespace Free Space screen*

# The Performance Manager—Building Your Own Charts

The Performance Manager also adds one extremely powerful tool—the option to build new charts or modify current ones. The chart's pull-down menu offers both a New Chart option as well as a Modify Chart option.

First, I built a custom chart that accesses the x$bh table, charting the buffers used for data (see Chapter 15 for more information regarding this query):

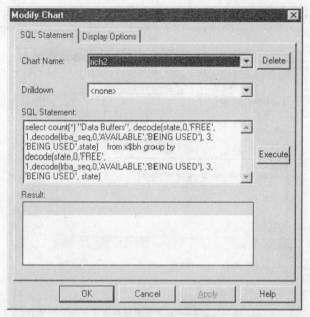

The following illustration shows the free buffers (never used), available (used but can be freed) and being used (currently in use) buffers. I must set the Display options for the chart, and the output is displayed here:

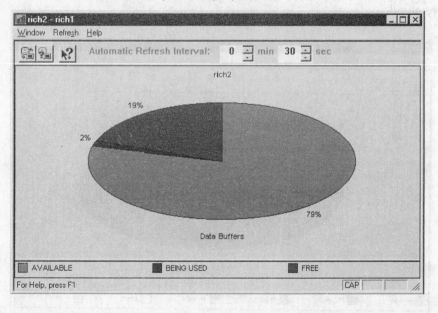

Next, I build a custom chart that accesses the x$ksmsp table, charting the shared pool buffer fragmentation (see Chapter 15 for more information regarding this query):

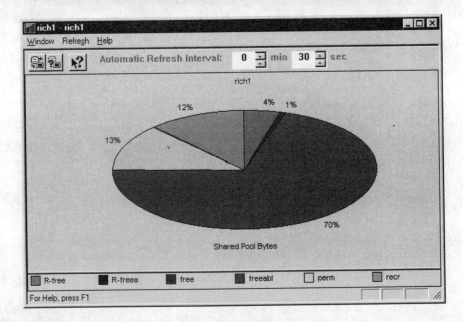

The chart, shown next, indicates the buffers that are free, can be freed, in use, and retained.

**TIP**
*One of the most powerful features of the Performance
Manager is the ability to create your own charts (note
that this feature does not exist in version 1.5.5).
Queries that are contained in various parts of this book
can be used to create custom charts. A couple of the
queries from Chapter 15 accessing the x$ tables are
displayed in this chapter as examples.*

# TopSessions Monitor

The TopSessions monitor tool within the Enterprise Manager is a powerful tool to
quickly find the most troublesome users and/or queries on a given system. The tool
is extremely versatile and can be used to find the "top" (or worst) session for a
number of different performance criteria. When the TopSessions monitor is running,
the first screen that appears is shown here:

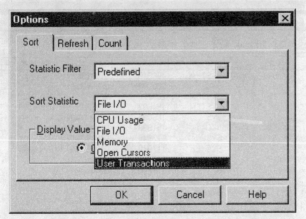

The Options screen can be used to sort the top sessions by largest resource use
by using a number of filters. The Predefined filter includes options for tracking top
CPU, file I/O, memory, open cursors, and user transactions. The User filter can be
used for tracking many statistics, including bytes sent/received from the client, CPU,
logons, open cursors, recursive calls, connect time, logical (memory) reads, and
SQL*Net roundtrips. The Cache and Redo options show a variety of ESTAT tracked
statistics. The Parallel Server filter shows a variety of options that track parallel
operations statistics. The SQL filter shows sorting statistics by session as well as
physical and memory reads. The Other filter shows a variety of global and remote
statistics and the All filter shows the statistics for all of these categories. The Count

tab, shown next, allows the setting of a limited amount of top sessions or the ability to display all sessions.

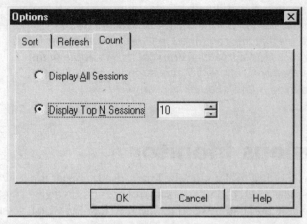

The next illustration shows an example listing of the top sessions.

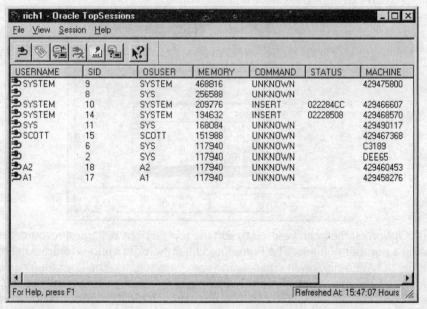

If TopSessions finds a problem user's session (perhaps an ad hoc query user), you can then click on the user (see the preceding illustration) and use the Session pull-down menu to choose kill. This will kill the problem user's session:

**TopSessions Monitor**

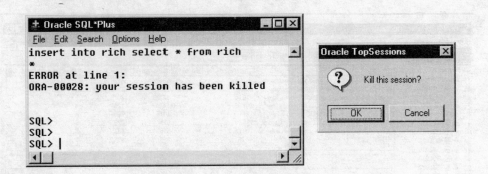

**TIP**
*Use the TopSessions monitor to find the sessions that are using the most resources on your system. By investigating a problem session in more detail, you can free up resources for other processes.*

**TIP**
*When a user finds that they have executed a problem query and need to end it, the Kill Session screen is an excellent tool.*

# Oracle Tuning Pack—SQL Analyze

Using SQL Analyze (version 1.6 in these examples), a DBA can identify the TopSQL for their system. The TopSQL screen displays a list, shown in Figure 5-11, of the worst SQL statements in the current cache based on several different SQL performance metrics, such as disk reads per execution. The DBA can drag the problem SQL from TopSQL into a tuning session to begin the process of analyzing and tuning the problem SQL. Version 2.0 of this product will allow the DBA to build a composite SQL history over time and use this as a target for identifying high-impact SQL. This same SQL history can be subsequently used with Oracle Expert (covered later in this chapter).

**TIP**
*By using SQL Analyze's TopSQL, you can identify the worst performing queries on your system. The next step is to use the SQL Analyze tool to generate EXPLAIN PLANs and alternative SQL for the problem queries.*

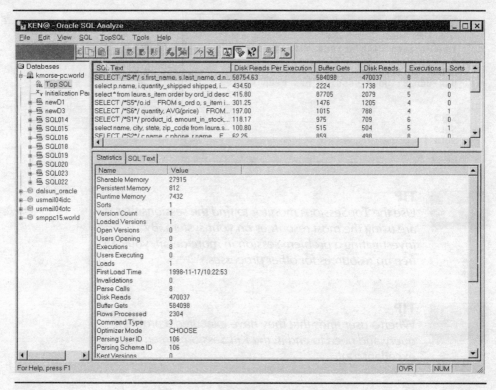

**FIGURE 5-11.** *SQL Analyze TopSQL (worst statements)*

## SQL Analyze—The EXPLAIN PLAN

The top SQL statement, S4 in Figure 5-12, based on disk reads per execution was dragged from the cache and the EXPLAIN PLAN was created using the Optimizer mode = "Choose." A plan was created for the option Cost All Rows. The plan can be examined executing the Plan Walk feature, which provides a description of each operation. See Chapter 6 for more information on reading and using the EXPLAIN PLAN tool.

**TIP**
*Use SQL Analyze to quickly view the EXPLAIN PLAN tree of a query.*

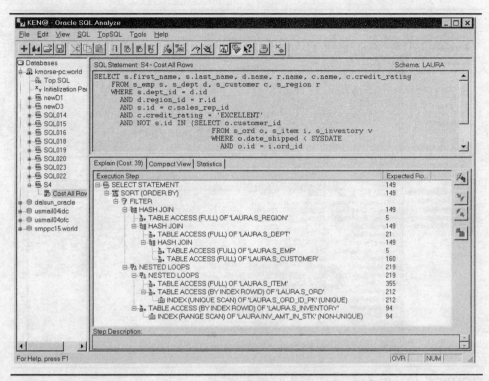

**FIGURE 5-12.**   *Performance Pack SQL Analyze EXPLAIN PLAIN*

# SQL Analyze—Execution Statistics

The user of the tool can then execute the statement from SQL Analyze to obtain execution statistics, as shown in Figure 5-13, and may choose to execute the query multiple times to obtain running average statistics for the query. This is executed to simulate the real-world environment where the query will often be in memory.

**TIP**

*Executing the statement in SQL Analyze will generate the query statistics quicker than using Oracle's SQL Trace (detailed in Chapter 6).*

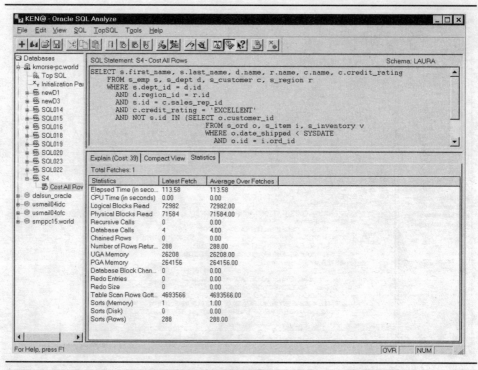

**SQL Analyze**

**FIGURE 5-13.** *Performance Pack SQL Analyze execution statistics*

## SQL Analyze—Comparing Different Plans

The user creates a different plan for the S4 statement using the FIRST_ROWS
optimizer mode, as shown in Figure 5-14; then, the SQL Analyze Comparison
feature can split the screen to examine and walk each plan side-by-side. The
comparison for this query displays whether using ALL_ROWS or FIRST_ROWS
will be a better solution when the query is executed.

**TIP**

*The SQL Analyze Comparison feature allows a
side-by-side comparison of SQL statements to help you
find the best execution path. By using these what-if
scenarios, you can find the best solution before
actually executing the query.*

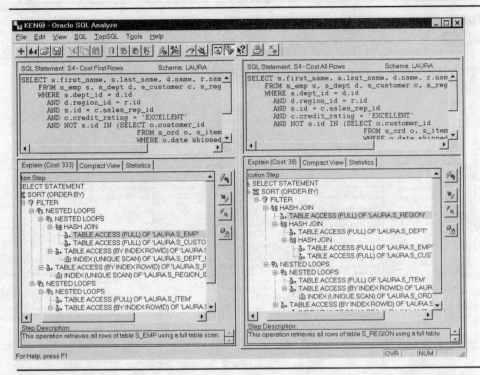

**FIGURE 5-14.** *SQL Analyze Comparison feature*

The user can exit the split screen mode (as shown in Figure 5-15), execute the S4 statement under ALL_ROWS (the better choice of the two in this case), and compare resulting statistics for both.

**TIP**
*After you have found the query path that seems to be the correct one, make sure that you execute it with statistics to ensure that it is the correct choice. The number given for the cost in the plan is not always an accurate reflection of how the query will perform.*

SQL Analyze

**SQL Analyze**

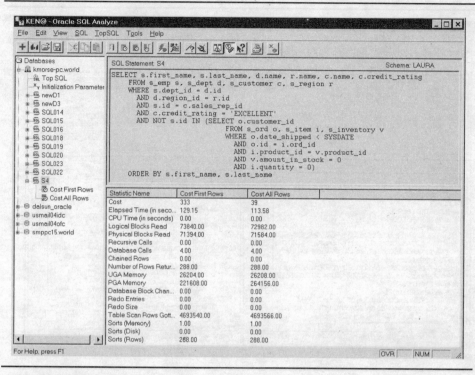

**FIGURE 5-15.** *SQL Analyze split screen mode*

## SQL Analyze—Tuning Wizard

Another excellent feature of the Tuning Pack is the SQL Analyze Tuning Wizard. This feature will walk the user through a SQL tuning process when evaluating a statement for potential performance impediments, such as the inadvertent disabling of an index. In Figure 5-16, the subquery contains a substring operation on an indexed column. The substring function has modified the column name and has prevented the optimizer from using the index. SQL Analyze generates an alternative statement (the "Modified SQL") that enables the use of the index (changing the SUBSTR to a LIKE), as shown through the new EXPLAIN PLAN for the modified SQL. Although it is not covered in great detail in this chapter, the Tuning Wizard also captures statistics for the objects used in the plan and evaluates the statement for alternative join optimization strategies. If the Tuning Wizard finds an alternative path, it will create a SQL hint to enforce, for example, a new join method and order if the user decides to use the suggested strategy.

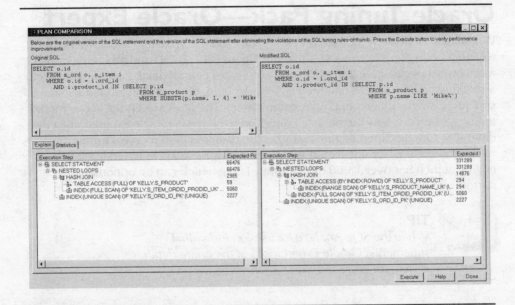

**FIGURE 5-16.** *SQL Analyze Tuning Wizard*

**TIP**
*The Tuning Wizard is a great tool for the beginner who is unfamiliar with how to tune problem SQL queries. The Tuning Wizard will provide an alternative SQL query that could lead to better performance for a problem query that needs to be tuned.*

The Tuning Wizard also provides statistics about the performance gain from the original statement to the modified statement. It is a simple way to get an improved query, and also illustrates the improvements made and in what areas they are affected.

**TIP**
*Optimizing the performance of one query is not as important as optimizing the performance of queries in the area of your system that is causing a bottleneck. The Tuning Wizard itemizes where the performance gain will be, enabling you to focus on the area that is hurting your system most.*

SQL Analyze

# Oracle Tuning Pack—Oracle Expert

Where SQL Analyze is focused on tuning individual SQL statements, Oracle Expert (version 1.6 in these examples), shown in Figure 5-17, is focused on tuning from a more global perspective. Oracle Expert automates overall database tuning in three areas: the top 25 instance parameters, indexes (add, drop, modify, rebuild) and structures (sizing, placement, OFA compliance). The DBA selects the scope for the tuning session and sets up the data collection (which has Oracle Expert collect the data). The Oracle Expert engine analyzes the data and then receives tuning recommendations. Oracle Expert is built on a proprietary rule-based inference engine, which has over 1,000 tuning rules, 1/3 of which can be optionally customized by the user.

**TIP**

*While the SQL Analyze focuses on individual statements, Oracle Expert looks at the entire database system for areas requiring improvement.*

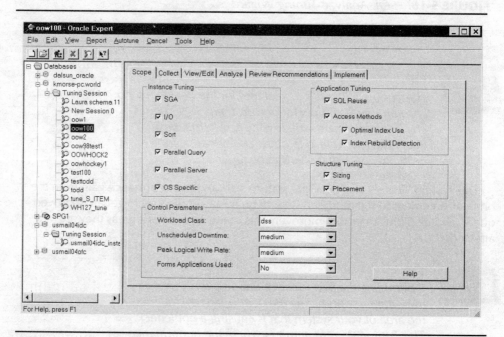

**FIGURE 5-17.** *Oracle Expert tuning session*

# Oracle Expert—Focusing on a Schema

A key part of setting the scope or focus of the tuning session is targeting a specific part of the database for index and structure tuning. Instance tuning will always be global for the entire instance, but index and structure tuning has to be focused on a schema, as it is the basis for all optimization. The DBA should pick a particular schema or set of tables for targeted tuning. This way, the engine (and DBA) is not overwhelmed with extraneous tables and indexes from another schema. The user should pick the hot tables (often used) to tune first, then move down the chain in subsequent tuning sessions. Note that in version 2.0, the product helps the DBA identify this table focus by providing the option of having the DBA identify the high-impact tables based on a workload analysis. In the example shown in Figure 5-18, the LAURA schema has been selected for tuning, and we will use the existing dictionary statistics. We could optionally use Expert's own statistics or run ANALYZE for selected objects.

Oracle Expert

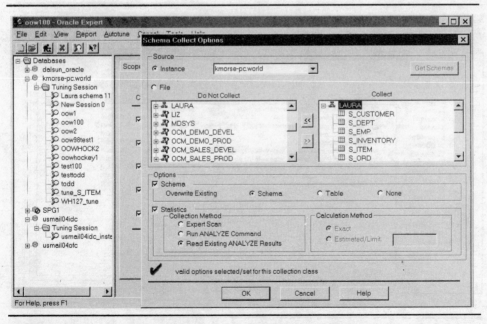

**FIGURE 5-18.** *Oracle Expert Schema Collect options*

## Oracle Expert—Set Up the Rules for the Tuning Session

After your data is collected for a schema, review it, edit it if desired, and customize some of the Oracle Expert rule values. This data editing and rule editing is an advanced feature. Figure 5-19 shows a screen shot of a Rule Description screen for the DB_FILE_SIMULTANEOUS_WRITES instance parameter. The user can easily receive access to the rule descriptions and can change the values, and "instantiate" the new values at certain levels in the product. For example, if you change a rule that applies to table tuning, you can instantiate that new value for a specific table, or for all tables. Again, *this is not an area that a beginner DBA could use.*

**TIP**
*There are expert-level tools that will allow the DBA to modify the Oracle Expert tool itself. The power of this tool becomes obvious for even the most knowledgeable DBAs.*

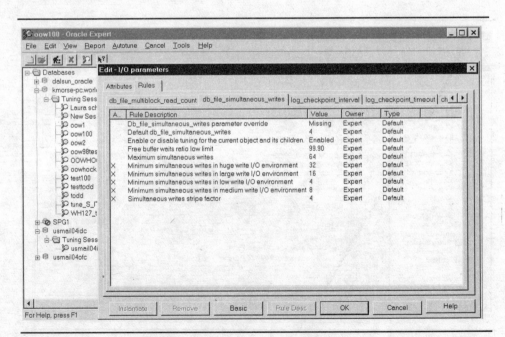

**FIGURE 5-19.** *Customizing Oracle Expert rule values*

# Oracle Expert—Making Changes and Measuring the Impact

Figure 5-20 illustrates an example of data editing. The user targets a workload for collection (either from a TRACE or from the SQL cache) and edits the workload SQL objects to impact the analysis. In the example—one SQL object that was collected—several variables can be changed, affecting this statement's impact during the Expert analysis: the frequency, resources used, the user-assigned importance rating, or the SQL statement itself can be edited. This helps model the impact of specific workloads on the assignment of database resources and decisions about dropping/modifying/adding indexes.

> **TIP**
>
> *An advanced DBA can edit the queries using a variety of methods—impacting analysis before and after modifications can show what effect the changes will have.*

Oracle Expert

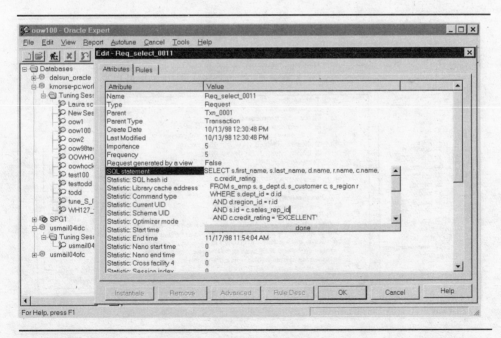

**FIGURE 5-20.**   *Performance Pack Oracle Expert impact analysis*

## Oracle Expert—Viewing the Recommendations

In Figure 5-21, a screen shot of Oracle Expert's Recommendation screen is displayed. It shows some index recommendations for one of our tables and some of our instance tuning recommendations. The DBA can scan them easily here and drill down into the details. We see that Oracle Expert is recommending two new indexes for Laura's S_ITEM table.

 **TIP**
*Oracle Expert provides a list of recommendations that can be clicked on to drill down into the detail before making the actual changes.*

## Oracle Expert—Drill Down to Recommendation Detail

In the illustration shown next, we have drilled down into the recommendation detail screen shot for one of the S_ITEM index recommendations. This screen shows a

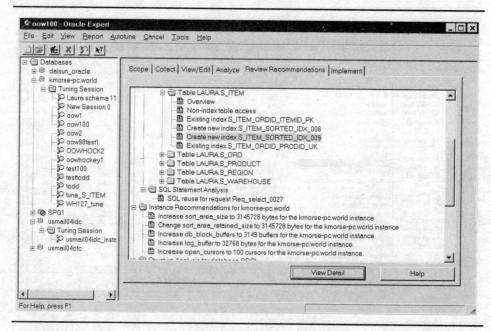

**FIGURE 5-21.** *Tuning Pack Oracle Expert Review Recommendations screen*

Oracle Expert

brief summary, but there is also an Analysis Report, which can be generated to display further detail. This recommendation calls for a new sorted index on three columns. The recommendation is based upon three requests (SELECT statements) from our workload comprising of predicate equality and inequality SELECTs on these columns. Oracle Expert rates each valid SQL request and assigns a rank value to each. Based on the rank order, it assigns a weighted value to the requests and develops an importance rating for the index recommendation. Oracle Expert also analyzed DML workload for this table and computed a table volatility rating that is used to balance the weighted value of the ranked SQL requests. This is executed in order to determine the best index strategy for the table. This is an oversimplified description of the complex process of the Oracle Expert.

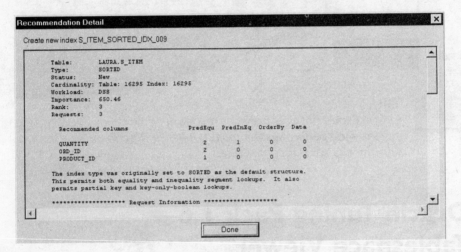

Oracle Expert

## Oracle Expert—Recommended System-Wide Changes

You can drill down into areas that are recommended for system-wide performance issues. The following illustration is a screen shot of the recommendation detail for an instance tuning recommendation calling for an increase to the SORT_AREA_SIZE.

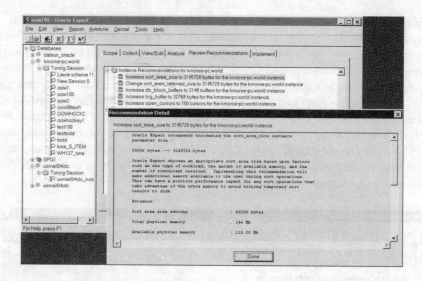

**Tablespace Viewer** *(vertical text, left margin)*

**TIP**

*Oracle Expert not only provides recommendations for system-wide performance tuning, but it also describes why the change is recommended.*

# Oracle Tuning Pack 1.6— Tablespace Viewer

The Oracle Tablespace Manager includes a Tablespace Viewer that provides a graphical view of all tablespaces, data files, segments, total data blocks, free data blocks, and percentage of free blocks available in the tablespace current storage allocation. (See Figure 5-22.) The tool provides the option of displaying all segments for a tablespace or all segments for a data file. The Tablespace Viewer also provides additional information for each segment, including average free space per block, chained rows, and the last date that the object was analyzed.

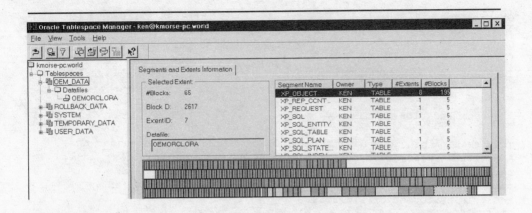

**FIGURE 5-22.** *Oracle Tablespace Viewer*

When reorganization is necessary, the DBA can use the Oracle Tablespace Manager Reorganization Wizard to automatically fix problem objects. The wizard uses Oracle's Export and Import (checking for sufficient space prior to executing) for the fragmented or problematic objects. The DBA can select a single segment, multiple segments, or the entire tablespace for defragmentation, including tables, indexes, and clusters. Segments can also be moved between tablespaces using the Tablespace Manager. There are also two new products to be included in Tuning Pack 2.0: the Index Tuning Wizard and the Auto-Analyze Wizard.

# Oracle Expert Analysis Report

Oracle Expert generates a report providing additional detail on the Oracle Expert tuning section. Listed next is a portion of the tuning analysis report (tuning_report.txt) generated by Oracle Expert for the tuning session used for the screen shots included in this chapter. The report generates a table of contents.

Analysis Report

```
Oracle Expert 1.6.0                        11/18/98 11:16:19 AM
                              Analysis Report
                          Recommendation Summary

Tune session: oow100                                        Page 1
------------------------------------------------------------------


1  Recommendation Summary

This section provides a summary of Oracle Expert's recommendations.
Additional information can be found in the remainder of this
report to explain Oracle Expert's reasoning for making each
recommendation. These recommendations were generated from an
analysis performed on 11/18/1998
11:11:35.

   Application Tuning for database ORCL

     Access Method Analysis

        o Overview

       Recommendation quality

          o Overview

       High impact index removals

          o Overview

        Table LAURA.S_WAREHOUSE

       High impact indexes

          o Overview

        Table LAURA.S_CUSTOMER

           o Create new index S_CUSTOMER_SORTED_IDX_001

        Table LAURA.S_DEPT

           o Create new index S_DEPT_SORTED_IDX_002

        Table LAURA.S_EMP

           o Create new index S_EMP_SORTED_IDX_004
           o Create new index S_EMP_SORTED_IDX_003
```

# Oracle Expert Implementation Script

Oracle Expert also generates an implementation script (tuning_script.sql) for the tuning session. This script usually requires a bit of customization by the DBA, depending on which recommendations that need to be implemented. The script can be very helpful when there are several index or structure changes to make. The following is a partial listing for the tuning session used for the screen shots in this chapter. The listing includes a section that explains how to use the file.

```
-- Oracle Expert 1.6.0                    11/18/98 11:19:17 AM
--                  Recommended SQL changes
--
-- Database User Recommendations
-----------------------------------------------------------------
ALTER USER KROUSE
    DEFAULT TABLESPACE "<tbs>"
    TEMPORARY TABLESPACE TEMPORARY_DATA;

ALTER USER OEMFMT
    DEFAULT TABLESPACE "<tbs>"
    TEMPORARY TABLESPACE TEMPORARY_DATA;


-----------------------------------------------------------------
-- CREATE Rollback Segment Recommendations
-----------------------------------------------------------------
CREATE ROLLBACK SEGMENT RB_TEMP
    TABLESPACE ROLLBACK_DATA
    STORAGE (
        INITIAL 100K
        NEXT 100K
        MINEXTENTS 2
        MAXEXTENTS 121);


-----------------------------------------------------------------
-  CREATE Index Recommendations
-----------------------------------------------------------------
CREATE BITMAP INDEX LAURA.S_CUSTOMER_PHONE_IDX
    ON LAURA.S_CUSTOMER
        (PHONE,
         REGION_ID)
    TABLESPACE USER_DATA
    PCTFREE 0
    INITRANS 2
    MAXTRANS 255
```

```
STORAGE (
    INITIAL 4K
    NEXT 4K
    PCTINCREASE 0
    MINEXTENTS 1
    MAXEXTENTS UNLIMITED
    FREELISTS 1
    FREELIST GROUPS 1);
```

# Tips Review

- The Schema Manager within the Enterprise Manager is a very quick way to look at tables and indexes when you are tuning your system. Use the Schema Manager to even view information about the SYS schema and internal tables that may be set up improperly for your size database.

- Use the Schema Manager to quickly find code to tune that is related to packages, procedures, and triggers for a given schema.

- Use profiles to limit ad hoc query users and/or other users that are typically unpredictable or problematic in their use of system resources.

- Use the Storage Manager to quickly find where database files and tablespaces are located so that you can strategically balance disk reads and writes.

- The Performance Manager includes many of the best performance queries to the V$ views. It shows a graphical look at the output to many of these strategic areas.

- Use the buffer cache hit ratio in Performance Manager to instantly see the ratio of memory reads to disk reads for your system. If the ratio is below 95 percent, tuning the DB_BLOCK_BUFFERS in the init.ora or finding queries that are causing a large amount of disk reads may be necessary.

- Use the library cache and row cache hit ratios in Performance Manager to instantly see the hit ratios that are related to the SHARED_POOL_SIZE init.ora parameter. Hit ratios that are below 95 percent indicate either a need to increase the SHARED_POOL_SIZE or it could indicate other problems. See Chapter 14 for more information.

- If the memory sort hit ratio is below 99 percent, it may indicate a need for an increase to the SORT_AREA_SIZE init.ora parameter. But be careful. Increasing the SORT_AREA_SIZE can cause problems if it is set too high.

- The Performance Manager Overview screen is probably the single most helpful screen within Enterprise Manager. It is a simple way to see the overall performance of your system in a single screen.

- One of the most powerful features of the Performance Manager is the ability to create your own charts. Queries that are contained in various parts of this book can be used to create custom charts.

- Use the TopSession Monitor to find the sessions that are using the most resources on your system. By investigating a problem session in more detail, you can free up resources for other processes.

- By using SQL Analyze's TopSQL, you can identify the worst performing queries on your system. The next step will be to use the SQL Analyze tool to generate EXPLAIN PLANs and alternative SQL for the problem queries.

- Use SQL Analyze to quickly view the EXPLAIN PLAN tree of a query.

- Executing the statement in SQL Analyze will generate the query statistics a lot quicker than using Oracle's SQL Trace (detailed in Chapter 6).

- The SQL Analyze comparison feature allows a side-by-side comparison of SQL statements to help you find the best execution path. By using these "what if" scenarios, you can find the best solution before actually executing the query.

- The Tuning Wizard within SQL Analyze is a great tool for the beginner who is unfamiliar with how to tune problem SQL queries. The Tuning Wizard will provide an alternative SQL query that could lead to better performance for a problem query that needs to be tuned.

- While the SQL Analyze focuses on individual statements, Oracle Expert looks at the entire database system for areas requiring improvement. There are expert-level tools that will even allow the DBA to modify the Oracle Expert tool itself.

- Oracle Expert provides a list of recommendations that can be "clicked on" to drill down into the detail before making the actual changes.

- Oracle Expert not only provides recommendations for system-wide performance tuning, but it also describes why the change is recommended. You can also generate a tuning report and implementation file for your tuning session.

Tips Review

# References

*Oracle Enterprise Manager Reference Manual*, Oracle Corporation

"Tuning Pack 2.0," Oracle White Paper

Many thanks to Ken Morse of Oracle for his assistance with this chapter (he's a great instructor, too).

# TIPS & TECHNIQUES

# CHAPTER
## 6

# Using EXPLAIN PLAN, TRACE, and TKPROF (Developer and DBA)

Finding and fixing problem queries has a lot to do with using the tools that are available. Different tools need to be used for different situations. The tools covered in this chapter are Oracle's provided utilities: TRACE, TKPROF, and EXPLAIN PLAN. Tips covered in this chapter include the following:

- Simple steps for using TRACE/TKPROF
- Sections of the TRACE output
- A more complex query TRACEd, and what to look for to help performance
- Using EXPLAIN PLAN
- Reading the EXPLAIN PLAN: Top to bottom or bottom to top?
- Yet another EXPLAIN PLAN method: The parent/child tree structure method
- TRACing in developer tools
- Important columns in the PLAN_TABLE table
- TRACing for errors and the undocumented init.ora parameters

# The Oracle TRACE Utility

The Oracle TRACE utility is used to measure timing statistics for a given query, a batch process, or an entire system. It is a fast method of finding where potential bottlenecks on the system reside. TRACE has the following functionality:

- TRACE runs the query and generates statistics about an Oracle query that is executed.
- TRACE helps developers analyze every section of a query.

## Simple Steps for TRACE with a Simple Query

The steps for setting up and running Oracle's TRACE utility are as follows:

1. Set the following init.ora parameters:
```
TIMED_STATISTICS = TRUE
MAX_DUMP_FILE_SIZE = 2000000 (Not 2M)
USER_DUMP_DEST = /oracle8/rich_trc
```

   In Oracle7, the database must be shut down and restarted for these parameters to take effect. In Oracle8, the TIMED_STATISTICS parameter may be set via an ALTER SESSION (for an individual session) or ALTER SYSTEM (for the entire system) command. The USER_DUMP_DEST specifies the location to put the files and the MAX_DUMP_FILE_SIZE specifies the maximum file size.

2. Enable TRACE for a SQL*Plus session (this starts TRACing for an individual session):
```
alter session set SQL_TRACE true;
```

3. Run the query to be TRACEd:
```
select    table_name, owner, initial_extent, uniqueness
from      ind2
where     owner || '' = 'SCOTT' ; (Note: An index
          on "OWNER" is suppressed)
```

4. Disable TRACE for the SQL*Plus session:
```
alter session set SQL_TRACE false;
```

5. You can also enable TRACE for *all* sessions by setting the SQL_TRACE parameter in the init.ora. You must shut down and restart the database for this to take effect. This is *not* suggested!

TRACE with a Simple Query

```
SQL_TRACE = TRUE
```

After running TRACE, your output file will look something like the following:

```
5_19554.trc
```

**TIP**

*Setting TIMED_STATISTICS=TRUE in the init.ora will begin TRACing upon the user's command. But, be careful;* setting SQL_TRACE=TRUE in the init.ora will cause the entire system and all queries to be TRACEd and could cause performance degradations.

6. Run TKPROF to put the TRACE file into readable format:

```
tkprof 5_19554.trc rich2.prf explain=system/manager
```

The TKPROF utility translates the TRACE file generated by the SQL_TRACE facility to a readable format. You can run TKPROF against a TRACE file that you have previously created, or you can run it while the program that is creating the TRACE file is still running. Options for TKPROF are listed next.

```
tkprof tracefile output_file [sort = parameters]
[print=number] [explain=username/password]
```

**Command-Line Options:**

| | |
|---|---|
| *TRACEfile* | The name of the TRACE file containing the statistics by SQL_TRACE. |
| *output_file* SORT=*parameters* | The name of the file where TKPROF writes its output. The order in which to display the statements in the output. There are about 20 different options for sorting the output—you can even combine these options. |
| PRINT=*number* | The number of statements to include in the output. If this statement is not included, TKPROF will list all statements in the output. |
| EXPLAIN= *username/ password* | Run the EXPLAIN PLAN on the user's SQL statements in the TRACE file. This option will create a PLAN_TABLE of its own, so the user will need to have privileges to create the table and space in which to create it. When TKPROF is finished, this table is dropped. |

*(left margin)* TRACE with a Simple Query

**New options in 7.3+:**

INSERT=*filename*    This option creates a script to create a table and store the TRACE file statistics for each SQL statement TRACEd.

RECORD=*filename*    This option will produce a file of all the user's SQL statements.

SYS=*YES*|*NO*    This option allows the user to request the recursive SQL statements not be displayed in the output. The default is set to YES.

SORT=*parameters*    There is a tremendous number of sorting options that are available. My favorites are FCHCPU (CPU time of fetch), FCHDSK (disk reads for fetch), FCHCU and FCHQRY (memory reads for fetch), FCHROW (number of rows fetched), EXEDSK (disk reads during execute), EXECU and EXEQRY (memory reads during execute), EXEROW (rows processed during execute), EXECPU (execute CPU time), and PRSCNT (times parsed).

**TIP**

*The TKPROF utility puts a TRACEd output into a readable format. Without running TKPROF, it would be difficult to read the output of a TRACE. By specifying "explain=username/password" (noted earlier), we are able to get the EXPLAIN PLAN execution path in addition to the execution statistics of the query.*

7a. The output of the file rich2.prf (query with the index suppressed):

```
select     table_name, owner, initial_extent, uniqueness
from       ind2
where      owner = 'SCOTT';
```

| | count | cpu | elap | disk | query | current | rows |
|---|---|---|---|---|---|---|---|
| Parse: | 1 | 1 | 2 | 0 | 0 | 0 | |
| Execute: | 1 | 0 | 0 | 0 | 0 | 2 | 0 |
| Fetch: | 2 | 69 | 113 | 142 | 430 | 0 | 36 |

**Execution Plan (no index used):**

```
TABLE ACCESS (FULL) OF 'IND2'
```

TRACE with a Simple Query

The output shows 142 disk reads and 430 memory reads (query + current). Having such a high number of disk reads compared to physical reads is certainly a potential problem. The execution path shows a full table scan confirming that we may have a potential problem.

**TIP**

*A TRACEd query with a large number of physical reads usually indicates a missing index. The disk column indicates the physical reads (usually where an index is not used) and the query added to the current columns indicates the memory reads (usually reads where an index is being used).*

**7b.** Here's what happens when I rerun the query (after restarting the system) to be TRACEd, now using an index on the owner table:

```
select     table_name, owner, initial_extent, uniqueness
from       ind2
where      owner = 'SCOTT' ;
(The index on "OWNER" is not suppressed)
```

**The output of the file rich2.prf:**

```
select     table_name, owner, initial_extent, uniqueness
from       ind2
where      owner = 'SCOTT' ;
```

|          | count | cpu | elap | disk | query | current | rows |
|----------|-------|-----|------|------|-------|---------|------|
| Parse:   | 2     | 0   | 0    | 0    | 0     | 0       |      |
| Execute: | 2     | 0   | 0    | 0    | 0     | 0       | 0    |
| Fetch:   | 4     | 6   | 6    | 0    | 148   | 0       | 72   |

**Execution Plan (index used):**

```
TABLE ACCESS (BY ROWID) OF 'IND2'
  INDEX (RANGE SCAN) OF 'IND2_1' (NON-UNIQUE)
```

**TIP**

*A TRACEd query output with only memory reads (query-consistent reads) indicates that an index is being used.*

# The Sections of a TRACE Output

The TRACE utility has multiple sections including the SQL statements, statistics, information, and the EXPLAIN PLAN. Each of these different topics are discussed in the following sections.

## The SQL Statement

The first section of a TKPROF statement is the SQL statement. This statement will be the exact same as the statement that was executed. If there were any hints or comments in the statement, they would be retained in this output. This can be helpful when you are reviewing the output from multiple sessions. If you find a statement causing problems, you would be able to search for the exact statement. Remember, some of the statements from Oracle forms are generated dynamically.

## The Statistics Section

This section contains all the statistics for this SQL statement and all the recursive SQL statements generated to satisfy this statement. In this section there are eight columns, the first being the type of call to the database. There are three types of calls, parse, execute, and fetch. Each type of call will generate a separate line of statistics. The other seven columns are the statistics for each type of call.

| | |
|---|---|
| count | The number of times this type of call was made. |
| cpu | The total CPU time for all of the calls of this type for this statement. If the TIMED_STATISTICS parameter in the init.ora is not set to TRUE, this statistic and the elapsed statistic will be 0. |
| elapsed | The total elapsed time for this call. |
| disk | The total number of data blocks retrieved from disk to satisfy this call. |
| query | The total number of data buffers retrieved from memory for this type of call. SELECT statements usually retrieve buffers in this mode. |
| current | The total number of data buffers retrieved from memory for this type of call. UPDATE, INSERT, or DELETE the usual access buffers in this mode. |
| rows | The total number of rows processed by this statement. The rows processed for SELECT statements will appear in the row of Fetch statistics. INSERTS, UPDATES, and DELETES will appear in the execute row. |

## Information Section

This section contains information about the number of misses in the library cache from parse and execute calls. If the number of misses is high, there may be a problem with the size of the Shared Pool. You should check the hit ratio and the reload rate of the library cache.

There is also information about the current optimizer mode setting. This section shows the username of the last user to parse this statement.

## The EXPLAIN PLAN

This is the section of the TKPROF I find to be the most useful. The first column of this section of the TRPROF output listing below, is the number of rows processed by each line of the execution plan. Here, you will be able to see how bad a statement is. If the total number of rows in the Fetch statistics is low compared to the number of rows being processed by each line of the EXPLAIN PLAN, you may want to review the statement.

It is also possible that there is only one line of the execution plan that is processing a large number of rows compared to the rest of the statement. This can be caused by full table scans or the use of a bad index.

# A More Complex TKPROF Output

The following example illustrates a TRACEd query with a slightly higher complexity.

```
select    Item_Item_Id, InitCap(Item_Description)
from      Item
where     Item_Classification = 1
and       Item_Item_Id Between 1000000 And 2700000
and       Item_Item_Id Not In (Select Invitem_Item_Id
from      Inventory_Item
where     Invitem_Location_Id = '405')


call      count      cpu     elapsed    disk     query    current    rows
Parse       1       0.00      0.00        0        0          0        0
Execute     1       0.00      0.00        0        0          0        0
Fetch      27      20.87     21.24        0      4408         0       399
Totals     29      20.87     21.24        0      4408         0       399

Misses in library cache during parse: 0
Optimizer hint: CHOOSE
Parsing user id: 106   (C12462)


Rows      Execution Plan
0             SELECT STATEMENT    OPTIMIZER HINT: CHOOSE
572               FILTER
```

```
598              TABLE ACCESS (BY ROWID) OF 'ITEM'
599                  INDEX (RANGE SCAN) OF 'ITEM_PK' (UNIQUE)
278790               INDEX (RANGE SCAN) OF 'INVITEM_PK' (UNIQUE)
```

Some of the things to look for in the TKPROF output are listed in this table:

| Problems | Solutions |
|---|---|
| High numbers for the parsing | The SHARED_POOL_SIZE may need to be increased. |
| The disk reads are very high The "query" and/or "current" (memory reads) are very high | Indexes are not used or may not exist. Indexes may be on columns with high cardinality (columns where an individual value generally makes up a large percentage of the table). Removing or suppressing the index may increase performance. |
| The parse elapse time is high | There may be a problem with the number of open cursors. |
| The number of rows processed by a row in the EXPLAIN PLAN is high compared to the other rows | This could be a sign of an index with a poor distribution of distinct keys (unique values for a column). Or This could also be a sign of a poorly written statement. |
| If the number of misses in the library cache during parse is greater than 1 | This is an indication that the statement had to be reloaded. You may need to increase the SHARED_POOL_SIZE in the init.ora. |

# Using EXPLAIN PLAN Alone

The EXPLAIN PLAN command allows a developer to view the query execution plan that the Oracle optimizer will use to execute a SQL statement. This command is very helpful in improving performance of SQL statements, since it does not actually execute the SQL statement—it only outlines the plan to use and inserts this execution plan in an Oracle table. Prior to using the EXPLAIN PLAN command, a file called UTLXPLAN.sql (located in the same directory as CATALOG.sql) must be executed under the Oracle account that will be executing the EXPLAIN PLAN command. The script creates a table called PLAN_TABLE that is used by the EXPLAIN PLAN command to insert the query execution plan in the form of records. This table can then be queried and viewed to determine if there needs to be any modifications to the SQL statement to force a different execution plan. An EXPLAIN PLAN example is shown next (executed in SQL*Plus).

**Q.** Why use EXPLAIN PLAN without TRACE?

**A.** The statement is *not* executed; it only shows what will happen if the statement is executed.

**Q.** When do you use EXPLAIN PLAN without TRACE?

**A.** When the query will take exceptionally long to run.

The following diagram demonstrates the procedures for running TRACE versus EXPLAIN PLAN:

Using EXPLAIN PLAN Alone

| TRACE | EXPLAIN PLAN |
|---|---|
| It takes four *hours* to TRACE a query that takes four hours to run. | It takes less than a *minute* to EXPLAIN PLAN a query that takes four hours to run. |

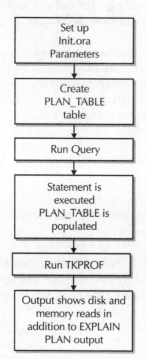

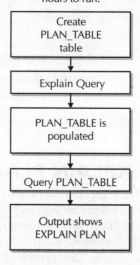

**Q.** How do I use EXPLAIN PLAN by itself?

**A.**  **I.** Find the script; it is usually in the ORACLE_HOME/rdbms/admin:
"utlxplan.sql"

   **2.** Execute the script XPLAINPL.sql in SQL*Plus:
```
@utlxplan
```
This creates the PLAN_TABLE for the user executing the script. You may create your own PLAN_TABLE, but use Oracle's syntax *or else*!!!

**3a.** Run EXPLAIN PLAN for the query to be optimized:
```
explain plan for
select      CUSTOMER_NUMBER
from        CUSTOMER
where       CUSTOMER_NUMBER = 111;
Explained.
```

**3b.** Run EXPLAIN PLAN for the query to be optimized (using a tag for the statement):
```
explain plan
set statement_id = 'CUSTOMER' for
select      CUSTOMER_NUMBER
from        CUSTOMER
where       CUSTOMER_NUMBER = 111;
```

**TIP**
*Use the SET STATEMENT_ID = 'your_identifier' when the PLAN_TABLE will be populated by many different developers. I rarely use the SET STATEMENT_ID statement. Instead, I EXPLAIN PLAN a query, look at the output, and then delete from the PLAN_TABLE table. I continue to do this (making changes to the query), until I see an execution plan that I think will be favorable. I then run the query to see if the performance has been improved. If multiple developers/DBAs are using the same PLAN_TABLE, then the SET STATEMENT_ID will be essential to identifying a statement.*

   **4.** Select the output from the PLAN_TABLE table:
```
select      operation, options, object_name, id, parent_id
from        plan_table
```

```
where     statement_id = 'CUSTOMER';
Operation              Options        Object Name    ID      Parent

select statement                                     0
Table Access           By ROWID       Customer       1
Index                  Range Scan     CUST_IDX       2         1
```

**TIP**
*Use EXPLAIN PLAN instead of TRACE so that you don't have to wait for the query to run. EXPLAIN☐PLAN will show the path of a query without actually running the query. Use TRACE only for multi-query batch jobs to find out which of the many queries in the batch job are slow.*

**Using EXPLAIN PLAN Alone**

## An Additional **EXPLAIN PLAN** Example for a Simple Query

1. Run the query with the EXPLAIN syntax embedded prior to the query:
```
explain plan
set statement_id = 'query 1' for
select    customer_number, name
from      customer
where     customer_number = '111';
```

2. Retrieve the output of EXPLAIN PLAN by querying the PLAN_TABLE:

   To retrieve the information for viewing, a SQL statement must be executed. Two scripts provided in the Oracle documentation are displayed in this step and in step 3, along with the results of each based on the previous EXPLAIN PLAN command. Note that this example varies from the last example. The customer_number column is an indexed number field, which in the second example is suppressed (by forcing a to_char) because of a data type mismatch ('111' is in quotes). In the first example, I treated the customer_number column correctly as a number field (111 is not in quotes).
```
select    operation, options, object_name, id, parent_id,
position
from      plan_table
where     statement_id = 'query 1'
order by  id;
Operation          Options   Object Name          ID   Parent ID

select Statement                                  0
Table Access       Full      Customer_Information  1          0
```

**3.** Retrieving a more intuitive and easy to read output of EXPLAIN PLAN:

```
select     lpad(' ', 2*(level-1)) || operation || ' ' || options || ' ' ||
           object_name || '.' || decode(id, 0, 'Cost = ' || position)
'Query Plan'
from       plan_table
start      with id = 0
and        statement_id = 'query 1'
connect by prior id = parent_id
and        statement_id = 'query 1';
```

**Output:**

```
Query Plan

select statement    Cost=220
    Table Access Full Customer
```

# EXPLAIN PLAN—Read It Top to Bottom or Bottom to Top?

Actually, it depends on how you write the query that retrieves the information from the PLAN_TABLE table. That is probably why many people differ on which way to read the result (all of them may be correct). Next, I give an example with the order of execution based on the query that retrieves the information. In this example, the output is read top to bottom with one caveat...you must read from the innermost to the outermost. The example here shows a method that should clear up any questions.

The SQL statement should be placed after the FOR clause of the EXPLAIN PLAN statement:

```
delete     from plan_table;
explain plan
set        statement_id = 'SQL1' for
select     to_char(sysdate, 'MM/DD/YY HH:MM AM'), to_char((trunc((sysdate -4 -1),
           'day') +1), 'DD-MON-YY'),
from       bk, ee
where      bk_shift_date >= to_char((trunc(( sysdate - 4 - 1), 'day') + 1), 'DD-
           MON- YY')
and        bk_shift_date <= to_char((sysdate - 4), 'DD-MON-YY')
and        bk_empno = ee_empno(+)
and        substr(ee_hierarchy_code, 1, 3) in ('PNA', 'PNB', 'PNC', 'PND', 'PNE',
           'PNF')
order by   ee_job_group, bk_empno, bk_shift_date
/
select     LPad(' ', 2*(Level-1)) || Level || '.' || Nvl(Position,0)|| ' ' ||
           Operation || ' ' || Options || ' ' || Object_Name || ' ' || Object_Type
```

```
            || ' ' || Decode(id, 0, Statement_Id || ' Cost = ' || Position) || Other
            || ' ' || Object_Node "Query Plan"
from       plan_table
start      with id = 0 And statement_id = 'SQL1'
connect by prior id = parent_id
and        statement_id = 'SQL1'
/
Query Plan
1.0 SELECT STATEMENT    SQL1  Cost =
    2.1 SORT ORDER BY
        3.1 FILTER
            4.1 NESTED LOOPS OUTER
                5.1 TABLE ACCESS BY ROWID BK
                    6.1 INDEX RANGE SCAN I_BK_06 NON-UNIQUE
                5.2 TABLE ACCESS BY ROWID EE
                    6.1 INDEX UNIQUE SCAN I_EE_01 UNIQUE
```

## Reading the EXPLAIN PLAN

Using the previous EXPLAIN PLAN, I will explain the steps below. A number located in the left column in the following table identifies each step. I will go in the order in which they were executed.

| Step | Action |
| --- | --- |
| 6.1 | This is the index range scan of I_BK_06. This is the first step. This index is on the bk_shift_dt column. This step performs a scan of this index to produce a list of ROWIDs that fall between the two dates. |
| 5.1 | Retrieve the rows from the BK table. |
| 6.1 | Scan of the I_EE_01 index. This index is on the ee_empno column. Using the bk_empno retrieved from the previous step, this index is scanned to retrieve the ROWIDs to produce a list of the ee_empnos that match the bk_empnos. |
| 5.2 | Retrieve the rows from the EE table. |
| 4.1 | NESTED LOOP. The two lists are joined, producing one list. |
| 3.1 | FILTER. The rest of the conditions of the WHERE clause are applied. |
| 2.1 | SORT ORDER BY. The remaining rows are sorted according to the ORDER BY clause. |
| 1.0 | This tells what type of statement it is. |

**TIP**
*Whether the EXPLAIN PLAN is read from top to bottom or from the bottom to the top is dependent entirely on the query used to select information from the PLAN_TABLE table. Both methods of reading the query may be correct, given the query selecting the information is correctly structured.*

## Setting AUTOTRACE On

There is also an easier method with SQL*Plus for generating an EXPLAIN PLAN and statistics about the performance of a query. The AUTOTRACE command (available in SQL*Plus 3.3 and later) generates similar information, as shown in this example:

```
SET AUTOTRACE ON
select      count(name)
from        emp7
where       name = 'branches';
```

**Output:**

```
COUNT(NAME)
100

Query Plan
    0       SELECT STATEMENT Optimizer=CHOOSE
    1    0  SORT (AGGREGATE)
    2    1   INDEX (RANGE SCAN) OF 'EMP7_I1' (NON-UNIQUE)

Statistics
        0  recursive calls
        0  db block gets
        1  consistent gets
        1  physical reads
        0  redo size
      223  bytes sent via SQL*Net to client
      274  bytes recd via SQL*Net from client
        2  SQL*Net roundtrips to/from client
        1  sorts (memory)
        0  sorts (disk)
        1  rows processed
```

**TIP**

*The AUTOTRACE option provides an EXPLAIN PLAN and statistics for a query. The AUTOTRACE provides many of the TRACE and TKPROF statistics such as disk reads (physical reads) and memory reads (consistent reads + db block gets).*

## EXPLAIN PLAN When Using Partitions

Table partitions yield different outputs for their EXPLAIN PLANs (as shown in the next example). In this example, we will create a partitioned table in three parts with a partitioned index. For more information on partitioning tables, refer to Chapter 13.

```
create table dept1
     (deptno      number(2),
      dept_name      varchar2(30))
      partition by range(deptno)
     (partition d1 values      less than (10),
      partition d2 values      less than (20),
      partition d3 values      less than (maxvalue));

insert into dept1 values (1, 'DEPT 1');
insert into dept1 values (7, 'DEPT 7');
insert into dept1 values (10, 'DEPT 10');
insert into dept1 values (15, 'DEPT 15');
insert into dept1 values (22, 'DEPT 22');

create index dept_index
     on dept1 (deptno)
     local
     (partition d1,
      partition  d2 ,
      partition  d3 );
```

We now generate an EXPLAIN PLAN for a forced full table scan accessing the first two partitions:

```
explain plan for
select      dept_name
from        dept1
where       deptno  ||  '' = 1
or          deptno  ||  '' = 15;
```

Reading EXPLAIN PLAN

When selecting from the plan table, you must select the additional columns partition_start (starting partition) and partition_stop (ending partition). For a full table scan, all partitions will be accessed:

```
select     operation, options, id, position , object_name,
partition_start,
           partition_stop
from       plan_table;
```

**Output (for the full table scan):**

| OPERATION | OPTIONS | ID | OBJECT NAME | PARTITION START | PARTITION STOP |
|---|---|---|---|---|---|
| SELECT STATEMENT | | | | | |
| PARTITION | CONCATENATED | 1 | | NUMBER(1) | NUMBER(3) |
| TABLE ACCESS | FULL | 2 | DEPT1 | NUMBER(1) | NUMBER(3) |

This example shows that a full table scan on the dept1 table is performed. All three partitions are scanned. The starting partition is 1 and the ending partition is 3.

Next, an EXPLAIN PLAN is generated for an indexed search of partitions 1 and 2 only:

```
explain plan for select dept_name
from       dept1
where      deptno    = 15;
Explained.
```

We now generate an EXPLAIN PLAN for a forced full table scan accessing the first two partitions:

```
select     operation, options, id, position , object_name, partition_start,
           partition_stop
from       plan_table;
```

**Output (for the full table scan):**

| OPERATION | OPTIONS | ID | OBJECT NAME | PARTITION START | PARTITION STOP |
|---|---|---|---|---|---|
| SELECT STATEMENT | | | | | |
| TABLE ACCESS | BY LOCAL INDEX ROWID | 1 | DEPT1 | NUMBER(2) | NUMBER(2) |
| TABLE ACCESS | RANGE SCAN | 2 | DEPTIDX | NUMBER(2) | NUMBER(2) |

The output shows that the only partition of the table OR index that is accessed is the second partition. This is because the value for "deptno=15" is within the second partition of the dept1 table. The deptno column is also indexed, and this value also is within the second partition of the index.

Reading EXPLAIN PLAN

**TIP**
*Partitions can also be viewed by the EXPLAIN PLAN by accessing the columns partition_start and partition_stop in the PLAN_TABLE table.*

## Finding High Disk and/or Memory Reads Without Using TRACE

Is there another method for retrieving problem disk and memory read information without tracing everything? The answer is yes! By using V$SQLAREA, you can find the problem queries on your system. The following example shows how to find the problem queries. In this query, I am searching for queries where the disk reads are greater than 10,000 (missing or suppressed index potentials). If your system is much larger, you may need to set this to a higher number.

```
select      disk_reads, sql_text
from        v$sqlarea
where       disk_reads > 10000
order by    disk_reads desc;
DISK READS       SQL TEXT
    12987        select      order#,columns,types from orders
                 where       substr(orderid,1,2)=:1
    11131        select      custid, city from customer
                 where       city = 'CHICAGO'
```

The output suggests that there are two problem queries causing heavy disk reads. The first has the index on ORDERID suppressed by the SUBSTR function and the second shows that there is a missing index on city.

In the next query, I am searching for queries where the memory reads are greater than 200,000 (overindexed query potentials). If your system is much larger, you may need to set this to a higher number.

```
select      buffer_gets, sql_text
from        v$sqlarea
where       buffer_gets > 200000
order by    buffer_gets desc;
BUFFER GETS      SQL TEXT
    300219       select order#,cust_no, from orders
                 where division = '1'
```

The output suggests that there is one problem query causing heavy memory reads. The index on division appears to have a high cardinality and should be suppressed for this statement to improve the performance.

# Yet Another EXPLAIN PLAN Output Method: Building the Tree Structure

While many people will find the earlier EXPLAIN PLAN methods sufficient, still
others require a more theoretical approach that ties to the parent/child relationships
of a query and the corresponding tree structure. For some people, this makes using
EXPLAIN easier to visualize and is included for that audience.

1. The query to be EXPLAINed:

```
explain plan
set statement_id = 'SQL2' for
select    cust_no ,cust_address ,cust_last_name, cust_first_name ,cust_mid_init
from      customer
where     cust_phone = '3035551234';
```

2. The query used for this approach:

```
select    LPAD(' ',2*(LEVEL-1))||operation "OPERATION", options "OPTIONS",
          DECODE(TO_CHAR(id),'0','COST = ' || NVL(TO_CHAR(position),'n/a'),
          object_name) "OBJECT NAME", id ||'-'|| NVL(parent_id, 0)||'-'||
          NVL(position, 0) "ORDER", SUBSTR(optimizer,1,6) "OPT"
from      plan_table
start     with id = 0
and       statement_id = 'SQL2'
connect by prior id = parent_id
and       statement_id = 'SQL2';
```

3. The output for this approach:

| OPERATION | OPTIONS | OBJECT NAME | ORDER | OPT |
|---|---|---|---|---|
| SELECT STATEMENT | | COST = n/a | 0-0-0 | RULE |
| TABLE ACCESS | BY ROWID | CUSTOMER | 1-0-1 | |
| INDEX | RANGE SCAN | IX_CUST_PHONE | 2-1-1 | |

Note that two new columns are introduced:

order     This column contains the ID, the parent ID, and the position of the step in the execution plan. The ID identifies the step but does not imply the order of execution. The parent ID identifies the parent step of the step. The position indicates the order in which children steps are executed that have the same parent ID.

opt       This column contains the current mode of the optimizer.

**4.** The execution tree.

Based on the execution plan in the diagram below, an execution tree can be constructed to get a better feel for how Oracle is going to process the statement. To construct the tree, simply start with Step 1, find all other steps whose parent step is 1 and draw them in. Repeat this until all the steps are accounted for. The execution tree for the execution plan for the query in this diagram is displayed here:

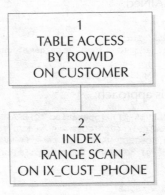

**5.** Execution plan interpretation.

To understand how Oracle is going to process a statement, you must understand what sequence Oracle is going to process the steps in and what Oracle is doing in each step.

The sequence is determined by the parent/child relationship of the steps. Basically, the child step is always performed first, at least once, and feeds the parent steps from there. When a parent has multiple children, children steps are performed in the order of the step position, which is the third number displayed in the order column of the execution plan. When the execution tree is constructed, if the lower-position children for a parent are arranged left to right, then the execution tree will read left to right, bottom to top.

# Another Example Using the Tree Approach

**1.** The query to be EXPLAINed:

```
select    a.cust_last_name, a.cust_first_name, a.cust_mid_init, b.order_desc,
          b.order_create_dt
from      customer a, ,order_hdr b
where     cust_phone = :host1
and       b.cust_no = a.cust_no
and       b.order_status = 'OPEN';
```

**2.** The execution plan:

| OPERATION | OPTIONS | OBJECT NAME | ORDER | OPT |
|---|---|---|---|---|
| SELECT STATEMENT | | COST = n/a | 0-0-0 | RULE |
| NESTED LOOPS | | | 1-0-1 | |
| TABLE ACCESS | BY ROWID | ORDER_HDR | 2-1-1 | |
| INDEX | RANGE SCAN | IX_ORDER_STATUS | 3-2-1 | |
| TABLE ACCESS | BY ROWID | CUSTOMER | 4-1-2 | |
| INDEX | UNIQUE SCAN | PK_CUSTOMER | 5-4-1 | |

**3.** The execution tree (diagrammed here):

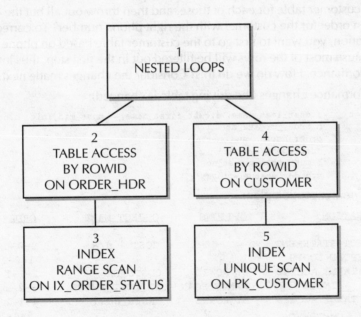

**4.** The execution plan sequence for the query.

This statement has five steps. Child Step 3 is executed first, because it is a range scan, it will return 0, 1, or many ROWIDs to Step 2. For each ROWID returned, Step 2 will access the order table by ROWID, get the requested data, and return the data to Step 1. For each row of data received from Step 2, Step 1 will send the cust_no to Step 5. Step 5 will use the customer number to perform a unique scan to get the ROWID. The ROWID will then be returned from Step 5 to Step 4. If no ROWID was found, Step 4 will tell Step 1 to eliminate that particular row. If a ROWID was found, Step 4 will access the table by ROWID and retrieve the data. Once it gets the data, if the phone number is correct, it will return the data to Step 1, where it will be merged with the result from Steps 2 and 3 for that row and returned to the user. If the phone number is incorrect, Step 4 will return no row and Step 1 will throw the row out.

5. Performance Review.

   Is this a good table access order? In most order entry systems where there are lots of customers and many open orders at a given time, why would you want to spin through all open orders first, get the data for each one, go to the customer table for each of those, and then throw out all but the one open order for the customer with the right phone number? To correct this situation, you want to first go to the customer table based on phone number because most of the rows will be filtered out in the first step, thus improving performance. How do we do this? Consider the changes made next.

**6a.** Performance changes (the driving table is changed):

```
select      a.cust_last_name, a.cust_first_name, a.cust_mid_init, b.order_desc,
            b.order_create_dt
from        order_hdr b, customer a
where       cust_phone = :host1
and         b.cust_no = a.cust_no
and         b.order_status = 'OPEN';
```

**6b.** The *new* execution plan:

| OPERATION | OPTIONS | OBJECT NAME | ORDER | OPT |
|---|---|---|---|---|
| SELECT STATEMENT | | COST = n/a | 0-0-0 | RULE |
|   NESTED LOOPS | | | 1-0-1 | |
|     TABLE ACCESS | BY ROWID | CUSTOMER | 2-1-1 | |
|       INDEX | RANGE SCAN | IX_CUST_PHONE | 3-2-1 | |
|     TABLE ACCESS | BY ROWID | ORDER_HDR | 4-1-2 | |
|       AND-EQUAL | | | 5-4-1 | |
|         INDEX | RANGE SCAN | IX_ORDER_CUST | 6-5-1 | |
|         INDEX | RANGE SCAN | IX_ORDER_STATUS | 7-5-2 | |

**6c.** Performance review of semituned query.

Why did the table order change? In rule-based optimization, when faced with multiple tables to join and identical access paths to enter into each (in this case, each table starts with an index range scan on a single-column index), the table lowest in the FROM clause gets accessed first. So by switching the FROM clause around, the execution plan changed. In cost-based optimization, it may have figured this out in the first place based on table and index statistics. If not, hints could have been used to achieve the same result.

Is this a good table access order? The table order is good because the customer half of the query is executed first and will probably return only one row to the order half of the query.

Is the AND-EQUAL optimal? In this case no. Why churn through 1,000 ROWIDs in the order_status index and all the ROWIDs in the cust_no index and only keep the ones that match? What we should do is either pick the most unique index of the two and use it, or create a composite index on cust_no and order status. Changing the driving table was the right thing to do. Now, we must stop Oracle from using the order status index to completely tune the query.

**7a.** The *tuned* query (the index on order_status is suppressed):

```
select      a.cust_last_name, a.cust_first_name, a.cust_mid_init, b.order_desc,
            b.order_create_dt
from        order_hdr b, customer a
where       cust_phone = :host1
and         b.cust_no = a.cust_no
and         b.order_status || '' = 'OPEN';
```

**7b.** The *tuned* execution plan:

| OPERATION | OPTIONS | OBJECT NAME | ORDER | OPT |
|---|---|---|---|---|
| SELECT STATEMENT | | COST = n/a | 0-0-0 | RULE |
| NESTED LOOPS | | | 1-0-1 | |
| TABLE ACCESS | BY ROWID | CUSTOMER | 2-1-1 | |
| INDEX | UNIQUE SCAN | PK_CUSTOMER | 3-2-1 | |
| TABLE ACCESS | BY ROWID | ORDER_HDR | 4-1-2 | |
| INDEX | RANGE SCAN | IX_ORDER_STATUS | 5-4-1 | |

**7c.** The *tuned* execution tree:

To determine how Oracle is going to process a SQL statement, you must generate and interpret an execution plan for the statement. With access to the tools that can generate execution plans for SQL, along with a rudimentary understanding of the information that is an execution plan and the knowledge of how to construct an execution tree, a developer or DBA can begin exploring the vast variety of EXPLAIN PLANs that their diverse SQL code will produce and learn fairly quickly how to tune and develop quality SQL.

Using the Tree Approach

## TRACing/EXPLAINing Problem Queries in Developer Products

While you can issue the ALTER SESSION SET SQL_TRACE TRUE; command on the SQL*Plus command line to TRACE SQL statements, this is tough when it comes to using developer products. One drawback to this option is that you are not able to TRACE a form or report. You will need to cut the code out of the form or report and run it from SQL*Plus. This can be very time-consuming if you do not know which statements you need to TRACE.

There is another way to produce a TRACE of the execution of a form. If you are using Forms 3.0, you can include a '-s' on the command line; when using Forms 4.xx, you can include 'statistics=yes' on the command line. This way you are able to TRACE individual forms.

```
f45run module=myform userid=username/password statistics=yes
runform30 -s myform username/password
```

Tracing reports is also possible, but it is done from inside the report. Please refer to the Reports documentation for an explanation of how to use the options.

**TIP**
*You can also use TRACE within the Developer/2000 products. You simply need to set "statistics=yes" on the command line for forms, or you may embed the tracing within an actual trigger to turn tracing on and off.*

## Important Columns in the PLAN_TABLE Table

The descriptions for some of the more important columns available in the PLAN_TABLE table are listed here:

| | |
|---|---|
| statement_id | The value of the option STATEMENT_ID parameter specified in the EXPLAIN PLAN statement. |
| timestamp | The date and time when the EXPLAIN PLAN statement was issued. |
| remarks | Any comment (of up to 80 bytes) you wish to associate with each step of the EXPLAIN PLAN. If you need to add or change a remark on any row of the PLAN_TABLE table, use the UPDATE statement to modify the rows of the PLAN_TABLE table. |

| operation | The name of the internal operation performed in this step. See Appendix A of *Oracle Server Tuning* for information on the contents of this column. In the first row generated for a statement, the column contains one of four values: DELETE, INSERT, SELECT, or UPDATE, depending on the type of the statement. |
|---|---|
| options | A variation on the operation described in the operation column. See Appendix A of *Oracle Server Tuning* for information on the contents of this column. |

**TIP**
*The operation and options columns of the PLAN_TABLE are the most important columns for tuning a query. The operation column shows the actual operation performed (including type of join), and the options column tells you when there is full table scan being performed (that may need an index).*

| object_node | The name of the database link used to reference the object (a table name or view name). For local queries using the parallel query option, this column describes the order in which output from operations is consumed. |
|---|---|
| object_owner | The name of the user that owns the schema containing the table or index. |
| object_name | The name of the table or index. |
| object_instance | A number corresponding to the ordinal position of the object as it appears in the original statement. The numbering proceeds from left to right, outer to inner with respect to the original statement text. Note that view expansion will result in unpredictable numbers. |
| object_type | A modifier that provides descriptive information about the object—for example, NON-UNIQUE for indexes. |
| optimizer | The current mode of the optimizer. |
| search_columns | Not currently used. |
| id | A number assigned to each step in the execution plan. |

**TIP**

*The ID column shows the order that a statement is processed. One of the basic rules of tuning a SQL statement is to change the query in a way such that the ID of the order that steps in the query execute is changed. Changing the order that steps execute in a query will usually change the performance of a query either positively or negatively. Using HINTS (see Chapter 7) will force a query to execute in a different statement order and will usually make a query faster or slower.*

parent_id      The ID of the next execution step that operates on the output of the ID step.

**TIP**

*The parent_id column is very important since it shows the dependencies of two steps in an EXPLAIN PLAN. If a section of the EXPLAIN PLAN has a parent_id, it implies that this statement must run prior to the parent_id that is specified.*

position      The order of processing for steps that all have the same parent_id.

other      Other information that is specific to the execution step that a user may find useful.

other_tag      Describes the contents of the other column.

cost      The cost of the operation as estimated by the optimizer's cost-based approach. For statements that use the rule-based approach, this column is NULL. Cost is not determined for table access operations. The value of this column does not have any particular unit of measurement; it is merely a weight value used to compare costs of execution plans.

cardinality      The cost-based approach's estimate of the number of rows accessed by the operation.

bytes      The cost-based approach's estimate of the number of bytes accessed by the operation.

**TIP**
*The bytes column is extremely important when evaluating how to tune a query. When an index is used and the number of bytes is great, it implies that perhaps doing a full table scan would be more efficient (i.e., reading the index and data is more costly than just reading the data in a full table scan). Also, the number of bytes helps us to determine which table should be accessed first in the query (driving table), as one table may limit the number of bytes needed from another. Choosing the driving table is covered in Chapter 9.*

## Helpful Oracle-Supplied Packages

You can also TRACE the sessions of other users by using their session information within the DBMS_SYSTEM package. First, you must get the user's information from the V$SESSION view. You then pass that information to the procedure to begin tracing.

```
select     sid, serial#
from       v$session
where      username = 'SCOTT';
```

**Output:**

```
SID      SERIAL#
  9         190
1 row selected.
```

Begin TRACing the username by using the following package (the sid and serial# for the user's session must be entered):

```
execute dbms_system.set_sql_trace_in_session(9,190,TRUE);
PL/SQL procedure successfully completed.
```

**TIP**
*It is also possible to enable TRACE by calling the procedure DBMS_ORACLE_TRACE_ USER.SET_ORACLE_TRACE.*

You can also initiate TRACE for the session that you are in using the DBMS_SESSION package. This package is particularly helpful for tracing queries within stored procedures, as well as use within PL/SQL code.

```
execute DBMS_SESSION.SET_SQL_TRACE (TRUE);
PL/SQL procedure successfully completed.
```

# init.ora Parameters for Undocumented TRACE

An area that the experts may investigate is the x$ksppi table. A brief listing for undocumented TRACE parameters in init.ora are listed next. Note that Oracle does not support use of undocumented features of the product.

```
select      ksppinm "Parameter Name", ksppivl "Value",ksppidf "Default"
from        x$ksppi
where       ksppinm like '%trace%';
```

| Parameter Name | Value | Default |
|---|---|---|
| _trace_files_public | FALSE | TRUE |
| _trace_buffers_per_process | 0 | TRUE |
| _trace_block_size | 2048 | TRUE |
| _trace_archive_start | FALSE | TRUE |
| _trace_flushing | FALSE | TRUE |
| _trace_enabled | TRUE | TRUE |
| _trace_events | | TRUE |
| _trace_archive_dest | %RDBMS70%\trace.dat | TRUE |
| _trace_file_size | 10000 | TRUE |
| _trace_write_batch_size | 32 | TRUE |
| sql_trace | FALSE | TRUE |

11 rows selected.

**TIP**
*The x$ksppi table can only be accessed by the SYS user. See Chapter 15 on tips for accessing the x$ tables and using some of these parameters. Do not use any undocumented parameters without consulting Oracle Corporation.*

## TRACing Errors Within Oracle for More Information

Before using undocumented init.ora parameters, please contact Oracle Corporation. The use of one of the undocumented features of TRACE is explained in this section. To TRACE errors for a session, you may alter and monitor the session (shown next) or you may set an event in the init.ora (see Chapter 15). Sessions can be TRACEd for errors by running the query shown next (use to TRACE a 4031 error). These queries will build a TRACE file in your _trace_archive_dest (found in x$ksppi) that contain a dump of the full error text.

Prior to v7.0.16, use the following command:

```
alter session set events ='4031 trace name errorstack';
```

On v7.0.16+, use the following command:

```
alter session set events='4031 trace name errorstack level 4';
```

**TIP**
*TRACing queries can help performance, but using the TRACE facility built within the undocumented TRACE init.ora parameters (discussed earlier) can give great insight to solving errors within Oracle.*

# Tips Review

- Setting SQL_TRACE=TRUE in the init.ora will cause the entire system and all queries to be TRACEd, and could cause performance degradations.

- By specifying "explain=username/password" in TKPROF, we are able to get the EXPLAIN execution path in addition to the execution statistics of the query.

- A TRACEd query with a large number of physical reads usually indicates a missing index.

- A TRACEd query output with only memory reads usually indicates that an index is being used.

- If multiple developers/DBAs are using the same PLAN_TABLE, then the SET STATEMENT_ID will be essential to identifying a statement.

- Use EXPLAIN instead of TRACE so that you don't have to wait for the query to run. EXPLAIN will show the path of a query without actually running the query. Use TRACE only for multi-query batch jobs to find out which of the many queries in the batch job are slow.

- Whether the EXPLAIN PLAN is read from top to bottom or from the bottom to the top is dependent entirely on the query used to select information from the PLAN_TABLE. See queries in this chapter for more information.

- The AUTOTRACE option also provides an EXPLAIN PLAN for a query. The AUTOTRACE also provides many of the TRACE and TKPROF statistics such as disk reads (physical reads) and memory reads (consistent reads + db block gets).

Tips Review

■ Partitions can also be viewed by the EXPLAIN PLAN by accessing the columns partition_start and partition_stop in the PLAN_TABLE table.

■ Accessing the V$SQLAREA view can give statistics that are often found when TRACing a query.

■ You can also use TRACE within the Developer/2000 products. You simply need to set "statistics=yes" on the command line for Oracle Forms.

■ The ID column shows the order that a statement is processed. One of the primary rules of tuning a SQL statement is to change the query in a way such that the ID of the order that steps in the query execute is changed. Changing the order that steps execute in a query will usually change the performance of a query either positively or negatively.

■ The bytes column is extremely important when evaluating how to tune a query. When an index is used and the number of bytes is great, it implies that perhaps doing a full table scan would be more efficient (i.e., reading the index and data is more costly than just reading the data in a full table scan). Also, the number of bytes helps us to determine which table should be accessed first in the query as one table may limit the number of bytes needed from another.

■ It is also possible to enable TRACE by calling the procedure DBMS_ORACLE_TRACE_USER.SET_ORACLE_TRACE.

■ TRACing queries can help performance, but using the TRACE facility built within the undocumented TRACE init.ora parameters can give great insight (and better information) to solving errors within Oracle.

# References

Many thanks to Dave Hathway, Jake Van der Vort, and Greg Pucka of TUSC for contributions to this chapter.

Tips Review

# TIPS

&

# TECHNIQUES

# CHAPTER
## 7

## Basic Hint Syntax
## (Developer and DBA)

W hile the optimizer is incredibly accurate in choosing the correct optimization path and use of indexes for thousands of queries on your system, the optimizer is not perfect. Oracle has provided hints that you can specify for a given query so that the optimizer is overridden, and hopefully better performance is achieved for a given query. This chapter will focus on the basic syntax and use of hints. The following chapters (Chapters 8 and 9) will have more complex examples, using various hints covered in this chapter.

The most useful hints that you use for your system may not be the same ones that I have found to be best, because of the diversity of each system. Common to all systems is the use of the FULL, INDEX, ALL_ROWS and FIRST_ROWS hints. A system with the parallel option will probably use the hints that are in the specific grouping. Tips covered in this chapter include the following:

- Available hints and groupings, and specifying multiple hints
- When using an alias, you *must* use the alias, *not* the table in the hint
- The CHOOSE hint to force cost-based optimization
- The RULE hint to force rule-based optimization
- The FIRST_ROWS hint to generally force the use of indexes
- The ALL_ROWS hint to generally force a full table scan
- Using the FULL hint to force a full table scan
- The INDEX hint to force the use of an index
- The INDEX_ASC hint to use and index ordered in ascending order
- The INDEX_DESC hint to use and index ordered in descending order
- Forcing fast full scans with the INDEX_FFS
- The ORDERED hint for specifying the driving order of tables
- Forcing the use of the ROWID
- Star queries and the STAR hint
- Queries involving multiple locations and the DRIVING_SITE hint
- The USE_MERGE to change how tables are joined internally
- Forcing the subquery to process earlier with PUSH_SUBQ
- The parallel query option and using PARALLEL and NO_PARALLEL
- Using APPEND and NO_APPEND with parallel options

- Caching and pinning a table into memory with the CACHE hint
- A table specified as CACHE, but you prevent the caching with NOCACHE
- Forcing clustering with the CLUSTER hint
- Forcing hashing with the HASH hint

For further information on Oracle8 hints, please refer to Chapter 12.

# Available Hints and Groupings

The available hints vary according to the version of the database installed. Since there are so many variations, I have included a list of only the hints that are available as of the release of Oracle8. While this chapter will focus on the hints that are used frequently, many of these hints that are not covered in detail may give great performance gains for someone with a particular system.

Hints are separated into different categories based on which type of operation is being modified by the hint.

## Execution Path

These hints modify the execution path when an optimizer processes a particular statement. The init.ora parameter OPTIMIZER_MODE may be used to modify all statements in the database to follow a specific execution path, but a hint to a different execution path overrides anything that is specified in the init.ora. However, cost-based optimization will not be used if tables have not been analyzed (we'll see how to do this in a later section of this chapter). Hints that change the execution path include the following:

- ALL_ROWS*
- CHOOSE*
- FIRST_ROWS*
- RULE*

## Access Methods

The hints that are grouped into access methods are hints that allow the coder to vary the way the actual query is accessed. This is the group that is most frequently used, especially the INDEX hint. It provides direction as to whether and how indexes are

*Covered in detail in this chapter

used, and how the corresponding indexes will be merged to get the final answer. The access method hints are listed here:

| | | |
|---|---|---|
| AND_EQUAL | CLUSTER* | FULL* |
| HASH* | HASH_AJ | INDEX* |
| INDEX_ASC* | INDEX_COMBINE | INDEX_DESC* |
| INDEX_FFS* | MERGE_AJ | ROWID* |
| USE_CONCAT | | |

## Join Orders

The join orders grouping shows the hints that cause a query to be driven by a particular table or to return results from one query back to another:

- ORDERED*
- STAR*
- STAR_TRANSFORMATION

## Join Operations

The join operations grouping shows how joined tables merge data together. A join operation, such as USE_MERGE, may be best for retrieving all rows for a query (throughput), while a USE_NL may be best for retrieving the first row (response time). See Chapter 9 for further information regarding table joins and join methods.

- DRIVING_SITE*
- USE_HASH
- USE_MERGE*
- NO_MERGE*
- USE_NL*
- PUSH_SUBQ*

*Covered in detail in this chapter

**Available Hints and Groupings**

## Parallel Execution

The parallel execution grouping applies to databases using the parallel query option. However, although the APPEND and NO_APPEND hints can be used without the parallel option, they are frequently used with it. See Chapter 11 for further information regarding parallel operations.

- NO_PARALLEL*
- PARALLEL*
- PARALLEL_INDEX
- APPEND*
- NO_APPEND*

## Cache Hints

The cache grouping pertains to the hints that will put items as Least Recently Used (CACHE) or most recently used (NOCACHE).

- CACHE*
- NOCACHE*

# Specifying a Hint

If you incorrectly specify a hint in any way, it will become a comment, and it will be ignored. Be very careful to get the hint syntax *exactly* correct. The best way to ensure that a hint has been correctly specified is to run an EXPLAIN PLAN, or set AUTOTRACE to on in SQL*Plus to see if the hint was used. Some hints are overridden by Oracle despite the fact that a hint is primarily to override Oracle. The basic hint syntax (in this example, it is for a FULL hint) is shown here:

**Syntax:**

```
select      /*+ FULL(table) */ column1,…
```

The *table* is the table name to perform a full table scan on.

**Example:**

```
select      /*+ FULL(emp) */ empno, ename, deptno
from        emp
where       deptno = 1;
```

*Covered in detail in this chapter

Specifying a Hint

In this query, if there was an index on the deptno column, a full table scan would be performed. The case of the hint is not required to be uppercase.

**Example (incorrect hint syntax):**

```
select      /* FULL(emp) */ empno, ename, deptno
from        emp
where       deptno = 1;
```

In the query, if there was an index on the deptno column, the index would be used since the hint is missing the **+**.

 **TIP**
*Incorrect hint syntax leads to the hint being interpreted as a comment.*

# Specifying Multiple Hints

You can also use more than one hint at a time, although this may cause some or all of the hints to be ignored. The basic syntax is to separate hints with spaces.

**Syntax:**

```
select      /*+ FULL(table) CACHE(table)*/ column1,…
```

The *table* is the table name to perform the full scan and cache on.

**Example:**

```
select      /*+ FULL(emp) CACHE(emp)*/ empno, ename, deptno
from        emp
where       deptno = 1;
```

 **TIP**
*Multiple hints are separated with a space. At times, specifying multiple hints can mysteriously cause the query to use none of the hints.*

# Hint the Alias, and Not the Table

When you use aliases on a given table that you want to use in a hint, you must specify the alias and *not* the table name in the hint. If you specify the table name in the hint when an alias is used, the hint will *not* be used.

**Syntax:**

```
select      /*+ FULL(table) */ column1,…
```

This *table* will have to be replaced with the following alias since the query uses an alias. If an alias is used, the alias *must* be used in the hint or it will *not* work.

**Example:**

```
select      /*+ FULL(A) */ empno, ename, deptno
from        emp A
where       deptno = 1;
```

**TIP**
*If an alias is used, the alias must be used in the hint or it will* not *work.*

# The CHOOSE Hint

When people think of cost-based optimization, they are often led to believe that the hint for cost-based optimization is COST. It is not! The hint for cost-based optimization is CHOOSE! The CHOOSE hint will cause the optimizer to choose the optimal plan for a given query. If CHOOSE is specified in the init.ora, it will cause cost-based optimization for the entire database unless overridden for a given query. If tables in a query have not been analyzed, then rule-based optimization will still be used. If one of the tables in a multi-table join has been analyzed, then cost-based optimization will be used for the entire query, and Oracle makes its best guess for the non-analyzed tables. In general, all tables in a join should be analyzed before you use cost-based optimization for the join. The syntax for the CHOOSE hint is displayed here.

**Syntax:**

```
select      /*+ CHOOSE */ column1, …
```

**Example:**

```
select      /*+ CHOOSE */ empno, ename, deptno
from        emp
where       deptno = 1;
```

**TIP**
*The CHOOSE hint will use cost-based optimization for the entire query unless all of the tables in the query have not been analyzed. If one table of a multi-table join query has been analyzed, then cost-based optimization will be used for all tables. Generally, you should choose an index if one is available on the non-analyzed tables. It will use rule-based optimization if none of the tables have been analyzed. The CHOOSE hint may set in the init.ora for the entire database, but query-level hints will override it on a given query.*

# The RULE Hint

Every hint that is issued causes the use of the cost-based optimizer with the exception of the RULE hint. The RULE hint will cause the optimizer to use rule-based optimization. This means that the distribution of data in the table or indexes is not taken into consideration. Instead, the optimizer will execute the query based on Oracle's predefined set of rules, such as using the ROWID or unique indexes before other options, which govern how a query will execute. The RULE hint also causes the statement to avoid any other use of hints in the statement other than the DRIVING_SITE and ORDERED hints, which will be used despite rule-based optimization.

**Syntax:**

```
select      /*+ RULE */ column1, …
```

**Example:**

```
select      /*+ RULE */ empno, ename, deptno
from        emp
where       deptno = 1;
```

If an index exists on the deptno column, it would be used for this statement even if the index was a poor choice for the query.

**TIP**
*The RULE hint forces Oracle to use predefined rules (such as using ROWID and UNIQUE indexes) over using the statistics about the data. The RULE hint may set in the init.ora for the entire database, but some query level hints will override it on a given query.*

# The FIRST_ROWS Hint

The FIRST_ROWS (response time) hint directs a query to optimize a query on the basis of retrieving the first row the fastest. This is especially helpful when users of the system are using Oracle Forms to retrieve a single record on their screen. This would be a poor choice for a batch-intensive environment where a lot of rows are generally retrieved by a query. The FIRST_ROWS hint will generally force the use of indexes, which under normal circumstances may not have been used. The FIRST_ROWS hint is used, even when statistics are not gathered when using cost-based optimization.

The FIRST_ROWS hint is ignored in UPDATE and DELETE statements, since all rows of the index must be updated or deleted. It is also ignored when any grouping statement is used (GROUP BY, DISTINCT, INTERSECT, MINUS, UNION), since all of the rows for the grouping will have to be retrieved for the grouping to occur. The statement may also choose to avoid a sort when there is an ORDER BY in the statement, if an index scan can do the actual sort. The optimizer may also choose NESTED LOOPS over a SORT-MERGE when an index scan is available and the index is on the inner table (nondriving table). The inner table would shorten the result set that will be joined back to the outside table (driving table) in the query, and specifying access paths will override this hint. See Chapter 9 for further information.

**Syntax:**

```
select    /*+ FIRST_ROWS */ column1, …
```

**Example:**

```
select    /*+ FIRST_ROWS */ empno, ename, deptno
from      emp
where     deptno = 1;
```

**TIP**

*The FIRST_ROWS hint will cause the optimizer to choose a path that will retrieve the first row of a query fastest, at the cost of retrieving multiple rows slower. The FIRST_ROWS hint may set in the init.ora for the entire database, but query-level hints will override it on a given query.*

# The ALL_ROWS Hint

The ALL_ROWS (best throughput) hint directs a query to optimize a query on the basis of retrieving all of the rows the fastest (best throughput). This is especially helpful when users of the system are in a heavy batch report environment and running reports that retrieve a lot of rows. This would be a poor choice for a heavy Oracle Forms environment where users are trying to view a single record on a screen. The ALL_ROWS hint may suppress the use of indexes that under normal circumstances would have been used. Specifying access path hints will override the use of this hint.

**Syntax:**

```
select      /*+ ALL_ROWS */ column1, …
```

**Example:**

```
select      /*+ ALL_ROWS */ empno, ename, deptno
from        emp
where       deptno = 1;
```

**TIP**

*The ALL_ROWS hint will cause the optimizer to choose a path that will retrieve all the rows of a query fastest, at the cost of retrieving one single row slower. The ALL_ROWS hint may set in the init.ora for the entire database, but query-level hints will override it on a given query.*

# The FULL Hint

The FULL hint directs a query to override the optimize and perform a full table scan on the specified table in the hint. The FULL hint has different functionality based on the query that you are tuning. You can use it to force a full table scan when a large portion of the table is being queried. The cost of retrieving the index *and* the rows may be larger than just retrieving the entire table. The FULL hint may also cause an unexpected result. Causing a full table scan may cause tables to be accessed in a different order, because a different driving table is used. This may lead to better performance, leading one to believe that the full table scan was the key benefit, when changing the order of the driving table was the real cause of the increased performance. The syntax for the FULL hint is displayed next.

**Syntax:**

```
select      /*+ FULL(table) */ column1,…
```

The *table* is the table name to perform the full scan on. If an alias is used, the alias *must* be used in the hint or it will *not* work.

**Example:**

```
select      /*+ FULL(emp) */ empno, ename, deptno
from        emp
where       deptno = 1;
```

The FULL hint in the preceding example would be particularly helpful if the only department in the company was 1. Going to an index on deptno and the emp table would be slower than simply performing a full table scan on the emp table.

The FULL hint is also a necessary part of using some of the other hints. The CACHE hint can only cause a table to be cached when the full table is accessed. Some of the hints in the parallel grouping also necessitate the use of a full table scan. We will look at each of these hints later in this chapter.

**TIP**
*The FULL hint performs a full table scan on the table that is specified, and not all tables in the query. The FULL hint may also lead to better performance, which is attributable to causing a change in the driving table of the query and not the actual full table scan.*

The FULL Hint

# The INDEX Hint

The INDEX hint is frequently used to force one or more indexes to be executed for a given query. Oracle will generally choose the correct index with the optimizer, but when the optimizer chooses the wrong index or no index at all, this hint is excellent. You may also use multiple indexes with this hint.

**Syntax:**

```
select      /*+ INDEX (table index1, index2…) */ column1, …
```

**Example:**

```
select      /*+ INDEX (emp deptno_idx) */ empno, ename, deptno
from        emp
where       deptno = 1;
```

In the example, the deptno_idx index on the emp table will be used.

**Example:**

```
select      /*+ INDEX (emp deptno_idx, empno_idx) */ empno, ename,
deptno
from        emp
where       deptno = 1
and         empno = 7750;
```

In the second example, Oracle may use the deptno_idx index, or the empno_idx index, or a merge of both of them. We have placed these choices in the optimizer's hands to decipher the best choice. It would have been best to only specify the index on the empno column (empno_idx) if this was the most restrictive statement (usually much more restrictive than the department).

**TIP**
*The INDEX hint will cause the optimizer to choose the index specified in the hint. Multiple indexes for a single table can be specified, but it is usually better to specify only the most restrictive index on a given query (avoiding the merging of the result of each index). If multiple indexes are specified, Oracle will choose which (one or more) to use so be careful or your hint will be potentially overridden.*

**Example:**

```
select    /*+ INDEX */ empno, ename, deptno
from      emp
where     deptno = 1
and       empno = 7750;
```

In the example, no index is specified. Oracle will now weigh all of the possible indexes that are available and choose one or more to be used. Since we have not specified a particular index, but we have specified the INDEX hint, the optimizer will *not* perform a full table scan.

**TIP**
*The INDEX hint, without a specified index, will not perform a full table scan, even though no indexes have been specified. The optimizer will choose the best index or indexes for the query.*

# The INDEX_ASC Hint

The INDEX_ASC hint currently does *exactly* the same thing as the INDEX hint. Since indexes are already sorted in ascending order, this does nothing more than the current INDEX hint. So what is it good for? Oracle does not guarantee that indexes will be sorted in ascending order in the future.

**Syntax:**

```
select    /*+ INDEX_ASC (table index1, index2…) */ column1, …
```

**Example:**

```
select    /*+ INDEX_ASC (emp deptno_idx) */ empno, ename, deptno
from      emp
where     deptno = 1;
```

In the example, the deptno_idx index on the emp table will be used.

**TIP**
*The INDEX_ASC does exactly what the INDEX hint does since indexes are already sorted in ascending order. It is used to guarantee this to be true, as Oracle may change this default in the future.*

# The INDEX_DESC Hint

The INDEX_DESC hint causes indexes to be sorted in descending order (of their indexed value or order), which is the opposite of the INDEX and INDEX_ASC hints. This index is overridden when the query has multiple tables, because the index will need to be used in the normal ascending order to go back to the other table in the query.

**Syntax:**

```
select      /*+ INDEX_DESC (table index1, index2...) */ column1, ...
```

**Example:**

```
select      /*+ INDEX_DESC (emp deptno_idx) */ empno, ename, deptno
from        emp
where       deptno = 1;
```

> **TIP**
> The INDEX_DESC will process an index in the descending order of how it was built. This hint will not be used if more than one table exists in the query.

# The INDEX_FFS Hint (Oracle8 Only)

The INDEX_FFS hint is a fast full scan of the index. This hint will access only the index and *not* the corresponding table. It will only be used if all of the information that the query needs to retrieve is in the index. This one can give great performance gains, especially when the table has a large number of columns.

**Syntax:**

```
select      /*+ INDEX_FFS (table index) */ column1, ...
```

**Example:**

```
select      /*+ INDEX_FFS (emp deptno_idx) */ deptno, empno
from        emp
where       deptno = 1;
```

The INDEX_FFS hint will only be used if the deptno_idx index contains both deptno and empno columns as a part of it.

**TIP**
*The INDEX_FFS will process only the index and will not take the result and access the table. All columns that are used and retrieved by the query must be contained in the index.*

# The ORDERED Hint

The ORDERED hint causes tables to be accessed in a particular order, based on the order of the tables in the FROM clause of the query, which is often referred to as the driving order for a query. Generally in rule-based optimization, the last table in the FROM clause is the driving table in queries; however, using the ORDERED hint causes the first table in the FROM clause to be the driver. The ORDERED hint also guarantees the driving order. When the ORDERED hint is not used, Oracle may internally switch the driving table when compared to how tables are listed in the FROM clause (EXPLAIN PLAN can show how tables are accessed). The complexity of possibilities when this hint is used is so great that much of the next chapter is focused on this subject (please see Chapter 9 for more information regarding tuning joins). This chapter will only briefly cover this hint, mainly for syntactical purposes. Contrary to the documentation, this hint can be used for cost- or rule-based optimization.

**Syntax:**

```
select      /*+ ORDERED */ column1, …
```

**Example:**

```
select      /*+ ORDERED */ empno, ename, deptno
from        emp, dept
where       emp.deptno = dept.deptno
and         dept.deptno = 1
and         emp.empno = 7747;
```

In the example, if both tables (emp and dept) have been analyzed (we are using the cost-based optimizer) *and* there are *no* indexes on either table *and* we are in Oracle8, then the emp table is accessed first and the dept table is accessed second.

The ORDERED Hint

There is a plethora of possible variations (covered in the next two chapters) that will cause this hint to work differently.

**Example:**

```
select      /*+ ORDERED */ empno, ename, deptno, itemno
from        emp, dept, orders
where       emp.deptno = dept.deptno
and         emp.empno = orders.empno
and         dept.deptno = 1
and         emp.empno = 7747
and         orders.ordno = 45;
```

In the example, if all three tables (emp, dept, and orders) have been analyzed (using cost-based optimization) *and* there are *no* indexes on any of the tables using Oracle8, then the emp table would be accessed first, then joined to the dept table, which would be accessed second. The result would be joined with the orders table, which is accessed last. There is a plethora of possible variations (covered Chapter 9) that will cause this to work differently.

**TIP**
*The ORDERED hint is one of the most powerful hints available. It processes the tables of the query in the order that they are listed in the FROM clause (the first table in the FROM clause is processed first). There are many variations that cause this to work differently. The version of Oracle, the existence of indexes on the tables, and which tables have been analyzed, will all cause this to work differently. However, when a multi-table join is slow and you don't know what to do…this should be one of the first hints that you should try!*

## The ROWID Hint

The ROWID hint will cause Oracle to use the ROWID (when possible) to go to the exact physical location (block address) to retrieve information that is desired.

**Syntax:**

```
select      /*+ ROWID (table) */ column1, …
```

Consider an emp table with the following records:

```
EMPNO       ENAME       HERO
1000        RICH        REGINA
1000        RICH        REGINA
1000        RICH        REGINA
2000        JOE         LORI
2000        JOE         LORI
3000        BRAD        KRISTEN
```

The following example has been included to demonstrate the use of the ROWID hint. This example provides a query for you to find duplicate values, in this case duplicate empno values:

```
select      /*+ ROWID (a) */ empno, count(*)
from        emp a
where       rowid not in
 (select      max(rowid)
  from        emp b
  where       a.empno = b.empno)
group by    empno;
```

**Output:**

```
EMPNO       COUNT(*)
1000        2
2000        1
```

The query must hint the alias (the alias is "a" for the emp table) in order to use the hint. This query finds duplicate empno values in the emp table. It does an AGGREGATE merge max()) and the ROWID hint in this scenario is actually not used (despite the correct syntax) because of the max() function performed. The real goal here is to give you a query to find duplicates and the syntax for the ROWID hint. It is *not* recommended that you reference actual ROWIDs.

**TIP**
*The ROWID hint will process a query using the ROWID, if it is possible, based on how the query is written.*

# The STAR Hint (Oracle 7.3+ Only)

The STAR hint forces a star query plan, which is identical to the ORDERED hint for a denormalized table at the center of a join. Designers often build star schemas

The STAR Hint

where you have multiple tables that need to be used together. You build a common table (at the center of the star—often called the "fact" table) that contains key columns from the other tables that are related. Accessing the smaller tables first and then accessing the largest fact (composite) table last causes an improvement in performance. The fact table must have a concatenated index of all of the keys from the other tables that it will be joined to at any given time. Although this has been popularized with data warehouses, people have been building composite (very denormalized) tables for years to achieve faster reports. The concatenated index on the fact table is then accessed last in the driving order so that it can be accessed using nested loops.

**Syntax:**

```
select      /*+ STAR */ column1, …
```

**Equivalent syntax:**

```
select      /*+ ORDERED USE_NL(table) INDEX(table concat_idx) */
                        column1, …
```

**Example:**

```
select      /*+ ORDERED USE_NL(orderfacts) INDEX(orderfacts of_idx) */ empno,
            ename, deptno, itemno
from        orders, emp, dept, orderfacts
where       orderfacts.empno = emp.empno
 and        orderfacts.deptno = dept.deptno
 and        orderfacts.ordno  = orders.ordno
 and        orderfacts.ordno = 317548813;
```

In the query, a concatenated index exists on the empno, deptno and ordno columns of the orderfacts table. The orders table is joined with the emp table. The result set is merged with the dept table and then that result set is joined with the concatenated index for orderfacts using NESTED LOOPS. The equivalent process would be to simply use the STAR hint.

**Example:**

```
select      /*+ STAR */ empno, ename, deptno, itemno
from        emp, dept, orders, orderfacts
where       orderfacts.empno = emp.empno
 and        orderfacts.deptno = dept.deptno
 and        orderfacts.ordno  = orders.ordno
 and        orderfacts.ordno = 317548813;
```

The STAR Hint

The STAR hint will assume the last table in the FROM clause is the fact table.

**TIP**
*The STAR hint is used to join multiple tables together. The central (facts) table is a denormalized combination of the key information of the other tables that it will join. The composite (fact) table is the "center of the star."*

# The DRIVING_SITE Hint (Oracle8 Only)

The DRIVING_SITE hint is identical to the ORDERED hint, except this hint is for processing data by driving it from a particular database. The table specified in the hint will be the driving site that will be used to process the actual join. This hint can be used with either cost- or rule-based optimization.

**Syntax:**

```
select      /*+ DRIVING_SITE (table) */ column1, …
```

**Example:**

```
select      /*+ DRIVING_SITE (deptremote) */ empno, ename,
                          deptremote.deptno
from        emp, dept@oratusc deptremote
where       emp.deptno = deptremote.deptno
  and       deptremote.deptno = 10
  and       empno = 7747;
```

Normally Oracle would have retrieved the rows from the remote site and joined them at the local site if this hint was not specified. Since the "empno = 7747" limits the query greatly, we would rather pass the small number of rows from the emp table to the remote site instead of pulling an entire dept table department back to our local site to process.

Limiting the rows that are retrieved from a remote site can also be achieved by creating a view locally for the remote table. The local view should have the WHERE clause that will be used, so that the view will limit the rows returned from the remote database before they are sent back to the local database. I have personally tuned queries from hours to seconds using this method.

The location specification is not specified in the hint (just the table name). However, if an alias were used, the alias would have to be used instead of the table name in the hint.

The DRIVING_SITE Hint

The USE_MERGE Hint

**TIP**
*The DRIVING_SITE hint is extremely powerful as it will potentially limit the amount of information that will be processed over your network. The table specified with the DRIVING_SITE hint will be the location for the join to be processed. Using views for remote tables can also lead to better performance by limiting the number of rows passed from the remote site before the records are sent to the local site.*

## The USE_MERGE Hint

The USE_MERGE hint is a hint that is generally used to achieve the best throughput for a given query. Assume you are joining two tables together, as shown next. The row set returned from each table is sorted and then merged (known as a sort-merged join) to form the final result set. Since each is sorted and then merged together, this action is fastest in retrieving all rows from a given query. If you wanted the first row faster instead, the USE_NL would be the hint to use.

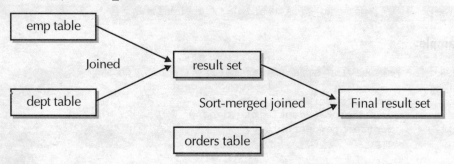

**Syntax:**

```
select      /*+ USE_MERGE (table) */ column1, …
```

**Example:**

```
select      /*+ USE_MERGE(orders) */ empno, ename, dept.deptno,
                    itemno
from        emp, dept, orders
where       emp.deptno = dept.deptno
 and        emp.empno = orders.empno
 and        dept.deptno = 1
 and        emp.empno = 7747
 and        orders.ordno = 45;
```

The USE_MERGE hint in the preceding query causes the orders table to be joined in a SORT-MERGE join to the resulting row source resulting from the join of the emp and dept tables. The rows are sorted and then merged together to find the final result.

**TIP**
*In a three or more table join, the USE_MERGE hint will cause the table(s) specified in the hint to be SORT-MERGE joined with the resulting row set from a join of the other tables in the join.*

## The USE_NL Hint

The USE_NL (use nested loops) is usually the fastest way to return a single row (response time); thus, it is consequently slower at returning all the rows. This hint causes a statement to be processed using nested loops, which will take the first matching row from one table based on the result from another table. This is the opposite of a MERGE join, which will retrieve rows that match the conditions from each table and then merge them together—this usually takes a lot longer to get the first row.

**Syntax:**

```
select      /*+ USE_NL (table index1, index2...) */ column1, …
```

**Example:**

```
select      /*+ ORDERED USE_NL(dept) */ empno, ename, deptno
from        emp, dept
where       emp.deptno = dept.deptno
and         dept.deptno = 1
and         emp.empno = 7747;
```

The USE_NL hint causes Oracle to take the resulting rows returned from the emp table (driving table) and process them with the matching rows from the dept table (the specified nested loop table). The first row that matches from the dept table can be returned to the user immediately (as in an Oracle Form), as opposed to waiting until all matching rows are found. The ORDERED hint will guarantee that the emp table is processed first.

**TIP**
*The USE_NL hint usually provides the best response time (first row comes back faster), whereas the USE_MERGE hint usually provides the best throughput.*

## The PUSH_SUBQ Hint (Oracle8 Only)

The PUSH_SUBQ hint can lead to dramatic performance gains (over an increase of 100 times in performance) when used in the appropriate situation. The best situation to use this hint is when the subquery will return a relatively small number of rows (quickly); then, those rows can be used to substantially limit the rows in the outer query. It will cause the subquery to be evaluated at the earliest possible time. This hint can *not* be used when the query uses a MERGE join and can *not* be used with remote tables. Moving the subquery to be part of the main query (when possible) can lead to the same gains when the tables are driven in the correct order (accessing the former subquery table first).

**Syntax:**

```
select      /*+ PUSH_SUBQ */ column1, …
```

**Example:**

```
select      /*+ PUSH_SUBQ */ emp.empno, emp.ename, orders.order_item
from        emp, orders
where       emp.empno = orders.empno
and         emp.deptno =
 (select    deptno
 from       dept
 where      location = 'BELMONT');
```

This query will process the subquery to be used by the outer query at its earliest possible time.

**TIP**
*The PUSH_SUBQ hint can improve performance greatly when the subquery will return only a few rows very fast, and those rows can be used to limit the rows returned in the outer query.*

## The PARALLEL Hint

The PARALLEL hint causes full table scan queries to break up a query into pieces (the degree of parallelism) and process each piece with a different process. It can only be used if you have Oracle's parallel query option installed with your database. The *Degree of Parallelism* is applied to each operation of a SQL statement. A query that requires a sort operation will cause the number of processes used to be double the degree specified. The operation that does the breaking up and putting back together of the pieces also requires a process. Therefore, if the degree you set for a query is 4, it may use 4 processes for the query plus 4 *more* processes for the sorting plus 1 *more* process for the breaking up and putting together of the 4 pieces. The total used with a degree of 4 is actually 4+4+1, or 9 total processes.

The PARALLEL hint allows you to specify the desired number of concurrent servers that can be used for a parallel operation. In Oracle8, the hint can now be applied to the INSERT, UPDATE, and DELETE portions of a statement (you have to commit immediately after if you use this) as well as to the table scan partition (parallel scanning of partitions). See Chapter 11 for an extremely detailed look at all of the requirements and rules that are associated with this powerful option.

**Syntax:**

```
/*+ PARALLEL (table, DEGREE,INSTANCES) */
```

The degree, as just discussed, is the number of pieces that the query is broken into. The instances (second number specified after the degree) are the number of instances that are used if Parallel Server is used.

**Example:**

```
select     /*+ PARALLEL (order_line_items) */ invoice_number, invoice_date
from       order_line_items
order by   invoice_date;
```

This statement does not specify a degree of parallelism. The *Default Degree of Parallelism* is dictated by the table definition when the table was created.

**Example:**

```
select     /*+ PARALLEL (order_line_items, 4)*/ invoice_number, invoice_date
from       order_line_items
order by   invoice_date;
```

The statement specifies a degree of parallelism of four. Per previous discussion, as many as nine query servers may be allocated or created to satisfy this query.

**Example:**

```
select     /*+ PARALLEL (oli, 4) */ invoice_number, invoice_date
from       order_line_items oli
order by   invoice_date;
```

In the example, an alias is used and now must be used in the hint instead of using the table name.

The PARALLEL Hint

**TIP**
*Using the PARALLEL hint will enable the use of parallel operations. If the degree is not specified with the hint, the default degree specified during the table creation will be used.*

# The NO_PARALLEL Hint

If a table is created with a parallel degree set, the table will use that degree for all full table scan queries. However, you may also "turn off" the use of parallel operations in any one given query on a table that has been specified to use parallel operations using the NO_PARALLEL hint. The NO_PARALLEL hint is a query with a degree of 1.

**Syntax:**

```
select       /*+ NO_PARALLEL (table) */
```

**Example:**

```
select       /*+ NO_PARALLEL (oli) */ invoice_number, invoice_date
from         order_line_items oli
order by     invoice_date;
```

The NO_PARALLEL hint is a query with a degree of 1.

**TIP**
*The use of the NO_PARALLEL hint will disable parallel operations in a statement that would otherwise utilize parallel processing due to a parallel object definition.*

# The APPEND Hint (Oracle8 Only)

The APPEND hint is a great hint if you have space to burn. The APPEND hint will not check to see if there is space within currently used blocks for inserts, but instead it will append the data into new blocks. Potentially, you may waste space, but you will not get the overhead of checking the current blocks to see if they have fallen below the PCTUSED (the minimum percent of free space in a block before you can reuse it). If you never delete rows from a table, you should definitely use the

APPEND, since the blocks will never get to the PCTUSED (only deleting rows will empty a current block to this level). PCTUSED is a storage parameter that is set when a table is created.

If parallel loading is used with SQL*Loader, then the APPEND option for SQL*Loader must be used. Also, if an INSERT is parallelized using the PARALLEL hint, the APPEND will be used by default. You can use the NO_APPEND hint (next section) to override this behavior.

**Syntax:**

```
insert /*+ APPEND */ …
```

**Example:**

```
insert /*+ APPEND */
into      emp (empno, deptno)
values    (7747, 10);
```

**TIP**
*The APPEND hint will insert values into a table without checking the free space in the currently used blocks, but instead it appends the data into new blocks.*

# The NO_APPEND Hint (Oracle8 Only)

The NO_APPEND hint is used to override the default for the PARALLEL inserts (the default, of course, is APPEND). The syntax is displayed next. The NO_APPEND hint is the opposite of the APPEND hint and will check for free space within current blocks (blocks with space less than the PCTUSED) before using new ones.

**Syntax:**

```
insert    /*+ NO_APPEND */ …
```

**Example:**

```
insert    /*+ PARALLEL(emp) NO_APPEND */
into      emp (empno, deptno)
values    (7747, 10);
```

**TIP**
*The NO_APPEND hint overrides a PARALLEL hint,
which normally will use the APPEND hint by default.*

## The CACHE Hint

The CACHE hint will cause a full table scan to be cached (pinned) into memory, so future users accessing the same table will find it in memory instead of going to disk. This creates one potentially very large problem. If the table is very large, it can take up an enormous amount of memory (DB_BLOCK_BUFFER memory space for data). For small lookup tables, however, this is an excellent option to use. Tables can be created with the CACHE option to be cached the first time they are accessed.

**Syntax:**

```
select     /*+ FULL(dept) CACHE(dept) */ column1, …
```

**Example:**

```
select     /*+ FULL(dept) CACHE(dept) */ deptno, location
from       dept;
```

The entire dept table is now cached in memory and is marked as a Most Recently Used (MRU) object.

**TIP**
*The CACHE hint should be used with small lookup
tables that are often accessed by users. This will ensure
that the table will remain in memory.*

## The NOCACHE Hint

The NOCACHE hint will cause a table that is specified to be cached at the database level to *not* get cached when you access it.

**Syntax:**

```
select     /*+ FULL(dept) NOCACHE(dept) */ column1, …
```

**Example:**

```
alter    table dept cache;
select   deptno, location
from     dept;
```

In the example, the table would be cached because the table was altered to use this option.

**Example:**

```
alter    table dept cache;
select   /*+ NOCACHE(dept) */ deptno, location
from     dept;
```

In the example, the table is not cached despite the ALTER statement and is put on the LRU list.

**TIP**
*The NOCACHE hint should be used to prevent caching a table specified with the CACHE option—basically, when you want to access the table but you don't want to cache it.*

# The CLUSTER Hint

The CLUSTER hint is used only for clusters. A cluster is usually created when tables are joined so often that it is faster to create an object containing information about the joined tables that is accessed most often. A cluster is identical to denormalizing a table or group of tables. The CLUSTER hint will force the use of the cluster. If hashing is used for the cluster (see the next section and Chapter 2 for more information), the HASH hint should be considered. I have not had much luck with using clusters and gaining performance.

**Syntax:**

```
select    /*+ CLUSTER (table) */ column1, …
```

**TIP**
*The CLUSTER hint forces the use of a cluster. It is good to have clusters if the joined tables are frequently accessed but not frequently modified.*

## The HASH Hint

HASH indexes require the use of hash clusters. When a cluster or hash cluster is created, a cluster key is defined. This key tells Oracle how to store the tables in the cluster. When data is stored, all of the rows relating to the cluster key are stored in the same database blocks. With the data being stored in the same database blocks, using the HASH index, Oracle can access the data by performing one hash function and one I/O—as opposed to accessing the data by using a b-tree index. HASH indexes can potentially be the fastest way to access data in the database, but they don't come without their drawbacks (see Chapter 2 for more information).

**Syntax:**

```
select      /*+ HASH(table) */ column1, …
```

**Example:**

```
select      /*+ HASH(emp) */ empno, deptno
from        emp, dept
where       emp.deptno = dept.deptno
where       empno = 7747;
```

In the query, Oracle will use the hash key to find the information in the emp table.

**TIP**
*Caution should be taken before implementing HASH clusters. The application should be reviewed fully to ensure that enough information is known about the tables and data before implementing this option. Generally speaking, hashing is best for static data with primarily sequential values.*

## Tips Review

- Incorrect hint syntax leads to the hint being interpreted as a comment.
- Multiple hints are separated with a space between each. At times, specifying multiple hints can cause the query to use *none* of the hints.

- If an alias is used, the alias *must* be used in the hint or it will *not* work.

- The CHOOSE hint will use cost-based optimization for the entire query if *any* of the tables in the query have been analyzed.

- The RULE hint forces Oracle to use predefined rules (such as using ROWID and UNIQUE indexes) over using the statistics about the data. The RULE hint may set in the init.ora for the entire database, but *some* query-level hints will override it on a given query.

- The FIRST_ROWS hint will cause the optimizer to choose a path that will retrieve the first row of a query fastest, at the cost of retrieving multiple rows slower.

- The ALL_ROWS hint will cause the optimizer to choose a path that will retrieve all rows of a query fastest, at the cost of retrieving one single row slower.

- The FULL hint performs a full table scan on the table that is specified (not all tables in the query).

- The INDEX hint will cause the optimizer to choose the index specified in the hint.

- The INDEX_ASC does exactly what the INDEX hint does since indexes are already sorted in ascending order. It is used to guarantee this to be true, as Oracle may change this default in the future.

- The INDEX_DESC will process an index in the descending order of how it was built. This hint will not be used if more than one table exists in the query.

- The INDEX_FFS will process *only* the index and will not take the result and access the table. All columns that are used and retrieved by the query *must* be contained in the index.

- The ROWID hint will process a query using the ROWID, if it is possible, based on how the query is written.

- The ORDERED hint is one of the most powerful hints provided. It processes the tables of the query in the order that they are listed in the FROM clause (the *first* table in the FROM clause is processed first). There are, however, many variations that cause this to work differently.

- The STAR hint is used to join multiple tables together. The central (facts) table is a denormalized combination of the key information of the other tables that it will join. The composite (fact) table is the "center of the star."

- The DRIVING_SITE hint is extremely powerful, as it will potentially limit the amount of information that will be processed over your network. The table specified with the DRIVING_SITE hint will be the location for the join to be processed.

- Using views for remote tables can also lead to better performance by limiting the number of rows passed from the remote site *before* the records are sent to the local site.

- In a three or more table join, the USE_MERGE hint will cause the table(s) specified in the hint to be SORT-MERGE joined with the resulting row set from a join of the other tables in the join.

- The USE_NL hint *usually* provides the best response time (first row comes back faster), whereas the USE_MERGE hint *usually* provides the best throughput.

- The PUSH_SUBQ hint can improve performance greatly when the subquery will return only a few rows very fast and those rows can be used to limit the rows returned in the outer query.

- Using the PARALLEL hint will enable the use of parallel operations. If the degree is not specified with the hint, the default degree specified during the table creation will be used.

- The use of the NO_PARALLEL hint will disable parallel operations in a statement that would otherwise use parallel processing due to a parallel object definition.

- The APPEND hint will insert values into a table without checking the free space in the currently used blocks, but instead appending the data into new blocks.

- The CACHE hint should be used with small lookup tables that are often accessed by users. This will ensure that the table will remain in memory.

- The NOCACHE hint should be used to prevent caching a table specified with the CACHE option—basically, when you want to access the table but you *don't* want to cache it.

- The CLUSTER hint forces the use of a cluster. It is good to have clusters if the joined tables are frequently accessed but *not* frequently modified.

- Caution should be taken before implementing hash clusters. The application should be reviewed fully to ensure that enough information is known about the tables and data before implementing this option. Generally speaking, hashing is best for static data with primarily sequential values.

# References

*Oracle7 Server Tuning*; Oracle Corporation

*Oracle8 Server Tuning*; Oracle Corporation

*Performance Tuning Guide Version 7.0*; Oracle Corporation

*Oracle8 DBA Handbook*; Kevin Loney, Oracle Press

*Tuning Tips: You Will Be Toast!*; Rich Niemiec

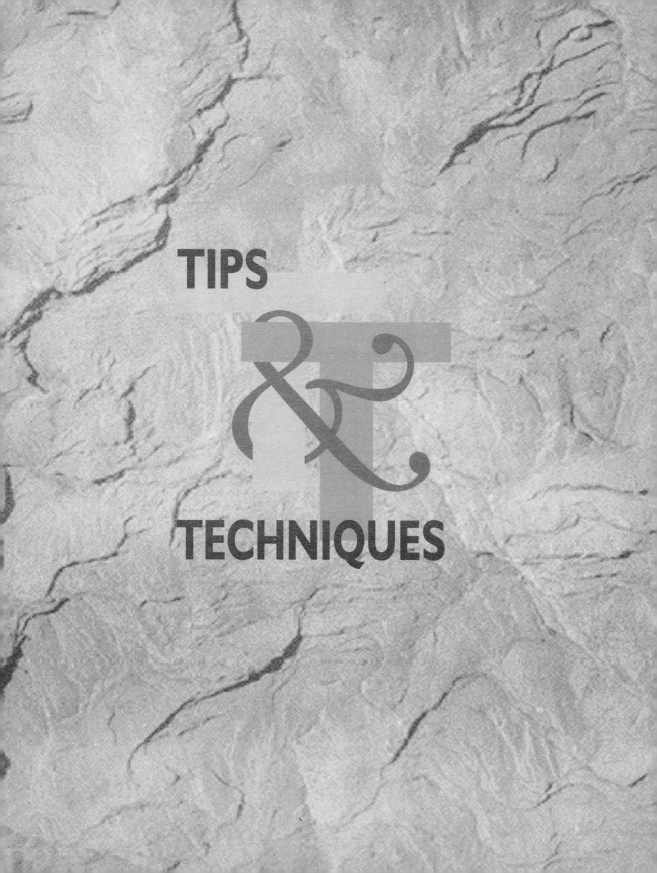

# TIPS & TECHNIQUES

# CHAPTER
# 8

## Query Tuning
## (Developer and DBA)

There is a vast number of examples spread throughout this book on various queries, and instructions to make them more effective based on the architecture of your system. This chapter will focus on some of the most common queries that can be tuned existing on *most* systems. There are several variations in behavior that can be displayed by a query, depending on the version of Oracle and whether cost- or rule-based optimization is used (the optimizer changes from version to version). This chapter will use strictly cost-based examples for timings and version 8 of the database (except where noted). No other queries were performed at the time of the tests in this chapter. Many hints are used throughout this chapter. For a detailed look at hints and the syntax and structure of hints, please refer to Chapter 7. Table joins and advance queries will be the focus of the next chapter and are not covered here.

Please note that this is not an all-inclusive chapter. There are many other queries throughout the book, which need to be investigated when trying to increase performance for a given query. Some of the most dramatic include using the parallel features of Oracle (Chapter 11), using partitioned tables and indexes (Chapter 13), and using PL/SQL to improve performance (Chapter 10). Also, note the benefits of EXPLAINing and TRACing queries (Chapter 4). Some advances with Oracle 8i are covered in Chapter 13. Tips covered in this chapter include the following:

- What queries do I tune? Querying the V$SQLAREA view
- When an index should be used
- What if I forget the index?
- Creating and checking an index
- If you create a bad index
- Dropping an index and caution to be exercised
- Increasing performance by indexing the SELECT and WHERE clause
- Use the fast full scan to guarantee success
- A concatenated index and using the leading edge
- Making queries "magically" faster
- Caching a table into memory
- Multiple indexes on a table (use the most selective)
- Indexes that get suppressed
- Avoiding full table scans when using the OR operation
- Inequalities and problems with the optimizer
- Using the EXISTS and the nested subquery

# What Queries Do I Tune? Querying the V$SQLAREA View

The V$SQLAREA view is your primary means to find the worst performing SQL statements that need optimization. The disk_reads signify the volume of disk reads that are being performed on the system. This combined with the executions (disk_reads/executions) returns the SQL statements that have the most disk hits per statement execution. Statements that make the top of this list are a problem and need to be tuned.

## Selecting from the V$SQLAREA View to Find the Worst Queries

The following query can be used to fix the worst queries existing in your database; this query alone is worth more than the price of this book.

```
select      b.username username, a.disk_reads reads,
            a.executions exec, a.disk_reads /decode
            (a.executions, 0, 1,a.executions) rds_exec_ratio,
            a.command_type, a.sql_text Statement
from        v$sqlarea a, dba_users b
where       a.parsing_user_id = b.user_id
and         a.disk_reads > 100000
order       by a.disk_reads desc;
```

| USERNAME | READS | EXEC | RDS EXEC RATIO | STATEMENT |
|----------|-------|------|----------------|-----------|
| ADHOC1 | 7281934 | 1 | 7281934 | select custno, ordno<br>from cust, orders |
| ADHOC5 | 4230044 | 4 | 1057511 | select ordno<br>from orders<br>where trunc(ordno)<br>= 721305 |
| ADHOC1 | 801716 | 2 | 400858 | select custno,<br>ordno from cust<br>where substr(custno,1,6)<br>= '314159' |

The disk_reads column in the preceding statement can be replaced with the buffer_gets column, to provide information on SQL statements possessing the largest number of memory. See Chapter 17 for an in-depth examination at PL/SQL procedures accessing the V$SQLAREA view.

**TIP**

*Query the V$SQLAREA view to find your problem queries that need to be tuned.*

# When Should an Index Be Used?

In Oracle version 5, many DBAs called the indexing rule the 80/20 Rule; you need to use an index if less than 20 percent of the rows are being returned by a query. In version 7, this number was reduced to about 7 percent on average. In version 8, the number is closer to 4 percent. Figure 8-1 shows when an index should generally be used (in V5 and V6 for rule-based optimization and in V7 and V8 for cost-based optimization). However, the distribution of data, whether parallel query can be used, and other factors need to be considered when contemplating the use of an index. In Chapter 9, you will see how to make this graph for your own queries. If the table has less than 1,000 records, then the graph is different. For small tables, Oracle V7 and V8 cost-based optimizer will generally use the index when only less than 1 percent of the table is queried.

**TIP**

*When a small number of rows ("small" is version dependent and roughly 1,000 rows) are to be returned based on a condition in a query, you generally want to use an index on that condition (column).*

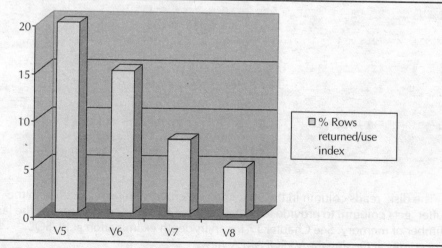

**FIGURE 8-1.** *The percent of records retrieved by a query*

# What Happens When I Forget the Index?

While it seems obvious that columns, which are generally restrictive, require indexes, it is not always common knowledge. I once went to a job where they were suffering incredibly poor performance. When I asked for a list of tables and indexes, they replied: "We have a list of tables, but we haven't figured out how to build indexes yet...do you think you can help our performance?" My first thought was, "Wow, can I ever." My second thought was that I had been training experts too long and forgot that not everyone is as far along in their performance education.

Even if you have built indexes correctly for most columns needing them, you may miss a crucial column here and there. If you forget to put an index on a column that is restrictive, then the speed of those queries will not be optimized. Consider the following example where the percent of rows returned by any given product_id is less than 1 percent. Under these circumstances, an index on the product_id column will be implemented. The query here does *not* have an index on product_id.

```
select    product_id, qty
from      product
where     product_id = 166;

Elapsed time: 405 seconds


OPERATION              OPTIONS     OBJECT NAME
SELECT STATEMENT
TABLE ACCESS           FULL        PRODUCT


49,825 consistent gets (memory reads)
41,562 physical reads (disk reads)
405 times slower than using an index (we'll see this later)
```

Not only is the query extremely slow, but it used a tremendous amount of memory and CPU to perform the query. This results in an impatient user and a frustrating wait for other users due to the lack of system resources. (Sound familiar?)

# Creating an Index

To accelerate the query in the preceding example, I built an index on the product_id column. The storage clause must be based on the size of the table and the column. The table is over 4 million rows, and all additional extents (beyond the initial extent) will be exactly 20M (pctincrease 0) should be retrieved.

```
Create index prod_idx1 on product(product_id)
Tablespace test1
Storage (initial 100M next 20M pctincrease 0);

Index Created.
```

# Check the Index on a Table

Before creating indexes, check for current indexes that exist on that table to ensure there will not be conflicts. Once you have created the index, verify that it exists by querying the DBA_IND_COLUMNS view.

## Query DBA_IND_COLUMNS to Find Indexes for a Table

```
select     table_name, index_name, column_name, column_position
from       dba_ind_columns
where      table_name = 'PRODUCT_LINES'
and        table_owner = 'RICH'
order by   table_name, index_name, column_position;

TABLE NAME       INDEX NAME    COLUMN NAME    COLUMN POSITION
PRODUCT_LINES    PROD_IDX1     PRODUCT_ID     1
```

The table_name is the table that is being indexed, the index_name is the name of the index, the column_name is the column being indexed and the column_position is the order of the columns in a multipart index. Since our index involved only one column, the column_position is 1. In the concatenated index section (later in this chapter), we will see how a multipart index will appear.

# Properly Indexed?

Rerun the same query that has the product_id properly indexed. The query is faster, and more importantly it will no longer "flood" the system with a tremendous amount of data to the SGA (low number of memory reads) and subsequently reduce the physical reads.

```
select     product_id, qty
from       product
where      product_id = 166;

Elapsed time: 1 second
```

```
OPERATION                OPTIONS        OBJECT NAME
SELECT STATEMENT
TABLE ACCESS             BY ROWID       PRODUCT
      INDEX              RANGE SCAN     PROD_IDX1

107 consistent gets (memory reads)
1 physical reads (disk reads)
1 second of elapsed time
```

**TIP**
*The first tip concerning slow queries is that you'll have a lot of them if you don't index columns that are restrictive (return a small percentage of the table). Building indexes on restrictive columns is the first step toward better system performance.*

# What If I Create a Bad Index?

In the product table, I also have a company_no column. Since this company's expansion has not occurred, all rows in the table have a company_no = 1. What if I am a beginner and I have heard that indexes are good, and have decided to index the company_no column?

In rule-based optimization, Oracle will automatically use the index that was created, and the following query would be extremely slow. The cost-based optimizer will analyze the index as bad and will suppress it internally. The table *must* be reanalyzed after the index is created for the cost-based optimizer to make the informed choice. The index created on company is suppressed by Oracle internally:

```
select     product_id, qty
from       product
where      company_no = 1;

Elapsed time: 405 seconds (all records are retrieved via a full table scan)

OPERATION                OPTIONS        OBJECT NAME
SELECT STATEMENT
TABLE ACCESS             FULL           PRODUCT

49,825 consistent gets (memory reads)
41,562 physical reads (disk reads)
```

I can override the suppression and force the use of the index (bad choice), as follows:

```
select    /*+ index(product company_idx1) */ product_id, qty
from      product
where     company_no = 1;

Elapsed time: 725 seconds  (all records retrieved using the index on company_no)

OPERATION             OPTIONS        OBJECT NAME
SELECT STATEMENT
TABLE ACCESS          BY ROWID       PRODUCT
    INDEX             RANGE SCAN     COMPANY_IDX1

4,626,725 consistent gets (memory reads)
80,513 physical reads (disk reads)
```

I can also suppress indexes myself that I deem to be poor, with the FULL hint:

```
select    /*+ FULL(product) */ product_id, qty
from      product
where     company_no = 1;

Elapsed time: 405 seconds (all records are retrieved via a full table scan)

OPERATION             OPTIONS        OBJECT NAME
SELECT STATEMENT
TABLE ACCESS          FULL           PRODUCT

49,825 consistent gets (memory reads)
41,562 physical reads (disk reads)
```

**TIP**
*Bad indexes (indexing the wrong columns) can cause
as much trouble as forgetting to use indexes on the
correct columns. While poor indexes are generally
suppressed by Oracle's cost-based optimizer, problems
can still develop when a bad index is used at the same
time as a good index.*

# Caution Should Be Exercised When Dropping Indexes

For some people, their first reaction when they find a query that is using a poor index is to drop the index. Suppressing the index should be the first reaction and investigating the impact of the index on other queries should be the next action. Consider the following query to an employee table that has over one million records and runs in 55 seconds with no indexes at all. The condition dept_no = 10 retrieves 10 percent of the records in the table. Consider the following query with no indexes:

```
select    emp_name, job
from      employees
where     dept_no = 10;

Elapsed time: 55 seconds (a full table scan is performed)

OPERATION              OPTIONS      OBJECT NAME
SELECT STATEMENT
TABLE ACCESS           FULL         EMPLOYEES
```

One day, you find that someone has created a concatenated index on the dept_no and emp_name columns of the table:

```
Create index emp_idx1 on employees (dept_no, emp_name)
Tablespace test1
Storage (initial 20M next 5M pctincrease 0);
```

The query is now slower with the added index. Since the dept_no = 10 condition returns 10 percent of the records in the query—too many for an index—the query that used to run in 55 seconds now runs in 70 seconds:

```
select    emp_name, job
from      employees
where     dept_no = 10;

Elapsed time: 70 seconds (the index on dept_no is used)

OPERATION              OPTIONS        OBJECT NAME
SELECT STATEMENT
TABLE ACCESS           BY ROWID       EMPLOYEES
    INDEX              RANGE SCAN     EMP_IDX1
```

An immediate reaction may be to drop the index that has caused this performance loss for the query. However, unless your query was the only one being performed against the employees table in the database, this might be a detrimental solution. The next section will explore the reasons why a new index was placed on the employees table, and investigate indexing the SELECT and WHERE clauses of the query.

# Indexing the SELECT and WHERE

The previous section illustrated how an index hurt performance for a query that we had. Consider the following query that the index was created to help. This query does not have indexes:

```
select      emp_name
from        employees
where       dept_no = 10;

Elapsed time: 55 seconds (a full table scan is performed)

OPERATION               OPTIONS        OBJECT NAME
SELECT STATEMENT
TABLE ACCESS            FULL           EMPLOYEES
```

First, we place an index on the dept_no column to try to improve performance:

```
Create index dept_idx1 on employees (dept_no)
Tablespace test1
Storage (initial 20M next 5M pctincrease 0);

select      emp_name
from        employees
where       dept_no = 10;

Elapsed time: 70 seconds (the index on dept_no is used but made things
worse)

OPERATION               OPTIONS        OBJECT NAME
SELECT STATEMENT
TABLE ACCESS            BY ROWID       EMPLOYEES
    INDEX               RANGE SCAN     DEPT_IDX1
```

This situation is now worse. In this query, only the emp_name is selected. If this is a crucial query on the system, choose to index that the columns contained in both the SELECT and the WHERE columns. By doing this, a concatenated index is created:

```
Drop index dept_idx1;

Create index emp_idx1 on employees (dept_no, emp_name)
Tablespace test1
Storage (initial 20M next 5M pctincrease 0);
```

The query is tremendously faster:

```
select      emp_name
from        employees
where       dept_no = 10;
```

Indexing SELECT and WHERE

```
Elapsed time: Less than 1 second (the index on dept_no AND emp_name is used)

OPERATION               OPTIONS        OBJECT NAME
SELECT STATEMENT
INDEX                   RANGE SCAN     EMP_IDX1
```

The table itself did not have to be accessed to increase the speed of the query. Indexing both the column contained in the SELECT clause and the column in the WHERE clause allows the query to only access the index.

**TIP**
*For crucial queries on your system, consider concatenated indexes on the columns contained in both the SELECT and the WHERE clauses.*

# The Fast Full Scan

The previous section demonstrated that if we index both the SELECT and the WHERE, the query is much faster. Oracle does not guarantee that only the index will be used under these circumstances. However, there is a hint that guarantees that only the index will be used under these circumstances. The INDEX_FFS hint is a fast full scan of the index. This hint will access only the index and not the corresponding table. Using the query from the previous section with the index on emp_name and dept_no yields the following:

```
select     /*+ index_ffs(employees emp_idx1) */ emp_name
from       employees
where      dept_no = 10;

Elapsed time: Less than 1 second (only the index is accessed)

OPERATION               OPTIONS        OBJECT NAME
SELECT STATEMENT
INDEX                   RANGE SCAN     EMP_IDX1
```

The query is now guaranteed to only access the index.

**TIP**
*The INDEX_FFS (available in Oracle8) will process only the index and will not access the table. All columns that are used and retrieved by the query must be contained in the index. This is a much better way to guarantee that the index will be used as the versions of Oracle change. Chapter 7 contains more information concerning the INDEX_FFS hint.*

# Concatenated Indexes Must Use the Leading Column

When a concatenated (composite or multipart) index is used, the leading part of the index must be used. Consider the following example to build a three-part index on the employees' table. Creating a concatenated index:

```
Create index emp_idx2 on employees (emp_no, dept_no, emp_name)
Tablespace test1
Storage (initial 30M next 5M pctincrease 0);

Index Created.
```

Viewing the concatenated index in the DBA_IND_COLUMNS view:

```
select     table_name, index_name, column_name, column_position
from       dba_ind_columns
where      table_name = 'EMPLOYEES'
and        table_owner = 'RICH'
order      by table_name, index_name, column_position;
```

| TABLE NAME | INDEX NAME | COLUMN NAME | COLUMN POSITION |
|---|---|---|---|
| EMPLOYEES | EMP_IDX2 | EMP_NO | 1 |
| EMPLOYEES | EMP_IDX2 | DEPT_NO | 2 |
| EMPLOYEES | EMP_IDX2 | EMP_NAME | 3 |

Consider the following queries where an index will or will not be used:

```
select     emp_name, job
from       employees
where      emp_no = 2213
and        dept_no = 10
and        emp_name = 'ADAMS';

Elapsed time: 1 second (one record is retrieved in this query using the index)
```

| OPERATION | OPTIONS | OBJECT NAME |
|---|---|---|
| SELECT STATEMENT | | |
| TABLE ACCESS | BY ROWID | EMPLOYEES |
|    INDEX | RANGE SCAN | EMP_IDX2 |

The full-concatenated index is used to return the record.

```
select     emp_name, job
from       employees
where      emp_no = 2213
and        dept_no = 10;
```

```
Elapsed time: 1 second (one record is retrieved in this query and part of the index used)

OPERATION              OPTIONS       OBJECT NAME
SELECT STATEMENT
TABLE ACCESS           BY ROWID      EMPLOYEES
    INDEX              RANGE SCAN    EMP_IDX2
```

Part of the index is used to return the records. Note that Oracle will not *always* use a portion of the index.

```
select      emp_name, job
from        employees
where       dept_no = 10
and         emp_name = 'ADAMS';

Elapsed time: 50 seconds (one record is retrieved in this query and index is NOT used)

OPERATION              OPTIONS       OBJECT NAME
SELECT STATEMENT
TABLE ACCESS           FULL          EMPLOYEES
```

The index in the preceding query cannot be used at all because the emp_no portion of the index is not used in the query. A full table scan is performed.

**TIP**
*For a concatenated index to be used in full or in part, the leading edge of the index must be present. If any column contained in the index is not present in the query, then all columns of the index following that column cannot use the index.*

# A "Magically" Faster Query

Consider the following query from the last example in which the user adds a hint called "richs_secret_hint." The user overheard a conversation about this hint at a recent user group and believes this hint (buried deep in the x$ tables) is the hidden secret to tuning. First, the query is run and no index can be used:

```
select      emp_name, job
from        employees
where       dept_no = 10
and         emp_name = 'ADAMS';

Elapsed time: 50 seconds (one record is retrieved in this query)

OPERATION              OPTIONS       OBJECT NAME
SELECT STATEMENT
TABLE ACCESS           FULL          EMPLOYEES
```

There is *no* index that can be used on these queries. A full table scan is performed. The user now adds Rich's secret hint to the query:

```
select     /*+ richs_secret_hint */ emp_name, job
from       employees
where      dept_no = 10
and        emp_name = 'ADAMS';

Elapsed time: 3 seconds (one record is retrieved in this query)

OPERATION              OPTIONS        OBJECT NAME
SELECT STATEMENT
TABLE ACCESS           FULL           EMPLOYEES
```

The hint worked and the query is "magically" faster, although a full table scan was still performed. Actually, the data is now stored in memory and querying the data from memory is now much faster than going to disk for the data—so much for the magic!

**TIP**
*When a query is executed multiple times in succession, it becomes faster since you have now cached the data in memory (although full table scans are aged out of memory quicker than indexed scans). At times, people are tricked into believing that they have made a query faster, when in actuality they are accessing data stored in memory.*

# Caching a Table in Memory

While it is disappointing that there is no "secret hint" for tuning, we can use this knowledge to our advantage. In the last section, the query ran faster the second time because it was cached in memory. What if the most often used tables were cached in memory? Well, the first problem is that we cannot cache every table in memory, so instead we will focus on the smaller and more often used tables. The following query is an unindexed customer table to return one of the rows:

```
select     cust_no, name
from       customer
where      cust_no = 1;

Elapsed time: 5 seconds (one record is retrieved in this query without an index)
```

```
OPERATION              OPTIONS        OBJECT NAME
SELECT STATEMENT
TABLE ACCESS           FULL           CUSTOMER
```

The database is then stopped and restarted as to not influence the timing statistics. The table is altered to cache the records:

```
Alter table customer cache;

Table altered.
```

Query the unindexed, but now cached customer table, to return one of the rows:

```
select     cust_no, name
from       customer
where      cust_no = 1;

Elapsed time: 5 seconds (one record is retrieved in this query without an index)

OPERATION              OPTIONS        OBJECT NAME
SELECT STATEMENT
TABLE ACCESS           FULL           CUSTOMER
```

Still 5 seconds? The table has been altered to be cached, but the data is not in memory yet. Every subsequent query will now be faster. I query the unindexed (but now cached) customer table to return one of the rows:

```
select     cust_no, name
from       customer
where      cust_no = 1;

Elapsed time: 1 second (one record is retrieved in this query without an index)

OPERATION              OPTIONS        OBJECT NAME
SELECT STATEMENT
TABLE ACCESS           FULL           CUSTOMER
```

The query is faster since the table is cached in memory; in fact, all queries to this table are now fast regardless of the condition used. A cached table is "pinned" into memory and will be placed at the "most recently used" end of the cache. A cached table will not be pushed out of memory until other full table scans to noncached tables are pushed out. Running a query multiple times places the data in memory so that subsequent queries are faster—only caching a table will ensure that the data is not later pushed out of memory. For more information on creating tables as cached, and other related topics, see the Chapter 7 section on caching.

**Caching Tables**

**TIP**
*Caching an often used, relatively small table into
memory will ensure that the data is not pushed out of
memory by other data. Also, be careful—cached tables
can alter the execution path normally chosen by the
optimizer, leading to an unexpected execution order
for the query (it can affect the driving table in NESTED
LOOP joins).*

# Using Multiple Indexes
# (Use the Most Selective)

Having multiple indexes on a table can cause problems when you execute a query
where there are choices that include using more than one of the indexes. Consider
the following example where the percent of rows returned by any given product_id
is less than 1 percent. Under these circumstances, place an index on the product_id
column. The following query has a single index on product_id.

```
select      product_id, qty
from        product
where       company_no = 1
and         product_id = 167;

Elapsed time: 1 second (one record is retrieved;
  the index on product_id is used)

OPERATION               OPTIONS        OBJECT NAME
SELECT STATEMENT
TABLE ACCESS            BY ROWID       PRODUCT
     INDEX             RANGE SCAN      PROD_IDX1

107 consistent gets (memory reads)
1 physical reads (disk reads)
```

Now create an additional index on the company column. In this example, all of
the records have a company = 1, an extremely poor index. Rerun the query with
both indexes (one on product_id and one on company) existing on the table.

```
select      product_id, qty
from        product
where       company_no = 1
```

```
and         product_id = 167;

Elapsed time: 725 seconds (one record is returned;
  a full table scan is performed)

OPERATION               OPTIONS       OBJECT NAME
SELECT STATEMENT
TABLE ACCESS            FULL          PRODUCT

4,626,725 consistent gets (memory reads)
80,513 physical reads (disk reads)
```

Oracle has chosen not to use either of the two indexes, and the query performed
a full table scan. Depending on the statistical data stored and version of Oracle
used, I have seen this same query use the right index, the wrong index, no index at
all, or a merge of both indexes. The correct choice is to force the use of the correct
index. The correct index is the most restrictive. Rewrite the query to force the use of
the most restrictive index, as follows:

```
select      /*+ index(product prod_idx1) */ product_id, qty
from        product
where       company_no = 1
and         product_id = 167;

Elapsed time: 1 second (one record is retrieved)

OPERATION               OPTIONS       OBJECT NAME
SELECT STATEMENT
TABLE ACCESS            BY ROWID      PRODUCT
      INDEX             RANGE SCAN    PROD_IDX1

107 consistent gets (memory reads)
1 physical reads (disk reads)
```

**TIP**
*When multiple indexes on a single table are used
within a query, use the most restrictive index. While
Oracle's cost-based optimizer will generally force the
use of the most restrictive index, variations will occur
based on the version of Oracle used and the structure
of the query. Forcing the use of the most restrictive
index will guarantee the best performance.*

Using Multiple Indexes

# Indexes That Get Suppressed

Building the perfect system with all of the correctly indexed columns does not guarantee success in the performance of the system. With the prevalence in business of the bright-eyed ad hoc query user, comes a variety of tuning challenges. One of the most common is the suppression of perfectly good indexes. Any modification of the column side of a WHERE clause will result in the suppression of that index (except in Oracle8i, where functional indexes are available). Alternative methods for writing the same query do not modify the column that is indexed. A couple of those examples are listed in the examples here.

A math function is performed on the column:

```
select      product_id, qty
from        product
where       product_id+12 = 166;

Elapsed time: 405 second
```

| OPERATION | OPTIONS | OBJECT NAME |
|-----------|---------|-------------|
| SELECT STATEMENT | | |
| TABLE ACCESS | FULL | PRODUCT |

The math function is performed on the other side of the clause:

```
select      product_id, qty
from        product
where       product_id = 166/12;

Elapsed time: 1 second
```

| OPERATION | OPTIONS | OBJECT NAME |
|-----------|---------|-------------|
| SELECT STATEMENT | | |
| TABLE ACCESS | BY ROWID | PRODUCT |
| INDEX | RANGE SCAN | PROD_IDX1 |

A function is performed on the column:

```
select      product_id, qty
from        product
where       substr(product_id,1,1) = 1;

Elapsed time: 405 second
```

```
OPERATION            OPTIONS      OBJECT NAME
SELECT STATEMENT
TABLE ACCESS         FULL         PRODUCT
```

The function is rewritten so that the column is not altered:

```
select    product_id, qty
from      product
where     product_id like '1%';

Elapsed time: 1 second

OPERATION              OPTIONS       OBJECT NAME
SELECT STATEMENT
TABLE ACCESS           BY ROWID      PRODUCT
     INDEX             RANGE SCAN    PROD_IDX1
```

**TIP**
*Any modification to the column side of the query results in the suppression of the index.*

**V8i TIP**
*Functions and operators on columns can now be indexed. See Chapter 13 for examples related to functional indexes. This is extraordinary!*

# The "Curious" OR

It seems that all index rules for the cost-based optimizer fall apart when we apply them to the OR statement. The best way to think of the OR is as multiple queries that are then merged. Depending on the indexes that are available and used, an increase in or hindrance of performance is achieved. Consider the following example: two separate indexes on product_id and item_id are being issued. Each of the conditions product_id = 167 and item_no = 95 return less than 1 percent of the rows in the table.

```
select    product_id, qty
from   .  product
where     product_id = 167
or        item_no = 95;

Elapsed time: 623 seconds (full table scan is performed)
```

```
OPERATION                  OPTIONS       OBJECT NAME
SELECT STATEMENT
TABLE ACCESS               FULL          PRODUCT


49,901 consistent gets (memory reads)
41,677 physical reads (disk reads)
```

The cost-based optimizer does not use the indexes even though the use of them would make the query faster. I attempt to override the optimizer as follows:

```
select    /*+ index(product prod_idx1 item_idx1) */ product_id, qty
from      product
where     product_id = 167
or        item_no = 95;

Elapsed time: 623 seconds (full table scan is STILL performed)

OPERATION                  OPTIONS       OBJECT NAME
SELECT STATEMENT
TABLE ACCESS               FULL          PRODUCT

49,901 consistent gets (memory reads)
41,677 physical reads (disk reads)
```

The optimizer has still outsmarted me, and actually overrides even the use of a hint (this is not always the case). I attempt to override the optimizer as follows:

```
select    /*+ RULE */ product_id, qty
from      product
where     product_id = 167
or        item_no = 95;

Elapsed time: 1 second (both indexes are used)

OPERATION                  OPTIONS       OBJECT NAME
SELECT STATEMENT
  CONCATENATION
    TABLE ACCESS           BY ROWID      PRODUCT
      INDEX                RANGE SCAN    PROD_IDX1
    TABLE ACCESS           BY ROWID      PRODUCT
      INDEX                RANGE SCAN    ITEM_IDX1

107 consistent gets (memory reads)
1 physical reads (disk reads)
```

The RULE hint overrides the use of the optimizer and automatically uses all indexes that exist on the table for the conditions specified in the WHERE clause.

> **TIP**
> *To fix queries that use the OR, force the use of the rule-based optimizer. This can be achieved with the RULE hint.*

# Inequalities and the Optimizer

A potential problem for the optimizer is the use of inequalities (< and >). This becomes most problematic when the distribution of the table is not linear between its high and low values. Consider the following example where the optimizer assumes that the values in the table are balanced. The order_line table has 10,000 rows between 1 and 10,000. The number of rows greater than 9,990 is assumed by the optimizer to be only 10. The actual distribution shows that the number of rows greater than 9,990 is 5,000 (or half of the table). There is an index called item_idx1 on the item_no (which the optimizer will think it should use for this query). The index on item_no is used by the optimizer:

```
select     size, item_no
from       order_line
where      item_no > 9990;

Execution Time: 53 Seconds
```

| OPERATION | OPTIONS | OBJECT NAME |
|---|---|---|
| SELECT STATEMENT | | |
| TABLE ACCESS | BY ROWID | ORDER_LINE |
|    INDEX | RANGE SCAN | ITEM_IDX1 |

We can override the optimizer (since we know that 50 percent of the rows are retrieved) as follows:

```
select     /*+ FULL(order_line) */  size, item_no
from       order_line
where      item_no > 9990;

Execution Time: 4 Seconds
```

| OPERATION | OPTIONS | OBJECT NAME |
|---|---|---|
| SELECT STATEMENT | | |
| TABLE ACCESS | FULL | ORDER_LINE |

**The Optimizer**

**TIP**
*The optimizer estimates the number of rows that will be returned for inequalities; the results are not always those that are desired. By understanding the true distribution of data (versus that estimated by the optimizer), the performance tuning professional can often get better performance than the optimizer can. You can also solve skewed data issues with the use of histograms (covered in Chapter 2).*

# The EXISTS Function

Another helpful tip to remember is to use the EXISTS function instead of the IN function. The EXISTS function checks to find a single matching row to return the result in a subquery. Since the IN function retrieves and checks all rows, it is slower. Consider this example where the IN function leads to very poor performance. This query is faster only if the items table is extremely small:

```
select     product_id, qty
from       product
where      product_id = 167
and        item_no in
(select    item_no
  from      items);

Elapsed time: 25 minutes (The items table is 10 million rows)

OPERATION                 OPTIONS        OBJECT NAME
SELECT STATEMENT
NESTED LOOPS
  TABLE ACCESS            BY ROWID       PRODUCT
    INDEX                 RANGE SCAN     PROD_IDX1
    SORT
      TABLE ACCESS        FULL           ITEMS
```

In this query, the entire items table is retrieved.

This query is faster when the condition product_id = 167 substantially limits the outside query:

```
select     product_id, qty
from       product a
where      product_id = 167
and        exists
```

```
(select    'x'
  from     items b
  where    b.item_no = a.item_no);

Elapsed time: 2 seconds (The items table query search is limited to 3
rows)

OPERATION                OPTIONS        OBJECT NAME
SELECT STATEMENT
FILTER
  TABLE ACCESS           BY ROWID       PRODUCT
    INDEX                RANGE SCAN     PROD_IDX1
  INDEX                  RANGE SCAN     ITEM_IDX1
```

In this query, only the items records that are retrieved in the outer query (from the product table) are checked against the items table. This query can be substantially faster than the first query if the item_no in the items table is indexed or if the items table is very large, yet the items are limited by the condition product_id = 167 in the outer query.

**TIP**

*Using the nested subquery with an EXISTS may make queries dramatically faster, depending on the data being retrieved from each part of the query.*

# Tips Review

- Query the V$SQLAREA view to find your problem queries that need to be tuned.

- When a small number of rows ("small" is version dependent) are to be returned based on a condition in a query, you generally want to use an index on the indexed columns condition.

- The first tip concerning poor queries is that you will have a lot of them if you are missing indexes on columns that are generally restrictive. Building indexes on restrictive columns is the first step toward better system performance.

- Bad indexes (indexing the wrong columns) can cause as much trouble (usually more) as forgetting to use indexes on the correct columns. While poor indexes are generally suppressed by Oracle's cost-based optimizer, we saw that problems can still develop when a bad index is used at the same time as a good index.

- For crucial queries on your system, consider concatenated indexes on the columns contained in both the SELECT and the WHERE clauses.

- The INDEX_FFS will process *only* the index and will not take the result and access the table. All columns that are used and retrieved by the query *must* be contained in the index. This is a much better way to guarantee that the index will be used as the versions of Oracle change.

- For a concatenated index to be used in full or in part, the leading edge of the index must be present. If any column contained in the index is not present in the query, then all columns of the index following that column cannot use the index.

- When a query is run multiple times in succession, it becomes faster since you have now cached the data in memory. At times, people are tricked into believing that they have actually made a query faster when in actuality they are accessing data stored in memory.

- Caching an often used but relatively small table into memory will ensure that the data is not pushed out of memory by other data.

- When multiple indexes on a single table are used within a query, use the most restrictive index. While Oracle's cost-based optimizer will generally force the use of the most restrictive index, variations occur based on the version of Oracle used and the structure of the query. Forcing the use of the most restrictive index will guarantee the best performance.

- Any modification to the column side of the query results in the suppression of the index.

- In Oracle8i, functions and operators on columns can now be indexed. See Chapter 13 for examples related to this new functionality.

- To fix queries that use the OR, you sometimes must force the use of the rule-based optimizer. This can be achieved with the RULE hint.

- Since the optimizer estimates the number of rows that will be returned for inequalities, the results are not always those that are desired. By understanding the true distribution of data (versus that estimated by the optimizer), the performance tuner can often get better performance than the optimizer can.

# References

*DBA Tips or a Job Is a Terrible Thing to Waste;* Deb Dudek; TUSC

*DBA Tuning Tips; Now YOU are the Expert;* Rich Niemiec; TUSC

# TIPS & TECHNIQUES

# CHAPTER
# 9

## Table Joins and Other Advanced Query Tuning

This chapter was very painful to write, and will hopefully be less painful to read. The complexities of Oracle come to light in this chapter. The driving table or the first table accessed in a query is an important aspect of superior performance. Having the wrong table designated as the driving table in a query can be the difference between hours and seconds. With only two or three tables, it's easy enough to use an ORDERED hint (guaranteeing the order of the tables) and then try variations of the order of the tables until the fastest outcome is achieved. However, in a ten-table join, there are over 1,000 possible combinations, making this method slightly time-consuming.

The complexity of the optimizer and all of the potential paths for joining and optimizing a query are mind boggling. Suppressing a single index in a query can change the driving table, the way Oracle joins tables in a query, and how other indexes are used or suppressed by Oracle. Trying to put driving tables in a useful format for a reader was one of the greatest challenges of this book. This chapter will focus on helping you make better decisions when choosing a driving table. While I have a good understanding of how Oracle performs these complexities, putting that understanding into words was a lot like ripping my brain out and trying to figure out how to put it in another person's body. It was not a fun task.

A special thanks to Roger Schrag and Joe Holmes, who contributed a large amounts of material to this chapter. The tips covered in this chapter include the following:

- Join methods (NESTED LOOPS, SORT-MERGE, CLUSTER, HASH (7.3), and INDEX joins (8.1))
- Table join init.ora parameters
- Comparing join methods
- Two-table joins in rule-based and cost-based optimization
- Forcing a join method using hints
- Eliminating join records (candidate rows) in multitable joins
- Two-table join between a large and small table
- Two-table join between a large and small table involving a concatenated index
- Three-table joins—not as much fun
- Index breakpoint for a small table
- The inlist iterator in Oracle8 using the IN operator
- Third-party product tuning
- Tuning distributed queries
- Tuning using simple mathematical techniques

# Join Methods

Since the days of Oracle6, the optimizer has used three different ways to join row sources together. These are the NESTED LOOPS join, the SORT-MERGE join, and the CLUSTER join. With Oracle 7.3, the HASH join was introduced, and in Oracle8i the INDEX join is introduced, making for a total of five primary join methods. Each has a unique set of features and limitations. Things that you need to know before you attack a potential join issue include the following:

■ What table will drive the query and when will each table be accessed given the path that is chosen for the query? What are the alternate driving paths?

■ What are the Oracle join possibilities (described in this section)? Remember, each join possibility for Oracle can yield different results depending on the join order, the selectivity of indexes, and available memory for sorting and/or hashing.

■ The indexes available and the selectivity of the indexes. The selectivity of an index not only can cause the use or suppression of the index by the optimizer but can change the way the query will drive, and may determine the use or suppression of other indexes in the query.

■ Hints that will provide alternate paths and hints that will suppress or force an index to be used. These will be used to change the driving order of the tables, and change how Oracle will perform the join and which indexes will be used or suppressed.

■ Which version of Oracle you are using. There are different choices depending on the version and release of Oracle you are using. The optimizer also works differently in different versions. In Oracle 7.3, the HASH join was available and is used instead of the SORT-MERGE join for many queries. In Oracle 8.1, the INDEX join is introduced as a way of eliminating full table scans by combining the use of all indexes on a table.

## NESTED LOOPS Joins

Suppose somebody gave you a telephone book and a list of 20 names to look up, and asked you to write down each person's name and corresponding telephone number. You would probably go down the list of names, looking each up in the telephone book one at a time. This would be pretty easy, because the telephone book is alphabetized by name. Moreover, somebody looking over your shoulder could begin calling the first few numbers you write down while you are still looking up the rest. This scene describes a NESTED LOOPS join.

In a NESTED LOOPS join, Oracle reads the first row from the first row source and then checks the second row source for matches. All matches are then placed in the result set and Oracle goes on to the next row from the first row source. This continues until all rows in the first row source have been processed. The first row source is often called the outer or *driving* table, while the second row source is called the inner table. This is one of the fastest methods of receiving the first records back from a join.

NESTED LOOPS joins are ideal when the driving row source (the records that you are looking for) is small and the joined columns of the inner row source are uniquely indexed or have a highly selective nonunique index. NESTED LOOPS joins have an advantage over other join methods in that they can quickly retrieve the first few rows of the result set without having to wait for the entire result set to be determined. This is ideal for query screens where an end user can read the first few records retrieved while the rest are being fetched. NESTED LOOPS joins are also flexible in that any two row sources can always be joined by NESTED LOOPS—regardless of join condition and schema definition.

However, NESTED LOOPS joins can be very inefficient if the inner row source (second table accessed) does not have an index on the joined columns or if the index is not highly selective. If the driving row source (the records retrieved from the driving table) is quite large, other join methods may be more efficient. The method of executing the following NESTED LOOPS join query is illustrated in Figure 9-1:

```
select      /*+ ordered */ ename, dept.deptno
from        dept, emp
where       dept.deptno = emp.deptno
```

## SORT-MERGE Joins

Suppose two people attend a conference and each collects over 100 business cards from potential new customers. Each salesperson now has a pile of cards in random order, and they want to see how many cards are duplicated in both piles. Each salesperson alphabetizes their pile, and then they call off names one at a time. Since both piles of cards have been sorted, it becomes much easier to find the names that appear in both piles. This scene describes a SORT-MERGE join.

In a SORT-MERGE join, Oracle sorts the first row source by its join columns, sorts the second row source by its join columns, and then merges the sorted row sources together. As matches are found, they are put into the result set.

SORT-MERGE joins can be effective when lack of data selectivity or useful indexes render a NESTED LOOPS join inefficient, or when both of the row sources are quite large (greater than 5 percent of the records). However, SORT-MERGE joins can only be used for equijoins (WHERE D.deptno = E.deptno, as opposed to WHERE D.deptno >= E.deptno). SORT-MERGE joins require temporary segments for sorting (if SORT_AREA_SIZE is set too small). This can lead to extra memory utilization and/or extra disk I/O in the temporary tablespace.

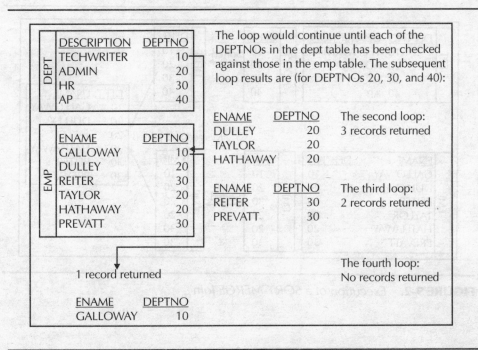

The loop would continue until each of the DEPTNOs in the dept table has been checked against those in the emp table. The subsequent loop results are (for DEPTNOs 20, 30, and 40):

| ENAME | DEPTNO | |
|---|---|---|
| DULLEY | 20 | The second loop: |
| TAYLOR | 20 | 3 records returned |
| HATHAWAY | 20 | |

| ENAME | DEPTNO | |
|---|---|---|
| REITER | 30 | The third loop: |
| PREVATT | 30 | 2 records returned |

The fourth loop:
No records returned

**FIGURE 9-1.**   *Execution of a NESTED LOOPS join*

The method of executing the following SORT-MERGE join query is illustrated in Figure 9-2:

```
select     /*+ ordered */ ename, dept.deptno
from       dept, emp
where      dept.deptno = emp.deptno
```

# CLUSTER Joins

A CLUSTER join is really just a special case of the NESTED LOOPS join. If the two row sources being joined are actually tables that are part of a cluster, and if the join is an equijoin between the cluster keys of the two tables, then Oracle can use a CLUSTER join. In this case, Oracle reads each row from the first row source and finds all matches in the second row source by using the CLUSTER index.

CLUSTER joins are extremely efficient, since the joining rows in the two row sources will actually be located in the same physical data block. However, clusters carry certain caveats of their own, and you cannot have a CLUSTER join without a cluster. Therefore, CLUSTER joins are not very commonly used.

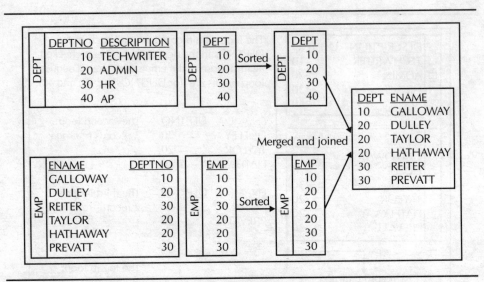

**FIGURE 9-2.** *Execution of a SORT-MERGE join*

# HASH Joins (Oracle 7.3+)

In a HASH join, Oracle reads all of the join column values from the second row source, builds a hash table (in memory if HASH_AREA_SIZE is large enough), then probes the hash table for each of the join column values from the first row source. This is identical to a NESTED LOOPS join—Oracle first builds a hash table to facilitate the operation. When using an ORDERED hint, the first table in the FROM clause is the driving table, but only after the second table is loaded in the hash table. The first table then accesses the hash table for matches. If enough memory is available (HASH_AREA_SIZE for the hash and DB_BLOCK_BUFFERS for the other table), then the join will be completely processed in memory.

HASH joins can be effective when the lack of a useful index renders NESTED LOOPS joins inefficient. The HASH join might be faster than a SORT-MERGE join, in this case, because only one row source needs to be sorted, and could possibly be faster than a NESTED LOOPS join because probing a hash table in memory can be faster than traversing a B-tree index. As with SORT-MERGE joins and CLUSTER joins, HASH joins only work on equijoins. As with SORT-MERGE joins, HASH joins use memory resources and can drive up I/O in the temporary tablespace if the HASH_AREA_SIZE is not set large enough. Finally, HASH joins are only available in Oracle 7.3 and subsequent releases, and only when cost-based optimization is used.

The method of executing the following HASH join query is illustrated in Figure 9-3:

```
select     /*+ ordered */ ename, dept.deptno
from       dept, emp
where      dept.deptno = emp.deptno
```

# INDEX Joins (Oracle8i)

In versions of Oracle prior to Oracle8i, you must always access the table unless the index contained all of the information required. In Oracle8i, if a set of indexes exists that collectively contain all of the information required by the query, then the optimizer can choose to generate a sequence of HASH joins between

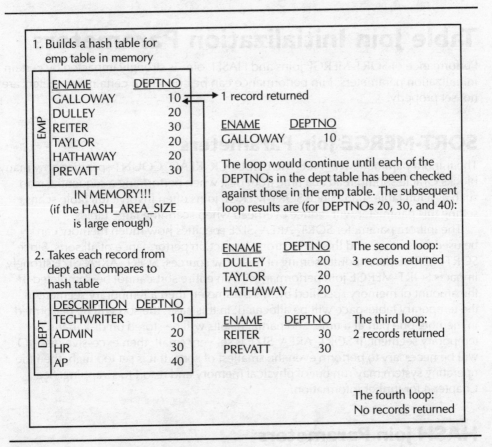

**FIGURE 9-3.** *Execution of a HASH join*

the indexes. Each of the indexes are accessed using a range scan or fast full scan, depending on the conditions available in the WHERE clause. This method is extremely efficient when a table has a large number of columns, but you only want to access a limited number of those columns. The more limiting the conditions in the WHERE clause, the faster the execution. In Oracle8i, the optimizer will evaluate this as an option when looking for the optimal path of execution.

You must create indexes on the appropriate columns (those that will satisfy the entire query) to ensure that the optimizer has the INDEX join as an available choice. This usually involves adding indexes on columns that may not be indexed or on columns that were not indexed together previously. Please consult the latest Oracle8i documentation for the latest information on this feature.

Also note that in Oracle8i, you can export statistics from a production database to be used in a test environment so that the entire database does not have to be re-created.

# Table Join Initialization Parameters

Performance of SORT-MERGE joins and HASH joins is strongly impacted by certain initialization parameters. Join performance can be crippled if certain parameters are not set properly.

## SORT-MERGE Join Parameters

The init.ora parameter DB_FILE_MULTIBLOCK_READ_COUNT specifies how many blocks Oracle should read at a time from disk when performing a sequential read such as a full table scan. Since SORT-MERGE joins often involve full table scans, setting this parameter will reduce overhead when scanning large tables.

The init.ora parameter SORT_AREA_SIZE specifies how much memory can be used for sorting, and this has a strong impact on performance of all sorts. Since SORT-MERGE joins require sorting of both row sources, SORT_AREA_SIZE strongly impacts SORT-MERGE join performance. If an entire sort cannot be completed in the amount of memory specified by this parameter, then a temporary segment in the temporary tablespace will be allocated. In this case, the sort will be performed in memory one part at a time, and partial results will be stored on disk in the temporary segment. If SORT_AREA_SIZE is set very small, then excessive disk I/O will be necessary to perform even the smallest of sorts. If it is set too high, then the operating system may run out of physical memory and resort to swapping. See Chapter 4 for further information.

## HASH join Parameters

The three parameters HASH_JOIN_ENABLED, HASH_AREA_SIZE, and HASH_MULTIBLOCK_IO_COUNT control HASH join behavior. Unlike most other initialization parameters, these three can also be dynamically altered with the ALTER SESSION command.

The init.ora parameter HASH_JOIN_ENABLED dictates whether the optimizer should consider using HASH joins. If you do not want HASH joins to be used, set this parameter to FALSE.

The init.ora parameter HASH_AREA_SIZE specifies how much memory can be used to build a hash table for a HASH join, and resembles the SORT_AREA_SIZE parameter. If this parameter is set too small, then partial hash tables will need to be stored in temporary segments. If this parameter is set too big, then physical memory may be exhausted. As with SORT_AREA_SIZE, HASH_AREA_SIZE indicates how much memory can be used per session. Many concurrent sessions can consume a lot of memory.

The init.ora parameter HASH_MULTIBLOCK_IO_COUNT specifies how many blocks should be read at a time when building the hash table, somewhat similar to DB_FILE_MULTIBLOCK_READ_COUNT for SORT-MERGE joins. However, the interplay between HASH_MULTIBLOCK_IO_COUNT and HASH_AREA_SIZE significantly impacts HASH join performance. Before changing either of these parameters, consult the formula listed in the Oracle 7.3 or 8.0 Server Reference Guide.

# Comparing the Primary Join Methods

| Category | NESTED LOOPS | SORT-MERGE Join | HASH Join |
|---|---|---|---|
| Optimizer hint | USE_NL | USE_MERGE | USE_HASH |
| When you can use it | Any join | Equijoins only | Equijoins only |
| Resource concerns | CPU, Disk I/O | Temporary segments | Memory |
| init.ora parameters | DB_BLOCK_BUFFERS | SORT_AREA_SIZE, DB_FILE_MULTIBLOCK _READ_COUNT | HASH_JOIN_ENABLED, SORT_AREA_SIZE, HASH_MULTIBLOCK_ IO_COUNT |
| Features | Efficient with highly selective indexes and restrictive searches. Returns the first row faster than SORT-MERGE or HASH without sorting. | Better than NESTED LOOPS when an index is missing or the search criteria is not very selective. Can work with limited memory. | Better than NESTED LOOPS when an index is missing or the search criteria is not very selective. It is usually faster than a SORT-MERGE. Available as of Oracle 7.3. |
| Drawbacks | Very inefficient when indexes are missing or if index criteria are not limiting. | Requires a sort on both tables. It is built for best optimal throughput and does not return the first row until all rows are found. | Can require a large amount of memory for the hash table to be built. Does not return the first rows quickly. |

# Two-Table Join—Equal-Size Tables—Rule-Based

Consider the following tables (not analyzed—rule-based optimization is used) that will be used for this example:

```
SMALL1    1000 rows    No Indexes
SMALL2    1000 rows    No Indexes
```

This is an important section of examples, as we look at how the rule-based optimizer works with all things being equal in a join (same size tables/no indexes).

## Situation 1

Neither table has an index and there are no other conditions.

### Query 1:

```
select    small1.col1, small2.col1
from      small1, small2
where     small1.col1 = small2.col1;
```

Join Method: SORT-MERGE Join

Although small2 would normally be the driving table (since it is last in the FROM clause and we are in rule-based optimization), a SORT-MERGE join forces the sorting of each of the tables before they are merged together (since there are no indexes). A full table scan is needed on both tables and the order in the FROM clause has no impact.

### Query 2:

```
select    small1.col1, small2.col1
from      small2, small1
where     small1.col1 = small2.col1;
```

Join Method: SORT-MERGE Join

Although small1 would normally be the driving table (since it is last in the FROM clause and we are in rule-based optimization), a SORT-MERGE join forces the sorting of each of the tables before they are merged together (since there are no indexes). A full table scan is needed on both tables and the order in the FROM clause has no impact.

**SITUATION 1 OUTCOMES**   Normally, the *last* table in the FROM clause in rule-based optimization is the driving table, but in a SORT-MERGE join this has no impact since each table must be sorted and then merged together.

## Situation 2
Neither table has an index and we will use the ORDERED hint.

**Query 1:**

```
select    /*+ ORDERED */ small1.col1, small2.col1
from      small1, small2
where     small1.col1 = small2.col1;
```

Join Method: SORT-MERGE Join (prior to 7.3); HASH Join (7.3 and later)

Although small1 would normally be the driving table (since it is first in the FROM clause and we are forcing cost-based optimization by using an ORDERED hint), a SORT-MERGE join forces the sorting of each of the tables before they are merged together (since there are no indexes). A full table scan is needed on both tables and the order in the FROM clause has no impact. In Oracle 7.3 and above, Oracle builds a hash table from the join values of the *second* table, small2, then probes that table for values from small1.

**Query 2:**

```
select    /*+ ORDERED */ small1.col1, small2.col1
from      small2, small1
where     small1.col1 = small2.col1;
```

Join Method: SORT-MERGE Join (prior to 7.3); HASH Join (7.3 and later)

Although small2 would normally be the driving table (since it is last in the FROM clause and we are forcing cost-based optimization by using an ORDERED hint), a SORT-MERGE join forces the sorting of each of the tables before they are merged together (since there are no indexes). A full table scan is needed on both tables and the order in the FROM clause has no impact. In Oracle 7.3 and above, Oracle builds a hash table from the join values of the *second* table, small1, then probes that table for values from small2.

**SITUATION 2 OUTCOMES**   All things being equal, the *first* table in the FROM clause in rule-based optimization is the driving table when the ORDERED hint is used. However, if no indexes can be used on the query, a SORT-MERGE join forces both tables to be scanned, sorted, and merged together. In Oracle7.3, a HASH join is used and the logic is almost completely reversed. In a HASH join, the second table in the FROM clause (when an ORDERED hint is used) is used to build a hash table of join values that is probed by the first table in the FROM clause.

**TIP**

*Using rule-based optimization, the last table in the FROM clause is the driving table when all other things are equal. If the ORDERED hint is used, then the first table in the FROM clause becomes the driving table and cost-based optimization is forced (since you have used a hint) if the tables are analyzed and the OPTIMIZER_MODE=CHOOSE. If a SORT-MERGE join must be used, then the order of the tables has no impact since neither will drive the query.*

**V7.3 TIP**

*In Oracle7.3, HASH joins are often used in lieu of SORT-MERGE joins by the optimizer. With HASH joins, the second table is used to build a hash table (in memory if available) and the first table in the FROM clause then probes for corresponding hashed table matches. The access order for HASH joins is opposite the access order of SORT-MERGE and NESTED LOOP joins where the first table in the FROM clause is the driving table (when using the ORDERED hint). Knowing which table is generally the driving table in small joins can help you to solve larger table join issues.*

# Two-Table Join—Equal-Size Tables—Cost-Based

Consider the following tables (they have been analyzed) that will be used for this example:

| | | |
|---|---|---|
| SMALL1 | 1000 rows | No Indexes |
| SMALL2 | 1000 rows | No Indexes |

This is an important section of examples, as we look at how the cost-based optimizer works with all things being equal in a join (same size tables/no indexes).

# Situation 1

Neither table has an index and there are no other conditions.

**Query 1:**

```
select      small1.col1, small2.col1
from        small1, small2
where       small1.col1 = small2.col1;
```

Join Method: SORT-MERGE Join (prior to 7.3); HASH Join (7.3 and later)

Although small1 would normally be the driving table (since it is first in the FROM clause and we are in cost-based optimization), a SORT-MERGE join forces the sorting of each of the tables before they are merged together (since there are no indexes). A full table scan is needed on both tables and the order in the FROM clause has no impact. In Oracle 7.3 and above, Oracle builds a hash table from the join values of the *second* table, small2, then probes that table for values from small1.

**Query 2:**

```
select      small1.col1, small2.col1
from        small2, small1
where       small1.col1 = small2.col1;
```

Join Method: SORT-MERGE Join (prior to 7.3); HASH Join (7.3 and later)

Although small2 would normally be the driving table (since it is first in the FROM clause and we are in cost-based optimization), a SORT-MERGE join forces the sorting of each of the tables before they are merged together (since there are no indexes). A full table scan is needed on both tables and the order in the FROM clause has no impact. In Oracle 7.3 and above, Oracle builds a hash table from the join values of the *second* table, small1, then probes that table for values from small2.

**SITUATION 1 OUTCOMES** Normally, the *first* table in the FROM clause in cost-based optimization is the driving table, but in a SORT-MERGE join this has no impact since each table must be sorted and then merged together. Also note that the order of tables cannot be guaranteed when all things are *not* equal (when we have tables of different sizes or with different indexes) since the optimizer will choose the order unless we specify the ORDERED hint. In Oracle 7.3 and above, Oracle builds a hash table from the join values of the *second* table, then probes that table for values from the first table.

## Situation 2

Neither table has an index and we will use the ORDERED hint.

**Query 1:**

```
select      /*+ ORDERED */ small1.col1, small2.col1
from        small1, small2
where       small1.col1 = small2.col1;
```

Join Method: SORT-MERGE Join (prior to 7.3); HASH Join (7.3 and later)

Although small1 would normally be the driving table (since it is first in the FROM clause and we are forcing the order by using an ORDERED hint), a SORT-MERGE join forces the sorting of each of the tables before they are merged together (since there are no indexes). A full table scan is needed on both tables and the order in the FROM clause has no impact. In Oracle 7.3 and above, Oracle builds a hash table from the join values of the *second* table, small2, then probes that table for values from small1.

**Query 2:**

```
select      /*+ ORDERED */ small1.col1, small2.col1
from        small2, small1
where       small1.col1 = small2.col1;
```

Join Method: SORT-MERGE Join (prior to 7.3); HASH Join (7.3 and later)

Although small2 would normally be the driving table (since it is first in the FROM clause and we are forcing the order by using an ORDERED hint), a SORT-MERGE join forces the sorting of each of the tables before they are merged together (since there are no indexes). A full table scan is needed on both tables and the order in the FROM clause has no impact. In Oracle 7.3 and above, Oracle builds a hash table from the join values of the *second* table, small1, then probes that table for values from small2.

**SITUATION 2 OUTCOMES**   Normally, the *first* table in the FROM clause in cost-based optimization is the driving table when an ORDERED hint is used, but in a SORT-MERGE join this has no impact since each table must be sorted and then merged together. In Oracle 7.3 and above, Oracle builds a hash table from the join values of the *second* table listed, then probes that table for values from the first table listed.

**TIP**

*Using cost-based optimization, the first table in the
FROM clause is the driving table when the ORDERED
hint is used. This overrides the optimizer from choosing
the driving table. If a SORT-MERGE join is used, then
the order of the tables has no impact since neither will
drive the query. Knowing which table is generally the
driving table when using an ORDERED hint in small
joins can help you to solve larger table join issues.*

**V7.3 TIP**

*In Oracle7.3, HASH joins are often used in lieu of
SORT-MERGE joins by the optimizer. With HASH
joins, the second table is used to build a hash table (in
memory if available) and the first table in the FROM
clause is then probed for corresponding matches. You
can still think of the first table in the FROM clause
(using the ORDERED hint) as being the driving table
in a HASH join, but only after the second is put
into a hash table in memory.*

# Two-Table INDEXED
# Join—Equal-Size Tables—Cost-Based

To get a better understanding of the driving table and how Oracle processes a
query, it is instructive to have an example where all things are equal in both tables.
While the queries in this section look strange, since we are trying to keep all things
equal, they are helpful in understanding the way joins work. Consider the following
tables (they have been analyzed) that will be used for this example:

```
SMALL1    1000 rows    Index on COL1
SMALL2    1000 rows    Index on COL1
```

   This is an important section of examples, as we look at how the cost-based
optimizer works using indexes. While the query in this section would *not* be one
that would normally be written, it is important to show how the driving table works,
when all things are equal, with a two-table join. In other words, it is for instructional
purposes only.

*Cost-Based Two-Table INDEXED
Join*

## Situation 1

Both tables have an index on the col1 column.

**Query 1:**

```
select    small1.col1, small2.col1
from      small1, small2
where     small1.col1 = small2.col1
and       small1.col1 = 77
and       small2.col1 = 77;
```

**EXPLAIN PLAN output:**

```
SELECT STATEMENT Optimizer=CHOOSE
  NESTED LOOPS (Cost=2 Card=3 Bytes=90)   (Each row from small1 is
  checked for matches in small2)
    INDEX (RANGE SCAN) OF 'SMALL1_IDX'   (This happens first / gets
    the first row to check)
    INDEX (RANGE SCAN) OF 'SMALL2_IDX'   (This happens second for
    each row matching small1)
```

Join Method: NESTED LOOPS Join

The small1 table (first table in the FROM clause) is the driving table of the query. Oracle will retrieve the records from the index on small1 and then take each record and check for matches in the small2 index. A NESTED LOOPS join will be faster when the source rows from the small1 table is a small set and there is a reasonably selective index on the small2 joining column.

**Query 2:**

```
select    small1.col1, small2.col1
from      small2, small1
where     small1.col1 = small2.col1
and       small1.col1 = 77
and       small2.col1 = 77;
```

**EXPLAIN PLAN output:**

```
SELECT STATEMENT Optimizer=CHOOSE
  NESTED LOOPS (Cost=2 Card=3 Bytes=90)   (Each row from small2 is
  checked for matches in small1)
    INDEX (RANGE SCAN) OF 'SMALL2_IDX'   (This happens first / gets
    the first row to check)
    INDEX (RANGE SCAN) OF 'SMALL1_IDX'   (This happens second for
    each row matching small2)
```

Join Method: NESTED LOOPS Join

The small2 table (first table in the FROM clause) is the driving table of the query. Oracle will retrieve the records from the index on small2 and then take each record and check for matches in the small1 index. A NESTED LOOPS join will be faster when the source rows from the small1 table is a small set and there is a reasonably selective index on the small1 joining column.

**SITUATION I OUTCOMES**   All things being equal, the *first* table in the FROM clause in cost-based optimization is the driving table. The index is used on the join condition for the second table. In the preceding examples, a NESTED LOOPS join was the way that Oracle joined the queries, but a HASH join or MERGE join was also possible depending on the number of records in the table and index.

# Situation 2

Both tables have an index on the col1 column and we use the ORDERED hint.

**Query 1:**

```
select    /*+ ORDERED */ small1.col1, small2.col1
from      small1, small2
where     small1.col1 = small2.col1
and       small1.col1 = 77
and       small2.col1 = 77;
```

**EXPLAIN PLAN output:**

```
SELECT STATEMENT Optimizer=CHOOSE
  NESTED LOOPS  (Each row from small1 is checked for matches in
```

```
small2)
    INDEX (RANGE SCAN) OF 'SMALL1_IDX'   (This happens first / gets
    the first row to check)
    INDEX (RANGE SCAN) OF 'SMALL2_IDX'   (This happens second for
    each row matching small1)
```

Join Method: NESTED LOOPS Join

The small1 table (first table in the FROM clause) is the driving table of the query. Oracle will retrieve the records from the index on small1 and then take each record and check for matches in the small2 index. A NESTED LOOPS join will be faster when the source rows from the small1 table is a small set and there is a reasonably selective index on the small2 joining column.

**Query 2:**

```
select     /*+ ORDERED */ small1.col1, small2.col1
from       small2, small1
where      small1.col1 = small2.col1
and        small1.col1 = 77
and        small2.col1 = 77;
```

**EXPLAIN PLAN output:**

```
SELECT STATEMENT Optimizer=CHOOSE
  NESTED LOOPS                                (Each row from small2 is
  checked for matches in small1)
    INDEX (RANGE SCAN) OF 'SMALL2_IDX'   (This happens first / gets
    the first row to check)
    INDEX (RANGE SCAN) OF 'SMALL1_IDX'   (This happens second for
    each row matching small2)
```

Join Method: NESTED LOOPS Join

The small2 table (first table in the FROM clause) is the driving table of the query. Oracle will retrieve the records from the index on small2 and then take each record and check for matches in the small1 index. A NESTED LOOPS join will be faster when the source rows from the small1 table is a small set and there is a reasonably selective index on the small1 joining column.

**SITUATION 2 OUTCOMES**   All things being equal, the *first* table in the FROM clause in cost-based optimization using NESTED LOOPS join is the driving table with or without the ORDERED hint. Only the ORDERED hint will guarantee the order the tables will be accessed. The index is used on the join condition for the second table.

**Cost-Based Two-Table INDEXED Join**

**TIP**
*Using cost-based optimization and a NESTED LOOPS join as the means of joining, the first table in the FROM clause is the driving table (all other things being equal), but only the ORDERED hint will guarantee this. In NESTED LOOPS joins, choosing a driving table that is the smaller result set (not always the smaller table) will make fewer loops to the other result set (from the nondriving table) and will usually result in the best performance.*

## Situation 3

Now we will select a nonindexed column (col2) other than col1 (which is indexed) so that the table will have to be accessed to see if it will change anything.

**Query 1:**

```
select    /*+ ORDERED */ small1.col2, small2.col2
from      small1, small2
where     small1.col1 = small2.col1
and       small1.col1 = 77
and       small2.col1 = 77;

Elapsed Time: 1.9 seconds
```

**EXPLAIN PLAN output:**

```
SELECT STATEMENT Optimizer=CHOOSE
  HASH JOIN
    TABLE ACCESS FULL OF 'SMALL1'        (The hash table is scanned
    with these rows)
    TABLE ACCESS FULL OF 'SMALL2'        (A hash table is built from
    this)
```

Join Method: HASH Join

This example was run with Oracle8 and a HASH join is performed. Oracle builds a hash table from the join values of the *second* table, small2, then probes that table for values from small1.

In the next query, we will try to improve the performance by forcing the indexes on both tables.

**Query 2:**

```
select    /*+ ORDERED INDEX (small1 col1_idx1) INDEX
          (small2 col1_idx) */
          small1.col2, small2.col2
from      small1, small2
where     small1.col1 = small2.col1
and       small1.col1 = 77
and       small2.col1 = 77;

Elapsed Time: 1.2 seconds (an improvement of over 35%)
```

**EXPLAIN PLAN output:**

```
SELECT STATEMENT Optimizer=CHOOSE
  HASH JOIN
    TABLE ACCESS (BY INDEX ROWID) OF 'SMALL1'
      INDEX (RANGE SCAN) OF 'SMALL1_IDX' (NON-UNIQUE)
    TABLE ACCESS (BY INDEX ROWID) OF 'SMALL2'
      INDEX (RANGE SCAN) OF 'SMALL2_IDX' (NON-UNIQUE)
```

Join Method: HASH Join

The preceding example was executed with Oracle8 and a HASH join is performed. Oracle scans the small2 index and gets the corresponding rows from small2 (the second table in the FROM clause). Small2 result set (after the index limited results) become the hash table. Oracle then scans the small1 table and probes small2 (the HASHed table) for matches.

**SITUATION 3 OUTCOMES**   Oracle chose to use a HASH join and also chose not to use the indexes on either table. By forcing the ORDERED and INDEX hints, we helped the performance of the query.

**TIP**
*The columns that are retrieved can change which indexes Oracle will use (in this case, they were suppressed by Oracle). This can change the way that Oracle will join the tables in the query (to a HASH join, in this case).*

## Situation 4

Moving from Oracle6 to Oracle7 caused many queries to behave differently. What if we change the preceding query to force the rule-based optimizer? The answer is the indexes used will change, as will the method of joining.

**Query 1:**

```
select     /*+ RULE */ small1.col2, small2.col2
from       small1, small2
where      small1.col1 = small2.col1
and        small1.col1 = 77
and        small2.col1 = 77;

Elapsed Time: 1.6 seconds
```

**EXPLAIN PLAN output:**

```
SELECT STATEMENT Optimizer=HINT: RULE
  NESTED LOOPS
    TABLE ACCESS (BY INDEX ROWID) OF 'SMALL2'
      INDEX (RANGE SCAN) OF 'SMALL2_IDX'
    TABLE ACCESS (BY INDEX ROWID) OF 'SMALL1'
      INDEX (RANGE SCAN) OF 'SMALL1_IDX'
```

**SITUATION 4 OUTCOMES**   The *last* table in the FROM clause in rule-based optimization using a NESTED LOOPS join is the driving table. In this case, the small2 index is accessed, then the small2 table is accessed to get the corresponding rows. Then, Oracle will take each record and check for matches in the small1 index. A NESTED LOOPS join will be fast when the source rows from the small1 table is a small set and there is a reasonably selective index on the small1 joining column.

**TIP**
*The RULE hint can change the way a query is joined and also change which indexes are used.*

Cost-Based Two-Table INDEXED Join

# Forcing a Specific Join Method

When choosing an execution plan for a query involving joins, the Oracle optimizer considers all possible join methods and table orders. The optimizer does its best to evaluate the merits of each option and to choose the optimal execution plan, but there are many times when the optimizer does not choose the best solution.

In these situations, the USE_NL, USE_MERGE, and USE_HASH hints can be used to request a specific join method, and the ORDERED hint can be used to request a specific join order. The optimizer will do its best to observe the wishes of these hints, but if you ask for something impossible (such as a SORT-MERGE join on an antijoin) the hint will be ignored. Note that there is no hint to request a CLUSTER join.

When tuning SQL that uses joins, you should run benchmark comparisons between different join methods and table execution order. For example, if a report joins two tables that form a master-detail relationship and the proper primary-key and foreign-key indexes are in place, the optimizer will probably choose to use a NESTED LOOPS join. However, if you know that this particular report joins all of the master records to all of the detail records, you might think it faster to use a SORT-MERGE join or HASH join instead. Run a benchmark to ensure that you have the best solution.

Query 1 shows an example query and its TKPROF output, query 2 shows the same query with a USE_MERGE hint, and query 3 shows it with a USE_HASH hint. In this example, the indexes were built so that a full table scan must be executed on the purchase_order_lines table (putting an index would have been the better choice but not as instructional). You can see that in this situation the HASH join cut CPU time by almost 40 percent and logical I/Os by about 98 percent.

**Query 1—NESTED LOOPS join:**

```
select    a.business_unit,a.po_number,a.vendor_type,b.line_number,
          b.line_amount,b.line_status,b.description
from      purchase_orders a,purchase_order_lines b
where     b.business_unit = a.business_unit
and       b.po_number = a.po_number
order by  a.business_unit,a.po_number,b.line_number
```

**TKPROF output:**

| call | count | cpu | elapsed | disk | query | current | rows |
|------|-------|-----|---------|------|-------|---------|------|
| Parse | 1 | 0.01 | 0.01 | 0 | 0 | 0 | 0 |
| Execute | 1 | 0.04 | 0.12 | 0 | 0 | 1 | 0 |
| Fetch | 73370 | 23.47 | 23.55 | 2071 | 298667 | 2089 | 73369 |
| total | 73372 | 23.52 | 23.68 | 2071 | 298667 | 2090 | 73369 |

```
Rows     Execution Plan
0        SELECT STATEMENT     GOAL: CHOOSE
73369     SORT (ORDER BY)
73369      NESTED LOOPS
73726        TABLE ACCESS    GOAL: ANALYZED (FULL) OF
                'PURCHASE_ORDER_LINES'
73369        TABLE ACCESS    GOAL: ANALYZED (BY ROWID) OF
                'PURCHASE_ORDERS'
73726          INDEX    GOAL: ANALYZED (UNIQUE SCAN) OF
                  'PURCHASE_ORDERS_PK' (UNIQUE)
```

The purchase_order_lines table is the driving table. Each record (one at a time) is taken from the purchase_order_lines table, and for each one, we loop through for matches in the purchase_order table. This is slow since the driving table list is large (the purchase_order_lines table has a large number of rows).

**Query 2—SORT-MERGE join:**

```
select    /*+ USE_MERGE (B)
          /a.business_unit,a.po_number,a.vendor_type,b.line_number,
          b.line_amount,b.line_status,b.description
from      purchase_orders a,purchase_order_lines b
where     b.business_unit = a.business_unit
and       b.po_number = a.po_number
order by  a.business_unit,a.po_number,b.line_number
```

**TKPROF output:**

| call | count | cpu | elapsed | disk | query | current | rows |
|------|-------|-----|---------|------|-------|---------|------|
| Parse | 1 | 0.01 | 0.01 | 0 | 0 | 0 | 0 |
| Execute | 1 | 0.02 | 0.15 | 0 | 0 | 2 | 0 |
| Fetch | 73370 | 17.49 | 19.57 | 3772 | 4165 | 3798 | 73369 |
| total | 73372 | 17.52 | 19.73 | 3772 | 4165 | 3800 | 73369 |

```
Rows     Execution Plan
0        SELECT STATEMENT    GOAL: CHOOSE
73369     SORT (ORDER BY)
73369      MERGE JOIN
886          SORT (JOIN)
886            TABLE ACCESS    GOAL: ANALYZED (FULL) OF
                  'PURCHASE_ORDERS'
73726        SORT (JOIN)
```

Forcing a Specific Join Method

```
73726          TABLE ACCESS    GOAL: ANALYZED (FULL) OF
               'PURCHASE_ORDER_LINES'
```

For the SORT-MERGE case, Oracle will sort both tables and then merge the result of each together. This is still not an efficient way to perform the query.

### Query 3—HASH join:

```
select    /*+ USE_HASH (B)
          /a.business_unit,a.po_number,a.vendor_type,b.line_number,
          b.line_amount,b.line_status,b.description
from      purchase_orders a,purchase_order_lines b
where     b.business_unit = a.business_unit
and       b.po_number = a.po_number
order by a.business_unit,a.po_number,b.line_number
```

### TKPROF output:

| call | count | cpu | elapsed | disk | query | current | rows |
|------|-------|-----|---------|------|-------|---------|------|
| Parse | 1 | 0.00 | 0.00 | 0 | 0 | 0 | 0 |
| Execute | 1 | 0.05 | 0.13 | 0 | 0 | 1 | 0 |
| Fetch | 73370 | 14.88 | 14.95 | 2071 | 4165 | 2093 | 73369 |
| total | 73372 | 14.93 | 15.08 | 2071 | 4165 | 2094 | 73369 |

```
Rows      Execution Plan
0         SELECT STATEMENT    GOAL: CHOOSE
73369       SORT (ORDER BY)
137807        HASH JOIN
886             TABLE ACCESS    GOAL: ANALYZED (FULL) OF
                  'PURCHASE_ORDERS'
73726           TABLE ACCESS    GOAL: ANALYZED (FULL) OF
                  'PURCHASE_ORDER_LINES'
```

The HASH join has proved to be the most efficient since it puts the purchase_order_lines table into a hash table, then scans to retrieve corresponding records. Since we must do a full table scan on purchase_order_lines (because we are retrieving almost all of the rows in this join), placing the table in a hash table becomes the most efficient manner to do this.

**SITUATION 3 OUTCOMES**   Oracle chose to do a NESTED LOOPS method of joining the tables, but this was not the most efficient way of joining in this case. Using the USE_HASH hint, we have cut CPU time by almost 40 percent and logical

I/Os by about 98 percent. While the CPU reduction is impressive, the reduction in logical I/Os (memory reads) is saving SGA memory for other users. There are times when you are retrieving a large amount of data, making a full table scan the most efficient method.

**TIP**
*To change the method that Oracle uses to join multiple tables, use the USE_MERGE, USE_NL, and USE_HASH hints.*

# Early Elimination of Candidate Rows

Suppose you have a list of 1,000 residents of your town along with each resident's street address, and you are asked to prepare an *alphabetized* list of residents who have the newspaper delivered to their home (only 50 get the newspaper). You could first alphabetize the list of 1,000 names (all residents in the town), then look up each street address in the list of 50 residents who get the newspaper (sort the 1,000 and then find the 50). A faster method would be to look up each street address of those that get the newspaper first, then get the names of the residents at that street and do the alphabetization last (find the 50 who get the newspaper from the list of 1,000, then sort the 50 matches). Either way, you will need to look at the 1,000 street addresses. However, these lookups will eliminate many names from the list, and the sorting will be faster when you only have a list of 50 to sort.

You can apply the same concept when writing SQL that joins tables together. The Oracle optimizer is pretty smart about choosing the most efficient order in which to do things, but how a query is written can constrain the options available to the optimizer.

The following query leaves the optimizer no choice but to read all of Acme's invoice lines (the large table), when in fact only the unpaid invoices (the small table) are of interest:

```
select     v.vendor_num, i.invoice_num, sum (l.amount)
from       vendors v, invoices i, invoice_lines l
where      v.vendor_name = 'ACME'
and        l.vendor_num = v.vendor_num
and        i.vendor_num = l.vendor_num
and        i.invoice_num = l.invoice_num
and        i.paid = 'N'
group by   v.vendor_num, i.invoice_num
order by   i.invoice_num
```

This query could be rewritten as follows:

```
select      v.vendor_num, i.invoice_num, sum (l.amount)
from        vendors v, invoices i, invoice_lines l
where       v.vendor_name = 'ACME'
and         i.vendor_num = v.vendor_num
and         i.paid = 'N'
and         l.vendor_num = i.vendor_num
and         l.invoice_num = i.invoice_num
group by    v.vendor_num, i.invoice_num
order by    i.invoice_num
```

In the rewritten query, the optimizer eliminates all of the paid invoices before joining to the invoice_lines table (the new intersection table). If most of the invoices in the database have already been paid, then the rewritten query will be significantly faster. (The schema design in this example is dubious, and is used for illustrative purposes only.)

**TIP**

*In a three-table join, the driving table is the intersection table or the table that has a join condition to each of the other two tables in the join. Try to use the most limiting table as the driving table (or intersection table) so that your result set from the join of the first two tables is small when you join it to the third table.*

# Two-Table Join—Large and Small Table

Consider the following tables that will be used for this example:

```
PRODUCT          70 thousand rows     Index on PRODUCT_ID
PRODUCT_LINES    4 million rows       Index on PRODUCT_ID
```

This section uses only cost-based optimization on Oracle8. This is an important section of examples, as it looks at a situation often encountered. It involves a two-table join between a small (business small) and a large table. The subsequent conditions (beyond the join itself) are on the column that we are joining. At times, the index on this column in the subsequent condition is suppressed. Unfortunately, this situation will lead to seven possible situations, based on various conditions. This section will cover those seven situations and summarize the results at the end of this section.

## Situation 1

Neither table can use an index (they are suppressed) and there are no other conditions.

**Query 1:**

```
select     product.name, product_lines.qty
from       product, product_lines
where      product.product_id || ''  =
           product_lines.product_id || '';
```

**EXPLAIN PLAN output:**

```
SELECT STATEMENT Optimizer=CHOOSE
  HASH JOIN
    TABLE ACCESS FULL OF 'PRODUCT'
    TABLE ACCESS FULL OF 'PRODUCT_LINES'
```

**Query 2:**

```
select     product.name, product_lines.qty
from       product_lines, product
where      product.product_id || ''  =
           product_lines.product_id || '' ;
```

**EXPLAIN PLAN output:**

```
SELECT STATEMENT Optimizer=CHOOSE
  HASH JOIN
    TABLE ACCESS FULL OF 'PRODUCT'
    TABLE ACCESS FULL OF 'PRODUCT_LINES'
```

**SITUATION 1 OUTCOME**   All things being equal, the *first* table in the FROM clause in cost-based optimization is the driving table. However, since these tables are different sizes, Oracle chooses the smaller table to be the driving table regardless of the order in the FROM clause. The product_lines table is put into a hash table and scanned with the product table. Since this is Oracle8, a HASH join is used for this join. Prior to Oracle7.3, a MERGE join would have been used. In rule-based optimization, Oracle would not have changed the order of the table based on its size.

Large and Small Table Two-Table Join

**V7.3 TIP**
*Using cost-based optimization, when a large and small table are joined, Oracle will put the larger table in a hash table and scan it with the first table regardless of the order in the FROM clause. If the ORDERED hint is specified, then the first table in the FROM clause will be the driving table and the second table will be put in a hash table.*

## Situation 2

There is a subsequent clause allowing the large table to use the PRODUCT_ID index.

**Query 1:**

```
select      product.name, product_lines.qty
from        product, product_lines
where       product.product_id = product_lines.product_id
and         product_lines.product_id = 4488;
```

**EXPLAIN PLAN output:**

```
SELECT STATEMENT Optimizer=CHOOSE
  HASH JOIN
    TABLE ACCESS BY INDEX ROWID PRODUCT_LINES
      INDEX RANGE SCAN PRODUCT_ID1
    TABLE ACCESS BY INDEX ROWID PRODUCT
      INDEX RANGE SCAN PRODUCT1
```

**Query 2:**

```
select      product.name, product_lines.qty
from        product_lines, product
where       product.product_id = product_lines.product_id
and         product_lines.product_id = 4488;
```

**EXPLAIN PLAN output:**

```
SELECT STATEMENT Optimizer=CHOOSE
  HASH JOIN
```

**Large and Small Table Two-Table Join**

```
TABLE ACCESS BY INDEX ROWID PRODUCT_LINES
  INDEX RANGE SCAN PRODUCT_ID1
TABLE ACCESS BY INDEX ROWID PRODUCT
  INDEX RANGE SCAN PRODUCT1
```

**SITUATION 2 OUTCOMES**    When a subsequent condition on PRODUCT_ID on the large table exists, the larger table is always the driving table regardless of the order in the FROM clause. The order of the tables in the FROM clause will not alter the order in which Oracle does this join unless an ORDERED hint is used.

> **TIP**
> *Using cost-based optimization, when a large and small table are joined, the larger table is the driving table if an index can be used on the large table. If the ORDERED hint is specified, then the first table in the FROM clause will be the driving table.*

## Situation 3

There is a subsequent clause allowing the small table to use the PRODUCT_ID index. Unexpectedly (to me, anyway), the large table will still drive the query after getting this condition (on PRODUCT_ID) passed to it by the join. Oracle is smart enough to figure out that PRODUCT_ID exists in both tables and it is more efficient to limit the product_lines table. In the "Three-Table Joins" section of this chapter, Oracle's internal processing will become more evident.

**Query 1:**

```
select      product.name, product_lines.qty
from        product, product_lines
where       product.product_id = product_lines.product_id
and         product.product_id = 4488;
```

**EXPLAIN PLAN output:**

```
SELECT STATEMENT Optimizer=CHOOSE
  HASH JOIN
    TABLE ACCESS BY INDEX ROWID PRODUCT_LINES
      INDEX RANGE SCAN PRODUCT_ID1
    TABLE ACCESS BY INDEX ROWID PRODUCT
      INDEX RANGE SCAN PRODUCT1
```

Large and Small Table Two-Table Join

**Query 2:**

```
select      product.name, product_lines.qty
from        product_lines, product
where       product.product_id = product_lines.product_id
and         product.product_id = 4488;
```

**EXPLAIN PLAN output:**

```
SELECT STATEMENT Optimizer=CHOOSE
  HASH JOIN
    TABLE ACCESS BY INDEX ROWID PRODUCT_LINES
      INDEX RANGE SCAN PRODUCT_ID1
    TABLE ACCESS BY INDEX ROWID PRODUCT
      INDEX RANGE SCAN PRODUCT1
```

**SITUATION 3 OUTCOMES**   When a subsequent condition on PRODUCT_ID on the small table exists, the larger table gets this passed to it via the join and *is still* the driving table. The order of the tables in the FROM clause will not alter the procedure unless an ORDERED hint is used.

## Situation 4

There is a subsequent clause on the large table to PRODUCT_ID, but the index is suppressed and cannot be used.

**Query 1:**

```
select      product.name, product_lines.qty
from        product, product_lines
where       product.product_id = product_lines.product_id
and         product_lines.product_id || '' = 4488;
```

**EXPLAIN PLAN output:**

```
SELECT STATEMENT Optimizer=CHOOSE
  HASH JOIN
    TABLE ACCESS FULL OF 'PRODUCT_LINES'
    TABLE ACCESS FULL OF 'PRODUCT'
```

**Query 2:**

```
select      product.name, product_lines.qty
from        product_lines, product
where       product.product_id = product_lines.product_id
and         product_lines.product_id || '' = 4488;
```

**EXPLAIN PLAN output:**

```
SELECT STATEMENT Optimizer=CHOOSE
  HASH JOIN
    TABLE ACCESS FULL OF 'PRODUCT_LINES'
    TABLE ACCESS FULL OF 'PRODUCT'
```

**SITUATION 4 OUTCOMES**   When a subsequent condition on PRODUCT_ID on the large table exists but is suppressed, it causes both tables to require a full table scan. This is *not* the desired result, as it leads to poor performance. The query is driven by the product_lines table in both cases after a hash table is built for the product table. The full table scans on one of the tables is unnecessary and should be altered with the following fix.

**SITUATION 4 SOLUTION**   The solution is to force the index on the product_lines table, rather than doing a full table scan on both tables. To do this, rewrite the subsequent statement (product_id = 4488) to go to the product table, rather than the product_lines table, and force the index on the large table to be used in the join. In the next section, the INDEX hint is actually not needed in this situation, while in other situations it guarantees some bit of safety. The reason that it is not needed is because when Oracle drives the query with product, it uses the index for the join on the product_id column of PRODUCT_LINES. More simply stated, since Oracle is driving the query with the table that it wants to, it uses the index on the other table. Although this may not sound logical, it is the way that things happen (Situation 5 will show this).

**Query 3:**

```
select    /*+ index(product_lines prodid_idx) */
          product.name, product_lines.qty
from      product_lines, product
```

```
where       product.product_id = product_lines.product_id
and         product.product_id || '' = 4488;
```

**EXPLAIN PLAN output:**

```
SELECT STATEMENT Optimizer=CHOOSE
  HASH JOIN
    TABLE ACCESS FULL OF 'PRODUCT'
    TABLE ACCESS BY INDEX ROWID PRODUCT_LINES
      INDEX RANGE SCAN PRODUCT_ID1
```

**TIP**

*Using cost-based optimization, when a large and small table are joined and the join condition is indexed but a subsequent statement on the large table suppresses the subsequent index, the larger table is accessed first and without using indexes on either table. This is undesirable! By using an INDEX hint, you should force the use of an index on the large table.*

## Situation 5

There is a subsequent clause (in addition to the join clause) referencing the column product_id, but the index is suppressed and cannot be used. This situation works itself to its own best solution by still using the index to the large table.

**Query 1:**

```
select     product.name, product_lines.qty
from       product, product_lines
where      product.product_id = product_lines.product_id
and        product.product_id || '' = 4488;
```

**EXPLAIN PLAN output:**

```
SELECT STATEMENT Optimizer=CHOOSE
  HASH JOIN
    TABLE ACCESS FULL OF 'PRODUCT'
    TABLE ACCESS BY INDEX ROWID PRODUCT_LINES
      INDEX RANGE SCAN PRODUCT_ID1
```

**Query 2:**

```
select      product.name, product_lines.qty
from        product_lines, product
where       product.product_id = product_lines.product_id
and         product.product_id || ''  = 4488;
```

**EXPLAIN PLAN output:**

```
SELECT STATEMENT Optimizer=CHOOSE
  HASH JOIN
    TABLE ACCESS FULL OF 'PRODUCT'
    TABLE ACCESS BY INDEX ROWID PRODUCT_LINES
      INDEX RANGE SCAN PRODUCT_ID1
```

**SITUATION 5 OUTCOMES**   When a subsequent condition on PRODUCT_ID on the small table exists (but must be suppressed for some reason), it causes the smaller table to be the driver with a full table scan and uses the index to the large table. This is the desired result compared to Situation 4 (where a full table scan on both tables was required).

## Situation 6

There is a subsequent clause on both tables to the PRODUCT_ID, but the index is suppressed in both cases and cannot be used. This situation works itself to its own best solution by still using the index to the large table. While you would *not* normally write a query that has conditions on both tables (product_id = 4488), it is important for instructional purposes.

**Query 1:**

```
select      product.name, product_lines.qty
from        product, product_lines
where       product.product_id = product_lines.product_id
and         product.product_id || ''  = 4488
and         product_lines.product_id || ''  = 4488;
```

**EXPLAIN PLAN output:**

```
SELECT STATEMENT Optimizer=CHOOSE
  HASH JOIN
```

```
TABLE ACCESS FULL OF 'PRODUCT'
TABLE ACCESS BY INDEX ROWID PRODUCT_LINES
   INDEX RANGE SCAN PRODUCT_ID1
```

**Query 2:**

```
select     product.name, product_lines.qty
from       product_lines, product
where      product.product_id = product_lines.product_id
and        product.product_id || '' = 4488
and        product_lines.product_id || '' = 4488;
```

**EXPLAIN PLAN output:**

```
SELECT STATEMENT Optimizer=CHOOSE
  HASH JOIN
    TABLE ACCESS FULL OF 'PRODUCT'
    TABLE ACCESS BY INDEX ROWID PRODUCT_LINES
       INDEX RANGE SCAN PRODUCT_ID1
```

**SITUATION 6 OUTCOMES**    When a subsequent condition on the product_id column exists on both tables but is suppressed, it causes the smaller table to be the driver with a full table scan and uses the index to the large table. This is the desired result, since the index is used for the larger table. The order of the last two AND statements does not alter the join method or sequence of the join.

## Situation 7

There is a subsequent clause on both tables to the product_id column, and the index can be used in both cases. This situation works itself to its own best solution by still using both indexes and driving with the large table.

**Query 1:**

```
select     product.name, product_lines.qty
from       product, product_lines
where      product.product_id = product_lines.product_id
and        product.product_id = 4488
and        product_lines.product_id = 4488;
```

**EXPLAIN PLAN output:**

```
HASH JOIN
    TABLE ACCESS BY INDEX ROWID PRODUCT_LINES
        INDEX RANGE SCAN PRODUCT_ID1
    TABLE ACCESS BY INDEX ROWID PRODUCT
        INDEX RANGE SCAN PRODUCT1
```

**Query 2:**

```
select      product.name, product_lines.qty
from        product_lines, product
where       product.product_id = product_lines.product_id
and         product.product_id = 4488
and         product_lines.product_id = 4488;
```

**EXPLAIN PLAN output:**

```
SELECT STATEMENT Optimizer=CHOOSE
  HASH JOIN
    TABLE ACCESS BY INDEX ROWID PRODUCT_LINES
        INDEX RANGE SCAN PRODUCT_ID1
    TABLE ACCESS BY INDEX ROWID PRODUCT
        INDEX RANGE SCAN PRODUCT1
```

**SITUATION 7 OUTCOMES**   When a subsequent condition on the product_id column exists on both tables, it causes the larger table to be the driver (regardless of the order of the FROM clause) with an indexed search and then does an indexed search on the smaller table. This is the desired result since an index is used on both tables and the limited large table is the driver.

## Summary

The situations in this section demonstrate the value of the optimizer. It is only wrong in one of the situations, when the small table index is suppressed. It chooses the correct path in all of the other situations:

- No indexes—Drives with the smaller table, but the larger table is put into a hash table in memory to be accessed by the smaller table. Need to fix this by adding an index.

- Indexes on both tables—Drives with the large table and small table result set put into a hash table in memory to be accessed by the larger table result set.

- If the index on the large table can be used, then only drive the query with the large table. The small table will be the hash table in memory to be accessed by the larger table result set.

- Index on small can be used only—If the column also exists on the large table, the value is passed to the large table and the query drives with the large table result set accessing the smaller table, which is put into the hash table in memory.

# Two-Table Join—Small and Large with Concatenated Index

A join of a small and a large table with concatenated indexes is another case that is handled in a sometimes inefficient manner by the cost-based optimizer. While the initial solution is to fix the indexes, that option does not always exist in all cases. Consider the following tables that will be used for this example:

```
CUSTOMER          600 rows            Index on CUST_NO
PRODUCT_LINES     4 million rows      Concatenated Index on
                                      (PRODUCT_ID, CUST_NO)
```

This is an important section of examples, as it looks at another situation that is often encountered. It involves a two-table join between a small and a very large table. The small table is indexed on the join condition (CUST_NO), but the large table is *not* indexed on the join condition (CUST_NO). Rather, this table has a concatenated index (see Chapter 8 for further details) on the combination of the subsequent clause and the join condition (PRODUCT_ID, CUST_NO). The subsequent conditions (beyond the join itself) will be *crucial* to attaining acceptable performance. The driving order of the tables will also be *crucial* to performance. The real problem is a poorly designed indexing strategy involving concatenated indexes that *do not* have the leading edge on the joined condition.

**SITUATION I**   Neither table will use an index (despite the fact there are indexes on both tables).

**Query 1:**

```
select    customer.name, product_lines.qty
from      customer, product_lines
where     customer.cust_no = product_lines.cust_no
and       product_lines.product_id = 4488;
```

**EXPLAIN PLAN output:**

```
SELECT STATEMENT Optimizer=CHOOSE
  HASH JOIN
    TABLE ACCESS FULL OF 'CUSTOMER'
    TABLE ACCESS FULL OF 'PRODUCT_LINES'

Elapsed Time: 15.5 MINUTES
```

**Query 2:**

```
select    customer.name, product_lines.qty
from      product_lines, customer
where     customer.cust_no = product_lines.cust_no
and       product_lines.product_id = 4488;
```

**EXPLAIN PLAN output:**

```
SELECT STATEMENT Optimizer=CHOOSE
  HASH JOIN
    TABLE ACCESS FULL OF 'CUSTOMER'
    TABLE ACCESS FULL OF 'PRODUCT_LINES'

Elapsed Time: 15.5 MINUTES
```

**SITUATION I OUTCOMES** When no indexes are used, the smaller table is always the driving table and the product_lines table is put into a hash table. The problem is that the PRODUCT_ID index *should be used*. This outcome is *not* the desired result. This query takes 15 minutes to process (as previously written), yet when fixed (following), it only takes 1 second.

**SITUATION I SOLUTIONS** The solution for this problem is to force the use of the index on the product_lines table. To do this, we can add an INDEX hint or add a RULE hint. The INDEX hint is suggested for forward compatibility.

**Query 3:**

```
select    /*+ index(product_lines prodid_cust_idx) */
          customer.name, product_lines.qty
from      product_lines, customer
where     customer.cust_no = product_lines.cust_no
and       product_lines.product_id = 4488;
```

Small and Large with
Concatenated Index

**EXPLAIN PLAN output:**

```
SELECT STATEMENT Optimizer=CHOOSE
  HASH JOIN
    TABLE ACCESS BY INDEX ROWID PRODUCT_LINES
      INDEX RANGE SCAN PRODID_CUST_IDX1
    TABLE ACCESS BY INDEX ROWID CUSTOMER
      INDEX RANGE SCAN CUST_IDX1

Elapsed Time: 1.2 SECONDS
```

**Query 4:**

```
select    /*+ rule */ customer.name, product_lines.qty
from      product_lines, customer
where     customer.cust_no = product_lines.cust_no
and       product_lines.product_id = 4488;
```

**EXPLAIN PLAN output:**

```
SELECT STATEMENT Optimizer=HINT: RULE
  NESTED LOOPS
    TABLE ACCESS BY INDEX ROWID PRODUCT_LINES
      INDEX RANGE SCAN PRODID_CUST_IDX1
    TABLE ACCESS BY INDEX ROWID CUSTOMER
      INDEX RANGE SCAN CUST_IDX1

Elapsed Time: 1.5 SECONDS
```

The solution in query 4 demonstrates the reason for the hesitation by some of moving from rule-based optimization to cost-based optimization. This solution is really a solution to an indexing problem. There should be an index on CUST_NO on the product_lines table. The RULE hint is the only hint that accommodates this design error.

**TIP**

*When a concatemnated index on the larger table of a join does not include the join condition as the leading edge of the index, that index on the subsequent part of the query must be forced or a full table scan on all tables could result.*

## Situation 2

Conditions beyond the join clause include columns of the full index on product_lines. The product_lines table will not use an index, despite the fact that both columns of the PRODUCT_LINES index are in the subsequent part of the query. Since the joined part of the PRODUCT_LINES index is the second part of the index, Oracle surrenders to do a full table scan on the product_lines table. A forced index on the product_lines table is much faster than Oracle's choice.

**Query 1:**

```
select    customer.name, product_lines.qty
from      customer, product_lines
where     customer.cust_no = product_lines.cust_no
and       product_lines.product_id = 4488
and       product_lines.cust_no = 5;
```

**EXPLAIN PLAN output:**

```
SELECT STATEMENT Optimizer=CHOOSE
  HASH JOIN
    TABLE ACCESS BY INDEX ROWID CUSTOMER
      INDEX RANGE SCAN CUST_IDX1
    TABLE ACCESS FULL OF 'PRODUCT_LINES'

Elapsed Time: 9.7 MINUTES
```

**Query 2:**

```
select    customer.name, product_lines.qty
from      product_lines, customer
where     customer.cust_no = product_lines.cust_no
and       product_lines.product_id = 4488
and       product_lines.cust_no = 5;
```

**EXPLAIN PLAN output:**

```
SELECT STATEMENT Optimizer=CHOOSE
  HASH JOIN
    TABLE ACCESS BY INDEX ROWID CUSTOMER
      INDEX RANGE SCAN CUST_IDX1
```

```
     TABLE ACCESS FULL OF 'PRODUCT_LINES'

Elapsed Time: 9.7 MINUTES
```

**SITUATION 2 OUTCOMES**   Since the PRODUCT_LINES concatenated index does not have cust_no as the first part, the PRODUCT_LINES index is not used at all. The problem is that the index *should be used*. This outcome is *not* the desired result. This query takes almost 10 minutes to process (as previously written), yet when fixed (following), it only takes 1 second. Note that using an ORDERED hint in either of the preceding two queries *will* cause the order of the FROM clause to be the order of the table execution, but will *still have poor performance* as the PRODUCT_LINES index will still *not* be used.

**SITUATION 2 SOLUTIONS**   The solution is to get the query to use the index on the large table instead of doing a full table scan. To do this, add an INDEX hint or add a RULE hint. The INDEX hint is a better choice for forward compatibility.

**Query 3:**

```
select     /*+ index(product_lines prodid_cust_idx) */
           customer.name, product_lines.qty
from       product_lines, customer
where      customer.cust_no = product_lines.cust_no
and        product_lines.product_id = 4488
and        product_lines.cust_no = 5;
```

**EXPLAIN PLAN output:**

```
SELECT STATEMENT Optimizer=CHOOSE
  HASH JOIN
    TABLE ACCESS BY INDEX ROWID PRODUCT_LINES
      INDEX RANGE SCAN PRODID_CUST_IDX1
    TABLE ACCESS BY INDEX ROWID CUSTOMER
      INDEX RANGE SCAN CUST_IDX1

Elapsed Time: 1.2 SECONDS
```

**Query 4:**

```
select     /*+ rule */ customer.name, product_lines.qty
from       product_lines, customer
where      customer.cust_no = product_lines.cust_no
```

```
and        product_lines.product_id = 4488
and        product_lines.cust_no = 5;
```

**EXPLAIN PLAN output:**

```
SELECT STATEMENT Optimizer=HINT: RULE
  NESTED LOOPS
    TABLE ACCESS BY INDEX ROWID PRODUCT_LINES
      INDEX RANGE SCAN PRODID_CUST_IDX1
    TABLE ACCESS BY INDEX ROWID CUSTOMER
      INDEX RANGE SCAN CUST_IDX1

Elapsed Time: 1.5 SECONDS
```

The concatenated (product_id, cust_no) index is used on the product_lines table and the cust_no column index is used on the customer. The order of the tables in the FROM clause does *not* matter, although we are forcing rule-based optimization. This is due to the fact that the join is executed after the conditions on product_lines (product_id = 4488, cust_no = 5) are searched and return a cust_no for the customer table to then use.

The solution in query 4 demonstrates the reason for the hesitation by some of moving from rule-based optimization to cost-based optimization. This solution is really a solution to an indexing problem. There should really be an index on cust_no on the product_lines table. Only the RULE or INDEX hints accommodate this design error.

# Three-Table Joins—Not as Much Fun (Cost-Based)

In a three-table join, Oracle joins two of the tables and joins the result with the third table. Which table is the driving table in a query? The answer that people give is often different and has a lot do with the query that accesses the plan_table. The following example shows an example query that has only one possible way to be accessed (the subqueries must be accessed first) and a query to the plan_table that will be used for the remainder of this chapter. This example is to ensure that you see how to read the output effectively.

```
explain plan for
 select    name
 from      customer
 where     cust_no =
  (select   cust_no
```

```
from       product_lines
where      qty = 1
and        product_id =
 (select   product_id
  from     product
  where    product.product_id = 807
  and      description = 'test'));
```

**A quick EXPLAIN PLAN:**

```
select    lpad(' ',2*level)||operation oper,options, object_name
from      plan_table
connect   by prior id = parent_id
start     with id = 1
order by  id
```

See Chapter 6 for a detailed EXPLAIN PLAN.

**EXPLAIN PLAN output:**

| OPER | OPTIONS | OBJECT NAME |
|------|---------|-------------|
| TABLE ACCESS | BY INDEX ROWID | CUSTOMER |
| INDEX | RANGE SCAN | CUST1 |
| TABLE ACCESS | BY INDEX ROWID | PRODUCT_LINES |
| INDEX | RANGE SCAN | PRODUCT_ID1 |
| TABLE ACCESS | BY INDEX ROWID | PRODUCT |
| INDEX | RANGE SCAN | PRODUCT1 |

Expected order of table access is based on the order in the FROM clause: product, product_lines, and customer
Actual order of access is product, product_lines, and customer

**WHY?** The innermost subquery (to the product table) must execute first so that it can return the product_id to be used in the product_lines (accessed second) table, which will in turn return the cust_no that the customer (accessed third) table needs.

**TIP**
*To ensure that you are reading your EXPLAIN PLAN correctly, run a query in which you are sure of the driving table (with nested subqueries).*

One exception to the preceding subquery:

```
explain plan for
 select      name
 from        customer
 where       cust_no =
  (select    cust_no
   from      product_lines
   where     product_lines.product_id = 807
   and       qty = 1
   and       product_id =
     (select     product_id
      from        product
      where       product.product_id = 807
      and         description = 'test'));
```

**EXPLAIN PLAN output:**

| OPER | OPTIONS | OBJECT NAME |
|------|---------|-------------|
| TABLE ACCESS | BY INDEX ROWID | CUSTOMER |
| INDEX | RANGE SCAN | CUST1 |
| FILTER | | |
| TABLE ACCESS | BY INDEX ROWID | PRODUCT_LINES |
| INDEX | RANGE SCAN | PRODUCT_ID1 |
| TABLE ACCESS | BY INDEX ROWID | PRODUCT |
| INDEX | RANGE SCAN | PRODUCT1 |

Expected order of table access is based on the order in the FROM clause: product, product_lines, and customer
Actual order of access is product_lines, product, and customer

**WHY?**   The product_lines query takes the product_id from the subquery to the product table and executes first.

# A Three-Table Join—Advanced (Cost-Based Optimizer)

The examples in this section show a three-table join. The order of access will be dependent on the order in the FROM clause, the intersection table, and the indexes that are used. In the following example , the first table accessed is product_lines, the cust_no is then used to access the customer table (using the CUST1 index on the customer table). Why is the product_lines table accessed first if the customer table is first in the FROM clause? The answer is that the index is suppressed (for instructional purposes) on the cust_no field in the product_lines table and there *is* an index on this field in the customer table. Oracle finds the optimal path to do the full table scan on the product_lines table so that it can use the index on the customer table in the join condition.

```
explain plan for
select     name, description, qty
from       customer, product_lines , product
where      customer.cust_no = product_lines.cust_no + 0
and        product.product_id = product_lines.product_id;
```

**EXPLAIN PLAN output:**

| OPER | OPTIONS | OBJECT NAME |
|---|---|---|
| NESTED LOOPS | | |
|   NESTED LOOPS | | |
|     TABLE ACCESS | FULL | PRODUCT_LINES |
|      TABLE ACCESS | BY INDEX ROWID | CUSTOMER |
|       INDEX | RANGE SCAN | CUST1 |
|     TABLE ACCESS | BY INDEX ROWID | PRODUCT |
|      INDEX | RANGE SCAN | PRODUCT1 |

Expected order of table access: customer, product_lines, and product
Actual order of access is product_lines, customer, and product

**WHY?** The index on the joining column of product_lines (cust_no) cannot be used, so the product_lines table is accessed first by a full table scan and then the customer table is accessed by the index.

## A Three-Table Join—Advanced

Here, we apply the same logic as the preceding example, but the index on the customer table is now suppressed in addition to the suppression on the product_lines table.

```
explain plan for
select     name, description, qty
from       customer, product_lines, product
where      customer.cust_no + 0 = product_lines.cust_no + 0
and        product.product_id = product_lines.product_id;
```

**EXPLAIN PLAN output:**

```
OPER                      OPTIONS              OBJECT NAME
NESTED LOOPS
   MERGE JOIN
      SORT                JOIN
         TABLE ACCESS     FULL                 CUSTOMER
      SORT                JOIN
         TABLE ACCESS     FULL                 PRODUCT_LINES
      TABLE ACCESS        BY INDEX ROWID       PRODUCT
         INDEX            RANGE SCAN           PRODUCT1
```

Expected order of table access is based on the order in the FROM clause: customer, product_lines, and product
Actual order of access is customer, product_lines, and product

**WHY?**    Unlike the last example, there is no reason for Oracle to change the driving order as listed in the FROM clause (since there are no helpful indexes on customer). The preceding EXPLAIN PLAN shows a query that you would *not* want running in production (it would be very slow with these full table scans). Also, the first two tables (customer, product_lines) are MERGE-joined together, so the order is irrelevant.

This is a better example with a more logical optimization path.

```
explain plan for
select    name, description, qty
from      product, product_lines , customer
where     customer.cust_no = product_lines.cust_no
and       product.product_id = product_lines.product_id
and       product.product_id = 777
```

**EXPLAIN PLAN output:**

```
OPER                      OPTIONS              OBJECT NAME
NESTED LOOPS
   NESTED LOOPS
      TABLE ACCESS        BY INDEX ROWID       PRODUCT
         INDEX            RANGE SCAN           PRODUCT1
      TABLE ACCESS        BY INDEX ROWID       PRODUCT_LINES
         INDEX            RANGE SCAN           PRODUCT_ID1
   TABLE ACCESS           BY INDEX ROWID       CUSTOMER
      INDEX               RANGE SCAN           CUST1
```

Expected order of table access is based on the order in the FROM clause: product, product_lines, and customer
Actual order of access is product, product_lines, and customer

**WHY?** The subsequent part of the WHERE clause (that part not related to the joining of tables) has a limiting condition on the product.product_id column (which is indexed) that will eliminate the need for a full table scan on any table. The table accessed is the product table. There is a join to the product_lines table (you need this to get to customer), and finally the customer table is accessed last.

**TIP**
*The order in the FROM clause determines the driving order of the tables, in general. However, the joining of the tables and the indexing regarding those joins will also change the order that Oracle accesses the tables. Only the ORDERED hint will guarantee a join order. The joining column on all tables should be indexed!*

# Index "Breakpoint" for a Small Table

With larger tables, Oracle will generally use an index when the percentage of returned rows of a query is around 4 percent (as discussed in the previous chapter). For smaller tables, Oracle is likely to do a full table scan even when as few as 1 percent of the rows are returned. There are some interesting caveats to these index tendencies, so don't take these to be the only possibilities. While a customer table would likely have unique values in the cust_no column, the customer table that we use (for instructional purposes) will not have unique values for cust_no. Consider the following table that will be used for this example:

```
CUSTOMER      600 rows      Index on CUST_NO
```

## Situation I
The makeup of the customer table is such that *any* condition will return 8 percent of the table. Generally, Oracle would *not* use the index on this table for larger tables—for example, cust_no = 8 (returns 8 percent of the table):

**Query 1:**

```
select    name
from      customer
where     cust_no = 8;
```

**Outcome:** The CUST_NO index is *not* used.

**Query 2:**

```
update     customer
set        cust_no = 77
where      cust_no = 8;
```

**SITUATION 1 OUTCOME**   The CUST_NO index is *not* used. Oracle follows its general guidelines of not using an index when retrieving a large amount of the table (8 percent in this case).

## Situation 2

The makeup of the customer table is such that *any* condition will return 4 percent of the table. Generally, Oracle would use the index on this table for larger tables—for example, cust_no = 4 (returns 4 percent of the table):

**Query 1:**

```
select     name
from       customer
where      cust_no = 4;
```

**Outcome:** The CUST_NO index is *not* used.

**Query 2:**

```
update     customer
set        cust_no = 77
where      cust_no = 4;
```

**Outcome:** The CUST_NO index *is* used.

**SITUATION 2 OUTCOME**   Oracle follows its general guidelines of using an index when retrieving a small amount of the table (4 percent in this case) for the UPDATE, yet does *not* follow that guideline for the SELECT statement.

## Situation 3

The makeup of the customer table is such that *any* condition will return 2 percent of the table. Generally, Oracle would use the index on this table for larger tables—for example, cust_no = 2 (returns 2 percent of the table):

**Query 1:**

```
select     name
from       customer
where      cust_no = 2;
```

**Outcome:** The CUST_NO index is *not* used.

**Query 2:**

```
update     customer
set        cust_no = 77
where      cust_no = 2;
```

**Outcome:** The CUST_NO index *is* used.

**SITUATION 3 OUTCOME**   Oracle follows its general guidelines of using an index when retrieving a small amount of the table (2 percent in this case) for the UPDATE, yet does not follow that guideline for the SELECT statement.

## Situation 4

The makeup of the customer table is such that *any* condition will return just less than 1 percent (0.833 percent to be exact, or 5 rows of the 600 total) of the table. Generally, Oracle would use the index on this table for larger tables—for example, cust_no = 1 (returns less than 1 percent of the table).

**Query 1:**

```
select     name
from       customer
where      cust_no = 1;
```

**Outcome:** The CUST_NO index *is* used.

**Query 2:**

```
update     customer
set        cust_no = 77
where      cust_no = 1;
```

**Outcome:** The CUST_NO index *is* used.

**SITUATION 4 OUTCOME**   Oracle follows its general guidelines of using an index when retrieving a small amount of the table (1 percent in this case) for the UPDATE, and finally uses the index for the SELECT statement.

## Summary

When you are working with smaller tables, Oracle will generally *not* use indexes for percentages (a large number of distinct keys) that it would under normal conditions. This would not be a problem, except the rules are different for UPDATE and DELETE operations. This can cause some inconsistencies (between SELECT, UPDATE, and DELETE operations) when writing queries to small tables. This also can cause problems with join conditions by internally causing a reordering of the tables. Using the ORDERED hint will solve this problem.

**TIP**
*When the cost-based optimizer will use an index depends on the size of the table. For larger tables, the breakpoint is around 4 percent. For smaller tables (less than 1,000 rows), the breakpoint is closer to 1 percent for SELECTs and still at 4 percent for UPDATEs and DELETEs.*

# The Inlist Iterator in Oracle8 (Using the IN)

In Oracle7 (prior to 7.3), Oracle transforms the IN operator into an OR clause and subsequently into a compound SQL statement, using the UNION ALL set operator. The execution plan doubles in size for a query with an IN operator that has two constant values in its inlist (for three it triples, and so on).

With release 7.3, Oracle apparently altered the optimizer's strategy for transforming SQL statements with large inlists (i.e., 200). Instead of transforming one query into 200 queries and using UNION ALL to bring the results together, Oracle 7.3 will often ignore the relevant index and instead perform one full table scan. Oracle reads every row of data from the table and compares each to all values listed in the inlist of the IN operator. If the underlying table is large, this full table scan can clobber performance, making performance on Oracle 7.3 worse than earlier versions of Oracle7.

Oracle8 handles IN operators with subqueries in much the same way as Oracle7 and 6. This was already efficient and needed no improvement. However, for IN operators with many constant values in the inlist, Oracle8 introduces the new *inlist iterator* data access path. This new method in the query optimizer makes handling of large inlists of constants extremely efficient and intuitive. For the following query, we can see each of the ways Oracle handles the IN operator for each of the three versions.

```
select   ord.order_id, ord.order_number,
         ord.total, cust.customer_name
from     orders ord, customers cust
where    ord.status in ('CANCELED', 'INVALID')
and      cust.customer_id = ord.customer_id
```

**EXPLAIN PLAN output (pre-Oracle7.3):**

```
Execution Plan (Version 7.2)
SELECT STATEMENT
 CONCATENATION
  NESTED LOOPS
   TABLE ACCESS BY ROWID (ORDERS)
    INDEX RANGE SCAN (ORDER_STATUS_IDX)
   TABLE ACCESS BY ROWID (CUSTOMERS)
    INDEX UNIQUE SCAN (CUSTOMERS_PK)
  NESTED LOOPS
   TABLE ACCESS BY ROWID (ORDERS)
    INDEX RANGE SCAN (ORDER_STATUS_IDX)
   TABLE ACCESS BY ROWID (CUSTOMERS)
    INDEX UNIQUE SCAN (CUSTOMERS_PK)
```

**EXPLAIN PLAN output (Oracle7.3):**

```
Execution Plan (Version 7.3)
SELECT STATEMENT
 NESTED LOOPS
  TABLE ACCESS BY ROWID (ORDERS)
   INDEX RANGE SCAN (ORDER_STATUS_IDX)
  TABLE ACCESS BY ROWID (CUSTOMERS)
   INDEX UNIQUE SCAN (CUSTOMERS_PK)
```

**EXPLAIN PLAN output (Oracle8):**

```
Execution Plan (Version 8)
SELECT STATEMENT
 NESTED LOOPS
  INLIST ITERATOR CONCATENATED
   TABLE ACCESS BY ROWID (ORDERS)
    INDEX RANGE SCAN (ORDER_STATUS_IDX)
   TABLE ACCESS BY ROWID (CUSTOMERS)
    INDEX UNIQUE SCAN (CUSTOMERS_PK)
```

# Third-Party Product Tuning

There are times when you are at the mercy of a third-party product. While you cannot modify the code, you can often modify the use of indexes. The following three examples are from a financials third-party product.

## Example 1

This query was taking 22 minutes to run. By providing a hint to a more efficient index, the query execution time was reduced to 15 seconds.

**Before hint is added:**

```
update PS_COMBO_DATA_TBL
set     EFFDT_FROM = TO_DATE ('1990-01-01', 'YYYY-MM-DD'),
        EFFDT_TO = TO_DATE ('2099-01-01', 'YYYY-MM-DD')
where   SETID = 'RRD'
and     PROCESS_GROUP = 'GROUP1'
and     COMBINATION = 'ACCT/NOLOC'
and     VALID_CODE = 'V'
and     EFFDT_OPEN = 'Y'
and     EXISTS
 (select    'X'
  from      PS_JRNL_LN
  where     BUSINESS_UNIT = '00003'
  and       PROCESS_INSTANCE = 0000085176
  and       JRNL_LINE_STATUS = '3'
  and       ACCOUNT = PS_COMBO_DATA_TBL.ACCOUNT
  and       PRODUCT = PS_COMBO_DATA_TBL.PRODUCT )
```

**After hint is added:**

```
update PS_COMBO_DATA_TBL
set    EFFDT_FROM = TO_DATE ('1990-01-01', 'YYYY-MM-DD'),
       EFFDT_TO = TO_DATE ('2099-01-01', 'YYYY-MM-DD')
where  SETID = 'RRD'
and    PROCESS_GROUP = 'GROUP1'
and    COMBINATION = 'ACCT/NOLOC'
and    VALID_CODE = 'V'
and    EFFDT_OPEN = 'Y'
and    EXISTS
 (select     /*+ INDEX(PS_JRNL_LN, PSGJRNL_LN) */  'X'
  from       PS_JRNL_LN
  where      BUSINESS_UNIT = '00003'
  and        PROCESS_INSTANCE = 0000085176
  and        JRNL_LINE_STATUS = '3'
  and        ACCOUNT = PS_COMBO_DATA_TBL.ACCOUNT
  and        PRODUCT = PS_COMBO_DATA_TBL.PRODUCT )
```

## Example 2

This query was taking 33 minutes to run. By creating a concatenated index on the ps_group_control table (columns: deposit_bu, deposit_id, payment_seq_num), the query execution time was reduced to 30 seconds.

**Index on ps_group_control helped performance:**

```
select     C.BUSINESS_UNIT, C.CUST_ID,  C.ITEM,
           C.ENTRY_TYPE, C.ENTRY_REASON, C.ENTRY_AMT,
           C.ENTRY_CURRENCY, C.ENTRY_AMT_BASE,
           C.CURRENCY_CD, C.POSTED_FLAG, D.PAYMENT_SEQ_NUM
from       PS_PENDING_ITEM C,
           PS_GROUP_CONTROL D
where      D.DEPOSIT_BU = :1
and        D.DEPOSIT_ID = :2
and        D.PAYMENT_SEQ_NUM = :3
and        D.GROUP_BU = C.GROUP_BU
and        D.GROUP_ID = C.GROUP_ID
order by   D.PAYMENT_SEQ_NUM
```

**EXPLAIN PLAN before index is added:**

```
Execution Plan
RULE SELECT STATEMENT
     SORT ORDER BY
```

```
    NESTED LOOPS
       ANALYZED TABLE ACCESS FULL PS_GROUP_CONTROL
       ANALYZED TABLE ACCESS BY ROWID PS_PENDING_ITEM
          ANALYZED INDEX RANGE SCAN PS_PENDING_ITEM
```

**EXPLAIN PLAN after index is added:**

```
Execution Plan
RULE SELECT STATEMENT
     SORT ORDER BY
       NESTED LOOPS
        ANALYZED TABLE ACCESS BY ROWID PS_GROUP_CONTROL
           INDEX RANGE SCAN PSAGROUP_CONTROL
         ANALYZED TABLE ACCESS BY ROWID PS_PENDING_ITEM
          ANALYZED INDEX RANGE SCAN PS_PENDING_ITEM
```

## Example 3

This query was taking 20 minutes to run, and was reduced to 30 seconds. We created a concatenated unique index on the ps_cust_option table (columns: cust_id, effdt) instead of the current index, which is on cust_id only. This forces Oracle to use a concatenated unique index rather than a single-column index.

**Unique concatenated index on ps_cust_option helped performance:**

```
INSERT INTO PS_PP_CUST_TMP  (PROCESS_INSTANCE, DEPOSIT_BU, DEPOSIT_ID,
PAYMENT_SEQ_NUM, CUST_ID, PAYMENT_AMT, PAYMENT_DT, PP_METHOD, SETID,
SUBCUST_QUAL1, SUBCUST_QUAL2, PP_HOLD, PP_MET_SW, PAYMENT_CURRENCY)

select    DISTINCT P.PROCESS_INSTANCE, P.DEPOSIT_BU,
          P.DEPOSIT_ID, P.PAYMENT_SEQ_NUM, C.CUST_ID,
          P.PAYMENT_AMT,  P.PAYMENT_DT, O.PP_METHOD,
          O.SETID, C.SUBCUST_QUAL1, C.SUBCUST_QUAL2,
          O.PP_HOLD, 'N', P.PAYMENT_CURRENCY
from      PS_CUST_OPTION O, PS_CUSTOMER C, PS_ITEM I,
          PS_SET_CNTRL_REC S, PS_PAYMENT_ID_ITEM X,
          PS_PP_PAYMENT_TMP P
where     P.PROCESS_INSTANCE = 85298
and       S.SETCNTRLVALUE = I.BUSINESS_UNIT
and       I.CUST_ID = C.CUST_ID
and       I.ITEM_STATUS = 'O'
and       (X.REF_VALUE = I.DOCUMENT
or        SUBSTR (X.REF_VALUE, 3, 7) = SUBSTR (I.DOCUMENT, 4, 7))
and       S.RECNAME = 'CUSTOMER'
and       S.SETID = C.SETID
```

**Third-Party Product Tuning**

```
and       O.SETID = C.REMIT_FROM_SETID
and       O.CUST_ID = C.REMIT_FROM_CUST_ID
and       O.EFFDT =
    (select   MAX (X.EFFDT)
     from     PS_CUST_OPTION X
     where    X.SETID = O.SETID
     and      X.CUST_ID = O.CUST_ID
     and      X.EFF_STATUS = 'A'
     and       X.EFFDT <= P.PAYMENT_DT)
and       O.PP_METHOD <> ' '
and       P.DEPOSIT_BU = X.DEPOSIT_BU
and       P.DEPOSIT_ID = X.DEPOSIT_ID
and       P.PAYMENT_SEQ_NUM = X.PAYMENT_SEQ_NUM
and       X.REF_QUALIFIER_CODE = 'D'
```

**EXPLAIN PLAN before index added:**

```
Execution Plan
RULE INSERT STATEMENT
    SORT UNIQUE
       NESTED LOOPS
          NESTED LOOPS
             NESTED LOOPS
                NESTED LOOPS
                   NESTED LOOPS
                      ANALYZED TABLE ACCESS BY ROWID PS_PP_PAYMENT_TMP
                         ANALYZED INDEX RANGE SCAN PSAPP_PAYMENT_TMP
                      ANALYZED INDEX RANGE SCAN PSAPAYMENT_ID_ITEM
                   ANALYZED INDEX RANGE SCAN PSDSET_CNTRL_REC
                ANALYZED INDEX RANGE SCAN PSEITEM
             ANALYZED TABLE ACCESS BY ROWID PS_CUSTOMER
                ANALYZED INDEX UNIQUE SCAN PS_CUSTOMER
          ANALYZED TABLE ACCESS BY ROWID PS_CUST_OPTION
             ANALYZED INDEX RANGE SCAN PSACUST_OPTION
       SORT AGGREGATE
          ANALYZED TABLE ACCESS BY ROWID PS_CUST_OPTION
             ANALYZED INDEX RANGE SCAN PSACUST_OPTION
```

**EXPLAIN PLAN after index added:**

```
Execution Plan
RULE INSERT STATEMENT
    SORT UNIQUE
       NESTED LOOPS
```

```
      NESTED LOOPS
         NESTED LOOPS
            NESTED LOOPS
               NESTED LOOPS
                  ANALYZED TABLE ACCESS BY ROWID PS_PP_PAYMENT_TMP
                     ANALYZED INDEX RANGE SCAN PSAPP_PAYMENT_TMP
                  ANALYZED INDEX RANGE SCAN PSAPAYMENT_ID_ITEM
               ANALYZED INDEX RANGE SCAN PSDSET_CNTRL_REC
            ANALYZED INDEX RANGE SCAN PS#ITEM
         ANALYZED TABLE ACCESS BY ROWID PS_CUSTOMER
            ANALYZED INDEX UNIQUE SCAN PS_CUSTOMER
      ANALYZED TABLE ACCESS BY ROWID PS_CUST_OPTION
         ANALYZED INDEX RANGE SCAN PS_CUST_OPTION
   SORT AGGREGATE
      ANALYZED TABLE ACCESS BY ROWID PS_CUST_OPTION
         ANALYZED INDEX RANGE SCAN PS_CUST_OPTION
```

**TIP**
*You may not be able to modify actual code for some third-party products, but you can often add, force, or suppress indexes to improve the performance.*

# Distributed Queries

When improperly written, distributed queries can sometimes be disastrous and lead to poor performance. In particular, a NESTED LOOPS join between two row sources on separate nodes of a distributed database can be very slow since Oracle will move all of the data to the local machine (depending on how the query is written). The first example below shows a simple distributed query and its execution plan. This query is slow because for each row retrieved from the customers table, a separate query will be dispatched to the remote node in order to retrieve records from the bookings table. This will result in many small network packets moving between the two nodes of the database, and the network latency and overhead will degrade performance.

**Distributed query example 1:**

```
select     customer_id, customer_name, class_code
from       customers cust
where      exists
(select    1
 from      bookings@book bkg
 where     bkg.customer_id = cust.customer_id
 and       bkg.status = 'OPEN' )
order by   customer_name;
```

**TKPROF output:**

| call | count | cpu | elapsed | disk | query | current | rows |
|------|-------|-----|---------|------|-------|---------|------|
| Parse | 1 | 0.00 | 0.01 | 0 | 0 | 0 | 0 |
| Execute | 1 | 0.00 | 0.00 | 0 | 0 | 0 | 0 |
| Fetch | 156 | 0.41 | 11.85 | 0 | 476 | 2 | 155 |
| total | 158 | 0.41 | 11.86 | 0 | 476 | 2 | 155 |

```
Rows    Execution Plan
0       SELECT STATEMENT    GOAL: CHOOSE
155       SORT (ORDER BY)
467         FILTER
467           TABLE ACCESS    GOAL: ANALYZED (FULL) OF 'CUSTOMERS'
0               REMOTE [BOOK.WORLD]
                    SELECT "CUSTOMER_ID","STATUS" FROM "BOOKINGS"
                BKG WHERE
                    "STATUS"='open' AND "CUSTOMER_ID"=:1
```

This query can be rewritten in a form that causes less network traffic. In the next example, one query is sent to the remote node to determine all customers with open bookings. The output is the same, but performance is greatly improved. Both versions of the query use roughly the same CPU time and logical I/Os on the local node, but the elapsed time is about 97 percent better in the following example. This gain is attributable to reduced network overhead.

**Distributed query example 2:**

```
select     customer_id, customer_name, class_code
from       customers
where      customer_id in
(select    customer_id
 from      bookings@book
 where     status = 'OPEN' )
order by   customer_name;
```

**TKPROF output:**

| call | count | cpu | elapsed | disk | query | current | rows |
|------|-------|-----|---------|------|-------|---------|------|
| Parse | 1 | 0.00 | 0.01 | 0 | 0 | 0 | 0 |
| Execute | 1 | 0.00 | 0.00 | 0 | 0 | 0 | 0 |
| Fetch | 156 | 0.07 | 0.27 | 0 | 467 | 0 | 155 |

```
total        158      0.07     0.28      0       467      0       155

Rows    Execution Plan
0       SELECT STATEMENT     GOAL: CHOOSE
155       SORT (ORDER BY)
155        NESTED LOOPS
156         VIEW
1000          SORT (UNIQUE)
1000           REMOTE [BOOK.WORLD]
                   SELECT "CUSTOMER_ID","STATUS" FROM "BOOKINGS"
                   BOOKINGS WHERE
                     "STATUS"='open'
155           TABLE ACCESS    GOAL: ANALYZED (BY ROWID) OF 'CUSTOMERS'
156            INDEX    GOAL: ANALYZED (UNIQUE SCAN) OF 'SYS_C002109'
                   (UNIQUE)
```

When distributed queries cannot be avoided, use IN clauses, set operators such as UNION and MINUS, and everything else you can to reduce the network traffic between nodes of the database. Using views that limit the records in a table can also improve performance by reducing what is sent from the remote client to the local client. With Oracle8, you can use the DRIVING_SITE hint to control which node of the distributed database drives the distributed query. In Oracle7, the driving site will always be the local node where the query originated.

**TIP**
*When distributed queries cannot be avoided, use IN clauses, set operators such as UNION and MINUS, and everything else you can to reduce the network traffic between nodes of the database. Queries written in a manner that cause looping between distributed nodes (distributed databases) can be extremely slow.*

# When You Have Everything Tuned

If you successfully tune all of *your* queries, then you can start working on those that go to the data dictionary views. The following example shows that even Oracle's own views have some highly complex joining schemes.

**Example query to data dictionary views:**

```
select    *
from      dba_ind_columns
where     table_name = 'PRODUCT_LINES';
```

**Execution Plan output:**

```
Execution Plan
   0        SELECT STATEMENT Optimizer=CHOOSE
   1     0   NESTED LOOPS
   2     1    NESTED LOOPS (OUTER)
   3     2     NESTED LOOPS
   4     3      NESTED LOOPS
   5     4       NESTED LOOPS
   6     5        NESTED LOOPS
   7     6         NESTED LOOPS
   8     7          TABLE ACCESS (FULL) OF 'IND$'
   9     7          TABLE ACCESS (BY INDEX ROWID) OF 'OBJ$'
  10     9           INDEX (UNIQUE SCAN) OF 'I_OBJ1' (UNIQUE)
  11     6         TABLE ACCESS (CLUSTER) OF 'USER$'
  12    11          INDEX (UNIQUE SCAN) OF 'I_USER#' (CLUSTER)
  13     5        TABLE ACCESS (BY INDEX ROWID) OF 'ICOL$'
  14    13         INDEX (RANGE SCAN) OF 'I_ICOL1' (NON-UNIQUE)
  15     4       TABLE ACCESS (BY INDEX ROWID) OF 'OBJ$'
  16    15        INDEX (UNIQUE SCAN) OF 'I_OBJ1' (UNIQUE)
  17     3      TABLE ACCESS (BY INDEX ROWID) OF 'COL$'
  18    17       INDEX (UNIQUE SCAN) OF 'I_COL3' (UNIQUE)
  19     2     TABLE ACCESS (CLUSTER) OF 'ATTRCOL$'
  20     1    TABLE ACCESS (CLUSTER) OF 'USER$'
  21    20     INDEX (UNIQUE SCAN) OF 'I_USER#' (CLUSTER)
```

# Tuning Using Simple Mathematical Techniques

This section discusses some simple but effective mathematical techniques you can use to significantly improve the performance of some Oracle SQL-based systems. These techniques can leverage the effectiveness of Oracle performance diagnostic tools and uncover hidden performance problems that can be overlooked by other methods. It also makes it easier to make performance predictions at higher loads. This section was provided by Joe A. Holmes. I am extremely grateful for his contribution, as I believe it ties all the chapters of this book together.

The methodology called Simple Mathematical Techniques involves isolating and testing the SQL process in question under ideal conditions, graphing the results of rows processed versus time, deriving equations using simple methods (without regression), predicting performance, and interpreting and applying performance patterns directly to tuning SQL code.

# Traditional Mathematical Analysis

First of all, do not be intimidated by this section. You *will* be able to understand this, and with this information provided, it will help you to predict response times for your queries as the size of the tables grow.

Traditional mathematical methods are very useful for analyzing performance. These may include graphing performance metrics on an *x*-*y* coordinate axis to obtain a picture of what a process is really doing and applying Least Squares Regression or Polynomial Interpolation to derive equations for predicting performance at higher loads. Computer science academics and specialists make extensive use of these techniques for performance analysis. There are problems with using mathematical techniques for performance analysis. First, textbook notation and explanations are often very complex and difficult to understand. The majority of math textbooks I have encountered regarding approximation and interpolation, for example, are steeped in theory rather than providing clear and practical examples.

Second, there is little or no information on how to apply this kind of analysis directly to tuning SQL code. This is likely because SQL analysis requires more specific interpretations to be useful rather than something more broad or general.

# Seven Steps of the Methodology

The following are seven steps in the methodology. Note that Deriving Performance Equations and Pattern Interpretation are discussed in more detail.

## 1. Isolating the SQL Code in Question

The SQL code in question is isolated from surrounding system code and placed in a SQL*Plus or PL/SQL script that can be run independently to duplicate the production process.

## 2. Running Tests under Ideal Conditions

In this context, "ideal" is defined as one SQL process running on a dedicated machine with hardware processing power fixed and executed under high-volume data.

## 3. Graphing Performance Observations on an *x*-*y* Coordinate Axis

From tests, the number of rows processed (*x*) versus time (*y*) for each SQL statement within a process is graphed on an *x*-*y* coordinate axis. We refer to this as a row-time metric. Under ideal conditions, the optimizer is for the most part more mechanical and less random, creating a more clearly defined and predictable trend line. The basic line shape can provide clues to the cause of underlying performance problems.

### 4. Using Simple Equation Determination

Once points are plotted on a graph, we assume that what appears straight is a linear function and what appears curved upwards is a quadratic function. (Other shapes may appear, but are treated as beyond the scope of this section.) From these observations, we can use either a simple two-point linear or three-point quadratic method to determine the equations. Both methods can be done easily by hand or with a basic calculator. Each separate SQL statement is graphed and analyzed individually.

### 5. Predicting Performance

Derived equations can be used to predict performance at much higher loads than are practical to test. Because the accuracy of the predictions may decrease as the predicted load increases, it is suggested that only ballpark predictions be made.

### 6. Interpreting Performance Patterns and Experimentation

The shape of the performance lines and the nature of the equations can provide clues to the cause of underlying performance problems and support (or sometimes contradict) the interpretations of diagnostic tools. Experiments can be conducted on SQL code based on pattern clues and the correction applied to production code. Tests of an improved process can be graphed again and the results compared with the original process.

### 7. Keeping a Record of Results to Build Expertise

It is important to keep a record of before and after performance graphs, what the true cause of performance problems were and what effective solutions were found in order to build up your expertise at using both these mathematical methods and your interpretation of Oracle diagnostic tools. Graphs provide hard evidence of performance problems that can be presented in a clear visual form to management and end users.

## Deriving Performance Equations

The following discusses two simple methods for equation determination based on simplified versions of Newton's Divided Difference Interpolating Polynomial [1]. These methods can be used if we assume what appears as a straight line is linear and what appears as upward sloping is quadratic.

## Simple Linear Equation Determination

The following is a simple two-point method for determining a linear best-performance line equation:

$y = a_0 + a_1 x$ (this is the final equation to use for linear queries)
$y$ = the number of rows in the table
$x$ = time to process the query
$a_1$ = the slope of the line (calculate this with two query tests)
$a_0$ = the y-intercept of the line (calculate this with two query tests)

Figure 9-4 shows points from an ideal test that appears linear. We visually select two points $(x_1, y_1)$ and $(x_2, y_2)$ that define a straight line of minimum slope where

slope: $a_1 = (y_2 - y_1)/(x_2 - x_1)$
y-intercept: $a_0 = y_1 - a_{1x1}$

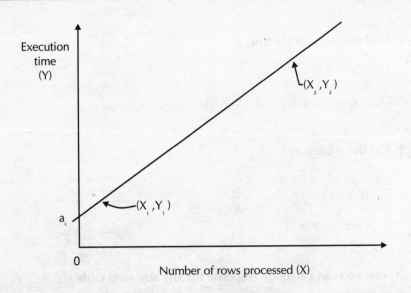

**FIGURE 9-4.** *Linear best-performance line*

**A SIMPLE EXAMPLE**   All of these equations look great, but let's look at a real-life query. We must time the query based on two different table sizes to get an equation for the line.

```
select     ename, deptno
from       emp
where      deptno = 10;
```

**For a very small system, consider the response for two tests:**
When there were 1,000 records in the emp table, this query took 2 seconds.
When there were 2,000 records in the emp table, this query took 3 seconds.

Therefore I know that:
$y_1 = 2$ (seconds)
$x_1 = 1000$ (records)
$y_2 = 3$ (seconds)
$x_2 = 2000$ (records)

**Step 1: Find the slope of the line.**

$a_1 = (y_2 - y_1)/(x_2 - x_1)$
$a_1 = (3 - 2)/(2,000 - 1,000)$
$a_1 = 0.001$ (the slope of the line is 0.001)

**Step 2: Get the _y_-intercept.**

$a_0 = y_1 - a_{1x1}$
$a_0 = 2 - (0.001)(1000)$
$a_0 = 2 - 1$
$a_0 = 1$ (the _y_-intercept is 1)

**Step 3: Now you can calculate response for any size emp table.**

We now have everything that we need for this query. We can now figure out how long this query will take as the number of rows in the emp table increases.

What will the response time be for 3,000 rows?
$y = a_0 + a_1x$ (_y_ is the response time and _x_ is the number of rows in the table)

$y = 1 + (0.001)(3,000)$
$y = 1 + 3$
$y = 4$ seconds (the response time for this query in a 3,000-row emp table will be 4 seconds)

What will the response time be for 100,000 rows?
$y = a_0 + a_1 x$
$y = 1 + (0.001)(100,000)$
$y = 101$ seconds (the response time for a 100,000-row emp table will be 1 minute and 41 seconds)

# Simple Quadratic Equation Determination

Unfortunately, many queries don't behave in a linear manner. Consequently, the previous section doesn't always help us. But never fear—a simple method for curved lines is next. Once again, do not be intimidated by this section. You *will* be able to understand this and with this information you will be able to predict query scaling (predict any response time for an increased number of rows). The following is a simple three-point method for determining a quadratic best-performance equation. This is the equation that you will use

$y = a_0 + a_1 x + a_2 x^2$ (this is the final equation to use for nonlinear queries)
$y$ = response time for a query
$x$ = number of rows
$a_0, a_1, a_2$ = are constants derived based on the curve the query creates.

Figure 9-5 shows points from an ideal test. We visually select three points, $(0, y_0)$, $(x_1, y_1)$, and $(x_2, y_2)$ that appear to be of minimum slope on a quadratic like curve. The midpoint between x0 and $x_1$ is $x_a$, and the midpoint between $x_1$ and $x_2$ is $x_b$ such that

$x_a = (x_1 + 0)/2$ and $x_b = (x_2 + x_1)/2$

When joined, $(0, y_0)$ and $(x_1, y_1)$ form a secant with slope $S_a$, and $(x_1, y_1)$ and $(x_2, y_2)$ form a secant with slope $S_b$. The x midpoints $(x_a, y_a)$ and $(xb, yb)$ lie on the desired curve with tangents having slopes $S_a$ and $S_b$, respectively. From the derivative of a quadratic equation, which gives the slope of the curve at the midpoints, we have

$S_a = (y_1 - y_0)/(x_1 - 0) = a_1 + 2a_{2xa}$
$S_a$ = slope of the lower part of the curve
$S_b = (y_2 - y_1)/(x_2 - x_1) = a_1 + 2a_{2xb}$
$S_b$ = slope of the upper part of the curve

Using Gauss elimination, we solve for the $a_i$ coefficients such that

$$a_2 = (S_{b-Sa})/[2(x_b - x_a)] = (S_b - S_a)/x_2$$
$$a_1 = S_a - 2a_{2xa} = S_a - a_{2x1}$$
$$a_0 = y_0$$

I'll have to use these three equations to get $a_0$, $a_1$, and $a_2$, and then I can use my final equation. These will be the constants in our equation that will give us the response time of a query as we vary the number of rows in the table.

Note that the preceding method will not work in all cases. If any $a_i$ coefficients are negative, the equation may dip below the x-axis and something else must be used. Often, the origin of $a_0 = y_0 = 0$ works best with this method.

**A SIMPLE EXAMPLE**   All of these equations look great, but let's look at a real-life query. We must time the query based on two different table sizes to get an equation for the line. The orders table has an index on ordno, but it is suppressed by the NVL function (causing the nonlinear response time). The real fix to this problem is to

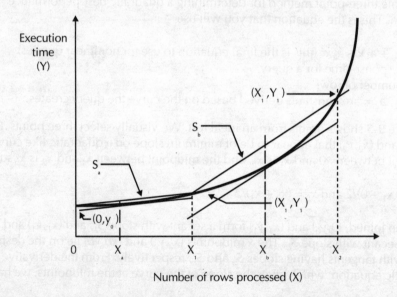

**FIGURE 9-5.**   *Quadratic best-performance curve*

eliminate nulls in the orders table and remove the NVL function from the query. However, this example is for instructional purposes to generate a quadratic equation.

```
select    ordno, total
from      orders
where     nvl(ordno,0) = 7777;
```

**For our system, consider the response of this query for two tests:**
When there were 100 records in the orders table, this query took 5 seconds.
When there were 2,000 records in the orders table, this query took 1,000 seconds.

I want to know how bad this query will be when I have 10,000 rows in the orders table.

Therefore, I know that:
$y_1 = 5$ (seconds)
$x_1 = 100$ (records)
$y_2 = 1000$ (seconds)
$x_2 = 2000$ (records)
$y_0 = 1$ (second - estimate); this is the $y$-intercept

I could calculate $y_0$ by using two points near the lower part of the curve (near 100 rows using the linear equations from the previous section), but since the lower part of the curve is small (5 seconds for 100 rows), I guesstimate this to be 1 second (you should calculate it).

## Step 1: Calculate $S_a$ and $S_b$.

$S_a = (y_1 - y_0)/ (x_1 - 0)$
$S_a = (5 - 1)/ (100 - 0)$
$S_a = 0.04$ (the slope of the lower part of the curve is almost horizontal)
$S_b = (y_2 - y_1)/ (x_2 - x_1)$
$S_b = (1,000 - 5)/ (2,000 - 100)$
$S_b = 0.52$ (the slope of the upper part of the curve; it's much higher than the lower part)

## Step 2: Calculate $a_0$, $a_1$, and $a_2$.

$a_2 = (S_b - S_a)/ x_2$
$a_2 = (0.52 - 0.04)/2,000$

$a_2 = 0.00024$
$a_1 = S_a - a_{2x1}$
$a_1 = 0.04 - (0.00024)(100)$
$a_1 = 0.016$
$a_0 = y_0$
$a_0 = 1$ (the $y$-intercept is 1)

**Step 3: Now create the equation to use as the table grows.**

$y = a_0 + a_{1x + a2x2}$
$y = 1 + (0.016)x + (0.00024)x^2$ (this is our equation to calculate future response)

**Step 4: Now calculate the *expected* response for 10,000 rows.**

$y = 1 + (0.016)x + (0.00024)x^2$
$y = 1 + (0.016)(10,000) + (0.00024)(10,000^2)$
$y = 24,161$ (the query will take 24,161 seconds or just under 7 hours…we have a problem)

I think that I'd better fix the NVL problem soon; I don't think that the users will want to wait 7 hours. But in reality, I have only calculated a couple of points, and this should really be extended out further to get a better future estimate of performance.

## Pattern Interpretation

Graphical performance patterns provide clues to underlying SQL problems and solutions, as seen in Figure 9-6. Our ultimate goal in using these methods is to convert a steep linear or quadratic best performance line to one that is both shallow and linear by optimizing the SQL process. This may involve experiments with indexes, temp tables, optimizer hint commands, or other methods of Oracle SQL performance tuning.

With pattern interpretation, it is important to do your own application-specific SQL experiments to develop an expertise at using these methods. The following are more specific interpretations—based on my personal experience—that provide a basic idea of how to apply what is observed directly to tuning SQL code. Provided the scale is correct, pattern interpretation will often provide a more accurate picture of what is actually happening to a process and may support or even contradict what a diagnostic tool may tell you.

| Pattern in Figure 9-6 | Possible Problem | Possible Solution |
|---|---|---|
| A | Missing index on a query SELECTing values | Create an index. Fix a suppressed index. |
| A | Overindexed table suffering during an INSERT | Delete some of the indexes or index fewer columns (or smaller columns) for the current indexes. |
| B | No problem | Don't touch it! |
| C | Missing index on a query SELECTing values | Create an index. Fix a suppressed index. |
| C | Overindexed table suffering during an INSERT | Delete some of the indexes or index fewer columns (or smaller columns) for the current indexes. |
| D | Doing a full table scan or using the ALL_ROWS hint when you shouldn't be | Try to do an indexed search. Try using the FIRST_ROWS hint to force the use of indexes. |
| E | The query was fine until some other limitation (such as disk I/O or memory) was encountered | You need to find which ceiling that you hit to cause this problem. Increasing the SGA may solve the problem, but this could be many things. |

## General Linear and Quadratic Interpretations

A shallow linear performance line usually indicates a relatively efficient process compared to something much steeper or curved. The slope $a_1$ indicates the rate $y$ increases for a given $x$. Scale is important since a shallow line on one scale can look steep on another and vice versa. A large $a_0$ coefficient always indicates an inefficient process.

An upward-sloping (concave) quadratic curve almost always indicates a problem with the process because as more rows are added, the time to process each additional row increases. Coefficient $a_2$ affects the bowing of the curve. If it is very small, the equation may be more linear. However, a very slight bowing may be an indicator of something more insidious under much higher volumes.

In rare cases, a quadratic curve might appear downward sloping (convex), indicating a process where as more rows are added the time to process each additional one decreases (i.e., economies of scale). This is desirable and may occur at a threshold, where a full table scan is more efficient than using an index.

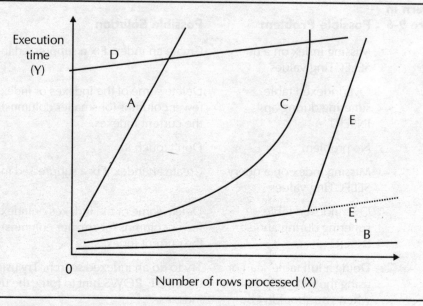

**FIGURE 9-6.** *Examples of performance patterns*

## Indexing

Missing indexes are a common cause of poor SQL performance. In Figure 9-6, line A or C could result from a missing index, depending on code complexity and data volume. Proper indexing improves performance to line B. Overindexing can be as bad as missing indexes. Line A or C could be a process that is forced to use an index whereas a full table scan would improve the process to B. Inserting into an indexed table is always slower than into an index-free table. Line A or C could be from an INSERT into a heavily indexed table versus line B with no indexing.

**INDEXING EXAMPLE**   The following illustrates what can happen with indexing analysis. Suppose we have two tables, table_a and table_b and there is a one-to-many relationship between them using key_field. There does not have to be a join between the two tables.

```
TABLE A
KEY_FIELD      NUMBER
TOTAL          NUMBER

TABLE B
KEY_FIELD      NUMBER
AMOUNT         NUMBER
```

We want to do the following update within a key_field:

```
table_a.total = table_a.total + sum(table_b.amount)
```

The following SQL statement will do this. Note that the EXISTS subquery must be used to prevent the NULLing out of any table_a.total fields where table_a.key_field does not match total_b.key_field.

```
update    table_a ta  set ta.total =
(select   ta.total + sum(tb.amount)
 from     table_b tb
 where    tb.key_field = ta.key_field
 group by ta.total)
where     exists
(select   null
 from     table_b tb2
 where    tb2.key_field = ta.key_field);
```

If there is a unique index on table_a.key_field and a nonunique index on table_b.key_field, then the performance will be similar to line B in Figure 9-6. However, if there is no index on table_b.key_field or the cost-based optimizer decides to shut it off, a line will be generated similar to A or C. The reason is that the EXISTS subquery is heavily dependent on indexing.

I have seen cases in Oracle7.3.2 of the preceding problem where the number of rows in table_a was small (< 2,000) but the cost-based optimizer shut off the index on table_b and reported a small EXPLAIN_PLAN cost. This was regardless of the number of rows in table_b (which was up to 800K rows). Actual tests showed a steep performance line that contradicted the EXPLAIN_PLAN cost. This is an example of uncovering a problem that may have been overlooked by a diagnostic tool.

When the optimizer (cost-based) finds a query to retrieve less than 5–6 percent (based on the average distribution) of the rows in a table, the optimizer will choose to drive the query with an index if one exists. Figure 9-7 shows how Oracle has evolved through the past years. While Oracle7 shows the best performance at all levels, the developer must know when to override the optimizer (see Chapter 8 for information about individual query tuning). Figure 9-7 shows the general curve of an indexed query.

## Optimizer Execution Plan

Graphing performance patterns can be used to leverage available diagnostic tools. For example, we analyzed a slow and complex SQL statement that used views, and ran high-volume data under the Oracle cost-based optimizer. Results showed a very high performance line identical to D in Figure 9-6. The Oracle EXPLAIN_PLAN also showed an inefficient execution plan. Once an effective optimizer HINT command

**Tuning Using Simple Mathematical Techniques**

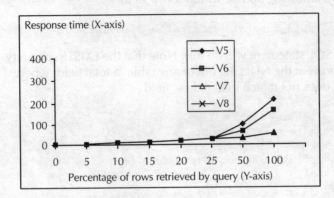

**FIGURE 9-7.** *Optimum percentage of rows for index for a given version of Oracle*

was found (i.e., FIRST_ROWS) and added directly to the SQL statements that defined the views, performance improved dramatically to line B.

## Multiple Table Joins

Complex multiple-table join statements often run poorly regardless of the conventional tuning used and may be similar to lines A or C in Figure 9-6. From past experience [2,3,4], rather than trying to only tune the statement with conventional techniques, a more effective solution is to decompose it into a series of simple SQL statements using temp tables. The final result would be the same but at much faster speed, represented by a composite line at B.

## Jackknifing

Jackknifing is a pattern where a performance line starts off shallow but then veers steeply upward at a certain threshold point, similar to E in Figure 9-6. Two linear equations may define the behavior; its cause could be anywhere from disk I/O or memory limitations to a switch in the optimizer execution plan due to changing data volumes. Possible solutions are to increase the systems limitations, run fresh optimizer statistics, use the rule-based optimizer, or break the statement into selection ranges. Proper tuning might either straighten out the line to $E_1$ or improve it further to line B.

## Riding the Quadratic Curve

Often, a poorly performing SQL process is designed and tested on low-volume data, but in production under higher volumes, its true and degrading quadratic nature is revealed, as shown by curve A in Figure 9-8. In this example, a process was created and tested up to $x_1$. Performance was believed to be close to line B, but once in production and the volume was increased to $x_3$, the line really turned out to be curve A.

If a proper tuning solution cannot be found, a quadratic process of unknown cause can still be improved by breaking the original statement into lower-volume selection ranges and riding the shallow part of the quadratic curve. Suppose in Figure 9-8 we break the process into three selection ranges, [0 to $x_0$] that rides the lower part of curve A, [from $x_1$ to $x_2$] that rides the lower part of curve $A_1$, and [from $x_2$ to $x_3$] that rides the lower part of curve $A_2$. The overall result is something closer to line B [from 0 to $x_3$] with $y_3$ a lot less time than the original $y_3$. While this technique may not be the best solution, it could still solve the problem.

## Mathematical Techniques Conclusions

Simple Mathematical Techniques is an effective Oracle SQL performance analysis and tuning methodology that involves running tests under ideal conditions, graphing performance observations, and using simple linear and quadratic equation determination for predicting performance at higher loads. It also includes the

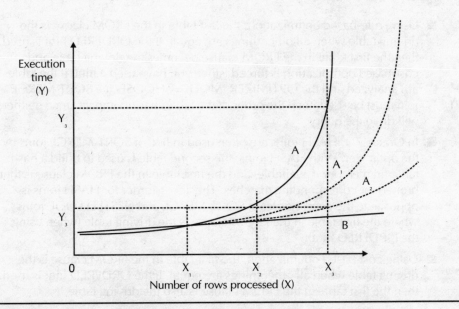

**FIGURE 9-8.** *Example of riding the quadratic curve*

interpretation of performance patterns that can be applied directly to tuning SQL code.

The methodology acts as a catalyst by combining the use of some traditional mathematical analysis with Oracle diagnostic tools in order to aid in their interpretation and to leverage their effectiveness. It can also help identify hidden problems that may be overlooked by other diagnostic methods by providing a broad picture of performance. The technique can also help overcome performance-tuning barriers such as inexperience with Oracle, lack of hard evidence, or difficulties with diagnostic tool interpretation that may prevent effective performance tuning. Graphs provide a visual picture of performance for presentation to management and end users.

**TIP**

*If you want an Oracle symphony as great as Beethoven's, you must learn and know how to apply mathematical techniques to your tuning efforts. You don't have to learn everything that you learned in college calculus; simply apply the simple equations in this chapter to tie everything in this book together. Thank you Joe Holmes for doing the math for us!*

# Tips Review

- Using rule-based optimization, the last table in the FROM clause is the driving table when all other things are equal. If the ORDERED hint is used, then the first table in the FROM clause becomes the driving table and cost-based optimization is forced (since you have used a hint) if the tables are analyzed and the OPTIMIZER_MODE=CHOOSE. If a SORT-MERGE join must be used, then the order of the tables has no impact since neither will drive the query.

- In Oracle 7.3, HASH joins are often used in lieu of SORT-MERGE joins by the optimizer. With HASH joins, the second table is used to build a hash table (in memory if available) and the first table in the FROM clause is then probed for corresponding matches. The access order for HASH joins is opposite to the access order of SORT-MERGE and NESTED LOOP joins where the first table in the FROM clause is the driving table (when using the ORDERED hint).

- Using cost-based optimization, the first table in the FROM clause is the driving table when all other things are equal. If the ORDERED hint is used, then the first table in the FROM clause is also the driving table.

■ Using cost-based optimization and NESTED LOOPS as the means of joining, the first table in the FROM clause is the driving table (all other things being equal), but only the ORDERED hint will guarantee this. In NESTED LOOPS joins, choosing a driving table that is the smaller result set (not always the smaller table) will mean making less loops to the other result set (from the nondriving table) and will usually result in the best performance.

■ The columns that are retrieved can change which indexes Oracle will use and also change the way that Oracle will join the tables in the query.

■ The RULE hint can change the way that a query is joined and also change which indexes are used.

■ To change the way that Oracle joins multiple tables, use the USE_MERGE, USE_NL, and USE_HASH hints.

■ In a three-table join, the driving table is the intersection table or the table that has a join condition to each of the other two tables in the join. Try to use the most limiting table as the driving table (or intersection table) so that your result set from the join of the first two tables is small when you join it to the third table. Also, ensure that all join conditions on all tables are indexed!

■ In Oracle 7.3 when using cost-based optimization, when a large and small table are joined, Oracle will put the larger table in a hash table and scan it with the small table regardless of the order in the FROM clause. If the ORDERED hint is specified, then the first table in the FROM clause will be the driving table and the second table will be put in a hash table.

■ Using cost-based optimization, when a large and small table are joined, the larger table is the driving table if an index can be used on the large table. If the ORDERED hint is specified, then the first table in the FROM clause will be the driving table.

■ Using cost-based optimization, when a large and small table are joined and the join condition is indexed but a subsequent statement on the large table suppresses the subsequent index, the larger table is accessed first and without using indexes on either table. This is undesirable! By using an INDEX hint, you should force the use of an index on the large table.

■ When a concatenated index on the larger table of a join does not include the join condition as the leading edge of the index, that index on the subsequent part of the query must be forced or a full table scan on all tables could result.

**Tips Review**

- To ensure that you are reading your EXPLAIN PLAN correctly, run a query for which you are sure of the driving table (with nested subqueries).

- The order in the FROM clause determines the driving order of the tables in general. However, the joining of the tables and the indexing regarding those joins will also change the order that Oracle accesses the tables. Only the ORDERED hint will guarantee a join order. The joining column on all tables should be indexed!

- When the cost-based optimizer will use an index depends on the size of the table. For larger tables, the breakpoint is around 4 percent. For smaller tables (less than 1,000 rows), the breakpoint is closer to 1 percent for SELECTs and still at 4 percent for UPDATE and DELETE operations.

- You may not be able to modify actual code for some third-party products, but you can often add, force, or suppress indexes to improve the performance.

- When distributed queries cannot be avoided, use IN clauses, set operators such as UNION and MINUS, and whatever else you can to reduce the network traffic between nodes of the database. Queries written in a manner that cause looping between distributed nodes (distributed databases) can be extremely slow.

- If you want an Oracle symphony as great as Beethoven's, you must learn and know how to apply mathematical techniques to your tuning efforts. You don't have to learn everything that you learned in college calculus; simply apply the simple equations in this chapter to tie everything in this book together. Thank you Joe Holmes!

- If you've read and understood this entire chapter, you probably represent 5 percent of all tuning professionals and you will see the heights and joys that exists with tuning Oracle.

## References

Tuning Joins: Roger Schrag, Database Specialists.

Chapra, S., & R. Canale, *Numerical Methods for Engineers; with Programming and Software Applications,* Third Edition, McGraw-Hill Book Co., 1998.

Holmes, J. A., "The path to better performance," *Database Programming & Design Magazine,* 8(4), Apr. 1995, Miller Freeman, pp. 47–49.

Holmes, J. A., "More paths to better performance," *Database Programming & Design Magazine,* 9(2), Feb. 1996, Miller Freeman, pp. 47–48.

Holmes, J. A., "Solve SQL Puzzles Using TEMP Tables (letter to the editor)," *Database Programming & Design Magazine*, 8(12), Nov. 1996, Miller Freeman, pp. 6–8.

Aronoff, E., K. Loney, & N. Sonawalla, "*Advanced Oracle Tuning and Administration,*" Oracle Press, Osborne/McGraw-Hill, 1997.

Corrigan, P. & M. Gurry, "Oracle Performance Tuning," O'Reilly & Associates, Inc., 1993.

Draper, N. & H. Smith, *Applied Regression Analysis*, Second Edition, John Wiley & Sons, Inc., 1980.

Holmes, J. A., "Canned Database Querying and Reporting," Paper presented at ECO92, Mar. 1992, Rockville, MD.

Holmes, J. A., "Boilerplate/Hotkey Bilingualization Using Row-wise Normal Form," *ECO93 Proceedings*, Philadelphia, PA, Mar. 1993, Oracle User Resource, Inc., pp. 163–166.

Holmes, J. A., "Dynamic boilerplate text and multilingual applications; The Row-wise Normal Form Solution," *Oracle Integrator Magazine*, Aug. 1993, Oracle Corp., pp. 25–26.

Holmes, J. A., "SQL Performance Analysis and Tuning Using Simple Mathematical Techniques," *The Carleton Journal of Computer Science*, No. 2, 1998, Carleton University Press, Inc., Ottawa, ON, pp. 9–14.

Jain, R., *The Art of Computer Systems Performance Analysis; Techniques for Experimental Design, Measurement, Simulation and Modelling*, John Wiley & Sons, Inc., 1991.

Lethbridge, T. C., "The Relevance of Software Education: A Survey and Some Recommendations," *11th Conference of Software Engineering Education and Training*, Atlanta, GA, 1998, (in press for the Annals of Software Engineering).

Special thanks to Joe Trezzo, Roger Schrag, Joe Holmes, Sean McGuire, Judy Corley, Greg Pucka, Jake Van der Vort, Randy Swanson, Bob Taylor, and Mark Greenhalgh for contributions to this chapter.

Tips Review

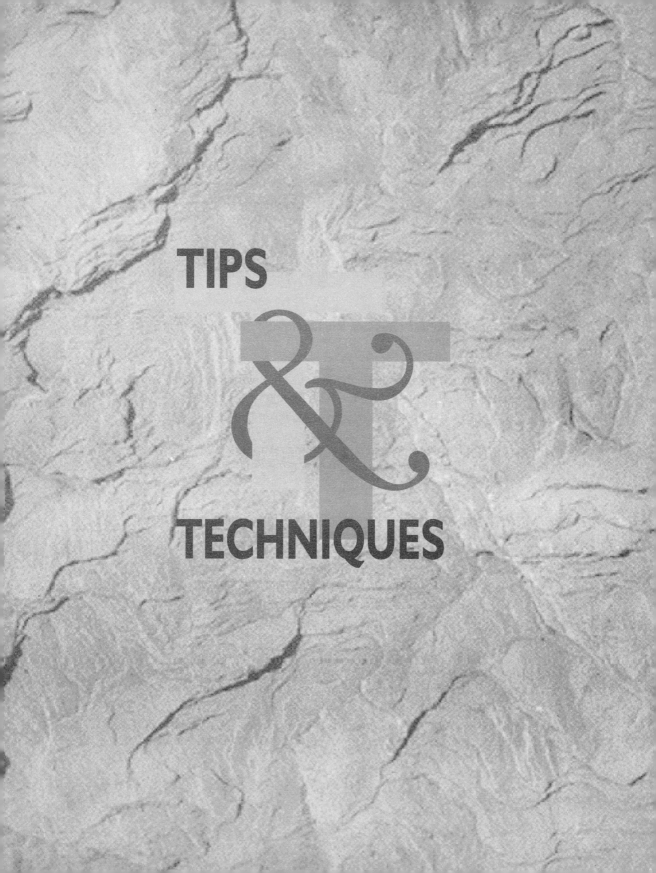

TIPS
&
TECHNIQUES

# CHAPTER
## 10

# Using PL/SQL to Enhance Performance (Developer and DBA)

TIPS
&
COVERED

The PL/SQL engine processes all PL/SQL requests and passes the statements to Oracle for execution. When PL/SQL is passed to Oracle, it is placed in Oracle's System Global Area (SGA), more particularly in the Shared Pool. In Oracle, PL/SQL source code can be stored in the database in the form of procedures, functions, packages, and triggers. Once these objects are stored in the database in compiled format, they can be executed from any Oracle tool by any user that has been granted EXECUTE privilege on that object. Upon execution, the p-code (executable code) is loaded into the SGA Shared Pool and executed by Oracle. A PL/SQL object remains in the SGA Shared Pool until the object is aged out with a Least Recently Used (LRU) algorithm. Therefore, if any processes call the object, it does not have to be reloaded into the SGA Shared Pool as long as it has not been aged out. Therefore, Oracle will look in the SGA Shared Pool (which is very efficient) for the object prior to going to disk (which is not as efficient) to load the object. How well the SQL within the PL/SQL is tuned is probably the biggest driving factor of performance, yet there are also other tuning enhancement considerations that will be covered in this chapter. The first portion of this chapter is dedicated to understanding and being able to locate the PL/SQL. Tips covered in this chapter include:

- Reusing memory with PL/SQL
- Finding PL/SQL *not* using bind variables
- Finding reusable PL/SQL with V$SQLAREA view
- Finding specific objects in the Shared Pool
- Flushing the Shared Pool when errors occur
- Pinning objects in the Shared Pool
- Identifying the PL/SQL that needs to be pinned
- Using PL/SQL to pin all packages into the Shared Pool
- Using and modifying DBMS_SHARED_POOL.SIZES
- Getting detailed object information from DBA_OBJECT_SIZE
- Finding invalid objects
- Finding disabled triggers
- Using PL/SQL for fast reference table lookups
- Accessing USER_SOURCE, USER_TRIGGERS, and USER_DEPENDENCIES
- PL/SQL and Oracle's DATE data type
- Using PL/SQL to tune PL/SQL

- PL/SQL location implications
- Don't reference form fields within the body of a trigger or program unit
- Specifying a rollback segment for a large cursor
- Modifying SQL.BSQ to avoid data dictionary fragmentation
- Samples just for the beginners (beginners start here)

# Reusing Memory with PL/SQL

If a PL/SQL block is written without the use of stored PL/SQL objects, when the PL/SQL block is executed, the block is passed to the Oracle kernal—where it is compiled into p-code and then compared to the SGA Shared Pool to determine if the p-code already exists in the SGA Shared Pool. If it already exists, the p-code is executed. If it does not exist, the p-code is loaded into the SGA Shared Pool and executed. The next time this PL/SQL block is executed by a user, the Oracle kernal will again process the execution request as described.

Oracle is very particular about its PL/SQL code-matching algorithm and will treat PL/SQL code as a new block unless the code is identical, including case, spacing, and carriage returns. The method in which the Oracle kernal processes PL/SQL code is the same as it processes SQL statements sent to the Oracle kernal, including the matching algorithm. Therefore, the following three examples illustrate this handling with a SQL statement:

1. Exact Match
   a. *UPDATE ORDER_MAIN SET ORDER_DATE = SYSDATE;*
   b. *UPDATE ORDER_MAIN SET ORDER_DATE = SYSDATE;*
2. Not Exact Match
   a. *UPDATE ORDER_MAIN SET ORDER_DATE = sysdate;*
   b. *UPDATE ORDER_MAIN SET ORDER_DATE = SYSDATE;*
3. Not Exact Match
   a. *UPDATE ORDER_MAIN SET ORDER_DATE = SYSDATE;*
   b. *UPDATE ORDER_MAIN*
   *SET ORDER_DATE = SYSDATE;*

In Example 1, both 1a and 1b are written *exactly* the same. The code that is in the Shared Pool after the first query (a) is run, is reused when the second query (b) is submitted. But in Examples 2 and 3, the code is not reused due to subtle differences.

**Resusing Memory**

In Example 2, the statements differ in the case (UPPER and lower) of the word sysdate. In Example 3, the statements differ only in terms of line spacing. By storing PL/SQL in the databases, problems like those of Examples 2 and 3 would be eliminated.

**TIP**
*For PL/SQL to be reused in memory, it must be written exactly the same. This is the benefit of storing code in packages, procedures, and triggers. Ensure that developers and DBAs call PL/SQL from the database to guarantee that the same piece of code is not reloaded due to differences in how it is written.*

# Finding PL/SQL *Not* Using Bind Variables

There are a couple of methods you can use to view the Shared Pool contents. One method is to query the V$SQLAREA view. This will provide access to the current contents of the Shared Pool at a point in time. Objects in the Shared Pool are aged out over time depending on the LRU algorithm. An object residing in the Shared Pool will not be aged out if currently in use by a session.

Many times, there is PL/SQL code that is exactly the same *except* there is a variable or value that changes from one statement to another. These are difficult to track down. Educating developers to use bind variables versus hard-coding constants into a statement is the key. Consider the three following statements:

```
select     line_no, cust_no, cust_type
from       orders
where      cust_no = 5571;

select     line_no, cust_no, cust_type
from       orders
where      cust_no = 7321;

select     line_no, cust_no, cust_type
from       orders
where      cust_no = 7777;
```

These statements should be replaced by using a bind variable for the constant. The replacement statement is displayed here:

```
select     line_no, cust_no, cust_type
from       orders
where      cust_no = :custno;
```

One way to find these types of statements is shown in the next example. By varying the length of the matching SQL_TEXT, you can find statements that are similar and that may be candidates for bind variables. You can also vary the HAVING clause to set how many matches will be retrieved.

```
select    substr(sql_text, 1, 20) sqltext, count(*)
from      v$sqlarea
group by  substr(sql_text, 1, 20)
having    count(*) > 10;
```

**TIP**
*Use bind variables instead of constants to avoid fragmenting the Shared Pool. By accessing V$SQLAREA view, you can find potential candidates that need bind variables.*

# Finding Reusable PL/SQL with V$SQLAREA and Specific Objects

Another problem area to identify is pieces of code that match except for differences in the case (UPPER or lower). This is a modification to the query in the previous section:

```
select    upper(substr(sql_text, 1, 20)) sqltext, count(*)
from      v$sqlarea
group by  upper(substr(sql_text, 1, 20))
having    count(*) > 10;
```

You can also use V$SQLAREA view to find references to particular objects. This is helpful to find statements that reference an object that you know has problems. Following is a query against the V$SQLAREA view that will search the contents of the SGA Shared Pool for references to particular objects. This example is searching for any reference to order_main.

```
select    sql_text
from      v$sqlarea
where     instr(upper(sql_text), 'ORDER_MAIN',1) > 0;
```

**TIP**
*Access V$SQLAREA view to find case (UPPER and lower) issues or to find a particular object that is problematic.*

# Shared Pool and Pinning PL/SQL Objects

The SHARED_POOL_SIZE sets the amount of Shared Pool allocated in the SGA (see Chapter 4 and Appendix A for a detailed look at SHARED_POOL_SIZE and closely related Shared Pool parameters). The Shared Pool stores all SQL statements and PL/SQL blocks executed under the Oracle database. Based on the method in which Oracle manages the SGA Shared Pool, as far as aging, the SGA Shared Pool can become fragmented. In addition, since Oracle will not age out any objects that are currently being processed by a session, there is the possibility that you can get an Oracle error indicating that the SGA Shared Pool does not have enough memory for a new object. The exact error message that a user will receive is "ORA-4031: unable to allocate $X$ bytes of shared memory" (where $X$ is the number of bytes it is attempting to allocate). If this error is ever received, it means that your SGA Shared Pool should be increased in size as soon as possible. To do this, modify the init.ora parameter SHARED_POOL_SIZE and then shut down and start up the database. The quick method of eliminating this error until the next database shutdown is to flush the SGA Shared Pool. This can be accomplished with the following command (only allowed if ALTER SYSTEM privilege is assigned to a user):

```
alter system flush shared_pool;
```

The key to never having to flush the Shared Pool is to pin the large objects into the Shared Pool when the database has started and make sure that the shared pool is large enough for all statements that will be cached.

 **TIP**
*When Shared Pool fragmentation errors occur, you can flush the Shared Pool using the ALTER SYSTEM FLUSH SHARED_POOL command.*

## Pinning (Caching) PL/SQL Object Statements into Memory

In the event that you cannot maintain a sufficient SHARED_POOL_SIZE, it may become important to keep the most important objects cached (pinned) in memory. The following example shows how to pin PL/SQL object statements (the procedure PROCESS_DATE is pinned in this example) in memory using the DBMS_SHARED_POOL.KEEP procedure (DBMS_SHARED_POOL is the package):

```
begin
dbms_shared_pool.keep('process_date','p');
end;
```

or

```
execute    dbms_shared_pool.keep ('SYS.STANDARD');
```

By pinning an object in memory, the object will not be aged out or flushed until the next database shutdown.

**TIP**
*Use the DBMS_SHARED_POOL.KEEP procedure to pin PL/SQL objects into the shared pool.*

## Pinning All Packages

To pin all packages in the system, execute the following (from Oracle's Metalink):

```
declare
own varchar2(100);
nam varchar2(100);
cursor pkgs is
    select     owner, object_name
    from       dba_objects
    where      object_type = 'PACKAGE';
begin
    open pkgs;
    loop
        fetch pkgs into own, nam;
        exit when pkgs%notfound;
        dbms_shared_pool.keep(own || '.' || nam, 'P');
    end loop;
end;
```

Common problem packages that are shipped with Oracle (and should be kept) include STANDARD, DBMS_STANDARD, and DIUTIL.

**TIP**
*Use the DBMS_SHARED_POOL.KEEP procedure to pin objecs into the Shared Pool. You can also use the PL/SQL procedure listed in this section to pin all packages into memory when the database is started (if memory/Shared Pool permits). This will help you to avoid errors involving loading packages when there isn't enough contiguous memory.*

**Shared Pool**

# Identifying PL/SQL Objects that Need to Be Pinned

Fragmentation that causes several small pieces to be available in the Shared Pool, and not enough large contiguous pieces, is a common occurrence. The key to eliminating Shared Pool errors (as noted in the previous section) is to recognize which of the objects will be large enough to cause problems when you attempt to load them. Once you know the problem PL/SQL, you can then pin this code when the database has started (and the shared pool is completely contiguous). This will guarantee that your large packages are already in the Shared Pool when they are called, instead of searching for a large contiguous piece of the Shared Pool (which may not be there later as the system is used). You can query the V$DB_OBJECT_CACHE view to determine the PL/SQL that is both large and currently not marked kept. This will only show the current statements in the cache. The example here searches for those objects requiring greater than 100K.

```
select    name, sharable_mem
from      v$db_object_cache
where     sharable_mem > 100000
and       type in ('PACKAGE', 'PACKAGE BODY', 'FUNCTION',
          'PROCEDURE')
and       kept = 'NO';
```

**TIP**
*Query the V$DB_OBJECT_CACHE view to find objects that are not pinned and are large enough to potentially cause problems.*

# Using and Modifying DBMS_SHARED_POOL.SIZES

An alternative and very precise indication of Shared Pool allocation can be viewed through the DBMS_SHARED_POOL.SIZES procedure. This call accepts a *minimum size* parameter and will display all cursors and objects within the Shared Pool of a size greater than that provided. The actual statement executed to retrieve this information is as follows:

```
select     to_char(sharable_mem / 1000 ,'999999') sz, decode
           (kept_versions,0,' ',rpad('yes(' || to_char(kept_versions)
           || ')' ,6)) keeped, rawtohex(address) || ',' || to_char
           (hash_value)  name, substr(sql_text,1,354) extra, 1 iscursor
from       v$sqlarea
where      sharable_mem > &min_ksize * 1000
union
select     to_char(sharable_mem / 1000 ,'999999') sz,
decode(kept,'yes',
           'yes   ','') keeped, owner || '.'  || name  || lpad(' ',29 -
           (length(owner) + length(name) ) )  || '(' || type || ')'
            name, null  extra, 0 iscursor
from       v$db_object_cache v
where      sharable_mem > &min_ksize * 1000
order by   1 desc;
```

This query can be placed into a procedure package, of your own construction, to display a formatted view of cursors and objects within the Shared Pool.

## Finding Large Objects

You can use DBMS_SHARED_POOL.SIZES procedure to view the objects using shareable memory higher than a threshold that you set. Execute this package as displayed here for a threshold of 100K (the output follows):

```
begin
dbms_shared_pool.sizes(100);
end;

SIZE(K)    KEPT       NAME
118        YES        SYS.STANDARD          (PACKAGE)
109                   SELECT    DT.OWNER,DT.TABLE_NAME,DT.TABLESPACE_NAME,
                                DT.INITIAL_EXTTENT,DT.NEXT_EXTENT,DT.NUM_ROWS,
                                DT.AVG_ROW_LEN,
                                SUM(DE.BYTES) PHY_SIZE
                      FROM      DBA_TABLES DT,DBA_SEGMENTS DE
                      WHERE     DT.OWNER = DE.OWNER
                      AND       DT.TABLE_NAME = DE.SEGMENT_NAME
                      AND       DT.TABLESPACE_NAME = DE.TABLESPACE_NAME
                      GROUP BY  DT.OWNER,DT.TABLE_NAME,DT.TABLESPACE_NAME,
                                DT.INITIAL_EXTENT,DT.NEX
                                (0B14559C,3380846737)    (CURSOR)
22                    RDBA.RDBA_GENERATE_STATISTICS (PACKAGE)

PL/SQL procedure successfully completed.
```

> **TIP**
> *Use the DBMS_SHARED_POOL.SIZES package procedure to find specific information about an object. This package may be modified to invent a package of your own.*

# Get Detailed Object Information from DBA_OBJECT_SIZE

Query the DBA_OBJECT_SIZE view to show the amount of memory used by a particular object, including detailed information concerning the object.

```
Compute sum of source_size on report
Compute sum of parsed_size on report
Compute sum of code_size on report
Break on report
select    *
from      dba_object_size
where     name = 'RDBA_GENERATE_STATISTICS';
```

| OWNER | NAME | TYPE | SOURCE SIZE | PARSED SIZE | CODE SIZE |
|-------|------|------|-------------|-------------|-----------|
| RDBA | RDBA_GENERATE_STATISTICS | PACKAGE | 5023 | 4309 | 3593 |
| RDBA | RDBA_GENERATE_STATISTICS | PACKAGE BODY | 85595 | 0 | 111755 |
| SUM | | | 90618 | 4309 | 115348 |

## Getting Contiguous Space Currently in the Shared Pool

Why does the Shared Pool return errors when an object is loaded? The answer is that a large enough piece of the Shared Pool is not available to fit the piece of code. We saw in the last section how to find the size of a piece of code. We also saw in a previous section how to pin pieces of code into the Shared Pool. Now, we must look at the query that will tell you which code, that has made it into the Shared Pool, is either very large and should be pinned or should be investigated and shortened if possible.

The following query accesses an x$ table (see Chapter 15), and you must be the SYS user to access these tables:

```
select    ksmchsiz, ksmchcom
from      x$ksmsp
where     ksmchsiz > 10000
and       ksmchcom like '%PL/SQL%'.
```

This query shows that the packages that have been accessed are very large and should be pinned at the time that the database has been started. If the last line of this query is eliminated, it will also show the large pieces of free memory (KSMCHCOM = 'free memory' and KSMCHCOM = 'permanent memory') that are still available (unfragmented) for future large pieces of code to be loaded. See Chapter 15 for further information regarding the x$ tables and example output.

**TIP**
*Query X$KSMSP to find all large pieces of PL/SQL that have appeared in the Shared Pool. These are candidates to be pinned when the database has been started.*

# Finding Invalid Objects

Developers often change a small section of PL/SQL code that fails to compile upon execution, forcing an application failure. A simple query, reviewed daily, will help you spot these failures before the end user does:

```
col        "Owner" format a12
col        "Object" format a20
col        "OType" format a12
col        "Change DTE" format a20
select     substr(owner,1,12) "Owner", substr(object_name,1,20)
           "Object", object_type "OType", to_char(last_ddl_time,
           'DD-MON-YYYY HH24:MI:SS') "Change Date"
from       dba_objects
where      status <> 'VALID'
order by   1, 2;
```

This example will display any objects that are INVALID, meaning they were never compiled successfully or changes in dependent objects have caused them to become INVALID. If we had a procedure PROCESS_DATE, for example, found to be INVALID, we could manually recompile this procedure with the following command:

```
alter procedure PROCESS_DATE compile;
```

Once this command is executed and the PROCESS_DATE passes the recompile, the procedure would be changed by Oracle automatically from INVALID to VALID. Another manual method that exists calls the DBMS_UTILITY.COMPILE_SCHEMA package procedure as outlined next to recompile all stored procedures, functions, and packages for a given schema:

```
begin
dbms_utility.compile_schema('USERA');
end;
```

To find the state of all objects for your schema, execute the following:

```
column     object_name  format a20
column     last_ddl_time heading 'last ddl time'
select     object_type, object_name, status, created, last_ddl_time
from       user_objects
where      object_type in ('procedure', 'function', 'package',
           'package body', 'trigger');
```

| OBJECT TYPE | OBJECT NAME | STATUS | CREATED | Last ddl |
|---|---|---|---|---|
| PACKAGE | DBMS_ALERT | VALID | 07-DEC-94 | 07-DEC-94 |
| PACKAGE | DBMS_DDL | VALID | 07-DEC-94 | 07-DEC-94 |
| PACKAGE | DBMS_DEFER_SYS | VALID | 07-DEC-94 | 07-DEC-94 |
| PACKAGE | DBMS_DESCRIBE | VALID | 07-DEC-94 | 07-DEC-94 |
| PACKAGE | DBMS_JOB | VALID | 07-DEC-94 | 07-DEC-94 |
| PACKAGE | DBMS_LOCK | VALID | 07-DEC-94 | 07-DEC-94 |
| PACKAGE | DBMS_OUTPUT | VALID | 07-DEC-94 | 07-DEC-94 |
| PACKAGE | DBMS_PIPE | VALID | 07-DEC-94 | 07-DEC-94 |
| PACKAGE | DBMS_REFRESH | VALID | 07-DEC-94 | 07-DEC-94 |
| PACKAGE | DBMS_SESSION | VALID | 07-DEC-94 | 07-DEC-94 |
| PACKAGE | DBMS_SNAPSHOT | VALID | 07-DEC-94 | 07-DEC-94 |
| PACKAGE | DBMS_SQL | VALID | 07-DEC-94 | 07-DEC-94 |
| PACKAGE | DBMS_STANDARD | VALID | 07-DEC-94 | 07-DEC-94 |
| PACKAGE | DBMS_SYS_ERROR | VALID | 07-DEC-94 | 07-DEC-94 |
| PACKAGE | DBMS_SYS_SQL | VALID | 07-DEC-94 | 07-DEC-94 |
| PACKAGE | DBMS_TRANSACTION | VALID | 07-DEC-94 | 07-DEC-94 |
| PACKAGE | DBMS_UTILITY | VALID | 07-DEC-94 | 07-DEC-94 |

 **TIP**
*Query DBA_OBJECTS (for system-wide objects) or
USER_OBJECT (for your schema only) to find the state
of objects and avoid errors and reloading by the user.
You can recompile individual objects or an entire
schema with the DBMS_UTILITY.COMPILE_SCHEMA
procedure.*

**Finding Invalid Objects**

# Finding Disabled Triggers

In some respects a disabled trigger is far more dangerous than an invalid object because it doesn't fail—*it just doesn't execute!* This can have severe consequences for applications, and consequently business processes, that depend on business logic stored within procedural code. The following script will identify disabled triggers:

```
col        "Owner/Table" format a30
col        "Trigger Name" format a20
col        "Event" format a12
select     substr(owner,12) "Owner", trigger_name "Trigger Name",
           trigger_type "Type", triggering_event "Event",
           table_owner||'.'||table_name "Owner/Table"
from       dba_triggers
where      status <> 'ENABLED'
order by   owner, trigger_name;
```

To find all triggers for your schema, execute the following:

```
column     trigger_name      format a15
column     trigger_type      format a15
column     triggering_event  format a15
column     table_name        format a15
column     trigger_body      format a25
select     trigger_name, trigger_type, triggering_event,
           table_name, status, trigger_body
from       user_triggers;
```

| TRIGGER NAME | TRIGGER TYPE | TRIGGERING EVENT | TABLE NAME | STATUS | TRIGGER BODY |
|---|---|---|---|---|---|
| UPDATE_TOTAL | AFTER STATEMENT | INSERT OR UPDATE OR DELETE | ORDER_MAIN | ENABLED | begin<br>  update total_orders<br>  set order_total = 10;<br>  end; |

**TIP**
*Query DBA_TRIGGERS (for system-wide objects) or
USER_TRIGGERS (for your schema only) to find the
state of triggers and avoid errors with disabled triggers.
Disabled triggers can have fatal results for an
application—they don't fail, they just don't execute.*

# Using PL/SQL Tables for Fast Reference Table Lookups

Programs that are designed to process data coming into a system usually incorporate numerous reference table lookups to properly validate and/or code the incoming data. When the reference tables are searched, using a unique key that is a numerical data type, the query performance against the reference tables can be drastically increased by loading the reference tables into PL/SQL tables. Consider an incoming data set that contains a single numerical column that must be translated to a coded string using a reference table. Following is a program to handle this task using the classic approach of repeated searches against the reference table:

```
declare
New_Code varchar2(10);
cursor C1 (The_Code IN number) is
    select      ref_string
    from        Ref_Table
    where       ref_num = The_Code;
  cursor CMain is
    select      *
    from        incoming_data;
begin
  -- Open a cursor to the incoming data.
  for In_Data in CMain loop
    begin
      -- Calculate the reference string from the
      -- reference data.
      open C1(In_Data.coded_value);
      fetch C1 into New_Code;
      if C1%notfound then
        close C1;
        raise NO_DATA_FOUND;
      end if;
      close C1;
      -- processing logic...
      -- Commit each record as it is processed.
      commit;
    exception
      when NO_DATA_FOUND then
        -- Appropriate steps...
      when OTHERS then
        -- Appropriate steps...
    end;
  end loop;
end;
```

While this program may appear to be written efficiently, it is in fact hampered by the repeated queries against the reference table. Even though Oracle may have the entire reference table in memory, due to pinning or prior queries, there is still a certain amount of overhead involved with processing the queries.

A more efficient technique is to load the entire reference table into a PL/SQL table. The numerical column (that the searches are performed against) is loaded as the array index. When a lookup against the reference data is required, the PL/SQL table is used instead of the actual reference table—the code in the incoming data that must be translated is used as the array index of the PL/SQL table. The inherent nature of working with PL/SQL tables is that if an INVALID array index is used (meaning the code in the incoming data does not match any value in the reference table), then the NO_DATA_FOUND exception will be raised. Next is the same processing program rewritten using a PL/SQL table to store the reference data:

```
declare
  type Ref_Dat_Array is table of varchar2(10)
  index by binary_integer;
  Ref_Dat  Ref_Dat_Array;
  New_Code varchar2(10);
  cursor C1 is
    select *
    from Ref_Table;
  cursor CMain is
    select *
    from incoming_data;
begin
  -- First, load the reference array
  -- with data from the reference table.
  for C1_Rec in C1 loop
    Ref_Dat(C1_Rec.Ref_Num) := C1_Rec.Ref_String;
  end loop;
  -- Open a cursor to the incoming data.
  for In_Data in CMain loop
    begin
      -- Calculate the reference string from the
      -- reference data.
      New_Code := Ref_Dat(In_Data.coded_value);
      -- processing logic...
      -- Commit each record as it is processed.
      commit;
    exception
      when NO_DATA_FOUND then
        -- Appropriate steps...
      when OTHERS then
        -- Appropriate steps...
    end;
  end loop;
end;
```

Fast Referencing

The result should be a drastic increase in processing speed due to the reduced overhead in working with the PL/SQL tables in comparison to the actual database table.

**TIP**
*Load reference tables into PL/SQL tables for faster lookups. This takes advantage of the performance of array indexes in PL/SQL.*

# Finding and Tuning the SQL When Objects Are Used

At times, the hardest part of tuning stored objects is finding the actual code that is stored in the database. This section will look at queries that will retrieve the SQL that can be tuned. We will query views that retrieve information about the actual source code that exists behind the stored objects.

Retrieving the code for a procedure you created called PROCESS_DATE:

```
column     text   format a80
select     text
from       user_source
where      name = 'PROCESS_DATE'
order by   line;

TEXT
procedure process_date is
  test_num number;
 begin
 test_num := 10;
 if test_num = 10 then
  update order_main
  set        process_date = sysdate
  where   order_num = 12345;
 end if;
 end;
```

Retrieving the code for the DBMS_JOB package:

```
column     text format a80
select     text
from       user_source
where      name  = 'DBMS_JOB'
and        type  = 'PACKAGE'
order by line;
```

```
TEXT
PACKAGE dbms_job IS
  -- Parameters are:
  -- JOB is the number of the job being executed.
  -- WHAT is the PL/SQL procedure to execute.
  --    The job must always be a single call to a procedure.  The
  --      routine may take any number of hardcoded parameters.
  --      Special parameter values recognized are:
  --        job:      an in parameter, the number of the current job
  --        next_date: in/out, the date of the next refresh
  --        broken:   in/out, is the job broken.  The IN values is FALSE.
PROCEDURE isubmit         ( job      IN  BINARY_INTEGER,
                            what      IN  VARCHAR2,
                            next_date IN  VARCHAR2,
                            interval  IN  VARCHAR2 DEFAULT 'null',
                            no_parse  IN  BOOLEAN DEFAULT FALSE );
  -- Submit a new job with a given job number.
```

Attempting to retrieve the package body for the DBMS_JOB package:

```
column    text  format a80
select    text
from      user_source
where     name = 'DBMS_JOB'
and       type = 'PACKAGE BODY'
order by  line;


TEXT
PACKAGE BODY dbms_job COMPRESS
0
abcd
abcd
     .        .        .
:2 a0 6b d a0 ac :3 a0 6b b2
ee :2 a0 7e b4 2e ac e5 d0
b2 e9 93 a0 7e 51 b4 2e
:2 a0 6b 7e 51 b4 2e 6e a5
57 b7 19 3c b0 46 :2 a0 6b
ac :2 a0 b2 ee ac e5 d0 b2
e9 :2 a0 6b :3 a0 6e :4 a0 :5 4d a5
57 :2 a0 a5 57 b7 :3 a0 7e 51
```

In this example, the package was wrapped (protected) and the output is unreadable. This is accomplished by using the WRAP command.

Retrieve the package body for the DBMS_OUTPUT package:

```
column    text  format a80
select    text
from      user_source
where     name = 'DBMS_OUTPUT'
and       type = 'PACKAGE BODY'
```

```
order by line;

TEXT
package body dbms_output as
  enabled          boolean := FALSE;
  buf_size         binary_integer;
  tmpbuf           varchar2(500)  := '';
  putidx           binary_integer := 1;
  amtleft          binary_integer := 0;
  getidx           binary_integer := 2;
  getpos           binary_integer := 1;
  get_in_progress boolean := TRUE;
  type char_arr is table of varchar2(512) index by binary_integer;
  buf  char_arr;
  idxlimit binary_integer;
procedure enable (buffer_size in integer default 20000) is
  lstatus integer;
```

In this example, the package is *not* wrapped and is viewable.

Retrieve the source code for a trigger:

```
column   trigger_name     format a15
column   trigger_type     format a15
column   triggering_event format a15
column   table_name       format a15
column   trigger_body     format a25
select   trigger_name, trigger_type, triggering_event, table_name, trigger_body
from     user_triggers;
```

| TRIGGER NAME | TRIGGER TYPE | TRIGGERING EVEN | TABLE NAME | TRIGGER BODY |
|---|---|---|---|---|
| UPDATE_TOTAL | AFTER STATEMENT | INSERT OR UPDATE OR DELETE | ORDER_MAIN | begin update order_main set order_total = 10; end; |

Finding the dependencies for PL/SQL objects:

```
column   name             format a20
column   referenced_owner format a15 heading R_OWNER
column   referenced_name  format a15 heading R_NAME
column   referenced_type  format a12 heading R_TYPE
select   name, type, referenced_owner,
         referenced_name,referenced_type
from     user_dependencies
order by type, name;
```

| NAME | TYPE | R OWNER | R NAME | R TYPE |
|---|---|---|---|---|
| INSERT_RECORD | PROCEDURE | USERA | ORDER_MAIN | TABLE |
| INSERT_RECORD | PROCEDURE | SYS | STANDARD | PACKAGE |
| PROCESS_DATE | PROCEDURE | SYS | STANDARD | PACKAGE |
| PROCESS_DATE | PROCEDURE | USERA | ORDER_MAIN | TABLE |

Tuning SQL

**TIP**
*Finding the source code behind PL/SQL package procedures involves querying the USER_SOURCE and DBA_SOURCE views. Finding the source code behind a trigger involves querying the USER_TRIGGERS and DBA_TRIGGERS views. Find dependencies by querying the USER_DEPENDENCIES and the DBA_DEPENDENCIES views.*

# The Time Component When Working with DATE Data Types

When working with the Oracle DATE data type, it is more accurate to think of it as a TIME data type. This is because the DATE data type always stores a complete temporal value, down to the second. It is impossible to insert a date value only into either a PL/SQL variable or database column that is defined as a DATE. If this behavior is not kept in mind during the design of an application, it is possible that the finished product will exhibit undesirable side effects. One of the most common side effects of improper date management within an application is when reports, which filter the data by a date value, return different results across multiple executions.

When a column or variable of this type (DATE) is initialized with a value, any missing component (if any) will be automatically supplied by Oracle. If the initialization value contains the date component, only then will Oracle supply the time component, and vice versa. This begs the question of how can one tell which component, if any, is missing during the initialization? Quite simply, both components are automatically present only when a date variable is initialized from another date variable. The system variable SYSDATE is one such date variable. Thus, whenever a column or variable is initialized from SYSDATE, it will contain a value representing the date and time when the initialization occurred.

If it is January 10, 1998 at 3:25:22 A.M., and you execute the command:

```
Date_Var_1 date := SYSDATE:
```

The value contained in the variable Date_Var_1 will be

```
10-JAN-1998 03:25:22.
```

It is also possible to initialize a date variable using a text string. For example:

```
Date_Var_2 date := '10-JAN-98';
```

The value contained in the variable Date_Var_2 will be

```
10-JAN-98 00:00:00.
```

Time Management

**TIP**
*A DATE data type always stores a complete temporal value, down to the second. It is impossible to insert a date value only into either a PL/SQL variable or database column that is defined as a DATE.*

At this point, it should be clear that Date_Var_1 and Date_Var_2 are not equal even though they both contain a date component of 10-JAN-98—their time components differ by almost three and a half hours. Herein lies the problem with a program that does not anticipate the time component that is inherent with date values. Consider an application that uses the SYSDATE variable to initialize the accounting date of records inserted into a database table. If a PL/SQL processing program (or a simple SQL SELECT statement for that matter) does not take the time component of the records into account, then records will be missed during processing.

Knowing that the date values in a table *contain time values* other than twelve midnight, the following statements would miss records.

**The problem**   The time is not the same and these statements all miss records:

```
select      *
from        table
where       date_column = SYSDATE;

select      *
from        table
where       date_column = trunc(SYSDATE);

select      *
from        table
where       date_column = '10-JAN-98';

select      *
from        table
where       date_column between '01-JAN-98' and '10-JAN-98';
```

**The solution**   Truncate the time on both sides of the WHERE clause.

One way to prevent this problem is to negate the difference in time components on both sides of the conditional test.

```
select      *
from        table
where       trunc(date_column) = trunc(SYSDATE);

select      *
from        table
where       trunc(date_column) = '10-JAN-98';
```

```
select     *
from       table
where      trunc(date_column) between '01-JAN-98' and '10-JAN-98';
```

**Tuned solution**   The time is truncated on the noncolumn side of the WHERE clause.
Of course, this technique has the undesired affect of suppressing any indexes that might otherwise improve query performance—the TRUNC function on the column_name suppresses the index on the column. The desired technique would be to adjust the filter conditions to include all possible times within a given date. Also note in the example here that .000011574 of one day is one second.

```
select     *
from       table
where      date_col between trunc(SYSDATE) and
           trunc(SYSDATE + 1) - .000011574;

select     *
from       table
where      date_col between to_date('10-JAN-98') and
           to_date('11-JAN-98') - .000011574;

select     *
from       table
where      date_col between to_date('01-JAN-98') and
           to_date('11-JAN-98') - .000011574;
```

**TIP**
*The Oracle DATE has both date and time included in it. Avoid suppressing indexes when trying to match dates. The key is to never modify the column side in the WHERE clause. Do all modifications on the noncolumn side.*

# Tuning and Testing PL/SQL

You can also use PL/SQL to time your PL/SQL and ensure that it is performing to your standards. Next is a simple example of how you can write a script that would allow you to test and tune your procedures (a procedure called "get_customer" in this example) directly from SQL*Plus (or PL/SQL within SQL*Plus):

```
set serveroutput    on
declare
cust_name char(100);
begin
dbms_output.put_line('Start Time:
    '||to_char(sysdate,'hh24:mi:ss'));
    get_customer(11111,cust_name);
```

```
    dbms_output.put_line('Complete Time:
    '||to_char(sysdate,'hh24:mi:ss'));
    dbms_output.put_line(cust_name);
end;
```

**TIP**
*Use PL/SQL to display the start and end time for your PL/SQL. Basically, don't forget to use PL/SQL to tune your PL/SQL.*

# PL/SQL Object Location: Implications

At TUSC, we generally recommend storing the PL/SQL objects on the server side, for many of the obvious reasons. The server is usually much more powerful and objects are reused much more often (especially when pinned into the shared pool). The security methods employed are also more straightforward. Sending the PL/SQL to be processed on the client side can be dependent on the power of the client and can lessen the number of round trips from client to server. However, when written correctly, the calls may be limited back to the server (see the next section for an example). There is certainly a continuing debate on this one, but with the evolving thin client, the server will probably be the only place to store the PL/SQL. Figure 10-1 diagrams how PL/SQL is executed when stored on the server side. Some additional reasons for storing code on the server are listed here:

- Performance is improved since the code is already compiled code (p-code).
- Allows the ability to pin objects in the Oracle SGA.
- It enables transaction-level security at the database level.
- Less redundant code and fewer version control issues.
- There is an ability to query source online since it is stored in the data dictionary.
- It is easier to determine impact analysis since it is stored in the data dictionary.
- It uses less memory since only one copy of the code is in memory.
- If packages are used, then the entire package is loaded upon initially being referenced.

**TIP**
*Where to store the PL/SQL code is an ongoing debate. Generally, the server side is the preferred place to store the code and may become the only choice as thin clients become more prevalent.*

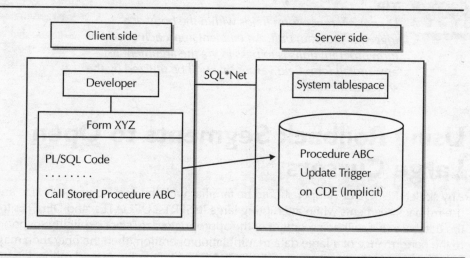

**FIGURE 10-1.** *Generally, executing an object on the server side is desirable for performance*

# Don't Bind PL/SQL Program Units in a Form to Form Fields

The Developer/2000 Forms module contains a PL/SQL engine that is independent of the one installed in the server database. Whenever possible, the Forms tool will attempt to use this local PL/SQL engine to process trigger statements and program units that have been coded into the form executable. The purpose of the behavior is to increase performance by limiting network communications when the statement is capable of being processed solely on the client side. If the local PL/SQL engine is incapable of processing the trigger or program unit on its own, then the code, or portions of it, will be passed off to the PL/SQL engine on the server side. To achieve maximum performance, when this handoff occurs, it is imperative that the communication between the client and server components be kept to a minimum.

One way to ensure that network communications are minimized is to not reference form fields within the body of a trigger or program unit. Doing so will generate network traffic to retrieve/set the form field each time the server-side PL/SQL engine encounters a reference to a field. A more efficient approach to coding form program units is to pass in via the argument list any and all form field values that will be utilized. The values for all pertinent form fields become simple program unit variables that can be utilized by the server-side engine without the need to reference the form.

**TIP**
*Do not reference form fields within the body of a trigger or program unit. An efficient approach to coding form program units is to pass in via the argument list any and all form field values that will be utilized by the server-side engine.*

# Using Rollback Segments to Open Large Cursors

Any skilled PL/SQL developer should be familiar with the need to properly size and use rollback segments when attempting large INSERTs, UPDATEs, and DELETEs to the database. If a rollback segment of the appropriate size is not explicitly set prior to the performance of a large data manipulation operation, then the operation may fail. The error code usually returned is "ORA-01562: failed to extend rollback segment." The reason for the failure is due to the transactions that do not explicitly set the rollback segment will have one randomly assigned by Oracle. If this randomly assigned rollback segment is of insufficient size to hold the entire transaction, then the operation will fail. Errors of this type can be eliminated by anticipating the amount of data that will be changed, choosing an appropriately sized rollback segment (the DBA_ROLLBACK_SEGS view is helpful in this regard), and setting this rollback segment just prior to the DML statement. The following example demonstrates the proper set of statements.

```
commit;

set transaction use rollback segment rbs1;

update big_table
set column_1 = column_1 * 0.234;

commit;
```

It is a little known fact that Oracle uses rollback segments during the usage of cursors—even if DML statements are not being issued from within the cursor loop. The rollback segments are being used as a type of work area as a cursor loop is executed. Thus, it is quite possible that a cursor loop will fail if a rollback segment of insufficient size is used to read the cursor. The failure does not occur immediately—only after numerous iterations of the cursor loop have been performed. The error message that is returned is the same message returned when a single DML statement fails; many developers are fooled into thinking that the error lies elsewhere in their code. Valiant efforts are made to properly manage transaction sizes *within* the cursor loops, but to no avail. To successfully open a large cursor, it is imperative that a large rollback segment be set just prior to the opening of the cursor.

```
commit;

set transaction use rollback segment rbs_big;

for C1_Rec in C1 loop
-- your processing logic goes here ...
end loop;
```

If large amounts of data are being manipulated within the cursor loop, the code should also be setting rollback segments within the cursor loop as well. This will prevent the DML statements from utilizing the same rollback segment that is being used to ensure that the large cursor can be read.

**TIP**
*Specify a large enough rollback segment when opening a large cursor.*

## Use Active Transaction Management to Process Large Quantities of Data

When coding procedures that will process large quantities of data, the developer must remember to take into account the size of the rollback segments. The rollback segments are the weak link in a program that performs mass data manipulation. A procedure that performs a single COMMIT statement at the end just won't do if it is to be used to process millions of rows of data. It could be argued that a single transaction could be used to process mass quantities of data, provided the rollback segments were large enough. There are two flaws in this logic: 1) rarely is it feasible to devote gigabytes of valuable drive space to serve as rollback space; and 2) should a hardware or software error occur, then the entire data set would have to be reprocessed. Thus, active transaction management is always the desired technique when processing large quantities of data; it yields efficient utilization of drive space (devoted to rollback segments) and provides for automatic recovery in the event of hardware/software failures.

Active transaction management is a coding technique that consists of three components: setting transactions for cursor and DML statements, performing intermittent database COMMITs, and utilizing a table column as a processing flag to indicate which records have been processed. Consider the following database procedure:

```
declare
  counter number;
  cursor C1 is
    select     rowid,column_1,column_2,column_3
    from       big_table
    where      process_time is NULL;
```

```
begin
  counter := 0;
  commit;
              set transaction use rollback segment rbs_big;
  for C1_Rec in C1 loop
    -- Commit every 1000 records processed.
    if (Counter = 0) or (Counter >= 1000)
      then
        commit;
        set transaction use rollback segment rbs_medium;
        Counter := 0;
      else
        Counter := Counter + 1;
    end if;
    Processing logic...
    update big_table
    set process_time = sysdate
    where rowid = C1_Rec.rowid;
  end loop;
  commit;
end;
```

The set transaction statements ensure that an appropriately sized rollback segment is used for both cursor reading and DML statements. The database COMMIT for every 1,000 records processed does two things: prevents the DML statements from exceeding the capacity of the rollback segment and divides the records being processed into discrete units, in the event of hardware/software failure. Finally, the process_time column serves as the processing flag that allows the procedure to identify records that have not yet been processed.

**TIP**
*Specify the correct size rollback segment for transactional processing. Limiting the amount of data manipulated between COMMITs is a key to avoiding rollback segment errors.*

# Modifying SQL.BSQ to Avoid Data Dictionary Fragmentation

Upon creation of an Oracle database, a file called sql.bsq is executed to create the underlying data dictionary tables. These tables are created under the SYS account and are stored in the SYSTEM tablespace. As programmers begin to utilize stored PL/SQL objects in the database, there is a shift of large amounts of source code from the application source files into the database. Therefore, efficient storage of these objects becomes very important. The default SYSTEM storage is an initial extent of 10K, a NEXT (incremental) extent of 10K and a PCTINCREASE (percent increase) of 50. Therefore, all tables created in the SYSTEM tablespace will be created with this storage unless a STORAGE clause is included in the table creation. In the sql.bsq file, several data dictionary tables related to the storage of PL/SQL objects are created with the default SYSTEM storage. These tables are listed here:

| | | | |
|---|---|---|---|
| *OBJ$[2]* | *PROCEDURE$[1]* | *ARGUMENT$[1]* | *SOURCE$[1]* |
| *DUC$[1]* | *EXPECT$* | *IDL_UB1$[1]* | *IDL_UB2$[1]* |
| *IDL_CHAR$[1]* | *IDL_SB4$[1]* | *ERROR$[1]* | *TRIGGERCOL$[1]* |
| *TRIGGER$[2]* | *DEPENDENCY$[2]* | *ACCESS$* | *JOB$[1]* |
| *USER$[1]* | *COL$[2]* | | |

[1]A table with one index
[2]A table with two indexes

The SOURCE$ table is often immediately fragmented from simply building the database and executing all of Oracle's scripts in some environments.

**TIP**
*If a large amount of PL/SQL is used for a given database, you may need to fix potential fragmentation problems in the data dictionary. Modifying the storage clause of sql.bsq prior to building the database can eliminate these problems. Be careful! Not all tables in sql.bsq can be modified and Oracle Corporation does not support this action.*

# Examples—The "Look and Feel" Just for the Beginners

Since many developers and DBAs reading this book are beginners at PL/SQL, I am also including an example of a piece of PL/SQL code, procedure, function, package, and trigger. I feel it is important that you have a feel for what these objects look like and how they differ, especially if you haven't seen some of them before. This section is intentionally placed as the last section of this chapter as a short reference section only and to give you a feel for how each looks. The goal is not to teach you how to write PL/SQL (please refer to the *Oracle PL/SQL Tips & Techniques* book for that).

Examples

Both procedures and functions can take parameters and can be called from PL/SQL. However, procedures typically perform an action. The parameters used in procedures can be in(put), out(put), and/or in(put)/out(put) parameters, whereas, functions typically compute a value and the parameters can only be in(put) parameters. As a matter of fact, you cannot even specify the "direction" of the parameters. Functions only permit the passing of one return value. Functions are "selectable," so you can create your own user-defined functions that return information. As of version 7.2 of Oracle, developers can create user-defined functions that can be used to process through a standard SQL-type function.

**PL/SQL example:**

```
declare
  acct_balance      NUMBER(11,2);
  acct              CONSTANT NUMBER(4)   := 3;
  debit_amt         CONSTANT NUMBER(5,2) := 500.00;
begin
 select  bal into acct_balance
 from    accounts
 where   account_id = acct
 for     update of bal;
   if acct_balance >= debit_amt THEN
   update       accounts
   set   bal = bal - debit_amt
   where         account_id = acct;
   else
   insert into temp values
        (acct, acct_balance, 'Insufficient funds');
            -- insert account, current balance, and message
   end if;
 commit;
end;
```

**Create a procedure example:**

```
create or replace procedure
    get_cust (in_cust_no in char, out_cust_name out char,
    out_cust_addr1 out char, out_cust_addr2 out char,
    out_cust_city out char, out_cust_st out char,
    out_cust_zip out char, out_cust_poc out char) IS
begin
 select  name, addr1, addr2, city, st, zip, poc
 into     out_cust_name, out_cust_addr1, out_cust_addr2,
          out_cust_city, out_cust_st, out_cust_zip,
          out_cust_poc
```

Examples

```
from      customer cust, address addr
where     cust.cust_no = addr.cust_no
and       addr.primary_flag = 'Y'
and       cust.cust_no = in_cust_no;
end       get_cust;
```

## Execute the procedure from PL/SQL example:

```
get_cust (12345, name, addr1, addr2, city, st, zip, poc);
```

## Create a function example:

```
create or replace function
get_cust_name (in_cust_no number)
returns
char IS
declare
out_cust_name customer.name%type;
begin
  select  name
  into    out_cust_name
  from    customer
  where   cust_no = in_cust_no;
  return  out_cust_name;
end get_cust_name;
```

## Execute the GET_CUST_NAME function from SQL:

```
select    get_cust_name(12345)
from      dual
```

## A Package example:

```
package emp_actions IS  -- package specification
   procedure hire_employee
        (empno NUMBER, ename CHAR, ...);
   procedure retired_employee (emp_id NUMBER);
end emp_actions;
package body emp_actions IS  -- package body
   procedure hire_employee
        (empno NUMBER, ename CHAR, ...)
is
   begin
      insert into emp VALUES (empno, ename, ...);
   end hire_employee;
```

Examples

```
    procedure fire_employee (emp_id NUMBER) IS
    begin
        delete from emp WHERE empno = emp_id;
    end fire_employee;
end emp_actions;
```

**Database trigger example using PL/SQL:**

```
create trigger audit_sal
    after update of sal ON emp
    for each row
begin
    insert into emp_audit VALUES( ...)
end;
```

# Tips Review

- For PL/SQL to be reused in memory, it must be written exactly the same.
- Use bind variables instead of constants to avoid fragmenting the shared pool.
- Access V$SQLAREA view to find case (UPPER and lower) issues or to find a particular object that is problematic.
- When shared pool fragmentation errors occur, you can flush the shared pool using the ALTER SYSTEM FLUSH SHARED_POOL command.
- Use the DBMS_SHARED_POOL.KEEP procedure to pin PL/SQL objects.
- Query the V$DB_OBJECT_CACHE view to find objects that are not pinned and are also large enough to potentially cause problems.
- Use the DBMS_SHARED_POOL.SIZES procedure to find specific information about an object.
- Query DBA_OBJECTS (for system-wide objects) *or* USER_OBJECT (for your schema only) to find the state of objects and avoid errors and reloading by the user.
- Query DBA_TRIGGERS (for system-wide objects) *or* USER_TRIGGERS (for your schema only) to find the state of triggers and avoid errors with disabled triggers. Disabled triggers can have fatal results for an application...they don't *fail*, they just *don't execute*.
- Load reference tables into PL/SQL tables for faster lookups.

- Finding the source code behind PL/SQL objects involves querying the USER_SOURCE, DBA_SOURCE, USER_TRIGGERS and DBA_TRIGGERS views. Find dependencies by querying the USER_DEPENDENCIES and the DBA_DEPENDENCIES views.

- The Oracle DATE has both date and time included in it. Avoid suppressing indexes when trying to match dates. The key is to never modify the column side in the WHERE clause. Do all modifications on the noncolumn side.

- Use PL/SQL to display the start and end time for your PL/SQL.

- Generally, the server side is the preferred place to store the PL/SQL.

- *Do not* reference form fields within the body of a trigger or program unit.

- Specify the correct size rollback segment within the PL/SQL for large cursors.

# References

*PL/SQL Tips and Techniques*; Oracle Press, Joe Trezzo

*Procedures, Functions, Packages and Triggers*; Joe Trezzo

*SQL Language Reference Manual*, Oracle Corporation

*Application Developer's Guide*, Oracle Corporation

Frank Naude's underground Oracle Web page

"OOPs-Objected Oriented PL/SQL," *Select Magazine*, April 1996, Bradley Brown

*Oracle PL/SQL Programming*, Oracle Press, Scott Urman

*Oracle DBA Handbook*, Oracle Press, Kevin Loney

*Oracle PL/SQL Programming*, O'Reilly & Associates, Steven Feuerstein

"Using SQL to Examine Stored Code," *Integrator*, February 1996, Steven Feuerstein

Many thanks to Joe Trezzo, Bob Taylor, Jake Van der Vort, and Dave Ventura of TUSC for contributions to this chapter.

Tips Review

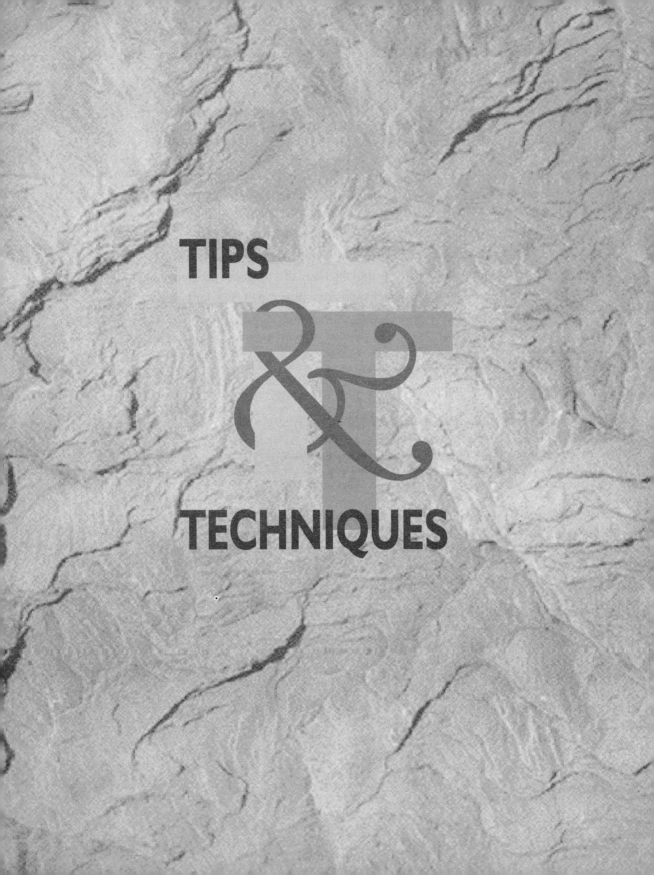

TIPS
&
TECHNIQUES

# CHAPTER
# 11

## Using Parallel Features to Improve Performance

TIPS
&
COVERED

Parallel Query Option was first introduced with the release of Oracle 7.1. This technology enabled DBAs to parallelize full table scan operations, effectively splitting a single, serial query into multiple processes with distinct result sets that are merged and returned to the end user. The Parallel Query Option has applicability to virtually every Oracle7 Server computing environment, and it has brought more applicability to Oracle8 with enhancements that have delivered parallel execution of DML statements and parallelized operations on table/index partitions. Whether you are running Oracle7 or Oracle8 instances, parallelized operations should be investigated. Significant performance enhancements have been made with each release of the RDBMS kernel.

Tips covered in this chapter:

- Basic concepts of parallel operations
- The number of processes used for a specified degree of parallelism
- Parallel query and operations with Oracle7
- Parallel DML statements and operations with Oracle8
- Parallel operations, partitions, and execution methods
- Producer/consumer relationship
- Inter- and intra-operations parallelization (PARALLEL and NOPARALLEL hints)
- Different statements are determined for parallel differently
- Create table and index examples of using parallel operations
- Real-world example of distributing data for effective parallel operations
- Oracle8 parallel DML statements
- Parallel DML statement examples
- Monitor parallel operations using V$PQ_SYSSTAT, V$PQ_SESSTAT, and V$PQ_TQSTAT views
- Using EXPLAIN PLAN on parallel operations
- Tuning parallel execution and the Oracle7 init.ora parameters
- Tuning parallel execution and the Oracle8 init.ora parameters
- Parallel loading
- Performance comparisons and monitoring parallel operations

# Basic Concepts of Parallel Operations

Utilizing parallel operations enables multiple processes (and potentially processors) to work together simultaneously to resolve a single SQL statement. This feature improves data-intensive operations, is dynamic (the execution path is determined at run time), and (when wisely implemented) makes use of all of your processors and disk drives. There's a small price to pay in all of this, but if your system is overwhelmed with ad hoc queries or long-running reports driven by SQL statements that scan table blocks or data/index partitions, this option may be the solution to your problems.

The most basic scenario is a full table scan. The variable to specify how many processes to break a query into is the parallel degree. The parallel degree can be set in a hint at table creation time or in other ways that will be specified in this chapter. In Figure 11-1, we see that a full table scan of table emp is broken into four separate processes (the parallel degree is 4). A total of five processes are used for this operation (one to break it up and four to process the query). The query could also access multiple disks (not shown), so balancing the actual data is also important (see Figure 11-2).

If the full table scan that is processed in Figure 11-1 also needs to be sorted, then the resulting operation will look like Figure 11-2 instead. Now you need one process

**Parallel Operations**

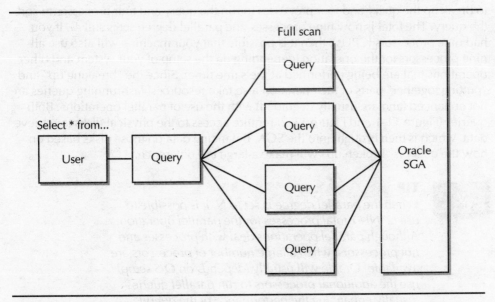

**FIGURE 11-1.**  *A simple full table scan with parallel execution (disk access not shown)*

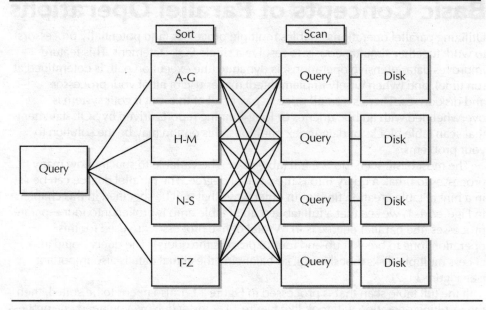

**FIGURE 11-2.** *A simple full table scan requiring a sort with parallel execution (SGA not shown)*

to break up the query and four processes to run the query and four processes to sort the query. The total is now nine processes (the parallel degree set is still 4). If you had nine processors (CPUs), then it is possible that your machine will also use all nine processors for the operation (depending on the setup of your system and other operations that are being performed at the same time). Since the "breaking up" and "putting together" parts of the operation also take resources, fast-running queries are not enhanced (and are usually degraded) with the use of parallel operations. Both queries (Figure 11-1 and Figure 11-2) require access to the physical disks to retrieve data, which is then brought into the SGA. Balancing data on those disks based on how the query is "broken up" will make a large I/O difference.

**TIP**
*When the parallel degree is set to N, it is possible to use (2\*N)+1 total processes for the parallel operation. Although parallel operations deal with processes and not processors, when a large number of processors are available, Oracle will usually (depends on O/S setup) use the additional processors to run parallel queries (usually enhancing the performance of the query).*

**TIP**
*Using parallel operations on very small tables or very fast queries can also degrade performance since the "breaking up" and "putting together" of the query also costs performance resources (at times the parallel cost is more than the query cost itself).*

# Parallel Query Option and Operations with Oracle7

Parallel Query Option in Oracle7 will *only* work on queries that contain at least one full table scan. If you are utilizing symmetric multiprocessor (SMP) architecture, Loosely Coupled Systems or Massively Parallel Systems, Parallel Query Option will take advantage of this processing power. If you are running Oracle7 Server on a single-processor system and your optimization is limited by I/O bound queries, you may achieve better performance by striping data across disk devices in multiple data files and utilizing Parallel Query. Recognize that Parallel Query or Oracle8 parallelized operations *may degrade performance* on a single processor system that does not suffer from I/O bottlenecks.

The following SQL statements within Oracle7 can take advantage of parallel operations:

- SELECT statements
- Subqueries of UPDATE, INSERT and DELETE statements
- CREATE TABLE (as SELECT...FROM) statements
- CREATE INDEX statements

These statements may embody one or more of the following *operations* that can be parallelized, all of which must include a full table scan:

- SORT operations: GROUP BY, ORDER BY, SELECT DISTINCT
- SORT/MERGE operations
- NESTED LOOP join operations to (full) scanned tables
- Aggregate functions: AVG, MIN, MAX

**TIP**
*In Oracle7, you must have at least one full table scan in order to take advantage of Parallel Query. Parallel DML statements are not allowed, but subqueries with a full table scan of the DML statements can use parallel operations.*

# Parallel DML Statements and Operations with Oracle8

Oracle8 introduced the parallel DML feature, allowing for parallel execution of INSERT, UPDATE, and DELETE operations. The following is a list of statements that are capable of parallel execution with Oracle8:

- SELECT
- UPDATE, INSERT
- DELETE
- CREATE TABLE as...
- CREATE INDEX
- REBUILD INDEX
- MOVE/SPLIT PARTITION
- ENABLE CONSTRAINT

The following operations can also be parallelized within a statement:

- select DISTINCT
- GROUP BY
- ORDER BY
- NOT IN
- UNION and UNION ALL
- NESTED LOOPS joins
- SORT/MERGE joins

**V8 TIP**

*In Oracle8, parallel DML statements are allowed. This functionality applies to partitioned tables and indexes. Parallelization still cannot be performed on an index operation but parallelization can be performed on a partitioned index.*

Additionally, Oracle8 utilizes cost-based optimization to determine whether to parallelize a statement and the degree of parallelism applied.

**Parallel DML Statements** *(side margin)*

# Parallel Operations, Partitions, and Execution Methods

Statements can be parallelized utilizing three distinct methods, which are determined dynamically when an execution plan is created for the SQL statement.

| | |
|---|---|
| Block Range (ROWID Range) | Utilized for SCAN operations on partitioned (V8 only) and nonpartitioned tables (V7 and V8). Scan operations are the only methods through which statements can be parallelized in Oracle7. |
| Partition | Servers are assigned per partition for partitioned tables and indexes. Partitions are a feature introduced with Oracle8. |
| Parallel Server Process | Servers assigned for INSERT operations on nonpartitioned tables only within Oracle8. |

Recalling the previous discussion of parallel statement operations, the following breakdowns for each execution method illustrate the parallel execution approach that will be applied to each type of operation:

- Block/ROWID Range
  - Queries using table scans
  - Move, split partition
  - Rebuild index partition
  - Create index (nonpartitioned)
  - Create table...as select
  - (nonpartitioned)
- Partition
  - UPDATE and DELETE
  - INSERT...SELECT
  - ALTER INDEX...REBUILD
  - Queries using a range scan on a partitioned index
  - CREATE INDEX
  - CREATE TABLE...as select
- Server process
  - INSERT on nonpartitioned tables

**Parallel Methods**

The Oracle8 partitioning feature has significant impact on parallel operations (as indicated earlier). Partitions are static, logical divisions of table data and indexes, and partitions of the same table/index can reside in multiple tablespaces. Given this architecture, the following important distinctions exist with Oracle8 parallel operations on partitions:

- There is no parallelism within a partition.
- Operations are performed in parallel on partitioned objects *only* when more than one partition is accessed.

Therefore, if a table is partitioned into 12 logical divisions by a dimension of the data, and a query posted against the table will only access six of those partitions (because the dimension of the data dictates the partition in which the data is stored), a maximum of six parallel server processes will be allocated to satisfy the query. This condition is known as "partition pruning" when an execution plan eliminates partitions of data based on the WHERE clause of the query.

### V8 TIP

*Operations are performed in parallel on partitioned objects only when more than one partition is accessed, and parallelism is not performed within a single partition. To use more parallel server processes, ensure that the table is partitioned into enough pieces.*

The differences in the processing model of executing the same SQL statement in parallel vs. a serial scan are illustrated in Figures 11-3 and 11-4. Figure 11-3 illustrates typical statement processing whether you operate under a dedicated server or multithreaded server Oracle7/8 architecture. SQL statements are executed and managed by a single server process. This results in a "serial" approach to data retrieval. Data "striping," whether implemented manually or via the operating system, can improve performance; however, a single server process is responsible for statement operations, including table scans and data sorting.

The processing model offered in Figure 11-4 illustrates the advantages of utilizing parallel processing. Multiple processes are "dispatched" to address each operation contained within a SQL statement. If data is "striped" or distributed across multiple disk drives, this processing model maximizes your investment in processing power *and* disk drives. Multiple server processes share the processing load and are each responsible for all or a portion of the statement operation(s). Table scans and temporary segment sorts can be processed concurrently and a single, dedicated server process coordinates the efforts of all server processes.

The coordinating process or *statement coordinator* dispatches the execution of discrete operations of a statement to parallel servers. As parallel servers return the

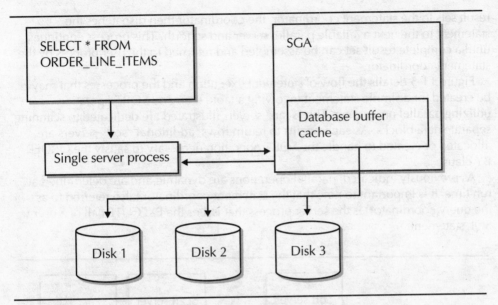

**FIGURE 11-3.** *Statement processing without parallel execution*

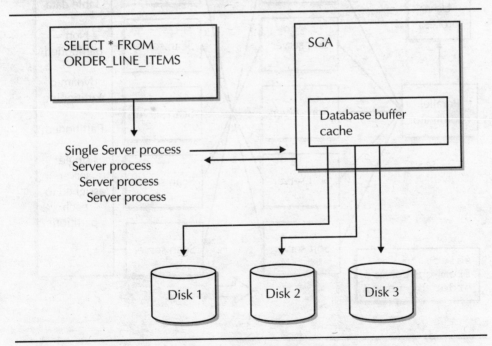

**FIGURE 11-4.** *Statement processing with parallel execution*

result sets to the statement coordinator, the coordinator then dispatches the statement to the next available parallel server and so forth. This process continues until a complete result set can be assembled and returned to the user process by the statement coordinator.

Figure 11-5 details the flow of statement execution and the processes that may be created for a simple statement involving a table scan and SORT operation utilizing parallel processing. The "scan" servers illustrated are dedicated to scanning separate data blocks. As each begins to return rows, additional "sort" servers are allocated or created to handle the SORT operation necessary to satisfy the ORDER BY clause.

As previously indicated, parallel operations are dynamic and are determined at run time. It is important to note that the statement coordinator (also referred to as the query coordinator) is the server process that issues the EXECUTE call of a user SQL statement.

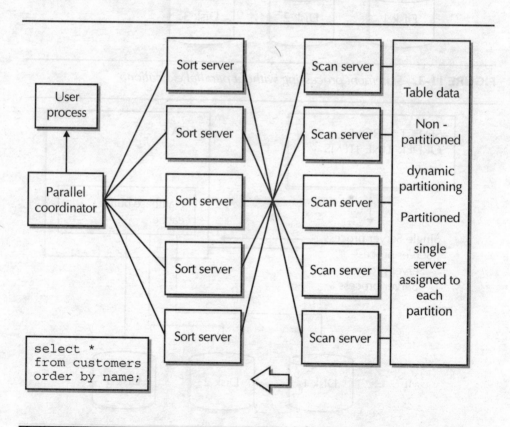

**FIGURE 11-5.** *Statement execution detail using parallel execution*

Parallel servers may exist at the time a user executes a parallelized statement or may be created dynamically to meet the demands of the *degree of parallelism* dictated by the execution path.

Figure 11-5 illustrates two important concepts of parallel execution: The producer/consumer relationship of parallel server processes, and the concept of inter- and intra-operation parallelism. Parallel server processes are allocated for each operation within a SQL statement.

# Producer/Consumer Relationship

The distribution of data, CPU allocation to each parallel server process, and the speed of devices servicing the parallel server data request may cause each server process to complete at different times. As each server process completes, it passes its result set to the next lower operation in the statement hierarchy. Thus any single parallel server process may handle or service statement operation requests from any other parallel server process at the next higher level in the statement hierarchy.

**V8 TIP**
*Any server process allocated for a statement may handle any request from a process within the same statement. Therefore, if some processes are faster than others are, the ones that are faster can assist with the ones that are slower (but only at the next higher statement hierarchy level).*

# Inter- and Intra-Operation Parallelization (PARALLEL and NOPARALLEL Hints)

The optimizer will evaluate a statement and determine how many and which parallel server processes will address a single SQL statement. This intra-operation parallelization is different from inter-operation parallelization, which is the process by which the statement coordinator distributes work between the server processes and consolidates the multiple result sets into a single result (all done automatically by Oracle).

The degree of parallelism is applied to each operation of a SQL statement that can be parallelized. This includes the SORT operation of data required by an ORDER BY clause. Figure 11-5 has depicted a degree of parallelism of 5. As many as 11 processes may be created on the system to process this query, five (5) each to the table SCAN operations and the SORT operations. An additional process, the query coordinator, may be allocated or created to administer the query.

# Examples of Using Inter- and Intra-Operations (PARALLEL and NOPARALLEL Hints)

Parallelizing SQL statements can be accomplished via a SQL statement hint or by the object definition itself. A statement hint is illustrated here:

```
select     /*+ PARALLEL (order_line_items) */ invoice_number, invoice_date
from       order_line_items
order by   invoice_date;
```

This statement *does not* specify a degree of parallelism. The *default degree of parallelism* dictated by the table definition or the init.ora parameters will be used:

```
select     /*+ PARALLEL (order_line_items, 4) */ invoice_number, invoice_date
from       order_line_items
order by   invoice_date;
```

This statement specifies a degree of parallelism of 4. Per our previous discussion, as many as nine query servers may be allocated or created to satisfy this query. The statement below must hint the alias.

```
select     /*+ PARALLEL (oli, 4) */ invoice_number, invoice_date
from       order_line_items oli
order by   invoice_date;
```

**TIP**

*Using the PARALLEL hint will enable the use of parallel operations. If the degree is not specified with the hint, the default degree during the table creation will be used. Using the alias for a table in the FROM clause means that you must use the alias for the table in the hint.*

You may also "turn off" the use of parallel operations in a given query on a table that has been specified to use parallel operations:

```
select     /*+ noPARALLEL */ invoice_number, invoice_date
from       order_line_items oli
order by   invoice_date;
```

**TIP**
*The use of the NOPARALLEL hint will disable parallel operations in a statement that would otherwise utilize parallel processing due to a parallel object definition.*

Queries against a table may be made candidates for parallel execution by creating or altering the table definition to include the PARALLEL clause, as in the following two statements, both of which are equivalent:

```
create table order_line_items
        (invoice_number   number(12) not null, invoice_date     date not null)
parallel 4;

create table order_line_items
        (invoice_number   number(12) not null, invoice_date     date not null);
alter table order_line_items
parallel (degree 4);
```

Conversely, a table can be removed from consideration for parallel operations by utilizing the ALTER TABLE command in the following manner:

```
alter table order_line_items
noparallel;
```

The coordinator process will evaluate the chronological order of the following, determining the degree of parallelism for a statement and whether parallel operations will be implemented in the execution path:

1. Hints contained in the SQL statement

2. Table definition

3. Default degree of parallelism dictated by init.ora parameters and table/index statistics

It is highly recommended that an explicit degree of parallelism be specified in either the SQL statement itself (preferred method) or in the table definition. Improvements have been made in later releases of Oracle7 (7.3) and in Oracle8 Server, providing more direct control over the number of default query servers created when a degree of parallelism is not available.

**TIP**
*Specify the degree of parallelism using a hint instead of relying on the table definition or the init.ora parameters. This will ensure that all operations are tuned for the given query as opposed to a "broad brush" method of tuning.*

**Parallelization**

# Different Statements Are Determined for PARALLEL Differently

The type of statement that is parallelized determines how the statement will actually be processed. SELECT statements behave differently from DML statements. This section will outline some of the different ways that SQL statements behave when parallel operations are used to process them.

## SELECT Statement Rules

This section shows rules concerning SELECT statement use with parallel options.

### SELECT Statements

Parallelization is determined by:

- Parallel hint or parallel object definition
- Table scan or index range scan

Degree of parallelization is determined by:

- Hints (always take precedence)
- Table or index with highest degree of parallelism

## SQL Statement DML Rules (Oracle8)

This section shows rules concerning DML statement use with parallel options.

### INSERT Statements

The INSERT/SELECT decision to parallelize a statement is performed independently; however, a single degree of parallelism applies to the entire statement.
Parallelization is determined by:

- Insert PARALLEL hint or parallel object definition

Degree of parallelization is determined by:

- PARALLEL hint of INSERT statement takes precedence
- Insert to table define with parallel definition
- Maximum *selected* table degree of parallelism

## UPDATE and DELETE Statements

Parallelization determined by:

- UPDATE/DELETE PARALLEL hint or parallel object definition

Degree of parallelization determined by:

- Hint of UPDATE/DELETE statement
- UPDATED/DELETED table definition
- *Only* applies to partitioned tables and hints (degree) apply to supporting scan operations
- Maximum degree equals number of partitions

# DDL Statement Rules (Oracle8)

This section shows rules concerning DDL statement use with parallel options. Parallelization determined by CREATE statement PARALLEL <*degree*> clause.

## CREATE TABLE as SELECT...FROM

CREATE portion of the statement:

- Parallelization is determined by PARALLEL clause
- Scan operation parallelized automatically, unless:
  - SELECT /*+ NOPARALLEL */
  - Index scan of nonpartitioned table

SELECT portion of the statement:

- Parallelization is determined by:
  - PARALLEL hint (no degree—ignored if specified) or
  - PARALLEL clause of the CREATE portion of the statement
  and
  - Full table scan, or
  - Index range scan of multiple partitions

- Degree of parallelism is determined by:
  - PARALLEL clause of CREATE statement
  - Number of system CPUs

### CREATE INDEX and ALTER INDEX

Parallelism is determined by PARALLEL clause:

- ALTER INDEX...REBUILD—nonpartitioned index only
- ALTER INDEX...REBUILD PARTITION—parallelized

Index scan operation utilizes parallelism definition of the REBUILD or CREATE operations.

- ALTER INDEX...MOVE PARTITION—parallelized
- ALTER INDEX...SPLIT PARTITION—parallelized

Index scan operation utilizes parallelism definition of the MOVE or SPLIT operations.

**TIP**
*The way that parallelism is determined depends on the statement that you are using. A SELECT statement is not considered the same way as an UPDATE statement would be considered. Review the previous section to see how all statements are determined.*

# Create Table and Index Examples of Using Parallel Operations

To further illustrate the application of parallelized operations in SQL statements, consider the following implementations of parallel operations for index and table creation:

```
create table order_line_items
tablespace tbsp1
storage (initial 75m next 75m pctincrease 0)
parallel (degree 4)
as
select     /*+ parallel (old_order_line_items,4) */ *
from       old_order_line_items;
```

and

```
create index order_key on order_line_items (order_id, item_id)
tablespace idx1
storage (initial 10m next 1m pctincrease 0)
parallel (degree 5);
```

The CREATE INDEX statement creates the order_key index using parallel SORT operations. The CREATE TABLE statement creates a new table ORDER_LINE_ITEMS with a degree of parallelism of 4 by selecting □from an existing OLD_ORDER_LINE_ITEMS table using a parallel operation. Clustered tables cannot be created and populated in parallel using parallel process. An important point to note is that although parallel queries increase the performance of queries that modify data, the redo log entries are written serially (not parallelized) and could cause a bottleneck. By using the UNRECOVERABLE (version 7.3) or the NOLOGGING (Oracle8+) options, this bottleneck is removed. These options are discussed in Chapter 13.

**TIP**
*Using UNRECOVERABLE (V7.3) or NOLOGGING (V8) can remove the bottleneck caused by parallel writes to the redo logs.*

Both of the preceding statements address an important aspect of table and index creation, referred to as storage parameters. To this point, we have ignored the physical location of the data queried in the example SELECT statements. If a full scanned table's data is all contained on a single disk, you may succeed only in creating a huge I/O bottleneck on the disk. An underlying principle of the performance gains that can be achieved utilizing parallel operations is that the data is stored on different devices, all capable of being addressed independently of one another. Returning to the CREATE INDEX statement, the following must be considered:

- Index creation will use temporary tablespace. Construct temporary tablespace in such a way that the physical data files are striped across as many (or more) disks as the degree of parallelism of the CREATE INDEX statement.

- In lieu of a PARALLEL clause in a CREATE INDEX statement, the table's degree of parallelism (if existing) will be used.

- Enabling a table constraint (PRIMARY, UNIQUE KEY) will not be performed in parallel unless the index is created first and the USING INDEX of the ALTER TABLE command is used.

Create Table

**TIP**
*The parallel degree specified by a table will be used for the CREATE INDEX statement when a parallel hint is not used on the CREATE INDEX.*

## Real-World Example of Distributing Data for Effective Parallel Operations

Returning to the CREATE TABLE statement example, the following conditions/ sequence of events might be pursued if this was an initial data load of a small but growing data warehouse:

■ A tablespace (TBSP1) is created composed of four data files each 100MB in size on separate disks.

■ The earlier CREATE TABLE statement is then executed, creating four extent allocations of 75MB each (and thus on four separate disks/devices).

■ The table storage definition is subsequently changed to a NEXT allocation of 25MB for subsequent, smaller data loads/population.

■ The temporary tablespace definition in this instance utilizes at least four data files to physically comprise the tablespace.

This method illustrates that careful planning and management of table and temporary tablespace construction can provide the underlying physical data distribution that is necessary to extract the most performance from parallel DDL operations.

**TIP**
*Effective parallel operations will depend greatly on how the data is physically located.*

## Oracle8 Parallel DML

The Oracle8 RDBMS introduced the capability to perform DML operations in parallel. Parallel DML mode must be enabled within a SQL session in order to perform a parallelized statement operation. The following conditions apply:

**Enabling parallel DML:**

- Session must be enabled via the command ALTER SESSION ENABLE PARALLEL DML.
- Parallel DML will *not* be performed if you have pending transactions before altering your session.
- Statement failure does not disable parallel DML within your session.
- Statement immediately following a parallel DML statement must be COMMIT or ROLLBACK.
- First DML statement in transaction must be parallel.
- Statements that will prevent parallel DML:
  - *Serial* UPDATEs/INSERTs/DELETEs performed
  - SELECT for UPDATE
  - LOCK TABLE
  - EXPLAIN PLAN
- Parallel DML mode does not affect parallel DDL or parallel queries.

# Parallel DML Rules, Exceptions, and Usage Notes

Here are some items to be considered when using parallel DML:

- PL/SQL statements that do not update/query the database are permitted after a parallel DML statement.
- If parallel DML statements are (accidentally) performed in serial, supporting scan operations may still be performed in parallel.
- If init.ora parameter ROW_LOCKING=INTENT is set, INSERTs, UPDATEs, and DELETEs are not parallelized.
- Triggers are not supported for parallel DML.
- Deletes on tables having a foreign key with DELETE CASCADE will not be parallelized.
- INSERTs/UPDATEs/DELETEs statements referencing a remote object will not be parallelized.
- Recovery from a system failure during parallel DML operations will be performed serially.

**Parallel DML**

### V8 TIP
*Parallel DML statements use an entirely different set of rules. You must know the rules for each scenario to effectively use parallel DML operations.*

## Parallel DML Statement Examples

This section illustrates examples concerning parallel DML statements.

```
alter session enable parallel dml;
Session altered.

update        /*+ PARALLEL (time_history,4) */time_history
set           fees = fees * 1.15
where         rank = 2;

150093 rows updated.

select        count(*)
from          time_history;
select count(*) from time_history
*

ERROR at line 1:
ORA-12830: Must COMMIT or ROLLBACK after
        executing parallel INSERT/UPDATE/DELETE

commit;

Commit complete.
```

### V8 TIP
*You must issue a COMMIT after using parallel DML statements. You will receive an error doing a SELECT statement that follows a parallel DML statement if you do not issue a COMMIT.*

**A parallel DDL statement:**

```
create table time_history_summary
tablespace thistory
storage   (initial 20M next 20M
          pctincrease 0)
```

Parallel DML

```
parallel 4
as select /*+ PARALLEL (time_history, 6) */
          rank, grpcode, sum(fees) fees
from      time_history
group by  rank, grpcode;

Table created.

commit;

Commit complete.

insert    /*+ PARALLEL (time_history_summary,2) */
into      time_history_summary
(rank, grpcode, fees)
(select   /*+ PARALLEL (time_history, 6) */
          rank, grpcode, sum(fees)
from      time_history
group by  rank, grpcode);

29093 rows created.
```

**TIP**
*The PARALLEL hint may be used in multiple sections of a query.*

```
commit;

Commit complete.

select  count(*)
from    time_history;

COUNT(*)
1493022

delete  /*+ PARALLEL (time_history ,6) */
where   rank = 2;

150093 Records deleted.

commit;

Commit complete.
```

Parallel DML

# Monitor Parallel Operations Using V$PQ_SYSSTAT, V$PQ_SESSTAT, and V$PQ_TQSTAT Views

The V$ fixed views are always a great place for instance monitoring and evaluating the current performance of the database, and this is no exception with parallel operations. The key performance views for monitoring parallel execution are as follows:

- V$PQ_SYSSTAT view
- V$PQ_SESSTAT view
- V$PQ_TQSTAT view

## V$PQ_SYSSTAT View

This view will provide parallel statistics for all parallelized statement operations within the instance. It is ideal for evaluating the number of servers executing currently, high-water mark levels, and the frequency of startup and shutdown of parallel servers.

```
select    statistic, value
from      v$pq_sysstat;

Statistic            Value
Servers Busy         12
Servers Idle         0
Servers High-water   12
Server Sessions      39
Servers Started      13
Servers Shut Down    7
Servers Cleaned Up   0
Queries Initiated    5
DFO Trees            5
Local Msgs Sent      91261
Distr Msgs Sent      0
Local Msgs Recv'd    91259
Distr Msgs Recv'd    0
```

**TIP**
*Querying the V$PQ_SYSSTAT view will display statistics for parallel operations. If the Servers Busy statistic is consistently higher than the init.ora parameter MIN_PARALLEL_SERVERS, you need to increase the this parameter in the init.ora file. Servers that high-water will display the maximum number of servers that have been in use.*

An example of the statistics found in this table on a freshly started instance is as follows. These statistics illustrate parallel servers executing during the UPDATE statement issued previously:

```
select      statistic, value
from        v$pq_sysstat;

Statistic              Value
Servers Busy           4
Servers Idle           0
Servers High-water     4
Server Sessions        4
Servers Started        0
Servers Shut Down      0
Servers Cleaned Up     0
Queries Initiated      0
DML Initiated          1
DFO Trees              1
Local Msgs Sent        8
Distr Msgs Sent        0
Local Msgs Recv'd      12
Distr Msgs Recv'd      0
```

Query PQ_SYSSTAT view after an INSERT operation specifying a parallel degree of 4. The subsequent execution of the INSERT statement illustrated previously produces the following statistics from the V$PQ_SYSSTAT view:

```
Statistic              Value
Servers Busy           4
Servers Idle           0
Servers High-water     8
```

```
Server Sessions         16
Servers Started          4
Servers Shut Down        4
Servers Cleaned Up       0
Queries Initiated        0
DML Initiated            2
DFO Trees                3
Local Msgs Sent        108
Distr Msgs Sent          0
Local Msgs Recv'd      122
Distr Msgs Recv'd        0
```

Query V$PQ_SYSSTAT view after a SELECT on a table defined with a parallel degree of 5. The following statement illustrates the SELECT COUNT(*)... statement execution. Note this table has a parallel degree object definition of 5:

```
select      statistic, value
from        v$pq_sysstat;

Statistic              Value
Servers Busy             5
Servers Idle             0
Servers High-water       8
Server Sessions         20
Servers Started          5
Servers Shut Down        4
Servers Cleaned Up       0
Queries Initiated        1
DML Initiated            2
DFO Trees                4
Local Msgs Sent        117
Distr Msgs Sent          0
Local Msgs Recv'd      136
Distr Msgs Recv'd        0
```

**TIP**
*A statement hint depicts the degree of parallelism first. If a hint is not present, the parallel object definition degree is used. If neither is available, the number of system CPUs determines the degree.*

Query V$PQ_SYSSTAT view after a DELETE on a table defined with a PARALLEL hint of 6. Even though the table queried is defined with a parallel degree of 5, the hint to use a parallel degree of 6 overrides the table definition.

Monitoring Parallel Operations

```
select      statistic, value
from        v$pq_sysstat;

Statistic            Value
Servers Busy         6
Servers Idle         0
Servers High-water   8
Server Sessions      24
Servers Started      7
Servers Shut Down    5
Servers Cleaned Up   0
Queries Initiated    1
DML Initiated        3
DFO Trees            5
Local Msgs Sent      175
Distr Msgs Sent      0
Local Msgs Recv'd    200
Distr Msgs Recv'd    0
```

**TIP**
*A PARALLEL hint overrides the parallel object definition when it comes to which degree of parallelism the operation will use. The selected degree of parallelism is applied to all statement operations that can be parallelized.*

## V$PQ_SESSTAT View

To provide the current session statistics, query the V$PQ_SESSTAT fixed view. This view should be utilized to see the number of queries executed within the current session, as well as the number of DML operations parallelized. Sample output of a simple SELECT from this view follows:

```
select      statistic, last_query, session_total
from        v$pq_sesstat;

Statistic              LAST QUERY   SESSION TOTAL
Queries Parallelized   0            1
DML Parallelized       1            2
DFO Trees              1            3
Server Threads         6            0
Allocation Height      6            0
Allocation Width       0            0
Local Msgs Sent        27           171
Distr Msgs Sent        0            0
Local Msgs Recv'd      27           167
Distr Msgs Recv'd      0            0
```

**Monitoring Parallel Operations**

## V$PQ_TQSTAT View

Detailed statistics on all parallel server processes and the producer/consumer relationship between them are presented in the v$pq_tqstat fixed view. Additional information is presented on the number of rows and bytes addressed by each server process. This view is best utilized by the DBA tuning long-running queries that require very specific tuning and evaluation of data distribution between server processes. An example of the data available from this fixed view follows:

```
select     *
from       v$pq_tqstat;
```

| DFO NUMBER | TQ ID | SERVER TYPE | NUM ROWS | BYTES | WAITS | TIMEOUTS | PROC |
|---|---|---|---|---|---|---|---|
| 1 | 0 | Consumer | 14315 | 123660 | 14 | 0 | P000 |
| 2 | 0 | Producer | 23657 | 232290 | 7 | 0 | P004 |
| 2 | 0 | Producer | 12323 | 90923 | 7 | 0 | P003 |
| 2 | 0 | Producer | 12321 | 92300 | 7 | 0 | P002 |
| 2 | 0 | Producer | 123212 | 1232222 | 9 | 0 | P001 |
| 2 | 0 | Producer | 330321 | 4333232 | 7 | 0 | P000 |
| 2 | 0 | Consumer | 190535 | 2234322 | 48 | 2 | QC |
| 3 | 0 | Consumer | 8754 | 12323 | 11 | 8 | P003 |
| 3 | 1 | Producer | 234323 | 2002322 | 0 | 0 | P003 |
| . . . | | | | | | | |

# Using EXPLAIN PLAN on Parallel Operations

Parallel statement tuning can be accomplished via the EXPLAIN PLAN facility utilizing the following statements. The other_tag column illustrates the producer/consumer relationship of the execution plan. The object_node column provides information that can be utilized to track the hierarchical, interoperation processing and dependencies between the result sets passed from each server process to the next operation within the execution plan. The EXPLAIN PLAN facility cannot illustrate the dynamics that occur when processes have been completed and become available to address additional result sets that are passed down from the operation level above. One approach utilizing an EXPLAIN PLAN view is illustrated here:

```
create or replace view plan_view
as
select     id, parent_id, lpad(' ',2*(level-1))||operation||'
           '||options||' '|| object_name||' '||object_node||'
           '||decode(id,0,'Cost= '||position) "Execution Plan",
           other_tag "Parallel Op", other "PQ Text"
from       plan_table
start      with id=0
and        statement_id = 'TEST'
```

```
connect by prior id=parent_id
and      statement_id = 'TEST'
/
col "Execution Plan" format a40
col "Parallel Op" format a30
col "PQ Text" format a40 word wrapped
set long 1000
delete    from plan_table
where     statement_id = 'TEST'
/
explain plan
set      statement_id = 'TEST' for
select   to_char(wedate,'YYYY') A, count(*) B
from     time_history
group by to_char(wedate,'YYYY')
order by to_number(to_char(wedate,'YYYY'))
/
select   *
from     plan_view
order by id, parent_id
/
```

| ID | PARENT ID | Execution Plan | Parallel Op | PQ Text |
|---|---|---|---|---|
| 0 | | SELECT STATEMENT | | Cost= 317653 |
| 1 | 0 | SORT ORDER BY | PARALLEL_TO_SERIAL | SELECT   A1.C0 C0,A1.C1 C1,A1.C2 C2 FROM :Q18001 A1 ORDER BY A1.C0 |
| 2 | 1 | SORT GROUP BY | PARALLEL_TO_PARALLEL | SELECT   /*+ CIV_GB */ TO_NUMBER(A1.C0) C0,A1.C0C1, COUNT(A1.C1) C2 FROM :Q18000 A1 GROUP BY A1.C0 |
| 3 | 2 | TABLE ACCESS FULL | PARALLEL_TO_PARALLEL | SELECT   /*+ PIV_GB*/ A1.C0 TIME_HISTORY C0,COUNT(*) C1 FROM (SELECT/*+ ROWID(A2) */ TO_CHAR(A2. WEDATE",'YYYY') C0 FROM "TIME_HISTORY" A2 WHERE ROWID BETWEEN :B1 AND :B2) A1 GROUP BY A1.C0 |

The key "other_tag" values to look for are PARALLEL_TO_SERIAL, PARALLEL_TO_PARALLEL, PARALLEL_COMBINED_WITH_PARENT, and PARALLEL_COMBINED_WITH_CHILD. If you see SERIAL_TO_SERIAL, you have effected a serial, nonparallelized execution plan. The primary operation, within the execution plan, will always be represented as PARALLEL_TO_SERIAL, and the last operation completed within the execution plan has the purpose of returning the result set to the process performing the EXECUTE call of the SQL statement.

**TIP**
*The other_tag and other columns of the plan_table are used to view information about a parallelized query.*

# Tuning Parallel Execution and the Oracle7 init.ora Parameters

Table 11-1 provides a listing of the init.ora parameters that are necessary for parallel operations or has an impact in Oracle7 and Oracle8. At the very least, the parameters PARALLEL_MAX_SERVERS and PARALLEL_MIN_SERVERS should be established in the init.ora.

Parameters related to physical memory are generally set much higher than in a nonparallel environment. These are general parameter settings, but your settings must be based on your specific business environment. The parameters that are noted with an "*" are those that are only indirectly related to parallel performance and must be set in accordance with the number of users and other environment issues that you have with your system.

| init.ora Parameter | Oracle7 Release | Meaning | Suggested Values |
|---|---|---|---|
| *ALWAYS_ANTI_JOIN | 7.3.1 | Setting this parameter enables hash antijoins. Meaningful to parallelize NOT IN clauses. | HASH |
| COMPATIBLE | ALL | Setting this parameter to the release level of the instance allows you to take advantage of all of the functionality built into the RDBMS engine. | Current Release (as in 7.2.3) |
| *DB_BLOCK_BUFFERS | ALL | Sets size of buffer cache in SGA; this parameter (expressed in blocks) multiplied by block size dictates size of buffer cache. | If BlkSize = 2K; 5000+ If BlkSize = 4K; 2500+ If BlkSize = 8K; 1200+ |

**TABLE 11-1.**   *Necessary init.ora Parameters for Parallel Operations*

| init.ora Parameter | Oracle7 Release | Meaning | Suggested Values |
|---|---|---|---|
| *DB_BLOCK_SIZE | ALL | Oracle block size expressed in bytes. Must be multiple of O/S block size. | 4096–8192 |
| *HASH_AREA_SIZE | 7.3.1 | Memory allocation expressed in bytes on a per-user basis for performing HASH joins. | 64K |
| *HASH_JOIN_ENABLED | 7.3.1 | Setting this parameter enables HASH joins. | TRUE |
| PARALLEL_DEFAULT_MAX_SCANS | 7.1.4 | Maximum degree of parallelism available to any single full table scan. | 4–8; this (only) limits each query. |
| PARALLEL_DEFAULT_SCANSIZE | 7.1.4 | Obsolete in 7.3.x. Parameter used to calculate the default degree of parallelism. Size of table in blocks divided by this parameter = default degree of parallelism. | Don't allow this to happen! Set this parameter high to approach size of largest tables. |
| PARALLEL_MAX_SERVERS | 7.1.4 | Maximum number of servers allowed existing simultaneously. | Calculate = (PQ Users * Max DOP * Avg # of Operations/statement). |
| PARALLEL_MIN_SERVERS | 7.1.4 | Minimum number of servers created when instance starts. As servers idle out, terminate, number of servers never falls below this number. | 0 - O/S limit. Realistically, start with 10–24. |
| PARALLEL_MIN_PERCENT | 7.3.1 | If the percentage of the degree of parallelism (number of servers) required by the query is not available, statement will terminate. | 0 = Always execute 100 = Only if servers can be acquired. Any value 0–100 valid. |
| PARALLEL_SERVER_IDLE_TIME | 7.1.4 | Number of minutes a server process remains idle before terminated by Oracle. | 1- unlimited. Depending on environment, 15–30 minutes is appropriate. |

**EXPLAIN PLAN**

**TABLE 11-1.** *Necessary init.ora Parameters for Parallel Operations* (continued)

| init.ora Parameter | Oracle7 Release | Meaning | Suggested Values |
|---|---|---|---|
| RECOVERY_PARALLELISM | 7.1.4 | Number of recovery processes that will be devoted to instance or media recovery. | 2 - value of PARALLEL_MAX_ SERVERS. |
| *SHARED_POOL_SIZE | ALL | Size of Oracle Shared Pool. Portion of Shared Pool is used for query server communication. | Increase existing parameter value by 5–10 percent for heavy, concurrent PQ use. |
| *SORT_DIRECT_WRITES | 7.2 | Bypass the buffer cache when writing sort data to temp tablespace. Set this parameter = TRUE, PQ or No PQ! | TRUE |
| *SORT_AREA_SIZE | ALL | Per-user maximum allocation of sort space. Each PQ server utilizes this amount of sort space as well. Set this value = SORT_AREA_RETAINED_SIZE as sort space will most often increase to this maximum. Be careful of physical memory limits! | 65K–1MB. Limited by physical memory. |
| *SORT_AREA_RETAINED_ SIZE | ALL | Set equal to SORT_AREA_ SIZE. Amount of sort space retained on a per-user basis. PQ server processes will be allocated and retain sort space. | 65K–1MB. Limited by physical memory. |

*An indirect effect on parallel options

**TABLE 11-1.** *Necessary init.ora Parameters for Parallel Operations* (continued)

# Tuning Parallel Execution and the Oracle8 init.ora Parameters

Parameters related to physical memory, shown in the following table, are generally set much higher than in a nonparallel environment. These are general parameter settings, but your settings must be based on your unique business environment.

| init.ora Parameter | Oracle8 Release | Meaning | Suggested Values |
|---|---|---|---|
| *ALWAYS_ANTI_JOIN | ALL | Enables HASH antijoins. Meaningful to parallelize NOT IN clauses; otherwise, they will be performed as sequential, correlated subquery. | HASH |
| *ALWAYS_SEMI_JOIN | 8.0.4 | Meaningful to parallelize EXISTS clauses using a view query block and semijoin evaluated in parallel. | HASH |
| COMPATIBLE | ALL | Setting this parameter to the release level of the instance allows you to take advantage of all of the functionality built into the RDBMS engine. Oracle recommends backing up the database *before* setting this parameter! | Set Value to 8.0.<x> |
| *DB_BLOCK_BUFFERS | ALL | Sets size of buffer cache in SGA; this parameter (expressed in blocks) multiplied by block size dictates bytes of memory available for actual data. | If BlkSize = 2K; 5000+ If BlkSize = 4K; 2500+ If BlkSize = 8K; 1200+ |
| *DB_BLOCK_SIZE | ALL | Oracle block size expressed in bytes. Must be multiple of O/S block size. | 4096–8192 |
| *DB_FILE_MULTIBLOCK_ READ_COUNT | ALL | The number of blocks that are read into the SGA in a single I/O. Data warehouses generally benefit from larger values while heavy TP environments with a lot of users may cause wasted memory with a high setting. | 2–16, but O/S dependent |
| *HASH_AREA_SIZE | ALL | Memory allocation expressed in bytes on a per-user basis for performing HASH joins. | Set to the square root of the larger of the two inputs. Then, divide this number by 2 times the number of processes. |

**Tuning Parallel Execution**

| init.ora Parameter | Oracle8 Release | Meaning | Suggested Values |
|---|---|---|---|
| OPTIMIZER_PERCENT_PARALLEL | ALL | This determines the probability that the optimizer will choose a parallel scan over an index scan. This is disabled if OPTIMIZER_MODE= FIRST_ROWS. | 0 = Use Index 1–99 = likelihood of a parallel scan choice 100 = Use parallel |
| PARALLEL_ADAPTIVE_MULTI_USER | 8.0.4 | Reduces the degree of parallelism based on number of active parallel users. | TRUE/FALSE False = default |
| PARALLEL_BROADCAST_ENABLE | 8.0.4 | Allows the optimizer to send a small table result set to each of the parallel servers handling pieces of the large table in a hash and merge join scenario. | TRUE/FALSE False = default |
| PARALLEL_MAX_SERVERS | ALL | Maximum number of ervers allowed existing simultaneously. *Set this parameter*! Attempts to initiate parallel operations beyond this amount cannot be executed in parallel. | 2 * Number CPUs + 1 |
| PARALLEL_MIN_SERVERS | ALL | Minimum number of servers created when instance originates. As servers idle out, terminate, number of servers never falls below this number. | 0 - O/S limit. Realistically, start with 10–24. Set to PARALLEL_MAX_SERVERS if PQO is prevalent. |
| PARALLEL_MIN_PERCENT | ALL | If this percentage of the degree of parallelism (number of servers) required by the query is not available, statement will terminate with an error. This is effective when a serial execution of the statement is undesired. | 0 = Always execute. 100 = Only if servers can be acquired. Any value 0–100 valid. |

| init.ora Parameter | Oracle8 Release | Meaning | Suggested Values |
|---|---|---|---|
| PARALLEL_SERVER_IDLE_TIME | ALL | Number of minutes a server process remains idle before terminated by Oracle. Will not go below the PARALLEL_MIN_SERVERS. | 1- unlimited. Depending on environment, 15–30 minutes is appropriate. |
| RECOVERY_PARALLELISM | ALL | Number of recovery processes that will be devoted to instance or media recovery. | 2 - value of PARALLEL_MAX_SERVERS. |
| *SHARED_POOL_SIZE | ALL | Size of Oracle Shared Pool. Portion of Shared Pool is used for query server communication. | Increase existing parameter value by 5–10 percent for heavy, concurrent PQ use. |
| *SORT_DIRECT_WRITES | ALL | Bypass the buffer cache when writing sort data to temp tablespace. | AUTO |
| *SORT_AREA_SIZE | ALL | Per-user maximum allocation of sort space. Each PQ server utilizes this amount of sort space as well. Set this value = SORT_AREA_RETAINED_SIZE as sort space will most often increase to this maximum. Be careful of physical memory limits! | 65K–1MB. Limited by physical memory. |
| *SORT_AREA_RETAINED_SIZE | ALL | Set equal to SORT_AREA_SIZE. Amount of sort space retained on a per-user basis. PQ server processes will be allocated and retain sort space. | 65K–1MB. Limited by physical memory. |

*An indirect effect on parallel options

The existence of the above parameters in the init.ora file will *not* initiate parallel *anything* on your system until you enable parallel operations! You enable

**Tuning Parallel Execution**

parallel operations by using a PARALLEL hint on a SQL statement or using a CREATE/ALTER...PARALLEL on a table definition. When giving consideration to adjusting any init.ora parameter, fully investigate the *Oracle Database Administrator's Guide* or the appropriate server installation guide for your system *prior* to experimenting with an Oracle7/8 Server instance.

### V8 TIP
*Version 8.0.4 new init.ora parameters: ALWAYS_SEMI_JOIN (helps queries using EXISTS), PARALLEL_ADAPTIVE_MULTI_USER (dynamically adjusts degree), and PARALLEL_BROADCAST_ENABLE (joins a small table with each piece of a parallelized large table).*

# Parallel Loading

Parallel loading can greatly increase the speed of loading data. When considering the use of parallel loading, you must first consider some of the issues that come along with the advantages. For example, indexes cannot be defined on the table that you are loading into, and you must size the initial extents of the table to accommodate each parallel session without wasting space. Each loader session will allocate a new extent, and space preallocated to the table that will be loaded into is not used. The parallel argument to SQL*Loader requires an APPEND directive in the control file.

**SQL*Loader command:**

```
sqlldr80 userid=scott/tiger DATA=file<x>.dat DIRECT=TRUE PARALLEL=TRUE
```

- Multiple Loads are executed at the same time.
- The PARALLEL argument is required because any single loader session can write into any partition. If you place partitions strategically in different tablespaces, the desired distribution is achieved.

### TIP
*The PARALLEL option for data loading improves performance of loads, but can also cause space to be wasted when not properly used.*

# Performance Comparisons and Monitoring Parallel Operations

We will perform the following test and display the following results:

1. Start the database with 12 parallel servers and check the background processes that are created.

2. Run a query without PARALLEL and check the speed.

3. Run a query with PARALLEL that requires sorting with a degree of 6.

4. Check the output of V$PQ_SYSSTAT and V$PQ_SESSTAT views.

   The following output shows the ps -ef output for 12 parallel servers running. We started the database with the init.ora parameter PARALLEL_MIN_SERVERS = 12. The name of the database is fdr1.

```
#ps -ef
oracle  2765     1  0 00:08:32    ?    0:00 ora_dbwr_fdr1
oracle  2764     1  0 17:08:30    ?    0:00 ora_pmon_fdr1
oracle  2766     1  0 17:08;34    ?    0:00 ora_lgwr_fdr1
oracle  2768     1  0 17:08:38    ?    0:00 ora_reco_fdr1
oracle  2770     1  0 17:08:42    ?    0:00 ora_d000_fdr1
oracle  2769     1  0 17:08:40    ?    0:00 ora_s000_fdr1
oracle  2767     1  0 17:08:36    ?    0:00 ora_smon_fdr1
oracle  2771     1  4 17:08:44    ?    0:33 ora_p000_fdr1
oracle  2772     1  5 17:08:46    ?    0:42 ora_p001_fdr1
oracle  2773     1  4 17:08:48    ?    0:33 ora_p002_fdr1
oracle  2774     1  4 17:08:50    ?    0:32 ora_p003_fdr1
oracle  2775     1  5 17:08:52    ?    0:40 ora_p004_fdr1
oracle  2776     1 14 17:08:54    ?    1:26 ora_p005_fdr1
oracle  2819  2802 13 17:12:39    ?    1:44 ora_p006_fdr1
oracle  2820  2802  1 17:12:41    ?    0:05 ora_p007_fdr1
oracle  2821  2802  0 17:12:43    ?    0:01 ora_p008_fdr1
oracle  2822  2802  0 17:12:45    ?    0:01 ora_p009_fdr1
oracle  2825  2802  2 17:12:47    ?    0:11 ora_p010_fdr1
oracle  2826  2802 10 17:12:49    ?    1:18 ora_p011_fdr1
```

5. Run the query *not* using PARALLEL:

```
select  job_sub_code, sum(amount_cost), sum(amount_credit),
        sum(amount_debit)
from    edap.job_order_line_items
group by job_sub_code;
```

Performance Comparisons

```
JO      SUM(AMOUNT COST)   SUM(AMOUNT CREDIT)   SUM(AMOUNT DEBIT)
02           9834013.62          20611471.9             0
04           38670782.7          43440986.1             0
05             252599.77          7139753.85            0
07              8899.66                   0             0
12           1689729.94          3355174.16            0
14            103089.64          3287384.45            0
...(only partial output)
Elapsed: 00:02:29.34
```

6. Run the query using PARALLEL:

```
select     /*+ PARALLEL (job_order_line_items,6) */
           sum(amount_cost), sum(amount_credit),
           sum(amount_debit)
from       edap.job_order_line_items
group by   job_sub_code;
```

```
JO   SUM(AMOUNT COST)   SUM(AMOUNT CREDIT)   SUM(AMOUNT DEBIT)
02   9834013.62          20611471.9            0
04   38670782.7          43440986.1            0
05   1252599.77          7139753.85            0
07   8899.66             0                     0
12   1689729.94          3355174.16            0
14   103089.64           3287384.45            0

...(only partial output)
Elapsed: 00:01:04.55
```

The query is over twice as fast, but this was with a degree of 6. Do not be fooled into believing that a degree of *N* will make a query *N* times faster.

**TIP**

*The degree of a parallel operation does not decrease the time of execution. It is entirely dependent on the complete setup of the system that you have. The degree only chooses the number of processes that will be used for the operation.*

7. The V$ output when using PARALLEL with degree 12 (for the previous query):

```
select     statistic, value
from       v$pq_sysstat;
```

```
Statistic            Value
Servers Busy         12
Servers Idle         0
Servers High-water   12
```

```
Server Sessions        39
Servers Started        13
Servers Shut Down      7
Servers Cleaned Up     0
Queries Initiated      5
DFO Trees              5
Local Msgs Sent        91261
Distr Msgs Sent        0
Local Msgs Recv'd      91259
Distr Msgs Recv'd      0

select      *
from        v$pq_sesstat

Statistic                  LAST QUERY    SESSION TOTAL
Queries Parallelized       1             4
DFO Trees                  1             4
Server Threads             12            0
Allocation Height          6             0
Allocation Width           1             0
Local Msgs Sent            20934         83722
Distr Msgs Sent            0             0
Local Msgs Recv'd          20934         83722
Distr Msgs Recv'd          0             0
```

Note that the output from the v$ views shows the degree used.

**Performance example (parallelism degree is 20):**

```
select      /*+ FULL(order)  PARALLEL(order,20) */
            ordno, ord_total
from        order
where       cust_id = 31754;
```

Note that once again the performance is not 20 times faster when the degree is set to 20. In this case, it is about 15 times faster. Your results will depend on your hardware and system setup.

```
Operation    Processors    Minutes
Scan         1             46.4
             20            3.1
```

# Summary

Planning (or reengineering) the physical location of data files is key to successful parallel data access. Determine an appropriate degree of parallelism for each parallelized SQL statement and parallelize the creation of your parallel-able physical design.

Don't let the init.ora parameters dictate how the degree of parallelism is determined. Remember, you're trying to optimize a few (OK, maybe a dozen or so), slow queries, not every table access. Databases perform optimally when *indexes* are used nearly exclusively! Experiment with conservative parameters and utilize parallel operations for table or index creations and hint the degree of parallelism you identify as optimal.

The parallel features offered in Oracle7/8 are incredibly powerful tools when utilized in a targeted fashion—most databases can be tuned to place indexes in the right quantity and location to deliver acceptable performance. Parallel operations should be used for those statements that cannot be written any other way but to scan an entire table or address a partitioned large table/index. The second most powerful application of parallelized operations is the creation of data warehouse or data store tables and indexes in nightly or weekly runs. Performance improvements for these operations can be dramatic.

# Tips Review

- When the parallel degree is set to *N*, it is possible to use $(2*N)+1$ total processes for the parallel operation.

- A statement hint dictates the degree of parallelism first. If a hint is not present, the parallel object definition degree is used. If neither is available, the number of system CPUs determines the degree.

- Using parallel operations on very small tables or very fast queries can also degrade performance since the "breaking up" and "putting together" part also costs performance resources.

- In Oracle7, you must have at least one full table scan in order to take advantage of Parallel Query Option. Parallel DML statements are *not* allowed, but subqueries with a full table scan of the DML statements can use parallel operations.

- In Oracle8, parallel DML statements *are* allowed.

- In Oracle8, operations are performed in parallel on partitioned objects *only* when more than one partition is accessed, and parallelism is *not* performed within a single partition.

- In Oracle8, any server process allocated for a statement may handle any request from a process within the same statement (but only at the next statement hierarchy level).

■ Using the PARALLEL hint will enable the use of parallel operations. If the degree is not specified with the hint, the default degree during the table creation will be used. Using the alias for a table in the FROM clause means that you must use the alias for the table in the hint.

■ The use of the NOPARALLEL hint will disable parallel operations in a statement that would otherwise utilize parallel processing due to a parallel object definition.

■ Specify the degree of parallelism using a hint instead of relying on the table definition or the init.ora parameters. This will ensure that all operations are tuned for the given query as opposed to a "broad brush" method of tuning.

■ Parallelism is determined by the statement that you are using. A SELECT and an UPDATE statement cannot be assumed to perform the same functions.

■ The parallel degree specified by a table will be used for the CREATE INDEX statement when a PARALLEL hint is not used on the CREATE INDEX.

■ Using UNRECOVERABLE (V7.3) or NOLOGGING (V8) can remove the bottleneck caused by parallel writes to the redo logs.

■ Effective parallel operations will depend greatly on how the data is physically located.

■ In Oracle8, parallel DML statements use an entirely different set of rules. You must know the rules for each scenario to effectively use parallel DML operations.

■ In Oracle8, an error statement will occur if a COMMIT is not issued after using parallel DML statements prior to issuing another query. You will receive an error doing a SELECT statement that follows a parallel DML statement if you do not issue a COMMIT.

■ The PARALLEL hint may be used in multiple sections of a query.

■ Querying the V$PQ_SYSSTAT view will display statistics for parallel operations. If the Servers Busy statistic is consistently higher than the init.ora parameter MIN_PARALLEL_SERVERS, you need to increase the parameter in the init.ora file.

■ The other_tag and other columns of the plan_table are used to view information about a parallelized query.

■ Version 8.0.4 new init.ora parameters: ALWAYS_SEMI_JOIN (helps queries using EXISTS), PARALLEL_ADAPTIVE_MULTI_USER (dynamically adjusts degree), and PARALLEL_BROADCAST_ENABLE (joins a small table with each piece of a parallelized large table).

**Tips Review**

- The PARALLEL option for data loading improves performance of loads, but can also cause space to be wasted when not properly used.

- The Parallel Query Option is not just for the 100GB-plus database crowd! Implementations scanning less than 1 million rows see anywhere from 10–100+ percent query performance improvements.

# References

*Oracle Parallel Query*; Jake Van der Vort, TUSC

*Oracle8 Server Tuning*; Oracle Corporation

*Oracle8 Server Concepts*; Oracle Corporation

*Oracle8 Server Reference*; Oracle Corporation

Thanks to R&R Donnelley and Sons, A. T. Kearney, Inc., and the TUSC DBA*Tech Team. Jake Van der Vort contributed the major portion of this chapter.

Tips Review

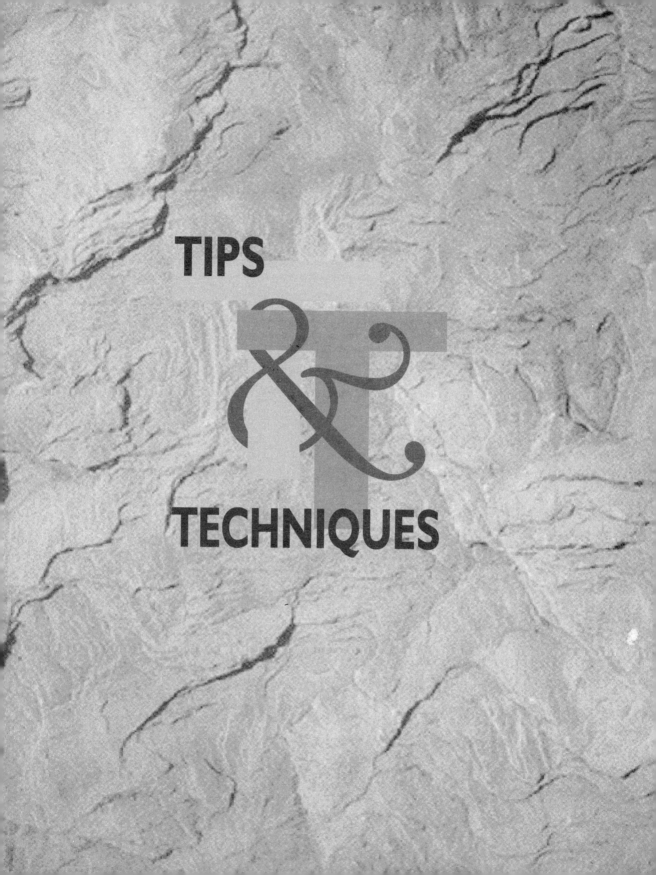

TIPS
&
T
TECHNIQUES

# CHAPTER
## 12

Oracle8 New Features
(Developer and DBA)

The goal of this chapter is to list some of the new features that are important when considering the migration of Oracle8. Chapter 13 will investigate some of the Oracle8 features and provide detailed examples that can lead to improvements in performance. The latest release of Oracle8 is a tremendous improvement over previous releases of Oracle RDBMS. The difficulty in understanding the new features of Oracle8 is in finding documentation that explains all of the new available options. Several features are well marketed by the Oracle Corporation and are featured in this book, but a comprehensive list is difficult to find. This chapter will focus on some of the more important features of Oracle8. Tips covered in this chapter include the following:

- Database scalability and the new limits of Oracle
- The Oracle Call Interface (OCI); fewer cursors for connections
- Large object support (BLOB, CLOB, NCLOB, and BFILE)
- Partitioning options and general overview
- Net8 replacing SQL*Net
- Constraints and the NOVALIDATE option
- Indexing organized tables and reverse-key indexes explained
- Parallel processing expands to DML statements in Oracle8
- Star query processing gets a new algorithm
- Security profiles and passwords have expanded options
- ROWID changes and new views in Oracle8
- What a parallel server is and what a distributed server is
- Notes on upgrading or migrating to Oracle8
- Network Computing Architecture (NCA) and the explosion of the Internet
- Develop for NCA: JDeveloper, Oracle Forms, and Internet Commerce Server (ICS)
- Desupported features from Oracle7

# Database Scalability

Everything just got bigger! As Oracle heads toward a revolution away from smaller distributed servers to larger, more centralized database powerhouses, the size limitations have gone through the roof. As smaller database vendors struggle to catch up to the functionality of Oracle, Oracle8 positions companies for a return to a more centralized computing and three-tier architecture. Those tiers that seem to be the next future for IS are the client (browser), the application server (applications), and the database server on the back end. Oracle8's ability to address scalability may push this to fruition.

The following table shows some of the incredible increases in the upper limits for Oracle's database.

| Name | Oracle8 New Upper Limit |
| --- | --- |
| Database size | 512PB (up from 32TB) |
| Maximum data files | 65,533 |
| Data files per tablespace | 1,022 |
| Blocks per data file | 4,000,000 |
| Block size | 32K |
| Maximum data file size | 128GB (4M*32K) |
| Maximum tablespace size | 128TB (1,022 *128GB) |
| DB_BLOCK_BUFFERS | Unlimited |
| SGA for 32-bit OS | 4GB |
| SGA for 64-bit OS | Beyond 4GB |
| User population | 10,000 |
| Table columns | 1,000 (up from 256) |
| B-tree index columns | 32 (up from 16) |
| Bitmap index columns | 30 |

Oracle also increased support for very large databases (VLDBs) with the addition of partitions, index-organized tables, and unlimited extents. The support of the 64-bit operating systems will provide increased performance.

**TIP**

*Knowing the upper limits of the Oracle database is paramount to successful implementation. The Oracle database can now be as large as 512 petabytes!*

Database Scalability

# Oracle Call Interface

A "free" and automatic benefit of moving to Oracle8 is the improvements to the Oracle Call Interface (OCI) that Oracle uses to manage cursors and connections. The shift from a cursor to a message-based connection allows OCI to use a handle instead of a cursor. This saves a tremendous amount of memory per user and reduces round-trips (from client to server) by piggybacking multiple commands in a single message. This is probably the best performance benefit of moving to Oracle8—other than the partitioning option, which I consider the best benefit of Oracle8. No additional coding is necessary for this to take effect in Oracle8; you just need to use the Oracle8 OCI in the client or the newer ODBC driver supplied by Oracle.

 **TIP**
*Upgrading to Oracle8 will yield immediate gains in performance as Oracle has moved from a cursor to message-based connection. This allows OCI to use a handle instead of a cursor.*

# Large Object Support

Large objects (LOBs) are data types that will help with large binary objects in addition to the LONG data type. LOBs are used for sound, images, and other large pieces of data. LOBs replace many of the Oracle7 uses of LONG and LONG RAW data types. LOB data can be indexed with access that starts at a specific byte (piece-wise access) of information. You can also access LOBs directly from disk, in addition to going through the Oracle buffer cache. LOBs can range up to 4GB in size and a single table may contain multiple LOBs. LOBs can also be replicated. The following LOBs are available:

- BLOB, for binary large objects
- CLOB, for character large objects
- NCLOB, for character large objects stored in the national character
- BFILE, for binary files stored outside of the database. The data type stores a locator within the Oracle8 table that points to an operating system file. This can be advantageous since these files would not need to be backed up with the database (if static).

 **TIP**
*The LONG and LONG RAW data types can be replaced with the more functional BLOB, CLOB, NCLOB, and BFILE data types.*

Oracle Call Interface

# Partitioning

One of the most powerful features of Oracle8 is the ability to partition tables and indexes, enabling you to break up tables and/or indexes into smaller pieces, by accessing strategically placed smaller pieces of a table and/or index (see Figure 12-1). The performance is greatly increased when compared to accessing the entire (large) table and/or index. In Figure 12-1, a large orders table may be broken into several logical partitions that reside in logical tablespaces, which in turn reside in the physical data files on the disks. Note that there are detailed examples in Chapter 13 on partitioning.

# Important Issues Concerning Partitioning

The following points should be considered when partitioning:

- Oracle recommends that any table greater than 2GB should be partitioned. Historical tables that are large should be considered for partitioning.

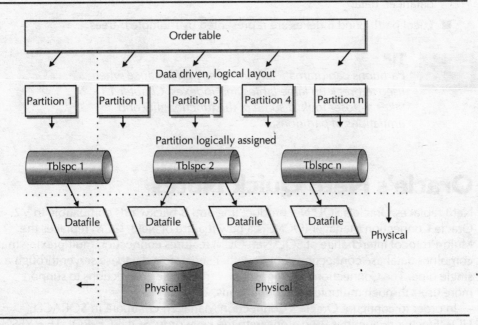

**FIGURE 12-1.** *Several partitions residing in logical tablespaces*

- Tables used to perform parallel DML *must* be partitioned, and the degree of parallelism will be equal to the number of partitions affected by the DML operation. Ensure that heavy I/O operations are split into multiple partitions so that the full effect of parallel DML is achieved. During a parallel INSERT, global unique indexes must be set to UNUSABLE prior to parallel UPDATEs and then rebuilt after the UPDATE. Parallel INSERTs *cannot* be performed on a partitioned table with a global index. Following recoveries of partitioned data, global indexes must be rebuilt. Indexes that are accessed in a parallel index scan should be partitioned.

- Large tables that are frequently accessed with a full table scan should be partitioned.

- EXPORT can now export a single table partition. You can also export in parallel and/or export a single partition.

- Partition the read data from the write data, and you can export only the changed data.

- You can analyze a partition of a table independently from others and run these simultaneously.

- Data imbalances that are often fixed with histograms can also be fixed by partitioning the data to unbalanced data separated into partitions that have balanced data.

- Local partitioned indexes are represented by multiple b-trees.

**TIP**
*Partitions can dramatically increase performance when used to break up large tables and indexes. Chapter 13 takes a closer look at some of the functionality and limitations of partitions.*

# Oracle's Net8 Quick Notes

Net8 replaces Oracle's SQL*Net product line and is backwards compatible to V2. Oracle Connection Manager (OCM) is a new feature of Net8. OCM replaces the Multi-Protocol Interchange of SQL*Net. OCM features connection multiplexing that combines database connections from another server to a database server through a single pipe. The Connection Pooling feature utilizes idle connections to support more users through multiplexing connections.

In order to configure Oracle's Connection Manager, cman.ora in $ORACLE_HOME/network/admin is used along with the keywords "SOURCE_ROUTE = YES" in tnsnames.ora for the database and "USE_CMAN = TRUE" in sqlnet.ora. OCM listens by default on port 1600. To start CM, use "cmctl start cman." This spawns both the cmadmin (CM admin) and cmgw (CM) background processes (cman is for both, cm is for CM, adm is for admin process only). MTS_MULTIPLE_LISTENERS in init.ora parameter enables listener load balancing for MTS in Oracle8 databases.

The Oracle Advanced Networking Option (ANO) is an add-on layer to Net8. This option integrates with third-party vendors of network security. This option uses RC4 from RSA Data Security, providing Advanced Cryptography, Data Modification and Disruption Protection, and Enhanced User Authentication and Authorization.

Some parameters and files that are obsolete or soon to be obsolete are as follows:

- COMMUNITY
- NAMES.DEFAULT_ZONE
- NAMES.PREFERRED_SERVERS
- SQLNET.AUTHENTICATION_SERVICES
- SQLNET.EXPIRE_TIME
- SQLNET.CRYPTO_SEED
- TNSNAV.ORA

**TIP**
*Net8 is replacing SQL*Net, and many of the original SQL*Net parameters are now obsolete. There is now a GUI front end for configuring and maintaining Net8. Oracle does not recommend manual editing of the TNSnames.ora file.*

# Constraint Options

Constraints can be enabled with a NOVALIDATE as part of the ENABLE CONSTRAINT command. This is an excellent feature for a data warehouse where large amounts of data are loaded. When the ENABLE CONSTRAINT is issued, the existing table data is not validated against the constraint, but all future data is checked. Don't forget to eventually issue the ENABLE CONSTRAINT...VALIDATE, so that all data is eventually validated (but all at once...which is faster).

**TIP**
*Using the NOVALIDATE option in the ENABLE CONSTRAINT command allows for a high-speed INSERT of large amounts of data. The data must be eventually validated, but this can be done all at once instead of one row at a time.*

Constraint Options

# Index Organized Tables

An index-organized table is when all of the table data is stored in a b-tree structure. Only one database object is used to store both the data and the index. All of the columns are stored as an index. B-tree indexes identify rows by primary keys, not by ROWIDs. A secondary index cannot be created on the table, and if UPDATEs are made, entire rows may be moved by the operation (costly). The performance gain is achieved when the data is accessed by the key in an exact match or range scan on the key.

# Reverse-Key Index

The bytes of the column data value are reversed in a reverse-key index that eliminates sequential values being stored in a sequential order. This allows sequential values to be distributed more accurately in the b-tree, when inserting values that are sequential, and hot spots are avoided.

# Parallel Operations with Oracle8

Parallel operations in Oracle7 and Oracle8 are covered in Chapter 11; this section will focus on new features in Oracle8. Oracle8 introduced the Parallel DML feature, allowing parallel execution of INSERT, UPDATE, and DELETE operations. The following is a list of statements that are capable of parallel execution with Oracle8:

- SELECT
- UPDATE, INSERT
- DELETE
- CREATE TABLE as...
- CREATE INDEX
- REBUILD INDEX
- MOVE/SPLIT PARTITION
- ENABLE CONSTRAINT

**TIP**

*In Oracle8, parallel DML statements are allowed. This functionality applies to partitioned tables and indexes. Parallelization still cannot be performed on an index operation, but parallelization can be performed on a partitioned index.*

Note that no parallel DML is allowed on the following:

- Triggers
- Tables with object columns
- Distributed transactions
- Delete cascade constraints
- Deferred integrity constraints

# Star Query Processing

Star query processing was officially introduced in version 7.3 of the database, but has been improved in version 8. One type of data warehouse design centers around what is known as a "star" schema. The star schema is characterized by one or more very large fact tables (the table that connects almost all others). The fact table contains the primary information in the data warehouse and a number of much smaller dimension tables (or "lookup" tables) contain information about the entries for a particular attribute in the fact table.

A star query is a join between a fact table and a number of lookup tables. Each lookup table is joined to the fact table using a primary-key to foreign-key join, but the lookup tables are not joined to each other. A typical fact table contains keys and measures. For example, a simple fact table might contain the measure sales, and keys time, product, and market. In this case, there would be corresponding dimension tables for time, product, and market. The product dimension table, for example, would typically contain information about each product number that appears in the fact table. A star join is a primary-key to foreign-key join of the dimension tables to a fact table. The fact table normally has a concatenated index on the key columns to facilitate this type of join.

The Oracle8 cost-based optimizer has a new algorithm for recognizing and optimizing star queries and generates more efficient execution plans than Oracle7. However, the rule-based optimizer does not recognize star queries.

**TIP**
*Oracle8 has an improved star query processing algorithm. Oracle has also added hints to facilitate the use of star query processing.*

# Security—Options

The Oracle security system has been enhanced in Oracle8 with a variety of helpful options. The Oracle Security Server offers a single sign-on environment complete with the means for global roles and user setup, password expiration, minimum password lengths, shared database links, privileged database links, and encryption from OCI and PL/SQL.

The init.ora parameter, DBLINK_ENCRYPT_LOGIN specifies whether attempts to connect to other Oracle servers through database links should use encrypted passwords. When you attempt to connect to a database using a password, Oracle encrypts the password before sending it to the database. If the DBLINK_ENCRYPT_ LOGIN parameter is TRUE and the connection fails, Oracle does not reattempt the connection. If this parameter is FALSE, Oracle will attempt the connections using an unencrypted version of the password.

## Security Data Dictionary Changes

The following tables illustrate detailed information regarding three security data dictionary parameters (an * denotes new columns in Oracle8).

**SYS.DBA_USERS:**

| Column Name | Null | Type |
| --- | --- | --- |
| username | NOT NULL | VARCHAR2(30) |
| user_id | NOT NULL | number |
| password | | VARCHAR2(30) |
| *account_status | NOT NULL | VARCHAR2(32) |
| *lock_date | | date |
| *expiry_date | | date |
| default_tablespace | NOT NULL | VARCHAR2(30) |
| temporary_tablespace | NOT NULL | VARCHAR2(30) |
| created | NOT NULL | date |
| profile | NOT NULL | VARCHAR2(30) |
| *external_name | | VARCHAR2(4000) |

**SYS.DBA_PROFILES:**

| Column Name | Null | Type |
| --- | --- | --- |
| profile | NOT NULL | VARCHAR2(30) |
| resource_name | NOT NULL | VARCHAR2(32) |
| **\*resource_type** | | **VARCHAR2(8) kernel/password** |
| limit | | VARCHAR2(40) |

**SYS.DBA_DB_LINKS:**

| Column Name | Null | Type |
| --- | --- | --- |
| owner | NOT NULL | VARCHAR2(30) |
| db_link | NOT NULL | VARCHAR2(128) |
| username | | VARCHAR2(30) |
| **\*host** | | **varchar2(2000) \*up from 255** |
| created | NOT NULL | date |

The following are new roles in Oracle8:

SELECT_CATALOG_ROLE
EXECUTE_CATALOG_ROLE
DELETE_CATALOG_ROLE
AQ_USER_ROLE
AQ_ADMINISTRATOR_ROLE
RECOVERY_CATALOG_OWNER
HS_ADMIN_ROLE

**TIP**
*New columns enin DBAz_USERS, DBA_PROFILES, and
DBA_DB_LINKS offer new information concerning user
account status and general security information.*

# Security—Profiles

Profiles are used in Oracle to prevent users from using inordinate amounts of resources and to enforce security regarding user passwords. The following profile options have been added in Oracle8 to enhance security:

```
FAILED_LOGIN_ATTEMPTS
PASSWORD_LIFE_TIME
PASSWORD_REUSE_TIME
PASSWORD_REUSE_MAX
PASSWORD_VERIFY_FUNCTION
PASSWORD_LOCK_TIME
PASSWORD_GRACE_TIME
```

Examples of creating a profile with explanations of each profile option are embedded within the command. Note that I have placed comments in parentheses for each of the parameters in the command. The command will not work as written here unless you remove the comments (for explanation purposes).

CREATE PROFILE *NEW_PROFILE* LIMIT

| | |
|---|---|
| SESSIONS_PER_USER | UNLIMITED (limits a user integer concurrent session) |
| CPU_PER_SESSION | UNLIMITED (limits the CPU time for a session) |
| CPU_PER_CALL | 3000 (limits CPU time for a parse, execute, or fetch) |
| CONNECT_TIME | 45 (limits the total elapsed time of a session) |
| IDLE_TIME | 120 (limits periods of continuous inactive time) |
| LOGICAL_READS_PER_SESSION | 1000 (limits the data blocks read in a session) |
| LOGICAL_READS_PER_CALL | 1000 (limits the data blocks read for a call) |
| PRIVATE_SGA | 15K (limits the bytes of Shared Pool for a session) |

| | |
|---|---|
| COMPOSITE_LIMIT | DEFAULT (limits the total resources cost for a session) |
| FAILED_LOGIN_ATTEMPTS | 5 (failed attempts allowed until the account is locked) |
| PASSWORD_LIFE_TIME | 60 (number of days the same password can be used) |
| PASSWORD_REUSE_TIME | 60 (days before a password can be reused) |
| PASSWORD_REUSE_MAX | UNLIMITED (password changes required before the current password can be reused) |
| PASSWORD_VERIFY_FUNCTION | VERIFY_FUNCTION (allows a PL/SQL password verification script to be passed as an argument to the CREATE PROFILE command) |
| PASSWORD_LOCK_TIME | 1/24 (days an account will be locked after specified number of consecutive failed login attempts) |
| PASSWORD_GRACE_TIME | 10 (specifies the number of days after the grace period begins during which a warning is issued and login is allowed) |

The default verification script is UTLPWDMG.sql. You can use fractions of days for all parameters with days as units. Fractions are expressed as x/y. For example, 1 hour is 1/24 and 1 minute is 1/1440.

The PASSWORD_VERIFY_FUNCTION script available in Oracle8 allows modifications to a profile. The script must be run manually as SYS and is located in the $ORACLE_HOME/rdbms/admin directory. It creates the sys.VERIFY_FUNCTION function and it can be customized.

If you plan to customize the script, follow these steps:

1. Copy script.
2. Edit and change FUNCTION_NAME.
3. Create function as SYS.
4. Alter or create a new profile to using this function.

**Security—Profiles**

**TIP**
*Use security profiles to manage user passwords and
limits to the user account. If profiles are not used, a
single user could take the memory of the entire system
for a given query. At times, the best performance
improvement is often the elimination of a potential
performance degradation.*

# Security—Passwords

There are several options for managing password security in the Oracle8 database.
Examples of expiring a password, locking a user out of the database, and changing a
password are listed in this section.

You can also immediately expire a password for the user, as displayed here:

```
connect SYSTEM/MANAGER
alter user SCOTT password expire;

User altered.

connect SCOTT/TIGER

ERROR:
ORA-28001: the account has expired
Changing password for SCOTT
Old password: *****
New password: ********
Retype new password: ********
Password changed

Connected.
```

You can also immediately lock a user out of the database as displayed here:

```
connect SYSTEM/MANAGER
alter user SCOTT account lock;

User altered.

connect SCOTT/TIGER

ERROR:
ORA-28000: the account is locked
Warning: You are no longer connected to ORACLE.
```

```
connect SYSTEM/MANAGER
alter user SCOTT account unlock;

User altered.

connect SCOTT/TIGER

Connected.
```

A user can change his or her password in SQL*Plus as shown here:

```
connect SCOTT/TIGER
Password
Changing password for SCOTT
Old password: ********
New password: *****
Retype new password: *****

Password changed.
```

The old way still works, too:

```
connect SYSTEM/MANAGER
alter user SCOTT identified by LION;
```

**TIP**
*Using the ALTER USER command enables you to lock
and expire passwords.*

# ROWID Changes in Oracle8

The format of Oracle's ROWID has completely changed. The expansion of the
ROWID to a Base 64 encoding in Oracle8 was needed to support partitioned tables
and indexes. DBAs or developers who have hard-coded ROWIDs into an
application must pay careful attention to the changes in Oracle8. The
DBMS_ROWID package (covered in Chapter 13) can be used to convert ROWIDs.
Note that the following formats of ROWIDs in Oracle7 and Oracle8 are different and
are not interchangeable:

- Oracle7 Restricted Format (BBBBBBBB.RRRR.FFFF)
- Oracle8 Extended Format (OOOOOOFFFBBBBBBSSS)

## New Views in Oracle8

The following views are new in Oracle8. I have separated them into those for data types, partitions, and PL/SQL. The new V$ views in Oracle8 are listed in Appendix B.

- **Data types**

  dba_coll_types
  dba_directories
  dba_lobs
  dba_method_params
  dba_method_results
  dba_nested_tables
  dba_refs
  dba_types
  dba_type_attrs
  dba_type_methods

- **Partitions**

  dba_ind_partitions
  dba_part_col_statistics
  dba_part_histograms
  dba_part_indexes
  dba_part_key_columns
  dba_part_tables
  dba_tab_col_statistics
  dba_tab_partitions

- **PL/SQL**

  dba_libraries

## Backup and Recovery

The backup and recovery management tools in Oracle8 have increased tremendously. These changes are well beyond the scope of this book, but note that these changes have caused changes in the data dictionary (for autorecovery capability). The Backup Manager and Recovery Manager help simplify the process, but the manual methods are still available in Oracle8.

# Parallel Server and Distributed Server

The Oracle Parallel Server (OPS) or the Oracle Distributed Server (ODS) is the center of most corporate database architectures. These options are beyond the scope of this book, but I would like to point out a few of the enhancements of OPS and ODS. As more companies move back toward centralized computing, they will find that single servers are not fast enough to handle all corporate data. The Parallel Server Option allows for a single database to be spread onto multiple pieces of hardware, while each piece of hardware can have its own SGA and other environment setups used to balance users. The distributed server uses multiple databases that can be kept in synch using replication or user-built scripts. The Oracle Distributed Database options allow for the coordination and/or replication of information among multiple servers, as shown here:

Parallel Server                                      Distributed Server

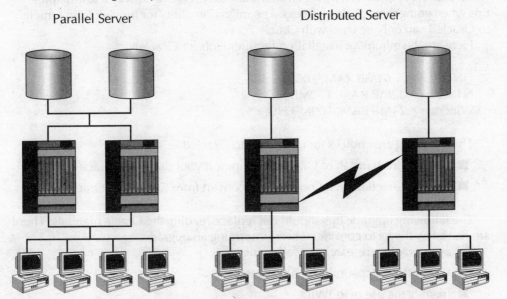

In Oracle8, Oracle offers transparent application failover for higher availability. Greater attention to clusters and MPP systems will also balance performance—the ability to use parallel processing with OPS.

**TIP**
*Oracle Parallel Server (OPS) may be the future of all IS systems. It allows multiple front-end SGAs and a back-end database that is shared by all instances (many instances, but one database). The distributed option offers a means of distributing systems to multiple smaller boxes that are linked via database links.*

# Notes on Upgrading to Oracle8

Please refer to the "Oracle Installation and Upgrade Guide" for your given system when moving to Oracle8. This section should only serve to convey a few helpful tips when going through this process. The migration utility for moving from Oracle7 to Oracle8 can only be used with Oracle 7.1+.

Here are the minimum installation requirements for Oracle8:

```
UNIX server    64MB RAM, 200MB HD
NT server      32MB RAM, 150MB HD
Windows        24MB RAM, 100MB HD
```

The following are choices for upgrading to Oracle8:

- Create a fresh install of Oracle8 and import your data from Oracle7
- Use the Oracle8 migration utility to convert from Oracle7 to Oracle8

The following upgrade tips should not replace reading the Oracle manuals. These are just a few things to consider when performing an upgrade.

Before upgrading, research the following:

- Check the compatibility in a test database.
- Identify the use of ROWID.
- Identify obsolete init.ora parameters.
- Identify new reserved words.

Before running the upgrade, check the following:

- Back up the database (do a cold backup and an export).
- Change DB_WRITERS to DBWR_IO_SLAVES in the init.ora.

- ■ . Copy init.ora to the pfile directory structure of the OFA configuration.
- ■ All dumps will write to cdump, bdump, and udump—not to $ORACLE_HOME/dbs.
- ■ All tablespaces are set to read/write to avoid future and constant ROWID conversions.
- ■ If the Migrate Utility is set, use the language to US7ASCII.

After upgrading, check the following:

- ■ Revalidate all objects.
- ■ Return tablespaces that were originally set to read-only back to their read-only state.
- ■ Test everything!

**TIP**
*Upgrading or migrating to Oracle8 requires many pre-and post-installation steps. Ensure that you read all of the installation guide for your particular hardware and operating system. The tips covered in this section are reminders and should not override anything that you find in your documentation. There are different steps, depending on whether you upgrade or migrate.*

# Network Computing Architecture (NCA)

Oracle8 is the foundation for Network Computing Architecture (NCA). Using a three-tier architecture, Oracle prepares the corporate database for the Internet age and commerce. One early adopter of Internet commerce, Amazon, has quickly and directly affected the likes of Barnes & Noble and Borders Books (both now have Internet commerce solutions after a loss of some market share to Amazon). Will the Internet send us back to the "glass house" of terminal host computing? The question of whether the Internet will be a complement or competitor to client/server depends not only on the business that you are in but also the speed at which the Web will permeate through society. Looking at the early numbers of Internet growth, a focus on the Web and writing business applications that focus on Internet commerce seems paramount to future success. If you're still not sure that the Web will catch on, consider the adoption rate displayed next.

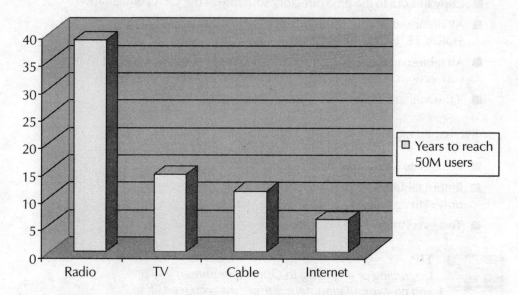

Where do you start, and which tools will help you toward faster Internet commerce solutions for your business? This chapter will focus on the tools provided by Oracle with the Oracle8 database. The Java and PL/SQL options that are contained in Oracle 8 are reviewed, with examples in Chapter 13.

**TIP**
*Get Internet and Java knowledgeable or join the ranks of the IS museum of underleveraged skills.*

# Web Development Products (JDeveloper and Oracle Developer)

JDeveloper (also known as JBuilder, AppBuilder, and Valhalla) is a product based on Borland's JBuilder technology. The original name for the effort was known as Project Valhalla. JBuilder is very similar in many ways to the look and feel of Developer/2000. It has several wizards and contains an Object Navigator-like window to view dynamic HTML. The product includes an HTML-Java Wizard for building the Java that will generate the dynamic HTML. It has a Deployment Wizard that packages all files needed for given applications. It consists of a PL/SQL Java Wizard for including calls to the database using PL/SQL. Wizards allow quick form creation and master-detail forms as easy as Dev/2000. The JDBC driver is included with JBuilder and is hidden so that connections to the database are made easily through Object Navigator-like windows. JDeveloper currently runs on Windows 95 and NT.

JDeveloper is very impressive in its early stages, and is a powerful tool geared toward the Java developer writing applications for the Oracle database. The Oracle developer will find that it is a reasonably easy transition from Developer/2000 to the look-and-feel aspects of JDeveloper. Knowing how to write the Java to generate the dynamic HTML is the learning transition that must be made for the non-Java Oracle developers.

**TIP**

*As of the writing of this book, Oracle's JDeveloper was the 4GL Java tool for writing applications in Java that access an Oracle database.*

# Oracle Developer (Dev/2000) and Web-Enabling

Retraining your staff from Oracle Developer to JBuilder is reasonably simple, but there is an even faster way to Web-enable your current forms and reports. The answer is the latest version of the Developer suite of tools. Forms 5.*x*+ (Oracle Forms) and Reports 3.*x*+ (Oracle Reports) now have the ability to run as Web pages by using an applet viewer. The biggest advantage to using this method over the JBuilder solution is that your application may already be written. With the tool, you can generate both Web-enabled and client/server versions of the application; users can utilize browsers or be in a typical PC client/server setup. I prefer the browser front end for the reduction of PC maintenance. With this solution, the need to learn Java, HTML, or JavaScript is eliminated. The same .FMX runs on the browser or in a client/server setup.

The user's HTML page retrieves a Java applet that is downloaded at run time from an application server to the user's Web browser. One issue that must be considered is the difference between how you write a screen when there is a constant connection (client/server) and the changes that you make for performance in writing screens for a stateless interface (the Internet or intranet).

Now that I can write my own application with a 4GL Web tool, is there a faster way to get Internet commerce up and running without writing the whole thing myself? The answer is to integrate tools like Oracle's ICS and others that can be used for the lion's share of the job.

**TIP**

*Oracle Forms and Oracle Reports have been core products for more than ten years. Memory requirements for these products may slow their Internet capability. A merge of Oracle Forms and JDeveloper may be the eventual product for the Web, but look for Oracle Applications to consistently be written in what Oracle considers its core developer products.*

## Oracle's Internet Commerce Server (OICS)

Oracle Internet Commerce Server (OICS) is an intuitive, easy product to use. The product is dependent on several products, both Oracle and third-party vendors. Once all the products have been gathered together and installed, the installation of OICS is relatively simple. OICS provides more out-of-the-box functionality. Through the use of the Store Manager GUI, a store can be created and populated with products. The look and feel of the store can be customized with graphics using the Store Manager, or modifying the HTML templates. Third-party products need to be utilized to calculate taxes and shipping and handling, as well as providing a method for customers to pay. Once all the pieces are put together, the store can be deployed, you can begin doing business on the Internet.

**V9 TIP**

*Oracle has said that the focus of Oracle9 will be expanded tools for Internet commerce.*

# Desupported Features in Oracle8

The SELECT privilege is needed in addition to the UPDATE/DELETE privilege for users to modify data. Previously, only the UPDATE/DELETE privilege was needed for a user to be allowed to update a table. Now, a user must have UPDATE/DELETE and DELETE/SELECT privileges to be able to update a table. Empty strings ('') are no longer equivalent to NULL.

## Nondeferred Linking

In Oracle6, Oracle separated the PARSE, BIND, and DEFINE calls of an SQL statement. Oracle7 and 8 allows deferred linking, which combines steps of this process and minimizes network traffic. While nondeferred linking is still supported in Oracle8, it will *not* be supported in Oracle9.

**V6 TIP**

*Nondeferred linking is the only choice.*

**V7 TIP**

*Nondeferred linking is still supported.*

**V8 TIP**

*Nondeferred linking will still be supported.*

**V9 TIP**
*Nondeferred linking will not* be supported.

# Features in Oracle8i (8.1)

Some of the tuning features that are included in Oracle8i (Oracle 8.1) are included in the next chapter. Please refer to Chapter 13 for all Oracle8i features that are referenced in this book.

# Tips Review

- The Oracle database can now be as large as 512,000,000,000,000,000 bytes!

- Upgrading to Oracle8 will yield immediate gains in performance as Oracle has moved from a cursor to message-based connection in managing connections.

- The LONG and LONG RAW data types can be replaced with the more functional BLOB, CLOB, NCLOB, and BFILE data types.

- Partitions can dramatically increase performance when used to break up large tables and indexes.

- Net8 is replacing SQL*Net, and many of the original SQL*Net parameters are now obsolete.

- Using the NOVALIDATE option in the ENABLE CONSTRAINT command allows a high-speed INSERT of large amounts of data.

- In Oracle8, parallel DML statements *are* allowed.

- Oracle8 has an improved star query processing algorithm.

- Use security profiles to manage user passwords and limits to the user account. If profiles are not used, a single user could take the memory of the entire system for a given query. At times, the best performance improvement is often the elimination of a potential performance degradation.

- Using the ALTER USER command, you can lock and expire passwords.

- Upgrading or migrating to Oracle8 requires many pre and post installation steps. Ensure that you read *all* of the installation guide for your particular hardware and operating system.

- Oracle's JDeveloper and Forms products can be used to generate Web-enabled applications that run under Network Computing Architecture (NCA).

Tips Review

- Gain Internet and Java knowledge or join the ranks of the IS museum of underleveraged skills.

- Nondeferred linking will *not* be supported in Oracle9, but is still supported in Oracle8 and Oracle7.

- Oracle has stated that the focus of Oracle9 will be expanded tools for Internet commerce.

# References

*Oracle8 Performance Tuning*; Eyal Aronoff, Kevin Loney, and Noorali Sonawalla; Osborne/McGraw-Hill

*Oracle8 DBA Handbook*; Kevin Loney; Osborne/McGraw-Hill

*Oracle8 Server Administrator's Guide Release 8.0*, Oracle Corporation, 1997

*Oracle8 Server Concepts Release 8.0*, Volumes 1&2, Oracle Corporation, 1997

*Oracle8 Server Reference Release 8.0*, Oracle Corporation, 1997

*Oracle8 Server SQL Reference Release 8.0*, Oracle Corporation, 1997

*Oracle8 Backup and Recovery Guide Release 8.0*, Oracle Corporation, 1997

*Oracle8 Server Utilities Guide Release 8.0*, Oracle Corporation, 1997

*Oracle8 Server Tuning Guide Release 8.0*, Oracle Corporation, 1997

*Oracle7 Server Tuning*; Oracle Corporation

*Tuning Tips: You will be Toast!*; Rich Niemiec, TUSC

http://www.oracle.com

http://www.tusc.com

Special thanks to Kim Austin, Jake Van der Vort, Jean Kuzniar, Sean McGuire, Greg Pucka, John Molinaro, Kevin Loney, and Netscape for contributions to this chapter.

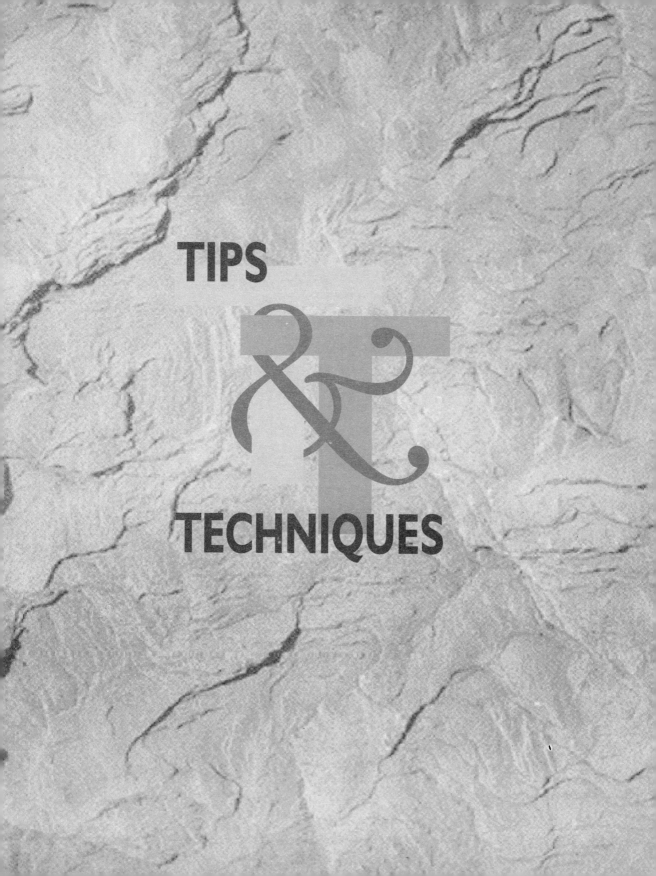

TIPS
&T
TECHNIQUES

# CHAPTER
## 13

Oracle8 and 8i
New Tips
(Developer and DBA)

The goal of this chapter is to explain some of the new Oracle8 features in detail and provide examples using those features. Chapter 12 was an overview of new features; this chapter looks into the new features that relate more closely to performance tuning. Tips covered in this chapter include the following:

- Changing init.ora parameters without a restart
- Using index-organized tables
- Oracle8 constraint options (deferring constraint checking)
- Using reverse-key indexes
- Table partitioning
- Index partitioning
- Exporting a single partition
- Desupported features in Oracle8
- Parallel operations in Oracle8
- Using ROWID and the DBMS_ROWID package
- The NOLOGGING feature
- Java, SQLJ, JDBC, and NCA
- Oracle objects, object_type, map and order members, refs, nested tables, and varrays
- New hints in Oracle8
- Using the BUFFER_POOL_KEEP and BUFFER_POOL_RECYCLE
- Using function-based indexes in Oracle 8.1
- The DROP COLUMN command is finally here in Oracle 8.1
- Transportable tablespaces in Oracle 8.1 and 8.2

# Changing the init.ora without a Restart

One of the new features of Oracle8 is an increase in the number of init.ora parameters that can be dynamically changed in a session (without shutting down the database). In earlier versions of Oracle, most of the init.ora parameters required a shutdown and restart of the database. In Oracle8, some very important parameters can be modified spontaneously without a restart. Be careful, because these parameters can be places of concern as much as they are a benefit. Knowledgeable developers can set individual parameters that positively affect their session at the expense of others on the system. The following query illustrates a list of init.ora parameters that can be set without shutting down and restarting the database.

There are two key fields in the V$PARAMETER view:

- *ISSES_MODIFIABLE* – Indicates if a user with the ALTER SESSION privilege can modify this init.ora parameter for their session. It may be modified if the value in the V$PARAMETER view is TRUE. The only possible values are TRUE and FALSE.

- *ISSYS_MODIFIABLE* – Indicates if someone with ALTER SYSTEM privilege can modify this particular parameter. The choices are IMMEDIATE, FALSE, and DEFERRED. IMMEDIATE means that the change will take effect immediately. FALSE means that the parameter cannot be modified without shutting down and restarting the database. DEFERRED means that the change will not take effect until your next session (you must log out of Oracle and come back in before this takes effect).

The following query will display the init.ora parameters that can be modified with an ALTER SYSTEM or ALTER SESSION command:

```
select    name, value, isdefault, isses_modifiable,
          issys_modifiable
from      v$parameter
where     issys_modifiable <> 'FALSE'
or        isses_modifiable <> 'FALSE'
order by  name;
```

The result of the query is all of the init.ora parameters that may be modified, as shown in this table:

| NAME | VALUE | ISDEFAULT | ISSES | ISSYS |
|------|-------|-----------|-------|-------|
| ALLOW_PARTIAL_SN_RESULTS | FALSE | TRUE | TRUE | DEFERRED |
| AQ_TM_PROCESSES | 0 | TRUE | FALSE | IMMEDIATE |
| B_TREE_BITMAP_PLANS | FALSE | TRUE | TRUE | FALSE |
| BACKUP_DISK_IO_SLAVES | 0 | TRUE | FALSE | DEFERRED |

Changing init.ora without a Restart

| Parameter | Value | | | |
|---|---|---|---|---|
| BACKUP_TAPE_IO_SLAVES | FALSE | TRUE | FALSE | DEFERRED |
| CONTROL_FILE_RECORD_KEEP_TIME | 7 | TRUE | FALSE | IMMEDIATE |
| DB_BLOCK_CHECKPOINT_BATCH | 8 | TRUE | FALSE | IMMEDIATE |
| DB_BLOCK_CHECKSUM | FALSE | TRUE | FALSE | IMMEDIATE |
| DB_BLOCK_MAX_DIRTY_TARGET | 4294967294 | TRUE | FALSE | IMMEDIATE |
| DB_FILE_DIRECT_IO_COUNT | 64 | TRUE | FALSE | DEFERRED |
| **\*DB_FILE_MULTIBLOCK_READ_COUNT** | **8** | **TRUE** | **TRUE** | **IMMEDIATE** |
| FIXED_DATE | | TRUE | FALSE | IMMEDIATE |
| FREEZE_DB_FOR_FAST_INSTANCE_RECOVERY | FALSE | TRUE | FALSE | IMMEDIATE |
| GC_DEFER_TIME | 10 | TRUE | FALSE | IMMEDIATE |
| GLOBAL_NAMES | TRUE | FALSE | TRUE | IMMEDIATE |
| **\*HASH_AREA_SIZE** | **0** | **TRUE** | **TRUE** | **FALSE** |
| **\*HASH_JOIN_ENABLED** | **TRUE** | **TRUE** | **TRUE** | **FALSE** |
| **\*HASH_MULTIBLOCK_IO_COUNT** | **8** | **TRUE** | **TRUE** | **IMMEDIATE** |
| LICENSE_MAX_SESSIONS | 0 | TRUE | FALSE | IMMEDIATE |
| LICENSE_MAX_USERS | 0 | TRUE | FALSE | IMMEDIATE |
| LICENSE_SESSIONS_WARNING | 0 | TRUE | FALSE | IMMEDIATE |
| LOG_ARCHIVE_DUPLEX_DEST | | TRUE | FALSE | IMMEDIATE |
| LOG_ARCHIVE_MIN_SUCCEED_DEST | 1 | TRUE | FALSE | IMMEDIATE |
| **\*LOG_CHECKPOINT_INTERVAL** | **10000** | **FALSE** | **FALSE** | **IMMEDIATE** |
| **\*LOG_CHECKPOINT_TIMEOUT** | **0** | **TRUE** | **FALSE** | **IMMEDIATE** |
| **\*LOG_SMALL_ENTRY_MAX_SIZE** | **80** | **TRUE** | **FALSE** | **IMMEDIATE** |
| MTS_DISPATCHERS | | TRUE | FALSE | IMMEDIATE |
| MTS_SERVERS | 0 | TRUE | FALSE | IMMEDIATE |
| OBJECT_CACHE_MAX_SIZE_PERCENT | 10 | TRUE | TRUE | DEFERRED |
| OBJECT_CACHE_OPTIMAL_SIZE | 102400 | TRUE | TRUE | DEFERRED |
| OPS_ADMIN_GROUP | | TRUE | TRUE | IMMEDIATE |
| OPTIMIZER_MODE | CHOOSE | TRUE | TRUE | FALSE |
| **\*OPTIMIZER_PERCENT_PARALLEL** | **0** | **TRUE** | **TRUE** | **FALSE** |
| OPTIMIZER_SEARCH_LIMIT | 5 | TRUE | TRUE | FALSE |
| PARALLEL_INSTANCE_GROUP | | TRUE | TRUE | IMMEDIATE |
| **\*PARALLEL_MIN_PERCENT** | **0** | **TRUE** | **TRUE** | **FALSE** |
| PARALLEL_TRANSACTION_RESOURCE_TIMEOUT | 300 | TRUE | FALSE | IMMEDIATE |
| **\*PARTITION_VIEW_ENABLED** | **FALSE** | **TRUE** | **TRUE** | **FALSE** |
| PLSQL_V2_COMPATIBILITY | FALSE | TRUE | TRUE | IMMEDIATE |
| REMOTE_DEPENDENCIES_MODE | TIMESTAMP | TRUE | TRUE | IMMEDIATE |
| RESOURCE_LIMIT | FALSE | TRUE | FALSE | IMMEDIATE |
| SORT_AREA_RETAINED_SIZE | 0 | TRUE | TRUE | DEFERRED |
| SORT_AREA_SIZE | 65536 | TRUE | TRUE | DEFERRED |
| SORT_DIRECT_WRITES | AUTO | TRUE | TRUE | DEFERRED |
| SORT_READ_FAC | 20 | TRUE | TRUE | DEFERRED |
| SORT_WRITE_BUFFER_SIZE | 32768 | TRUE | TRUE | DEFERRED |
| SORT_WRITE_BUFFERS | 2 | TRUE | TRUE | DEFERRED |
| SPIN_COUNT | 1 | TRUE | TRUE | IMMEDIATE |
| STAR_TRANSFORMATION_ENABLED | FALSE | TRUE | TRUE | FALSE |
| **\*TEXT_ENABLE** | **FALSE** | **TRUE** | **TRUE** | **IMMEDIATE** |
| TIMED_OS_STATISTICS | 0 | TRUE | FALSE | IMMEDIATE |
| **\*\*TIMED_STATISTICS** | **FALSE** | **TRUE** | **TRUE** | **IMMEDIATE** |
| TRANSACTION_AUDITING | TRUE | TRUE | FALSE | DEFERRED |

53 rows selected.

\*available since Oracle 7.3

\*\*available since Oracle 6

Here's an example of what a developer with ALTER SESSION privilege can do:

```
Alter session set sort_area_size=100000000;

Session altered.
```

The problem in the preceding query is the developer has granted the session the capability of using 100M of memory for a sorting in this session.

**TIP**
*Changing init.ora parameters spontaneously is a powerful feature for both developers and DBAs. Consequently, a user with the ALTER SESSION privilege is capable of irresponsibly allocating 100M+ for the SORT_AREA_SIZE for a given session if it is not restricted.*

# Index-Organized Tables

An index-organized table is where all of the table data is stored in a b-tree structure. Only one database object is used to store both the data and the index. All of the columns are stored as an index. B-tree indexes uniquely identify rows by primary keys, not by ROWIDs. A secondary index cannot be created on the table, and if updates are made, entire rows may be moved by the operation, and could be costly in terms of performance. The performance advantage is achieved when the key in an exact match or range scan on the key accesses the data. The query here shows how to create an index-organized table:

```
create table order_idx
  ( name char(20), id integer,  description varchar(500),
   constraint pk_temp_tab_idx primary key (name, id) )
  ORGANIZATION INDEX tablespace users
  pctthreshold 20 including temp_data  OVERFLOW TABLESPACE users2;
```

In this example, the *order_idx* organization index (index-organized table) is constructed. The combination of the *name* and *id* columns makes up the primary key. The references to this table should use, at a minimum, the name column, so that at least the leading edge of the primary key is used. It would be best written when the name *and* ID columns are referenced in selecting data with a query. If many queries accessed the data based on the description column, then this would not make a good organizational index. If future rows are added that are widely distributed, rows may have to be redistributed to maintain proper order in the organizational index. The options for an organization index are as follows:

- *ORGANIZATION INDEX* – Specifies that a table is created as an index-organized table. In an index-organized table, the data rows are held in an index defined on the primary key for the table. There is an optional row overflow specification clause that defines physical attributes of the overflow area. The data row will be placed in the overflow tablespace if its size exceeds the threshold. The threshold is specified as a percentage of the block size.

- *ORGANIZATION HEAP* – Specifies that the data rows of the table are not stored in a particular order. This is the default.

- *PCTTHRESHOLD integer* – Specifies the percentage of space reserved in the index block for an index-organized table row. A portion of the row that exceeds the defined threshold is stored in the area. If OVERFLOW is not defined, then rows exceeding the THRESHOLD limit are rejected. PCTTHRESHOLD must be a value from 0 to 50.

- *INCLUDING column_name* – Specifies a column to divide an index-organized table row into index and overflow portions. All columns that follow column_name are stored in the overflow data segment. A column_name is either the name of the last primary-key column or nonprimary-key column.

Organizational indexes are best used for tables that are frequently accessed by known values and where there are *not* frequent INSERTs.

**TIP**
*Index-organized tables are best used for frequently accessed tables that are usually accessed by the same columns. A table that has frequent INSERTs into it is not a good candidate.*

# Oracle8 Constraint Options

When large volumes of data are inserted into a table, validating data using constraints can be costly. This can be a particularly troublesome cost in data warehouses, where these types of INSERTs are completed frequently. Oracle has provided an option in the release of Oracle8 that allows the checking of constraints to be deferred to a later time. The new options provided are listed next. Deferring a constraint waits until the end of the transaction, where nondeferred constraints perform the checking after each statement.

- *DEFERRABLE* – Indicates that constraint checking can be deferred until the end of the transaction by using the SET CONSTRAINT(S) command.

- *NOT DEFERRABLE* – Indicates that this constraint is checked at the end of each DML statement. You cannot defer a NOT DEFERRABLE constraint with the SET CONSTRAINT(S) command. If you do not specify DEFERRABLE or NOT DEFERRABLE, then NOT DEFERRABLE is the default.

- *INITIALLY IMMEDIATE* – Indicates that at the start of every transaction, the default checks this constraint at the end of every DML statement. If no INITIALLY clause is specified, INITIALLY IMMEDIATE is the default.

- *INITIALLY DEFERRED* – Implies that this constraint is DEFERRABLE and by default specifies the constraint to be checked only at the end of each transaction.

- *ENABLE NOVALIDATE* – Ensures that all new INSERT, UPDATE, and DELETE operations on the constrained data comply with the constraint. Oracle does not verify that existing data in the table complies with the constraint.

The following two examples illustrate the procedure to enable a constraint to be deferrable and then actually setting the constraint to be deferred for a given transaction:

```
alter constraint s_dept_id_pk INITIALLY DEFERRED DEFERRABLE;

set constraint s_dept_name_region_id_uk DEFERRED;
```

This example illustrates the ability to set *all* deferrable constraints *in this transaction* to be checked immediately following each DML statement. The ALTER will change the way the constraint works overall, while the SET will change the way the constraint works for a given transaction.

```
set constraints ALL IMMEDIATE;
```

**TIP**
*Constraints can now be checked for a statement or for an entire transaction. Altering a constraint to be deferrable will allow individual users to defer the constraint until after the entire transaction is completed.*

# Reverse-Key Indexes

In a reverse-key index, the bytes of the column data value are what eliminate sequential values being stored in a sequential order. This allows sequential values to be more distributed in the b-tree when inserting values that are sequential, and hot spots are avoided. In a table containing months, for example, this would distribute values of a given month more evenly in the table. Instead of hitting the same block for a group of values (months), those values (months) may be in different blocks or on different partitions. When data from a month is DELETEd, instead of deleting a plurality of blocks, DELETE rows from many blocks; the result is that the data left over is better distributed. Consider the following order numbers and how they appear in a reverse-key index:

| Order# | Stored as (Reversed) |
| --- | --- |
| 79001 | 10097 |
| 79002 | 20097 |
| 79003 | 30099 |

The example data shows that the orders from 79001-79003 would normally be stored together, yet in a reverse-key index they would appear independently. If the data is sufficiently distributed, the three order numbers could be accessed simultaneously from different physical drives, instead of residing next to each other.

**TIP**
*Reverse-key indexes are an excellent resource for sequential data that you do not want to index in a sequential manner. This type of index allows a more suitable distribution of data, often residing close together in the same physical block.*

# Partitions

Partitioning is a way to increase efficiency by accessing smaller pieces of a table or index instead of accessing the full table or index. When an object is partitioned, all of the partitions must contain the same columns, constraints, and other attributes. However, partitions can have different storage attributes such as INITIAL_EXTENT, TABLESPACE_NAME (that the data is stored in), in addition to other storage attributes. Partitions can be backed up and recovered independently of each other. Only when partitions are properly implemented are the best performance-enhancing features of Oracle8 realized. The best way to understand partitioning is to look at an example. Consider the following simple example where we partition the dept table into three partitions (pieces) using the deptno column.

**The table dept is created with three partitions:**

```
create     table dept
    (deptno          number(2),
     dept_name     varchar2(30))
partition by range(deptno)
 (partition d1 values less than (10) tablespace dept1,
  partition d2 values  less than (20) tablespace dept2,
  partition d3 values  less than (maxvalue) tablespace dept3);
```

**Data is entered into all three partitions of the table:**

```
insert into dept values (1,   'ADMIN');
insert into dept values (7,   'MGMT');
insert into dept values (10, 'MANUF');
insert into dept values (15, 'ACCT');
insert into dept values (22, 'SALES');
```

**The dept table still looks like a single table when we select from it:**

```
select     *
from       dept;

DEPTNO     DEPT NAME
1          ADMIN
7          MGMT
10         MANUF
15         ACCT
22         SALES
```

We selected all records from all of the partitions in this example. In the next three examples, we SELECT individually from each partition.

**We SELECT from a single partition and access only a *single* partition:**

```
select     *
from       dept partition (d1);

DEPTNO     DEPT NAME
1          ADMIN
7          MGMT

select     *
from       dept partition (d2);
```

```
DEPTNO    DEPT NAME
10        MANUF
15        ACCT


select    *
from      dept partition (d3);

DEPTNO    DEPT NAME
22        SALES
```

## Dropping a Partition

As seen in the preceding example, we drop the d3 partition in the previously-referenced example and we can observe the effect when we select data from the table.

```
alter table dept drop partition d3;

Table altered.

select    *
from      dept;

DEPTNO    DEPT NAME
1         ADMIN
7         MGMT
10        MANUF
15        ACCT
```

The preceding record (deptno = 22) from the third partition (d3) is eliminated from the dept table.

### Getting More Information About Partitions

We can retrieve the information regarding partitions by accessing USER_TABLES, DBA_PART_TABLES, and USER_SEGMENTS. Example queries to these three views are displayed here with corresponding output for the examples in the previous section.

```
select    table_name, partitioned
from      dba_tables
where     table_name in ('DEPT','EMP');

TABLE NAME    PAR
DEPT          YES
EMP           NO
```

In the previous example, the par column indicates whether a table is partitioned.

```
select     owner, table_name, partition_count
from       dba_part_tables
where      table_name = 'DEPT';

OWNER    TABLE NAME   PARTITION COUNT
KEVIN    DEPT            3
```

In the preceding and following examples, the number of partitions on the dept table is 3; this is before we dropped the third partition.

```
select     segment_name, partition_name, segment_type, tablespace_name
from       user_segments;

SEGMENT NAME   PARTITION NAME   SEGMENT TYPE        TABLESPACE NAME
EMP                             TABLE               USER_DATA
DEPT           D1               TABLE PARTITION     DEPT1
DEPT           D2               TABLE PARTITION     DEPT2
DEPT           D3               TABLE PARTITION     DEPT3
```

**TIP**
*Tables can be easily partitioned for individual pieces to be accessed and/or manipulated; you can still access the entire table of a partitioned index. Accessing the views DBA_TABLES, DBA_PART_TABLE, and DBA_SEGMENTS provides additional information concerning tables that have been partitioned.*

The following example features a table with five partitions that will be placed in five different tablespaces (each tablespace points to a data file on a different physical disk). The column id has values between 1 and 100. We have decided to break the table up, with each partition holding 20 values. In the last partition, we use MAXVALUE instead of using 100 so that a value entered greater than 100 will not cause errors to occur.

```
create table s_dept1
(id        number(7)       constraint s_dept1_id_nn NOT NULL,
 name      varchar2(25)    constraint s_dept1_name_nn NOT NULL,
                           constraint s_dept1_id_pk primary key (id)
 using index   storage (initial 10K next 10K pctincrease 0),
                           constraint s_dept1_name_region_id_uk UNIQUE (name)
 using index   storage (initial 10K next 10K pctincrease 0))
           storage (initial 10K next 10K pctincrease 0)
partition by range (id)
```

**Dropping a Partition**

```
(partition p1 values less than (20) tablespace users1,
 partition p2 values less than (40) tablespace users2,
 partition p3 values less than (50) tablespace users3,
 partition p4 values less than (80) tablespace users4,
 partition p5 values less than (maxvalue) tablespace users5);
```

Some of the options used in partitioning and their definitions are listed here:

- *PARTITION BY RANGE* – Specifies that the table is partitioned on ranges of values from column_list.

- *column_list* – An ordered list of columns used to determine into which partition a row belongs. You cannot specify more than 16 columns in column_list. The column_list cannot contain the ROWID pseudocolumn or any columns of data type ROWID or LONG.

- *PARTITION partition_name* – Specifies the physical partition clause. If partition_name is omitted, Oracle generates a name with the form SYS_Pn for the partition. The partition_name must conform to the rules for naming schema objects.

- *VALUES LESS THAN* – Specifies the noninclusive upper bound for the current partition.

- *value_list* – An ordered list of literal values corresponding to column_list in the PARTITION BY RANGE clause. You can substitute the keyword MAXVALUE for any literal in value_list. Specifying a value other than MAXVALUE for the highest partition bound imposes an implicit integrity constraint on the table. See *Oracle8 Server Concepts* for more information about partition bounds.

- *MAXVALUE* – Specifies a maximum value that will always sort higher than any other value, including NULL. For partitioned tables, the logging attribute value specified is the default physical attribute of the segments associated with the table partitions. The default logging value applies to all partitions specified in the CREATE statement, and on subsequent ALTER TABLE ADD PARTITION statements, unless you specify LOGGING/ NOLOGGING in the PARTITION description clause.

## An Additional Example Using Multiple Columns for a Date

You can use multiple columns to distinguish how you will partition a table. In the following example, the table is partitioned by the year, month, and day (all are separate columns):

```
create table cust_sales
(acct_no      number(5),
 cust_name    char(30),
 item_id      number(9),
 sale_day     integer not null,
 sale_mth     integer not null,
 sale_yr      integer not null)
partition by range (sale_yr, sale_mth, sale_day)
     partition cust_sales_q1 values less than (1998, 04, 01) tablespace users,
     partition cust_sales_q2 values less than (1998, 07, 01) tablespace users2,
     partition cust_sales_q3 values less than (1998, 10, 01) tablespace users,
     partition cust_sales_q4 values less than (1999, 01, 01) tablespace users2);
```

**TIP**
*You can also partition tables using multiple columns as the criteria.*

# Other Partitioning Options

This section covers some of the many options that can be used with partitioning. You will see that many of the options that are available for operations on tables are also available for partitions:

- *MODIFY PARTITION partition_name* – Modifies the real physical attributes of a table partition. You can specify any of the following as new physical attributes for the partition: LOGGING, ATTRIBUTE, PCTFREE, PCTUSED, INITRANS, MAXTRANS, STORAGE.

- *RENAME PARTITION partition_name to new_partition_name* – Renames table partition PARTITION_NAME to NEW_PARTITION_NAME.

- *MOVE PARTITION partition_name* – Moves table partition PARTITION_NAME to another segment. You can move partition data to another tablespace, recluster data to reduce fragmentation, or change a create-time physical attribute:

```
alter table dept move partition d3 tablespace dept4 nologging;
```

In the preceding example, the d3 partition and all corresponding data is moved from the dept3 tablespace, where it originally resided, to the dept4 tablespace.

**TIP**
*When moving a partition, use the NOLOGGING option for speed.*

**Other Partitioning Options**

- *ADD PARTITION new_partition_name* – Adds a new partition new_partition_name to the "high" end of a partitioned table. You can specify any of the following as new physical attributes for the partition: logging, attribute, PCTFREE, PCTUSED, INITRANS, MAXTRANS, STORAGE.

- *VALUES LESS THAN (value_list)* – Specifies the upper bound for the new partition. The value_list is a comma-separated, ordered list of literal values corresponding to column_list. The value_list must collate greater than the partition bound for the highest existing partition in the table.

- *DROP PARTITION partition_name* – Removes partition partition_name, and the data in that partition, from a partitioned table:

```
alter table dept drop partition d3;
```

**TIP**

*Dropping a table partition causes its local index (but not the other local partition indexes) to be dropped and a global index (one that exists on the entire table) to be unavailable. Don't use global indexes if you desire to drop partitions of a table.*

- *TRUNCATE PARTITION partition_name* – Removes all rows from a partition in a table.

- *SPLIT PARTITION partition_name_old* – Creates two new partitions, each with a new segment, new physical attributes, and new initial extents. The segment associated with the old partition is discarded.

- *UNUSABLE LOCAL INDEXES* – Marks all the local index partitions associated with partition_name as unusable.

- *REBUILD UNUSABLE LOCAL INDEXES* – Rebuilds the unusable local index partitions associated with partition_name.

- *UNUSABLE* – Marks the index or index partition(s) as unusable. An unusable index must be rebuilt, or dropped and re-created before it can be used. While one partition is marked unusable, the other partitions of the index are still valid, and you can execute statements that require the index if the statements do not access the unusable partition. You can also split or rename the unusable partition before rebuilding it.

- *REBUILD PARTITION* – Rebuilds one partition of an index. You can also use this option to move an index partition to another tablespace, or to change a create-time physical attribute.

# Index Partitioning

Partitioned indexes have the same advantages as partitioned tables. Accessing smaller pieces instead of one index on the entire table increases performance when properly executed. There are local and global indexes, and prefixed on nonprefixed indexes. When a local index has been partitioned, each piece is a local index. A global index is a nonpartitioned index, used before partitioning existed. A prefixed index is when the leftmost part of the index is the partition key, whereas a nonprefixed index can be costly to access since the partition key is not indexed. If a partition of a table with a global index is dropped, then the corresponding global index is invalidated. If a partition of a table with a local index is dropped, then the local index is also dropped.

The following is an example of a local partitioned index. The index name is dept_index and the index is on the deptno column of the dept table. The index is split into three pieces (d1, d2, and d3) that are located in three tablespaces (dept1, dept2, and dept3) that are striped differently from the location of the corresponding data. This will ensure that accessing information from a partition of a table and its corresponding index partition will result in accessing two physical disk drives instead of one—given that dept1-dept3 are tablespaces that correspond to data files on different physical disks.

```
create index dept_index on dept (deptno)
  local
 (partition d1 tablespace dept2,
  partition d2 tablespace dept3,
  partition d3 tablespace dept1);

Index Created.
```

We can get the information regarding partitioned indexes by accessing dba_indexes:

```
select    index_name, partition_name, tablespace_name
from      dba_indexes
where     index_name = 'DEPT_INDEX'
order by  partition_name;
```

*Index Partitioning*

| INDEX NAME | PARTITION NAME | TABLESPACE NAME |
|---|---|---|
| DEPT_INDEX | D1 | DEPT2 |
| DEPT_INDEX | D2 | DEPT3 |
| DEPT_INDEX | D3 | DEPT1 |

**TIP**
*Indexes that are partitioned (local indexes) should also be prefixed; the partitioning key is the leading edge of the index.*

# Exporting Partitions

Partitions can be effortlessly exported. If the data in your table is segmented carefully, it is possible to keep all new information in a single partition to export. This eliminates the need to export data from partitions that have not changed and have been previously exported. By using the EXPORT command and giving the owner.table. partition_name for the table to be exported, only the partition is exported.

```
exp user/pass file=tab.dmp tables=(owner.table.partition_name)
```

**TIP**
*If data is partitioned correctly, all the new information falls into a single partition, enabling an EXPORT of a single partition of a large table during backups. This could save you time in your backup plan scenarios.*

# Desupported Feature in Oracle8

An important change that was made in Oracle8 altered the way that improperly written statements were translated. Oracle previously had assumed what you "meant" in certain syntax errors. In Oracle8, improperly written TO_DATE functions will cause an error instead of translating what Oracle thinks you want. In the following example, the TO_DATE value is '1299' and the string is 'MM/YY', which has a slash (/) that is not in the '1299' portion. In Oracle7, Oracle knew that you meant '12' to be the month and '99' to be the year.

```
select    to_char(to_date('1299', 'MM/YY'), 'MM/YY')
from      system.dual;

Oracle7 Result:
12/99


Oracle8 Result:
ORA-1861 Error
```

**TIP**
*In moving to Oracle8, testing will be your best tool in finding problem code that Oracle no longer automatically translates. Oracle8's stricter syntax rules could cause errors after the conversion. Test!*

# Parallel Operations with Oracle8

For a complete look at parallel operations, please turn to Chapter 11, which is completely devoted to this subject.

Oracle8 introduced the parallel DML feature, allowing for parallel execution of INSERT, UPDATE, and DELETE operations. The following is a list of statements that are capable of parallel execution with Oracle8:

- SELECT
- UPDATE, INSERT
- DELETE
- CREATE TABLE as...
- CREATE INDEX
- REBUILD INDEX
- MOVE/SPLIT PARTITION
- ENABLE CONSTRAINT

The following operations can also be parallelized within a statement:

- select DISTINCT
- GROUP BY
- ORDER BY
- NOT IN
- UNION and UNION ALL
- NESTED LOOP joins
- SORT/MERGE joins

**TIP**
*In Oracle8, parallel DML statements are allowed. This functionality applies to partitioned tables and indexes. Parallelization still* cannot *be performed on an index operation, but parallelization* can *be performed on a partitioned index.*

Additionally, Oracle8 utilizes cost-based optimization to determine to parallelize a statement and the degree of parallelism applied.

**Parallel DML statement example:**

```
alter session enable parallel dml;

Session altered.

update     /*+ PARALLEL (time_history,4) */
           time_history
set        fees = fees * 1.15
where      rank = 2;

150093 rows updated.

select     count(*)
from       time_history;

select     count(*)
from       time_history
*

ERROR at line 1:
ORA-12830: Must COMMIT or ROLLBACK after
      executing parallel INSERT/UPDATE/DELETE

commit;

Commit complete.
```

**TIP**
*You must issue a COMMIT after using parallel DML statements. You will receive an error executing a SELECT statement that follows a parallel DML statement if you do not issue a COMMIT.*

## Parallel Execution Methods

Statements can be parallelized utilizing three distinct methods, determined when an execution plan is created for the SQL statement:

- *Block Range (ROWID Range)* – Utilized for SCAN operations on partitioned (V8 only) and nonpartitioned tables (V7 and V8). Scan operations are the only method for statements to be parallelized in Oracle7.

- *Partition* – Servers are assigned per partition for partitioned tables and indexes. Partitions are a feature introduced with Oracle8.

- *Parallel Server Process* – Servers assigned for INSERT operations on nonpartitioned tables only within Oracle8.

The Oracle8 Partitioning feature has significant impact on parallel operations (as just indicated). Partitions are static, physical divisions of table data, indexes, and partitions of the same table/index that can reside in multiple tablespaces. Given this architecture, the following important distinctions exist with Oracle8 parallel operations on partitions:

- There is no parallelism within a partition.

- Operations are performed in parallel on partitioned objects *only* when more than one partition is accessed.

**TIP**
*Operations are performed in parallel on partitioned objects only when more than one partition is accessed and parallelism is not performed within a single partition. To use more parallel server processes, ensure that the table is partitioned into enough pieces.*

# ROWID in Oracle8

Oracle8 introduces a new ROWID format. In version 7, Oracle stored three numbers in the ROWID, as shown in the following example.

**Restricted format (BBBBBBBB.RRRR.FFFF) (V7):**

| | |
|---|---|
| BBBBBBBB | Block in hex |
| RRRR | Row number within block |
| FFFF | File number |

In version 8, Oracle has an extended format, which stores four different numbers to accommodate the changes in Oracle8. The new extended format is shown in the following example:

**Extended format (OOOOOOFFFBBBBBBSSS) (V8):**

| | |
|---|---|
| OOOOOO | Data object number identifying segment |
| FFF | Data file containing row |
| BBBBBB | Data block containing row |
| SSS | Row within block |

Oracle8 can support more files per database, and blocks per file, because of the extended format. Oracle can expand from terabytes to petabytes (1 petabyte = 1,024 terabytes = 1,048,576 gigabytes).

# DBMS_ROWID Package

Along with the new ROWID structure, Oracle has also provided a package that assists you in conversions and other desired functions using ROWID. The DBMS_ROWID package is installed by DBMSUTIL.sql, called by CATPROC.sql, at database installation time. The following examples show some of the many uses of the DBMS_ROWID package:

■ *ROWID_TO_RESTRICTED* – This will display restricted V7 format.

```
select      dbms_rowid.rowid_to_restricted(rowid,0)
from        emp;
```

■ *ROWID_OBJECT* – These two queries will find the OBJECT_ID for an object in dba_extents.

```
select      dbms_rowid.rowid_object(rowid)
from        emp
where       rownum=1;

select      object_name
from        sys.dba_objects
where       object_id = (value returned by above query);
```

■ *ROWID_RELATIVE_FNO* – These two queries will find the relative file number.

```
select    dbms_rowid.rowid_relative_fno(rowid)
from      emp
where     rownum=1;

select    file_name, file_id
from      sys.dba_data_files
where     relative_fno = (value returned by above query);
```

■ *ROWID_TO_ABSOLUTE_FNO* – This will find the absolute file number of a table.

```
select    dbms_rowid.rowid_to_absolute_fno
          (rowid,'TABLE_OWNER','TABLE')
from      TABLE
where     rownum=1;
```

■ *ROWID_BLOCK_NUMBER* – This query will provide the block number. You can also verify this by accessing dba_extents (in the second query).

```
select    dbms_rowid.rowid_block_number(rowid)
from      emp
where     rownum=1;

select    relative_fno, block_id
from      sys.dba_extents
where     segment_name = 'EMP';
```

■ *ROWID_ROW_NUMBER* – This query will find the row sequence number. There may be multiple rows per block, and the sequence number starts at zero.

```
select    dbms_rowid.rowid_row_number(rowid)
from      emp;
```

You can combine many of the queries specified in the preceding list. The following example will display both the relative file number and the block number:

```
select    dbms_rowid.rowid_relative_fno(rowid),
          dbms_rowid.rowid_block_number(rowid)
from      emp
where     rownum=1;
```

**TIP**
*The DBMS_ROWID package provides a DBA with excellent information about the storage of data within the database. It can be used in lieu of the normal DBA tables and views for many operations.*

**DBMS_ROWID Package**

# The **NOLOGGING** Feature

The NOLOGGING feature in Oracle8 on tables and indexes replaces the UNRECOVERABLE parameter in Oracle7. This allows a quicker table and index creation, avoiding overhead associated by writing records to the redo logs.

The NOLOGGING option specifies whether the creation of the table (and any indexes required because of constraints), partition, or LOB storage characteristics will be logged in the redo log file. It specifies whether subsequent direct loader (SQL*Loader) and direct-load INSERT operations against the table, partition, or LOB storage are logged. If you omit the LOGGING/NOLOGGING clause, the logging attribute of the table or table partition defaults to the logging attribute of the tablespace where it resides.

In NOLOGGING mode, data is modified with minimal logging (to mark new extents invalid and to record dictionary changes). When applied during media recovery, the extent invalidation records mark a range of blocks as logically corrupt, because the redo data is not fully logged. If you cannot afford to lose this table, you should take a backup after the NOLOGGING operation. The size of a redo log generated for an operation in NOLOGGING mode is significantly smaller than the log generated with the LOGGING option set. If the database runs in ARCHIVELOG mode, media recovery from a backup taken before the LOGGING operation restores the table. However, media recovery from a backup taken before the NOLOGGING operation does not restore the table.

Here's an example of creating a table with NOLOGGING:

```
Create table orders_temp
As select * from orders
nologging;

Table created.
```

Here's an example of creating an index with NOLOGGING:

```
Create index ot_idx1 on orders_temp (order_no) nologging;

Index created.
```

**TIP**
*The NOLOGGING option for creating tables and indexes is a tremendous performance gain and provides redo log space savings. Make sure you use this powerful option!*

# Network Computing

Note that as of the writing of this section, Oracle8i (Oracle version 8.1.*x*) was not officially released into production. Changes to the features and their implementation that may be made may affect information in this section. Refer to your current re!ease documentation when conflicts arise. Chapter 12 gave a brief description of Network Computing Architecture (NCA) and some of the tools that will enable this architecture to succeed. In this chapter, I will cover the most powerful aspect of NCA as it relates to the incorporation of Java and the Internet-enabling functionality of Oracle8i.

There is always the question how "pure" the Java needs to be. Sun's CEO, Scott McNealy, sums it up this way: "What do you get when you take a cup of coffee and add three drops of poison?" Answer: "Windows."

While it appears to be a minor attack of words at a competitor (a large one), it echoes the desire by some developers (especially McNealy) to have Java as a nonproprietary and standard vanilla language. Anyone who has written a Web application using Java understands the difficulty with subtle differences in Java and the browsers that support them. These differences lead to different responses on different browsers.

In an effort to move more developers into Oracle, and expand the capabilities and speed of Web-enabled applications, Oracle has integrated Java with the Oracle database. Oracle has done this in two ways. The first allows Java developers the ability to embed SQL within Java (SQLJ), and the second embeds Java within PL/SQL. JDBC offers a Java equivalent to ODBC for speed on the Internet. Oracle is providing many of the packages that are stored in Oracle to be written in Java, ensuring less traffic on the wire and greater speed for the user. As Larry Ellison often puts it, "Put the complexity of the application on the Application Server and the Database Server and not on the user's PC or browser."

## The Integration of Java with SQL (SQLJ and JDBC)

The two primary tools that allow Java to work with Oracle are JDBC and SQLJ. SQLJ is an integration of Oracle's SQL within Java code. JDBC is much like ODBC for Java. JDBC is a call level library interface, further enhanced by SQLJ's ability to access the database at compile time. Although both of these methods allow using the combination of Java with Oracle, there are distinct differences and benefits. At times when you use JDBC, it is both complementary and advantageous to use SQLJ.

SQLJ is perfect for simple SQL calls to the database, and embedding SQL within Java. The SQLJ preprocessor is written in Java and the precompiler changes the SQLJ to Java classes. Commonly used SQL statements that can be included in Java include the following:

Integration of Java with SQL

■ **Queries**  SELECT statements and expressions

■ **Data Manipulation Language (DML)**  INSERT, UPDATE, and DELETE

■ **Data statements**  FETCH, SELECT INTO

■ **Transaction control**  COMMIT, ROLLBACK, etc.

■ **Data Definition Language (DDL)**  CREATE, DROP, etc.

■ **Calls to stored procedures**  e.g., CALL MYPROC(:x, :y, :z)

■ **Calls to stored functions**  e.g., VALUES( MYFUN(:x) )

The simplest SQLJ executable clauses consist of the token #sql followed by a SQL statement enclosed in "curly braces". The following example shows a Java routine with a SQL statement embedded within it. The simple Java print routine is displayed here:

```
void print_ordno (String name) {
  String addr;
  #sql { SELECT ORDNO, PRICE INTO :ord, :price FROM ORDERS WHERE :custno = CUST };
  System.out.println( cust + "has order no" + ord + "at a price of" + price );
  }
```

You can call a stored procedure from Java. An example of a SQL Persistent Stored Modules (SQL/PSM) statement of a stored procedure call is listed here (the host variable arg can be varied for the program):

```
#sql { CALL MY_PROCEDURE(:arg) };
```

JDBC stands for Java Database Connectivity and is a standard set of Java classes specified by JavaSoft, so all vendors can access the database in the same manner. JDBC classes provide the standard features that ODBC did, such as transaction management, simple queries, manipulation of precompiled statements with bind variables, calls to stored procedures, access to the database dictionary, and other basic database access functionality. For the user, it is a matter of typing in the Web page desired, and the necessary JDBC driver is downloaded to the browser from the Web server. There is no client-side installation. There is a thin JDBC driver that only works with TCP/IP, which is much faster. Both the Oracle JDBC and thin JDBC drivers are JDK (Java Development Kit) 1.0.2. and 1.1 compliant. These drivers work with SQL*Net along with firewalls certified with SQL*Net: firewalls from Checkpoint, SunSoft, Cisco Systems, Milkyway Networks, Trusted Information Systems, Raptor, Secure Computing Corporation, and Global Internet.

**Integration of Java with SQL**

# Comparing SQLJ and JDBC

Consider the following comparison from Oracle's OTN (www.technet.oracle.com; I highly recommend this site) Web site that has the same piece of code written with SQLJ and then written using the JDBC driver.

In the following, the types PreparedStatement and ResultSet, and their methods (prepareStatement, setFloat, setInt, and executeQuery) are defined by JDBC. The variable *recs* contains the connection object of JDBC type java.sql.Connection:

```
java.sql.PreparedStatement ps =
    recs.prepareStatement(
    "SELECT STUDENT, SCORE "
    + "  FROM GRADE_REPORTS "
    + "  WHERE SCORE >= ? "
    + "    AND ATTENDED >= ? "
    + "    AND DEMERITS <= ? "
    + "ORDER BY SCORE DESCENDING");
ps.setFloat(1, limit);
ps.setInt(2, days);
ps.setInt(3, offences);
java.sql.ResultSet honor = ps.executeQuery();
while (honor.next()) {
 System.out.println(honor.getString(1) + " has grade " +
 honor.getFloat(2));
}
```

The following is the *equivalent SQLJ program*. In contrast to the preceding dynamic SQL example, it defines a type for the result set to be returned, binds host data by name rather than by position, and provides named accessors for the returned data.

```
#sql iterator Honors ( String name, float grade );
Honors honor;
#sql (recs) honor =
    { SELECT   STUDENT AS "name", SCORE AS "grade"
      FROM     GRADE_REPORTS
      WHERE    SCORE >= :limit
      AND      ATTENDED >= :days
      AND      DEMERITS <= :offenses
      ORDER BY SCORE DESCENDING };
while (honor.next()) {
  System.out.println( honor.name() + " has grade " + honor.grade() );
}
```

While the likes of HTML, Java, and JavaScript get us to the Web in time for a likely Internet commerce explosion, I still consider them 3GLs that are maintenance and support nightmares that I remember having about 10 years ago. There is a desperate need for a 4GL that achieves the same result without the 3GL programming, and the tools in Chapter 12 will provide the 4GL answer. The functionality of Java with Oracle provides for the special needs that a 3GL offers.

**TIP**
*Oracle has provided a means for utilizing Java with the Oracle database. SQLJ and JDBC will give you the means for moving complexity off the desktop and back to the database server. This will eliminate much of the network traffic and improve performance.*

# Oracle Objects

With Oracle8, Oracle has embraced object-oriented programming and offers several options in the area of objects. This section provides some of the definitions related to objects. To explain objects would take a complete book. The world of objects has a unique vocabulary. Consider some of the following terms and definitions that are "tossed around" (and rarely defined) by object experts:

- *Object* – An attribute or variable that consists of attributes, operational information, and therefore other objects.

- *Extensibility* – The ability to conform to new requirements using existing structures. Oracle8 is extensible because it allows for the assembly of new, abstract data types based on its predefined primitive types such as number, VARCHAR2, and date.

- *Varray* – An ordered list of data elements; useful for a nonsearchable finite data set.

- *Nested Table* – Unordered set of data elements; useful for searchable, indexable, and unlimited data.

- *Method* – Procedure or function that is a part of the object type definition and can operate on the data attributes of the object type. Loosely defined, a trigger on a table could be viewed as a method for a table.

- *Object View* – Allows the use of relational data in object-oriented applications.

- *Encapsulation* – The mechanism that data and their methods can be bound and protected. An object is a logical entity that encapsulates both the data and the code that manipulates that data.

- *Inheritance* – The process by which one object can acquire the properties of another object.

- *Class* – Related, hierarchical groupings or categorization of objects.

- *Polymorphism* – An object's ability to react to or interface with a general class of actions, achieved through overloading. DBMS_OUTPUT.PUT_LINE does not care whether a character string, number, or date (or any combination thereof) are sent as parameters to the procedure.

- *Metadata* – The data that is comprised of all of the information about all of the data on your system—how it is stored, where it is stored, etc. It's the "data about the data."

# New Hints in Oracle8

There are a variety of new hints in Oracle8. The four hints (DRIVING_SITE, INDEX_FFS, APPEND, and NO_APPEND) listed in this section are particularly worth noting. This section will give a brief description of each, but please see Chapter 7 (a chapter on hints) for detailed descriptions and examples of each.

## The DRIVING_SITE Hint

The DRIVING_SITE hint is identical to the ORDERED hint, except this hint is for processing data by driving it from a particular database. The table specified in the hint will be the driving site that will be used to process the actual join. This hint can be used with either cost- or rule-based optimization.

## The INDEX_FFS Hint

The INDEX_FFS hint is a fast full scan of the index. This hint will access only the index and *not* the corresponding table. It will only be used if all of the information that the query needs to retrieve is in the index. This one can give great performance gains, especially when the table has a large number of columns.

## The APPEND Hint

The APPEND hint is a great hint if you have an abundance of space to burn. The APPEND hint will not check to see if there is space within currently used blocks for INSERTs, but instead it will append the data into new blocks. Potentially, you may waste space, but you will not get the overhead of checking the current blocks to see if they have fallen below the PCTUSED (the minimum percent of free space in a block before you can reuse it). If you never DELETE rows from a table, you should definitely use the APPEND since the blocks will never get to the PCTUSED (only deleting rows will empty a current block to this level). Note that PCTUSED is a storage parameter that is set when a table is created.

If PARALLEL loading is used with SQL*Loader, then the APPEND option for SQL*Loader must be used. Also, if an INSERT is parallelized using the PARALLEL hint, the APPEND will be used by default. Note that you can use the NOAPPEND hint (next section) to override this behavior.

## The NO_APPEND Hint

The NO_APPEND hint is used to override the default for the PARALLEL inserts (the default, of course, is APPEND). The NO_APPEND hint is the opposite of the APPEND and will check free space within current blocks (blocks with space less than the PCTUSED) before using new ones.

# Using the Buffer Pools in Oracle8

The Shared Pool parameters are covered in Appendix A. In this section, we will focus on the pools that are used to store the actual data in memory. The init.ora parameters DB_BLOCK_BUFFERS, DB_BLOCK_SIZE, BUFFER_POOL_KEEP, and BUFFER_POOL_RECYCLE will be the determining factors for memory used to store data.

DB_BLOCK_BUFFERS times the DB_BLOCK_SIZE refers to the total size in bytes of the main buffer cache (or memory for data) in the SGA. In Oracle8, two new buffer pools are introduced: BUFFER_POOL_KEEP and BUFFER_POOL_RECYCLE. These additional two pools serve the same purpose as the main buffer cache (used to store data in memory), with the exception that the algorithm to maintain the pool is different for all three available pools.

The *main buffer cache* (defined by DB_BLOCK_BUFFERS) maintains the LRU (Least Recently Used) list and flushes the oldest buffers in the list. The number of blocks specified in DB_BLOCK_BUFFERS make up all three pools. The main buffer cache is what is left over from the BUFFER_POOL_KEEP and the BUFFER_POOL_RECYCLE.

### Keep Pool

The *Keep Pool* (defined by BUFFER_POOL_KEEP) is never flushed, and is intended for buffers that need to be "pinned" indefinitely (buffers that are very important and need to stay in memory). Use the Keep Pool for small tables that are frequently accessed and need to be in memory at all times.

## Recycle Pool

The *Recycle Pool* (defined by BUFFER_POOL_RECYCLE) is instantly flushed in order to reduce contention and waits for memory in the pool. Overhead searching for a LRU list is avoided using this pool. Use the Recycle Pool for large, less important data that is usually accessed only once in a long while.

To create a table that will be stored in the Keep Pool upon being accessed:

```
Create table state_list (state_abbrev varchar2(2), state_desc varchar2(25))
Storage (buffer_pool keep);
```

To alter the table to the Recycle Pool:

```
Alter table state_list storage (buffer_pool recycle);
```

To alter the table back to the Keep Pool:

```
Alter table state_list storage (buffer_pool keep);
```

To find the disk and memory reads in the Keep Pool:

```
select   physical_reads "Disk Reads",
         block_gets + consistent_gets "Memory Reads"
from     v$buffer_pool
where    name = 'KEEP';
```

Use the example here to query the V$PARAMETER view and list the various buffer pool settings.

```
select    name, value, isdefault, isses_modifiable, issys_modifiable
from      v$parameter
where     name like '%pool%';
```

| NAME | VALUE | ISDEFAULT | ISSES | ISSYS |
|------|-------|-----------|-------|-------|
| SHARED_POOL_SIZE | 10,000,000 | FALSE | FALSE | FALSE |
| SHARED_POOL_RESERVED_SIZE | 500,000 | TRUE | FALSE | FALSE |
| SHARED_POOL_RESERVED_MIN_ALLOC | 5K | TRUE | FALSE | FALSE |
| LARGE_POOL_SIZE | 0 | TRUE | FALSE | FALSE |
| LARGE_POOL_MIN_ALLOC | 16K | TRUE | FALSE | FALSE |
| BUFFER_POOL_KEEP | | TRUE | FALSE | FALSE |
| BUFFER_POOL_RECYCLE | | TRUE | FALSE | FALSE |
| PARALLEL_MIN_MESSAGE_POOL | 48,330 | TRUE | FALSE | FALSE |

```
8 rows selected.
```

**Using Buffer Pools**

**V8 TIP**
*The additional buffer pools (memory for data) available in Oracle8 are initially set to zero. By setting values for the BUFFER_POOL_KEEP and BUFFER_POOL_ RECYCLE, we eliminate from the blocks set by DB_BLOCK_BUFFERS that are allocated for the main memory for data and give them to the other two pools.*

# Features in Oracle8i (8.1)

This section will focus on a few of the new features in Oracle8i that are related to performance tuning. As of the writing of this book, Oracle8i (Oracle version 8.1.*x*) was not in production, so these features must be viewed with that in mind. Oracle always reserves the right to change things before they go to production, so check the latest Oracle documentation before using these features.

## Function-Based Indexes

One of the largest problems with indexes is that the indexes are often suppressed by developers. Developers using the UPPER function can suppress an index on a column for a given query. In Oracle8i, there is now a way to combat this problem. Function-based indexes allow you to create an index based on a function or expression. The value of the function or expression is specified by the person creating the index and is stored in the index. Function-based indexes can involve multiple columns or arithmetic expressions, or may be a PL/SQL function or C callout. The following example shows a function-based index.

To create the function-based index:

```
CREATE INDEX emp_idx ON emp (UPPER(ename));
```

An index has been created on the ename column when the UPPER function is used on this column.

To query the emp table using the function-based index:

```
select    ename, job, deptno
from      emp
where     upper(ename) = 'ELLISON';
```

The function-based index can be used for this query. For large tables where the condition retrieves a small number of records, the query yields substantial performance gains over a full table scan.

**V8i TIP**
*Function-based indexes can lead to dramatic*
*performance gains when used to create indexes on*
*functions often used on selective columns.*

## Enable/Disable All Triggers

It is often helpful to enable or disable all of the triggers associated with a given table. The following commands show how to perform this powerful operation.

To enable all triggers for the customer table:

```
ALTER TABLE customer ENABLE ALL TRIGGERS;
```

To disable all triggers for the customer table:

```
ALTER TABLE customer DISABLE ALL TRIGGERS;
```

## The NO_INDEX Hint

The Optimizer, in its infinite wisdom, often uses indexes that are undesirable despite efforts to override the use of the indexes. Now there is a hint that specifically disallows one or more indexes to be used by the optimizer but does not suppress the use of all indexes (as with the FULL hint). This hint applies to b-tree, bitmap, cluster, and domain indexes. If no indexes are specified with this hint, a full table scan will result (all indexes are disallowed).

To query the emp table using the function-based index created earlier:

```
select     /*+ NO_INDEX(emp emp_idx) */ ename, job, deptno
from       emp
where      upper(ename) = 'ELLISON';
```

Although there is a function-based index that can be used on the "upper(ename)" condition, it is disallowed by the NO_INDEX hint.

## The DROP COLUMN Command

I remember Oracle DBAs and developers asking since version 5 for a way to drop a column from a table. I remember hearing that it was coming as a future enhancement. Well, ten years later we finally have the command I have most heard asked for over the years. The DROP COLUMN command allows you to remove a column from a table.

To alter the emp table and drop the ename and job columns:

```
ALTER TABLE emp DROP (ename, job);
```

This statement removes the ename and job columns as well as any constraints on either of these columns.

To alter the orders table and drop the primary key:

```
ALTER TABLE orders DROP (orderid) CASCADE CONSTRAINTS;
```

This statement would drop the primary-key column called orderid and any other constraints that reference this column. If the orderid column was referenced in other constraints, the CASCADE CONSTRAINTS must be used or an error would result.

To drop the orders table and CASCADE CONSTRAINTS:

```
DROP TABLE orders CASCADE CONSTRAINTS;
```

**V8i TIP**
*The DROP COLUMN command is finally here. The DROP COLUMN command also contains an option for CASCADE CONSTRAINTS.*

## The DBMS_REPAIR Package

In Oracle8i, Oracle has made it easier to find and repair block corruptions without losing the entire object that is corrupted. The DBMS_REPAIR package detects and repairs lost data while making the object usable even when there is a block corruption. While some data (the corrupted data) may be lost, this feature will allow you to skip the corrupted blocks without errors. There are also additional reporting features with this package.

## ALTER SYSTEM SUSPEND/RESUME

The ALTER SYSTEM command now has options to suspend all I/O for a specified period. This can be helpful when disk mirrors are broken or put back together. While this command is not used for backup purposes, it could be used for instance or crash recovery. When the database is suspended, you can make copies without worrying about ongoing transactions. The commands for suspending and resuming are listed next.

To alter the system and SUSPEND all I/O:

```
ALTER SYSTEM SUSPEND;
```

This command suspends all I/O to datafiles, control files, and file headers. It suspends any I/O by any query on the system.

To alter the system and RESUME all I/O:

```
ALTER SYSTEM RESUME;
```

This command resumes normal operation of the system.

## Reading Multiple Blocks for Disk Sorts

In prior versions of Oracle, we could use the DB_MULTIBLOCK_READ_COUNT parameter in the init.ora to read multiple blocks in a single I/O. With the new init.ora parameter SORT_MULTIBLOCK_READ_COUNT, we can read multiple blocks for sorting operations that will occur on disk.

```
SORTep_MULTIBLOCK_READ_COUNT = 16
```

This set parameter (in the init.ora) specifies 16 database blocks to read each time a sort performs a read from temporary segments.

## Transportable Tablespaces

The feature Transportable Tablespaces allows the DBA to move tablespaces and data files to another Oracle instance. The way this is performed is by using the TABLESPACES and DATAFILES parameters with the IMP and EXP Oracle utilities. The power of this new feature can be realized as you can now clone large portions of one database to another instance. Please see the Oracle 8.1 documentation for the full process.

There are several limitations, the largest one being that this feature only works between database instances that are version 8.1 or higher. However, you can move objects from Oracle 8.1 and Oracle 8.2. You can also move objects from Oracle 8.2 running at an 8.1 compatibility level to Oracle 8.1. Both databases must be on the same platform, have the same block size, and have the same character set. Bitmap indexes, nested tables, varrays cannot be transported, and must be deleted before transporting a tablespace. There are additional limitations that should be investigated before using this option.

**V8i TIP**
*Transportable tablespaces and data files are powerful
features in Oracle 8.1 and 8.2, but be aware that there
are several limitations associated with this feature.*

# Tips Review

- Changing init.ora parameters spontaneously is a powerful feature for both developers and DBAs. Consequently, a user with the ALTER SESSION privilege is capable of irresponsibly allocating 100M+ for the SORT_AREA_SIZE (dangerous) for a given session if not restricted.

- Index-organized tables are best used for frequently accessed tables that are usually accessed by the same columns.

- Constraints can now be checked for a statement or for an entire transaction. Altering a constraint to be deferrable will allow individual users to defer the constraint until after the entire transaction is completed.

- Reverse-key indexes are an excellent resource for sequential data that you do not want to index in a sequential manner. This type of index allows a more suitable distribution of data, frequently residing close together—often in the same physical block.

- Tables can be easily partitioned for individual pieces to be accessed and/or manipulated. Accessing the views DBA_TABLES, DBA_PART_TABLE, and DBA_SEGMENTS provides additional information concerning tables that have been partitioned.

- You can also partition tables using multiple columns as the partitioning criteria.

- Dropping a table partition causes its local index (but not the other local partition indexes) to be dropped and a global index (one that exists on the entire table) to be unavailable. Don't use global indexes if you desire to drop partitions of a table.

- Indexes that are partitioned (local indexes) should also be prefixed (the partitioning key is the leading edge of the index).

- If data is partitioned correctly, all the new information falls into a single partition, enabling an export of a single partition of every table during backups.

■ In moving to Oracle8, testing will be your best tool in finding problem code that Oracle no longer automatically translates. Oracle8's stricter syntax rules could cause errors after the conversion. Test!

■ In Oracle8, parallel DML statements *are* allowed. This functionality applies to partitioned tables and indexes. Parallelization still *cannot* be performed on an index operation, but parallelization *can* be performed on a partitioned index.

■ You *must* issue a COMMIT after using parallel DML statements. You will receive an error executing a SELECT statement that follows a parallel DML statement if you do not issue a COMMIT.

■ Operations are performed in parallel on partitioned objects *only* when more than one partition is accessed and parallelism is *not* performed within a single partition. To use more parallel server processes, ensure that the table is partitioned into enough pieces.

■ The DBMS_ROWID package provides a DBA with excellent information about the storage of data within the database. It can be used in lieu of the normal DBA tables and views for many operations.

■ The NOLOGGING option for creating tables and indexes is a tremendous performance gain and results in redo log space savings. Make sure you use this powerful option!

■ Oracle has provided a means for utilizing Java with the Oracle database. SQLJ and JDBC will give you the means for moving complexity off the desktop and back to the database server. This will eliminate much of the network traffic and improve performance.

■ Object types are the backbone of using Oracle objects. Objects can be nested within each other, causing major complexity in your design. Be careful to use the benefits of objects without causing the larger problem of not knowing how everything fits together because the complexity is too great.

■ When a query uses a table alias, the hint must specify the alias and not the table.

■ The additional buffer pools (memory for data) available in Oracle8 are initially set to zero. By setting values for the BUFFER_POOL_KEEP and BUFFER_POOL_RECYCLE, we take away from the blocks set by DB_BLOCK_BUFFERS that are allocated for the main memory for data and give them to the other two pools.

Tips Review

**V8i TIP**

*Function-based indexes can lead to dramatic
performance gains when used to create indexes on
functions often used on selective columns.*

 **V8i TIP**

*The DROP COLUMN command is finally here. The
DROP COLUMN command also contains an option for
CASCADE CONSTRAINTS.*

 **V8i TIP**

*Transportable tablespaces and data files are powerful
features in Oracle 8.1 and 8.2, but be aware that there
are several limitations associated with this feature.*

# References

*Oracle8 Server: SQL Language Reference Manual*; Oracle Corporation

*Oracle7 Server Tuning*; Oracle Corporation

*Oracle8 Server Tuning*; Oracle Corporation

*Performance Tuning Guide Version 7.0*; Oracle Corporation

*Performance Tuning*; Eyal Aronoff, Kevin Loney, Noorali Sonawalla; Osborne/
McGraw-Hill

*Oracle8 DBA Handbook*; Kevin Loney, Osborne/McGraw-Hill

*Oracle8 Server Administrators Guide Release 8.0*, Oracle Corporation, 1997

*Oracle8 Server Concepts Release 8.0*, Volumes 1&2, Oracle Corporation, 1997

*Oracle8 Server Reference Release 8.0*, Oracle Corporation, 1997

*Oracle8 Server SQL Reference Release 8.0*, Oracle Corporation, 1997

*Oracle8 Backup and Recovery Guide Release 8.0*, Oracle Corporation, 1997

*Oracle8 Server Utilities Guide Release 8.0*, Oracle Corporation, 1997

*Oracle8 Server Tuning Guide Release 8.0*, Oracle Corporation, 1997

http://www.oracle.com

*Tuning Tips: You will be Toast!*; Rich Niemiec, TUSC

Thanks to Joe Trezzo, Dave Ventura, Sean McGuire, Greg Pucka, and
John Molinaro who all contributed to this chapter.

**Tips Review**

# TIPS

# &T

# TECHNIQUES

# CHAPTER
# 14

The V$ Views
(Developer and DBA)

A lmost every great tuning or DBA product has one thing in common. Most of them access the V$ view information to get the insightful information that is retrieved about the database, individual queries, or an individual user. Accessing the V$ views has become quite prevalent due to the numerous presentations by Joe Trezzo and other V$ gurus. If you currently don't look at the V$ views, you don't know what you're missing. The V$ views are unfiltered and unbiased looks into the heart of the Oracle database. They are the link to moving from the average to the expert DBA. In Chapter 15 we will explore a more extensive look at the underlying tables of the V$ views. Appendices B and C provide information about the V$ views and also the creation scripts from the X$ tables. Unfortunately, I can't show every great V$ script due to space limitations. Please check our Web site (www.tusc.com) for the latest V$ scripts available. Tips covered in this chapter include the following:

- V$ view creation and granting access to the V$ views

- Getting a listing of all V$ views

- Getting a listing of the x$ scripts that make up the V$ views

- Indexes on the x$ tables make V$ views access faster

- Querying V$DATABASE view to get database creation time and archiving information

- Querying V$LICENSE view to view licensing limits and warning settings

- Accessing V$OPTIONS view to view all options that have been installed

- Accessing V$NLS_PARAMETER view for language support and Y2K compliance settings

- Basic memory allocation for Oracle can be found by querying V$SGA view

- Detailed memory allocation for Oracle can be found by querying V$SGASTAT view

- Init.ora settings can be found in V$PARAMETER view

- Hit ratio for data (V$SYSSTAT view)

- Hit ratio for the data dictionary (V$ROWCACHE view)

- Hit ratio for the shared SQL and PL/SQL (V$LIBRARYCACHE view)

- Which objects need to be pinned and whether there is contiguous free memory (V$DB_OBJECT_CACHE view)

- Finding the problem queries accessing V$SQLAREA, V$SQLTEXT, V$SESSION, and V$SESS_IO views

- Finding out what users are doing and the resources they are using

- Identifying locking problems and killing the corresponding session

- Finding users with multiple sessions

- Balancing I/O using the views V$DATAFILE, V$FILESTAT, and DBA_DATA_FILES views

- Querying V$ROLLNAME, V$ROLLSTAT, and V$TRANSACTION views for rollback segment information

- Checking to see if free lists is sufficient

- A table grouping the V$ views by category

# V$ View Creation and Access

These V$ views are created by the catalog.sql script. As of the release of Oracle8, there are approximately 132 views. The actual number varies by the version, but they are all created with the prefix of V_$. Two of the views are created by the catldr.sql script, which is used for SQL*Loader direct load statistical information. The underlying view creations for each V$ view can be seen in the V$ view named V$FIXED_VIEW_DEFINITION. The views are created by selecting from one or more X$ tables. There is a view created for each V_$ view to allow users to access the view. Users cannot access the V_$ views and therefore, this method provides access to these views via a view on a view. The view name changes the prefix of each view to V$. Lastly, there is a public synonym created on each view since the SYS user owns the tables. An example of a V$ view creation in the catalog.sql script is shown here:

```
create     or replace view v_$datafile as
select     *
from       v$datafile;
drop       public synonym v$datafile;
create     public synonym v$datafile for v_$datafile;
```

The complete sequence of events is detailed in the following steps:

1. The V$ views are created from the X$ tables when the database is created:
```
create     or replace view v$fixed_table as
select     kqftanam, kqftaobj, 'TABLE'
from       x$kqfta
union all
select     kqfvinam, kqfviobj, 'VIEW'
```

V$ View Creation

```
from      x$kqfvi
union all
select    kqfdtnam, kqfdtobj, 'TABLE'
from      x$kqfdt;
```

2. The catalog.sql script is executed:

```
SQL> @catalog
```

3. A V_$ view is created from the V$ view:

```
create or replace view v_$fixed_table
as
select    *
from      v$fixed_table;
```

The original synonym for the V$ views is dropped:

```
drop public synonym v$fixed_table;
```

4. A new V$ synonym is created on the V_$ view:

```
create public synonym v$fixed_table for v_$fixed_table;
```

**TIP**
*The V$ views that are accessed by SYSTEM are actually synonyms that point to the V_$ views that are views of the original V$ views based on the x$ tables (better read that one again).*

The only operation that can be performed on these views is a SELECT. In order to provide access to the V$ views, you must grant access to the underlying V_$ view.

**You cannot grant access to the V$ tables (even as the SYS user):**

```
connect        sys/ change_on_install
Grant select on v$fixed_table to richn;
ORA-02030: can only select fixed tables/views
```

Although the error message for attempting to grant access to V$FIXED_TABLE view is erroneous, the grant will not be allowed. You may, however, grant access to the underlying V_$ view that is behind the V$ view.

**In order to connect to the SYS superuser, use the following:**

```
Connect        sys/change_on_install
Connected.
```

**To grant access to underlying view to the desired user, use the following:**

```
grant select on v_$fixed_table to richn;
Grant succeeded.
```

**To connect as the desired user, use this:**

```
conn     richn/tusc
Connected.
```

**Access the V$FIXED_TABLE view via the synonym V$FIXED_TABLE created for V_$FIXED_TABLE with the following:**

```
select    count(*)
from      v$fixed_table;

COUNT(*)
464
```

**You still *can't* access the V_$FIXED_TABLE even though that was the grant made:**

```
select    count(*)
from      v_$fixed_table;

Object does not exist.
```

**You *can* access the V_$FIXED_VIEW if you preface it with SYS:**

```
conn      richn/tusc
select    count(*)
from      SYS.v_$fixed_table;

COUNT(*)
464
```

To avoid confusion, it is better to give access to the V_$ tables and notify the DBA that users have access to the V$ views. Using this method, you may give access to the V$ view information without giving out the password for the SYS or SYSTEM accounts. The key is granting SELECT access to the original SYS owned V_$ view.

**TIP**
*When other DBAs need access to the V$ view information, but not the SYS or SYSTEM passwords, grant the user access to the V_$ views. The user may then access the V$ views that have public synonyms to the V_$ views.*

Granting privilege to the V$ views to non-DBA users should be provided on an as-needed basis and used with caution. Remember, there are performance costs that come with querying the V$ views and the larger your environment, the greater those costs.

## Getting a Count and Listing of All V$ Views

To get a count of all V$ views for a given version of Oracle, query the V$FIXED_TABLE view. The number of V$ views continues to change even within the same version. The examples that follow display the V$ view queries for both Oracle7 and Oracle8. The frontier in the world of the V$ views continues to expand with each version of Oracle.

**Version 7 query to get a count of V$ views:**

```
select      count(*)
from        v$fixed_table
where       name like 'V%';


COUNT(*)
72
```

**Version 8 query to get a count of V$ views:**

```
select      count(*)
from        v$fixed_table
where       name like 'V%';


COUNT(*)
132
```

The number of V$ views has increased substantially from Oracle7 to Oracle8.
Many of the V$ views continue to be undocumented. The possibilities for information to be explored are continually changing for Oracle, because the number of views continues to expand. In Oracle8, the GV$ views are introduced. The GV$ (global V$) views are the same as the V$ views with an additional column for the instance ID.

**Version 7 query to get a list of V$ views:**

```
select      name
from        v$fixed_table
where       name like 'V%'
order by    name;
```

```
NAME
v$access
v$archive
v$backup
v$bgprocess
v$circuit
v$compatibility
v$compatseg
v$controlfile
v$database
v$datafile
v$dbfile
v$dblink
```

Note that this is a partial listing only; a complete listing is in Appendix B.

**TIP**
*Query V$FIXED_TABLE view to get a listing of all V$
views in the database.*

**Version 8 query to get a list of GV$ views:**

```
select      name
from        v$fixed_table
where       name like 'GV%'
order by    name;

NAME
gv$access
gv$active_instances
gv$archive
gv$archived_log
gv$archived_dest
gv$backup
gv$backup_corruption
gv$backup_datafile
gv$backup_device
gv$backup_piece
gv$backup_redolog
gv$backup_set
gv$bgprocess
gv$bh
gv$buffer_pool
```

Note that this is a partial listing only; a complete listing is in Appendix B.

**Getting a Count**

**V8 TIP**

*Query V$FIXED_TABLE to get a listing of all GV$ and V$ views in the database. The GV$ views are the exact same as the V$ views, except the instance ID contains an identifier.*

# Finding the x$ Tables Used in the Creation of the V$ Views

To understand where the V$ view information comes from, query the underlying x$ tables (see Chapter 15 for x$ table information). At times, it may be advantageous to query the underlying x$ table since the V$ views are often the join of several x$ tables. The x$ tables are very cryptic in nature because they are very similar to the underlying table constructs of the Oracle data dictionary. Oracle creates V$ views in the SGA to allow users to examine the information stored in the x$ tables in a more readable format. In fact, when SELECTs are performed against the V$ views, the SELECTs are actually retrieving information out of the SGA—and more specifically, out of the x$ tables. With the knowledge of the V$ view underlying a given SELECT statement, you have the capability to create customized views; simply copy the existing V$ view underlying SELECT statement and modify it or create a new customized SELECT on the x$ tables. This technique allows more selective and more optimized queries. The following queries are used to access the underlying query to the x$ tables.

**Version 7 query to get the CREATE statement for the V$ views:**

```
select    'View Name: '||view_name, substr(view_definition,1,
          (instr(view_definition, 'from')-1)) def1,
          substr(view_definition,(instr(view_definition,'from'))) def2
from      v$fixed_view_definition
order by  view_name;
```

**View name, V$ACCESS view:**

```
select    distinct s.ksusenum,o.kglnaown,o.kglnaobj,o.kglobtyp
from      x$ksuse s,x$kglob o,x$kgldp d, x$kgllk l
where     l.kgllkuse=s.addr
and       l.kgllkhdl=d.kglhdadr
and       o.kglhdadr=d.kglrfhdl
/
```

**View name, V$ARCHIVE view:**

```
select    le.indx+1,le.lethr,le.leseq, decode
          (bitand(le.leflg,8),0,'NO','YES'), to_number(le.lelos)
from      x$kccle le,x$kccdi di
where     bitand(di.diflg,1)!=0
and       le.ledup!=0
and       bitand(le.leflg,1)=0
and       (to_number(le.lelos)<= to_number(di.difas)
          or bitand(le.leflg,8)=0)
/
```

Note that this is a partial listing only; a complete listing is in Appendix B.

**Version 8 query to get the CREATE statement for the V$ views:**

```
select    'View Name: '||view_name, substr(view_definition,1,
          (instr (view _definition,'from')-1)) def1,substr
          (view_definition, (instr(view _definition,'from')))
          def2
from      v$fixed_view_definition
order by  view_name;
```

**View name, GV$ACCESS view:**

```
select    distinct s.inst_id,s.ksusenum,o.kglnaown,o.kglnaobj,
          decode(o.kglobtyp,     0, 'CURSOR',    1, 'INDEX',
          2, 'TABLE',    3, 'CLUSTER',    4, 'VIEW',    5, 'SYNONYM',
          6, 'SEQUENCE',    7, 'PROCEDURE',    8, 'FUNCTION',
          9, 'PACKAGE',    10,'NON-EXISTENT',    11,'PACKAGE BODY',
          12,'TRIGGER',    13,'CLASS',    14,'SET',    15,'OBJECT',
          16,'USER',    17,'DBLINK',    'INVALID TYPE')
from      x$ksuse s,x$kglob o,x$kgldp d,x$kgllk l
where     l.kgllkuse=s.addr
and       l.kgllkhdl=d.kglhdadr
and       l.kglnahsh=d.kglnahsh
and       o.kglnahsh=d.kglrfhsh
and       o.kglhdadr=d.kglrfhdl
/
```

**View name, GV$ACTIVE_INSTANCES view:**

```
select    inst_id, ksiminum, rpad(ksimstr,60)
from      x$ksimsi
/
```

Note that this is a partial listing only; a complete listing is in Appendix B.

**Finding the x$ Tables**

**TIP**
*Query V$FIXED_VIEW_DEFINITION retrieves the query
that creates the V$ and GV$ views from the x$ tables.*

In the future, the V$ views and x$ tables are expected to change. Oracle is expected to add indexes to the underlying x$ tables to improve the performance of SELECTs on the V$ views and x$ tables. This will make it much easier to optimize x$ SELECTs by providing the ability to SELECT directly from the x$ tables.

## Indexes on the x$ Tables Make the V$ Views Faster in Oracle8

In Oracle8, there are indexes on the underlying x$ tables to provide faster execution of queries performed on the V$ views. The index information on the underlying x$ tables can be viewed through the V$INDEXED_FIXED_COLUMN view (see Chapter 15 for more information). This information can be viewed by executing the following query:

```
select     table_name, column_name, index_number
from       v$indexed_fixed_column
order by   table_name, column_name;

TABLE NAME       COLUMN NAME    INDEX NUMBER
X$BH             INDX           1
X$KCBCBH         ADDR           1
X$KCBCBH         INDX           2
X$KCBFWAIT       ADDR           1
X$KCBFWAIT       INDX           2
X$KCBRBH         ADDR           1
X$KCBRBH         INDX           2
```

Note that this is a partial listing only; a complete listing is in Appendix C.

**TIP**
*Query V$INDEXED_FIXED_COLUMN view to retrieve
the indexes on the x$ tables that ultimately make the
x$ views faster in Oracle8. You are not allowed to
create your own indexes on the x$ tables.*

## Helpful V$ Scripts

The rest of this chapter is dedicated to scripts that are very helpful in analyzing different areas of the Oracle database. Many of these scripts are dynamic and provide valuable insight into areas of the database that may need to be analyzed to determine resource contention at a point in time. Typically, the result is that the DBA performs some operation to immediately eliminate the contention by tuning a query or increasing an init.ora parameter to reduce the resource contention in the future. Revoking access to a given ad hoc query user, or restricting their system resource use with profiles, could be an emergency option as well. These sections include scripts that retrieve the following:

- Basic database information
- Memory settings and hit ratio information
- User and session information
- File distribution and redo log information

## Basic Database Information

Accessing V$DATABASE view will give you basic information concerning the database. The most important information in the output is to ensure that you are in the desired archivelog mode. The output will also give you the exact date when the database was created.

```
select     *
from       v$database;

NAME       CREATED             LOG MODE       CHKPT CHANGE#     ARCH CHANGE#
ORACLE     05/03/97 07:00:06   NOARCHIVELOG   11791             11591
```

**TIP**
*Query the V$DATABASE view to find out when your database was created and also basic archiving information.*

## Basic Licensing Information

The V$LICENSE view allows a DBA to monitor the system activity in terms of overall database numbers at any time. It provides a DBA with a log of the maximum number of concurrent sessions at any time, which allows a company to ensure they are licensed properly. The current number of sessions is displayed along with the session warning level and session maximum level. A session warning level of 0 indicates that the init.ora session warning parameter was not set; therefore, no warning message displays. A session maximum level of 0 indicates that the init.ora session maximum parameter was not set; therefore, there is no limit as to the number of sessions. This script should be executed on a periodic basis to provide a DBA with the actual number of sessions on the system throughout the day and to ensure proper licensing. Setting the init.ora parameter

LICENSE_MAX_SESSIONS = 110 would limit the sessions to 110. Setting the init.ora parameter LICENSE_SESSIONS_WARNING = 100 would give every user past the 100th a warning message so that they would (hopefully) notify the DBA that the system is closing in on a problem. The LICENSE_MAX_USERS init.ora parameter is used to set the number of named users that can be created in the database. In the example here, there is no limit and the value is set to zero.

```
select     *
from       v$license;

SESS MAX   SESS WARNING   SESS CURRENT   SESS HIGHWATER   USERS MAX
110        100            44             105              0
```

**TIP**
*Query the V$LICENSE view to see the maximum sessions that you are allowed. You can also set warnings when you get close to the maximum.*

## Database Options Installed in Your Database

The following script describes what options are installed on your database and available for use. If you have purchased a product that does not show up in this list, you may have incorrectly installed it. Query the V$option table to check for installed products or log on to SQL*Plus to see the products that are installed.

```
select     *
from       v$option;

PARAMETER          VALUE
Procedural         TRUE
Distributed        TRUE
Replication        TRUE
Parallel query     FALSE
Parallel Server    FALSE
Spatial Data       FALSE
```

This database has the Procedural, Distributed, and Replication options. It does not have any of the Parallel or the Special Data options.

**TIP**
*Query the V$OPTION view to retrieve the Oracle options that you have installed. The V$VERSION view will give the versions of the products installed.*

# Y2K Compliance and the NLS_DATE_FORMAT

NLS_DATE_FORMAT provides information related to natural language parameter values. This statement is a basic query, but one that helps the actual language settings based on a country. While the values associated with languages and currencies are beyond the scope of this book, one parameter is quite crucial for Y2K compliance. The NLS_DATE_FORMAT value needs to be set correctly for Y2K compliance (depending on how Y2K dates will be handled). The setting of this parameter will not solve the entire Y2K compliance problem, but it is one important piece to becoming Y2K compliant. Any other Y2K issues related to Oracle should be addressed to Oracle Corporation. I will not even begin to address this vast subject.

```
select     *
from       v$nls_parameter;


PARAMETER                       VALUE
NLS_LANGUAGE                    AMERICAN
NLS_TERRITORY                   AMERICA
NLS_CURRENCY                    $
NLS_ISO_CURRENCY                AMERICA
NLS_NUMERIC_CHARACTERS          ,
NLS_DATE_FORMAT                 DD-MON-RR
NLS_DATE_LANGUAGE               AMERICAN
NLS_CHARACTERSET                WE8ISO8859P1
NLS_SORT                        BINARY
NLS_CALENDAR                    GREGORIAN
```

**TIP**
*One important part of being Y2K (Year 2000) compliant is correctly setting the init.ora parameter NLS_DATE_FORMAT. This does not solve all Y2K issues, but it is one important aspect for Y2K compliance.*

# Summary of Memory Allocated (V$SGA)

V$SGA view gives the summary information for the System Global Area (SGA) memory structures of your system. The database buffers is the number of bytes allocated to memory for data. It is calculated from the init.ora parameters DB_BLOCK_BUFFERS multiplied by DB_BLOCK_SIZE. The redo buffers is the value of the init.ora parameter LOG_BUFFER.

Allocated Memory

```
select    *
from      v$sga;


NAME                    VALUE
Fixed Size              45,584
Variable Size           11,226,428
Database Buffers        8,192,000
Redo Buffers            524,288
```

This output indicates a relatively small SGA with memory allocated to data as 8M (DB_BLOCK_BUFFER x DB_BLOCK_SIZE = 8M). The predominant part of the variable size category is the shared pool (the shared pool for this SGA was 11M). This SGA is using about 20M of the actual physical system memory in the preceding example.

**TIP**
*Access the V$SGA view to get a baseline idea of the system's physical memory that is allocated for data, shared pool, and log buffering of Oracle. But, don't forget that each session will require additional memory, as will each session that is sorting.*

## Detail of Memory Allocated (V$SGASTAT)

A more detailed V$ view query to retrieve the information about memory allocation for the SGA is in the V$SGASTAT view. This view gives dynamic (it changes as the database is accessed) information about SGA and memory resources. This statement describes the SGA sizes at a detailed level. The records FIXED_SIZE, DATABASE_ BUFFERS and REDO_BUFFERS are the same for both the V$SGA and V$SGASTAT views. The remaining records in V$SGASTAT view make up the only other V$SGA view record (the variable size or Shared Pool record). The variable size is made up of 33 memory structures in Oracle7 and 36 memory structures in Oracle8. Oracle chooses how the Shared Pool (variable size) will be allocated among the buckets (33 and 36 buckets for V7 and V8 respectively).

Of particular importance are the free memory, dictionary cache, and library cache records. The free memory is an indicator of the free contiguous memory in the Shared Pool. If this value is constantly low or is reduced in a short period of time after database startup, it is a good indicator that your Shared Pool should be increased (the later section on viewing V$DB_OBJECT_CACHE view will show if this is sufficient). In such a case where free memory is low, a stored package or procedure may result in an error, since there may not be enough contiguous memory to load the object into the Shared Pool. Whether the dictionary and library

cache parameters are sufficient will also be reviewed in the coming sections
(V$LIBRARYCACHE and V$ROWCACHE).

### In V7, the V$SGASTAT view has 36 total records:

| | |
|---|---|
| Fixed Size (V$SGA) | = FIXED_SGA (V$SGASTAT) |
| Database Buffers (V$SGA) | = DB_BLOCK_BUFFERS (V$SGASTAT) |
| Redo Buffers (V$SGA) | = LOG_BUFFER (V$SGASTAT) |
| Variable Size (V$SGA) | = 33 Other Records (V$SGASTAT) |

### In V8, the V$SGASTAT view has 39 total records:

| | |
|---|---|
| Fixed Size (V$SGA) | = FIXED_SGA (V$SGASTAT) |
| Database Buffers (V$SGA) | = DB_BLOCK_BUFFERS (V$SGASTAT) |
| Redo Buffers (V$SGA) | = LOG_BUFFER (V$SGASTAT) |
| Variable Size (V$SGA) | = 36 Other Records (V$SGASTAT) |

## Version 8 Query of V$SGASTAT View

V7 does not have the pool column in V$SGASTAT view and has three less records:

```
select      *
from        v$sgastat;

POOL              NAME                      BYTES
                  fixed_sga                 45584
                  db_block_buffers          2048000
                  log_buffer                524288
shared pool       free memory               594780
shared pool       miscellaneous             157512
shared pool       network connections       16700
shared pool       fixed allocation callback 256
shared pool       PLS non-lib hp            2096
shared pool       db_block_buffers          208000
shared pool       PL/SQL MPCODE             883520
shared pool       latch nowait fails or sleeps 12048
shared pool       branches                  16080
shared pool       db_handles                21000
shared pool       node map                  16384
shared pool       KGFF heap                 3192
shared pool       transaction branches      11776
```

Allocated Memory

```
shared pool      SYSTEM PARAMETERS          42328
shared pool      transactions               57024
shared pool      ktlbk state objects        28248
shared pool      file # translation table   32812
shared pool      checkpoint queue           20500
shared pool      PL/SQL DIANA             2139708
shared pool      KGK heap                    9364
shared pool      enqueue_locks             105312
shared pool      table columns              23300
shared pool      dictionary cache          617624
shared pool      db_files                  251940
shared pool      KQLS heap                 852704
shared pool      character set memory       28220
shared pool      enqueue_resources          20448
shared pool      library cache            2543008
shared pool      dlo fib struct             20500
shared pool      sql area                 2139116
shared pool      Processes                  40200
shared pool      Sessions                  127920
shared pool      db_block_hash_buckets      39156
shared pool      event statistics per sess  97920
shared pool      DML locks                  30624
shared pool      state objects              21380
shared pool      LRMPD SGA Table            17472

40 rows selected (this would be 36 in Oracle7).
```

**TIP**
*Accessing V$SGASTAT view gives us a detailed
breakdown for the Oracle SGA and breaks down all
buckets for the Shared Pool allocation.*

## Init.ora Settings Can Be Found in V$PARAMETER View

This script displays the init.ora parameters for your system. It also provides information on each parameter that identifies if the current value was the default value (ISDEFAULT=TRUE). It also shows if the parameter is modifiable with the ALTER SESSION command, and with the ALTER SYSTEM command (ISSYS_MODIFIABLE=IMMEDIATE). These can be modified with the ALTER SESSION and ALTER SYSTEM commands vs. modifying the init.ora file and shutting down and restarting the instance. The example that follows displays some of the init.ora parameters that can be modified with one of the ALTER commands (IMMEDIATE means it can be modified and it will take effect immediately):

```
select     name, value, isdefault, isses_modifiable,
           issys_modifiable
from       v$parameter
order by   name;
```

**Version 8 query of V$PARAMETER view:**

| NAME | VALUE | ISDEFAULT | ISSES | ISSYS MOD |
|------|-------|-----------|-------|-----------|
| DB_FILE_MULTIBLOCK_ READ_COUNT | 8 | TRUE | TRUE | IMMEDIATE |
| HASH_AREA_SIZE | 0 | TRUE | TRUE | FALSE |
| HASH_JOIN_ENABLED | TRUE | TRUE | TRUE | FALSE |
| HASH_MULTIBLOCK_IO_ COUNT | 8 | TRUE | TRUE | IMMEDIATE |
| IFILE | | TRUE | FALSE | FALSE |
| LOG_CHECKPOINT_ INTERVAL | 10000 | FALSE | FALSE | IMMEDIATE |
| LOG_CHECKPOINT_ TIMEOUT | 0 | TRUE | FALSE | IMMEDIATE |
| LOG_SMALL_ENTRY_ MAX_SIZE | 80 | TRUE | FALSE | IMMEDIATE |
| PARALLEL_MIN_PERCENT | 0 | TRUE | TRUE | FALSE |
| PARTITION_VIEW_ ENABLED | FALSE | TRUE | TRUE | FALSE |
| TEXT_ENABLE | FALSE | TRUE | TRUE | FALSE |
| TIMED_STATISTICS | FALSE | TRUE | TRUE | IMMEDIATE |

(...partial output listing)

There are also version-dependent columns available.

**TIP**
*Query V$PARAMETER view and find out the current values for the init.ora parameters. It will also show which init.ora parameters have been changed from their original defaults (ISDEFAULT = FALSE) and which parameters may be changed without shutting down and restarting the database (ISSYS_MODIFIABLE = IMMEDIATE).*

# Hit Ratio for Data (V$SYSSTAT View)

Query V$SYSSTAT view to see how often your data is being read from memory. It gives the hit ratio for the setting of the database block buffers. This information can be a helpful indicator to identify when your system needs more database block buffers or when a system is not tuned very well (both lead to low hit ratios). If your system is highly interactive, ensure the read hit ratio is greater than 95 percent. If your system is highly batch oriented, ensure the read hit ratio is greater than 85 percent. If your system is a data warehouse, then the hit ratio should be generally greater than 98 percent. Data warehouses with hit ratios less than 98 percent could mean that the metadata has not been summarized optimally. Increasing the hit ratio on your system from 98 percent to 99 percent could mean performance that is 100 percent+ faster (as half of all accesses to disk would have been eliminated).

```
select    1-(sum(decode(name, 'physical reads', value,0))/
          (sum(decode(name, 'db block gets', value,0)) +
          (sum(decode(name, 'consistent gets', value,0))))))
          "Read Hit Ratio"
from      v$sysstat;

Read Hit Ratio
.98415926
```

The hit ratio in the preceding example is very good, but that does not mean that it can't be improved. If this hit ratio is low, you may need to increase the init.ora parameter DB_BLOCK_BUFFERS or tune some of the queries that are causing the disk reads.

**TIP**

*This is crucial! Query V$SYSSTAT view to see how often your data is being read from memory. Memory is about 14,000 times faster than most disks. This hit ratio is crucial to performance and should generally range between 95 percent to 99.99 percent.*

## Hit Ratio for the Data Dictionary (V$ROWCACHE View)

The V$ROWCACHE view is used to find how often the data dictionary calls are effectively hitting the memory cache allocated by the SHARED_POOL_SIZE init.ora parameter. Every time a statement is processed by Oracle, it uses the dictionary cache to find required information in the data dictionary in order to execute the statement. The dictionary cache is a component of the Shared Pool and the statement must go here before it gets the corresponding data. Therefore, if the dictionary hit ratio is not adequate, the overall system performance will suffer greatly.

```
select    sum(gets), sum(getmisses),(1 - (sum(getmisses) /
          (sum(gets) + sum(getmisses)))) * 100 HitRate
from      v$rowcache;
```

| SUM(GETS) | SUM(GETMISSES) | HITRATE |
|---|---|---|
| 10233 | 508 | 95.270459 |

The recommended hit ratio is 90 to 95 percent. If the hit ratio falls below this percentage, it indicates that the SHARED_POOL_SIZE init.ora parameter may need to be increased. But remember, we saw in the V$SGASTAT view that the shared pool is made up of many pieces, of which this is only one.

**TIP**
*This is crucial! Query V$ROWCACHE view to see how often your data dictionary is being read from memory. Memory is about 14,000 times faster than most disks. This hit ratio is crucial to performance and should optimally be at 95 percent or better.*

## Hit Ratio for the Shared SQL and PL/SQL (V$LIBRARYCACHE View)

Accessing the V$LIBRARYCACHE view will show how well the actual statements (SQL and PL/SQL) are accessing memory. If the SHARED_POOL_SIZE in the init.ora is too small, enough room may not be available to store all of the statements into memory. If the Shared Pool becomes fragmented to a large degree, large PL/SQL may not fit into the Shared Pool. The following script will indicate how often statements are being accessed from memory.

There is an execution (pin) hit ratio and a reload hit ratio. The recommended hit ratio for pin hits is 95 percent+ and the reload hit ratio should be 99 percent+ (less than 1 percent reloads). If either of the hit ratios falls below these percentages, it indicates that the Shared Pool may need to be increased to improve overall performance. In the next example, the reload hit ratio is over 99 percent (99.83 percent) and the execution hit ratio is above 95 percent (96.43 percent). Both are within the recommended values.

```
select    sum(pins) "Executions", sum(pinhits) "Hits",
          ((sum(pinhits) / sum(pins)) * 100) "PinHitRatio",
          sum(reloads) "Misses", ((sum(pins) / (sum(pins)
          + sum(reloads))) * 100)  "RelHitRatio"
from      v$librarycache;

Executions    Hits   PinHitRatio    Misses   RelHitRatio
     3,582   3,454         96.43         6         99.83
```

**TIP**
*This is crucial! Query V$LIBRARYCACHE view to see
how often your SQL and PL/SQL are being read from
memory. The pin hit ratio should optimally be at 95
percent or better, and the number of reloads should not
be greater than 1 percent.*

## Identifying PL/SQL Objects that Need to Be Pinned

Fragmentation that causes several small pieces to be available in the Shared Pool, and not enough large contiguous pieces, is a common occurrence in the Shared Pool. The key to eliminating Shared Pool errors (see Chapter 10 for more information) is to understand which objects will be large enough to cause problems when you attempt to load them. Once you know the potential problem PL/SQL objects, you can then pin this code when the database is started (and the Shared Pool is completely contiguous). You can query the V$DB_OBJECT_CACHE view to determine PL/SQL that is both large and currently not marked 'kept'. This query will only show the current statements in the cache. The example that follows searches for those objects requiring greater than 100K:

```
select      name, sharable_mem
from        v$db_object_cache
where       sharable_mem > 100000
and         type in ('PACKAGE', 'PACKAGE BODY',
            'FUNCTION', 'PROCEDURE')
and         kept = 'NO';
```

**TIP**
*Query the V$DB_OBJECT_CACHE view to find objects
that are not pinned and are also large enough to
potentially cause problems.*

## Finding the Problem Queries by Querying V$SQLAREA View

V$SQLAREA view provides a means of identifying the *potential* problem SQL statements or SQL statements needing optimization to improve overall database optimization by reducing disk access. The *disk_reads* signify the volume of disk reads that are being performed on the system. This combined with the executions (disk_reads/executions) returns the SQL statements that have the most disk hits per statement execution. The *disk_reads* was set to 30 in the preceding example, but should typically be set much larger on production systems (10,000 or 100,000, depending on the database) to reveal only the greater problem statements on your system. Once identified, the top statements should be reviewed and optimized to improve overall performance. Typically, the statement that is not using an index or the execution path is forcing the statement not to use the proper indexes.

One potentially misleading part of the next query is the rds_exec_ratio. This is the number of disk reads divided by the executions. In reality, a statement may be read once using 100 disk reads and then forced out of memory (if memory is insufficient). If it is read again, then it will read 100 disk reads again and the rds_exec_ratio will be 100 (or 100+100 reads divided by 2 executions). But, if the statement happens to be in memory the second time (memory is sufficient), the disk reads will be zero (the second time) and the rds_exec_ratio will only be 50 (or 100+0 divided by 2 executions). Any statement that makes the top of this list is a problem and needs to be tuned. Period!

```
select     b.username username, a.disk_reads reads,
           a.executions exec, a.disk_reads /decode
           (a.executions, 0, 1,a.executions) rds_exec_ratio,
           a.command_type, a.sql_text Statement
from       v$sqlarea a, dba_users b
where      a.parsing_user_id = b.user_id
and        a.disk_reads      > 100000
order by   a.disk_reads desc;


USERNAME   READS      EXEC   RDS EXEC RATIO   STATEMENT
ADHOC1     7281934    1      7281934          select  custno, ordno
                                              from    cust, orders

ADHOC5     4230044    4      1057511          select  ordno
                                              from    orders
                                              where   trunc(ordno) = 721305

ADHOC1     801715     2      499858           select  custno, ordno
                                              from    cust
                                              where   decode(custno,1,6) = 314159
```

The disk_reads column in the preceding statement can be replaced with the buffer_gets column, to provide information on SQL statements that may not possess the large disk hits (although they usually do), but possess a large number of memory hits (higher than normally desired). These are statements that are using a large amount of memory that is allocated for the data (DB_BLOCK_BUFFERS). The problem is not that the statement is being executed in memory (which is good), but that the statement is "hogging up" a lot of the memory. Many times, this is attributable to a SQL statement using an index when it should be doing a full table scan or a join. These types of SQL statements can also involve a join operation that is forcing the path to utilize a different index than desired, or using multiple indexes and forcing index merging or volumes of data merging. Remember, the bulk of system performance problems are attributable to poorly written SQL and PL/SQL statements.

**TIP**
*Query the V$SQLAREA view to find problem queries (and users).*

# Find Out what Users Are Doing and the Resources They Are Using

Joining V$SESSION and V$SQLTEXT views will display the SQL statement that is currently being executed by each session. It is extremely useful when a DBA is trying to determine what is happening in the system at a point in time.

```
select    a.sid, a.username, s.sql_text
from      v$session a, v$sqltext s
where     a.sql_address      = s.address
and       a.sql_hash_value = s.hash_value
order by  a.username, a.sid, s.piece;


SID   USERNAME      SQL TEXT
11    PLSQL_USER    update s_employee set salary = 10000
9     SYS           select a.sid, a.username, s.sql_text
9     SYS           from v$session a, v$sqltext
9     SYS           where a.sql_address   = s.address
9     SYS           and a.sql_hash_value  = s.hash_value
9     SYS           order by a.username, a.sid, s.piece
```

(...partial output listing)

The sql_text column displays the entire SQL statement, but the statement is stored in the V$SQLTEXT view as a VARCHAR2(2000) datatype (in version 8, the length is increased to 4000) and therefore spans multiple records. The piece column is used to order the statement in version 8.

To view the resources being used by each of the users, we simply use the following query. The goal of this statement is to highlight the physical disk and memory hits for each session. It is very easy to recognize users that are performing a large number of physical disk or memory reads.

```
select     a.username, b.block_gets, b.consistent_gets,
           B.PHYSICAL_READS, B.BLOCK_CHANGES, b.consistent_changes
from       v$session a, v$sess_io b
where      a.sid = b.sid
order by   a.username;
```

| USERNAME | BLOCK GETS | CONSISTENT GETS | PHYSICAL READS | BLOCK CHANGES | CONSISTENT CHANGES |
|----------|-----------|-----------------|----------------|---------------|--------------------|
| PLSQL_USER | 39 | 72 | 11 | 53 | 1 |
| SCOTT | 11 | 53 | 12 | 0 | 0 |
| SYS | 14 | 409 | 26 | 0 | 0 |
| SYSTEM | 8340 | 10197 | 291 | 2558 | 419 |

**TIP**
*Query V$SESSION, V$SQLTEXT, and V$SESS_IO views
to find the problem users and what they are executing
at a given point in time.*

## Find the Objects a User Is Accessing

Querying V$ACCESS view can point us to potential problem objects (potentially
missing indexes) once we have found the problem user or query on our system. It
can also be helpful when you want to modify a particular object and need to know
who is using it at a given point in time.

```
select     a.sid, a.username, b.owner, b.object, b.type
from       v$session a, v$access b
where      a.sid = b.sid;
```

| SID | USERNAME | OWNER | OBJECT | TYPE |
|-----|----------|-------|--------|------|
| 8 | SCOTT | SYS | DBMS_APPLICATION_INFO | PACKAGE |
| 9 | SYS | SYS | DBMS_APPLICATION_INFO | PACKAGE |
| 9 | SYS | SYS | X$BH | TABLE |
| 10 | SYSTEM | PUBLIC | V$ACCESS | SYNONYM |
| 10 | SYSTEM | PUBLIC | V$SESSION | SYNONYM |
| 10 | SYSTEM | SYS | DBMS_APPLICATION_INFO | PACKAGE |
| 10 | SYSTEM | SYS | V$ACCESS | VIEW |
| 10 | SYSTEM | SYS | V$SESSION | VIEW |
| 10 | SYSTEM | SYS | V_$ACCESS | VIEW |

This script displays all objects being accessed, including synonyms, views,
stored source code, etc.

Checking Up on Users

**TIP**
*Query V$ACCESS view to find all objects that are being accessed by a user at a given time. This can help to pinpoint problem objects, while also being helpful when modifying a particular object (find out who is accessing it).*

## Getting Detailed User Information

A method for analyzing user statistics is extremely valuable when a new or updated application module is being tested to determine the overhead. It also is a window into the problems of a user that is having performance problems, since it provides statistics on a variety of areas for each user. It can also serve as a guideline for setting profiles to limit a particular user. The following script limits the statistics to only areas that have a value (b.value != 0):

```
select     a.sid, a.username, c.name, b.value
from       v$session a, v$sesstat b, v$statname c
where      a.sid          = b.sid
and        b.statistic#   = c.statistic#
and        b.value        != 0
group by   name;
```

| USERNAME | NAME | VALUE |
|----------|------|-------|
| PLSQL_USER | logons cumulative | 1 |
| PLSQL_USER | opened cursors cumulative | 14 |
| PLSQL_USER | session uga memory max | 31508 |
| PLSQL_USER | table fetch by rowid | 10 |
| PLSQL_USER | SQL*Net roundtrips to/from client | 64 |
| PLSQL_USER | bytes received via SQL*Net from client | 5441 |
| PLSQL_USER | bytes sent via SQL*Net to client | 2632 |
| PLSQL_USER | db block changes | 53 |
| PLSQL_USER | physical reads | 11 |
| PLSQL_USER | consistent gets | 72 |
| PLSQL_USER | db block gets | 39 |
| PLSQL_USER | enqueue requests | 2 |
| PLSQL_USER | session pga memory max | 76592 |
| PLSQL_USER | session pga memory | 76592 |
| PLSQL_USER | session uga memory | 31508 |
| PLSQL_USER | recursive calls | 69 |
| PLSQL_USER | user calls | 57 |
| PLSQL_USER | opened cursors current | 1 |
| PLSQL_USER | logons current | 1 |

# Identifying Locking Issues

Identifying locking issues is instrumental in locating the user that is waiting for someone or something else. It is used to identify users that are currently being locked in the system. This allows DBAs to ensure if an Oracle-related process is truly locked or just running slow. It also identifies the current statement that the locked user(s) are executing at the current time.

```
select    b.username, b.serial#, d.id1, a.sql_text
from      v$session b, v$lock d, v$sqltext a
where     b.lockwait    = d.kaddr
and       a.address     = b.sql_address
and       a.hash_value = b.sql_hash_value;


USERNAME    SERIAL#  ID1        SOL TEXT
AUTHUSER    53       393242     update  emp
                                set     salary = 5000
                                where   empname = 'JOHNSON'
```

You also need to identify the user in the system that is causing the problem of locking the user above (usually this is the user/developer that presses CTRL/ALT/DEL as you approach his or her desk).

```
select    a.serial#, a.sid, a.username, b.id1, c.sql_text
from      v$session a, v$lock b, v$sqltext c
where     b.id1 in
(select   distinct e.id1
 from     v$session d, v$lock e
 where    d.lockwait    = e.kaddr)
 and      a.sid          = b.sid
 and      c.hash_value = a.sql_hash_value
 and      b.request     = 0;


SERIAL#  SID   USERNAME   ID1      SOL TEXT
18       11    JOHNSON    393242   update  authuser.emp
                                   set     salary=90000
```

In the preceding example, 'JOHNSON' will make everyone happy by forgetting a crucial WHERE clause. Unfortunately, 'JOHNSON' has locked the authorized user of this table.

# Kill the Problem User

A user may have run something that they really didn't want to run, or there may be a problem query that needs to be eliminated during business hours and rerun at night. If the operation in the previous section needed to be aborted, the following statement could be executed:

```
alter system kill session '11,18';
```

The order of the parameters is *sid*, then *serial#*.

**TIP**
*Identify users that are locking others and kill their session (if necessary).*

## Finding Users with Multiple Sessions

Users, at times, enjoy using multiple sessions to get several things done at once, and this can be a problem. The problem may also be a developer that has built a poor application that begins spawning multiple processes. Either of these could degrade the overall performance of the system. The following query to the V$SESSION view will display these types of issues:

```
select     username, count(*)
from       v$session
group by   username;

USERNAME       COUNT(*)
PLSQL_USER     1
SCOTT          1
JOHNSON        9
SYS            1
SYSTEM         1
               6
```

On certain O/S platforms, if a user starts a session and reboots his or her PC, oftentimes the process will continue in the background as the user starts another session. If the user is running multiple reports on multiple terminals or PCs, this could also affect the overall performance of the system. Note: The NULL username and count of 6 are the Oracle background processes.

**TIP**
*Identify users that are holding multiple sessions and determine if it is an administrative problem (the user is using multiple terminals) or a system problem (sessions are not being cleaned or are spawning runaway processes).*

Finding Users

## Query for Current Profiles

Profiles are limits on a given schema (user). To view the profiles for your system, execute the following query:

```
column c0 heading "Profile";
column c1 heading "Resource";
column c2 heading "Limit";
select    substr(profile,1,10) Profile, substr
          (resource_name,1,30) Resource,
          substr(limit,1,10) Limit
from      dba_profiles
group by  substr(profile,1,10), substr(resource_name,1,30),
          substr(limit,1,10);
```

# Finding Disk I/O Issues

The views V$DATAFILE, V$FILESTAT and DBA_DATA_FILES views provide file I/O activity across all data files and disks of your database. Ideally, the distribution of physical reads and writes should be distributed equally. If the system is not configured properly, overall performance will suffer. This script identifies the actual distribution and makes it easy to identify where an imbalance exists. Chapter 3 looks at this topic in great detail; this section just shows the quick hit query to get a baseline.

```
select    a.file#, a.name, a.status, a.bytes,
          b.phyrds, b.phywrts
from      v$datafile a, v$filestat b
where     a.file# = b.file#;
```

| FILE# | NAME | STATUS | BYTES | PHYRDS | PHYWRTS |
|-------|------|--------|-------|--------|---------|
| 1 | D:\ORAWIN95\DB\SYS1ORCL.ORA | SYSTEM | 10485760 | 946 | 82 |
| 2 | D:\ORAWIN95\DB\USR1ORCL.ORA | ONLINE | 3145728 | 1 | 0 |
| 3 | D:\ORAWIN95\DB\RBS1ORCL.ORA | ONLINE | 10485760 | 18 | 209 |
| 4 | D:\ORAWIN95\DB\TMP1ORCL.ORA | ONLINE | 2097152 | 0 | 457 |
| 6 | D:\ORAWIN95\DB\SYS2ORCL.ORA | SYSTEM | 52428800 | 10 | 11 |

If the output reveals that the balance is not distributed properly, then it is the responsibility of the DBA to reconfigure the system to ensure proper balancing. Any time there is a significant imbalance, there will be overall system performance degradation. This script should be executed any time a configuration modification is made, on a periodic basis to ensure the disk balancing that is expected is truly happening on your system, when there is a large amount of data growth (interactive or batch loading), or when tables or indexes are added to your system.

The following two queries give an improved formatted report for file and data distribution issues. The first gets the data file I/O and the second gets the disk I/O.

### Getting the data file I/O:

```
Set TrimSpool On
Set Line     142
Set Pages     57
Set NewPage    0
Set FeedBack Off
Set Verify   Off
Set Term     Off
TTitle       Off
BTitle       Off
Clear Breaks
Break On Tablespace_Name
Column TableSpace_Name For A12      Head "Tablespace"
Column Name      For A45           Head "File Name"
Column Total     For 999,999,990   Head "Total"
Column Phyrds    For 999,999,990   Head "Physical|Reads  "
Column Phywrts   For 999,999,990   Head "Physical| Writes "
Column Phyblkrd  For 999,999,990   Head "Physical |Block Reads"
Column Phyblkwrt For 999,999,990   Head "Physical |Block Writes"
Column Avg_Rd_Time  For 90.9999999 Head "Average |Read Time|Per Block"
Column Avg_Wrt_Time For 90.9999999 Head "Average |Write Time|Per Block"
Column Instance        New_Value _Instance   NoPrint
Column Today           New_Value _Date       NoPrint
select   Global_Name Instance, To_Char(SysDate, 'FXDay DD, YYYY HH:MI') Today
from     Global_Name;
TTitle On
TTitle Left 'Date Run: ' _Date Skip 1-
     Center 'Data File I/O' Skip 1 -
     Center 'Instance Name: ' _Instance Skip 1
select    C.TableSpace_Name, B.Name, A.Phyblkrd +
          A.Phyblkwrt Total, A.Phyrds, A.Phywrts,
          A.Phyblkrd, A.Phyblkwrt
from      V$FileStat A, V$DataFile B, Sys.DBA_Data_Files C
where     B.File# = A.File#
and       B.File# = C.File_Id
order by  TableSpace_Name, A.File#
/
```

### Getting the disk I/O:

```
Column TableSpace_Name For A12      Head "Tablespace"
Column Total      For 9,999,999,990 Head "Total"
Column Phyrds     For 9,999,999,990 Head "Physical|Reads  "
Column Phywrts    For 9,999,999,990 Head "Physical| Writes "
Column Phyblkrd   For 9,999,999,990 Head "Physical |Block Reads"
Column Phyblkwrt  For 9,999,999,990 Head "Physical |Block Writes"
Column Avg_Rd_Time   For 9,999,990.9999  Head "Average |Read Time|Per Block"
Column Avg_Wrt_Time  For 9,999,990.9999  Head "Average |Write Time|Per Block"
Clear Breaks
Break on Disk Skip 1
Compute Sum Of Total On Disk
Compute Sum Of Phyrds On Disk
```

```
Compute Sum Of Phywrts On Disk
Compute Sum Of Phyblkrd On Disk
Compute Sum Of Phyblkwrt On Disk
TTitle Left 'Date Run: ' _Date Skip 1-
       Center 'Disk I/O' Skip 1 -
       Center 'Instance Name: ' _Instance Skip 2
select     SubStr(B.Name, 1, 13) Disk, C.TableSpace_Name,
           A.Phyblkrd + A.Phyblkwrt Total, A.Phyrds, A.Phywrts,
           A.Phyblkrd, A.Phyblkwrt, ((A.ReadTim /
           Decode(A.Phyrds,0,1,A.Phyblkrd))/100) Avg_Rd_Time,
           ((A.WriteTim / Decode(A.PhyWrts,0,1,A.PhyblkWrt)) /
           100) Avg_Wrt_Time
from       V$FileStat A, V$DataFile B, Sys.DBA_Data_Files C
where      B.File# = A.File#
and        B.File# = C.File_Id
order by   Disk,C.Tablespace_Name, A.File#
/
Set FeedBack   On
Set Verify     On
Set Term       On
TTitle         Off
BTitle         Off
```

**TIP**
*The views V$DATAFILE, V$FILESTAT, and
DBA_DATA_FILES views provide file I/O activity across
all data files and disks of your database. Ensure that
both data file and disks are properly balanced for
optimal performance.*

# Finding Rollback Segment Contention

The following query will identify the activity in the rollback segments and if there is
contention. To increase efficiency, only one user should exist in a given rollback
segment at a time (for efficiency); however, more than one user may be accessing
the same rollback segment depending on the size of the transaction. The query
provides a picture of the current activity of each rollback segment.

```
select     a.name, b.xacts, c.sid, c.serial#,
           c.username, d.sql_text
from       v$rollname a, v$rollstat b, v$session c,
           v$sqltext d,v$transaction e
where      a.usn            = b.usn
and        b.usn            = e.xidusn
and        c.taddr          = e.addr
and        c.sql_address    = d.address
and        c.sql_hash_value = d.hash_value
order by   a.name, c.sid, d.piece;
```

| NAME | XACTS | SID | SERIAL# | USERNAME | SQL TEXT |
|------|-------|-----|---------|----------|----------|
| RB3 | 1 | 11 | 11 | PLSQL_USER | update   emp |
| | | | | | set    salary='10000' |

Another helpful query shows the actual waits on a rollback segment. You can display rollback information and determine if more segments are needed. If the waits-to-retrieve ratio goes over 1 percent on a regular basis, add more rollback segments. Shrinks and wraps can also be queried from the views shown here:

```
select    a.name, b.extents, b.rssize, b.xacts,
          b.waits, b.gets, optsize, status
from      v$rollname a, v$rollstat b;
```

**TIP**

*Querying V$ROLLNAME, V$ROLLSTAT, and V$TRANSACTION view can provide information on how users are using rollback segments. Generally, more than one person should not be accessing a rollback segment at one time (although this is allowed). Placing rollback segments on multiple disks will also help limit disk I/O issues when multiple DML statements are being issued.*

**Finding waits on the entire system:**

```
select    A.Class, Count, Sum(Value) Con_Get,
          ((Count / Sum(Value)) * 100) pct
from      V$WaitStat A, V$SysStat B
where     Name In ('db block gets', 'consistent gets')
group by  A.Class, Count
```

The count column in V$WAITSTAT view is the number of misses and the class is the type of miss (or get) that is being measured. The pct alias is a measure of the memory gets to waits (misses).

**Query to get the system waits on the entire system:**

```
Set TrimSpool On
Set NewPage    0
Set Pages      57
Set Line       132
Set FeedBack Off
Set Verify    Off
Set Term      Off
TTitle        Off
BTitle        Off
Clear Breaks
Column Event       For A40 Heading "Wait Event"
Column Total_Waits For 999,999,990 Head Total Number| Of Waits    "
```

Finding Contention

```
Column Total_Timeouts For 999,999,990 Head "Total Number|Of TimeOuts"
Column Tot_Time    For 999,999,990 Head "Total Time|Waited  "
Column Avg_Time    For  99,990.999 Head "Average Time|Per Wait   "
Column Instance New_Value _Instance    NoPrint
Column Today    New_Value _Date        NoPrint
select    Global_Name Instance, To_Char(SysDate,
          'FXDay DD, YYYY HH:MI') Today
from      Global_Name;
TTitle On
TTitle Left 'Date Run: ' _Date Skip 1-
       Center 'System Wide Wait Events' Skip 1 -
       Center 'Instance Name: ' _Instance Skip 2
select    event, total_waits, total_timeouts,
          (time_waited / 100)  tot_time, (average_wait / 100)
          Avg_time
from      v$system_event
order by  total_waits desc
/
```

## Check to See If Free Lists Is Sufficient

If you have multiple processes doing large inserts, a default free lists of 1 may not be
enough. To check if the free lists (list of free database blocks) storage parameter is
sufficient, run the following report.

```
Set TrimSpool    On
Set Line         132
Set Pages        57
Set NewPage      0
Set FeedBack     Off
Set Verify       Off
Set Term         Off
TTitle           Off
BTitle           Off
Column Pct Format 990.99 Heading "% Of      |Free List Waits"
Column Instance New_Value _Instance NoPrint
Column Today    New_Value _Date NoPrint
select   Global_Name Instance, To_Char
         (SysDate, 'FXDay DD, YYYY HH:MI') Today
from     Global_Name;

TTitle On
TTitle Left 'Date Run: ' _Date Skip 1-
       Center 'Free list Contention' Skip 1 -
       Center 'If Percentage is Greater then 1%' Skip 1 -
       Center 'Consider increasing the number of free lists' Skip 1 -
       Center 'Instance Name: ' _Instance
select    ((A.Count / (B.Value + C.Value)) * 100) Pct
from      V$WaitStat A, V$SysStat B, V$SysStat C
where     A.Class = 'free list'
```

```
and         B.Statistic# =  (select    Statistic#
                            from       V$StatName
                            where      Name = 'db block gets')
and         C.Statistic# =  (select    Statistic#
                            from       V$StatName
                            where      Name = 'consistent gets')
/
Column Total_Waits   Format 999,999,999,990 Heading "Buffer Busy Waits"
Column DB_Get        Format 999,999,999,990 Heading "DB Block Gets"
Column Con_Get       Format 999,999,999,990 Heading "Consistent Gets"
Column Busy_Rate     Format 990.999          Heading "Busy Rate"
TTitle Left 'Date Run: ' _Date Skip 1-
       Center 'Buffer Busy Waits Rate' Skip 1 -
       Center 'If >5% review V$WaitStat' Skip 1 -
       Center 'Instance Name: ' _Instance Skip 2
select   Total_Waits, B.Value DB_Get, C.Value Con_Get,
         ((A.Total_Waits / (B.Value + C.Value)) * 100) Busy
from     V$System_Event A, V$SysStat B, V$SysStat C
where    A.Event = 'buffer busy waits'
and          B.Statistic#  = (select  Statistic#
                             from      V$StatName
                             where     Name = 'db block gets')
and          C.Statistic#  = (select  Statistic#
                             from      V$StatName
                             where     Name = 'consistent gets')
/
```

If the activity rate is greater than 1 percent, then freelists needs to be increased.

**TIP**
*Ensure that free lists is sufficient when using multiple processes to do inserts. The default storage value is 1.*

## V$ View Categories

The views in this section are categorized according to their primary function. You will often need to join one category to another category to retrieve the desired information. The V$ views can be queried the same as any other Oracle view, but keep in mind that the information in these tables changes rapidly. You can insert the information from the V$ views into a precreated table to allow for the compilation of data over a period of time, to be analyzed later or to build statistical reports and alerts based on different conditions in your database.

The V$ view (and x$ table) information is utilized by most DBA monitoring tools on the market today. Querying this database information without a DBA monitoring tool requires that you have an in-depth understanding of the information stored in each view and how to query the view properly. Table 14-1 contains a list of V$

| Category | Description and Associated V$ Tables |
|---|---|
| Backup/recovery | Information related to database backups and recovery, including last backup, archive logs, state of files for backup, and recovery<br>**V$ Tables:** V$ARCHIVE, V$ARCHIVED_LOG (V8), V$ARCHIVE_DEST (V8), V$BACKUP, V$BACKUP_CORRUPTION (V8), V$BACKUP_DATAFILE(V8), V$BACKUP_DEVICE (V8), V$BACKUP_PIECE (V8), V$BACKUP_REDOLOG (V8), V$BACKUP_SET (V8), V$DELETED_OBJECT (V8), V$RECOVERY_FILE_STATUS, V$RECOVERY_LOG, V$RECOVERY_STATUS, V$RECOVER_FILE |
| Caches | Information related to the various caches, including objects, library, cursors, and the dictionary<br>**V$ Tables:** V$CACHE (V8), V$DB_OBJECT_CACHE, V$LIBRARYCACHE, V$ROWCACHE, V$SUBCACHE[1] |
| Control files | Information related to instance control files<br>**V$ Tables:** V$CONTROLFILE, V$CONTROLFILE_RECORD_SECTION[1] |
| Cursors/SQL statements | Information related to cursors and SQL statements, including the open cursors, statistics, and actual SQL text<br>**V$ Tables:** V$OPEN_CURSOR, V$SQL, V$SQLAREA, V$SQLTEXT, V$SQLTEXT_WITH_NEWLINES, V$SQL_BIND_DATA[1], V$SQL_BIND_METADATA[1], V$SQL_CURSOR, V$SQL_SHARED_MEMORY |
| Database instances | Information related to the actual database instance<br>**V$ Tables:** V$ACTIVE_INSTANCES, V$BGPROCESS, V$BH[1], V$COMPATIBILITY, V$COMPATSEG, V$COPY_CORRUPTION[1], V$DATABASE, V$DATAFILE, V$DATAFILE_COPY[1], V$DATAFILE_HEADER[1], V$DBFILE, V$DBLINK, V$DB_PIPES, V$INSTANCE, V$LICENSE, V$OFFLINE_RANGE[1], V$OPTION, V$SGA, V$SGASTAT, V$TABLESPACE[1], V$VERSION |
| Direct loader | Information related to the SQL*Loader direct load option<br>**V$ Tables:** V$LOADCSTAT, V$LOADPSTAT[1], V$LOADTSTAT |

**V$ View Categories**

**TABLE 14-1.** *V$ Views Categories*

| Category | Description and Associated V$ Tables |
|---|---|
| Fixed view | Information related to the v$ tables themselves<br>**V$ Tables:** V$FIXED_TABLE, V$FIXED_VIEW_DEFINITION, V$INDEXED_FIXED_COLUMN |
| General | General information related to various system information<br>**V$ Tables:** V$TIMER, V$TYPE_SIZE, V$_SEQUENCES[1] |
| I/O | Information related to I/O, including files, and statistics<br>**V$ Tables:** V$FILESTAT, V$WAITSTAT |
| Latches/locks | Information related to latches and locks<br>**V$ Tables:** V$BUFFER_POOL[1], V$CACHE_LOCK, V$CLASS_PING[1], V$DLM_CONVERT_LOCAL[1], V$DLM_CONVERT_REMOTE[1], V$DLM_LATCH[1], V$DLM_MISC (V8), V$ENQUEUE_LOCK[1], V$EVENT_NAME, V$FALSE_PING, V$FILE_PING[1], V$LATCH, V$LATCHHOLDER, V$LATCHNAME, V$LATCH_CHILDREN, V$LATCH_MISSES, V$LATCH_PARENT, V$LOCK, V$LOCK_ACTIVITY, V$LOCK_ELEMENT, V$LOCKED_OBJECT, V$LOCKS_WITH_COLLISIONS, V$PING, V$RESOURCE, V$RESOURCE_LIMIT[1], V$TRANSACTION_ENQUEUE[1], V$_LOCK, V$_LOCK1 |
| Multithreaded/ parallel server | Information related to multithreaded and parallel servers, including connections, queues, dispatchers, and shared servers<br>**V$ Tables:** V$CIRCUIT, V$DISPATCHER, V$DISPATCHER_RATE[1], V$MTS, V$QUEUE, V$REQDIST, V$SHARED_SERVER, V$THREAD |
| Overall system | Information related to the overall system performance<br>**V$ Tables:** V$GLOBAL_TRANSACTION[1], V$OBJECT_DEPENDENCY, V$SHARED_POOL_RESERVED, V$SORT_SEGMENT, V$SORT_USAGE[1], V$STATNAME, V$SYSSTAT, V$SYSTEM_CURSOR_CACHE, V$SYSTEM_EVENT, V$TRANSACTION |

**TABLE 14-1.** *V$ Views Categories* (continued)

| Category | Description and Associated V$ Tables |
|---|---|
| Parallel Query | Information related to the Parallel Query option<br>**V$ Tables:** V$EXECUTION, V$EXECUTION_LOCATION[1], V$PQ_SESSTAT, V$PQ_SLAVE, V$PQ_SYSSTAT, V$PQ_TQSTAT |
| Parameters | Information related to various Oracle parameters, including initialization and NLS per session<br>**V$ Tables:** V$NLS_PARAMETER, V$NLS_VALID_VALUES, V$PARAMETER, V$SYSTEM_PARAMETER |
| Redo logs | Information related to redo logs, including statistics and history<br>**V$ Tables:** V$LOG, V$LOGFILE, V$LOGHIST, V$LOG_HISTORY |
| Rollback segments | Information on rollback segments, including statistics and transactions<br>**V$ Tables:** V$ROLLNAME, V$ROLLSTAT, V$TRANSACTION |
| Security/privileges | Information related to security<br>**V$ Tables:** V$ENABLEDPRIVS, V$PWFILE_USERS<br>SessionsInformation related to a session, including object access, cursors, processes, and statistics<br>**V$ Tables:** V$ACCESS, V$MYSTAT, V$PROCESS, V$SESSION, V$SESSION_CONNECT_INFO, V$SESSION_CURSOR_CACHE, V$SESSION_EVENT, V$SESSION_LONGOPS[1], V$SESSION_OBJECT_CACHE[1], V$SESSION_WAIT, V$SESSTAT, V$SESS_IO |

[1]Signifies views that are Oracle8 views. Also, the V$ROLLNAME and V$MLS_PARAMETERS views are created slightly different than the other V$ views. The V$ROLLNAME is a join of an X$ table and the undo$ table. The V$MLS_PARAMETERS view is a subset of the V$NLS_PARAMETERS view. Note some of the V$ timing fields are dependent on the timed_statistics init.ora parameter being set to TRUE; otherwise, there will be no timing in these fields.

**TABLE 14-1.** *V$ Views Categories (continued)*

views categorized according to their primary function. The views are listed in categories related to the operation that they monitor. This is not an exhaustive list. It only contains the most commonly used views.

# Summary

Oracle explicitly states in their manuals that the V$ views may change in the future, and as evidenced from the modifications from version 7 to version 8 this is definitely true. Not only has there been an increase in the number of V$ views and X$ tables, but some of the tables have changed columns as well. The V$ views and X$ tables are continually being enhanced as more and more features are added to Oracle.

The queries in this chapter are by no means all-encompassing. There is much more that can be obtained from these tables, but the intent of this chapter is to provide a solid starting point. See Appendix B for a complete listing.

# Tips Review

- The V$ views that are accessed by SYSTEM are actually synonyms that point to the V_$ views that are views of the original V$ views based on the x$ tables (better read that one again).

- When other DBAs need access to the V$ view information, but *not* the SYS or SYSTEM passwords, grant the user access to the V_$ views. The user may then access the V$ views that have public synonyms to the V_$ views.

- In Oracle7, query V$FIXED_TABLE view to get a listing of all V$ views in the database.

- In Oracle8, query V$FIXED_TABLE view to get a listing of all GV$ and V$ views in the database. The GV$ views are exactly the same as the V$ views except the instance ID contains an identifier.

- Query V$FIXED_VIEW_DEFINITION views to retrieve the query that creates the V$ and GV$ views from the x$ tables.

- Query V$INDEXED_FIXED_COLUMN view to retrieve the indexes on the x$ tables that ultimately make the V$ views faster in Oracle8. You are *not* allowed to create your own indexes on the x$ tables.

- Query the V$DATABASE view to find out when your database was created and also basic archiving information.

- Query the V$LICENSE view to see the maximum sessions that you are allowed. You can also set warnings when you get close to the maximum.

- Query the V$OPTION view to retrieve the Oracle options that you have installed. The V$VERSION view will give you the actual versions of products installed.

■ One important part of being Y2K (Year 2000) compliant is correctly setting the init.ora parameter NLS_DATE_FORMAT. This does not solve all Y2K issues, but is one important aspect for Y2K compliance.

■ Access the V$SGA view to get a baseline idea of the system's physical memory that is allocated for data, shared pool and log buffering of Oracle.

■ Accessing V$SGASTAT view gives us a detailed breakdown for the Oracle SGA and breaks down all buckets for the shared pool allocation.

■ Query V$PARAMETER view and find out the current values for the init.ora parameters. It will also show which init.ora parameters have been changed from their original defaults (ISDEFAULT = FALSE) and which parameters may be changed without shutting down and restarting the database (ISSYS_MODIFIABLE = IMMEDIATE).

■ This is crucial! Query V$SYSSTAT view to see how often your data is being read from memory. Memory is about 14,000 times faster than most disks. This hit ratio is crucial to performance and should optimally be at 95 percent or better.

■ This is crucial! Query V$ROWCACHE view to see how often your data dictionary is being read from memory. This hit ratio should optimally be at 95 percent or better.

■ This is crucial! Query V$LIBRARYCACHE view to see how often your SQL and PL/SQL is being read from memory. The pin hit ratio should generally range between 90 to 95 percent and optimally at 95 percent or better, and the number of reloads should not be greater than 1 percent.

■ Query the V$DB_OBJECT_CACHE view to find objects that are not pinned and are also large enough to potentially cause problems.

■ Query the V$SQLAREA view to find problem queries (and users).

■ Query V$SESSION, V$SQLTEXT, and V$SESS_IO views to find the problem users and what they are executing at a given point in time.

■ Query V$ACCESS view to find all objects that are being accessed by a user at a given time. This can help to pinpoint problem objects, while also being helpful when modifying a particular object (find out who is accessing it).

■ Identify users that are locking others and kill their session (if necessary).

■ Identify users that are holding multiple sessions and determine if it is an administrative problem (the user is using multiple terminals) or a system problem (sessions are not being cleaned or spawning runaway processes).

Tips Review

■ The views V$DATAFILE, V$FILESTAT, and DBA_DATA_FILES provide file I/O activity across all data files and disks of your database. Ensure that both data file and disks are properly balanced for optimal performance.

■ Querying V$ROLLNAME, V$ROLLSTAT, and V$TRANSACTION views can provide information on how users are using rollback segments.

■ Ensure that freelists is sufficient when using multiple processes to do inserts. The default storage value is 1.

# References

*The V$ Arsenal: Key V$ Scripts Every DBA Should Use Regularly*; Joe Trezzo

*Oracle7 Server: SQL Language Reference Manual*; Oracle Corporation

*Oracle7 Server: Application Developer's Guide*; Oracle Corporation

TUSC, 1997 IOUG-A Proceedings, *The V$ Views – A DBA's Best Friend*; Joseph C. Trezzo

Many thanks to Joe Trezzo who wrote the majority of this chapter. Also, thanks to Allen Peterson and Greg Pucka who also made contributions to this chapter.

A poster that contains the V$ view definitions grouped by category can be obtained from TUSC by calling TUSC and requesting a V$ poster. This poster is currently (as of the writing of this book) a listing of the Oracle8 V$ views.

**Tips Review**

# TIPS & TECHNIQUES

# CHAPTER
## 15

The x$ Tables (DBA)

The x$ tables are the last frontier for the expert DBA to explore and analyze the deepest cavern of the Oracle database. Querying the x$ tables can give secrets to undocumented init.ora parameters, information about future Oracle versions, and shorter or faster routes to database information. The x$ tables are usually not mentioned in the Oracle documentation or the Oracle user community. For this reason, I am including them in this book as one of the only references available. Tips covered in this chapter include:

- Misconceptions about the x$ tables
- Granting access to view the x$ tables
- V$ views and x$ table creation
- How to get a listing of the V$ views (x$kqfvi)
- The x$ tables that make up the V$ views
- How to get a listing of all the x$ tables (x$kqfvi)
- How to get a listing of all the x$ indexes
- Using hints with the x$ tables and indexes
- Data cached in memory (x$bh)
- Oracle8 takes more startup resources
- What memory is still in use?
- A better query for memory in use
- Information cached in the SHARED_POOL memory (x$ksmsp)
- When to pin objects in the SHARED_POOL (x$ksmlru)
- Accessing the undocumented init.ora parameters (x$ksppi and x$ksppcv)
- Finding the init.ora parameters for undocumented TRACE
- How many init.ora parameters are there, and how many are documented? (x$ksppi & v$parameter)
- What is the block size and how much of the block can be used? (x$kvis)

# Misconceptions About the x$ Tables

"Do not use the x$ tables if you have a heart condition or are an inexperienced DBA, or you may ruin the entire database" (at least this is what most people will tell you...sounds pretty scary).

The most common misconception about the x$ tables is that the DBA can drop one or update one, causing the database to be ruined. Can the x$ tables be ruined? The answer is no. The only user that can select from these tables is the SYS user. A SELECT statement is the only command available to be performed on these x$ tables. An error occurs if an attempt is made to grant SELECT access to a user. Consider the following attempts to drop or alter an x$ table.

**You will not be able to drop any of the x$ tables (even as the SYS user):**

```
connect sys/change_on_install
drop table x$ksppi;

ORA-02030: can only select fixed tables/views
```

**You will not be able to update, insert, or delete any data in the x$ tables (even as the SYS user):**

```
update   x$ksppi
set      ksppidf = 'FALSE'
where    ksppidf = 'TRUE';

ORA-02030: can only select fixed tables/views
```

### TIP
*When you mention the x$ tables, most people say "ooh...pretty scary, I would never touch those tables." The fact is, DML commands (UPDATE, INSERT, and DELETE) are not allowed on the x$ tables, even as the SYS superuser.*

### TIP
*Only the SYS superuser can select from the x$ tables. An error occurs if an attempt is made to grant select access to a user.*

# Granting Access to View the x$ Tables

**You cannot grant access to the x$ tables (even as the SYS user):**

```
connect richn/tusc
connect sys/manager
grant select on x$ksppi to richn;

ORA-02030: can only select fixed tables/views
```

Although the error message for attempting to grant access to x$ksppi (above) is erroneous, the grant will not be allowed. However, you may build your own x$ views from the original x$ tables and then grant access to those views. Consider the following example, which gives access to the x$ksppi table via a view called x$_ksppi and a synonym called x$ksppi.

**Connect to the SYS superuser:**

```
Connect sys/change_on_install;

Connected.
```

**Create a view mirroring the x$ksppi table:**

```
create view x_$ksppi as
select      *
from        x$ksppi;

View created.
```

**Create a synonym for the newly created view:**

```
create public synonym x$ksppi for x_$ksppi;

Synonym created.
```

**Grant access to the newly created view to the desired user:**

```
grant select on x$_ksppi to richn;

Grant succeeded.
```

**Connect as the desired user:**

```
conn richn/tusc;

Connected.
```

**Access the x$ksppi table via the synonym created for x$_ksppi:**

```
select     count(*)
from       x$ksppi;

COUNT(*)
312
```

You may now give access to the x$ table information without giving the password to the SYS account. The key was creating a view that referenced the original SYS-owned x$ tables.

**TIP**
*A DBA may need access to the x$ table information, but not the SYS password. Create a view under a different name that mirrors the desired tables. Name these tables according to the appropriate synonyms of the original tables.*

# V$ Views and x$ Table Creation

The x$ tables are virtual or fixed tables, which are created in memory at database startup and maintained real-time in memory. These tables store up-to-date information on the current activity of the database at a current point in time, or since the last database startup. In the SGA, there are V$ views created (see Chapter 14) on these x$ tables to allow users to view this information in a more readable format. The x$ tables are fixed tables, and since they have been created in memory, there is a very limited access to these tables.

The V$ views are known as the virtual tables, fixed tables, V$ tables, dynamic performance tables, and a half-dozen other names. The first hurdle to understanding the x$ tables is to become familiar with their creation, security, content, and relationship to the V$ views.

In addition, these x$ tables are very cryptic in nature. They are very similar to the underlying table construction of the Oracle data dictionary. Therefore, Oracle creates V$ views that are more readable and practical. In addition, Oracle has built

other views (USER, DBA, ALL) within the CATALOG.sql script for easier use. Oracle
has also created a public synonym on V_$ views in the CATALOG.sql file that
changes the name back to a view with a prefix of V$. An example of a V_$ view
and V$ public synonym creation in the CATALOG.sql is shown below:

```
create or replace view v_$datafile
as select * from v$datafile;

drop public synonym v$datafile;

create public synonym v$datafile for v_$datafile;
```

**TIP**
*See Chapter 14 and Appendix B for detailed
V$ view information, and Appendix C for
detailed x$ table information.*

Once the CATALOG.sql file has been executed, the V$ views are available to
only the SYS user. At this point, access can be granted to V$ views by granting
SELECT access on the V$ view. Therefore, all SELECTs performed against the V$
views are actually retrieving information out of the SGA, more specifically out of the
x$ tables. The X$ tables cannot be modified in any manner, and indexes cannot be
created on these tables by the DBA. Oracle now provides indexes on the x$ tables in
version 8. In addition, the V$ views are the underlying views that are used for
Oracle monitoring tools.

Note that Oracle has explicitly stated in their manuals that the V$ views may
change in the future, and as evidenced from the modifications from version 7 to
version 8, this is definitely true. Not only has there been an increase in the number
of V$ views and x$ tables, but some of the tables have changed columns as well.
This is also evident by the modifications to the V$ views and x$ tables between
incremental version upgrades within version 7.0 and 7.1.

**To get a listing of all V$ views:**

```
select     kqfvinam name
from       x$kqfvi
order by   kqfvinam;
```

**Partial output shown here (on Oracle8):**

```
NAME
GV$ACCESS
```

```
GV$ACTIVE_INSTANCES
GV$ARCHIVE
GV$ARCHIVED_LOG
GV$ARCHIVE_DEST
GV$BACKUP
GV$BACKUP_CORRUPTION
GV$BACKUP_DATAFILE
GV$BACKUP_DEVICE
GV$BACKUP_PIECE
GV$BACKUP_REDOLOG
GV$BACKUP_SET
GV$BGPROCESS
GV$BH
...
V$ACCESS
V$ACTIVE_INSTANCES
V$ARCHIVE
V$ARCHIVED_LOG
V$ARCHIVE_DEST
V$BACKUP
...
```

V$ Views and
x$ Table Creation

Note that the GV$ views are the same as the V$ tables except that you can see multiple instances with Oracle parallel server. The only difference between the GV$ and the V$ tables is a column that shows the instance ID.

## The x$ Tables That Make Up the V$ Views

To get a listing of the x$ tables that make up the V$ views, you must access the V$FIXED_TABLE_DEFINITION view. This view shows how the V$ views were created. By knowing which x$ tables make up a V$ view, you may be able to build a faster query that goes directly to the x$ tables.

```
select    *
from      v$fixed_view_definition
where     view_name = 'GV$FIXED_TABLE';
```

**Output:**

| VIEW NAME | VIEW DEFINITION |
|---|---|
| GV$FIXED_TABLE | select  inst_id,kqftanam, kqftaobj, 'TABLE', indx<br>from    x$kqfta<br>union all |

```
select   inst_id,kqfvinam, kqfviobj, 'VIEW', 65537
from     x$kqfvi
union all

select   inst_id,kqfdtnam, kqfdtobj, 'TABLE', 65537
from     x$kqfdt
```

**TIP**
*Access the x$kqfvi table for a listing of all V$ and GV$ views.*

**TIP**
*Access the V$FIXED_VIEW_DEFINITION view to get all of the information of the underlying x$ tables that make up a V$ view.*

# How to Get a Listing of All x$ Tables

The names of the x$ tables are in the x$kqfta (contains 192 of the x$ V8 tables) and x$kqftd (contains the other eight x$ V8 tables) tables. As shown earlier, the V$ names can be found in the x$kqfvi (contains the 132 V$ and 132 GV$ V8 views) table. The V$FIXED_TABLE view combines all three of these tables (shown in the example in the last section) so that you can get a listing of any desired grouping. The next query shows how this is accomplished.

**Query the V$FIXED_TABLE view for the names of the x$ tables:**

```
select     name
from       v$fixed_table
where      name like 'X%'
order by   name;
```

**Partial output shown here (on Oracle8):**

```
NAME
X$ACTIVECKPT
X$BH
X$CKPTBUF
X$CLASS_STAT
```

```
X$DUAL
X$K2GTE
X$K2GTE2
X$KCBBF
X$KCBBMC
X$KCBCBH
X$KCBFWAIT
X$KCBRBH
X$KCBSW
X$KCBWAIT
X$KCBWBPD
X$KCBWDS
X$KCBWH
X$KCCAL
X$KCCBF
X$KCCBL
X$KCCBP
....
```

**Query x$kqfta or x$kqfdt for a partial group of x$ tables:**

```
select       *
from         x$kqfdt;

ADDR              KQFDTNAM
010DD878          X$KCVFHONL
010DD8BC          X$KCVFHMRR
010DD900          X$KGLTABLE
010DD944          X$KGLBODY
010DD988          X$KGLTRIGGER
010DD9CC          X$KGLINDEX
010DDA10          X$KGLCLUSTER
010DDA54          X$KGLCURSOR

8 rows selected.
```

**TIP**
*Query the V$FIXED_TABLE view for the names of the
x$ tables, or you may also access the two x$ tables,
x$kqfta and x$kqftd, for partial listings that when
combined make up the full list.*

Getting All x$ Tables

# How to Get a Listing of All the x$ Indexes

If you often query the V$ views or x$ tables for information, it is helpful to understand what indexes are being used.

```
select     table_name, column_name, index_number
from       v$indexed_fixed_column
order by   table_name;
```

**Partial output shown here (on Oracle8):**

| TABLE NAME | COLUMN NAME | INDEX NUMBER |
|------------|-------------|--------------|
| X$BH | INDX | 1 |
| X$CLASS_STAT | ADDR | 1 |
| X$CLASS_STAT | INDX | 2 |
| X$DUAL | ADDR | 1 |
| X$DUAL | INDX | 2 |
| X$KCBBF | ADDR | 1 |
| X$KCBBF | INDX | 2 |
| X$KCBBMC | ADDR | 1 |
| X$KCBBMC | INDX | 2 |
| X$KCBCBH | ADDR | 1 |
| X$KCBCBH | INDX | 2 |
| X$KCBFWAIT | ADDR | 1 |
| X$KCBFWAIT | INDX | 2 |
| X$KCBRBH | ADDR | 1 |
| X$KCBRBH | INDX | 2 |
| X$KCBSW | ADDR | 1 |
| X$KCBSW | INDX | 2 |
| X$KCBWAIT | ADDR | 1 |
| X$KCBWAIT | INDX | 2 |

....

To see the data concerning which x$ tables the information is retrieved from, perform the query to the V$FIXED_VIEW DEFINITION view (displayed here).

```
select    *
from      v$fixed_view_definition
where     view_name = 'GV$INDEXED_FIXED_COLUMN';
```

Getting All the x$ Indexes

**Output:**

```
VIEW NAME                   VIEW DEFINITION
GV$INDEXED_FIXED_COLUMN  select  c.inst_id,    kqftanam,   kqfcoidx,
                                 kqfconam,    kqfcoipo
                         from    x$kqfco c,   x$kqftat
                         where   t.indx = c.kqfcotab
                         and     kqfcoidx != 0
```

**TIP**
*Access the V$INDEXED_FIXED_COLUMN view for a
listing of all x$ table indexes.*

# Using Hints with the x$ Tables and Indexes

As with other tables, you may also use hints, with the x$ tables, to achieve greater performance. The following three queries will show the EXPLAIN PLAN and statistics while forcing the use of an index and changing the driving tables. Note that I am using aliases for the tables and must hint the alias and not the table.

**The index on the x$ksbdp table is forced:**

```
select    /*+ index p(p.indx)  */ p.ksbdppro, p.ksbdpnam,
          d.ksbdddsc,p.ksbdperr
from      x$ksbdp p, x$ksbdd d
where     p.indx = d.indx
and       p.indx = 1;

Execution Plan
0        SELECT STATEMENT Optimizer=CHOOSE
1    0   MERGE JOIN
2    1   FIXED TABLE (FULL) OF 'X$KSBDD'
3    1   SORT (JOIN)
4    3   FIXED TABLE (FIXED INDEX #1) OF 'X$KSBDP'

Statistics
2  sorts (memory)
0  sorts (disk)
1  rows processed
```

**The ordered hint is used to force the driving table to be x$ksbdp:**

```
select    /*+ ordered */ p.ksbdppro, p.ksbdpnam,
          d.ksbdddsc,p.ksbdperr
from      x$ksbdp p, x$ksbdd d
where     p.indx = d.indx
and       p.indx = 1;

Execution Plan
0         SELECT STATEMENT Optimizer=CHOOSE (Cost=2 Card=1 Bytes=40)
1    0    NESTED LOOPS (Cost=2 Card=1 Bytes=40)
2    1    FIXED TABLE (FIXED INDEX #1) OF 'X$KSBDP'
3    1    FIXED TABLE (FIXED INDEX #2) OF 'X$KSBDD'

Statistics
1    sorts (memory)
0    sorts (disk)
1    rows processed
```

**The ordered hint is used to force the driving table to be x$ksbdd:**

```
select    /*+ ordered */ p.ksbdppro, p.ksbdpnam,
d.ksbdddsc,p.ksbdperr
from      x$ksbdd d, x$ksbdp p
where     p.indx = d.indx
and       p.indx = 1;

Execution Plan
0         SELECT STATEMENT Optimizer=CHOOSE (Cost=2 Card=1 Bytes=40)
1    0    NESTED LOOPS (Cost=2 Card=1 Bytes=40)
2    1    FIXED TABLE (FIXED INDEX #2) OF 'X$KSBDD'
3    1    FIXED TABLE (FIXED INDEX #1) OF 'X$KSBDP'

Statistics
1    sorts (memory)
0    sorts (disk)
1    rows processed
```

**TIP**

*Indexes are not available on version 7 x$ tables, but there are indexes on version 8 x$ tables. Oracle will generally use the indexes as needed, but from time to time you may use hints to achieve a desired result.*

**V8 TIP**

*There is never more than one column to an index on an x$ table.*

# Data Cached in Memory (x$bh)

To find out how fast memory is being depleted upon starting the database, run the following query of the x$bh table:

**To see how fast the SGA is depleting using x$bh:**

```
select      state, count(*)
from        x$bh
group by    state;


STATE       COUNT(*)
0                371
1                429


In the above result:
Total DB_BLOCK_BUFFERS = 800 (371+429)
Total buffers that have been used = 429
Total buffers that have NOT been used = 371
```

**TIP**

*If free buffers are not available (none with state=0) within the first 30 minutes of business hours, you probably need to set DB_BLOCK_BUFFERS higher. Remember, x$bh relates to memory that is allocated for the actual data of a query.*

**V8 TIP**

*In Oracle8, the results are adjusted more frequently and, as a result, the query is more accurate.*

# Oracle8 Takes More Startup Resources

Oracle8 takes more DB_BLOCK_BUFFERS upon startup than Oracle 7. Consider the following with identical init.ora files immediately upon starting the database. This example includes two systems, each with their DB_BLOCK_BUFFERS in the init.ora file set to 1000. The Oracle8 database will require 401 buffers upon startup, and Oracle7 will only require 160 buffers. Keep in mind, included in this number is a session that logs in to SQL*Plus to perform the actual query to the x$bh table.

**Version 7 upon startup:**

```
select     state, count(*)
from       x$bh
group by   state;

STATE      COUNT(*)
0          840
1          160
```

There are 840 blocks free of our original 1,000 blocks after starting the version 7 database.

**Version 8 upon startup:**

```
select     state, count(*)
from       x$bh
group by   state;

STATE      COUNT(*)
0          599
1          401
```

We can see here, there are 599 blocks free of our original 1,000 blocks after starting the version 8 database.

# What Memory Is Still in Use?

While the queries in the previous section show how fast memory is used at the start of the day, it does not tell us how much is being used at any given time. A popular way of doing this is to take the number of blocks with state=3, and call these the currently used blocks of memory. After weeks of testing, I found this to be not completely true. Through the examples in this section, we will see how to find memory currently in use (for the data) while also mapping that memory back to physical objects. These queries were performed while inserting data into the product and product2 tables.

**Finding the memory in use from x$bh table:**

```
select     state, count(*)
from       x$bh
group by   state;
```

| STATE | COUNT(*) |
|-------|----------|
| 0     | 186      |
| 1     | 760      |
| 3     | 20       |

The results seem to show 186 blocks (state=0) of memory were never used, 760 blocks (state=1) of memory that have been used once but are available if needed, and 20 blocks (state=3) that are being held while in use. We will see next why this is not actually the correct answer:

```
select     dbablk, state, lrba_seq
from       x$bh
where      lrba_seq <> 0
or         state = 3;
```

The output is listed next. The blocks (dbablk) with a state=3 are currently in use, while the blocks with a state=1 and lrba_seq=178 are the records for an INSERT into one particular segment.

| DBABLK | STATE | LRBA_SEQ |
|--------|-------|----------|
| 9749   | 3     | 0        |
| 10063  | 1     | 177      |
| 10064  | 1     | 177      |
| 10065  | 1     | 177      |
| 10066  | 1     | 177      |
| ...    |       |          |
| 10783  | 1     | 178      |
| 10784  | 1     | 178      |
| 10785  | 1     | 178      |
| 10786  | 1     | 178      |
| 10787  | 1     | 178      |
| 10788  | 1     | 178      |
| ...    |       |          |
| 10107  | 3     | 0        |
| 123    | 3     | 167      |
| ...    |       |          |

```
89 rows selected (partial list is shown).
```

**Finding the table for the corresponding memory blocks that are in question:**

```
select     segment_name, block_id, blocks
from       dba_extents
```

```
where     block_id > 9500
order by  block_id;

SEGMENT NAME      BLOCK ID        BLOCKS
SOURCE$           9530            100
I_SOURCE1         9630            100
PRODUCT           9730            30
PRODUCT           9760            15
PRODUCT           9775            20
PRODUCT           9795            15
PRODUCT           9810            30
PRODUCT           9840            20
PRODUCT           9860            45
PRODUCT           9905            30
PRODUCT           9935            65
PRODUCT2          10000           45
PRODUCT2          10045           45
PRODUCT2          10090           65
PRODUCT2          10155           95
PRODUCT2          10250           140
PRODUCT2          10390           210
PRODUCT2          10600           315
```

**What these queries tell us (or seem to tell us):**

- The extent sizes for product and product2 were too small and had to extend.

- The product table extent is in use (block 9749) because the BLOCK_ID 9730 has 30 blocks. The product table extends from 9730-9935, covering many extents.

- The product2 table has its last extent in use (the one that starts at 10600 and is 315 blocks long). This block goes from 10600-10914. Several extents are being used (10783 to 10788). Note that the state is set to 1 for these blocks.

- A state of 3 is a block being used, but a state of 1 can also be in use.

- A state of 0 is a block that has not been used before.

- Mapping actual memory being used back to tables is not that easy!

## A Better Query for Memory in Use

**The original query:**

```
select      state, count(*)
from        x$bh
group by    state;

STATE     COUNT(*)
0         167
1         741
3         92
```

**The problem records in use but seemingly not previously counted:**

```
select      count(*)
from        x$bh
where       state=1
and         lrba_seq <> 0;

COUNT(*)
62
```

**A query that fixes the problem (Use this query!):**

```
select      decode(state,0, 'FREE',
            1,decode(lrba_seq,0,'AVAILABLE','BEING USED'),
            3, 'BEING USED', state) "BLOCK STATUS",
            count(*)
from        x$bh
group by    decode(state,0,'FREE',1,decode(lrba_seq,0,'AVAILABLE',
            'BEING USED'),3, 'BEING USED', state);

BLOCK STATUS      COUNT(*)
AVAILABLE         779
BEING USED        154
FREE              167
```

This query takes the 62 records that were at a state=1, but also with a lrba_seq<>0, and placed them with the records that were set to a state=3 or BEING

USED. Is this the final answer? Probably not, but there are not any sources to give any additional information in this area. These results came from several weeks of testing and give a rough estimate of only memory that is in use.

A final point of interest comes from some of Oracle's "bh" creation scripts that show a DECODE with the following undocumented statuses (make your own conclusions):

| STATE | STATUS |
|-------|--------|
| 0 | free |
| 1 | xcurr |
| 2 | scurr |
| 3 | cr |
| 4 | read |
| 5 | mrec |
| 6 | irec |

**TIP**
*Accessing x$bh gives a hazy picture of memory use.*
*Checking blocks with a state of 1 that also have values for*
*lrba_seq and combining them with the blocks in a state of*
*3 gives a much closer picture of memory that is in use.*

# Information Cached in the SHARED_POOL Memory (x$ksmsp)

To find out how fast memory in the SHARED_POOL is being depleted (made noncontiguous) and also what percent is unused (and still contiguous), run the following query after starting the database and running production queries for a short period of time (after the first hour of the day):

```
col value for 999,999,999,999 heading "Shared Pool Size"
col bytes for 999,999,999,999 heading "Free Bytes"
select    to_number(v$parameter.value) value, v$sgastat.bytes,
          (v$sgastat.bytes/v$parameter.value)*100 "Percent Free"
from      v$sgastat, v$parameter
where     v$sgastat.name = 'free memory'
and       v$ parameter .name = 'shared_pool_size;

Shared Pool Size       Free Bytes           Percent Free
100,000,000            82,278,960            82.27896
```

If there is plenty of contiguous free memory (greater than 2MB) after running most queries in your production system (you'll have to determine how long this takes), there is no need to increase the SHARED_POOL_SIZE parameter. I have never seen this parameter go all the way to zero (Oracle saves a portion for emergency operations via the SHARED_POOL_RESERVED_SIZE parameter). I have seen it go to 2GB (with a shared pool of only 100MB) when the Shared Pool started approaching zero (an indicator that the SHARED_POOL_RESERVED_SIZE is set too low). Consider the following two queries to versions 7 and 8 of the database to see how fast a 7MB SHARED_POOL_SIZE drops when the database is started.

**Version 7 upon startup:**

```
select      *
from        v$sgastat
where       name = 'free memory'


NAME                BYTES
free memory         6,691,044
```

**Version 8 upon startup:**

```
select      *
from        v$sgastat
where       name = 'free memory';

POOL            NAME            BYTES
shared pool     free memory     5,647,092
```

**TIP**

*When you access the V$SGASTAT view for "free memory," it does not actually show you the current amount of memory that is free. It shows you any memory that has never been used combined with any piece of memory that has been reused. It is not using the entire piece of memory that the original query using it needed. Free memory will go up and down as the day goes on based on how the pieces are fragmented.*

**Use the x$ksmsp table to get a detailed look at the Shared Pool:**

The x$ksmsp table is a method of looking at the total breakdown for the init.ora file. This table will show the amount of memory that is free or freeable, and memory that is retained for large statements that won't fit into the current Shared Pool.

Consider the following queries that access the x$ksmsp table, noting how different sizes for the Shared Pool are allocated in different ways.

**A Shared Pool of 1MB upon startup:**

```
select      sum(ksmchsiz) Bytes, ksmchcls Status
from        x$ksmsp
group by    ksmchcls

BTYES       STATUS
54,912      R-free
10,460      R-freea
22,272      free
545,764     freeabl
1,406,568   perm
186,444     recr
```

**A Shared Pool of 10MB upon startup:**

```
select      sum(ksmchsiz) Bytes, ksmchcls Status
from        x$ksmsp
group by    ksmchcls;

BYTES       STATUS
500,000     R-free
40          R-freea
3,940,956   free
823,016     freeabl
5,613,872   perm
348,536     recr
```

**A Shared Pool of 100MB upon startup:**

```
select      sum(ksmchsiz) Bytes, ksmchcls Status
from        x$ksmsp
group by    ksmchcls;

BYTES       STATUS
5,000,000   R-free
40          R-freea
0,932,132   free
824,596     freeabl
34,117,560  perm
352,084     recr
```

Information Cached in the SHARED_POOL Memory

**A Shared Pool of 1,000MB upon startup:**

```
select      sum(ksmchsiz) Bytes, ksmchcls Status
from        x$ksmsp
group by    ksmchcls;

BYTES            STATUS
50,000,000       R-free
40               R-freea
888,326,956      free
837,924          freeabl
61,702,380       perm
359,008          recr
```

Oracle does not state anywhere what the values for status in the x$ksmsp table mean. I offer the following possible descriptions based on the behavior of these values:

| Status | Possible Meaning |
|--------|------------------|
| R-free | This is SHARED_POOL_RESERVED_SIZE (default 5 percent of SP). |
| R-freea | This is probably reserved memory that has been used but freeable. |
| free | This is the amount of contiguous free memory available. |
| freeabl | This is probably memory that has been used but is freeable. |
| perm | This is free memory not yet moved to the free area for use. |
| recr | I am not sure what this is—possibly reserved memory for Oracle. |

**Portions of memory are moved from perm to free when free is depleted:**

The following two queries show how loading a large procedure causes the insufficient memory with a status of free to be refreshed with a portion of the memory from perm. In this case, about 1.3MB was moved from perm to free.

```
select      sum(ksmchsiz) Bytes, ksmchcls Status
from        x$ksmsp
group by    ksmchcls;

BYTES         STATUS
350,000       R-free
40            R-freea
25,056        free
```

```
2,571,948    freeabl
4,113,872    perm
1,165,504    recr
```

## A large package is loaded and x$ksmsp is requeried:

```
select      sum(ksmchsiz) Bytes, ksmchcls Status
from        x$ksmsp
group by    ksmchcls;

BYTES        STATUS
350,000      R-free
40           R-freea
1,367,448    free
2,573,672    freeabl
2,766,596    perm
1,168,664    recr
```

We see here that more bytes of memory than needed are moved from perm to free to satisfy the query. Why Oracle reserves a portion of the memory in perm (instead of keeping all of it in free) and why larger portions than needed are moved from perm to free is a mystery. One possible explanation is so that the free memory list is not too great at any given time.

**TIP**
*By accessing the x$ksmsp table, you get a better breakdown of the memory that is free and used. The ksmchcls column that is set up R-free shows the SORT_AREA_RETAINED_SIZE that is set for the large objects. The memory breakdown varies based on the total size of the Shared Pool.*

## The SHARED_POOL_SIZE is overfull and causing errors:

In the event the SHARED_POOL_SIZE was set too small and is overfragmented to the point where an ORA-4031 is encountered, there is a way to flush everything out and refresh the Shared Pool. Using the following statement, you can survive this problem, but this means that you need to take a serious look at increasing the SHARED_POOL_SIZE (or loading large procedures first) and physical memory (if necessary for an increased SHARED_POOL_SIZE). Also, note that flushing the Shared Pool also clears out any cached sequence values. If ten sequence numbers are cached and you have only used the first five when the flush occurs, your next sequence number will be 11 on the next access (sequence numbers 6-10 are lost).

```
SQL> ALTER SYSTEM FLUSH SHARED_POOL;
```

**TIP**
*Don't flush the Shared Pool unless you are getting errors. Flushing the Shared Pool pushes everything out of memory, which will cause degradation to all users, who must then reread everything back in. A low amount of free memory is not necessarily the precursor to an error.*

**TIP**
*An ORA-4031 is usually caused when the Shared Pool gets fragmented into smaller pieces over the course of a day and a request for a large piece of memory is issued that cannot be filled.*

# When to Pin Objects in the Shared Pool

In the event that you cannot maintain a sufficient SHARED_POOL_SIZE, it may become important to keep the most important (and largest) objects cached (pinned) in memory. If there is not enough contiguous space (due to Shared Pool fragmentation), you may receive errors. The following query will help you find the PL/SQL objects that are too large and need to be loaded first.

The following two examples show how to pin PL/SQL object statements in memory using the DBMS_SHARED_POOL.KEEP procedure.

```
begin
DBMS_SHARED_POOL.KEEP('PROCESS_DATE','P');
end
```

```
execute dbms_shared_pool.keep('SYS.STANDARD');
      (often a source of ORA-4031 errors)
```

**TIP**
*Pin PL/SQL objects into memory immediately upon starting the database to avoid insufficient memory errors later in the day. To accomplish this, use the DBMS_SHARED_POOL.KEEP procedure for PL/SQL object statements. Ensure that the STANDARD procedure is pinned soon after startup since it is so large.*

Pinning Objects

**Finding which large objects are causing others to be aged out (ksmlru):**

```
select     ksm1rhon, ksmlrsiz
from       x$ksmlru
where      ksmlrsiz > 1000;
```

The output will display the PL/SQL object in the ksmlrhon column and the size of that object in the ksmlrsiz column. The larger the value for ksmlrsiz, the larger the potential problem.

**TIP**

*Query the x$ksmlru table to view problem objects that are aging others out of the Shared Pool.*

# Accessing the Undocumented init.ora Parameters

Using parameters that are undocumented or unsupported by Oracle can lead to corruption or unexpected results. I have personally corrupted our test system on several occasions testing parameters from the x$ksppi table. Be careful! I also believe that people should know all of the possibilities that exist within Oracle so that they can make choices regarding these parameters for themselves. Be careful! I will be showing some of the more commonly used parameters in this section.

**In version 7, execute the following query:**

```
select     ksppinm, ksppivl, ksppidf
from       x$ksppi
where      substr(ksppinm,1,1) = '_';
```

Ksppidf tells you if the value has been altered from the Oracle default. If ksppidf = TRUE, the setting is the original value. If ksppidf = FALSE, the value has been altered in the init.ora.

**In Oracle8, you must also access the x$ksppcv table in addition to the x$ksppi table:**

```
select     a.ksppinm, b.ksppstvl, b.ksppstdf
from       x$ksppi a, x$ksppcv b
where      a.indx = b.indx
and        substr(ksppinm,1,1) = '_'
order by a.ksppinm;
```

**A partial output listing is displayed here:**

| KSPPINM | KSPPSTVL | KSPPSTDF |
|---|---|---|
| _advanced_dss_features | FALSE | TRUE |
| _affinity_on | TRUE | TRUE |
| _all_shared_dblinks | | TRUE |
| _allow_resetlogs_corruption | FALSE | TRUE |
| _always_star_transformation | FALSE | TRUE |
| _bump_highwater_mark_count | 0 | TRUE |
| _column_elimination_off | FALSE | TRUE |
| _controlfile_enqueue_timeout | 900 | TRUE |
| _corrupt_blocks_on_stuck_recovery | 0 | TRUE |
| _corrupted_rollback_segments | | TRUE |
| _cr_deadtime | 6 | TRUE |
| _cursor_db_buffers_pinned | 18 | TRUE |
| _db_block_cache_clone | FALSE | TRUE |
| ... | | |

In this output, ksppinm is the name of the init.ora parameter, ksppstvl is the current value, and ksppstdf tells you if the current setting for ksppstvl is the original default for that parameter.

**An Oracle8 example shows how to find the database-creating file that is executed:**

```
select     a.ksppinm, b.ksppstvl
from       x$ksppi a, x$ksppcv b
where      a.indx = b.indx
and        ksppinm = '_init_sql_file';


KSPPINM                    KSPPSTVL
_init_sql_file             %RDBMS80%\ADMIN\SQL.BSQ
```

**TIP**

*In Oracle 7.3 and higher, the INIT_SQL_FILE init.ora parameter no longer exists; therefore, the option to change the default initial files executed upon database creation no longer exists. In actuality, Oracle has changed the name and hidden it from the V$PARAMETER query. By querying the x$ksppi table and joining by the indx column to the x$ksppcv table, the value of the new parameter _init_sql_file can be obtained.*

Accessing init.ora

### Finding the init.ora parameters for undocumented TRACE:

```
select     ksppinm, ksppivl,ksppidf
from       x$ksppi
where      ksppinm like '%_trace%';
```

### Version 7 output here:

| KSPPINM | KSPPIVL | KSPPIDF |
| --- | --- | --- |
| _trace_files_public | FALSE | TRUE |
| _trace_buffers_per_process | 0 | TRUE |
| _trace_block_size | 2048 | TRUE |
| _trace_archive_start | FALSE | TRUE |
| _trace_flushing | FALSE | TRUE |
| _trace_enabled | TRUE | TRUE |
| _trace_events | | TRUE |
| _trace_archive_dest | %RDBMS70%\trace.dat | TRUE |
| _trace_file_size | 10000 | TRUE |
| _trace_write_batch_size | 32 | TRUE |
| sql_trace | FALSE | TRUE |

The _TRACE_FILES_PUBLIC undocumented init.ora parameter will allow everybody to read the TRACE files. Place the following statement in your init.ora file and restart the database for this to take effect.

```
_trace_files_public = true
```

**TIP**
*The x$ksppi table can be used to find undocumented TRACE settings. The _TRACE_FILES_PUBLIC parameter can be set for all user access to TRACE files.*

To TRACE errors, you may place certain event settings in the init.ora. These can be TRACEd by setting the init.ora parameter in the example shown next (used to TRACE a 4031 error).

### Prior to V7.0.16:

```
event="4031 trace name errorstack"
```

**On V7.0.16+ use the following command:**

```
event="4031 trace name errorstack level 4"
(Where "4031" is the ora-04031 error that you want to trace.)
```

This builds a TRACE file in your _trace_archive_dest (found in x$ksppi).

**TIP**
*TRACing queries can help performance, but using the TRACE facility built within the undocumented TRACE init.ora parameters (discussed earlier and later) can give great insight (and better information) to solving errors within Oracle.*

# How Many init.ora Parameters Are There and How Many Are Documented?

Query the V$PARAMETER view to see the total number of documented init.ora parameters in either version 7 or 8 of the database. Querying the x$ksppi table will show the total number of init.ora parameters in the Oracle databases. The four queries shown next will show the number of documented and total init.ora parameters in both versions 7 and 8. Note that these numbers will vary by database version and release number.

**Documented number of init.ora parameters in version 7:**

```
select      count(*)
from        v$parameter;

Count(*)
117
```

**Total number of init.ora parameters in version 7:**

```
select      count(*)
from        x$ksppi;

Count(*)
185
```

Finding init.ora

**Finding init.ora**

**Documented number of init.ora parameters in version 8.0.4 (varies by release):**

```
select      count(*)
from        v$parameter;

Count(*)
193
```

**Total number of init.ora parameters in version 8.0.4 (varies by release):**

```
select      count(*)
from        x$ksppi;

Count(*)
312
```

### TIP
*Access the V$PARAMETER view and the x$ksppi table to see the documented and undocumented init.ora parameters. All undocumented parameters should be extensively tested before contemplating use. The number of init.ora parameters in Oracle7 and 8.0.4 (varies by release) are listed here:*

*Total documented init.ora parameters in version 7: 117*
*Total undocumented init.ora parameters in version 7: 68*
*Grand total init.ora parameters in version 7: 185*

*Total documented init.ora parameters in version 8: 193*
*Total undocumented init.ora parameters in version 8: 119*
*Grand total init.ora parameters in version 8: 312*

## What Is the Block Size and How Much of the Block Can Be Used?
Accessing the x$kvis table can give you the current block size while also showing you the available area for data within the block. A query accessing this table is shown here:

```
select kvisval, kvisdsc
from x$kvis;

KVISVAL     KVISDSC
2048        size of physical block
2024        data area available in each physical block
```

## x$ Tables: A Closer Look

There are 126 x$ tables in version 7 and 200 x$ tables in version 8. Appendix C has a listing of all V7 and V8 x$ tables along with all indexes in version 8. There is also a cross listing of x$ to v$ tables and the x$ tables used in the V$ creation scripts. A listing for all version 7 and version 8.0.4 x$ tables is displayed next. Note that these numbers will vary by database version and release number.

**Version 8.0.4 x$ tables ordered by name (200 total; varies by release):**

| | | | |
|---|---|---|---|
| x$activeckpt | x$bh | x$ckptbuf | x$class_stat |
| x$dual | x$k2gte | x$k2gte2 | x$kcbbf |
| x$kcbbmc | x$kcbcbh | x$kcbfwait | x$kcbrbh |
| x$kcbsw | x$kcbwait | x$kcbwbpd | x$kcbwds |
| x$kcbwh | x$kccal | x$kccbf | x$kccbl |
| x$kccbp | x$kccbs | x$kcccc | x$kcccf |
| x$kcccp | x$kccdc | x$kccdi | x$kccdl |
| x$kccfc | x$kccfe | x$kccfn | x$kccle |
| x$kcclh | x$kccor | x$kccrs | x$kccrt |
| x$kccts | x$kcfio | x$kckce | x$kckfm |
| x$kckty | x$kclfh | x$kclfi | x$kclfx |
| x$kclls | x$kclqn | x$kcluh | x$kclui |
| x$kcrfx | x$kcrmf | x$kcrmt | x$kcrmx |
| x$kcrrdest | x$kcvfh | x$kcvfhmrr | x$kcvfhonl |
| x$kdnssf | x$kdxhs | x$kdxst | x$kghlu |
| x$kgicc | x$kgics | x$kglau | x$kglbody |
| x$kglcluster | x$kglcursor | x$kgldp | x$kglindex |
| x$kgllc | x$kgllk | x$kglna | x$kglna1 |
| x$kglob | x$kglpn | x$kglrd | x$kglsn |
| x$kglst | x$kgltable | x$kgltr | x$kgltrigger |
| x$kglxs | x$kjicvt | x$kjilft | x$kjisft |
| x$kksai | x$kksbv | x$kllcnt | x$klltab |
| x$klpt | x$kmcqs | x$kmcvc | x$kmmdi |
| x$kmmdp | x$kmmrd | x$kmmsg | x$kmmsi |

Finding init.ora

| | | | |
|---|---|---|---|
| x$kocst | x$kqdpg | x$kqfco | x$kqfdt |
| x$kqfp | x$kqfsz | x$kqfta | x$kqfvi |
| x$kqfvt | x$kqlset | x$kqrpd | x$kqrsd |
| x$kqrst | x$ksbdd | x$ksbdp | x$ksfhdvnt |
| x$ksfvsl | x$ksfvsta | x$ksimat | x$ksimav |
| x$ksimsi | x$ksled | x$kslei | x$ksles |
| x$kslld | x$ksllt | x$ksllw | x$kslpo |
| x$kslwsc | x$ksmfs | x$ksmfsv | x$ksmhp |
| x$ksmlru | x$ksmls | x$ksmmem | x$ksmpp |
| x$ksmsd | x$ksmsp | x$ksmspr | x$ksmss |
| x$ksmup | x$ksppcv | x$ksppi | x$ksppsv |
| x$ksqdn | x$ksqeq | x$ksqrs | x$ksqst |
| x$kstex | x$ksucf | x$ksull | x$ksulop |
| x$ksulv | x$ksumysta | x$ksupl | x$ksupr |
| x$ksuprlat | x$ksurlmt | x$ksuru | x$ksusd |
| x$ksuse | x$ksusecon | x$ksusecst | x$ksusesta |
| x$ksusex | x$ksusgsta | x$ksusio | x$ksutm |
| x$ksuxsinst | x$ksxafa | x$ktadm | x$ktcxb |
| x$ktsso | x$ktstssd | x$kttvs | x$kturd |
| x$ktuxe | x$kvii | x$kvis | x$kvit |
| x$kxfpcds | x$kxfpcms | x$kxfpcst | x$kxfpdp |
| x$kxfpsds | x$kxfpsms | x$kxfpsst | x$kxfpys |
| x$kxfqsrow | x$kxsbd | x$kxscc | x$kzdos |
| x$kzspr | x$kzsro | x$kzsrt | x$le |
| x$le_stat | x$messages | x$nls_parameters | x$option |
| x$trace | x$traces | x$uganco | x$version |

**Version 7 x$ tables ordered by name (126 total; varies by release):**

| | | | |
|---|---|---|---|
| x$bh | x$k2gte | x$k2gte2 | x$kcbcbh |
| x$kcbfwait | x$kcbrbh | x$kcbwait | x$kcccf |
| x$kccdi | x$kccfe | x$kccfn | x$kccle |
| x$kcclh | x$kccrt | x$kcfio | x$kckce |
| x$kckfm | x$kckty | x$kcvfh | x$kcvfhmrr |
| x$kcvfhonl | x$kdnce | x$kdnssc | x$kdnssf |
| x$kdnst | x$kdxhs | x$kdxst | x$kghlu |
| x$kgicc | x$kgics | x$kglau | x$kglbody |
| x$kglcluster | x$kglcursor | x$kgldp | x$kglindex |
| x$kgllc | x$kgllk | x$kglna | x$kglob |
| x$kglpn | x$kglst | x$kgltable | x$kgltr |
| x$kgltrigger | x$kglxs | x$kksbv | x$kllcnt |
| x$klltab | x$kmcqs | x$kmcvc | x$kmmdi |
| x$kmmdp | x$kmmrd | x$kmmsg | x$kmmsi |
| x$kqdpg | x$kqfco | x$kqfdt | x$kqfsz |
| x$kqfta | x$kqfvi | x$kqrpd | x$kqrsd |
| x$kqrst | x$ksbdd | x$ksbdp | x$ksled |
| x$kslei | x$ksles | x$kslld | x$ksllt |
| x$ksmcx | x$ksmlru | x$ksmsd | x$ksmsp |
| x$ksmss | x$ksppi | x$ksqdn | x$ksqeq |
| x$ksqrs | x$ksqst | x$ksucf | x$ksull |
| x$ksulv | x$ksumysta | x$ksupl | x$ksupr |
| x$ksuprlat | x$ksuru | x$ksusd | x$ksuse |
| x$ksusecst | x$ksusesta | x$ksusgsta | x$ksusio |
| x$ksutm | x$ksuxsinst | x$ktadm | x$ktcxb |

Finding init.ora

| | | | |
|---|---|---|---|
| x$kttvs | x$kturd | x$kvii | x$kvis |
| x$kvit | x$kxfpcds | x$kxfpcms | x$kxfpcst |
| x$kxfpdp | x$kxfpsds | x$kxfpsms | x$kxfpsst |
| x$kxfpys | x$kzdos | x$kzspr | x$kzsro |
| x$kzsrt | x$le | x$le_stat | x$messages |
| x$nls_parameters | x$option | x$trace | x$traces |
| x$uganco | x$version | | |

# Future Version Impact

As noted several times in this chapter, the V$ views and x$ tables are continually being enhanced as more and more features are added to Oracle. Based on information obtained currently on version 8 of Oracle, the V$ views and x$ tables have changed from version 7. Performance of SELECTs on V$ views and x$ tables has improved as Oracle has added indexes (in V8) on the underlying x$ tables. As in the past, consider more changes to come in the future!

# Tips Review

When you mention the x$ tables, most people say "ooh…pretty scary, I would never touch those tables." The fact is that DML commands (UPDATE, INSERT, DELETE) are not allowed on the x$ tables, even as the SYS superuser.

Only the SYS superuser can SELECT from the x$ tables. An error occurs if an attempt is made to grant SELECT access to a user. A DBA may need access to the x$ table information, but *not* the SYS password. Create a view under a different name that mirrors the desired tables. Name these tables according to the appropriate synonyms of the original tables.

- Access the x$kqfvi table for a listing of all V$ and GV$ views.
- Access the V$FIXED_VIEW_DEFINITION view to get all of the information of the underlying x$ tables that make up a V$ view.
- Query the V$FIXED_TABLE view for the names of the x$ tables, or you may also access the two x$ tables, x$kqfta and x$kqftd, for partial listings that when combined make up the full list.
- Access the V$INDEXED_FIXED_COLUMN view for a listing of all x$table indexes. There are *not* any indexes on version 7 x$. There is never more

than one part to an index on an x$ table. There can be multiple indexes on an x$ table.

■ Oracle will generally use the indexes as needed for the x$ tables, but from time to time you may use hints to achieve a desired result.

■ If free buffers are not available (none with state=0) within the first 30 minutes of business hours, you probably need to set DB_BLOCK_BUFFERS higher. Remember, x$bh relates to memory that is allocated for the actual data of a query.

■ Accessing x$bh gives a hazy picture of memory use. Checking blocks with a state of 1 that also have values for lrba_seq and combining them with the blocks in a state of 3 gives a much closer picture of memory that is in use.

■ By accessing the x$ksmsp table, you get a better breakdown of the memory that is free and used. The ksmchcls column that is set up R-free shows the sort_area_retained_size that is set for the large objects. The memory breakdown varies based on the total size of the Shared Pool.

■ Don't flush the Shared Pool unless you are getting errors. Flushing the Shared Pool pushes everything out of memory, which will cause degradation to all users, who must then reread everything back in. A low amount of free memory is not necessarily the precursor to an error.

■ An ORA-4031 is usually caused when the Shared Pool gets fragmented into smaller pieces over the course of a day and a request for a large piece of memory is issued that cannot be filled.

■ Pin PL/SQL objects into memory immediately upon starting the database to avoid insufficient memory errors later in the day. To accomplish this, use the DBMS_SHARED_POOL.KEEP procedure for PL/SQL object statements. Ensure that the STANDARD procedure is pinned soon after startup since it is so large.

■ Query the x$ksmlru table to view problem objects that are aging others out of the Shared Pool.

■ The x$ksppi table can be used to find undocumented TRACE settings. The trace_files_public parameter can be set for *all* user access to TRACE files.

■ Access the V$PARAMETER and the x$ksppi table to see the documented and undocumented init.ora parameters.

See Appendix C for x$ detailed listings. See Chapter 14 and Appendix B for detailed V$ view information.

# References

*Journey to the Center of the x$ Tables*; Joe Trezzo, TUSC

*Oracle7 Server: SQL Language Reference Manual*; Oracle Corporation

*Oracle7 Server: Application Developer's Guide*; Oracle Corporation

*Get the Most out of Your Money: Utilize the V$ Views*; IOUG 1994, Joseph Trezzo

*Monitoring Oracle Database: The Challenge;* IOUG 1994, Eyal Aronoff
& Noorali Sonawalla

Frank Naude's underground Oracle Web page

Tony Jambu, *Select Magazine* column

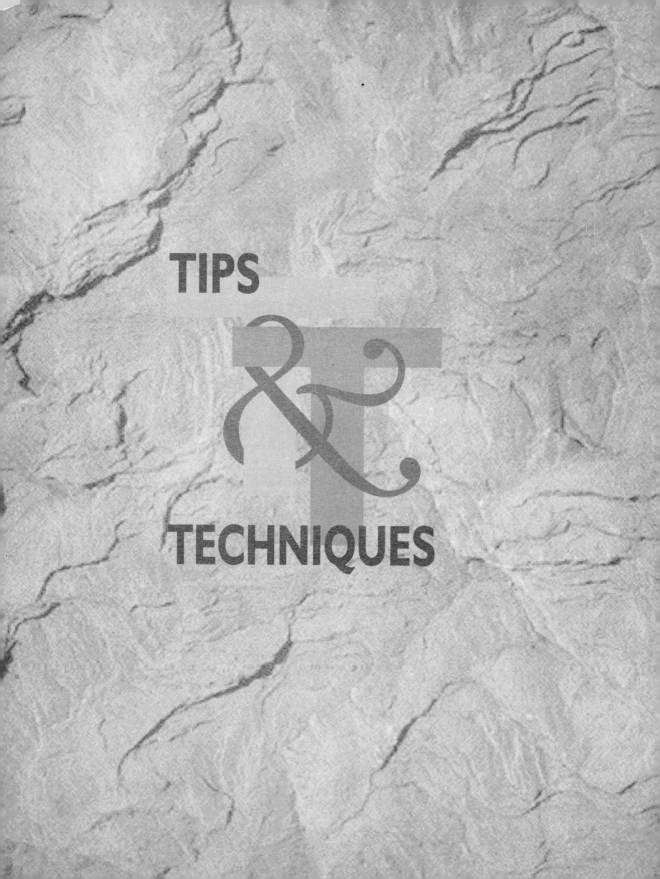

# TIPS & TECHNIQUES

# CHAPTER
## 16

Using and Interpreting
UTLESTAT/UTLBSTAT
(Advanced DBA)

The UTLBSTAT.sql and UTLESTAT.sql are scripts provided by Oracle that are used to gain insight into the Oracle database. They can be found in the ORACLE_HOME/rdbms/admin directory. Together, these scripts are used to generate a report (report.txt) that can be used to determine how well the Oracle database has been tuned. Many DBAs are unfamiliar with these scripts or are unaware how to use the information provided in the report generated by these scripts. This chapter will focus on the best information provided by these scripts. The sections of this chapter will coincide with the order of output generated to build report.txt. This chapter contains the following tips designed to achieve the greatest performance by focusing on the most important information provided within this report:

- How to run UTLESTAT/UTLBSTAT
- What tables are populated by the queries
- When to run the report
- Checking the library cache hit ratio
- Checking the database statistics like buffer cache hit ratio, free buffers, and physical sorts
- Checking the dirty buffer write queue and blocks that can be written at once
- Checking system-wide wait events to see where the bottlenecks are
- Checking the latches and latch contention
- Find out what class of blocks are causing contention
- Checking the rollback segments and shrinks
- Generate a list of init.ora parameters that have been modified from their defaults
- Check the dictionary cache and all parameters that make up the dc cache
- Check the file I/O and tablespace I/O to see disk and other I/O contention
- Generate reporting dates and times as well as the versions of products installed at the time

# Running the Utilities

The UTLBSTAT.sql Oracle script creates statistics tables and collects beginning statistics. The UTLESTAT.sql Oracle script collects ending statistics and a report called report.txt in the working directory of the person running the UTLESTAT.sql script.

In order to collect and report the statistics, complete the actions described here.

■ The database should be started up with the TIMED_STATISTICS init.ora parameter set to TRUE. If you do not set this parameter, the scripts will still run but the timing-related statistics will not be generated.

■ Once the buffers and cache have stabilized (wait until after the database has been started and has stabilized from the start process), the UTLBSTAT script can be run as the SYS superuser by using SVRMGR or Enterprise Manager to create statistics tables and collect beginning statistics. You can also run the scripts through SQL*Plus (only as the SYS user), but you must take out the "connect internal" line in the scripts.

■ Run the application(s) through their paces, with a full compliment of users.

■ Run the UTLESTAT script to end the statistics gathering and to also generate a report called report.txt. This report will include results from all areas of the database monitored.

**TIP**
*The UTLBSTAT.sql and UTLESTAT.sql can be found in your Oracle Home directory under the subdirectory "rdbms/admin." UTLESTAT will generate a report called report.txt (in your working directory) that should be reviewed for database changes.*

**TIP**
*Wait until the database has stabilized before running UTLBSTAT (the start of statistics gathering) or the results may be erroneously affected by the database startup process; all of the cache areas are loaded at start time, and this will skew the results of your reports.*

# Frequency of Monitoring

The frequency of monitoring will depend on the number of problem performance times that your individual system has. The key is to run the report whenever you have a specific problem time period (e.g., between 1 P.M. and 3 P.M. during the heaviest order entry). These reports will show the difference between the data at the beginning of the time period and the data at the end of the time period. Some of the best times to run these scripts are during the peak production hours and during batch runs. This gives you a good look at how the database is performing during the times of heaviest use.

**TIP**
*Run UTLBSTAT.sql and UTLESTAT.sql at problem performance times for your system so that the results can be used to measure system problems at the worst possible time.*

## The Tables That Are Populated by the Scripts

UTLBSTAT.sql will create and populate the following tables as the SYS user. This script will also create a view that will be used by the UTLESTAT.sql when it is generating the reports. The stats$end_ tables are only created, they are not populated.

| | |
|---|---|
| stats$begin_stats | System statistics from the V$SYSSTAT view |
| stats$end_stats | |
| stats$begin_latch | Latch statistics from the V$LATCH view |
| stats$end_latch | |
| stats$begin_roll | Rollback statistics from the V$ROLLSTAT view |
| stats$end_roll | |
| stats$begin_lib | Library cache statistics from the V$LIBRARYCACHE view |
| stats$end_lib | |
| stats$begin_dc | Dictionary cache statistics from the V$ROWCACHE view |
| stats$end_dc | |
| stats$begin_event | System-Wide Wait Event statistics from the V$SYSTEM_EVENT |
| stats$end_event | view |
| stats$dates | Contains a Date/Time stamp of the start of the report |
| stats$file_view | A view of the V$FILESTAT, V$DATAFILE, TS$, and FILE$ |
| stats$begin_file | File I/O statistics from the stat$file_view |

stats$end_file

| | |
|---|---|
| stats$begin_waitstat | Returns the class (rollback, freelist) of any block |
| stats$end_waitstat | contention from V$WAITSTAT, V$ROLLSTAT, and V$ROLLCACHE |

**TIP**
*The SYS user owns the tables that are populated. You may write your own reports to these tables if you have privileges to the SYS user account.*

When the UTLESTAT.sql script is run, the following tables will be created. The first section of this script will populate the stats$end_ tables with the current information in the database. After the ending statistics have been gathered, the tables are populated with the differences between the stats$begin_ and the stats$end_ tables.

| | |
|---|---|
| stats$stats | System statistics |
| stats$latches | Latch statistics |
| stats$roll | Rollback segment statistics |
| stats$files | Data file I/O statistics |
| stats$dc | Dictionary cache statistics |
| stats$lib | Library cache statistics |
| stats$event | System-wide wait event statistics |
| stats$waitstat | Block contention waits |
| stats$dates | Stores the date and time for running begin and end statistics |

These tables will be used to generate the report.txt report produced by the UTLESTAT.sql.

**TIP**
*If the database happens to go down at any time between the start and end of the report, the report will contain meaningless data and should be ignored.*

# The Library Cache

The first section of the report deals with the performance of the library cache. These statistics are generated from the V$LIBRARYCACHE view. The library cache contains the shared SQL and PL/SQL areas. These areas are represented by the body, sql area, table/procedure, and the trigger. They contain all of the SQL and PL/SQL statements that are cached in memory. The other names are areas that Oracle uses. The following query is the one that is run by UTLESTAT for the library section of the report:

```
select      namespace library, gets,
            round(decode(gethits,0,1,gethits)/decode
            (gets,0,1,gets),3) gethitratio,
            pins, round(decode(pinhits,0,1,pinhits)
            /decode(pins,0,1,pins),3)
            pinhitratio, reloads, invalidations
from        stats$lib;
```

**Example output:**

| LIBRARY | GETS | GETHITRATIO | PINS | PINHITRATIO | RELOADS | INVALIDATIONS |
|---------|------|-------------|------|-------------|---------|---------------|
| BODY | 3180 | .999 | 3183 | .992 | 25 | 0 |
| CLUSTER | 0 | 1 | 0 | 1 | 0 | 0 |
| INDEX | 146 | .007 | 218 | .335 | 0 | 0 |
| OBJECT | 0 | 1 | 0 | 1 | 0 | 0 |
| PIPE | 0 | 1 | 0 | 1 | 0 | 0 |
| SQL AREA | 287513 | .955 | 2353969 | .985 | 5387 | 539 |
| TABLE/PROCEED | 203065 | .992 | 1606163 | .996 | 4998 | 0 |
| TRIGGER | 4632 | .996 | 4631 | .987 | 39 | 0 |

| | |
|---|---|
| Library | The name of the library namespace. |
| Gets | The number of times the system requested a handle to an object in this namespace. |
| Gethitratio | The number of gethits divided by the number of gets. The gethits are the number of times a request was made for an object and the object was already in the cache. This ratio should be as close to 1 as possible. |
| Pins | The number of times an item in the cache was executed. A high number is what you are after since these are statements that are in memory when called. |
| Pinhitratio | The number of pinhits divided by the number of pins. Pinhits are the number of times that objects the system is pinning are already in the cache. This ratio should be as close to 1 as possible. |

| | |
|---|---|
| Reloads | The number of library cache misses on an execution step. These are statements that were in memory at one time, but had to be reloaded when called. The ratio of reloads divided by the number of pins should be 0 percent. If greater than 1 percent, you should increase the size of the Shared Pool. |
| Invalidations | The number of times nonexistent library objects have been invalidated. |

**TIP**
*If the PINHITRATIO is less than .95 when the report is run for an extended period of time, the SHARED_POOL_SIZE is probably too small for your best system performance. If the reloads are greater than 1 percent, this also points to a SHARED_POOL_SIZE that is too small.*

# Database Statistics

This section contains all of the system-wide statistics. Only the statistics related to the largest performance issues will be covered. The following query is the one that is run by UTLESTAT for this section of the report:

```
select      n1.name "Statistic", n1.change "Total",
            round(n1.change/trans.change,2) "Per Transaction",
            round(n1.change/logs.change,2)  "Per Logon",
            round(n1.change/(to_number(to_char(end_time, 'J'))*60*60*24 -
            to_number(to_char(start_time, 'J'))*60*60*24 +
            to_number(to_char(end_time,   'SSSSS')) -
            to_number(to_char(start_time, 'SSSSS'))), 2) "Per Second"
from        stats$stats n1, stats$stats trans, stats$stats logs, stats$dates
where       trans.name='user commits'
and         logs.name='logons cumulative'
and         n1.change != 0
order by    n1.name;
```

**Example output (partial listing only):**

| Statistic | Total | Per Transaction | Per Logon | Per Second |
|---|---|---|---|---|
| CR blocks created | 7 | .58 | .03 | 0 |
| DBWR buffers scanned | 12954 | 1079.5 | 50.4 | 1.7 |
| DBWR free buffers found | 289 | | 24.08 | |
| buffer is not pinned count | 6435 | 536.25 | 25.04 | .84 |
| buffer is pinned count | 7005 | 583.75 | 27.26 | .92 |
| consistent gets | 8394 | 699.5 | 32.66 | 1.1 |

```
db block gets               16214     1351.17        63.09       2.13
free buffer inspected       467                       38.92
free buffer requested       2954      246.17         11.49       .39
physical reads              121       10.08           .47        .02
physical writes             1849      154.08          7.19       .24
session pga memory          43927668  3660639     170924.78    5764.03
session pga memory max      43927668  3660639     170924.78    5764.03
sorts (disk)                9         .75             .04        0
sorts (memory)              488       40.67           1.9        .06
sorts (rows)                11982     998.5          46.62       1.57
table fetch by rowid        1479      123.25          5.75       .19
table scan blocks gotten    1023      85.25           3.98       .13
table scan rows gotten      8061      671.75         31.37       1.06
table scans (long tables)   2         .17             .01        0
table scans (short tables)  382       31.83          1.49        .05

89 rows selected (only partial number of key rows are displayed)
```

consistent gets — The number of blocks accessed in the buffer cache for queries without the SELECT FOR UPDATE clause. The value for this statistic plus the value of the "db block gets" statistic constitute what is referred to as a logical read.

db block gets — The number of blocks in the buffer cache that were accessed for INSERT, UPDATE, DELETE, and SELECT for UPDATE statements.

dirty buffers inspected — This is the number of dirty (modified) data buffers that were aged out on the LRU list. A value here indicates that the DBWR is not keeping up. You may benefit by adding more DBWRs.

physical reads — The number of data blocks that were read from disks to satisfy a SELECT, SELECT FOR UPDATE, INSERT, UPDATE, or DELETE statements.

By adding the "consistent gets" and "db block gets," you get the number of logical reads (memory reads). Using the following equation, you can calculate the data cache hit ratio.

```
Hit Ratio = (Logical Reads - Physical Reads) / Logical Reads
```

**Database Statistics**

**TIP**
*The buffer hit ratio should be above 95 percent. If it is less than 95 percent, you should increase the size of the data cache by increasing the DB_BLOCK_BUFFERS parameter in the init.ora (given that physical memory is available to do this).*

**TIP**
*If the dirty buffers inspected is greater than 0, increase the init.ora parameter DB_WRITERS in Oracle7 or DBWR_IO_SLAVES in Oracle8.*

**V8 TIP**
*Lowering the init.ora parameter LOG_CHECKPOINT_ INTERVAL or making the redo log sizes smaller will also reduce dirty buffers (causing a write more often), but this action will hurt performance on large-volume INSERT, UPDATE, and DELETE operations. It may also cause these actions to error if the redo space is insufficient.*

| enqueue timeouts | The number of times that an enqueue lock was requested and one was not available. If this statistic is above 0, increasing the Enqueue_Resource parameter in the init.ora can help improve performance. |
|---|---|
| free buffer inspected | Indicates the number of buffers skipped in the buffer cache to find a free buffer. By dividing this statistic by the free buffer scans statistic, you can get an indication of if your data cache is too small. A high percentage is an indication of too many modified blocks in the data cache. |

**Database Statistics**

**Database Statistics**

**TIP**
*If the free buffers inspected divided by the free buffer scans is less than 1, the DB_BLOCK_BUFFERS parameter in the init.ora needs to be increased (given that physical memory is available to do this). Check the hit ratios described earlier in this chapter to be sure.*

| | |
|---|---|
| parse count | The number of times a SQL statement was parsed. |
| recursive calls | The number of recursive calls to the database. This type of call occurs for a few reasons—misses in the dictionary cache, dynamic storage extension, and when PL/SQL statements are executed. Generally, if the number of recursive classes is more than 4 per process, you should check the dictionary cache hit ratio, and look to see if there are tables or indexes with a large number of extents. Unless there is a significant use of PL/SQL, the ratio of recursive calls to user calls should be 10 percent or less. |
| redo buffer allocation retries | The number of attempts to allocate space in the redo buffer. A value other then 0 indicates that the redo writer is falling behind. This could be caused by log switches or checkpoints. By adjusting the LOG_CHECKPOINT_ INTERVAL and LOG_CHECKPOINT_ TIMEOUT parameters in the init.ora, you will be able to minimize the number of checkpoints. You can also increase the number of LGWR writers. These parameters are new in Oracle8 and are defined by the init.ora parameters LGWR_IO_SLAVES and ARCH_IO_SLAVES. |
| redo entries | The number of entries in the redo log buffer. |
| redo log space requests | The number of times a user process waited for a space in the redo log buffer. This statistic should be as close to 0 as possible. Increasing the size of the LOG_BUFFER parameter in the init.ora will help reduce this number. |
| redo size | The size in bytes of the amount of redo information that was written to the redo logs. This information can be used to help size the redo logs and the LOG_SMALL_ENTRY_ MAX_ SIZE parameter in the init.ora. |

redo small copies     The number of redo entries that were copied to the redo buffer using the redo allocation latch. By dividing this statistic by the number of redo entries, you will get the percentage of entries that used the allocation latch. This percentage should be less then 10 percent. If it is above 10 percent, try decreasing the size of the LOG_SMALL_ENTRY_MAX_SIZE parameter in the init.ora.

sorts (disk)     The number of sorts that were unable to be performed in memory and therefore required the creation of a temp segment in the temporary tablespace. This statistic divided by the sorts (memory) should not be above 5 percent. If it is, you should increase the SORT_AREA_SIZE parameter in the init.ora.

sorts (memory)     The number of sorts that were performed in memory.

sorts (rows)     The total number of rows that were sorted.

**TIP**

*The sorts (disk) statistic divided by the sorts (memory) should not be above 5 percent. If it is, you should increase the SORT_AREA_SIZE parameter in the init.ora (given that physical memory is available to do this). Remember that the memory allocated for SORT_AREA_SIZE is a per-user value that is outside the SGA.*

summed dirty queue length     This statistic is the sum of the buffers left in the write queue after every write request. Dividing this parameter by the "write requests" statistic will give you the average number of buffers left in the queue after the write.

table fetch by ROWID     Indicates the number of rows that were accessed by using a ROWID. This ROWID either came from an index or a 'where rowid = ' statement. A high number *usually* indicates a well-tuned application.

table fetch continued row     The number of rows that were fetched that were chained or migrated.

**TIP**
*If chained rows are indicated as before, the problem needs to be fixed as soon as possible. Chained rows can cause severe degradation to performance if there is a large number of rows that are chained. See Chapter 3 for tips on chaining.*

table scans (long tables)
The total number of full table scans on tables that have more than five data blocks. If the number of table scans per transaction is above 0, you may wish to review the application SQL statements to try and increase the use of indexes.

**TIP**
*If full table scans are being performed, serious performance issues may be prevalent and data hit ratios will be low. These tables need to be identified so that the appropriate indexes are created or used. See Chapters 8 and 9 on query tuning for more information.*

table scans (short tables)
The number of full table scans on tables with less than five data blocks. Full table scans on tables are preferred. Oracle can read the table with one I/O, whereas the use of an index would require an I/O to read the index and an I/O to read the table.

user calls
The number of times a call was made to the Oracle kernel. To calculate the number of calls to the kernel per parse divide this statistic by the "parse count" statistic.

## Dirty Buffer Write Queue

Dividing the summed dirty queue length statistic by the write requests statistic generates these statistics. A possible cause for this statistic to be high is having one or two data files that are extremely active. Having more modified blocks than can be written at once will require multiple I/Os; this causes blocks to wait in the queue to be written. Increasing the number of blocks that can be written simultaneously decreases the number of blocks that will have to wait in the queue. It is possible to decrease this statistic by increasing the DB_BLOCK_SIMULTANEOUS_WRITES parameter in the init.ora. The query here is the one that is run by UTLESTAT for this section of the report:

```
select     queue.change/writes.change "Average Write Queue Length"
from       stats$stats queue, stats$stats writes
where      queue.name  = 'summed dirty queue length'
and        writes.name = 'write requests';
```

**Example output:**

```
Average Write Queue Length
.160756501182033096927 1395
```

# System-Wide Wait Events

These events can also be viewed by querying the V$SYSTEM_EVENT view. There is also a V$SESSION_EVENT view that can be used to see events as they are occurring. There are two queries that are run by ESTAT. The first is the nonbackground system-wide waits and the second is the background (PMON, SMON…etc.) waits. The first query shown next is the one that is run by UTLESTAT to get the nonbackground waits and the second is for the background waits section of the report.

### Query for nonbackground waits:

```
select     n1.event "Event Name", n1.event_count "Count",
           n1.time_waited "Total Time",
           round(n1.time_waited/n1.event_count, 2) "Avg Time"
from       stats$event n1
where      n1.event_count > 0
order by   n1.time_waited desc;
```

### Example output (partial listing only):

| Event Name | Count | Total Time | Avg Time |
|---|---|---|---|
| SQL*Net break/reset to client | 68 | 0 | 0 |
| SQL*Net message from client | 875 | 0 | 0 |
| control file parallel write | 15 | 0 | 0 |
| control file sequential read | 42 | 0 | 0 |
| db file sequential read | 89 | 0 | 0 |
| direct path write | 8 | 0 | 0 |

### Query for background waits:

```
select     n1.event "Event Name", n1.event_count "Count",
           n1.time_waited "Total Time",
```

```
              round(n1.time_waited/n1.event_count, 2) "Avg Time"
from          stats$bck_event n1
where         n1.event_count > 0
order by      n1.time_waited desc;
```

**Example output (partial listing only):**

| Event Name | Count | Total Time | Avg Time |
|---|---|---|---|
| control file parallel write | 191 | 0 | 0 |
| control file sequential read | 98 | 0 | 0 |
| file open | 14 | 0 | 0 |
| latch free | 6 | 0 | 0 |
| pmon timer | 2532 | 0 | 0 |
| smon timer | 25 | 0 | 0 |

| | |
|---|---|
| Event name | The name of the event. |
| Count | The number of times the event occurred. |
| Total time | The total amount of time processes had to wait on the event. This time is in hundredths of a second. |
| Average time | The average time per event. This is also in hundredths of a second. |

Some of the events that will normally be here are the smon timer, pmon timer, client message, and rdbms ipc message. There are a few that you would hope not to find listed—the free buffer waits, buffer busy waits, and enqueue.

- The free buffer waits event is an indication that either the DBWR(s) could not keep up or you may need to adjust how often checkpoints are occurring.

- The buffer busy waits event indicates contention for a buffer in the SGA. You are able to get more information about this event by querying the V$SESSION_WAIT view. In this view, you will find the p1 and p2 columns. When the event is a buffer busy waits the p1 column will indicate the file ID of a segment and the p2 column will indicate the block ID causing the contention. Using these two IDs, you are able to query the DBA_EXTENTS view and get the name of the segment causing the contention. If the segment is a table or index, you may want to increase the INITRANS parameter to allow more transactions per data block.

**System-Wide Wait Events**

Note that this also increases the amount of storage space needed for the table.

- One other way to use the "buffer busy waits" event is to calculate the ratio to the number of logical reads. If the ratio is greater then 5 percent, you should review the V$WAITSTAT view to see what types of blocks are causing the contention.

```
(buffer busy waits / logical reads)  * 100 = busy rate
```

- An "enqueue" event can be an indication of a couple of things. There may be too many DDL locks or DML locks, or there could be an excessive use of sequences.

## Latches Willing to Wait

Processes that are trying to acquire these latches are willing to sleep if the latch is unavailable. By querying the V$LATCH view, you can see how many processes had to sleep, and the number of times they had to sleep. The following query is the one that is run by UTLESTAT for this section of the report.

```
select     name latch_name, gets, misses,
           round((gets-misses)/decode(gets,0,1,gets),3) hit_ratio,
           sleeps, round(sleeps/decode(misses,0,1,misses),3)
               "SLEEPS/MISS"
from       stats$latches
where      gets != 0
order by   name;
```

**Example output (partial listing only):**

| LATCH NAME | GETS | MISSES | HIT RATIO | SLEEPS | SLEEPS/MISS |
|---|---|---|---|---|---|
| cache buffer handles | 298 | 0 | 1 | 0 | 0 |
| cache buffers lru chain | 5755 | 0 | 1 | | |
| dml lock allocation | 1999 | 0 | 1 | 0 | 0 |
| library cache | 50013 | 0 | 1 | 0 | 0 |
| redo allocation | 14673 | 6 | 1 | 6 | 1 |
| session allocation | 2128 | 0 | 1 | 0 | 0 |
| shared pool | 10583 | 0 | 1 | 0 | 0 |

```
32 rows selected (only a partial number of key rows are displayed).
```

One thing to remember about processes that are sleeping: These processes may also be holding other latches that will not be released until the process is finished with them. This will cause even more processes to sleep, waiting for those latches. So, you can see how important it is to reduce contention as much as possible.

System-Wide Wait Events

| | |
|---|---|
| Latch_Name | The name of the latch. |
| Gets | The number of times a latch was requested and it was available. |
| Misses | The number of times a latch was initially requested but was not available. |
| Hit_Ratio | The ratio of gets to misses (gets - misses) / gets—this ratio should be as close to 1 as possible. |
| Sleeps | The number of processes that waited and then requested the latch again. The number of sleeps may be higher than the misses. Processes may sleep multiple times before obtaining the latch. |
| Sleeps/Misses | The ratio of sleeps to misses—sleeps / misses. A value higher than 1 indicates that there were processes that had to sleep more than once before acquiring the latch. |

Any of the latches that have a hit ratio below .99 should be looked at. Some of the more common latches on this list would be the redo allocation, redo copy, library cache, and the cache buffers lru.

**TIP**
*Latches are like locks on pieces of memory (or memory buffers). If the latch hit ratio is below 99 percent, there is a serious problem since not even the lock to get memory could be gotten.*

■ Contention for the redo allocation latch can be reduced, by decreasing the size of the LOG_SMALL_ENTRY_MAX_SIZE parameter. This parameter controls the maximum size of a redo entry that can be copied to the redo log using the redo allocation latch.

■ The number of redo copy latches is determined by the LOG_SIMULTANEOUS_COPIES parameter. Increasing this parameter helps to reduce contention for these latches.

■ Contention for the library cache latch occurs mostly when space is needed in the library cache. While space is being freed up in order to load a SQL or PL/SQL statement, the latch is being held exclusively and other users must wait. You can help to reduce contention by increasing the size of the Shared Pool or by pinning large SQL and PL/SQL statements in memory using the DBMS_SHARED_POOL.KEEP (see Chapter 10) procedure.

**TIP**
*Increasing the SPIN_COUNT and/or _LATCH_SPIN_
COUNT parameters can be set to increase the amount
of time a process will spend in the CPU trying to
acquire the latch before it sleeps. These two parameters
should not be increased if your application is already
bound by the CPU. In this case, you may wish to
decrease these parameters to cause processes to sleep
faster. This would help to free up some of the CPU
for other processes. Note that Oracle does not
recommend changes to the SPIN_COUNT, and the
_LATCH_SPIN_COUNT is an undocumented init.ora.
Consult with Oracle before changing these parameters.*

## Latches Not Willing to Wait

This type of latch does not wait for the latch to become available. They immediately
time out and retry to obtain the latch. These statistics are generated using the
immediate_gets and the immediate_misses columns of the V$LATCH view. The
query here is the one that is run by UTLESTAT for this section of the report:

```
select      name latch_name, immed_gets nowait_gets,
            immed_miss nowait_misses,
            round((immed_gets/immed_gets+immed_miss), 3) nowait_hit_ratio
from        stats$latches
where       immed_gets + immed_miss != 0
order by    name;
```

**Example output:**

| LATCH NAME | NOWAIT GETS | NOWAIT MISSES | NOWAIT HIT RATIO |
|---|---|---|---|
| cache buffers chains | 1168281 | 0 | 1 |
| cache buffers lru chain | 6124 | 0 | 1 |
| process allocation | 3 | 0 | 1 |

| | |
|---|---|
| Latch_Name | The name of the latch. |
| NoWait_Gets | The number of times an immediate request for a latch was made and it was available. |
| NoWait_Misses | The number of times immediate request for a latch was unsuccessful. |
| NoWait_Hit_Ratio | The ratio of nowait_misses to nowait_gets (nowait_gets – nowait_misses) / nowait_gets. This ratio should be as close to 1 as possible. |

**System-Wide Wait Events**

See the earlier section for some hints on ways to reduce contention for these latches. The hit ratio for these latches should also approach 1 and the misses should never fall below 1 percent misses.

## Buffer Busy Wait Statistics

The buffer busy wait statistics section of report.txt will show the class of buffer that is found to be busy when an attempt to access it is made. Only the class of the buffer is given, but you may access V$SESSION_WAIT to get the address of the actual block causing the problem. The following query is the one that is run by UTLESTAT for this section of the report:

```
select      *
from        stats$waitstat
where       count != 0
order by    count desc;

no rows selected.
```

Class The class of the latch. Possible classes of blocks are data block, sort block, save undo block, segment header, save undo header, free list, extent map, bitmap block, bitmap index block, unused, system undo header, system undo block, undo header and undo block. These can be seen by querying the full V$WAITSTAT view.

Count The number of times a request for a block was made and it was busy.

Time The amount of time waited.

If the value for buffer busy wait in the wait event statistics is high, this section will help you identify where the problem is. If this table identifies problems with undo header, you can add more rollback segments. If the contention is data block, you may need to increase the SGA. If there are segment header waits, you may need to add more freelists.

# Rollback Segments

These statistics are generated by using the V$ROLLSTAT view:

```
select      *
from        stats$roll;
```

**Example output:**

| UNDO_SEGMENT | TRANS_TBL_GETS | TRANS_TBL_WAITS | UNDO_BYTES_WRITTEN | SEGMENT_SIZE_BYTES | XACTS | SHRINKS | WRAPS |
|---|---|---|---|---|---|---|---|
| 0 | 2705 | 1 | 0 | 407552 | 0 | 0 | 0 |
| 2 | 78 | 0 | 13568 | 4554752 | 0 | 0 | 0 |
| 3 | 304 | 0 | 251186 | 4554752 | 0 | 0 | 6 |
| 4 | 395 | 0 | 81544 | 2455552 | 0 | 0 | 2 |
| 5 | 78 | 0 | 33286 | 663552 | 0 | 0 | 0 |
| 6 | 83 | 0 | 12146 | 1585152 | 0 | 0 | 1 |
| 7 | 94 | 0 | 58890 | 2301952 | 0 | 0 | 1 |

7 rows selected.

| Undo_Segment | Rollback segment number |
|---|---|
| Trans_Tbl_Gets | The number of requests for a segment header in the rollback segment |
| Trans_Tbl_Waits | The number of requests that had to wait |
| Undo_Bytes_Written | The total number of bytes written to this rollback segment |
| Segment_Size_Bytes | The current size of the rollback segment |
| Xacts | The current number of active transactions in the rollback segment |
| Shrinks | The number of times the rollback segment eliminated one or more extents because it was larger than the optimal size |
| Wraps | The number of times the rollback segment wrapped from one extent to another |

- The optimal size of the rollbacks should be set to a value that will help keep the number of shrinks down but does not waste a lot of disk space.

- The ratio of trans_tbl_waits to trans_tbl_gets should be less then 5 percent. If it is above 5 percent, you should increase the number of rollback segments ((trans_tbl_waits / trans_tbl_gets) * 100).

**Rollback Segments**

**TIP**

*If the number of "shrinks" of the rollback segment is greater than 1 per rollback segment per day, the optimal size is set too low. Shrinks to a rollback segment take resources, and an inordinate amount of shrinks implies rollback segments that are too small.*

## Nondefault init.ora Parameters

These are the parameters in the init.ora that are set to a value other than the default. The list is generated by querying the V$PARAMETER view where the default column is equal to FALSE. This list can be used as a reference. While you are tuning the database, these parameters can provide a record of how the database performed with certain values. The following query is the one that is run by UTLESTAT for this section of the report:

```
select      name, value
from        v$parameter
where       isdefault = 'FALSE'
order by    name;
```

**Example output:**

```
NAME                VALUE
db_block_size       8192
db_files            1024
nls_date_format     DD-MON-RR
shared_pool_size    100000000
db_block_buffers    12000

19 rows selected.
```

One drawback is that the parameters that begin with an '_' will not be displayed in this list. You need to query the x$ksppi table to get these parameters. Select the ksppinm and ksppivl columns where the ksppidf is equal to FALSE.

**TIP**

*See Chapter 15 and Appendix C for more information on querying x$ksppi and the undocumented init.ora parameters. See Appendix A for a complete listing of all documented init.ora parameters.*

# The Dictionary Cache

This section contains all of the data dictionary information. This data pertains to all of the objects in the database. This information is accessed for every SQL that gets parsed and again when the statement is executed. The activity in this area can be very heavy. Maintaining a good hit ratio is very important to prevent recursive calls back to the database to verify privileges. You can evaluate the efficiency of the dictionary cache by querying the V$ROWCACHE view. The following query is the one that is run by UTLESTAT for this section of the report:

```
select      *
from        stats$dc
where       get_reqs != 0
or          scan_reqs != 0
or          mod_reqs != 0;
```

**Example output:**

| NAME | GET_REQS | GET_MISS | SCAN_REQS | SCAN_MISS | MOD_REQS | COUNT | CUR_USAGE |
|---|---|---|---|---|---|---|---|
| dc_tablespaces | 1324 | 0 | 0 | 0 | 0 | 8 | 5 |
| dc_free_extents | 731 | 171 | 79 | 0 | 432 | 54 | 14 |
| dc_segments | 308 | 20 | 0 | 0 | 154 | 107 | 65 |
| dc_rollback_segments | 900 | 0 | 0 | 0 | 0 | 24 | 19 |
| dc_used_extents | 194 | 80 | 0 | 0 | 169 | 70 | 38 |
| dc_tablespace_quotas | 47 | 0 | 0 | 0 | 39 | 2 | 1 |
| dc_users | 171 | 0 | 0 | 0 | 0 | 14 | 13 |
| dc_user_grants | 120 | 0 | 0 | 0 | 0 | 30 | 12 |
| dc_objects | 586 | 34 | 0 | 0 | 41 | 284 | 254 |
| dc_synonyms | 36 | 4 | 0 | 0 | 0 | 23 | 20 |
| dc_usernames | 64 | 0 | 0 | 0 | 0 | 21 | 5 |
| dc_object_ids | 165 | 11 | 0 | 0 | 8 | 154 | 128 |
| dc_profiles | 3 | 0 | 0 | 0 | 0 | 2 | 1 |
| dc_histogram_defs | 9 | 0 | 25 | 0 | 0 | 13 | 8 |

```
14 rows selected.
```

| | |
|---|---|
| Name | Name of the cache area |
| Get_Reqs | Total number of requests for an object |
| Get_Miss | The total number of times an object was requested and it was not in the cache |
| Scan_Reqs | The total number of times the cache was scanned for an object |
| Scan_Miss | The total number of times the cache was scanned for an object and it was not found |

| | |
|---|---|
| Mod_Reqs | The total number of INSERTs, UPDATEs, and DELETEs to the cache area |
| Count | The total number of entries in the cache area |
| Cur_Usage | The total number of cache entries that contain valid data |

There are a couple of ways to calculate the hit ratio for the dictionary cache. First, you can calculate the hit ratio for the individual cache areas, and second, you can calculate the hit ratio for the entire dictionary cache. The following query can be used to calculate the hit ratio of the dictionary row cache:

```
select      sum(gets), sum(getmisses),
            (1 - (sum(getmisses) / (sum(gets) )))
            * 100 HitRate
from        v$rowcache;
```

Example output:

```
SUM(GETS)    SUM(GETMISSES)      Hit Ratio
10233        508                 95.270459
```

**TIP**

*Measure hit ratios for the rowcache of the Shared Pool with V$ROWCACHE. A hit ratio of over 95 percent should be achieved. However, when the database is initially started, hit ratios will be around 85 percent. If the hit ratio is less than 95 percent after the database has been running over the course of a day, then SHARED_POOL_SIZE may be too small for your best system performance.*

# Tablespace I/O

This part of the report sums the I/O by tablespace. There are a couple of parameters that can be set in the init.ora that can help to improve the read and write time. These are the DB_FILE_MULTIBLOCK_READ_COUNT and DB_FILE_SIMULTANEOUS_WRITES parameters. The following query is the one that is run by UTLESTAT for this section of the report:

```
select        table_space||'        ' table_space,
           sum(phys_reads) reads,  sum(phys_blks_rd) blks_read,
           sum(phys_rd_time) read_time,  sum(phys_writes) writes,
           sum(phys_blks_wr) blks_wrt,
           sum(phys_wrt_tim) write_time,
           sum(megabytes_size) megabytes
from        stats$files
group by    table_space
order by    table_space;
```

### Example output (simplified partial listing only):

| TABLE SPACE | READS | BLKS READ | READ TIME | WRITES | BLKS WRT | WRITE TIME | MEGABYTES RB DATA |
|---|---|---|---|---|---|---|---|
| SYSTEM | 79 | 99 | 0 | 298 | 298 | 0 | 31 |
| TEMPORARY_DATA | 0 | 0 | 0 | 724 | 724 | 0 | 2 |
| USER_DATA | 18 | 22 | 0 | 334 | 338 | 0 | 8 |

The DB_FILE_MULTIBLOCK_READ_COUNT parameter controls the number of blocks that can be read in one I/O when a full table scan is being performed. This can reduce the number of I/Os needed to scan a table, thus improving the performance of the full table scan. The DB_FILE_SIMULTANEOUS_WRITES controls the number of data blocks in a data file that can be written to simultaneously. This helps to reduce the number of I/Os required to write the data blocks back to the disk after they have been modified.

| | |
|---|---|
| Table_Space | The name of the tablespace. |
| phys_reads | The number of physical reads that were performed on the data file to retrieve data. |
| phys_blks_rd | The number of blocks that were read from the data file to satisfy all of the reads. |
| phys_rd_time | The total amount of time it took to read all of the blocks from the data file. This time is in hundredths of a second. (If this value is 0, it is because the timed_statistics parameter in the init.ora is set to FALSE or not set at all; the default is FALSE.) |
| phys_writes | The number of writes to the data file. |
| phys_blks_wrt | The number of blocks written. |

phys_wrt_tim              The total amount of time it took to write all of the blocks to the data file. This time is in hundredths of a second. (If this value is 0, it is because the timed_statistics parameter in the init.ora is set to FALSE or not set at all; the default is FALSE.)

If the number of physical block reads is significantly higher than the number of physical reads, this is an indication that the indexes on these tables may need to be reviewed, or there may be full table scans being performed on the tables within the tablespace. In general, if the number of block reads is equal to the number of reads, the tables in the tablespace were more than likely being accessed by a ROWID, requiring the database to read only one data block. See Chapter 3 for more information on tuning I/O.

# Data File I/O

This is a very granular look at how the I/O is being distributed across the data files. If one of the data files is getting a majority of the reads and writes, you may be able to improve performance by creating multiple data files on separate disks or by striping the data file across multiple disks. The following query is the one that is run by UTLESTAT for this section of the report:

```
select       table_space, file_name, phys_reads reads,
             phys_blks_rd blks_read, phys_rd_time read_time,
             phys_writes writes, phys_blks_wr blks_wrt,
             phys_wrt_tim write_time, megabytes_size megabytes
from         stats$files
order by     table_space, file_name;
```

**Example output (simplified partial listing only):**

| TABLE SPACE | FILE NAME | READS | BLKS READ | READ TIME | WRITES | BLKS WRT | WRITE TIME | MEGABYTES |
|---|---|---|---|---|---|---|---|---|
| ROLLBACK_DATA | C:\ORAWIN95\DATABASE\RBS1ORCL.ORA | 0 | 0 | 0 | 495 | 495 | 0 | 16 |
| SYSTEM | C:\ORAWIN95\DATABASE\SYS1ORCL.ORA | 79 | 99 | 0 | 298 | 298 | 0 | 31 |
| TEMPORARY_DATA | C:\ORAWIN95\DATABASE\TMP1ORCL.ORA | 0 | 0 | 0 | 724 | 724 | 0 | 2 |
| USER_DATA | C:\ORAWIN95\DATABASE\USR1ORCL.ORA | 10 | 12 | 0 | 232 | 208 | 0 | 6 |
| USER_DATA | C:\ORAWIN95\DATABASE\USR2ORCL.ORA | 8 | 10 | 0 | 102 | 130 | 0 | 2 |

table_space              The name of the tablespace that owns the data file.

file_name                The name of the data file.

phys_reads               The number of physical reads that were performed on the data file to retrieve data.

| phys_blks_rd | The number of blocks that were read from the data file to satisfy all of the reads. |
|---|---|
| phys_rd_time | The total amount of time it took to read all of the blocks from the data file. This time is in hundredths of a second. (If this value is 0, it is because the TIMED_STATISTICS parameter in the init.ora is set to FALSE or not set at all; the default is FALSE.) |
| phys_writes | The number of writes to the data file. |
| phys_blks_wrt | The number of blocks written. |
| phys_wrt_time | The total amount of time it took to write all of the blocks to the data file. This time is in hundredths of a second. (If this value is 0, it is because the TIMED_STATISTICS parameter in the init.ora is set to FALSE or not set at all; the default is FALSE.) |

**TIP**
*If the number of physical reads is heavier on one physical disk, proper balancing of data will probably increase performance. See Chapter 3 for tips on fixing I/O problems with either data files or tablespaces.*

# Date/Time

This section of the report lists the date and time the report was started and when it is finished. By running the report at peak times, the optimal use of this report can be achieved. The following query is the one that is run by UTLESTAT for this section of the report:

```
select      to_char(start_time, 'dd-mon-yy hh24:mi:ss') start_time,
            to_char(end_time,   'dd-mon-yy hh24:mi:ss') end_time
from        stats$dates;
```

**Example output:**

```
START TIME           END TIME
12-oct-98 23:24:34   13-oct-98 01:31:35
```

Date/Time

>  **TIP**
> *You may execute UTLESTAT multiple times to generate a new report without rerunning UTLBSTAT. So, you can run UTLBSTAT at the beginning of the day and then run UTLESTAT every hour to get an hourly report that will have statistics since the beginning of the day. You could also run both UTLBSTAT and UTLESTAT every hour to get only an hourly picture for each portion of the day. The report start time and statistics are not reset until UTLBSTAT is executed again.*

## Oracle Versions from the V$VERSION View

The last section of the report shows all of the products and versions that you are running. The following query is the one that is run by UTLESTAT for this section of the report:

```
select    *
from      v$version;
```

**Example output (partial listing):**

```
BANNER
Oracle8 Release 8.0.3.0.0 - Production
PL/SQL Release 8.0.3.0.0 - Production
CORE Version 4.0.3.0.0 - Production
```

## Summary Listing of Sections That Are Created

These reports, although listed separately here, are dumped into a single file called report.txt (which also includes hints for interpreting the output). The format of this file leaves a lot to be desired.

| | |
|---|---|
| Library report | This section contains a list of library cache statistics. |
| Database statistics | This section contains data on every aspect of the database. |
| Dirty buffer write queue | Shows if you have more blocks than can be written at once. |

| | |
|---|---|
| Event report | This section contains data on system-wide wait events. |
| Latch statistics reports | These two sections show latch use and contention. |
| Waits report | This section shows the class of the block being waited on. |
| Rollback segment report | This section monitors rollback segment use. |
| Changed init.ora report | This section shows init.ora parameters that have been changed. |
| Dictionary cache report | This section shows data dictionary usage and hit ratios. |
| Tablespace I/O report | This section shows contention for tablespaces. |
| Data File I/O Report | This section shows contention for data files. |
| Date/Time report | This section shows the beginning and ending time for the monitoring. |
| Version report | This section shows the versions of all products for the database. |

# Tips Review

- The UTLBSTAT.sql and UTLESTAT.sql can be found in your Oracle Home directory under the rdbms/admin subdirectory. UTLESTAT will generate a report called report.txt (in your working directory) that should be reviewed for database changes.

- Wait until the database has stabilized before running UTLBSTAT (the start of statistics gathering) or the results may be erroneously affected by the database startup process.

- Run UTLBSTAT.sql and UTLESTAT.sql at problem performance times for your system so that the results can be used to measure system problems at the worst possible time.

- The SYS user owns the tables that are populated. You may write your own reports to these tables if you have privileges to the SYS user account.

- If the database happens to go down at any time between the start and end of the report, the report will contain meaningless data and should be ignored.

■ If the PINHITRATIO is less than .95 when the report is run for an extended period of time, the SHARED_POOL_SIZE is probably too small for your best system performance. If the reloads are greater than 1 percent, this also points to a SHARED_POOL_SIZE that is too small.

■ The buffer hit ratio should be above 95. If it is less than 95 percent, you should increase the size of the data cache by increasing the DB_BLOCK_BUFFERS parameter in the init.ora (given that physical memory is available to do this).

■ If the number of dirty buffers inspected is greater than 0, increase the init.ora parameter DB_WRITERS in Oracle7 or DBWR_IO_SLAVES in Oracle8.

■ In V8, lowering the init.ora parameter Log_Checkpoint_Interval or making the redo log sizes smaller will also reduce dirty buffers (causing a write more often), but this action will hurt performance on large volume INSERT, UPDATE, and DELETE actions. It may also cause these actions to error if the redo space is insufficient.

■ If the free buffers inspected divided by the free buffer scans are less than 1, the DB_BLOCK_BUFFERS parameter in the init.ora needs to be increased (given that physical memory is available to do this). Check the buffer hit ratios described earlier in this chapter to be sure.

■ The "sorts (disk)" statistic divided by the "sorts (memory)" should not be above 5 percent. If it is, you should consider increasing the SORT_AREA_SIZE parameter in the init.ora (given that physical memory is available to do this). Remember: The memory allocated for SORT_AREA_SIZE is a per-user value that is *outside* the SGA.

■ If chained rows are indicated, the problem needs to be fixed as soon as possible. Chained rows can cause severe degradation to performance if there is a large number of rows that are chained. See Chapter 3 for tips on chaining.

■ If full table scans are being performed, serious performance issues may result and data hit ratios will be distorted. These tables need to be identified so that the appropriate indexes are created or used. See Chapters 8 and 9 on query tuning for more information.

■ Latches are like locks on pieces of memory (or memory buffers). If the latch-hit ratio is below 99 percent, there is a serious problem since not even the lock to get memory could be gotten.

**Tips Review**

- If the number of "shrinks" of the rollback segment is greater than 2-5 per rollback segment per day, the optimal size is set too low.

- Measure hit ratios for the row cache of the Shared Pool with the V$ROWCACHE view. A hit ratio of over 95 percent should be achieved. However, when the database is initially started, hit ratios will be around 85 percent. If the hit ratio is less than 95 percent after the database has been running over the course of a day, SHARED_POOL_SIZE may be too small for your best system performance.

- If the number of physical reads is heavier on one physical disk, then proper balancing of data will probably increase performance. See Chapter 3 for tips on fixing I/O problems with either data files or tablespaces.

- You may execute UTLESTAT multiple times to generate a new report without rerunning UTLBSTAT. The report start time and statistics are *not* reset until UTLBSTAT is executed again.

# References

Many thanks to Greg Pucka and Burk Sherva of TUSC for contributions to this chapter.

Tips Review

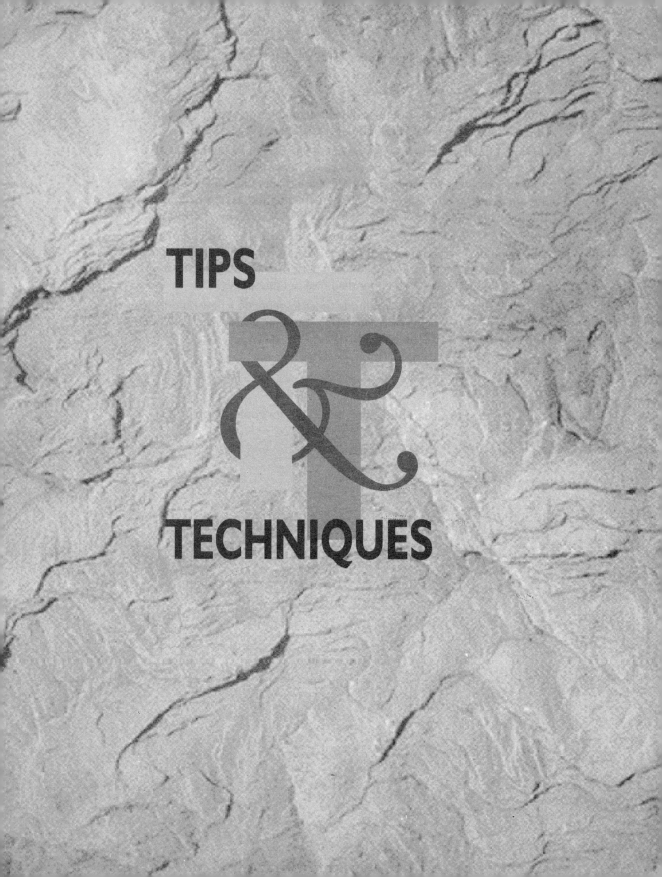

TIPS
& T
TECHNIQUES

# CHAPTER

## 17

## Performing a Quick System Review (DBA)

O ne of the key approaches to achieving a focus toward improving and maintaining excellent system performance requires a system review on an annual basis. This could be an internal or external review of your system performance. Many companies have come up with methods of measuring system performance and overall system speed. This chapter will not be the six-month process that many propose, but will serve as a simple barometer of how your system rates compared to others in the industry. Variations in your business processes may cause your score to be slightly higher or lower using this simple review. Tips covered in this chapter include the following:

- The Total Performance Index (TPI) and reasons why you should use it
- How to get your Memory Performance Index (MPI)
- How to get your Disk Performance Index (DPI)
- How to get your Education Performance Index (EPI)
- How to get your System Performance Index (SPI)
- How to get your Total Performance Index (TPI)
- An overall system review example template
- The immediate action items list
- Gathering the system information list
- Rating the DBA by an impartial expert
- The remote DBA and building a GUI interface for intuitive representations

## Total Performance Index (TPI)

TUSC invented the Total Performance Index (TPI) to help Oracle DBAs measure their system with other systems, using a quick and simple scoring method. Many systems differ in categories based on their business case, but this system tells you how close or far your system is from others in the industry. There are four categories: memory, disk, knowledge (education), and overall system. This chapter will show how you can measure your TPI using several simple queries. For detailed information on a particular category, please refer to the chapter in this book related to that issue. To help identify how your system is progressing, use your TPI to compare future growth in the number of users or changes in hardware and software.

| Category Index | Maximum Score |
| --- | --- |
| Memory Performance Index (MPI) | 250 |
| Disk Performance Index (DPI) | 250 |

| Category Index | Maximum Score |
|---|---|
| Education Performance Index (EPI) | 250 |
| System Performance Index (SPI) | 250 |
| **Total Performance Index (TPI)** | **1000** |

# Memory Performance Index (MPI)

This section measures memory use and allocation. The following table illustrates how to receive a perfect MPI score. This rating system is not meant to be an all-encompassing benchmark of memory use and allocation; rather, it is a barometer to see if memory use and allocation improvements could be beneficial.

| Category | Level Required | Maximum Score |
|---|---|---|
| Buffer hit ratio | > 98 percent | 30 |
| Dictionary hit ratio | > 98 percent | 30 |
| Library hit ratio | > 98 percent | 30 |
| Sorts in memory | > 98 percent | 30 |
| Buffers in x$bh at state=0 | 10-25 percent | 30 |
| Shared pool buffers contiguous | 10-25 percent | 30 |
| Top 10 statements memory use | < 5 percent | 30 |
| Top 25 (worst memory) statements tuned | Yes | 30 |
| Pin/cache frequently used objects | Yes | 10 |
| **Memory Performance Index (MPI)** | **Section Total** | **250** |

# Buffer Hit Ratio

The buffer hit ratio displays the percentage of data memory hits versus disk reads.

**Query for buffer hit ratio:**

```
select    (1 - (sum(decode(name, 'physical reads',value,0)) /
          (sum(decode(name, 'db block gets',value,0)) +
```

**Buffer Hit Ratio**

```
          sum(decode(name, 'consistent gets',value,0))))) * 100
          "Hit Ratio"
from      v$sysstat;
```

**Sample output:**

```
Hit Ratio
99.08%
```

**Rate your system:**

| What is your buffer hit ratio? | Points | Score |
|---|---|---|
| < 90% | 0 | |
| 90–94% | 10 | |
| 95–98% | 20 | |
| > 98% | 30 | **30** |

**Alternate query for buffer hit ratio (includes the rating):**

You can also expand the previous query to include the actual ratings in your result. The following query shows how this is accomplished using the DECODE function. You can also apply this to the remainder of the queries in this chapter if you would like the score in your results. At TUSC, we use a PL/SQL procedure to accomplish the results (we also display them graphically).

```
select   (1 - (sum(decode(name, 'physical reads',value,0)) /
         (sum(decode(name, 'db block gets',value,0)) +
         sum(decode(name, 'consistent gets',value,0))))) * 100 "Hit Ratio",
         decode(sign((1-(sum(decode(name, 'physical reads',value,0)) /
         (sum(decode(name, 'db block gets',value,0)) +
         sum(decode(name, 'consistent gets',value,0))))) * 100 - 98,1,30
         decode(sign((1-(sum(decode(name, 'physical reads',value,0)) /
         (sum(decode(name, 'db block gets',value,0)) +
         sum(decode(name, 'consistent gets',value,0))))) * 100 - 95,1,20
         decode(sign((1-(sum(decode(name, 'physical reads',value,0)) /
         (sum(decode(name, 'db block gets',value,0)) +
         sum(decode(name, 'consistent gets',value,0))))) * 100 - 90,1,10,0)))
         "Score"
from     v$sysstat;
```

**Sample output:**

```
Hit Ratio      Score
99.08%           30
```

# Dictionary Cache Hit Ratio

The dictionary hit ratio displays the percentage of memory reads for the data dictionary and other objects.

**Query for dictionary hit ratio:**

```
select     (1-(sum(getmisses)/sum(gets))) * 100 "Hit Ratio"
from       v$rowcache;
```

**Sample output:**

```
Hit Ratio
95.40%
```

**Rate your system:**

| What is your dictionary cache hit ratio? | Points | Score |
|---|---|---|
| < 85% | 0 | |
| 86–92% | 10 | |
| 92–98% | 20 | |
| > 98% | 30 | **20** |

# Library Cache Hit Ratio

The library cache hit ratio reveals the percentage of memory reads for actual statements and PL/SQL objects.

**Query for library hit ratio:**

```
select     Sum(Pins) / (Sum(Pins) + Sum(Reloads)) * 100  "Hit Ratio"
from       V$LibraryCache;
```

**Sample output:**

```
Hit Ratio
99.40%
```

**Rate your system:**

| What is your library cache hit ratio? | Points | Score |
|---|---|---|
| < 90% | 0 | |
| 90–95% | 10 | |
| 95–98% | 20 | |
| > 98% | 30 | **30** |

# Sorting in Memory Hit Ratio

Based on the value of the init.ora SORT_AREA_SIZE, user sorts may fit into memory or be performed on disk in a specified temporary tablespace.

## Query for Sort Hit Ratio

You can receive specific sorting statistics (memory, disk, and rows) by running the following queries, or go to the UTLESTAT.sql output file (report.txt) to receive these statistics (see Chapter 16 for more information on UTLBSTAT).

**Query to get memory and disk sorts:**

```
select    a.value "Disk Sorts", b.value "Memory Sorts",
          round(100*b.value)/decode((a.value+b.value),0,1,(a.value+b.value)),2)
          "Pct Memory Sorts"
from      v$sysstat a, v$sysstat b
where     a.name = 'sorts (disk)'
and       b.name = 'sorts (memory)';
```

**Sample output:**

| Disk Sorts | Memory Sorts | Pct Memory Sorts |
|---|---|---|
| 16 | 66977 | 99.98 |

**Rate your system:**

| What percent of sorts are performed in memory? | Points | Score |
|---|---|---|
| < 90% | 0 | |
| 90–94% | 10 | |

| What percent of sorts are performed in memory? | Points | Score |
|---|---|---|
| 95–98% | 20 | |
| > 98% | 30 | **30** |

# Percent of Data Buffers Still Free

When you start the Oracle database at the beginning of the day, users start using memory for their queries. Although this memory is reusable when the user's query is complete, when the following query runs on a system after 2 hours of processing, it is a good indication of how quickly the buffers are being used up. Also note that you have to run this query as SYS.

**Query for free data buffers:**

```
select    decode(state,0, 'FREE',
          1,decode(1rba_seq,0,'AVAILABLE','BEING USED'),
          3, 'BEING USED', state) "BLOCK STATUS",
          count(*)
from      x$bh
group by decode(state,0,'FREE',1,decode(1rba_seq,0,'AVAILABLE',
          'BEING USED'),3, 'BEING USED', state);
```

**Sample output (see Chapter 15 for more information):**

| BLOCK STATUS | COUNT(*) |
|---|---|
| AVAILABLE | 7790 |
| BEING USED | 1540 |
| FREE | 1670 |

**Rate your system:**

| What percent of buffers in x$bh are at a state=0 (free) after two hours of running in production? | Points | Score |
|---|---|---|
| < 5% | 0 | |
| 5–10% | 10 | |
| 10–25% | 30 | |
| > 25% | 20 | **30** |

Note that the reason that you only get 20 points for greater than 25 percent free is because the data buffers are probably oversized and potentially wasting memory. The scoring should be tailored to your individual system use. Remember that this is only a general guideline.

## Shared Pool Still Contiguous

As statements and packages are accessed and loaded into memory, the Shared Pool becomes used and the pieces of memory available for reuse become fragmented. When the following query runs on a system after about more hours of processing, it is a good indication of how quickly the Shared Pool is being used. See Chapter 15 for information about this query (you have to run this query as SYS).

**Query for Shared Pool memory:**

```
select    sum(ksmchsiz) Bytes, ksmchcls Status
from      x$ksmsp
group by ksmchcls;
```

**Sample output (see Chapter 15 for more information):**

```
BYTES         STATUS
5,000,000     R-free
40            R-freea
60,932,132    free
824,596       freeabl
34,117,560    perm
352,084       recr

Percent Free = ((free+perm)/(Rfree+Rfreea+free+freeabl+
               perm+recr))*100
Percent Free = 93.90%
```

**Rate your system:**

| What percent of shared pool memory is available and contiguous after four hours in production? | Points | Score |
|---|---|---|
| < 5% | 0 | |
| 5–10% | 10 | |
| 10–25% | 30 | |
| > 25% | 20 | **20** |

Note that the reason that you only get 20 points for greater than 25 percent free is because the Shared Pool is probably oversized and potentially wasting memory. The scoring should be tailored to your individual system use. Remember that this is only a general guideline.

# Top 10 "Memory Abusers" as a Percent of All Statements

I have found that the top 10 statements accessed on most systems when left untuned, make up over 50 percent of all memory reads of the entire system. This section measures how severe the most harmful statements are, as a percentage of the entire system.

**Script to retrieve this percentage:**

```
set serverout on
DECLARE
 CURSOR c1 is
  select    buffer_gets
  from      v$sqlarea
  order by buffer_gets DESC;
 CURSOR c2 is
  select    sum(buffer_gets)
  from      v$sqlarea;

 sumof10 NUMBER:=0;
 mybg NUMBER;
 mytotbg NUMBER;

BEGIN
 dbms_output.put_line('Percent');
 dbms_output.put_line('-------');
 OPEN c1;
 FOR i IN 1..10 LOOP
  FETCH c1 INTO mybg;
  sumof10 := sumof10 + mybg;
 END
 LOOP;
 CLOSE c1;
 OPEN c2;
 FETCH c2 INTO mytotbg;
 CLOSE c2;
 dbms_output.put_line(sumof10/mytotbg*100);
END;
/
```

**Sample output:**

```
Percent
7.1415926
```

**Rate your system:**

| Take your top 10 memory read statements in the V$SQLAREA view. What percent are they of all memory reads? | Points | Score |
| --- | --- | --- |
| > 25% | 0 | |
| 20–25% | 10 | |
| 10–19% | 20 | |
| < 5% | 30 | **30** |

## Top 25 "Memory Abusers" Statements Tuned

I have found that the top 25 statements accessed on most systems when left untuned make up over 75 percent of all memory reads of the entire system. The following code rates and illustrates how to find the greatest 25 memory abusers.

**Query to get the 25 worst memory abusers:**

```
set serverout on size 1000000
DECLARE
 top25 number;
 text1 varchar2(4000);
 x number;
 len1 number;
CURSOR c1 is
   select buffer_gets, substr(sql_text,1,4000)
   from v$sqlarea
   order by buffer_gets desc;
BEGIN
 dbms_output.put_line('Gets'||'    '||'Text');
 dbms_output.put_line('----------'||'  '||'----------------------');
 OPEN c1;
 for i in 1..25 loop
   fetch c1 into top25, text1;
```

**Top Memory Abusers**

```
  dbms_output.put_line(rpad(to_char(top25),9)||'
'||substr(text1,1,66));
  len1:=length(text1);
  x:=66;
  while len1 > x-1 loop
    dbms_output.put_line('"            '||substr(text1,x,66));
  x:=x+66;
  end loop;
 end loop;
end;
/
```

**Sample partial output:**

```
SQL> @pl4

Gets       Text
16409      select f.file#, f.block#, f.ts#, f.length from fet$ f, ts$ t where
"          e t.ts#=f.ts# and t.dflextpct!=0
6868       select job from sys.job$  where next_date < sysdate  order by next
"          t_date, job
6487       SELECT BUFFER_GETS,SUBSTR(SQL_TEXT,1,3500)    FROM V$SQLAREA ORDER
"              BY BUFFER_GETS DESC
3450       SELECT BUFFER_GETS,SUBSTR(SQL_TEXT,1,4000)    FROM V$SQLAREA ORDER
"              BY BUFFER_GETS DESC
(...Simplistic Partial Listing Displayed)
```

**Rate your system:**

| How many of your top 25 memory statements in the V$SQLAREA view have you attempted to tune? | Points | Score |
|---|---|---|
| 0 | 0 | |
| 1–5 | 10 | |
| 6–15 | 20 | |
| 16–25 | 30 | **30** |

# Pinning/Caching Objects

Objects can be pinned into memory if they are often-used objects, as shown in Chapter 10. Tables can also be pinned into memory by caching the table when it is created, or by using the ALTER command to cache a table. See Chapter 7 for more information on caching tables.

Pinning/Caching Objects

**Rate your system:**

| Do you pin PL/SQL objects or cache tables when needed? | Points | Score |
|---|---|---|
| Yes/No Need | 10 | |
| No | 0 | **10** |

| **Total of all MPI sections:** | | |
|---|---|---|
| Example Memory Performance Index (MPI) | **Total Score** | **230 (A)** |

**Grade your system:**

| MPI Grade | Comments | Score |
|---|---|---|
| A+ | Top 10 percent of most systems | > 230 |
| A | Top 20 percent of most systems | 200–230 |
| B | Top 40 percent of most systems | 160–199 |
| C | Top 70 percent of most systems | 100–159 |
| Needs help now | Bottom 30 percent of most systems | < 100 |

**TIP**

*Measuring your MPI (Memory Performance Index) can be helpful in identifying potential memory allocation and usage improvements that could be beneficial.*

# Disk Performance Index (DPI)

This section measures disk use. The following table illustrates how to receive a perfect DPI score. This rating system is not meant to be an all-encompassing benchmark of disk use; rather, it is a barometer to see if disk use improvements could be beneficial.

| Category | Level Required | Maximum Score |
|---|---|---|
| Top 25 (worst disk) statements tuned | Yes | 30 |
| Top 10 statements disk use | < 5 percent | 30 |
| Tables/indexes collocated | No | 30 |
| Mission-critical tables with chaining | No | 30 |
| redo logs/rollbacks/Data Separated | Yes | 30 |
| Disks used for rollback segments | > 4 | 30 |
| Disks used for temporary tablespaces | > 2 | 30 |
| Number of tables fragmented > 5 extents | 10 or fewer | 20 |
| Number of tables fragmented > 30 extents | 2 or fewer | 20 |
| **Disk Performance Index (DPI)** | **Section Total** | **250** |

# Top 25 "Disk-Read Abuser" Statements Tuned

I have found that the top 25 statements accessed on most systems when left untuned make up over 75 percent of all memory reads of the entire system when left untuned. This section measures how severe the most harmful statements are as a percentage of the entire system. The following example shows a tuned system where only data dictionary queries show up.

**Query to get the 25 worst disk-read abusers:**

```
set serverout on size 1000000
DECLARE
 top25 number;
 text1 varchar2(4000);
 x number;
 len1 number;
CURSOR c1 is
  select disk_reads, substr(sql_text,1,4000)
  from   v$sqlarea
  order  by disk_reads desc;
BEGIN
 dbms_output.put_line('Reads'||'    '||'Text');
```

```
dbms_output.put_line('----------'||' '||'---------------------');
OPEN c1;
for i in 1..25 loop
  fetch c1 into top25, text1;
  dbms_output.put_line(rpad(to_char(top25),9)||' '||substr
    (text1,1,66));
  len1:=length(text1);
  x:=66;
  while len1 > x-1 loop
    dbms_output.put_line('"            '||substr(text1,x,66));
  x:=x+66;
  END LOOP;
 END LOOP;
END;
/
```

**Sample partial output:**

```
Reads    Text
1156       select file#, block#, ts# from seg$ where type# = 3
122        select distinct d.p_obj#,d.p_timestamp from sys.dependency$ d, obj
"          j$ o where d.p_obj#>=:1 and d.d_obj#=o.obj# and o.status!=5
111        BEGIN sys.dbms_ijob.remove(:job); END;
(...Simplistic Partial Listing Displayed)
```

**Rate your system:**

| How many of your top 25 disk read statements in the V$SQLAREA view have you attempted to tune? | Points | Score |
|---|---|---|
| 0 | 0 | |
| 1–5 | 10 | |
| 6–15 | 20 | |
| 16–25 | 30 | **30** |

# Top 10 Disk-Read Abusers as Percent of All Statements

I have found that the top 10–25 statements accessed on most systems when left untuned make up over 75 percent of all disk reads of the entire system. This section measures how severe the most harmful statements are as a percentage of the entire system.

**Script to retrieve this percentage:**

```
Set serverout on;
DECLARE
 CURSOR c1 is
  selelct   disk_reads
  from      v$sqlarea
  order by  disk_reads DESC;
 CURSOR c2 is
  select    sum(disk_reads)
  from      v$sqlarea;
 Sumof10 NUMBER:=0;
 mydr NUMBER;
 mytotdr NUMBER;
BEGIN
 dbms_output.put_line('Percent');
 dbms_output.put_line('-------');
 OPEN c1;
 FOR i IN 1..10 LOOP
  FETCH c1 INTO mydr;
  sumof10 := sumof10 + mydr;
 END LOOP;
 CLOSE c1;
 OPEN c2;
 FETCH c2 INTO mytotdr;
 CLOSE c2;
 dbms_output.put_line(sumof10/mytotdr*100);
END;
/
```

**Sample output:**

```
Percent
5.5183036
```

**Rate your system:**

| Take your top 10 disk read statements in the **V$SQLAREA** view. What percent are they of all disk reads? | Points | Score |
|---|---|---|
| > 25% | 0 | |
| 20–25% | 10 | |

Top 10 Disk-Read Abusers

| Take your top 10 disk read statements in the V$SQLAREA view. What percent are they of all disk reads? | Points | Score |
|---|---|---|
| 10–19% | 20 | |
| < 5% | 30 | **20** |

## Tables/Indexes Separated

Tables and their corresponding indexes should be located on separate physical disks to decrease file I/O. Chapter 3 covers this topic and provides queries to assist in this matter.

Rate your system:

| Are tables and their corresponding indexes located on the same physical disk? | Points | Score |
|---|---|---|
| Yes | 0 | |
| Disk Array | 20 | |
| No | 30 | **30** |

## Chaining in Mission-Critical Tables

When a table is updated and the block of the record updated does not have enough room to fit the changes, a record is "chained" to another block. A record spans more than one block. By analyzing a table for chained rows and querying the chained_rows table (covered in Chapter 2), you identify tables that are chained (note that you must first run the UTLCHAIN.sql script located in the /rdbms/admin subdirectory of your Oracle software home directory to build the chained_rows table). You must decide which tables are mission-critical.

Rate your system:

| Are there mission critical tables that have records that are chained? | Points | Score |
|---|---|---|
| Yes | 0 | |
| No | 30 | **30** |

## Key Oracle Files Separated

Redo logs should be separated from rollback segments and DML data for maximum disk I/O performance.

**Rate your system:**

| Are redo logs separated from rollback segments? Are both of these separated from DML data? | Points | Score |
|---|---|---|
| Yes | 30 | |
| Disk Array | 20 | |
| No | 0 | **20** |

## Rollback Segment Balance

Rollback segments should be separated from each other and, optimally, from the disks that hold the tables and indexes they are performing operations on. If your system is very small, then separating rollback segments may not be possible. Also, the number of DML statements that users are executing should determine the true number of rollback segments that are optimal. My rule of thumb is that the number of rollback segments should be a number where there is *never* (or extremely rarely) more than one user using a single rollback segment at the same time. My rule of thumb varies greatly from those of others (please use whichever you feel is best for your system). Adjust the scoring in this section based on your system size and number of users that use rollback segments.

**Query:**

```
select    segment_name, file_name
from      dba_data_files, dba_rollback_segs
where     dba_data_files.file_id = dba_rollback_segs.file_id;
```

**Sample output:**

```
SEGMENT NAME    FILE NAME
RBS1            /disk1/oracle/rbs1.dbf
RBS2            /disk2/oracle/rbs2.dbf
RBS3            /disk3/oracle/rbs3.dbf
RBS4            /disk4/oracle/rbs4.dbf
```

```
RBS5              /disk1/oracle/rbs1.dbf
RBS6              /disk2/oracle/rbs2.dbf
RBS7              /disk3/oracle/rbs3.dbf
RBS8              /disk4/oracle/rbs4.dbf
```

**Rate your system:**

| How many different disks do rollback segments occupy? | Points | Score |
|---|---|---|
| 1 | 0 | |
| 2 | 10 | |
| 3–4 | 20 | |
| > 4 | 30 | **20** |

# Temporary Segment Balance

When the SORT_AREA_SIZE specified in the init.ora is not sufficient for sorting, users will sort in their predefined temporary tablespace. If a large amount of sorting on disk is prevalent, you need to ensure that users are sorting on different disks.

**Query:**

```
select    username, file_name
from      dba_data_files, dba_users
where     dba_data_files.tablespace_name =
          dba_users.temporary_tablespace;
```

**Sample output:**

```
USERNAME     FILE NAME
SYS          /disk1/oracle/sys1orcl.dbf
TEDP         /disk1/oracle/tmp1orcl.dbf
SANDRA       /disk1/oracle/tmp1orcl.dbf
TEDR         /disk1/oracle/tmp2orcl.dbf
ROB          /disk1/oracle/tmp2orcl.dbf
DIANNE       /disk1/oracle/tmp2orcl.dbf
RICH         /disk1/oracle/tmp2orcl.dbf
DONNA        /disk1/oracle/tmp3orcl.dbf
DAVE         /disk1/oracle/tmp3orcl.dbf
ANDREA       /disk1/oracle/tmp3orcl.dbf
MIKE         /disk1/oracle/tmp3ora.dbf
```

**Rate your system:**

| The users in your system can be altered to use a temporary tablespace for sorting. How many disks (other than SYSTEM) are used for this? | Points | Score |
|---|---|---|
| All in System | 0 | |
| 1 | 10 | |
| 2 | 20 | |
| > 2 | 30 | **10** |

# Minor Fragmentation Issues

Fragmentation and the perceived costs due to fragmentation are debated issues. Depending on if the fragmentation of an object consists of blocks that are next to each other (not very costly), or in a table where only a single block is any accessed at one time (also not very costly), the true cost of fragmentation is tough to assess. Since fragmentation is generally a reasonable cost to the performance of most systems, I included it in the rating system.

**Query:**

```
select     segment_name, extents
from       dba_extents
where      extents > 5
order by   extents  desc;
```

**Sample output:**

```
SEGMENT_NAME    EXTENTS
RB1             89
RICH2           55
RB3             48
SOURCE$         39
RICH            19
RB4             13
IDL_UB2$        12
C_OBJ#           6
```

**Rate your system:**

| How many tables are fragmented into 5 or more pieces? | Points | Score |
|---|---|---|
| > 31 | 0 | |
| 21–30 | 10 | |
| 11–20 | 15 | |
| 10 or fewer | 20 | **20** |

## Major Fragmentation Issues

This section finds the objects with a larger degree of fragmentation than the preceding section.

**Query:**

```
select      segment_name, extents
from        dba_segments
where       extents > 30
order by    extents  desc;
```

**Sample output:**

```
SEGMENT NAME      EXTENTS
RB1               89
RICH2             55
```

**Rate your system:**

| How many tables are fragmented into 30 or more extents? | Points | Score |
|---|---|---|
| > 10 | 0 | |
| 6–10 | 10 | |
| 3–5 | 15 | |
| 2 or fewer | 20 | **20** |
| **Total of all DPI sections:** Example Disk Performance Index (DPI) | **Total Score** | **200(B)** |

**Grade your system:**

| DPI Grade | Comments | Score |
|---|---|---|
| A+ | Top 10 percent of most systems | > 235 |
| A | Top 20 percent of most systems | 205–235 |
| B | Top 40 percent of most systems | 170–204 |
| C | Top 70 percent of most systems | 110–169 |
| Needs help now | Bottom 30 percent of most systems | < 110 |

**TIP**
*Measuring your DPI (Disk Performance Index) can be helpful in identifying potential disk improvements that could be beneficial.*

# Education Performance Index (EPI)

This section measures the knowledge and education of your technical staff members. The following table illustrates how to receive a perfect EPI score. This rating system is not meant to be an all-encompassing benchmark of knowledge and education, but rather a barometer to see if educational improvements could be beneficial.

| Category | Level Required | Maximum Score |
|---|---|---|
| DBAs required to tune database | Yes | 30 |
| Developers required to tune code written | Yes | 30 |
| DBAs last trained in tuning | Less than 1 year | 30 |
| Developers last trained in tuning | Less than 1 year | 30 |
| DBAs proficient in V$ views | Yes | 30 |
| DBAs proficient in Enterprise Manager | Yes | 20 |
| DBAs trained in EXPLAIN PLAN | Yes | 20 |
| Developers trained in EXPLAIN PLAN | Yes | 20 |

| Category | Level Required | Maximum Score |
|---|---|---|
| DBAs trained in use of hints | Yes | 20 |
| Developers trained in use of hints | Yes | 20 |

| | | |
|---|---|---|
| Education Performance Index (EPI) | Section Total | 250 |

**Rate your system:**

| | | | |
|---|---|---|---|
| Are DBAs *required* to tune the database? | Yes | 30 | |
| | No | 0 | **30** |
| Are developers *required* to tune the code that they write? | Yes | 30 | |
| | No | 0 | **0** |
| When is the last time that your DBAs attended a training course that included tuning? | < 1 year | 30 | |
| | 1-2 years | 20 | |
| | > 2 years | 0 | **20** |
| When is the last time that your developers attended a training course that included tuning? | < 1 year | 30 | |
| | 1–2 years | 20 | |
| | > 2 years | 0 | **20** |
| Are DBAs proficient in using the V$ views? | Yes | 30 | |
| | No | 0 | **20** |
| Are DBAs proficient in using Enterprise Manager or an equivalent performance tool? | Yes | 20 | |
| | No | 0 | **20** |

| | | | |
|---|---|---|---|
| Have DBAs been trained on the use of EXPLAIN PLAN? (See Chapter 6 on EXPLAIN PLAN.) | Yes<br>No | 20<br>0 | **20** |
| Have developers been trained on the use of EXPLAIN PLAN? | Yes<br>No | 20<br>0 | **0** |
| Have DBAs been trained on the use of hints? (See Chapter 7 on hints.) | Yes<br>No | 20<br>0 | **20** |
| Have developers been trained on the use of hints? | Yes<br>No | 20<br>0 | **0** |

---

**Total of all EPI sections:**
Example Education Performance
Index (EPI)                                                    **Total Score    150 (B)**

### Grade your system:

| EPI Grade | Comments | Score |
|---|---|---|
| A+ | Top 10 percent of most systems | 250 |
| A | Top 20 percent of most systems | 210–249 |
| B | Top 40 percent of most systems | 150–209 |
| C | Top 70 percent of most systems | 90–149 |
| Needs help now | Bottom 30 percent of most systems | < 90 |

**TIP**
*Measuring your EPI (Education Performance Index) can be helpful in identifying educational improvements that could be beneficial.*

Education Performance Index
(EPI)

# System Performance Index (SPI)

This section measures overall system issues. The following table illustrates how to receive a perfect SPI score. This rating system is not meant to be an all-encompassing benchmark of overall system issues; rather, it is a barometer to see if improvements could be beneficial.

| Category | Level Required | Maximum Score |
|---|---|---|
| Inside party database review | < 1 year | 50 |
| Ran UTLBSTAT/UTLESTAT last | < 1 month | 30 |
| Users asked about performance issues | < 2 months | 30 |
| Backup tested for recovery speed | Yes | 30 |
| Outside party database review | < 1 year | 30 |
| Outside party operating system review | < 1 year | 30 |
| Optimizer used | Cost-based | 20 |
| Design is strictly normalized or partially denormalized | Denormalized | 20 |
| Parallel query used or tested for gains | Yes | 10 |
| **System Performance Index (SPI)** | **Section Total** | **250** |

**Rate your system:**

| | | Points | Score |
|---|---|---|---|
| When is the last time that database was reviewed by an inside party other than the DBA? | < 1 year | 50 | |
| | 1–2 years | 30 | |
| | > 2 years | 0 | **50** |

|  |  | **Points** | **Score** |
|---|---|---|---|
| When is the last time that you ran *and* analyzed UTLESTAT/UTLBSTAT ? (See Chapter 16 on ULTBSTAT/UTLESTAT.) | < 1 month | 30 | |
| | 1–3 months | 20 | |
| | 4–6 months | 10 | |
| | > 6 months | 0 | **20** |
| When is the last time that users of your system were asked about system performance or where things could be improved? | < 2 months | 30 | |
| | 3–6 months | 20 | |
| | 7–12 months | 10 | |
| | > 1 year | 0 | **20** |
| Has your backup plan been tested to determine the time that it will take to recover? | Yes | 30 | |
| | No | 0 | **30** |
| When is the last time that your database was reviewed by an outside party? | < 1 year | 30 | |
| | 1–2 years | 20 | |
| | > 2 years | 0 | **20** |
| When is the last time that your operating system was reviewed by an outside party? | < 1 year | 30 | |
| | 1–2 years | 20 | |
| | > 2 years | 0 | **30** |
| What optimizer do you use? | Cost-based | 20 | |
| | Rule-based | 10 | |
| | Unsure | 0 | **20** |

System Performance Index (SPI)

System Performance Index (SPI)

| | | Points | Score |
|---|---|---|---|
| Do designers adhere *strictly* to 3<sup>rd</sup> normal form or higher in their design of the database? | Yes | 10 | |
| | *Denormalize | 20 | |
| | No designer | 0 | 20 |
| Has Parallel Query been evaluated and is it in use where advantageous? | Yes | 10 | |
| | Not needed | 10 | |
| | Not tested | 0 | 20 |

**Total of all SPI sections:**
Example System Performance
Index (SPI)

| | | **Total Score** | 220 (A+) |
|---|---|---|---|

*Denormalized only where needed.

## Grade your system:

| SPI Grade | Comments | Score |
|---|---|---|
| A+ | Top 10 percent of most systems | > 210 |
| A | Top 20 percent of most systems | 180–210 |
| B | Top 40 percent of most systems | 140–179 |
| C | Top 70 percent of most systems | 80–139 |
| Needs help now | Bottom 30 percent of most systems | < 80 |

 **TIP**
*Measuring your SPI (System Performance Index) can be
helpful in identifying overall system improvements that
could be beneficial.*

# Total Performance Index (TPI)

The Total Performance Index is the composite score of the memory, disk, education and system indices.

| Category Index | Maximum Score |
|---|---|
| Memory Performance Index (MPI) | 250 |
| Disk Performance Index (DPI) | 250 |
| Education Performance Index (EPI) | 250 |
| System Performance Index (SPI) | 250 |
| **Total Performance Index (TPI)** | **1000** |

**Rate your system:**

| | | |
|---|---|---|
| Example Disk Performance Index (DPI) | Total Score | 200 (B ) |
| Example Memory Performance Index (MPI) | Total Score | 230 (A ) |
| Example Education Performance Index (EPI) | Total Score | 150 (B ) |
| Example System Performance Index (SPI) | Total Score | 220 (A+) |
| **Example Total Performance Index (SPI)** | **Total Score** | **800 (A )** |

**Grade your system:**

| TPI Grade | Comments | Score |
|---|---|---|
| A+ | Top 10 percent of most systems | > 925 |
| A | Top 20 percent of most systems | 795–924 |
| B | Top 40 percent of most systems | 620–794 |
| C | Top 70 percent of most systems | 380–619 |
| Needs help now | Bottom 30 percent of most systems | < 380 |

**TIP**
*Measuring your TPI (Total Performance Index) can be helpful in identifying bottlenecks; it is a simple barometer rating your overall system performance as it compares to others in the industry.*

Total Performance Index (TPI)

# Overall System Review Example

The following is an example rating scale, the example rating results that you could use to generate a yearly review for your system. Some of the items (such as backup and recovery ratings) are not covered in depth. The goal of this section is to give you ideas of some of the areas that you might consider reviewing. This is not an actual client system review, but a slightly modified version of several reviews to help generate discussion items for your review template. The goal is to give you a "feel" of a review.

# Rating System

This is the rating system that TUSC uses for doing overall ratings. Having a review that includes a rating for items that desperately need improvement or attention (where appropriate) is important in generating manager support. In many cases, a DBA needs managerial support to receive the time to address major issues with their system. At times, if the system is up and running, upper management does not see a need for change. This review can be a catalyst for change as issues are identified.

| Grade | Ranking | Comments |
|---|---|---|
| A+ | Top 5 percent of systems reviewed | Excellent |
| A | Top 10 percent | Very good to excellent |
| A- | Top 15 percent | Very good |
| B, B+, B- | Top 25 percent | Good/could be improved |
| C, C+, C- | Top 50 percent | Requires Improvement |
| D, D+, D- | Bottom 50 percent | Desperately requires improvement |
| F | Bottom 10 percent | Immediately needs to be corrected |

**TIP**
*Have your system reviewed on an annual basis by an outside party or at the minimum by someone inside your company.*

# Example System Review Rating

The following table summarizes the results of a sample system review. While some of the categories of the TPI are discussed, this section is an addition to the TPI that goes into greater depth. An overview of the recommended changes should follow this section, and the TPI rating could precede or follow this section. This section is more subjective, so an experienced person that you respect should make these judgements. The ratings should include more detailed comments than those given here as an example. The recommended changes should be detailed with supporting documentation. (Note: This is not an actual review, but an example.)

| Category | Grade | Comments |
| --- | --- | --- |
| Overall review | C- | The system is running very poorly due to an insufficient amount of memory allocated for the data processing. Several areas need to be corrected immediately for substantially improved system performance, especially as additional users are added. |
| Architecture | B | The overall architecture is good. Several data files need to be moved to improve I/O. |
| Hardware sizing | A- | The hardware is well sized for the business activity, but the system is not tuned to take full advantage of the hardware. |
| Security | F | The passwords are never changed, even when employees leave the company. Several unprotected files have hard-coded passwords. The SYSTEM password is MANAGER and the SYS password is CHANGE_ON_INSTALL. This is unacceptable! |
| Memory allocation | B+ | Hit ratios are very good. However, they could be improved with increases to the shared pool. |
| Database tuning | D- | The top 25 queries make up 98 percent of all resource usage. No effort has been made to tune these queries. |
| Disk configuration | B | Disk I/O is reasonably balanced, but could be improved by moving a few of the hardest hit files. |

Example System Review Rating

| Category | Grade | Comments |
|---|---|---|
| Redo logs | B+ | Redo logs are sized well, but the LOG_BUFFER is set too low. Increasing the LOG_BUFFER will allow writes to the redo logs less often. As the business grows and users are added, additional redo log files will need to be added. |
| Archived log files | A+ | File systems containing the archive log files are independent of other Oracle file systems. Archives are archived to tape, but also kept on disk for fast recoveries. |
| Rollback segments | A+ | Rollback segments are sized well and spread across multiple disks. |
| Control files | A- | Multiple control files are located on different physical disks, but a backup of control file to TRACE does not exist. |
| init.ora parameters | D- | There is 2GB of memory available on the system. The database is 2 terabytes and there are 1,000 users on the system. A Shared Pool of 500M appears to be reasonable, but the default of 200 DB_BLOCK_BUFFERS is *too low* and is the current major bottleneck of the system. |
| Table design | C- | There is no database-level referential integrity. |
| Tables | C- | The number of extents is set to unlimited on all tables. PCTUSED is set to 90 percent, causing reuse of blocks at an incredible performance-costly rate. Tables are also sized poorly. Too many extents or too much wasted space. |
| Indexes | C- | Indexes are sized poorly. Too many extents or too much wasted space. |
| Tablespaces | C+ | Tablespaces are severely undersized for growth. |
| Data dictionary sizing | A | Fewer than five tables have more than five extents. |

## Items Requiring Immediate Action

Once you have reviewed your system, you need to make a comprehensive list of items that need to be addressed immediately. The following list is a summary of some of the issues that could warrant immediate action:

- Change the SYS and SYSTEM passwords immediately! Let's do it now.
- All other passwords should be changed, as the security is currently compromised.
- DB_BLOCK_BUFFERS needs to be increased immediately! Let's do it when the system can be brought down.
- The top 25 queries causing disk and memory reads need to be tuned.
- Tables and indexes need to be resized for effective space usage. Indexes need to be added for some of the poorly running queries. PCTFREE on tables needs to be changed immediately. Ten percent is a more appropriate number for most of the tables.
- After the DB_BLOCK_BUFFER problem is corrected, the init.ora will need to be resized again, prior to additional user increase from the East Coast branch. The number of concurrent users will increase by 25 percent by the end of the year. The init.ora will need to be resized accordingly.
- The NLS_DATE_FORMAT needs to be set for year 2000 compliance in the registry (regedit) on all client PCs.

**TIP**
*A system review should always include immediate action items. This ensures that the time needed for improvements will be allocated.*

## Other Items Requiring Action

The second list that you should make lists items needing attention, after the most pressing issues have been addressed. A summary example list is shown next. Your list should include more detail on how the action will be corrected. At the end of this list, I have included sample memory changes that could be made to a UNIX kernel and sample init.ora changes that could be made (see Appendix A for a detailed list of init.ora parameters).

- Monitor the items detailed in this document at least once per quarter, along with the current growth rate of the system.
- SYSTEM and SYS passwords in production should be different in development.
- Resize the database objects that are currently oversized and undersized.

- Change all passwords at least once per quarter.
- Fix file protection so that users are unable to delete Oracle software.
- Remove hard-coded passwords from scripts and backup jobs.
- Balance I/O across data files and file systems.
- Relocate the data files on the system to better isolate the tablespaces to minimize disk contention.
- Consider adding additional indexes for the top 25 worst disk read queries to improve query performance.
- Configure multiple dedicated temporary tablespaces.
- Rebuild the UNIX kernel as described next.

By default, the UNIX kernel is not configured for a database of any size to be run on the server. Several parameters need to be modified to allow the database to get the amount of memory, the number of open files, and the number of semaphores required for the database to start and run correctly. The following table outlines the parameters that should be reviewed.

| Name | Current Value | Suggested Value | Description |
| --- | --- | --- | --- |
| MAXFILES | 512 | 512 | Maximum number of open files that can be associated with a process. This parameter needs to be large enough to allow the database to increase the number of data files associated with the database. |
| SEMMNI | 64 | 256 | The maximum number of semaphore identifiers. This parameter controls the number of semaphore groups allowed on the system. |
| SEMMNS | 200 | 1000 | The maximum number of semaphores allowed on the system. Semaphores are used for interprocess communication. Every process that connects to the shared memory for the database will require a semaphore. The database is not the only process on the system that uses semaphores, so additional semaphores need to be available. |

**Items Requiring Immediate Action**

| Name | Current Value | Suggested Value | Description |
|---|---|---|---|
| SEMMNU | 30 | 256 | The number of semaphore undo structures. |
| SHMMAX | 134,217,728 | 268,435,456 | The maximum size of a single shared memory segment. Oracle's System Global Area (SGA) is all shared memory. Oracle will use multiple segments for the SGA, but performance is better if there is only one segment. |
| SHMMNI | 200 | 200 | The maximum number of shared memory segment identifiers. |
| SHMSEG | 120 | 120 | The maximum number of shared memory segments that can be attached to one process. |

If init.ora changes are to be made, you should compile a list like the one displayed next. This list shows some examples of init.ora changes and why they should be changed. It poses some suggestions for your system review recommendations, and is for that purpose only. Refer to Appendix A for a complete list of init.ora parameters with detailed descriptions.

| Name | Current Value | Suggested Value | Description |
|---|---|---|---|
| COMPATIBLE | 7.3.2.0.0 | 7.3.3.6 | Controls what options are available within the database. |
| DB_BLOCK_BUFFERS | 3200 | 25600 | Controls the amount of memory available for the data cache. |
| DB_BLOCK_LRU_LATCHES | 1 | 2 | Allows Oracle more locking mechanisms for the data cache. |
| DB_FILE_MULTIBLOCK_READ_COUNT | 24 | 32 | Allows Oracle to read more data in a single I/O when doing full table scans. |

Items Requiring Immediate Action

| Name | Current Value | Suggested Value | Description |
|------|------|------|------|
| DB_FILE_SIMULTANEOUS_WRITES | 4 | 24 | Allows Oracle to write to more blocks within a data file at the same time. |
| LOG_BUFFER | 8192 | 5342880 | Oracle stores modifications to data in the log buffer until the user commits the changes. Long transactions can cause contention for space if the buffer is too small. |
| LOG_CHECKPOINTS_TO_ALERT | FALSE | TRUE | Allows Oracle to make an entry in the alert log when a checkpoint is triggered. Used for monitoring to help determine redo log sizes. |
| SHARED_POOL_SIZE | 9000000 | 20971520 | Controls the amount of memory allocated to the Shared Pool. The Shared Pool contains the dictionary cache and library cache. Both areas can become bottlenecks for performance. |
| SORT_AREA_RETAINED_SIZE | 65536 | 1048576 | Controls the amount of memory Oracle maintains after a user finishes sorting the data. |
| SORT_AREA_SIZE | 65536 | 1048576 | Controls the amount of memory available to Oracle to do sorts. |

# System Information List

This section describes some of the system information that you should gather and keep with the review. As you look back on a review, you need to know what the parameters of the system were at the time of the review. Any ratings of specific items (such as backup and recovery) could be placed in this section. I also have included a sample DBA review that illustrates some of the areas that may be reviewed. It is wise to have someone else rate your DBA skills so that you can continue to improve. This section has been greatly simplified for the book. It is a quick list designed to give a "picture" of the system as whole.

# Memory-Related Values

The following are memory-related questions that should be asked about the system:

| Question | Answer |
| --- | --- |
| What is the current memory for the hardware? | 2GB |
| What is the current number of users? | 500 total/50 concurrent |
| What will be the future number of users? | 100–150 concurrent in the next three months |
| What other software is used on the system? | None that is a major influence |
| Is the system terminal/host or client/server? | terminal/host |
| What response times are required? | Subsecond, OLTP transactions make up main mix |
| How large is the database? | Currently 104GB with 42GB currently free in the database |
| How large are often-accessed tables? | One million rows is the average |
| Future software that will affect memory? | None |

# Disk-Related Values

The following are disk-related questions that should be asked about the system:

| Question | Answer |
| --- | --- |
| What is the maximum disk capacity for the hardware? | Eight times current capacity |
| What disk sizes are available? | 2GB and 4GB |
| What will be the size of the database in one year? | Double the current level |

| Question | Answer |
|---|---|
| Is there a RAID (striping) level for database files/OS? | Yes; RAID 1 and RAID 5 |
| Will there be multiplexed redo Logs? | No, but they are RAID 1 (mirrored at the OS) |
| All software that will be installed? | No additions in near future |
| System utilities that will be installed? | BMC's Patrol and Platinum's TSReorg |
| What EDI transfers will happen nightly? | Bulk order transfers |

## Miscellaneous Disk-Related Values

| | |
|---|---|
| Logical volume(s) | Check the distribution of key Oracle components |
| Tables | On one logical volume |
| Indexes | On one logical volume |
| Redo logs | On one logical volume |
| Rollback segments | On one logical volume |
| Control files | Need to make additional copies on separate disks |
| Archive files | Currently not archiving |

The following shows the layout of actual files on the system:

| Mount Point | File |
|---|---|
| /oracle | Control01.ctl |
| | System01.dbf |
| | Temp01.dbf |
| | Tools01.dbf |
| | Users01.dbf |
| /disk01 | Redo01.log |
| | Redo02.log |
| | Redo03.log |
| | Control02.ctl |

**Disk-Related Values**

| Mount Point | File |
|---|---|
| | Roll01.dbf |
| | Temp01.dbf |
| /disk02 | Control03.ct |
| | Temp01.dbf |
| | Temp02.dbf |
| /disk03 | Table02.dbf |
| /disk04 | Roll02.dbf |
| | Index01.dbf |
| /disk05 | Roll03.dbf |
| | Index02.dbf |

**TIP**
*Showing a layout of files on the system can be particularly helpful as you review queries that have I/O contention issues.*

## CPU-Related Values

The following are CPU-related questions that should be asked about the system (see Chapter 18 for more information on this area):

| Question | Answer |
|---|---|
| What is the number of processors/ maximum for the hardware? | 6 currently/12 maximum |
| Is there a future upgrade path? | Yes; path to an HP T600 |
| What is the transaction processing load? | 40 percent CPU average/90 percent sustained maximum |
| What is the batch load? | Some heavy at night/OK during the day |

| Question | Answer |
|---|---|
| Are hot backups employed? | Omniback cold backups are employed with archiving |
| Are batch processes running during the day? | None that are affecting performance |
| Will Parallel Query be used in the future? | Currently being used on some processes |
| Will there be a future distributed setup? | Probable, given the multisite setup |

## Backup and Recovery-Related Information

The following are backup and recovery-related questions that should be asked about the system:

| Question | Answer |
|---|---|
| Does the system require 24-hour use? | No, it is 6x24 |
| How fast will recovery need to be made (on disk backup)? | 12-hour maximum |
| Are there "standby" disks in case of failure? | No, 4-hour turnaround from HP |
| How much data is "backed up"? Is it being "tape-striped" with parity? | 180G/no tape striping |
| Has the UPS been established? | Yes |
| Are export files also taken? | No |
| How are the cold backup procedures? | Excellent |
| How are the export procedures? | Needs improvement |
| How are the hot backup procedures? | Not applicable |
| How are the disaster recovery procedures? | Needs improvement |

The following is an example of some of the areas that you may evaluate in a backup and recovery rating. The layout should be identical to your system review.

| Category | Grade | Comments |
|---|---|---|
| Backup and recovery overall | A | A script to replace all of the backed up files should also be generated |

| Category | Grade | Comments |
|---|---|---|
| Backup procedures | A | Excellent |
| Archiving procedures | A | Excellent |
| Recovery procedures | A- | Should have scripts ready to go for a recovery |
| Backup knowledge | A | Very good |
| Recovery knowledge | A | Very good |
| Disaster backup | A+ | Excellent |
| Disaster recovery | A | Very good, rolling forward was still being worked on |

# Naming Conventions and/or OFA Standards and Security Information

A.  Review naming conventions used: **Excellent, but not OFA**
B.  Check file protections on key Oracle files: **Poor**
C.  Check database security procedures: **Poor**
D.  Check password procedures: **Poor**

# DBA Knowledge Rating

Having all DBAs reviewed by an impartial expert is paramount to identifying and improving the skills for a DBA. Often, the primary DBA is too busy to attend training sessions or improve skills on new versions of Oracle. This area will help identify areas of strengths and weaknesses. This process will fail if this review is used against a person. It *must* be used with the goal of identifying and improving.

| Category | Rating |
|---|---|
| DBA knowledge overall | A |
| Oracle architecture | A- |
| Oracle objects | B+ |
| Oracle internals | B+ |
| Oracle init.ora | B+ |

| Category | Rating |
| --- | --- |
| Oracle query tuning | A |
| Oracle database tuning | A |
| Oracle backup | A |
| Oracle recovery | A |
| Oracle utilities | A |
| Operating system | B+ |

**TIP**
*Reviewing a DBA's ability should only be done if the review will be used as a means of improving the skills of the DBA. Reviewing a person is a very sensitive issue and must be done by someone who has the goal of improvement first and foremost.*

**DBA Knowledge Rating**

# Remote TUSC DBA

One way to bottle-up the system review in an intuitive review mechanism is by using Oracle GUI products accessing the dictionary tables. TUSC accomplished this by using the Oracle GUI tools for monitoring client sites.

**TIP**
*If you can't effectively monitor your own system, then contract someone who can. The cost of maintaining a database is usually far less than the cost of downtime when problems occur.*

## Building the Graphical View Using Oracle Reports

You can use a graphical tool such as Oracle Reports to access data dictionary information. Displaying the information in a graphical form can be more helpful than using scripts to retrieve tabular results. The graphical means of displaying results are often more intuitive to those evaluating the results. The example shown in Figure 17-1 is the number of each type of statement that is being performed on a system. Oracle's Enterprise Manager (see Chapter 5) shows some of the database information graphically. The output of the query text is displayed next.

**The text output is not as intuitive:**

| COMMAND TYPE | COUNT | EXECUTIONS | BUFFERGETS | DISKREADS |
|---|---|---|---|---|
| INSERT | 22 | 16022 | 148973 | 82 |
| SELECT | 203 | 101013 | 1085182 | 4498 |
| UPDATE | 12 | 1386 | 18155 | 304 |
| DELETE | 21 | 1137 | 98732 | 75 |
| ALTER SESSION | 3 | 383 | 0 | 0 |
| COMMIT | 2 | 53 | 26 | 0 |
| ROLLBACK | 1 | 17 | 0 | 0 |
| PL/SQL EXECUTE | 21 | 21018 | 1101755 | 1093 |
| SET ROLE | 1 | 20 | 3860 | 1 |
| ALTER PACKAGE BODY | 1 | 27 | 0 | 0 |

10 rows selected.

# Building the Screen View

You can also use a graphical tool such as Oracle Forms to access data dictionary information. The graphical means of displaying results are often more insightful than evaluating the results. Using Oracle Forms also gives the user the opportunity to

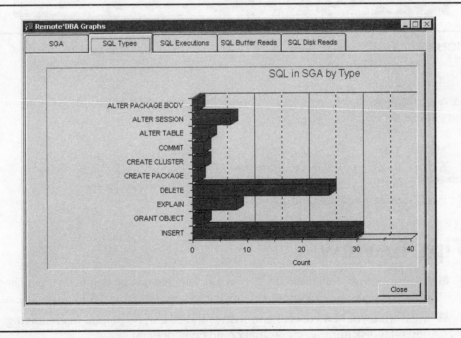

**FIGURE 17.1.** *Graphical view using Oracle Reports of statements performed on a system*

Building the Screen View

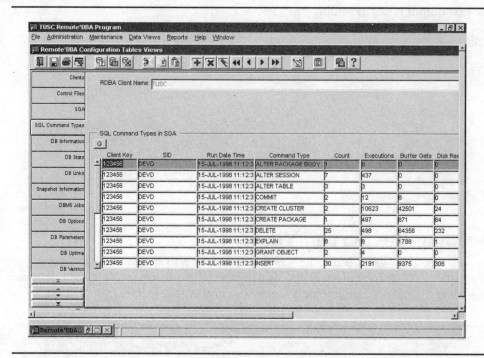

**FIGURE 17.2.** *Graphical view using Oracle Forms of statements performed on a system*

query on different items. Figure 17-2 shows the statements performed on the system and various statistics for each statement.

**TIP**

*By using Oracle's graphical products (Reports and Forms), you can display data dictionary information in a more graphical and intuitive manner.*

# Tips Review

- Measuring your MPI (Memory Performance Index) can be helpful in identifying potential memory allocation and usage improvements that could be beneficial.
- Measuring your DPI (Disk Performance Index) can be helpful in identifying potential disk improvements that could be beneficial.

■ Measuring your EPI (Education Performance Index) can be helpful in identifying educational improvements that could be beneficial.

■ Measuring your SPI (System Performance Index) can be helpful in identifying overall system improvements that could be beneficial.

■ Measuring your TPI (Total Performance Index) can be helpful in identifying bottlenecks and is a simple barometer rating your overall system performance as it compares to others in the industry.

■ Have your system reviewed on an annual basis by an outside party or, at a minimum, by someone inside your company.

■ A system review should always include immediate action items. This ensures that the time needed for improvements will be allocated.

■ Reviewing a DBA's ability should only be done if the review will be used as a means of improving the skills of the DBA. Reviewing a person is a very sensitive issue and must be done by someone who has the goal of improvement first and foremost.

■ If you can't effectively monitor your own system, then contract someone who can. The cost of maintaining a database is usually far less than the cost of downtime when problems occur.

■ By using Oracle's graphical products (Reports and Forms), you can display data dictionary information in a more graphical and intuitive manner.

# References

*SQL Language Reference Manual*, Oracle Corporation

Memory Performance Index, Disk Performance Index, Education Performance Index, Total Performance Index, MPI, DPI, EPI, SPI and TPI; copyright TUSC 1998.

Many thanks to Jake van der Vort, Randy Swanson, Allen Peterson, Judy Corley, Sean McGuire, and Greg Pucka of TUSC for contributions to this chapter.

Tips Review

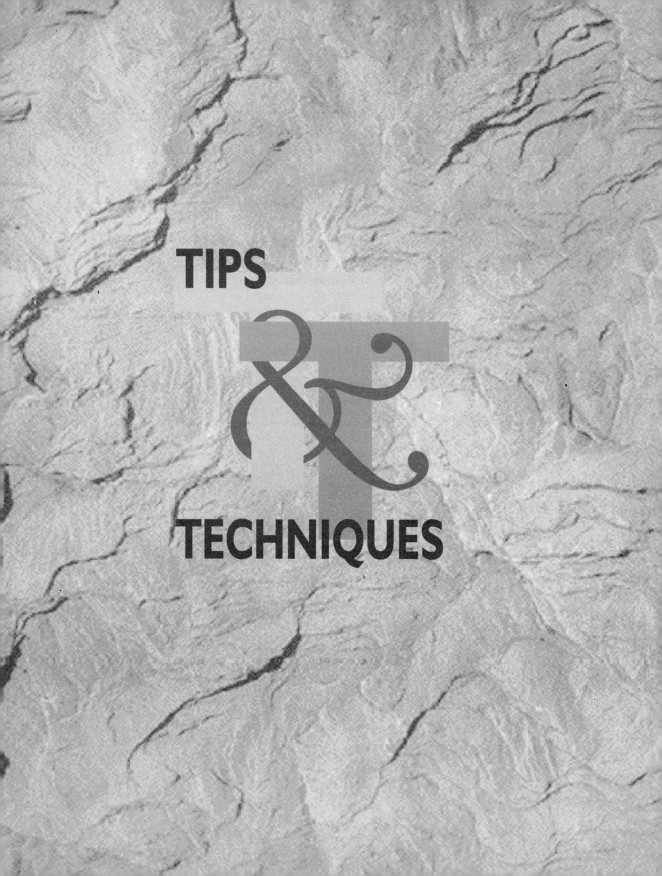

TIPS
&
TECHNIQUES

# CHAPTER

## 18

Monitor the System
Using UNIX Utilities
(DBA)

Part of being able to solve performance problems includes being able to effectively use operating utilities. Using the correct utilities to find CPU, memory, and disk I/O issues is crucial to identifying where performance problems exist. This chapter will focus on tips related to UNIX utilities that can be used to find these problems.

Most of the utilities in this chapter are UNIX utilities. The focus of this chapter will be UNIX tools that monitor CPU, memory, and disk issues. Tips covered in this chapter are as follows:

- Using the sar command to monitor CPU usage
- Finding the worst user on the system using the top command
- Using the uptime command to monitor the CPU load
- Using the mpstat command to identify CPU bottlenecks
- Combining ps with selected V$ views
- Using the sar command to monitor disk I/O problems
- Using iostat to identify disk I/O bottlenecks
- Monitoring memory issues using sar
- Determining shared memory usage using ipcs
- Monitoring all system activity using vmstat
- The Task Manager tool for NT
- The Proctool from Sun UNIX

# Using the sar Command to Monitor CPU Usage

The sar command has many different switches that can be set to display different pieces of performance information. With the -u switch, sar can be used to monitor CPU utilization. The sar utility is an effective way to see a quick snapshot of how heavily the CPU is "bogged down." Run this utility on a regular basis to get a baseline for your system, enabling you to identify when your system is running poorly. Of the two numbers following the switch for sar (-u in the following example), the first is to display the number of seconds between readings. The second is the number of times you want sar to run.

**Report CPU utilization (10 seconds apart; 8 times):**

```
# sar -u 10 8
HP-UX sch1p197 B.10.20 E 9000/893     01/23/98

            %usr      %sys      %wio      %idle
11:55:53     80        14         3         3
11:56:03     70        14        12         4
11:56:13     72        13        21         4
11:56:23     76        14         6         3
11:56:33     73        10        13         4
11:56:43     71         8        17         4
11:56:53     67         9        20         4
11:57:03     69        10        17         4
Average      73        11        13         4
```

%usr    Percent of CPU running in user mode

%sys    Percent of CPU running in system mode

%wio    Percent of CPU running idle with a process waiting for block I/O

%idle   Percent of CPU that is idle

A low %idle time could point to a CPU-intensive job or an underpowered CPU. Use the ps or top command (later in this chapter) to find a CPU-intensive job. A poorly written query requiring a large amount of disk access can also cause a large amount of CPU usage as well.

In the following sar output, the cause for concern is the large values being returned for %wio (waiting for block I/O) vs. actual heavy CPU usage:

```
# sar -u 5 4
```

|          | %usr | %sys | %wio | %idle |
|----------|------|------|------|-------|
| 14:29:58 | 20   | 20   | 60   | 0     |
| 14:30:03 | 17   | 23 . | 60   | 0     |
| 14:30:08 | 19   | 14   | 67   | 0     |
| 14:30:13 | 22   | 11   | 67   | 0     |
| Average  | 21   | 16   | 64   | 0     |

This list shows a high %wio, waiting for I/O time. This would point towards a disk contention problem. Iostat (discussed later in this chapter) can be used to pinpoint disk contention. See Chapter 3 for methods to combat I/0 issues.

**TIP**
*Use the sar -u command to see a quick snapshot of how heavily the CPU is "bogged down." Run sar on a regular basis to get a baseline for your system so that you can identify when your system is running poorly. However, at times low CPU idle time can also be an I/O issue and not a CPU issue.*

# What's a Good Idle Percentage for the CPU?

It really depends on the system size and variation in time accessed. For instance, a system that is accessed with heavy CPU usage for short periods of time may have an 80 percent average CPU idle time. In contrast, a system with very small jobs, but many of them, may have the same 80 percent average CPU idle time. The idle percentage is not as important as what is available when you run a job that must complete immediately (and is very important to the business). A 50 percent idle CPU may be a problem for the company with a large CPU-bound job that must complete quickly, while a 10 percent idle CPU may be more than enough for a company that has a very small job (requiring little CPU) that must complete quickly. Oracle will generally try to use the entire CPU available to complete a job.

# Finding the Worst User on the System Using the UNIX top Command

The top command shows a continuous display of the most active processes. (Chapter 5 shows the Enterprise Mangager Top Session screen.) DBAs and operations experts often run this (or similar utilities) at the first sign of system performance issues. This display will automatically update itself on the screen every few seconds. The first lines give general system information, while the rest of the display is arranged in order of decreasing current CPU usage (the worst user is on "top").

```
# top
Cpu states:  0.0% idle, 81.0% user, 17.7% kernel,  0.8% wait,  0.5% swap
Memory: 765M real, 12M free, 318M swap, 1586M free swap

PID    USERNAME  PRI  NICE   SIZE    RES  STATE  TIME    WCPU     CPU  COMMAND
23626  psoft     -25     2   208M  4980K  cpu    1:20  22.47%  99.63%  oracle
15819  root      -15     4  2372K   716K  sleep 22:19   0.61%   3.81%  pmon
20434  oracle     33     0   207M  2340K  sleep  2:47   0.23%   1.14%  oracle
20404  oracle     33     0    93M  2300K  sleep  2:28   0.23%   1.14%  oracle
23650  root       33     0  2052K  1584K  cpu    0:00   0.23%   0.95%  top
23625  psoft      27     2  5080K  3420K  sleep  0:17   1.59%   0.38%  sqr
23554  root       27     2  2288K  1500K  sleep  0:01   0.06%   0.38%  brxpu2.1.adm
15818  root       21     4  6160K  2416K  sleep  2:05   0.04%   0.19%  proctool
  897  root       34     0  8140K  1620K  sleep 55:46   0.00%   0.00%  Xsun
20830  psoft      -9     2  7856K  2748K  sleep  7:14   0.67%   0.00%  PSRUN
20854  psoft      -8     2   208M  4664K  sleep  4:21   0.52%   0.00%  oracle
  737  oracle     23     0  3844K  1756K  sleep  2:56   0.00%   0.00%  tnslsnr
 2749  root       28     0  1512K   736K  sleep  1:03   0.00%   0.00%  lpNet
18529  root       14    10  2232K  1136K  sleep  0:56   0.00%   0.00%  xlock
    1  root       33     0   412K   100K  sleep  0:55   0.00%   0.00%  init
```

This display shows the top user to be psoft with a PID of 23626. This user is using 99.63 percent of one CPU. If this output persisted for any length of time, it would be imperative to find out *who* this is and *what* they are doing. I will show how to link this back to an Oracle user using the ps command and querying the V$ views later in this chapter.

### TIP
*Use the top command to find the worst user on the system at a given point in time (the kill command often follows for many DBAs). If the worst query only lasts a short period of time, it may not be a problem; but if it persists, additional investigation may be necessary.*

## Monitoring Tools

There are GUI monitoring tools available on most platforms that either come bundled with the software or are available on the Internet. The Task Manager process monitor is available on NT, Proctool is available for Solaris, and Glance is available for HP.

Finding the Worst User

These monitoring tools will show a number of activities including CPU and I/O activity. A display of Proctool is shown in Figure 18-1. This particular screen does many of the commands that are available with the sar or top command.

### CPU Monitoring Tool

Proctool can also show the CPU utilization. The screen shown here depicts a six-processor system. The first processor is buried and the other five are relatively idle.

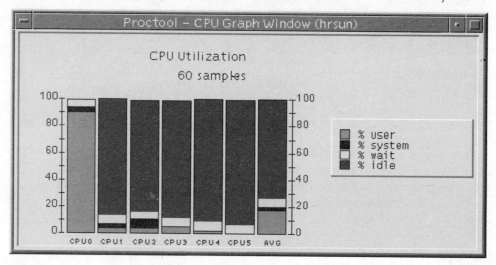

# Using the uptime Command to Monitor CPU Load

The uptime command is an excellent utility to find a quick 1, 5, and 15 minute CPU load of all jobs (including those currently running). You would want to look at the load average. This is the *number of jobs* in the CPU run queue for the last 1, 5, and 15 minutes. Note that this is not the percentage of CPU being used.

```
# uptime
  3:10pm  up 5 day(s), 19:04,  2 users,  load average: 2.10, 2.50, 2.20
```

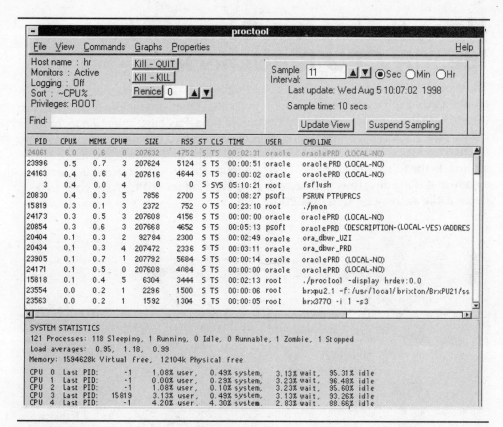

**FIGURE 18-1.** *Solaris Proctool utility*

I have found that a system with an average run queue of 2-3 is acceptable. If you add the following script to your cron table to run every hour, you will be mailed your average system load every two hours.

```
{uptime; sleep 120; uptime; sleep 120; uptime;} | mailx -s uptime  you@company.com
```

**TIP**
*Use cron and uptime to get your system load mailed to you on a regular basis.*

# Using the mpstat Command to Identify CPU Bottlenecks

The mpstat command is a Sun Solaris tool that reports per-processor statistics in tabular form. Each row of the table represents the activity of one processor. The first table shows the summary of activity since boot time. Pay close attention to the smtx measurement. Smtx measures the number of times the CPU failed to obtain a mutex (mutual exclusion lock). Mutex stalls waste CPU time and degrade multiprocessor scaling. In the following example, there are four processors numbered 0-3, and a system that is heading toward disaster is displayed (all four CPUs have gone to 0 percent idle and smtx is well over 200).

**Identifying CPU Bottlenecks**

```
# mpstat 10 5
CPU minf mjf xcal intr ithr  csw icsw migr smtx srw syscl usr sys wt idl
0    1    0    0    110   9    75   2    2     9    0   302   4   4  11  81
1    1    0    0    111  109   72   2    2    11    0   247   3   4  11  82
2    1    0    0     65   63   73   2    2     9    0   317   4   4  11  82
3    1    0    0      2    0   78   2    2     9    0   337   4   5  10  81
CPU minf mjf xcal intr ithr  csw icsw migr smtx srw syscl usr sys wt idl
0    2    8    0    198  12   236  113  35   203   60  1004  74  26  0   0
1    1   17    0    371  286  225  107  39   194   48  1087  60  40  0   0
2    0   22    0    194  82   267  127  38   227   49  1197  63  37  0   0
3    0   14    0    103   0   218  107  35   188   46  1075  71  29  0   0
CPU minf mjf xcal intr ithr  csw icsw migr smtx srw syscl usr sys wt idl
0   17   22    0    247  12   353  170  26   199   21  1263  54  46  0   0
1    8   14    0    406  265  361  165  27   200   25  1242  53  47  0   0
2    6   15    0    408  280  306  151  23   199   24  1229  56  44  0   0
3   10   19    0    156   0   379  174  28   163   27  1104  63  37  0   0
CPU minf mjf xcal intr ithr  csw icsw migr smtx srw syscl usr sys wt idl
0    0   19    0    256  12   385  180  24   446   19  1167  48  52  0   0
1    0   13    0    416  279  341  161  24   424   20  1376  45  55  0   0
2    0   13    0    411  290  293  144  22   354   15   931  54  46  0   0
3    0   14    0    140   0   320  159  22   362   14  1312  58  42  0   0
CPU minf mjf xcal intr ithr  csw icsw migr smtx srw syscl usr sys wt idl
0   23   15    0    264  12   416  194  31   365   25  1146  52  48  0   0
1   20   10    0    353  197  402  184  29   341   25  1157  41  59  0   0
2   24    5    0    616  486  360  170  30   376   20  1363  41  59  0   0
3   20    9    0    145   0   352  165  27   412   26  1359  50  50  0   0
```

**TIP**

*If the smtx column for the mpstat output is greater than 200, you are heading toward CPU bottleneck problems.*

# Combining ps with Selected V$ Views

Which process is using the most CPU? The following UNIX command will list the top nine CPU users (much like the top command earlier in this chapter).

```
ps -e -o pcpu¹,pid,user,args | sort -k 3 -r | tail

%CPU   PID    USER     COMMAND
0.3    1337   oracle   oraclePRD
0.3    4888   oracle   oraclePRD (LOCAL=NO)
0.4    3      root     fsflush
0.4    1333   psoft    PSRUN PTPUPRCS
0.4    3532   root     ./pmon
0.4    4932   oracle   oraclePRD (LOCAL=NO)
0.4    4941   oracle   oraclePRD (LOCAL=NO)
2.6    4943   oracle   oraclePRD (LOCAL=NO)
16.3   4699   oracle   oraclePRD
```

This command lists the %CPU[2] used, the pid, the UNIX username, and the command that was executed. If the top user was an Oracle user, you could then get the information on the process from Oracle using the queries listed next. This is done by passing the system pid obtained from the ps command into the following queries:

```
rem this is ps_view.sql
col username format a15
col osuser   format a10
col program  format a20
set verify off
select    a.username, a.osuser, a.program, spid, sid, a.serial#
from      v$session a, v$process b
where     a.paddr = b.addr
and       spid = '&pid';

rem this is ps_sql.sql
set verify off
column username format a15
column sql_text format a60
```

[1]This command should work on any POSIX Compatible version of UNIX.
[2]PCPU is defined by SunOS 5.5 as "The ratio of CPU time used recently to CPU time available in the same period, expressed as a percentage. The meaning of 'recently' in this context is unspecified. The CPU time available is determined in an unspecified manner."

**Combining ps with Selected V$ Views**

```
undefine sid
undefine serial#
accept sid prompt 'sid: '
accept serial prompt 'serial#: '
select     'SQL Currently Executing: '
from       dual;

select     b.username, a.sql_text
from       v$sql a, v$session b
where      b.sql_address       = a.address
and        b.sql_hash_value = a.hash_value
and        b.sid        = &sid
and        b.serial# = '&serial';

select     'Open Cursors:'
from       dual;

select     b.username 'USERNAME', a.sql_text 'SQL_TEXT'
from       v$open_cursor a, v$session b
where      b.sql_address       = a.address
and        b.sql_hash_value = a.hash_value
and        b.sid        = &sid
and        b.serial# = '&serial';
```

**Running an example (one step at a time):**

```
$ ps -e -o pcpu,pid,user,args | sort -k 3 -r | tail

%CPU    PID    USER        COMMAND
0.4     650    'nobody     /opt/SUNWsymon/sbin/sm_logscand
0.4     3242   oracle      ora_dbwr_DM6
0.4     3264   oracle      ora_dbwr_DMO
0.4     3316   oracle      ora_dbwr_CNV
0.4     4383   oracle      ora_dbwr_QAT
0.5     3      root        fsflush
0.8     654    root        /opt/SUNWsymon/sbin/sm_krd -i 10
1.7     652    root        /opt/SUNWsymon/sbin/sm_configd -i 10
3.6     4602   oracle      oracleCNV (LOCAL=NO)
$ sqlplus system/manager
SQL> @ps_view
Enter value for pid: 4602
```

Note that we use 4602 as the input as it is the PID for the worst CPU from the ps command:

```
old   4:         and spid='&pid'
new   4:         and spid='4602'

USERNAME   OSUSER    PROGRAM              SPID    SID     SERIAL#
DBAENT     mag       sqlplus@hrtest       4602    10      105

SQL> @ps_sql
sid: 10
serial#: 105
```

Note that we use 10 as the SID and 105 as the serial# as they were the values retrieved in the previous query (ps_view.sql).

```
'SQLCURRENTLYEXECUTING:'
------------------------
SQL Currently Executing:
old   5: and b.sid=&sid
new   5: and b.sid=10
old   6: and b.serial#='&serial'
new   6: and b.serial#='105'

USERNAME   SQL TEXT
DBAENT     select sum(bytes),sum(blocks) from dba_segments

Open Cursors:
old   5: and b.sid=&sid
new   5: and b.sid=10
old   6: and b.serial#='&serial'
new   6: and b.serial#='105'

USERNAME   SQL TEXT
DBAENT     select sum(bytes),sum(blocks) from dba_segments
```

**Putting it all together (setting headings off), you get**

```
DBAENT     mag       sqlplus@hrtest       4602    10      105
SQL Currently Executing:
DBAENT     select sum(bytes),sum(blocks) from dba_segments
Open Cursors:
DBAENT     select sum(bytes),sum(blocks) from dba_segments
```

**Combining ps with Selected V$ Views**

If we had an ad hoc query user problem and received problem queries that showed up in this result on a regular basis, we could add an automated kill command at the end to completely automate our job.

 **TIP**
*Combine operating system utilities with Oracle utilities to quickly and effectively find problematic users.*

### CPU/Memory Monitoring Tool on NT

Task Manager can be used for monitoring CPU and memory use under NT. The screen shown next depicts a two-processor system under NT:

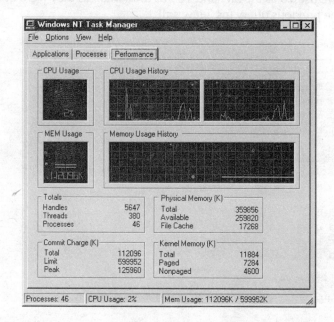

# Using the sar Command to Monitor Disk I/O Problems

Using sar with the -d switch will show us potential disk I/O bottlenecks. This command will list the %busy, avque (average queue length), r+w/s (read and write activity), blks/s (number of blocks transferred), avwait, and avserv. A high %busy and high avque would indicate a disk I/O bottleneck. Consider the following output where disk sd17 is a problem (it is 100 percent busy). If this condition persisted, an analysis of disk sd17 should lead to a reorganization of information from sd17 to a less-used disk. The sar command allows two significant numerical inputs (as shown next), the first is the number of seconds between running sar and the second is how many times to run it (below 5 is 5 seconds and 2 is sar runs twice).

```
# sar  -d 5 2
```

| | device | %busy | avque | r+w/s | blks/s | avwait | avserv |
|---|---|---|---|---|---|---|---|
| 13:37:11 | fd0 | 0 | 0.0 | 0 | 0 | 0.0 | 0.0 |
| | sd1 | 0 | 0.0 | 0 | 0 | 0.0 | 0.0 |
| | sd3 | 0 | 0.0 | 0 | 0 | 0.0 | 0.0 |
| | sd6 | 0 | 0.0 | 0 | 0 | 0.0 | 0.0 |
| | sd15 | 0 | 0.0 | 0 | 0 | 0.0 | 0.0 |
| | sd16 | 13 | 0.1 | 5 | 537 | 0.0 | 26.4 |
| | sd17 | 100 | 6.1 | 84 | 1951 | 0.0 | 72.4 |
| | sd18 | 0 | 0.0 | 0 | 0 | 0.0 | 0.0 |
| 13:37:16 | fd0 | 0 | 0.0 | 0 | 0 | 0.0 | 0.0 |
| | sd1 | 0 | 0.0 | 0 | 0 | 0.0 | 0.0 |
| | sd3 | 1 | 0.0 | 1 | 16 | 0.0 | 32.7 |
| | sd6 | 0 | 0.0 | 0 | 0 | 0.0 | 0.0 |
| | sd15 | 3 | 0.1 | 1 | 22 | 0.0 | 92.3 |
| | sd16 | 13 | 0.1 | 5 | 537 | 0.0 | 26.4 |
| | sd17 | 100 | 6.1 | 85 | 1955 | 0.0 | 71.5 |
| | sd18 | 0 | 0.0 | 0 | 0 | 0.0 | 0.0 |
| Average | fd0 | 0 | 0.0 | 0 | 0 | 0.0 | 0.0 |
| | sd1 | 0 | 0.0 | 0 | 0 | 0.0 | 0.0 |
| | sd3 | 0 | 0.0 | 0 | 3 | 0.0 | 32.7 |
| | sd6 | 0 | 0.0 | 0 | 0 | 0.0 | 0.0 |
| | sd15 | 1 | 0.0 | 0 | 4 | 0.0 | 92.3 |
| | sd16 | 13 | 0.1 | 5 | 570 | 0.0 | 25.3 |
| | sd17 | 100 | 6.1 | 85 | 1962 | 0.0 | 71.2 |
| | sd18 | 0 | 0.0 | 0 | 0 | 0.0 | 0.0 |

Refer to Chapter 3 for additional information on tuning disk I/O when it is at the database level.

# Using iostat Command to Identify Disk I/O Bottlenecks

The UNIX tool iostat can also be used to identify a disk bottleneck. Iostat reports terminal and disk I/O activity, as well as CPU utilization. The first line of the output is for everything since booting the system, whereas each subsequent line shows only the prior interval specified.

**Monitoring Disk I/O Problems**

Depending on the flavor of UNIX, this command has several options (switches). The most useful switches are usually the -d, -x, -D, and -c (cpu load).

```
Format:     iostat [option] [disk] [interval] [count]
```

Using the -d switch, we are able to list the number of kilobytes transferred per second, the number of transfers per second, and the average service time in milliseconds. This displays I/O only; it doesn't distinguish between read and writes.

**Using the -d switch of iostat:**

```
# iostat -d sd15 sd16 sd17 sd18 5 5
```

| | sd15 | | | sd16 | | | sd17 | | | sd18 | |
|---|---|---|---|---|---|---|---|---|---|---|---|
| Kps | tps | serv | Kps | tps | serv | Kps | tps | serv | Kps | tps | serv |
| 1 | 0 | 53 | 57 | 5 | 145 | 19 | 1 | 89 | 0 | 0 | 14 |
| 140 | 14 | 16 | 0 | 0 | 0 | 785 | 31 | 21 | 0 | 0 | 0 |
| 8 | 1 | 15 | 0 | 0 | 0 | 814 | 36 | 18 | 0 | 0 | 0 |
| 11 | 1 | 82 | 0 | 0 | 26 | 818 | 36 | 19 | 0 | 0 | 0 |
| 0 | 0 | 0 | 1 | 0 | 22 | 856 | 37 | 20 | 0 | 0 | 0 |

This output shows that sd17 is severely overloaded compared to the other drives. Moving information from sd17 to one of the other drives would be a good idea if this information is representative of disk I/O on a consistent basis.

**Using the -D switch of iostat:**

The -D switch will report the reads per second, writes per second, and percentage of disk utilization.

```
# iostat -D sd15 sd16 sd17 sd18 5 5
```

| | sd15 | | | sd16 | | | sd17 | | | sd18 | |
|---|---|---|---|---|---|---|---|---|---|---|---|
| rps | wps | util | rps | wps | util | rps | wps | util | rps | wps | util |
| 0 | 0 | 0.3 | 4 | 0 | 6.2 | 1 | 1 | 1.8 | 0 | 0 | 0.0 |
| 0 | 0 | 0.0 | 0 | 35 | 90.6 | 237 | 0 | 97.8 | 0 | 0 | 0.0 |
| 0 | 0 | 0.0 | 0 | 34 | 84.7 | 218 | 0 | 98.2 | 0 | 0 | 0.0 |
| 0 | 0 | 0.0 | 0 | 34 | 88.3 | 230 | 0 | 98.2 | 0 | 0 | 0.0 |
| 0 | 2 | 4.4 | 0 | 37 | 91.3 | 225 | 0 | 97.7 | 0 | 0 | 0.0 |

This shows that the activity on sd17 is completely read activity, while the activity on sd16 is strictly write activity. Both drives are at a peak level of utilization and there may be I/O problems. These statistics were gathered during a backup of sd17 to sd16. Your system should never look this bad!

## Using the -x switch of iostat:

Using the -x switch will report extended disk statistics for all disks. This combines many of the switches previously discussed.

```
extended disk statistics
disk    r/s    w/s    Kr/s    Kw/s    wait    actv    svc_t    %w    %b
fd0     0.0    0.0    0.0     0.0     0.0     0.0     0.0      0     0
sd1     0.0    0.2    0.0     23.2    0.0     0.0     37.4     0     1
sd3     0.0    1.2    0.0     8.4     0.0     0.0     31.3     0     1
sd6     0.0    0.0    0.0     0.0     0.0     0.0     0.0      0     0
sd15    0.0    1.6    0.0     12.8    0.0     0.1     93.3     0     3
sd16    0.0    5.8    0.0     315.2   0.0     0.1     25.0     0     15
sd17    73.0   2.8    941.1   117.2   0.0     6.9     90.8     0     100
sd18    0.0    0.0    0.0     0.0     0.0     0.0     0.0      0     0
extended disk statistics
disk    r/s    w/s    Kr/s    Kw/s    wait    actv    svc_t    %w    %b
fd0     0.0    0.0    0.0     0.0     0.0     0.0     0.0      0     0
sd1     0.0    0.0    0.0     0.0     0.0     0.0     0.0      0     0
sd3     0.0    0.0    0.0     0.0     0.0     0.0     0.0      0     0
sd6     0.0    0.0    0.0     0.0     0.0     0.0     0.0      0     0
sd15    0.0    0.0    0.0     0.0     0.0     0.0     0.0      0     0
sd16    0.0    4.6    0.0     257.6   0.0     0.1     26.4     0     12
sd17    69.0   3.2    993.6   179.2   0.0     7.6     105.3    0     100
sd18    0.0    0.0    0.0     0.0     0.0     0.0     0.0      0     0
```

Once again disks sd16 and sd17 are problems that need to be investigated and monitored further.

## Combining -x switch of iostat with logic in a shell script:

This script will take the iostat -x output and sort it by the % busy field and print out the 10 busiest disks for the listed interval. Some options for this script are listed here, followed by the script example and output.

- This is the diskbusy script built on 1/1/2000.
- The shell this example is running in is !/bin/ksh.
- This script will get an iostat -x listing and sort it by % busy field.
- Change print $10 to sort by a different field.
- Change iostat -x 5 5 to get a different interval and count.
- Change tail to tail -20 to get the top 20 busiest disks.

Identifying Disk I/O Bottlenecks

```
iostat -x | awk '/^disk/'
iostat -x 5 5|grep -v '^    ' |grep -v '^disk'| awk '{
        print $10 ", " $0
        }' $* |
sort -n |
awk -F, '{
        print $2
        }' |
tail
```

**Running the preceding shell script, we receive the following output:**

```
# ./diskbusy

disk      r/s     w/s    Kr/s    Kw/s    wait    actv    svc_t    %w    %b
sd6       0.0     0.0     0.0     0.0     0.0     0.0      0.0     0     0
sd3       0.2     0.6     0.2     2.0     0.0     0.0      8.1     0     1
sd6       0.1     0.0     2.0     0.0     0.0     0.0    176.3     0     1
sd1       3.0     0.1    11.9    10.4     6.0     1.9   2555.3     3     3
sd17      3.4     0.7    37.4    17.2     0.0     0.2     54.6     0     4
sd16      4.1     0.8    38.6    26.0     0.0     0.6    129.5     0    -6
sd17     99.0    14.2   790.8   795.2     0.0     3.6     31.4     0    99
sd17    100.0    14.0   798.8   784.0     0.0     3.5     30.8     0   100
sd17     95.0    14.2   760.0   772.8     0.0     3.6     32.7     0   100
sd17     95.5    14.0   764.3   762.7     0.0     3.5     31.6     0   100
```

In this example, iostat is run five times and the top 10 busiest disks are displayed over all five runs. The disk sd17 is listed five times because it hits the combined top 10 all five times that iostat is run.

**TIP**
*The sar and iostat commands can be used to find potential disk I/O problem areas. Utilizing the capabilities of shell scripting with these commands embedded can further enhance these commands.*

## Disk I/O Monitoring Tools

There are GUI monitoring tools for disk I/O available on most platforms that either come bundled with the software or are available on the Internet. A display of Proctool, as shown next, depicts much of the same data that the iostat command returns.

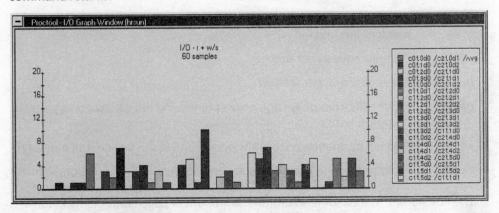

# Using the sar Command to Monitor System Paging/Swapping

The sar command can also be used to check for system paging/swapping. Depending on the system, any paging and swapping could be a sign of trouble. In a virtual memory system, paging is when users that *are not* currently active are moved from memory to disk (a small issue). Swapping is when users that *are* currently active are moved to disk due to insufficient memory (very large issue). Swapping and paging could easily take an entire book due to the depth of the subject. Simple and fast commands to get a general picture of the state of your system will be covered in this section.

**Using the -p switch of sar to report paging activities:**

```
#sar -p 5 4

           atch/s    pgin/s    ppgin/s    pflt/s    vflt/s    slock/s
14:37:41   13.15     20.12     179.08     11.16     2.19      58.57
14:37:46   34.33     20.56     186.23      4.19     1.40      57.49
14:37:51   22.36     19.56     151.30      2.20     0.00      60.88
14:37:56   24.75     22.36     147.90      1.80     0.00      60.28
Average    27.37     20.11     161.81      7.58     8.14      60.85
```

The following table gives a description for the fields that are displayed with sar's -p switch:

| | |
|---|---|
| *atch/s* | Page faults per second that are satisfied by reclaiming a page currently in memory (per second) |
| *pgin/s* | Page-in requests per second |
| *ppgin/s* | Pages paged-in per second |
| *pflt/s* | Page faults from protection errors per second (illegal access to page) or "copy-on-writes" |
| *vflt/s* | Address translation page faults per second (valid page not in memory) |
| *slock/s* | Faults per second caused by software lock requests requiring physical I/O |

The key statistic to look for is an inordinate amount of page faults of any kind. This usually indicates a high degree of paging. Remember that paging is not nearly as bad as swapping, but as paging increases, swapping will soon follow.

**Using the -w switch of sar to report swapping and switching activities:**

The -w switch of sar shows swapping activity. This command will display the fields swpin/s, swpot/s, bswin/s, bswot/s, which are the number of transfers and number of 512-byte units transferred for swapins and swapouts (including initial loading of some programs). The field pswch/s illustrates the process switches.

```
#sar -w 5 4
SunOS hrdev 5.5.1 Generic sun4m    08/05/98

          swpin/s   bswin/s   swpot/s   bswot/s   pswch/s
14:45:22    0.00      0.0       0.00      0.0       294
14:45:27    0.00      0.0       0.00      0.0       312
14:45:32    0.00      0.0       0.00      0.0       322
14:45:37    0.00      .0.0      0.00      0.0       327
Average     0.00      0.0       0.00      0.0       315
```

A high count for process switching would point towards a memory deficiency, because actual process memory is being paged. There is not a problem with swapping in the preceding example.

**Using the -r switch of sar to report free memory and free swap:**

```
# sar -r 5 4

             freemem    freeswap
14:45:21     517        1645911
14:45:26     294        1645907
14:45:36     378        1645919
14:45:41     299        1642633
Average      367        1644597
```

When freemem (free memory--listed here in 512-byte blocks) falls below a certain level, the system will start to page. If it continues to fall, the system will then start to swap processes out. This is a sign of a rapidly degrading system. Look for processes taking an extreme amount or memory or an excessive number of process.

**Using the -g switch of sar to report paging activities:**

```
#sar -g
           pgout/s    ppgout/s    pgfree/s    pgscan/s    %ufs ipf
14:58:34    2.40       74.40      132.80      466.40       0.00
14:58:39    1.80       55.69       90.62      263.87       0.00
14:58:44    2.20       62.32       98.00      298.00       0.00
14:58:49    4.59      142.32      186.43      465.07       0.00
14:58:54    0.80       24.75       24.15        0.00       0.00
```

The following table gives a description for the fields that are displayed with sar's -p switch:

*pgout/s*   Page-out requests per second.

*ppgout/s*  Pages paged-out per second.

*pgfree/s*  Pages per second placed on the free list by the page-stealing daemon.

*pgscan/s*  Pages per second scanned by the page-stealing daemon.

*%ufs_ipf*  The percentage of UFS inodes taken off the free list by iget that had reusable pages associated with them. These pages are flushed and cannot be reclaimed by processes. Thus, this is the percentage of igets with page flushes.

A high ppgout (pages being moved out of memory) also points towards a memory deficiency.

**TIP**
*The sar command can be used to monitor and evaluate memory use and a potential need for additional memory. Paging is generally the movement of inactive processes from memory to disk. A high degree of paging is usually the predecessor to swapping. Swapping is the movement of active processes from memory to disk. If swapping starts to escalate, your system begins the downward "death spiral." Fixing memory hogs or adding memory is the correct solution.*

# Using the ipcs Command to Determine Shared Memory

Another helpful memory command that can be used to monitor the Oracle SGA is the ipcs command. The ipcs command will show the size of each shared memory segment for the SGA. If there is not enough memory for the entire SGA to fit in a contiguous piece of memory, the SGA will be built in noncontiguous memory segments. In the event of an instant crash, there is a possibility that the memory will not be released. If this happens to you, note that the ipcrm command will remove the segments (ipcrm -m for memory segments and ipcrm -s for semaphore segments).

```
# ipcs -b
Shared Memory:
m    204 0x171053d8 --rw-r-----    oracle    dba      65536
m    205 0x1f1053d8 --rw-r-----    oracle    dba 100659200
m    206 0x271053d8 --rw-r-----    oracle    dba   1740800
Semaphores:
s 393218 00000000   --ra-r-----    oracle    dba        300
```

In this example, the SGA is built in three noncontiguous segments (making up the 100M+ SGA). The instance is then shut down and started with a smaller SGA (so that contiguous pieces of memory will make up the SGA). The SGA has been lowered to 70M. The ipcs command is again issued.

```
# ipcs -b
Shared Memory:
m   4403 0x0f1053d8 --rw-r-----    oracle    dba 71118848
Semaphores:
s 393218 00000000   --ra-r-----    oracle    dba      300
```

**TIP**
*Use the ipcs command to see if your SGA is built using multiple noncontiguous pieces of memory. A crash of your database can render this to be a problem with releasing the memory. Use the ipcrm command (only if the SGA pieces are not released after a database crash) to then remove the SGA pieces from memory. Do not issue the ipcrm command with a running database!*

# Using the vmstat Command to Monitor System Load

The vmstat command is a conglomeration of many of the other commands listed in this chapter. The difference with vmstat is you get to see everything at once. The problem with vmstat is that you see everything at once and must evaluate it.

**Procs:**

r    Processes that are currently running

b    Processes that are able to run, but are waiting on a resource

w    Processes that are able to run, but have been swapped out

**CPU information:**

us    Percentage of user time for normal and priority processes

sy    Percentage of system time

id    Percentage of idle time

```
#vmstat 5 3

procs memory     page        disk    faults      cpu
r b w  swap    free   re mf pi po fr de  sr s0 s1 s6 s9    in    sy   cs us sy
19 5 0 1372992 26296  0 2  363 0 0  0   70 31 0  0  703   4846  662  64 36 0
23 3 0 1372952 27024  0 42 287 0 0  0   68 22 0  0  778   4619  780  63 37 0
16 4 0 1381236 36276  0 43 290 0 0  0   59 23 0  0 1149  4560 1393  56 44 0
```

Having any process in the *b* or *w* column is usually a sign of a problem system (the system here has a problem if this continues). If processes are blocked from running, the CPU is likely to be overburdened. The CPU idle time of 0 is a reflection of the overburdening processes that are running and is a serious problem since some processes are blocked and people are waiting for CPU time. On the reverse side, if the idle time was high, you may not be using your system to its full capacity (not balancing activities efficiently) or the system may be oversized for the task. I like to see an idle time of 5-20 percent for a static (not adding new users) system.

The vmstat command is also used to view system paging and swapping. The po (page out) and pi (page in) indicate the amount of paging that is occurring on your system. A small amount of paging is acceptable during a heavy usage cycle, but should not occur for a prolonged period of time. On most systems, paging will occur during Oracle startup.

**TIP**
*Use the vmstat command to find blocked processes (users waiting for CPU time) and also for paging or swapping problems. The vmstat command is a great way to see many of the sar options in one screen.*

## Tips Review

- Use the sar -u command to see a quick snapshot of how heavily the CPU is "bogged down."

- Use the top command to find the worst user on the system at a given point in time.

- Use cron and uptime to get your system load mailed to you on a regular basis.

- If the smtx column for the mpstat output is greater than 200, you are heading toward CPU bottleneck problems.

- Combining operating system utilities with Oracle V$ views can lead to fast and effective answers to problem users. An example using the ps command is given in this chapter.

- The sar and iostat commands can be used to find potential disk I/O problem areas. These commands are further enhanced by utilizing the capabilities of shell scripting. An example is given in this chapter.

- Paging is generally the movement of inactive processes from memory to disk. A high degree of paging is usually the predecessor to swapping. Swapping is the movement of active processes from memory to disk. If swapping starts to escalate, your system begins the downward "death spiral." Fixing memory hogs or adding memory is the correct solution.

■ Use the ipcs command to see if your SGA is built using multiple noncontiguous pieces of memory. A crash of your database can render this to be a problem with releasing the memory.

■ Use the ipcrm command (only if the SGA pieces are not released after a database crash) to then remove the SGA pieces from memory. Do *not* issue the ipcrm command with a running database!

■ Use the vmstat command to find blocked processes (users waiting for CPU time) and also for paging or swapping problems. The vmstat command is a great way to see many of the sar options in one screen.

# References

*Oracle Performance Tuning*; Mark Gurry and Peter Corrigan

*Sun Performance and Tuning*; Adrian Cockcroft

**Tips Review**

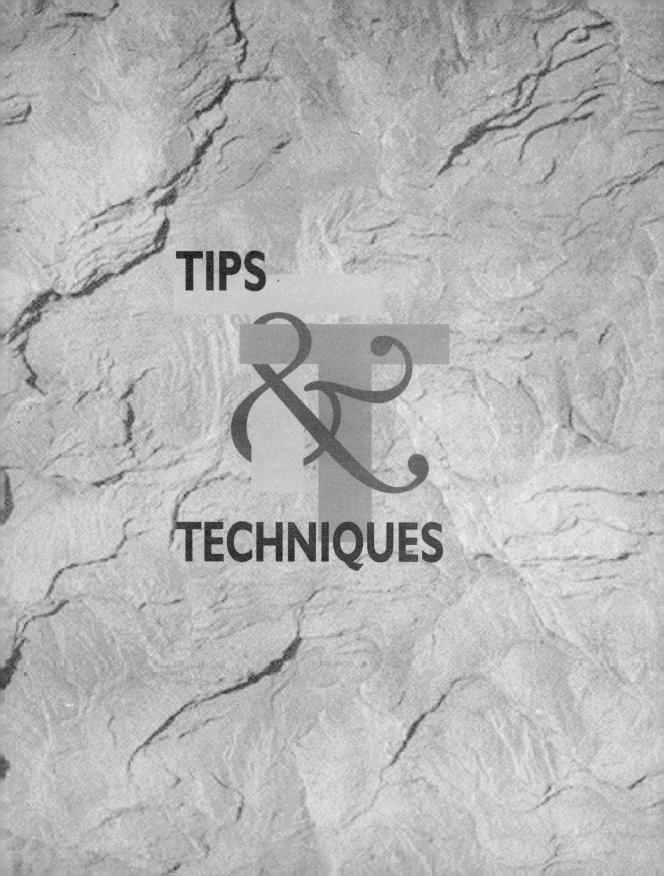

# TIPS & TECHNIQUES

# APPENDIX
# A

Key init.ora
Parameters (DBA)

T here are 193 different documented and 119 different undocumented init.ora parameters in Oracle 8.0.4. Even these numbers vary on different versions of Oracle8. The init.ora parameters vary (in both name and number) based on the database version and release used. Run the queries at the end of this appendix (accessing the V$PARAMETER view and the x$ksppi table) on your version of the database to get the number of views and structure for your specific version. Tips covered in this appendix:

- Top 25 documented init.ora parameters with descriptions and suggested settings

- Top 10 documented init.ora parameters that you better not forget (option dependent)

- Top 13 undocumented init.ora parameters (Shhh!)

- Top 13 undocumented init.ora parameters that I have no idea what they do (??)

- Complete list of documented init.ora parameters (there are 193)

- Complete list of undocumented init.ora parameters (there are 119)

- Top 10 reasons why *not* to write a book

Since every system is set up differently, my top 25 may not be the same as your top 25 (so feel free to write in this book if it is yours). Hopefully this will give you a place to start until someone writes the 1,000 page book on *all* of the init.ora parameters. Please refer to Chapter 4 for a detailed look at the most important tuning parameters.

# The Top 25 init.ora Parameters

The following list is *my* list of the top 25 most important init.ora parameters. Your top 25 may vary somewhat from my top 25 since everyone has a unique business, applications, and experiences.

**TIP**
*Setting certain init.ora parameters correctly could be the difference between a report taking two seconds and two hours. Test changes on a test system thoroughly before implementing those changes in a production environment!*

| init.ora Parameter (My Top 25 Only) | Version of Oracle / Units | Meaning | Suggested Values |
|---|---|---|---|
| NLS_DATE_FORMAT | ALL / Date format | Sets the default date specification for the database. Any display TO_CHAR () or TO_DATE () function will use this display by default. There is no setting that guarantees Y2K compliance. | "DD-MON-RR", "DD-MON-YYYY", or "FXDD-MON-YYYY" Note: You need to put the quotes! Which setting you should use depends on your system. See the Oracle Y2K Web site for additional information. |

| init.ora Parameter (My Top 25 Only) | Version of Oracle / Units | Meaning | Suggested Values |
|---|---|---|---|
| DB_BLOCK_BUFFERS | ALL / Oracle blocks | These are the number of buffers in the SGA cache that will be available for user data to be stored in memory. This number times the DB_BLOCK_SIZE gives the total memory allocated for data. The recommended values on the right are only rough estimates. See Chapter 4 for additional information. This is the total space including space allocated to the default, keep, and Recycle Buffer Pools (if used). | Depends on the database size, number of users, system memory. MINIMUM sizes: If BlkSize = 2K; 5000+ If BlkSize = 4K; 2500+ If BlkSize = 8K; 1200+ |
| SHARED_POOL_SIZE | ALL / Bytes | Size of Oracle Shared Pool. Portion of Shared Pool is used for query server communication. The estimate is on the right. Check Chapter 4 for more information setting this parameter. | Depends on the database size, number of users, system memory. MINIMUM size: Increase existing parameter value by 50–100+ percent for heavy PL/SQL use. |

| init.ora Parameter (My Top 25 Only) | Version of Oracle / Units | Meaning | Suggested Values |
| --- | --- | --- | --- |
| OPTIMIZER_MODE | All / CHOOSE RULE ALL_ROWS FIRST_ ROWS | The choices for this are CHOOSE (generally set to this for cost-based optimization), RULE (set this for rule-based optimization), ALL_ROWS (for best response time), FIRST_ROWS (for best throughput). | CHOOSE |
| SORT_AREA_SIZE | ALL / Bytes per user | *Per user* maximum allocation of sort space (but only allocated when the user executes a sort). For a full description, see Chapter 4. This memory comes from O/S memory *except* when using MTS (comes from SGA), so be careful when using MTS! | 65K–1MB - Limit this based on physical memory and users that need to do sorts. |

| init.ora Parameter (My Top 25 Only) | Version of Oracle / Units | Meaning | Suggested Values |
|---|---|---|---|
| SORT_AREA_RETAINED_SIZE | ALL / Bytes per user | Amount of sort space retained on a *per user* basis in the UGA. Generally, set this equal to SORT_AREA_SIZE. If SORT_AREA_SIZE is 65K+ and there are a lot of users sorting on your system, then I would keep this at 65K. Remember that the SORT_AREA_RETAINED_SIZE value is maintained for *each* sort operation in a query (with a lot of subqueries, this can be trouble). | Set equal to SORT_AREA_SIZE but less than or equal to 65K when a reasonable number of users access the system. |

| init.ora Parameter (My Top 25 Only) | Version of Oracle / Units | Meaning | Suggested Values |
|---|---|---|---|
| LOG_CHECKPOINT_ INTERVAL | ALL / O/S blocks | Sets number of redo blocks that can be written to the redo logs before the DBWR will write blocks from memory to the database. DBAs used to set this to 0; however, a zero value can cause problems (can cause interval checkpoints), so many people set this to 9999999 (10M) so that a checkpoint happens when the redo logs are switched and archived. But, this is not the only parameter that affects when blocks are written to disk. Also, this is O/S blocks and not Oracle blocks! | 9999999 I could have set it to 10,000,000 except everyone else uses 999.... Don't set it to zero! |

The Top 25 init.ora Parameters

| init.ora Parameter (My Top 25 Only) | Version of Oracle / Units | Meaning | Suggested Values |
| --- | --- | --- | --- |
| OPEN_CURSORS | ALL / Number per user | The maximum number of open cursors (context area/statement holding areas) that a SESSION can have at once. There is no cost for setting this too high (it's not preallocated), but you get an ORA-Error if it is too low. | O/S maximum |
| SHARED_POOL_ RESERVED_SIZE | ALL / Bytes | This is a holding area of bytes in the Shared Pool for large requests that the Shared Pool doesn't have enough contiguous blocks to meet. This is only used if the request is *larger* than the SHARED_POOL_ MIN_ALLOCATION. When this parameter is set below 1M, I have seen strange Oracle errors and behavior. If you make this 10 percent, then *do not* change the SHARED_POOL_ MIN_ALLOCATION (5K). | 10 percent of the SHARED_POOL_ SIZE but not less than 1M. |

| init.ora Parameter (My Top 25 Only) | Version of Oracle / Units | Meaning | Suggested Values |
|---|---|---|---|
| DB_BLOCK_SIZE | ALL / Bytes | ORACLE block size expressed in bytes. Must be a multiple of O/S block size. The database must be rebuilt to change this value. | 4096–8192 Smaller for transaction processing systems and larger for data warehouses. |
| DBWR_IO_SLAVES | Oracle8 In Oracle7, this is db_writers/ number of writers | This is the number of writers to write data from the SGA to disk. It simulates asynch I/O for systems that don't have it. It also works for systems that *do* have asynch I/O. | The lesser of 2*CPU and number of disk drives. Monitor this after setting it as it could cause I/O bottlenecks. |
| DB_FILE_MULTIBLOCK_ READ_ COUNT | ALL / Blocks | The number of blocks that are read into the SGA in a single I/O. Data warehouses generally benefit from larger values while heavy TP environments with a lot of users may cause wasted memory with a high setting. | 2–16, but O/S dependent |
| SORT_DIRECT_WRITES | Oracle 7.2+ AUTO, True or False | Writing to temporary segments bypasses the buffer cache. | True Auto = default |

| init.ora Parameter (My Top 25 Only) | Version of Oracle / Units | Meaning | Suggested Values |
|---|---|---|---|
| LOG_BUFFER | ALL / Bytes | Number of bytes for buffering data to the redo logs. The LGWR writes from the log buffers to the redo logs. Larger values are needed if you are executing large DMLs (INSERT, UPDATE, and DELETE). | At least 1M. Increase to a value great enough to eliminate redo request problems when you run bstat/estat. |
| BUFFER_POOL_KEEP | Oracle8 / Oracle blocks | This is the part of DB_BLOCK_BUFFERS that are allocated for data that users access that has been specified to be in the Keep Pool (either by a CREATE or ALTER statement). This is a special area for objects that you hope will be pinned into memory. | Zero / Don't Set, unless you have thoroughly investigated which data and how much needs to be allocated for this. (See Chapter 13 for more information.) |
| BUFFER_POOL_ RECYCLE | Oracle8 / Oracle blocks | This is the part of DB_BLOCK_BUFFERS that is allocated for data that will be reused or recycled. Any table/index…etc., that has been specified for the Recycle Pool will be put here. It is for data of queries that will probably not be needed again. | Zero / Don't Set, unless you have thoroughly investigated which data and how much needs to be allocated for this. |

| init.ora Parameter (My Top 25 Only) | Version of Oracle / Units | Meaning | Suggested Values |
|---|---|---|---|
| LOG_ARCHIVE_ DUPLEX_DEST | Oracle8 / Directory Location with archive prefix (arch) | A location to write an additional copy of archive logs (as redo logs are filled and are archived in ARCHIVELOG mode only). | If you have the space, this is a nice safety net. |
| LOG_ARCHIVE_MIN_ SUCCEED_DEST | Oracle8 / 1 or 2 | The minimum number of successful archives written for a redo log. It is either 1 or 2. | 1; in my opinion, setting this to 2 defeats the benefit. |
| LOCK_SGA | Oracle8 on some O/S / True or False | Locks SGA in physical memory. This prevents the SGA from being paged out to disk. This can help a memory-deficient system, but can also be dangerous is the SGA if built too large. | True; this parameter is not available on all O/S systems. |
| PRE_PAGE_SGA | ALL / True or False | Slows down instance startup, because it "touches" the entire SGA that is built so that the parameter is in memory. This makes users accessing the SGA not used yet, faster. | True |

| init.ora Parameter (My Top 25 Only) | Version of Oracle / Units | Meaning | Suggested Values |
|---|---|---|---|
| LOCK_SGA_AREAS | Oracle8 on some O/S / True or False | Locks certain SGA areas in physical memory. This prevents parts of the SGA from being paged out to disk. This can help a memory-deficient system, but can also be dangerous if the SGA is built too large. | False; this parameter is not available on all O/S systems. |
| LARGE_POOL_SIZE | Oracle8 / Bytes Default = 0 Min. = 300K | The size set aside within the SHARED_POOL_SIZE for large allocations in the Shared Pool. Minimum is 300K, but actually must be at least as big as the LARGE_POOL_MIN_ALLOC. | 10 percent of SHARED_POOL_SIZE but dependent on amount of large blocks of PL/SQL used. |
| LARGE_POOL_MIN_ALLOC | Oracle8 / bytes | Amount allocated from the LARGE_POOL_SIZE. | Set based on size of large PL/SQL that will need to be loaded. |
| LOG_SIMULTANEOUS_COPIES | ALL / Number, Min = cpu_count | The maximum number of redo buffer copy latches for the simultaneous writes. | 2*CPUs |

# The Top 10 init.ora Parameters Not to Forget

This section details some other important init.ora parameters. However, these parameters may be important only in certain cases or only if you are using a certain feature or version of Oracle:

1. COMPATIBLE    Set this to the correct version or you could miss things in the new version.
2. OPTIMIZER_FEATURES_ENABLED    If not set, you are missing out on new features.
3. JOB_QUEUE_PROCESSES    If you want to use DBMS_JOB, you must set this parameter.
4. UTL_FILE_DIR    This must be set to use the utl_file package.
5. DB_FILES    The maximum number of data files that you'll ever have.
6. RECOVERY_PARALLELISM    Recover using the Parallel Query Option, a faster solution.
7. LICENSE_MAX_SESSIONS and LICENSE_MAX_USERS    These limit concurrent and named users.
8. LICENSE_SESSIONS_WARNING    Here, you specify at which session you get a warning.
9. LOG_SMALL_ENTRY_MAX_SIZE    Set this to zero—writes made without copy latch.
10. PARALLEL_ADAPTIVE_MULTI_USER    This prevents parallel query session from taking over.

**TIP**
*There are some excellent options within Oracle. Unfortunately, some of them do not work unless you have the init.ora parameter set correctly.*

# The Top 13 Undocumented init.ora Parameters (as I See It)

1. _ALLOW_RESETLOGS_CORRUPTION   This saves you when you have corrupted redo logs.

2. _CORRUPTED_ROLLBACK_SEGMENTS   This saves you when you have corrupted RB segments.

3. _SPIN_COUNT   This shows how often the processor will take a new request (reduce CPU time-outs).

4. _LOG_ENTRY_PREBUILD_THRESHOLD = 30;   Redo entries larger than this will be prebuilt.

5. _LATCH_SPIN_COUNT   This shows how often a latch request will be taken (reduce latch timeouts).

6. _DB_BLOCK_WRITE_BATCH = 256;   Number of blocks to group in each DB Writer I/O.

7. _CPU_COUNT   Number of CPUs that you have (causes bugs with Parallel Query option). Check with Oracle support for restrictions on some versions and O/S.

8. _INIT_SQL_FILE   %RDBMS80%\ADMIN\SQL.BSQ (where the sql.bsq file is located).

9. _TRACE_FILES_PUBLIC   This allows users to see the TRACE output without major privileges.

10. _FAST_FULL_SCAN_ENABLED   This allows indexed fast full scans if only indexes are needed.

11. \_CORRUPT_BLOCKS_ON_STUCK_RECOVERY    This sometimes gets a corrupted database up.

12. \_ALWAYS_STAR_TRANSFORMATION    This is a fast method for DWHSE if you have a good designer.

13. \_SMALL_TABLE_THRESHOLD    Small tables are pinned into memory if smaller than this.

For a complete listing of all undocumented parameters, their default values, and descriptions, see the section later in this appendix.

**TIP**
*Undocumented init.ora parameters can corrupt your database! Some of them can also save a corrupted database. Try to use these only when all other choices have failed.*

# The *Other* Top 13 Undocumented init.ora  Parameters

I do *not* know what these do but they seem like they should do something that is great. Here's where you make the next discovery!

1. \_DEBUG_SGA    I tried this and didn't see anything happen.

2. \_LOG_BUFFERS_DEBUG    The note on this one is that it "slows things down."

3. \_REUSE_INDEX_LOOPS    These are the blocks to examine for index block reuse.

4. \_SAVE_ESCALATES    The default is True; I'm not sure what escalates are.

5. \_OPTIMIZER_UNDO_CHANGES    Oracle changed (in V6.03) queries with an in operation that is used in a subquery to be changed into a straight join. Setting this parameter to True will use the specific rule-based activity established prior to that version.

6. \_DSS_CACHE_FLUSH    This enables a full cache flush for parallel; can't measure effect.

7. \_DB_NO_MOUNT_LOCK    This does not get a mount lock; it didn't help me when I tried.

8. _AFFINITY   This defaults to TRUE and enables/disables affinity at run time.

9. _CORRUPT_BLOCKS_ON_STUCK_RECOVERY   This was tried in a corrupt recovery; it didn't do anything.

10. _CURSOR_DB_BUFFERS_PINNED   This lists additional buffers a cursor can pin; can't measure its effect.

11. _DB_BLOCK_NO_IDLE_WRITES   This disables writes of buffers when idle; sounds dangerous.

12. _DISABLE_LOGGING   You can do nologging in Oracle8 now; this corrupted my DB.

13. _IO_SLAVES_DISABLED   This disables I/O slaves; seems like there's a safer way to do this.

For a complete listing of all undocumented parameters, their default values, and descriptions, see the section later in this appendix.

**TIP**
*Undocumented init.ora parameters often show a glimpse of things coming in the next version of Oracle. However, some of them don't work or cause severe problems.*

# Listing of Documented init.ora Parameters (V$PARAMETER)

The following query will retrieve this listing. The listing is accurate output for 8.0.4.

```
select     name, value, ismodified,  description
from       v$parameter
order      by name;
```

| Name | Val | Ismodified | Description |
| --- | --- | --- | --- |
| O7_DICTIONARY_ ACCESSIBILITY | TRUE | FALSE | Version 7 Dictionary Accessibility Support |
| ALLOW_PARTIAL_SN_ RESULTS | FALSE | FALSE | Allow partial results when processing gv$ views |
| ALWAYS_ANTI_JOIN | NESTED_ LOOPS | FALSE | Always use this anti-join when possible |

| Name | Val | Ismodified | Description |
|---|---|---|---|
| AQ_TM_PROCESSES | 0 | FALSE | Number of AQ Time Managers to start |
| ARCH_IO_SLAVES | 0 | FALSE | ARCH I/O slaves |
| AUDIT_TRAIL | NONE | FALSE | Enable system auditing |
| B_TREE_BITMAP_PLANS | FALSE | FALSE | Enable the use of bitmap plans for tables with only B-tree indexes |
| BACKGROUND_DUMP_DEST | %rdbm s 80%\trace | FALSE | Detached process dump directory |
| BACKUP_DISK_IO_SLAVES | 0 | FALSE | BACKUP Disk I/O slaves |
| BACKUP_TAPE_IO_SLAVES | FALSE | FALSE | BACKUP Tape I/O slaves |
| BITMAP_MERGE_AREA_SIZE | 1048576 | FALSE | Maximum memory allowed for BITMAP MERGE |
| BLANK_TRIMMING | FALSE | FALSE | Blank trimming semantics parameter |
| BUFFER_POOL_KEEP | | FALSE | Number of database blocks/latches in keep buffer pool |
| BUFFER_POOL_RECYCLE | | FALSE | Number of database blocks/latches in recycle buffer pool |
| CACHE_SIZE_THRESHOLD | 100 | FALSE | Maximum size of table or piece to be cached (in blocks) |
| CLEANUP_ROLLBACK_ENTRIES | 20 | FALSE | Number of undo entries to apply per transaction cleanup |
| CLOSE_CACHED_OPEN_CURSORS | FALSE | FALSE | Close cursors cached by PL/SQL at each commit |
| COMMIT_POINT_STRENGTH | 1 | FALSE | Bias this node has toward not preparing in a two-phase commit |

| Name | Val | Ismodified | Description |
| --- | --- | --- | --- |
| COMPATIBLE | 8.0.0 | FALSE | Database will be completely compatibl with this software versio |
| COMPATIBLE_NO_ RECOVERY | 8.0.0 | FALSE | Database will be compatible unless crash or media recovery is ne |
| CONTROL_FILE_RECORD_ KEEP | 7 | FALSE | Control file record keep time in days time |
| CONTROL_FILES | c:\ orawin95\ database\ ctl1orcl.ora | FALSE | Control file names list |
| CPU_COUNT | 1 | FALSE | Number of cpu's for this instance |
| CREATE_BITMAP_AREA_SIZE | 8388608 | FALSE | Size of create bitmap buffer for bitmap index |
| CURSOR_SPACE_FOR_TIME | FALSE | FALSE | Use more memory in order to get faster execution |
| DB_BLOCK_BUFFERS | 1000 | FALSE | Number of database blocks cached in memory |
| DB_BLOCK_CHECKPOINT_ BATCH | 8 | FALSE | Max number of blocks to checkpoint in a DB Writer IO |
| DB_BLOCK_CHECKSUM | FALSE | FALSE | Store checksum in db blocks and check during reads |
| DB_BLOCK_LRU_EXTENDED_ STATISTICS | 0 | FALSE | Maintain buffer cache LRU statistics for last $N$ blocks discarded |
| DB_BLOCK_LRU_LATCHES | 1 | FALSE | Number of lru latches |
| DB_BLOCK_LRU_STATISTICS | FALSE | FALSE | Maintain buffer cache LRU hits-by-position statistics (slow) |

| Name | Val | Ismodified | Description |
| --- | --- | --- | --- |
| DB_BLOCK_MAX_DIRTY_ TARGET | 4294967294 | FALSE | Target upper bound on number of buffers that can be dirty |
| DB_BLOCK_SIZE | 2048 | FALSE | Size of database block in bytes |
| DB_DOMAIN | WORLD | FALSE | Directory part of global database name stored with CREATE DATABASE |
| DB_FILE_DIRECT_IO_ COUNT | 64 | FALSE | Sequential I/O block count |
| DB_FILE_MULTIBLOCK_ READ_COUNT | 8 | FALSE | Db block to be read each IO |
| DB_FILE_NAME_CONVERT | | FALSE | Datafile name convert pattern and string for standby/clone database |
| DB_FILE_SIMULTANEOUS_ WRITES | 4 | FALSE | Max simultaneous (overlaped) writes per db file |
| DB_FILES | 1024 | FALSE | Max allowable # db files |
| DB_NAME | oracle | FALSE | Database name specified in CREATE DATABASE |
| DBLINK_ENCRYPT_LOGIN | FALSE | FALSE | Enforce password for distributed login always be encrypted |
| DBWR_IO_SLAVES | 0 | FALSE | DBWR I/O slaves |
| DELAYED_LOGGING_ BLOCK_CLEANOUTS | TRUE | FALSE | Turn on delayed-logging block cleanouts feature |
| DISCRETE_TRANSACTIONS_ ENABLED | FALSE | FALSE | Enable OLTP mode |
| DISK_ASYNCH_IO | FALSE | FALSE | Use asynch I/O for random access devices |
| DISTRIBUTED_LOCK_ TIMEOUT | 60 | FALSE | Number of seconds a distributed transaction waits for a lock |

| Name | Val | Ismodified | Description |
|---|---|---|---|
| DISTRIBUTED_RECOVERY_CONNECTION_HOLD_TIME | 200 | FALSE | Number of seconds RECO holds outbound connections open |
| DISTRIBUTED_TRANSACTIONS | 16 | FALSE | Max. number of concurrent distributed transactions |
| DML_LOCKS | 264 | FALSE | Dml locks—one for each table modified in a transaction |
| ENQUEUE_RESOURCES | 284 | FALSE | Resources for enqueues |
| EVENT | | FALSE | Debug event control—default null string |
| FIXED_DATE | FALSE | fixed | SYSDATE value |
| FREEZE_DB_FOR_FAST_INSTANCE_RECOVERY | FALSE | FALSE | Freeze database during instance recovery |
| GC_DEFER_TIME | 10 | FALSE | How long to defer forced writes for hot buffers (DFS) |
| GC_FILES_TO_LOCKS | | FALSE | Mapping between file numbers and lock buckets (DFS) |
| GC_LCK_PROCS | 1 | FALSE | Number of background parallel server lock processes to start |
| GC_RELEASABLE_LOCKS | 0 | FALSE | Number of releasable locks (DFS) |
| GC_ROLLBACK_LOCKS | | FALSE | Number of undo locks (DFS) |
| GLOBAL_NAME | TRUE | FALSE | Enforce that database links have same name as remote database |
| HASH_AREA_SIZE | 0 | FALSE | Size of in-memory hash work area |
| HASH_JOIN_ENABLED | TRUE | FALSE | Enable/disable hash join |

| Name | Val | Ismodified | Description |
|---|---|---|---|
| HASH_MULTIBLOCK_IO_COUNT | 8 | FALSE | Number of blocks hash join will read/write at once |
| IFILE | | FALSE | Include file in init.ora |
| INSTANCE_GROUPS | | FALSE | List of instance group names |
| INSTANCE_NUMBER | 0 | FALSE | Instance number |
| JOB_QUEUE_INTERVAL | 60 | FALSE | Wakeup interval in seconds for job queue processes |
| JOB_QUEUE_KEEP_CONNECTIONS | FALSE | FALSE | Keep network connections between execution of jobs |
| JOB_QUEUE_PROCESSES | 2 | FALSE | Number of job queue processes to start |
| LARGE_POOL_MIN_ALLOC | 16K | FALSE | Minimum allocation size in bytes for the large allocation pool |
| LARGE_POOL_SIZE | 0 | FALSE | Size in bytes of the large allocation pool |
| LGWR_IO_SLAVES | 0 | FALSE | LGWR I/O slaves |
| LICENSE_MAX_SESSIONS | 0 | FALSE | Maximum number of non-system user sessions allowed |
| LICENSE_MAX_USERS | 0 | FALSE | Maximum number of named users that can be created in the database |
| LICENSE_SESSIONS_WARNING | 0 | FALSE | Warning level for number of non-system user sessions |
| LM_LOCKS | 12000 | FALSE | Number of locks configured for the lock manager |

| Name | Val | Ismodified | Description |
|---|---|---|---|
| LM_PROCS | 127 | FALSE | Number of client processes configured for the lock manager |
| LM_RESS | 6000 | FALSE | Number of resources configured for the lock manager |
| LOCAL_LISTENER | | FALSE | Local listener |
| LOCK_NAME_SPACE | | FALSE | Lock name space used for generating lock names for standby/clone |
| LOG_ARCHIVE_BUFFER_SIZE | 127 | FALSE | Size of each archival buffer in log file blocks |
| LOG_ARCHIVE_BUFFERS | 4 | FALSE | Number of buffers to allocate for archiving |
| LOG_ARCHIVE_DEST | %rdbms 80%\ | FALSE | Archival destination text string |
| LOG_ARCHIVE_DUPLEX_DEST | | FALSE | Duplex archival destination text string |
| LOG_ARCHIVE_FORMAT | arc%s%t | FALSE | Archival destination format |
| LOG_ARCHIVE_MIN_SUCCEED_DEST | 1 | FALSE | Minimum number of archive destinations that must succeed |
| LOG_ARCHIVE_START | FALSE | FALSE | Start archival process on SGA initialization |
| LOG_BLOCK_CHECKSUM | FALSE | FALSE | Calculate checksum for redo blocks when writing |
| LOG_BUFFER | 8192 | FALSE | Redo circular buffer size |
| LOG_CHECKPOINT_INTERVAL | 10000 | FALSE | Number redo blocks checkpoint threshold |
| LOG_CHECKPOINT_TIMEOUT | 0 | FALSE | Maximum time interval between checkpoints in seconds |

| Name | Val | Ismodified | Description |
|---|---|---|---|
| LOG_CHECKPOINTS_TO_ALERT | FALSE | FALSE | Log checkpoint begin/end to alert file |
| LOG_FILE_NAME_CONVERT | | FALSE | Logfile name convert pattern and string for standby/clone databa |
| LOG_FILES | 255 | FALSE | Max allowable log files |
| LOG_SIMULTANEOUS_COPIES | 0 | FALSE | Number of simultaneous copies into redo buffer (of copy latches) |
| LOG_SMALL_ENTRY_MAX_SIZE | 80 | FALSE | Redo entries larger than this will acquire the redo copy latch |
| MAX_COMMIT_PROPAGATION_DELAY | 90000 | FALSE | Max age of new snapshot in .01 seconds |
| MAX_DUMP_FILE_SIZE | 10240 | FALSE | Maximum size (blocks) of dump file |
| MAX_ENABLED_ROLES | 20 | FALSE | Max number of roles a user can have enabled |
| MAX_ROLLBACK_SEGMENTS | 30 | FALSE | Max number of rollback segments in SGA cache |
| MAX_TRANSACTION_BRANCHES | 8 | FALSE | Max number of branches per distributed transaction |
| MTS_DISPATCHERS | | FALSE | Specifications of dispatchers |
| MTS_LISTENER_ADDRESS | | FALSE | Address(es) of network listener |
| MTS_MAX_DISPATCHERS | 5 | FALSE | Max number of dispatchers |
| MTS_MAX_SERVERS | 20 | FALSE | Max number of servers |
| MTS_MULTIPLE_LISTENERS | FALSE | FALSE | Are multiple listeners enabled? |

Listing of Documented init.ora Parameters

| Name | Val | Ismodified | Description |
|---|---|---|---|
| MTS_RATE_LOG_SIZE | | FALSE | Number of rate statistic events to log |
| MTS_RATE_SCALE | | FALSE | Scale to display rate statistic (100ths of a second) |
| MTS_SERVERS | 0 | FALSE | Number of servers to start up |
| MTS_SERVICE | oracle | FALSE | Service supported by dispatchers |
| NLS_CURRENCY | | FALSE | NLS local currency symbol |
| NLS_DATE_FORMAT | dd-mon-rr | FALSE | NLS Oracle date format |
| NLS_DATE_LANGUAGE | | FALSE | NLS date language name |
| NLS_ISO_CURRENCY | | FALSE | NLS ISO currency territory name |
| NLS_LANGUAGE | American | FALSE | NLS language name |
| NLS_NUMERIC_CHARACTERS | | FALSE | NLS numeric characters |
| NLS_SORT | | FALSE | NLS linguistic definition name |
| NLS_TERRITORY | a | FALSE | NLS territory name |
| OBJECT_CACHE_MAX_SIZE_PERCENT | 10 | FALSE | Percentage of maximum size over optimal of the user session's ob |
| OBJECT_CACHE_OPTIMAL_SIZE | 102400 | FALSE | Optimal size of the user session's object cache in bytes |
| OPEN_CURSORS | 50 | FALSE | Max number cursors per process |
| OPEN_LINKS | 4 | FALSE | Max number open links per session |
| OPEN_LINKS_PER_INSTANCE | 4 | FALSE | Max number open links per instance |

| Name | Val | Ismodified | Description |
| --- | --- | --- | --- |
| OPS_ADMIN_GROUP | | FALSE | Instance group to use for global v$ queries |
| OPTIMIZER_MODE | choose | FALSE | Optimizer mode |
| OPTIMIZER_PERCENT_PARALLEL | 0 | FALSE | Optimizer percent parallel |
| OPTIMIZER_SEARCH_LIMIT | 5 | FALSE | Optimizer search limit |
| ORACLE_TRACE_COLLECTION_NAME | | FALSE | Oracle TRACE default collection name |
| ORACLE_TRACE_COLLECTION_PATH | %otrace80%\admin\cdf\ | FALSE | Oracle TRACE collection path |
| ORACLE_TRACE_COLLECTION_SIZE | 5242880 | FALSE | Oracle TRACE collection file max size |
| ORACLE_TRACE_ENABLE | FALSE | FALSE | Oracle TRACE instance wide enable/disable |
| ORACLE_TRACE_FACILITY_NAMED | Oracle | FALSE | Oracle TRACE default facility name |
| ORACLE_TRACE_FACILITY_PATH | %otrace80%\admin\fdf\ | FALSE | Oracle TRACE facility path |
| OS_AUTHENT_PREFIX | OPS$ | FALSE | Prefix for auto-logon accounts |
| OS_ROLES | FALSE | FALSE | Retrieve roles from the operating system |
| PARALLEL_DEFAULT_MAX_INSTANCES | 0 | FALSE | Default maximum number of instances for parallel query |
| PARALLEL_INSTANCE_GROUP | | FALSE | Instance group to use for all parallel operations |
| PARALLEL_MAX_SERVERS | 5 | FALSE | Maximum parallel query servers per instance |
| PARALLEL_MIN_MESSAGE_POOL | 48330 | FALSE | Minimum size of shared pool memory to reserve for pq servers |
| PARALLEL_MIN_PERCENT | 0 | FALSE | Minimum percent of threads required for parallel query |

**Listing of Documented init.ora Parameters**

| Name | Val | Ismodified | Description |
| --- | --- | --- | --- |
| PARALLEL_MIN_SERVERS | 0 | FALSE | Minimum parallel query servers per instance |
| PARALLEL_SERVER | FALSE | FALSE | If TRUE startup in parallel server mode |
| PARALLEL_SERVER_IDLE_TIME | 5 | FALSE | Idle time before parallel query server dies |
| PARALLEL_TRANSACTION_RESOURCE_TIMEOUT | 300 | FALSE | Global parallel transaction resource deadlock timeout in seconds |
| PARTITION_VIEW_ENABLED | FALSE | FALSE | Enable/disable partitioned views |
| PLSQL_V2_COMPATIBILITY | FALSE | FALSE | PL/SQL version 2.x compatibility flag |
| PRE_PAGE_SGA | FALSE | FALSE | Pre-page sga for process |
| PROCESSES | 50 | FALSE | User processes |
| RECOVERY_PARALLELISM | 0 | FALSE | Number of server processes to use for parallel recovery |
| REMOTE_DEPENDENCIES_MODE | timestamp | FALSE | Remote-procedure-call dependencies mode parameter |
| REMOTE_LOGIN_PASSWORDFILE | shared | FALSE | Password file usage parameter |
| REMOTE_OS_AUTHENT | FALSE | FALSE | Allow non-secure remote clients to use auto-logon accounts |
| REMOTE_OS_ROLES | FALSE | FALSE | Allow non-secure remote clients to use os roles |
| REPLICATION_DEPENDENCY_TRACKING | TRUE | FALSE | Tracking dependency for Replication parallel propagation |
| RESOURCE_LIMIT | FALSE | FALSE | Master switch for resource limit |

| Name | Val | Ismodified | Description |
| --- | --- | --- | --- |
| ROLLBACK_SEGMENTS | | FALSE | Undo segment list |
| ROW_CACHE_CURSORS | 10 | FALSE | Number of cached cursors for row cache management |
| ROW_LOCKING | always | FALSE | Row-locking |
| SEQUENCE_CACHE_ENTRIES | 10 | FALSE | Number of sequence cache entries |
| SEQUENCE_CACHE_HASH_ BUCKETS | 10 | FALSE | Number of sequence cache hash buckets |
| SERIAL_REUSE | disable | FALSE | Reuse the frame segments |
| SERIALIZABLE | FALSE | FALSE | Serializable |
| SESSION_CACHED_ CURSORS | 0 | FALSE | Number of cursors to save in the session cursor cache |
| SESSION_MAX_OPEN_FILES | 0 | FALSE | Maximum number of open files allowed per session |
| SESSIONS | 60 | FALSE | User and system sessions |
| SHARED_POOL_RESERVED_ MIN_ALLOC | 5K | FALSE | Minimum allocation size in bytes for reserved area of shared pool |
| SHARED_POOL_RESERVED_ SIZE | 500000 | FALSE | Size in bytes of reserved area of shared pool |
| SHARED_POOL_SIZE | 10000000 | FALSE | Size in bytes of shared pool |
| SNAPSHOT_REFRESH_ INTERVAL | 60 | FALSE | Wakeup interval in seconds for job queue processes |
| SNAPSHOT_REFRESH_KEEP_ CONNECTIONS | FALSE | FALSE | Keep network connections between execution of jobs |
| SNAPSHOT_REFRESH_ PROCESSES | 0 | FALSE | Number of job queue processes to start |

| Name | Val | Ismodified | Description |
|---|---|---|---|
| SORT_AREA_RETAINED_SIZE | 0 | FALSE | Size of in-memory sort work area retained between fetch calls |
| SORT_AREA_SIZE | 65536 | FALSE | Size of in-memory sort work area |
| SORT_DIRECT_WRITES | AUTO | FALSE | Use direct write |
| SORT_READ_FAC | 20 | FALSE | Multi-block read factor for sort |
| SORT_SPACEMAP_SIZE | 512 | FALSE | Size of sort disk area space map |
| SORT_WRITE_BUFFER_SIZE | 32768 | FALSE | Size of each sort direct write buffer |
| SORT_WRITE_BUFFERS | 2 | FALSE | Number of sort direct write buffers |
| SPIN_COUNT | 1 | FALSE | Amount to spin waiting for a latch |
| SPREAD_EXTENTS | TRUE | FALSE | Should extents be spread across files in the tablespace |
| SQL92_SECURITY | FALSE | FALSE | Require select privilege for searched update/ delete |
| SQL_TRACE | FALSE | FALSE | Enable SQL trace |
| STAR_TRANSFORMATION_ENABLED | FALSE | FALSE | Enable the use of star transformation |
| TAPE_ASYNCH_IO | TRUE | FALSE | Use asynch I/O requests for tape devices |
| TEMPORARY_TABLE_LOCKS | 60 | FALSE | Temporary table locks |
| TEXT_ENABLE | FALSE | FALSE | Enable text searching |
| THREAD | 0 | FALSE | Redo thread to mount |
| TIMED_OS_STATISTICS | 0 | FALSE | Internal os statistic gathering interval in seconds |

| Name | Val | Ismodified | Description |
|---|---|---|---|
| TIMED_STATISTICS | FALSE | FALSE | Maintain internal timing statistics |
| TRANSACTION_AUDITING | TRUE | FALSE | Transaction auditing records generated in the redo log |
| TRANSACTIONS | 66 | FALSE | Max number of concurrent active transactions |
| TRANSACTIONS_PER_ROLLBACK_SEGMENT | 11 | FALSE | Number of active transactions per rollback segment |
| USER_DUMP_DEST | %rdbms80%\ trace | FALSE | User process dump directory |
| UTL_FILE_DIR | | FALSE | Utl_file accessible directories list |

193 rows selected.

# Listing of Undocumented init.ora Parameters (x$ksppi/x$ksppcv)

**Warning:** Using these parameters is not supported by Oracle, nor do I recommend them on a production system. Only use them if you have thoroughly tested them on your crash and burn system. Undocumented init.ora parameters can lead to database corruption (although many of them can get your database back up when you have corruption). Use at your own risk.

The following query will retrieve the listing below. The listing is accurate output for version 8.0.4.

```
select      a.ksppinm, b.ksppstvl, b.ksppstdf, a.ksppdesc
from        x$ksppi a, x$ksppcv b
where       a.indx = b.indx
and         substr(ksppinm,1,1) = '_'
order       by ksppinm;
```

| Name | Val | Defit | Description |
|---|---|---|---|
| _ADVANCED_DSS_FEATURES | FALSE | TRUE | Enable advanced dss features |

| Name | Val | Defit | Description |
|---|---|---|---|
| _AFFINITY_ON | TRUE | TRUE | Enable/disable affinity at run time |
| _ALL_SHARED_DBLINKS | | TRUE | Treat all dblinks as shared |
| _ALLOW_RESETLOGS_CORRUPTION | FALSE | TRUE | Allow resetlogs even if it will cause corruption |
| _ALWAYS_STAR_TRANSFORMATION | FALSE | TRUE | Always favor use of star transformation |
| _BUMP_HIGHWATER_MARK_COUNT | 0 | TRUE | How many blocks should we allocate per free list on advancing HW |
| _COLUMN_ELIMINATION_OFF | FALSE | TRUE | Turn off predicate-only column elimination |
| _CONTROLFILE_ENQUEUE_TIMEOUT | 900 | TRUE | Control file enqueue timeout in seconds |
| _CORRUPT_BLOCKS_ON_STUCK_RECOVERY | 0 | TRUE | Number of times to corrupt a block when media recovery stuck |
| _CORRUPTED_ROLLBACK_SEGMENTS | | TRUE | Corrupted undo segment list |
| _CR_DEADTIME | 6 | TRUE | Global cache lock CR deadlock timeout in seconds |
| _CURSOR_DB_BUFFERS_PINNED | 18 | TRUE | Additional number of buffers a cursor can pin at once |
| _DB_BLOCK_CACHE_CLONE | FALSE | TRUE | Always clone data blocks on get (for debugging) |
| _DB_BLOCK_CACHE_MAP | 0 | TRUE | Map / unmap and track reference counts on blocks (for debugging) |
| _DB_BLOCK_CACHE_PROTECT | FALSE | TRUE | Protect database blocks (true only when debugging) |
| _DB_BLOCK_HASH_BUCKETS | 250 | TRUE | Number of database block hash buckets |
| _DB_BLOCK_HI_PRIORITY_BATCH_SIZE | 80 | TRUE | Percentage of write batch used for high priority ckpts |
| _DB_BLOCK_MAX_CR_DBA | 10 | TRUE | Maximum Allowed Number of CR buffers per dba |
| _DB_BLOCK_MAX_SCAN_CNT | 0 | TRUE | Maximum number of buffers to inspect when looking for free one |

| Name | Val | Defit | Description |
| --- | --- | --- | --- |
| _DB_BLOCK_ MED_PRIORITY_ BATCH_SIZE | 40 | TRUE | Percentage of write batch used for medium priority ckpts |
| _DB_BLOCK_NO_ IDLE_WRITES | FALSE | TRUE | Disable periodic writes of buffers when idle |
| _DB_BLOCK_ WRITE_BATCH | 0 | TRUE | Number of blocks to group in each DB Writer IO |
| _DB_HANDLES | 210 | TRUE | System-wide simultaneous buffer operations |
| _DB_HANDLES_ CACHED | 3 | TRUE | Buffer handles cached each process |
| _DB_LARGE_ DIRTY_QUEUE | 0 | TRUE | Number of buffers which force dirty queue to be written |
| _DB_NO_MOUNT_ LOCK | FALSE | TRUE | Do not get a mount lock |
| _DB_WRITER_SCAN_ DEPTH | 0 | TRUE | Number of LRU buffers for dbwr to scan when looking for dirty |
| _DB_WRITER_ SCAN_DEPTH_ DECREMENT | 0 | TRUE | Subtract from dbwr scan depth when dbwr is working too hard |
| _DB_WRITER_ SCAN_DEPTH_ INCREMENT | 0 | TRUE | Add to dbwr scan depth when dbwr is behind |
| _DEBUG_SGA | FALSE | TRUE | Debug sga |
| _DISABLE_ INCREMENTAL_ CHECKPOINTS | FALSE | TRUE | Disable incremental checkpoints for thread recovery |
| _DISABLE_LATCH_ FREE_SCN_WRITES_ VIA_32CAS | FALSE | TRUE | Disable latch-free SCN writes using 32-bit compare & swap |
| _DISABLE_LATCH_ FREE_SCN_WRITES_ VIA_64CAS | TRUE | TRUE | Disable latch-free SCN writes using64-bit compare & swap |
| _DISABLE_LOGGING | FALSE | TRUE | Disable logging |
| _DSS_CACHE_FLUSH | FALSE | TRUE | Enable full cache flush for parallel execution |

| Name | Val | Defit | Description |
|---|---|---|---|
| _DYNAMIC_STATS_THRESHOLD | 30 | TRUE | Delay threshold (in seconds) between sending statistics messages |
| _ENABLE_CSCN_CACHING | TRUE | TRUE | Enable commit SCN caching for all transactions |
| _ENABLE_MULTI_STATEMENT_PDML | TRUE | TRUE | Enable multi statement parallel DML operations |
| _ENQUEUE_DEBUG_MULTI_INSTANCE | FALSE | TRUE | Debug enqueue multi instance |
| _ENQUEUE_HASH | 155 | TRUE | Enqueue hash table length |
| _ENQUEUE_HASH_CHAIN_LATCHES | 1 | TRUE | Enqueue hash chain latches |
| _ENQUEUE_LOCKS | 1755 | TRUE | Locks for managed enqueues |
| _FAST_FULL_SCAN_ENABLED | TRUE | TRUE | If TRUE, enabled fast full scan |
| _GC_CLASS_LOCKS | 0 | TRUE | Set locks for the minor classes (DFS) |
| _IDL_CONVENTIONAL_INDEX_MAINTENANCE | TRUE | TRUE | Enable conventional index maintenance for insert direct load |
| _IGNORE_FAILED_ESCALATES | TRUE | TRUE | If TRUE, ignore failed escalates immediately (DFS) |
| _INIT_SQL_FILE | %rdbms80%\admin\sql.bsq | TRUE | File containing SQL statements to execute upon database creation |
| _IO_SLAVES_DISABLED | FALSE | TRUE | Do not use I/O slaves |
| _IOSLAVE_BATCH_COUNT | 1 | TRUE | Per attempt ios picked |
| _IOSLAVE_ISSUE_COUNT | 500 | TRUE | Ios issued before completion check |
| _KGL_BUCKET_COUNT | 0 | TRUE | Index to the bucket count array |
| _KGL_LATCH_COUNT | 0 | TRUE | Number of library cache latches |
| _KGL_MULTI_INSTANCE_INVALIDATION | TRUE | TRUE | Whether KGL to support multi-instance in validations |

| Name | Val | Defit | Description |
|---|---|---|---|
| _KGL_MULTI_INSTANCE_LOCK | TRUE | TRUE | Whether KGL to support multi-instance locks |
| _KGL_MULTI_INSTANCE_PIN | TRUE | TRUE | Whether KGL to support multi-instance pins |
| _LATCH_RECOVERY_ALIGNMENT | 80 | TRUE | Align latch recovery structures |
| _LATCH_WAIT_POSTING | 1 | TRUE | Post sleeping processes when free latch |
| _LM_AST_OPTION | FALSE | TRUE | Enable ast passthrough option |
| _LM_DIRECT_SENDS | lkmgr | TRUE | Processes which will do direct lock manager sends |
| _LM_DLMD_PROCS | 1 | TRUE | Number of background lock manager daemon processes to start |
| _LM_DOMAINS | 2 | TRUE | Number of groups configured for the lock manager |
| _LM_GROUPS | 20 | TRUE | Number of groups configured for the lock manager |
| _LM_NON_FAULT_TOLERANT | FALSE | TRUE | Disable lock manager fault-tolerance mode |
| _LM_SEND_BUFFERS | 10000 | TRUE | Number of lock manager send buffers |
| _LM_STATISTICS | FALSE | TRUE | Enable lock manager statistics collection |
| _LM_XIDS | 139 | TRUE | Number of transaction ids configured for the lock manager |
| _LOG_BLOCKS_DURING_BACKUP | TRUE | TRUE | Log block images when changed during backup |
| _LOG_BUFFERS_DEBUG | FALSE | TRUE | Debug redo buffers (slows things down) |
| _LOG_CHECKPOINT_RECOVERY_CHECK | 0 | TRUE | # Redo blocks to verify after checkpoint |
| _LOG_DEBUG_MULTI_INSTANCE | FALSE | TRUE | Debug redo multi instance code |
| _LOG_ENTRY_PREBUILD_THRESHOLD | 0 | TRUE | Redo entries larger than this will be prebuilt before getting la |

**Undocumented init.ora Parameters**

| Name | Val | Defit | Description |
|------|-----|-------|-------------|
| _LOG_IO_SIZE | 0 | TRUE | Automatically initiate log write if this many redo blocks in buf |
| _LOG_SPACE_ERRORS | TRUE | TRUE | Should we report space errors to alert log |
| _MAX_EXPONENTIAL_SLEEP | 0 | TRUE | Max sleep during exponential backoff |
| _MAX_SLEEP_HOLDING_LATCH | 4 | TRUE | Max time to sleep while holding a latch |
| _MESSAGES | 100 | TRUE | Message queue resources - dependent on # processes & # buffers |
| _MINIMUM_GIGA_SCN | 0 | TRUE | Minimum SCN to start with in 2^30 units |
| _MTS_LOAD_CONSTANTS | 3,0.75, 0.25,0.1 | TRUE | Server load balancing constants (S,P,D,I) |
| _NO_OBJECTS | FALSE | TRUE | No object features are used |
| _NUMBER_CACHED_ATTRIBUTES | 10 | TRUE | Maximum number of cached attributes per instance |
| _OFFLINE_ROLLBACK_SEGMENTS | | TRUE | Offline undo segment list |
| _OPEN_FILES_LIMIT | 4294967294 | TRUE | Limit on number of files opened by I/O subsystem |
| _OPTIMIZER_UNDO_CHANGES | FALSE | TRUE | Undo changes to query optimizer |
| _ORACLE_TRACE_EVENTS | | TRUE | Oracle TRACE event flags |
| _ORACLE_TRACE_FACILITY_VERSION | | TRUE | Oracle TRACE facility version |
| _PARALLEL_SERVER_SLEEP_TIME | 10 | TRUE | Sleep time between dequeue timeouts (in 1/100ths) |
| _PASSWORDFILE_ENQUEUE_TIMEOUT | 900 | TRUE | Password file enqueue timeout in seconds |
| _PREDICATE_ELIMINATION_ENABLED | TRUE | TRUE | Allow predicate elimination if set to TRUE |
| _PX_DISABLE_BROADCAST | FALSE | TRUE | Disable broadcasting of small inputs to joins except when necessary |

| Name | Val | Deflt | Description |
|------|-----|-------|-------------|
| _RELEASE_INSERT_ THRESHOLD | 5 | TRUE | Maximum number of unusable blocks to unlink from freelist |
| _REUSE_INDEX_LOOP | 5 | TRUE | Number of blocks being examine for index block reuse |
| _ROLLBACK_SEGMENT_CO UNT | 0 | TRUE | Number of undo segments |
| _ROLLBACK_SEGMENT_INITIAL | 1 | TRUE | Starting undo segment number |
| _ROW_CACHE_BUFFER_SIZE | 200 | TRUE | Size of row cache circular buffer |
| _ROW_CACHE_ INSTANCE_LOCKS | 100 | TRUE | Number of row cache instance locks |
| _SAVE_ESCALATE | TRUE | TRUE | If TRUE, save escalates from basts (DFS) |
| _SESSION_IDLE_BIT_ LATCHES | 0 | TRUE | One latch per session or a latch per group of sessions |
| _SHARED_SESSION_ SORT_FETCH_BUFFER | 0 | TRUE | Size of in-memory merge buffer for mts or xa fetch calls |
| _SINGLE_PROCESS | FALSE | TRUE | Run without detached processes |
| _SMALL_TABLE_ THRESHOLD | 20 | TRUE | Threshold level of table size for forget-bit enabled during scan |
| _SQL_CONNECT_ CAPABILITY_OVERRIDE | 0 | TRUE | Sql connect capability table override |
| _SQL_CONNECT_ CAPABILITY_TABLE | | TRUE | SQL Connect Capability Table (testing only) |
| _TEST_PARAM_1 | 25 | TRUE | Test parmeter 1 |
| _TEST_PARAM_2 | | TRUE | Test parameter 2 |
| _TEST_PARAM_3 | | TRUE | Test parameter 3 |
| _TRACE_ARCHIVE_DEST | %rdbms8 0%\ trace.dat | TRUE | Trace archival destination |
| _TRACE_ARCHIVE_ START | FALSE | TRUE | Start trace process on SGA initialization |
| _TRACE_BLOCK_SIZE | 2048 | TRUE | Trace block size |
| _TRACE_BUFFERS_PER_ PROCESS | 0 | TRUE | Trace buffers per process |

**Undocumented init.ora Parameters**

| Name | Val | Defit | Description |
|------|-----|-------|-------------|
| _TRACE_ENABLED | TRUE | TRUE | Should tracing be enabled at startup |
| _TRACE_EVENTS | | TRUE | Turns on and off trace events |
| _TRACE_FILE_SIZE | 10000 | TRUE | Trace file size |
| _TRACE_FILES_PUBLIC | FALSE | TRUE | Create publicly accessible trace files |
| _TRACE_FLUSHING | FALSE | TRUE | TRWR should try to keep tracing buffers clean |
| _TRACE_WRITE_BATCH_SIZE | 32 | TRUE | Trace write batch size |
| _UPCONVERT_FROM_AST | TRUE | TRUE | If TRUE, attempt to up-convert from an AST (DFS) |
| _USE_VECTOR_POST | FALSE | TRUE | Use vector post |
| _WAIT_FOR_SYNC | TRUE | TRUE | Wait for sync on commit MUST BE ALWAYS TRUE |
| _WALK_INSERT_THRESHOLD | 0 | TRUE | Maximum number of unusable blocks to walk across freelist |

119 rows selected.

The Top 10 reasons Not to Write a Book

# The Top 10 reasons *Not to* Write a Book

1. You require sleep and caffeine-enhanced water clogs your coffee maker.

2. You have enough trouble getting the time to read books, let alone write one.

3. You enjoy getting together with your family from time to time.

4. You're tired of being the first one in the office (actually you've been there all night).

5. You prefer golf, tennis, basketball, or some other sport more than speed typing.

6. You enjoy noticing the world around you versus a purple haze all through your mind.

7. Kevin Loney will write on that subject eventually…you'll wait for his book.

8. You don't want to "show-off" how much you know …you're far too humble.

9. Your PC is out of disk space already...you've just loaded Windows 99.1415926.

10. You just got your LIFE back after the last Oracle conversion—No way!

**TIP**
*Retirement is a good time to write a book, not* during the fastest growth of technology in history.

# Tips Review

- Setting certain init.ora parameters correctly could be the difference between a report taking two seconds and two hours. Try changes out on a test system thoroughly *before* implementing those changes in a production environment!

- There are some excellent options within Oracle. Unfortunately, some of them do *not* work unless the init.ora parameter is set correctly.

- Undocumented init.ora parameters can corrupt your database! Some of them can also save a corrupted database. Try to use these only when all other choices have failed.

- Undocumented init.ora parameters often show a glimpse of things coming in the next version of Oracle, but many of them don't work at all.

- Retirement is a good time to write a book. Writing a book during the fastest growth in the history of technology is *not*.

# References

*Oracle7 Server Tuning*; Oracle Corporation

*Oracle8 Server Tuning*; Oracle Corporation

*Performance Tuning Guide Version 7.0*; Oracle Corporation

*Oracle8 DBA Handbook*; Kevin Loney

*Oracle8 Advanced Tuning & Administration;* Aronoff, Loney, Sonawalla

*Oracle8 Tuning*; Corey, Abbey, Dechichio, and Abramson

Thanks to Brad Brown, Joe Trezzo, Sean McGuire, Randy Swanson, Greg Pucka, Mike Broullette, and Kevin Loney who made contributions to this chapter.

# TIPS & TECHNIQUES

# APPENDIX B

## The V$ Views
## (DBA and Developer)

T he V\$ views are very helpful in analyzing database issues. This appendix lists all views and creation scripts used to actually build the V\$ and GV\$ views. The V\$ views vary in structure and number based on the database version and release used. Run the queries on your version of the database to get the number of views and structure for your specific version. Areas covered in this appendix include the following:

- A list of all the V7 V\$ views
- A list of all V8 GV\$ and V\$ views
- V7 script listing of the x\$ tables used in the creation of the V\$ views
- V8 script listing of the x\$ tables used in the creation of the V\$ views
- V\$ view, x\$ table, and dictionary creation

**NOTE**
*V\$ to x\$ and x\$ to V\$ cross-references can be found in Appendix C.*

# A List of All the V7 V\$ Views

Here is the version 7 query to get this listing:

```
select    name
from      v$fixed_table
where     name like 'V%'
order by  name;
```

| | | | |
|---|---|---|---|
| V\$ACCESS | V\$ARCHIVE | V\$BACKUP | V\$BGPROCESS |
| V\$CIRCUIT | V\$COMPATIBILITY | V\$COMPATSEG | V\$CONTROLFILE |
| V\$DATABASE | V\$DATAFILE | V\$DBFILE | V\$DBLINK |
| V\$DB_OBJECT_CACHE | V\$DISPATCHER | V\$ENABLEDPRIVS | V\$FILESTAT |
| V\$FIXED_TABLE | V\$INSTANCE | V\$LATCH | V\$LATCHHOLDER |
| V\$LATCHNAME | V\$LIBRARYCACHE | V\$LICENSE | V\$LOADCSTAT |
| V\$LOADTSTAT | V\$_LOCK1 | V\$_LOCK | V\$LOCK |
| V\$LOG | V\$LOGFILE | V\$LOGHIST | V\$LOG_HISTORY |
| V\$MLS_PARAMETERS | V\$MTS | V\$MYSTAT | V\$NLS_PARAMETERS |
| V\$NLS_VALID_VALUES | V\$OPEN_CURSOR | V\$OPTION | V\$PARAMETER |
| V\$PQ_SESSTAT | V\$PQ_SLAVE | V\$PQ_SYSSTAT | V\$PROCESS |

| | | | |
|---|---|---|---|
| V$PWFILE_USERS | V$QUEUE | V$RECOVERY_LOG | V$RECOVER_FILE |
| V$REQDIST | V$RESOURCE | V$ROLLNAME | V$ROLLSTAT |
| V$ROWCACHE | V$SESSION | V$SESSION_CURSOR_<br>CACHE | V$SESSION_EVENT |
| V$SESSION_WAIT | V$SESSTAT | V$SESS_IO | V$SGA |
| V$SGASTAT | V$SHARED_SERVER | V$SQLAREA | V$SQLTEXT |
| V$STATNAME | V$SYSSTAT | V$SYSTEM_CURSOR_<br>CACHE | V$SYSTEM_EVENT |
| V$THREAD | V$TIMER | V$TRANSACTION | V$TYPE_SIZE |
| V$VERSION | V$WAITSTAT | | |

# A List of All the V8 GV$ and V$ Views

**NOTE**
*The V8 V$ views are the same as the GV$ views less
instance ID.*

Here is the version 8 query to get this listing:

```
select    name
from      v$fixed_table
where     name like 'GV%'
order by  name;
```

| | | |
|---|---|---|
| GV$ACCESS | GV$ACTIVE_INSTANCES | GV$ARCHIVE |
| GV$ARCHIVED_LOG | GV$ARCHIVED_DEST | GV$BACKUP |
| GV$BACKUP_CORRUPTION | GV$BACKUP_DATAFILE | GV$BACKUP_DEVICE |
| GV$BACKUP_PIECE | GV$BACKUP_REDOLOG | GV$BACKUP_SET |
| GV$BGPROCESS | GV$BH | GV$BUFFER_POOL |
| GV$CIRCUIT | GV$CLASS_PING | GV$COMPATIBILITY |
| GV$COMPATSEG | GV$CONTROLFILE | GV$CONTROLFILE_RECORD_<br>SECTION |
| GV$COPY_CORRUPTION | GV$DATABASE | GV$DATAFILE |
| GV$DATAFILE_COPY | GV$DATAFILE_HEADER | GV$DBFILE |
| GV$DBLINK | GV$DB_OBJECT_CACHE | GV$DB_PIPES |

| | | |
|---|---|---|
| GV$DELETED_OBJECT | GV$DISPATCHER | GV$DISPATCHER_RATE |
| GV$DLM_CONVERT_LOCAL | GV$DLM_CONVERT_REMOTE | GV$DLM_LATCH |
| GV$DLM_MISC | GV$ENABLEDPRIVS | GV$ENQUEUE_LOCK |
| GV$EVENT_NAME | GV$EXECUTION | GV$FILESTAT |
| GV$FILE_PING | GV$FIXED_TABLE | GV$FIXED_VIEW_DEFINITION |
| GV$GLOBAL_TRANSACTION | GV$INDEXED_FIXED_COLUMN | GV$INSTANCE |
| GV$LATCH | GV$LATCHHOLDER | GV$LATCHNAME |
| GV$LATCH_CHILDREN | GV$LATCH_MISSES | GV$LATCH_PARENT |
| GV$LIBRARYCACHE | GV$LICENSE | GV$LOADCSTAT |
| GV$LOADPSTAT | GV$LOADTSTAT | GV$_LOCK |
| GV$_LOCK1 | GV$LOCK | GV$LOCKED_OBJECT |
| GV$LOCKS_WITH_COLLISIONS | GV$LOCK_ELEMENT | GV$LOG |
| GV$LOGFILE | GV$LOGHIST | GV$LOG_HISTORY |
| GV$MTS | GV$MYSTAT | GV$NLS_PARAMETERS |
| GV$NLS_VALID_VALUES | GV$OBJECT_DEPENDENCY | GV$OFFLINE_RANGE |
| GV$OPEN_CURSOR | GV$OPTION | GV$PARAMETER |
| GV$PQ_SESSTAT | GV$PQ_SLAVE | GV$PQ_SYSSTAT |
| GV$PQ_TQSTAT | GV$PROCESS | GV$PWFILE_USERS |
| GV$QUEUE | GV$RECOVERY_FILE_STATUS | GV$RECOVERY_LOG |
| GV$RECOVERY_STATUS | GV$RECOVER_FILE | GV$REQDIST |
| GV$RESOURCE | GV$RESOURCE_LIMIT | GV$ROLLSTAT |
| GV$ROWCACHE | GV$_SEQUENCES | GV$SESSION |
| GV$SESSION_CONNECT_INFO | GV$SESSION_CURSOR_CACHE | GV$SESSION_EVENT |
| GV$SESSION_LONGOPS | GV$SESSION_OBJECT_CACHE | GV$SESSION_WAIT |
| GV$SESSTAT | GV$SESS_IO | GV$SGA |
| GV$SGASTAT | GV$SHARED_POOL_RESERVED | GV$SHARED_SERVER |
| GV$SORT_SEGMENT | GV$SORT_USAGE | GV$SQL |
| GV$SQLAREA | GV$SQLTEXT | GV$SQLTEXT_WITH_NEWLINES |
| GV$SQL_BIND_DATA | GV$SQL_BIND_METADATA | GV$SQL_CURSOR |
| GV$SQL_SHARED_MEMORY | GV$STATNAME | GV$SUBCACHE |
| GV$SYSSTAT | GV$SYSTEM_CURSOR_CACHE | GV$SYSTEM_EVENT |
| GV$SYSTEM_PARAMETER | GV$TABLESPACE | GV$THREAD |
| GV$TIMER | GV$TRANSACTION | GV$TRANSACTION_ENQUEUE |
| GV$TYPE_SIZE | GV$VERSION | GV$WAITSTAT |

# The V8 V$ Views

Here is the version 8.0.4 query to get this listing:

```
select    name
from      v$fixed_table
where     name like 'V%'
order by  name;
```

| | | |
|---|---|---|
| V$ACCESS | V$ACTIVE_INSTANCES | V$ARCHIVE |
| V$ARCHIVED_LOG | V$ARCHIVED_DEST | V$BACKUP |
| V$BACKUP_CORRUPTION | V$BACKUP_DATAFILE | V$BACKUP_DEVICE |
| V$BACKUP_PIECE | V$BACKUP_REDOLOG | V$BACKUP_SET |
| V$BGPROCESS | V$BH | V$BUFFER_POOL |
| V$CIRCUIT | V$CLASS_PING | V$COMPATIBILITY |
| V$COMPATSEG SECTION | V$CONTROLFILE | V$CONTROLFILE_RECORD_ |
| V$COPY_CORRUPTION | V$DATABASE | V$DATAFILE |
| V$DATAFILE_COPY | V$DATAFILE_HEADER | V$DBFILE |
| V$DBLINK | V$DB_OBJECT_CACHE | V$DB_PIPES |
| V$DELETED_OBJECT | V$DISPATCHER | V$DISPATCHER_RATE |
| V$DLM_CONVERT_LOCAL | V$DLM_CONVERT_REMOTE | V$DLM_LATCH |
| V$DLM_MISC | V$ENABLEDPRIVS | V$ENQUEUE_LOCK |
| V$EVENT_NAME | V$EXECUTION | V$FILESTAT |
| V$FILE_PING | V$FIXED_TABLE | V$FIXED_VIEW_DEFINITION |
| V$GLOBAL_TRANSACTION | V$INDEXED_FIXED_COLUMN | V$INSTANCE |
| V$LATCH | V$LATCHHOLDER | V$LATCHNAME |
| V$LATCH_CHILDREN | V$LATCH_MISSES | V$LATCH_PARENT |
| V$LIBRARYCACHE | V$LICENSE | V$LOADCSTAT |
| V$LOADPSTAT | V$LOADTSTAT | V$_LOCK |
| V$_LOCK1 | V$LOCK | V$LOCKED_OBJECT |
| V$LOCKS_WITH_COLLISIONS | V$LOCK_ELEMENT | V$LOG |
| V$LOGFILE | V$LOGHIST | V$LOG_HISTORY |
| V$MTS | V$MYSTAT | V$NLS_PARAMETERS |
| V$NLS_VALID_VALUES | V$OBJECT_DEPENDENCY | V$OFFLINE_RANGE |
| V$OPEN_CURSOR | V$OPTION | V$PARAMETER |
| V$PQ_SESSTAT | V$PQ_SLAVE | V$PQ_SYSSTAT |

| | | |
|---|---|---|
| V$PQ_TQSTAT | V$PROCESS | V$PWFILE_USERS |
| V$QUEUE | V$RECOVERY_FILE_STATUS | V$RECOVERY_LOG |
| V$RECOVERY_STATUS | V$RECOVER_FILE | V$REQDIST |
| V$RESOURCE | V$RESOURCE_LIMIT | V$ROLLSTAT |
| V$ROWCACHE | V$_SEQUENCES | V$SESSION |
| V$SESSION_CONNECT_INFO | V$SESSION_CURSOR_CACHE | V$SESSION_EVENT |
| V$SESSION_LONGOPS | V$SESSION_OBJECT_CACHE | V$SESSION_WAIT |
| V$SESSTAT | V$SESS_IO | V$SGA |
| V$SGASTAT | V$SHARED_POOL_RESERVED | V$SHARED_SERVER |
| V$SORT_SEGMENT | V$SORT_USAGE | V$SQL |
| V$SQLAREA | V$SQLTEXT | V$SQLTEXT_WITH_NEWLINES |
| V$SQL_BIND_DATA | V$SQL_BIND_METADATA | V$SQL_CURSOR |
| V$SQL_SHARED_MEMORY | V$STATNAME | V$SUBCACHE |
| V$SYSSTAT | V$SYSTEM_CURSOR_CACHE | V$SYSTEM_EVENT |
| V$SYSTEM_PARAMETER | V$TABLESPACE | V$THREAD |
| V$TIMER | V$TRANSACTION | V$TRANSACTION_ENQUEUE |
| V$TYPE_SIZE | V$VERSION | V$WAITSTAT |

# V7 Scripts of the x$ Tables Used to Create the V$ Views

Here is the version 7 query to get this listing:

```
select      'View Name: '||view_name,
            substr(view_definition,1,(instr(view_definition,'from')-1)) def1,
            substr(view_definition,(instr(view_definition,'from'))) def2
from        v$fixed_view_definition
order       by view_name;
```

### View Name: V$ACCESS

```
select  distinct s.ksusenum,o.kglnaown,o.kglnaobj,o.kglobtyp
from     x$ksuse s,x$kglob o,x$kgldp d, x$kgllk l
where     l.kgllkuse=s.addr
and       l.kgllkhdl=d.kglhdadr
and       o.kglhdadr=d.kglrfhdl
/
```

## View Name: **V$ARCHIVE**

```
select     le.indx+1,le.lethr,le.leseq, decode(bitand(le.leflg,8),0,'NO','YES'),
           to_number(le.lelos)
from       x$kccle le,x$kccdi di
where      bitand(di.diflg,1)!=0
and        le.ledup!=0
and        bitand(le.leflg,1)=0
and        (to_number(le.lelos)< = to_number(di.difas) or bitand(le.leflg,8)0)= 0)
```

## View Name: **V$BACKUP**

```
select     hxfil, decode(hxerr, 0, decode(bitand(fhsta, 1),
           0,'NOT ACTIVE','ACTIVE'), 1,'FILE MISSING', 2,
           'OFFLINE NORMAL', 3,'NOT VERIFIED', 4,'FILE NOT FOUND',
           5,'CANNOT OPEN FILE', 6,'CANNOT READ HEADER', 7,
           'CORRUPT HEADER', 8,'WRONG FILE TYPE', 9,'WRONG DATABASE',
           10,'WRONG FILE NUMBER', 11,'WRONG FILE CREATE', 12,
           'WRONG FILE CREATE', 13,'WRONG FILE SIZE', 'UNKNOWN ERROR'),
           to_number(fhbsc), fhbti
from       x$kcvfhonl
/
```

## View Name: **V$BGPROCESS**

```
select     p.ksbdppro,p.ksbdpnam,d.ksbdddsc, p.ksbdperr
from       x$ksbdp p,x$ksbdd d
where      p.indx=d.indx
/
```

## View Name: **V$CIRCUIT**

```
select     addr,kmcvcdpc, decode(kmcvcpro, kmcvcdpc,
           hextoraw('00'),kmcvcpro), kmcvcwat, kmcvcses,
           kmcvcsta,kmcvcque, kmcvcsz0,kmcvcsz1,kmcvcnmg,
           kmcvcnmb,kmcvcbrk
from       x$kmcvc
where      bitand(ksspaflg,1)!=0
/
```

## View Name: **V$COMPATIBILITY**

```
select     kcktyid, kcktyrls, kcktydsc
from       x$kckty
/
```

### View Name: V$COMPATSEG

```
select    kckceid, kckcer1, kckcevsn
from      x$kckce
/
```

### View Name: V$CONTROLFILE

```
select    decode(bitand(cfflg,1),0,'',1, 'INVALID'),cfnam
from      x$kcccf
/
```

### View Name: V$DATABASE

```
select    didbn,dicts,decode(bitand(diflg,1), 0,'NOARCHIVELOG',
          'ARCHIVELOG'), to_number(discn),to_number(difas)
from      x$kccdi
/
```

### View Name: V$DATAFILE

```
select    fe.indx+1,decode(bitand(fe.festa, 19),0,'OFFLINE',1,
          'SYSOFF', 2,'ONLINE', 3,'SYSTEM', 16,'RECOVER', 18,
          'RECOVER','UNKNOWN'), decode(bitand(fe.festa, 12), 0,
          'DISABLED', 4,'READ ONLY', 12,'READ WRITE','UNKNOWN'),
          to_number(fe.fecps), fe.fesiz*fe.febsz, fn.fnnam
from      x$kccfe fe,x$kccfn fn
where     fe.fedup!=0
and       fe.indx+1=fn.fnfno
and       fn.fntyp=3
/
```

### View Name: V$DBFILE

```
select    fnfno,fnnam
from      x$kccfn
where     fnnam is not null
and       fntyp=3
/
```

### View Name: V$DBLINK

```
select    nconam, ncouid, decode(bitand(hstflg, 32), 0, 'NO',
          'YES'), decode(bitand(hstflg, 8), 0, 'NO', 'YES'),
          decode(hstpro, 1, 'V5', 2, 'V6', 3, 'V6_NLS', 4, 'V7',
```

```
                'UNKN'), ncouct, decode(bitand(ncoflg, 2), 0, 'NO',
                'YES'), decode(bitand(ncoflg, 8), 0, 'NO', 'YES'), nco2pstr
from            x$uganco
where           bitand(hstflg, 1) != 0
/
```

## View Name: **V$DB_OBJECT_CACHE**

```
select          kglnaown,kglnaobj,kglnadlk, decode(kglhdnsp,1,
                'TABLE/PROCEDURE', 2,'BODY', 3,'TRIGGER', 4,'INDEX',
                5,'CLUSTER',6,'OBJECT'), decode(bitand(kglobflg,3),0,
                'NOT LOADED', 2,'NON-EXISTENT', 3,'INVALID STATUS',
                decode(kglobtyp, 1,'INDEX', 2,'TABLE', 3,'CLUSTER', 4,
                'VIEW', 5,'SYNONYM',6,'SEQUENCE', 7,'PROCEDURE',8,'FUNCTION',
                9,'PACKAGE',10, 'NON-EXISTENT',11, 'PACKAGE BODY',12,
                'TRIGGER', 13,'CLASS',14,'SET', 15,'OBJECT', 16, 'USER',
                17,'DBLINK','INVALID TYPE')),
                kglobhs0+kglobhs1+kglobhs2+kglobhs3+kglobhs4+kglobhs5+kglobhs6,
                kglhdldc,kglhdexc,kglhdlkc,kglobpc0, decode(kglhdkmk,0,'NO','YES')
from            x$kglob
where           kglhdnsp between 1 and 6
/
```

## View Name: **V$DISPATCHER**

```
select          kmmdinam,kmmdinet,kmmdipro,kmmdista,
                decode(kmmdiacc,0,'NO','YES'), kmmdinmg,
                kmmdinmb,kmmdibrk,kmmdinvo,kmmditnc,
                kmmdiidl,kmmdibsy,kmmdiler
from            x$kmmdi
where           kmmdiflg!=0
/
```

## View Name: **V$ENABLEDPRIVS**

```
select          -indx
from            x$kzspr
where           x$kzspr.kzsprprv=1
/
```

## View Name: **V$FILESTAT**

```
select          k.kcfiofno,k.kcfiopyr,k.kcfiopyw, k.kcfiopbr,
                k.kcfiopbw,k.kcfioprt, k.kcfiopwt
from            x$kcfio k,x$kccfe f
where           f.fedup <> 0
and             f.indx+1=k.kcfiofno
/
```

V7 Scripts Used to
Create the V$ Views

### View Name: V$FIXED_TABLE

```
select     kqftanam, kqftaobj, 'TABLE'
from       x$kqfta
union      all
select     kqfvinam, kqfviobj, 'VIEW'
from       x$kqfvi
union      all
select     kqfdtnam, kqfdtobj, 'TABLE'
from       x$kqfdt
/
```

### View Name: V$INSTANCE

```
select     key,value
from       x$ksuxsinst
/
```

### View Name: V$LATCH

```
select     addr,kslltnum,kslltlvl,kslltnam,kslltwgt,kslltwff,
           kslltwsl,kslltngt,kslltnfa,kslltwkc,kslltwth,ksllthst0,
           ksllthst1,ksllthst2,ksllthst3,ksllthst4,ksllthst5,
           ksllthst6,ksllthst7,ksllthst8,ksllthst9,ksllthst10,
           ksllthst11
from       x$ksllt
/
```

### View Name: V$LATCHHOLDER

```
select     indx,ksuprlat
from       x$ksuprlat
where      ksuprlat!=hextoraw('00')
/
```

### View Name: V$LATCHNAME

```
select     indx,kslldnam
from       x$kslld
/
```

## View Name: V$LIBRARYCACHE

```
select     decode(indx,0,'SQL AREA', 1,'TABLE/PROCEDURE',2,
           'BODY',3,'TRIGGER', 4,'INDEX', 5,'CLUSTER',6,
           'OBJECT',7,'PIPE','?'),kglstget,kglstght,
           decode(kglstget,0,1,kglstght/kglstget),kglstpin,
           kglstpht,decode (kglstpin,0,1,kglstpht/kglstpin),
           kglstrld,kglstinv
from       x$kglst
where      indx<8
/
```

## View Name: V$LICENSE

```
select     ksullms,ksullws,ksullcs,ksullhs,ksullmu
from       x$ksull
/
```

## View Name: V$LOADCSTAT

```
select     kllcntnrd,kllcntnrj,kllcnttds,kllcntnds,kllcntsdt
from       x$kllcnt
/
```

## View Name: V$LOADTSTAT

```
select     klltabnld,klltabnrj,klltabnfw,klltabnan,klltabnls
from       x$klltab
/
```

## View Name: V$_LOCK1

```
select     addr,ksqlkadr,ksqlkses,ksqlkres,ksqlkmod,ksqlkreq
from       x$kdnssc
where      bitand(kssobflg,1)!=0
and        (ksqlkmod!=0 or ksqlkreq!=0)
union      all
select     addr,ksqlkadr,ksqlkses,ksqlkres,ksqlkmod,ksqlkreq
from       x$kdnssf
where      bitand(kssobflg,1)!=0
```

V7 Scripts Used to
Create the V$ Views

```
and        (ksqlkmod!=0 or ksqlkreq!=0)
union      all
select     addr,ksqlkadr,ksqlkses,ksqlkres,ksqlkmod,ksqlkreq
from       x$ksqeq
where      bitand(kssobflg,1)!=0
and        (ksqlkmod!=0 or ksqlkreq!=0)
/
```

### View Name: V$_LOCK

```
select     laddr,kaddr,saddr,raddr,lmode,request
from       v$_lock1
union      all
select     addr,ksqlkadr,ksqlkses,ksqlkres,ksqlkmod,ksqlkreq
from       x$ktadm
where      bitand(kssobflg,1)!=0
and        (ksqlkmod!=0 or ksqlkreq!=0)
union      all
select     addr,ksqlkadr,ksqlkses,ksqlkres,ksqlkmod,ksqlkreq
from       x$ktcxb
where      bitand(ksspaflg,1)!=0
and        (ksqlkmod!=0 or ksqlkreq!=0)
/
```

### View Name: V$LOCK

```
select     l.laddr,l.kaddr,s.ksusenum,r.ksqrsidt,r.ksqrsid1,
           r.ksqrsid2,l.lmode, l.request
from       v$_lock l,x$ksuse s,x$ksqrs r
where      l.saddr=s.addr
and        l.raddr=r.addr
/
```

### View Name: V$LOG

```
select     le.indx+1,le.lethr,le.leseq,le.lesiz*le.lebsz,ledup,
           decode(bitand (le.leflg,1),0,'NO','YES'),
           decode(sign(leseq),0,'UNUSED',decode
           (bitand(le.leflg,8),8,'CURRENT', decode(sign(to_number(rt.rtckp_scn)-
           to_number(le.lenxs)), - 1,'ACTIVE','INACTIVE'))),to_number(le.lelos),
           le.lelot
fromx$kcccle le, x$kccrt rt
where      le.ledup!=0
and        le.lethr=rt.indx+1
/
```

## View Name: **V$LOGFILE**

```
select     fnfno, decode(fnfly,0,'',1,'INVALID',2,'STALE',4,
           'DELETED','UNKNOWN'), fnnam
from       x$kccfn
where      fnnam is not null
and        fntyp=2
/
```

## View Name: **V$LOGHIST**

```
select     lhthr,lhseq,to_number(lhlos),lhlot,to_number(lhnxs)
from       x$kcclh
/
```

## View Name: **V$LOG_HISTORY**

```
select     lhthr, lhseq, lhlot, to_number(lhlos),
           to_number(lhnxs)-1, lhnam
from       x$kcclh
/
```

## View Name: **V$MLS_PARAMETERS**

```
select     *
from       v$parameter
where      name like 'mls%'
/
```

## View Name: **V$MTS**

```
select     kmmsgcmx,kmmsgsta+kmmsgutr,kmmsgtrm,kmmsgsmx
from       x$kmmsg
/
```

## View Name: **V$MYSTAT**

```
select     ksusenum,ksusestn,ksusestv
from       x$ksumysta
where      bitand(ksspaflg,1)!=0
and        bitand(ksuseflg,1)!=0
and        ksusestn<
  (select    count(*)
   from      x$ksusd)
/
```

### View Name: V$NLS_PARAMETERS

```
select      parameter, value
from        x$nls_parameters
where       parameter != 'NLS_SPECIAL_CHARS'
/
```

### View Name: V$NLS_VALID_VALUES

```
select      parameter, value
from        x$ksulv
/
```

### View Name: V$OPEN_CURSOR

```
select      kgllkuse, user_name, kglhdpar, kglnahsh, kglnaobj
from        x$kgllk
where       kglhdnsp = 0
and         kglhdpar != kgllkhdl
/
```

### View Name: V$OPTION

```
select      parameter, value
from        x$option
/
```

### View Name: V$PARAMETER

```
select indx+1,ksppinm,ksppity,ksppivl,ksppidf
from        x$ksppi
where       translate(ksppinm,'_','#') not like '#%'
/
```

### View Name: V$PQ_SESSTAT

```
select      kxfpssnam, kxfpssval, kxfpsstot
from        x$kxfpsst
/
```

### View Name: V$PQ_SLAVE

```
select    kxfpdpnam, decode(bitand(kxfpdpflg,16), 0, 'BUSY',
          'IDLE'), kxfpdpses, floor(kxfpdpcit /   6000),
       floor(kxfpdpcbt / 6000), floor(kxfpdpcct / 100),
          kxfpdpclsnt + kxfpdpcrsnt, kxfpdpclrcv + kxfpdpcrrcv,
```

```
        floor((kxfpdptit + kxfpdpcit) / 6000), floor(
           (kxfpdptbt + kxfpdpcbt) / 6000), floor(
           (kxfpdptct + kxfpdpcct) / 100), kxfpdptlsnt + kxfpdpclsnt
           + kxfpdptrsnt + kxfpdpcrsnt, kxfpdptlrcv + kxfpdpclrcv
           + kxfpdptrrcv + kxfpdpcrrcv
from       x$kxfpdp
where      bitand(kxfpdpflg, 8) != 0
/
```

## View Name: V$PQ_SYSSTAT

```
select   rpad(kxfpysnam,30), kxfpysval
from     x$kxfpys
/
```

## View Name: V$PROCESS

```
select   addr,indx,ksuprpid,ksuprunm,ksuprser,ksuprtid,ksuprpnm,
         decode (bitand(ksuprflg,2),0, null,1),decode(ksllawat,
         hextoraw('00'), null,ksllawat)
from     x$ksupr
where    bitand(ksspaflg,1)!=0
/
```

## View Name: V$PWFILE_USERS

```
select   username,decode(sysdba,1,'TRUE','FALSE'), decode
         (sysoper,1,'TRUE', 'FALSE')
from     x$kzsrt
where    valid=1
/
```

## View Name: V$QUEUE

```
select   kmcqspro,decode(indx,0,'COMMON',1,'OUTBOUND',
         'DISPATCHER'), kmcqsncq,kmcqswat,kmcqstnc
from     x$kmcqs
where    indx in (0,1)
or       kmcqspro!=hextoraw('00')
/
```

## View Name: V$RECOVERY_LOG

```
select   lhthr, lhseq, lhlot, lhnam
from     x$kcclh
where    to_number(lhnxs) >
   (select   min(to_number(fhscn))
```

V7 Scripts Used to
Create the V$ Views

```
    from       x$kcvfhmrr
    where      hxerr = 0)
and        lhseq not in
    (select    leseq
    from       x$kccle
    where      lethr = lhthr)
and        to_number(lhlos) <
    (select    max(to_number(hxsts))
    from       x$kcvfhmrr
    where      hxerr = 0)
/
```

## View Name: V$RECOVER_FILE

```
select     hxfil, decode(hxons, 0, 'OFFLINE', 'ONLINE'),
           decode(hxerr, 0,'',1, 'FILE MISSING', 2,'OFFLINE NORMAL',
           3,'NOT VERIFIED', 4,'FILE NOT FOUND', 5,'CANNOT OPEN FILE',
           6,'CANNOT READ HEADER', 7,'CORRUPT HEADER', 8,
           'WRONG FILE TYPE', 9,'WRONG DATABASE', 10,
           'WRONG FILE NUMBER', 11,'WRONG FILE CREATE', 12,
           'WRONG FILE CREATE', 13,'WRONG FILE SIZE','UNKNOWN ERROR'),
           to_number(fhscn), fhtim
from       x$kcvfhmrr
/
```

## View Name: V$REQDIST

```
select     kmmrdbuc,sum(kmmrdcnt)
from       x$kmmrd
where      kmmrdpro!=hextoraw('00')
group by   kmmrdbuc
/
```

## View Name: V$RESOURCE

```
select     addr,ksqrsidt,ksqrsid1,ksqrsid2
from       x$ksqrs
where      bitand(ksqrsflg,2)!=0
/
```

## View Name: V$ROLLNAME (Joins to the undo$)

```
select     x$kturd.kturdusn usn,undo$.name
from       x$kturd, undo$
where      x$kturd.kturdusn=undo$.us#
and        x$kturd.kturdsiz!=0
/
```

### View Name: **V$ROLLSTAT**

```
select    kturdusn,kturdext,kturdsiz,kturdwrt,kturdnax,kturdget,
          kturdwat, decode(kturdopt, -1,      to_number(null),
          kturdopt), kturdhwm,kturdnsh, kturdnwp,kturdnex,
          kturdash,kturdaae, decode(kturdflg, 0,'ONLINE', 2,
          'PENDING OFFLINE', 3,'OFFLINE', 'UNKNOWN')
from      x$kturd
where     kturdsiz!=0
and       kturdflg != 3
/
```

### View Name: **V$ROWCACHE**

```
select    kqrstcid,decode(kqrsttyp,1,'PARENT','SUBORDINATE'),
          decode(kqrsttyp, 2, kqrstsno, null), kqrsttxt, kqrstcsz,
          kqrstusg,kqrstfcs,kqrstgrq,kqrstgmi,kqrstsrq,kqrstsmi,
          kqrstsco,kqrstmrq,kqrstmfl
from      x$kqrst
/
```

### View Name: **V$SESSION**

```
select    addr,ksusenum,ksuseser,ksuudses,ksusepro,ksuudlui,
          ksuudlna,ksuudoct, decode(ksusetrn,hextoraw('00'),
          null,ksusetrn), decode(ksqpswat, hextoraw('00'),
          null,ksqpswat), decode(bitand(ksuseidl,9),1,'ACTIVE',0,
          decode(bitand(ksuseflg,4096), 0,'INACTIVE', 'CACHED'),
          'KILLED'), decode(ksspatyp,1,'DEDICATED', 2,'SHARED',3,
          'PSEUDO','NONE'), ksuudsid,ksuudsna,ksuseunm,ksusepid,
          ksusemnm,ksusetid,ksusepnm, decode(bitand(ksuseflg,
          19),17,'BACKGROUND',1,'USER',2,'RECURSIVE','?'),
          ksusesql,ksusesqh
from      x$ksuse
where     bitand(ksspaflg,1)!=0
and       bitand(ksuseflg,1)!=0
/
```

### View Name: **V$SESSION_CURSOR_CACHE**

```
select    kgiccmax,kgicccnt,kgiccopd,kgiccope,kgiccopn,kgicchit,
          decode(kgiccopn,0, 1,kgicchit/kgiccopn)
from      x$kgicc
/
```

### View Name: **V$SESSION_EVENT**

```
select      s.kslessid, d.kslednam, s.ksleswts, s.kslestmo,
            s.kslestim, s.kslestim / s.ksleswts
from        x$ksles s, x$ksled d
where       s.ksleswts != 0
and         s.kslesenm = d.indx
/
```

### View Name: **V$SESSION_WAIT**

```
select      s.ksusenum,s.ksussseq,e.kslednam,e.ksledp1,s.ksussp1,
            e.ksledp2, s.ksussp2, e.ksledp3, s.ksussp3,s.ksusstim
from        x$ksusecst s, x$ksled e
where       bitand(s.ksspaflg,1)!=0
and         bitand(s.ksuseflg,1)!=0
and         s.ksussseq!=0
and         s.ksussopc=e.indx
/
```

### View Name: **V$SESSTAT**

```
select      ksusenum,ksusestn,ksusestv
from        x$ksusesta
where       bitand(ksspaflg,1)!=0
and         bitand(ksuseflg,1)!=0
and         ksusestn<
   (select    count(*)
    from      x$ksusd)
/
```

### View Name: **V$SESS_IO**

```
select      ksusenum, ksusesbg, ksusescg, ksusespr, ksusesbc, ksusescc
from        x$ksusio
where       bitand(ksspaflg,1)!=0
and         bitand(ksuseflg,1)!=0
/
```

### View Name: **V$SGA**

```
select      ksmsdnam,ksmsdval
from        x$ksmsd
/
```

## View Name: V$SGASTAT

```
select    ksmssnam,ksmsslen
from      x$ksmss
where     ksmsslen>1
/
```

## View Name: V$SHARED_SERVER

```
select    kmmsinam,kmmsiprp,kmmsista,kmmsinmg,kmmsinmb,kmmsibrk,
          kmmsivcp, kmmsiidl,kmmsibsy,kmmsitnc
from      x$kmmsi
where     bitand(kmmsiflg,1)!=0
/
```

## View Name: V$SQLAREA

```
select    kglnaobj,sum(kglobhs0+kglobhs1+kglobhs2+kglobhs3+
          kglobhs4+kglobhs5+kglobhs6),
          sum(kglobpsz+kglobpus),sum(kglobmsz),sum(kglobsor),
          count(*)-1,sum(decode(kglobhs6,0,0,1)),decode(sum(decode
          (kglhdlmd,0,0,1)),0,0, sum(decode(kglhdlmd,0,0,1))-1),
          sum(kglhdlkc)/2, sum(kglhdexc),sum (kglobpc6),
          sum(kglhdldc)-1,substr(to_char(kglnatim,
          'YYYY-MM-DD/HH24:MI:SS'),1,19), sum(kglhdivc),
          sum(kglobprs),sum(kglobdsk), sum(kglobbuf),
          sum(kgloboct),sum(decode(kglobcnu,0,kglobuid,0)),
          sum(decode(kglobcnu,0,kglobsid,0)),decode(sum(decode
          (kglhdkmk,0,0,1)), 0,0,sum(decode(kglhdkmk,0,0,1))-1),
          kglhdpar,kglnahsh
from      x$kglcursor
group by  kglnaobj,kglhdpar,kglnahsh,kglnatim
/
```

## View Name: V$SQLTEXT

```
select    kglhdadr, kglnahsh, piece, name
from      x$kglna
/
```

## View Name: V$STATNAME

```
select    indx,ksusdnam,ksusdcls
from      x$ksusd
/
```

### View Name: V$SYSSTAT

```
select    ksusgstn,ksusdnam,ksusdcls,ksusgstv
from      x$ksusgsta
/
```

### View Name: V$SYSTEM_CURSOR_CACHE

```
select    kgicsopn,kgicshit,decode(kgicsopn,0,1,kgicshit/kgicsopn)
from      x$kgics
/
```

### View Name: V$SYSTEM_EVENT

```
select    d.kslednam, s.ksleswts, s.kslestmo, s.kslestim,
          s.kslestim / s.ksleswts
from      x$kslei s, x$ksled d
where     s.ksleswts != 0
and       s.indx = d.indx
/
```

### View Name: V$THREAD

```
select    indx+1,decode(bitand(rtsta,1),1,'OPEN','CLOSED'),
          decode(bitand(rtsta,6),0,'DISABLED',2,'PRIVATE',6,
          'PUBLIC','UNKNOWN'), rtnlf,rtsid,rtots,rtcln,rtseq,
          to_number(rtckp_scn),rtckp_tim
from      x$kccrt
where     rtnlf!=0
/
```

### View Name: V$TIMER

```
select    ksutmtim
from      x$ksutm
/
```

### View Name: V$TRANSACTION

```
select    addr,kxidusn,kxidslt,kxidsqn,kubafil,kubablk,kubaseq,
          kubarec
from      x$ktcxb
where     bitand(ksspaflg,1)!=0
and       bitand(ktcxbflg,2)!=0
/
```

### View Name: V$TYPE_SIZE

```
select     kqfszcom,kqfsztyp,kqfszdsc,kqfszsiz
from       x$kqfsz
/
```

### View Name: V$VERSION

```
select     banner
from       x$version
/
```

### View Name: V$WAITSTAT

```
select     decode(indx,1,'data block',2,'sort block',3,
           'save undo block', 4,'segment header', 5,
           'save undo header',6,'free list',7,'system undo header',
           8,'system undo block', 9,'undo header',10,'undo block'),
           count,time
from       x$kcbwait
where      indx!=0
/
```

# V8 Scripts of the x$ Tables Used to Create the V$ Views

**V8 Scripts Used to Create the V$ Views**

Here is the version 8 query to get this listing:

```
select     'View Name: '||view_name,
           substr(view_definition,1,(instr(view_definition,'from')
           -1)) def1,
           substr(view_definition,(instr(view_definition,'from'))) def2
from       v$fixed_view_definition
order      by view_name;
```

### View Name: GV$ACCESS

```
select     distinct s.inst_id,s.ksusenum,o.kglnaown,o.kglnaobj,
           decode(o.kglobtyp, 0, 'CURSOR', 1, 'INDEX', 2, 'TABLE',
           3, 'CLUSTER', 4, 'VIEW', 5, 'SYNONYM', 6, 'SEQUENCE', 7,
           'PROCEDURE', 8, 'FUNCTION', 9, 'PACKAGE', 10,
           'NON-EXISTENT', 11,'PACKAGE BODY', 12,'TRIGGER', 13,
           'CLASS', 14,'SET', 15,'OBJECT', 16,'USER', 17,'DBLINK',
           'INVALID TYPE')
```

```
from      x$ksuse s,x$kglob o,x$kgldp d,x$kgllk l
where     l.kgllkuse=s.addr
and       l.kgllkhdl=d.kglhdadr
and       l.kglnahsh=d.kglnahsh
and       o.kglnahsh=d.kglrfhsh
and       o.kglhdadr=d.kglrfhdl
/
```

## View Name: GV$ACTIVE_INSTANCES

```
select    inst_id, ksiminum, rpad(ksimstr,60)
from      x$ksimsi
/
```

## View Name: GV$ARCHIVE

```
select    le.inst_id,le.lenum,le.lethr,le.leseq,decode
          (bitand(le.leflg,8),0, 'NO','YES'),to_number(le.lelos)
from      x$kccle le,x$kccdi di
where     bitand(di.diflg,1)!=0
and       le.ledup!=0
and       bitand(le.leflg,1)=0
and       (to_number(le.lelos)< to_number(di.difas)
or        bitand(le.leflg,8)=0)
/
```

## View Name: GV$ARCHIVED_LOG

```
select    inst_id,alrid,alstm,alnam,althp,alseq,to_number(alrls),
          to_date(alrlc, 'MM/DD/RR HH24:MI:SS'),to_number(allos),
          to_date(allot,'MM/DD/RR HH24:MI:SS'), to_number(alnxs),
          to_date(alnxt,'MM/DD/RR HH24:MI:SS'),albct,albsz,decode
          (bitand(alflg, 2),0,'NO','YES'), decode(bitand(alflg,
          1),0,'NO','YES'),to_date(altsm,'MM/DD/RR HH24:MI:SS')
from      x$kccal
/
```

## View Name: GV$ARCHIVE_DEST

```
select    inst_id, decode(kcrrdmod,1,'MUST SUCCEED',2,
          'BEST-EFFORT'), decode (kcrrdsta,1,'NORMAL',2,
          'DISABLED'),kcrrdest
from      x$kcrrdest
/
```

### View Name: **GV$BACKUP**

```
select     inst_id,hxfil, decode(hxerr, 0,decode(bitand(fhsta, 1),
           0,'NOT ACTIVE' ,'ACTIVE'), 1,'FILE MISSING', 2,
           'OFFLINE NORMAL', 3,'NOT VERIFIED', 4,'FILE NOT FOUND',
           5,'CANNOT OPEN FILE', 6,'CANNOT READ HEADER', 7,
           'CORRUPT HEADER', 8,'WRONG FILE TYPE', 9,
           'WRONG DATABASE', 10,'WRONG FILE NUMBER', 11,
           'WRONG FILE CREATE', 12,'WRONG FILE CREATE', 13,
           'WRONG FILE SIZE', 'UNKNOWN ERROR'), to_number(fhbsc),
           to_date(fhbti,'MM/DD/RR HH24:MI:SS')
from       x$kcvfhonl
/
```

### View Name: **GV$BACKUP_CORRUPTION**

```
select     inst_id,fcrid,fcstm,fcbss,fcbsc,fcpno,fcdfp,fcblk,fccnt,
           to_number(fcscn),decode(bitand(fcflg,1),1,'YES','NO')
from       x$kccfc
/
```

### View Name: **GV$BACKUP_DATAFILE**

```
select  inst_id,bfrid,bfstm,bfbss,bfbsc,bfdfp,to_number(bfcrs),
        to_date (bfcrt,'MM/DD/RR HH24:MI:SS'),to_number(bfrls),
        to_date(bfrlc,'MM/DD/RR HH24:MI:SS'),decode(bitand(bfflg,1),
        1,bflvl,NULL),to_number(bfics),to_number(bfcps),to_date(bfcpt,
        'MM/DD/RR HH24:MI:SS'),to_number(bfafs),bfncb,bfmcb,bflcb,
        bffsz,bfbct,bfbsz,bflor,to_date(bftsm, 'MM/DD/RR HH24:MI:SS')
from    x$kccbf
/
```

### View Name: **GV$BACKUP_DEVICE**

```
select     inst_id, devtype, devname
from       x$ksfhdvnt
/
```

### View Name: **GV$BACKUP_PIECE**

```
select     inst_id,bprid,bpstm,bpbss,bpbsc,bpnum,bpdev,bphdl,bpcmt,
           bpmdh,decode(bitand(bpflg,2),1,'YES','NO'),bptag,decode
           (bitand(bpflg,1),1,'YES','NO'),to_date(bptsm,'MM/DD/RR
```

V8 Scripts Used to
Create the V$ Views

```
            HH24:MI:SS'),to_date(bptim,'MM/DD/RR HH24:MI:SS'),
            (to_date(bptim,'MM/DD/RR HH24:MI:SS')-to_date
            (bptsm,'MM/DD/RR HH24:MI:SS'))*86400
from        x$kccbp
/
```

### View Name: GV$BACKUP_REDOLOG

```
select      inst_id,blrid,blstm,blbss,blbsc,blthp,blseq,to_number
            (blrls),to_date(blrlc,'MM/DD/RR HH24:MI:SS'),
            to_number(bllos),to_date(bllot, 'MM/DD/RR HH24:MI:SS'),
            to_number(blnxs),to_date(blnxt,'MM/DD/RR HH24:MI:SS'),
            blbct,blbsz
from        x$kccbl
/
```

### View Name: GV$BACKUP_SET

```
select      inst_id,bsrid,bsstm,bsbss,bsbsc,decode(bitand(bstyp,11),
            1,'D',2,'I' ,8,'L'),decode(bitand(bstyp,4),4,'YES','NO'),
            decode(bitand(bstyp,16),16,bslvl,NULL),bspct,to_date
            (bsbst,'MM/DD/RR HH24:MI:SS'),to_date(bstsm, 'MM/DD/RR
            HH24:MI:SS'),(to_date(bstsm,'MM/DD/RR HH24:MI:SS')
            -to_date (bsbst,'MM/DD/RR HH24:MI:SS'))*86400,bsbsz
from        x$kccbs
/
```

### View Name: GV$BGPROCESS

```
select      p.inst_id, p.ksbdppro,p.ksbdpnam,d.ksbdddsc,p.ksbdperr
from        x$ksbdp p,x$ksbdd d
where       p.indx=d.indx
/
```

### (3)View Name: GV$BH

```
select      bh.inst_id, file#, dbablk, class, decode(state,0,
            'free',1,'xcur', 2,'scur',3,'cr',4,'read',5,'mrec',6,
            'irec'), x_to_null, forced_reads, forced_writes,
            bh.le_addr, name,le_class, decode(bitand(flag,1), 0,
            'N', 'Y'), decode(bitand(flag,16), 0, 'N', 'Y'),
            decode(bitand(flag,1536), 0, 'N', 'Y'), decode
            (bitand(flag,16384), 0, 'N', 'Y'), decode(bitand
            (flag,65536), 0, 'N', 'Y'), 'N', obj
from        x$bh bh, x$le le
where       bh.le_addr = le.le_addr
/
```

## View Name: **GV$BUFFER_POOL**

```
select    inst_id, bp_id, bp_name, bp_lo_sid, bp_hi_sid,
          bp_set_ct, bp_size, bp_lo_bnum, bp_hi_bnum
from      x$kcbwbpd
/
```

## View Name: **GV$CIRCUIT**

```
select    inst_id,addr,kmcvcdpc, decode(kmcvcpro,kmcvcdpc,
          hextoraw('00'),kmcvcpro),kmcvcwat,kmcvcses,kmcvcsta,
          kmcvcque,kmcvcsz0,kmcvcsz1,kmcvcnmg, kmcvcnmb,kmcvcbrk
from      x$kmcvc
where     bitand(ksspaflg,1)!=0/
```

## View Name: **GV$CLASS_PING**

```
select    inst_id,  decode(indx,1,'data block',2,'sort block',3,
          'save undo block', 4,'segment header',5,
          'save undo header',6,'free list',7,'extent map', 8,
          'bitmap block',9,'bitmap index block',10,'unused',11,
          'undo header', 12,'undo block'), CLASS_X2NC,
          CLASS_X2NFWC,CLASS_X2NFSC, CLASS_X2SC,CLASS_X2SFWC,
          CLASS_X2SSXC,CLASS_X2SSXFWC, CLASS_S2NC, CLASS_S2NFSC,
          CLASS_SS2NC, CLASS_N2XC, CLASS_S2XC, CLASS_SSX2XC,
          CLASS_N2SC, CLASS_N2SSC
from      x$class_stat
/
```

## View Name: **GV$COMPATIBILITY**

```
select    inst_id,kcktyid, kcktyrls, kcktydsc
from      x$kckty
/
```

## View Name: **GV$COMPATSEG**

```
select    inst_id,kckceid, kckcerl, kckcevsn
from      x$kckce
/
```

## View Name: **GV$CONTROLFILE**

```
select    inst_id,decode(bitand(cfflg,1),0,'',1,'INVALID'),cfnam
from      x$kcccf
/
```

V8 Scripts Used to Create the V$ Views

### View Name: GV$CONTROLFILE_RECORD_SECTION

```
select    inst_id,decode(indx,0,'DATABASE',1, 'CKPT PROGRESS',2,
          'REDO THREAD',3,'REDO LOG',4,'DATAFILE',5,'FILENAME',6,
          'TABLESPACE',7,'RESERVED1',8,'RESERVED2',9,
          'LOG HISTORY',10,'OFFLINE RANGE',11,'ARCHIVED LOG',12,
          'BACKUP SET',13,'BACKUP PIECE',14,'BACKUP DATAFILE',15,
          'BACKUP REDOLOG',16,'DATAFILE COPY',17,
          'BACKUP CORRUPTION',18,'COPY CORRUPTION',19,
          'DELETED OBJECT',20,'RESERVED3',21,'RESERVED4',
          'UNKNOWN'),rsrsz,rsnum,rsnus,rsiol,rsilw,rsrlw
from      x$kccrs
/
```

### View Name: GV$COPY_CORRUPTION

```
select    inst_id,ccrid,ccstm,ccdcp,ccdcs,ccdfp,ccblk,cccnt,
          to_number (ccscn),decode(bitand(ccflg,1),1,'YES','NO')
from      x$kcccc
/
```

### View Name: GV$DATABASE

```
select    inst_id,didbi,didbn,to_date(dicts,'MM/DD/RR HH24:MI:SS'),
          to_number (dirls),to_date(dirlc,'MM/DD/RR HH24:MI:SS'),
          to_number(diprs),to_date (diprc,'MM/DD/RR HH24:MI:SS'),
          decode(bitand(diflg,1),0,'NOARCHIVELOG', 'ARCHIVELOG'),
          to_number(discn),to_number(difas),decode(bitand
          (diflg,256),256,'CREATED',decode(bitand(diflg,1024),
          1024,'STANDBY',decode(bitand(diflg,32768),32768,'CLONE',
          decode(bitand(diflg,4096),4096,'BACKUP','CURRENT')))),
          to_date(dicct, 'MM/DD/RR HH24:MI:SS'),dicsq,to_number
          (dickp_scn),to_date(dickp_tim, 'MM/DD/RR HH24:MI:SS'),
          decode(bitand(diflg,4),4, 'REQUIRED',decode(diirs,0,
          'NOT ALLOWED','ALLOWED')), to_date
          (divts, 'MM/DD/RR HH24:MI:SS')
from      x$kccdi
/
```

### View Name: GV$DATAFILE

```
select    fe.inst_id,fe.fenum,to_number(fe.fecrc_scn),
          to_date(fe.fecrc_tim,'MM/DD/RR HH24:MI:SS'),fe.fetsn,
          fe.ferfn,decode (fe.fetsn,0,decode(bitand(fe.festa,2),0,
          'SYSOFF','SYSTEM'),decode(bitand(fe.festa,18),0,
          'OFFLINE',2,'ONLINE','RECOVER')), decode(bitand
          (fe.festa, 12),0,'DISABLED',4,'READ ONLY',12,
```

```
            'READ WRITE','UNKNOWN'), to_number(fe.fecps),to_date
            (fe.fecpt,'MM/DD/RR HH24:MI:SS'),to_number(fe.feurs),
            to_date(fe.feurt,'MM/DD/RR HH24:MI:SS'),
            to_number(fe.fests), decode(fe.fests,NULL,to_date(NULL),
            to_date (fe.festt,'MM/DD/RR HH24:MI:SS')), to_number
            (fe.feofs),to_number (fe.feonc_scn), to_date
            (fe.feonc_tim,'MM/DD/RR HH24:MI:SS'), fh.fhfsz*fe.febsz,
            fh.fhfsz,fe.fecsz*fe.febsz,fe.febsz,fn.fnnam
from        x$kccfe fe, x$kccfn fn, x$kcvfh fh
where       fn.fnfno=fe.fenum
and         fn.fnfno=fh.hxfil
and         fe.fefnh=fn.fnnum
and         fe.fedup!=0
and         fn.fntyp=4
and         fn.fnnam is not null
/
```

## View Name: GV$DATAFILE_COPY

```
select      inst_id,dcrid,dcstm,dcnam,dctag,dcdfp,dcrfn,
            to_number(dccrs), to_date(dccrt,'MM/DD/RR
            HH24:MI:SS'),to_number(dcrls),to_date(dcrlc,
            'MM/DD/RR HH24:MI:SS'),decode(bitand(dcflg,8),
            8,0,NULL),to_number (dccps),to_date(dccpt,'MM/DD/RR
            HH24:MI:SS'),to_number(dcafs),to_number (dcrfs),
            to_date(dcrft,'MM/DD/RR HH24:MI:SS'),decode(bitand(dcflg,
            2),0,'NO','YES'),decode(bitand(dcflg,4),0,'NO','YES'),
            dcncb,dcmcb,dclcb,dcbct,dcbsz,dclor,
            decode(bitand(dcflg,1),0,'NO','YES'),to_date
            (dctsm, 'MM/DD/RR HH24:MI:SS')
from        x$kccdc
/
```

## View Name: GV$DATAFILE_HEADER

```
select      inst_id,hxfil,decode(hxons, 0, 'OFFLINE', 'ONLINE'),
            decode(hxerr, 0, NULL, 1,'FILE MISSING',2,'OFFLINE NORMAL',
            3,'NOT VERIFIED', 4,'FILE NOT FOUND',5,'CANNOT OPEN FILE',
            6,'CANNOT READ HEADER', 7,'CORRUPT HEADER',8,'WRONG FILE TYPE',
            9,'WRONG DATABASE', 10,'WRONG FILE NUMBER',11,'WRONG FILE CREATE',
            12,'WRONG FILE CREATE', 13,'WRONG FILE SIZE',14, 'WRONG RESETLOGS',
            15,'OLD CONTROLFILE', 'UNKNOWN ERROR'), hxver,decode(hxnrcv, 0,'NO',
            1,'YES', NULL),decode(hxifz, 0,'NO', 1,'YES',
            NULL),to_number(fhcrs),to_date(fhcrt,'MM/DD/RR HH24:MI:SS'),
            fhtnm,fhtsn,fhrfn,to_number(fhrls),to_date(fhrlc,'MM/DD/RR HH24:MI:SS'),
            to_number(fhscn),to_date(fhtim,'MM/DD/RR HH24:MI:SS'),
            fhcpc,fhfsz*fhbsz,fhfsz,hxfnm
from        x$kcvfh
/
```

### View Name: GV$DBFILE

```
select     inst_id,fnfno,fnnam
from       x$kccfn
where      fnnam is not null
and        fntyp=4
/
```

### View Name: GV$DBLINK

```
select   inst_id,nconam, ncouid, decode(bitand(hstflg, 32), 0,
         'NO', 'YES'),  decode(bitand(hstflg, 8), 0, 'NO', 'YES'),
         decode(hstpro, 1, 'V5', 2, 'V6', 3, 'V6_NLS', 4, 'V7', 'UNKN'),
         ncouct, decode(bitand(ncoflg, 2), 0, 'NO', 'YES'),
         decode(bitand(ncoflg, 8), 0, 'NO', 'YES'), nco2pstr
from     x$uganco
where    bitand(hstflg, 1) != 0
/
```

### View Name: GV$DB_OBJECT_CACHE

```
select   inst_id,kglnaown,kglnaobj,kglnadlk,decode(kglhdnsp,1,
         'TABLE/PROCEDURE',2,'BODY',3,'TRIGGER',4,'INDEX',5,'CLUSTER',
         6,'OBJECT'),decode(bitand(kglobflg,3),0,'NOT LOADED',
         2,'NON-EXISTENT',3,'INVALID STATUS',decode (kglobtyp,
         1,'INDEX',2,'TABLE',3,'CLUSTER',4,'VIEW', 5,'SYNONYM',6,
         'SEQUENCE',7,'PROCEDURE',8,'FUNCTION',9,'PACKAGE',10,
         'NON-EXISTENT',11, 'PACKAGE BODY',12,'TRIGGER',13,'CLASS',14,'SET',
         15,'OBJECT',16,'USER',17, 'DBLINK','INVALID TYPE')),
         kglobhs0+kglobhs1+kglobhs2+kglobhs3+kglobhs4+ kglobhs5+kglobhs6,
         kglhdldc,kglhdexc,kglhdlkc,kglobpc0,decode(kglhdkmk,0, 'NO','YES')
from     x$kglob
where    kglhdnsp between 1 and 6
/
```

### View Name: GV$DB_PIPES

```
seeplect  inst_id,decode(kglobt00,1,kglobt17,null),kglnaobj,
          decode(kglobt00,1, 'PRIVATE','PUBLIC'),
          kglobhs0+kglobhs1+kglobhs2+kglobhs3+kglobhs4+ kglobhs5+kglobhs6
from      x$kglob
where     kglhdnsp=7
/
```

### View Name: GV$DELETED_OBJECT

```
select   inst_id,dlrid,dlstm,decode(dltyp,11,'ARCHIVED LOG',13,'BACKUP
         PIECE',16,'DATAFILE COPY','UNKNOWN'),dlobp,dlosm
from     x$kccdl
/
```

## View Name: GV$DISPATCHER

```
select      inst_id,kmmdinam,kmmdinet,kmmdipro,kmmdista,
            decode(kmmdiacc,0,'NO','YES'),kmmdinmg,kmmdinmb,kmmdibrk,
            kmmdinvo,kmmditnc,kmmdiidl,kmmdibsy,kmmdiler
from        x$kmmdi
where       kmmdiflg!=0
/
```

## View Name: GV$DISPATCHER_RATE

```
select      inst_id,kmmdinam,kmmdipro,kmmdicrle,kmmdicre,kmmdicepl,
            kmmdicrm,  kmmdicrus,kmmdicrys,kmmdicyus,kmmdicruc,
            kmmdicryc,kmmdicyuc,kmmdicru,  kmmdicry,kmmdicyu,
            kmmdicic,kmmdicoc,kmmdicrr,kmmdimrle,kmmdimre,kmmdimepl,
            kmmdimrm,kmmdimrus,kmmdimrys,kmmdimyus,kmmdimruc,kmmdimryc
            kmmdimyuc,  kmmdimru,kmmdimry,kmmdimyu,kmmdimic,
            kmmdimoc,kmmdimrr,kmmdiarle,kmmdiare,  kmmdiaepl,
            kmmdiarm,kmmdiarus,kmmdiarys,kmmdiayus,kmmdiaruc,kmmdiaryc,
            kmmdiayuc,kmmdiaru,kmmdiary,kmmdiayu,kmmdiaic,
            kmmdiaoc,kmmdiarr,kmmdinrle,kmmdinrm,kmmdinrus,kmmdinruc,
            kmmdinru,kmmdinic,kmmdinoc,kmmdinrr,kmmdisrle,kmmdisrm,
            kmmdisrus,kmmdisruc,kmmdisru,kmmdisic,kmmdisoc,kmmdisrr
from        x$kmmdi
where       kmmdiflg!=0
/
```

## View Name: GV$DLM_CONVERT_LOCAL

```
select      inst_id, kjicvtnam, kjicvtalt, kjicvtalc
from        x$kjicvt
/
```

## View Name: GV$DLM_CONVERT_REMOTE

```
select      inst_id, kjicvtnam, kjicvtart, kjicvtarc
from        x$kjicvt
/
```

## View Name: GV$DLM_LATCH

```
select      inst_id, kjilftdesc, kjilftimgt, kjilfttlgt
from        x$kjilft
/
```

## View Name: GV$DLM_MISC

```
select      inst_id, indx, kjisftdesc, kjisftval
from        x$kjisft
/
```

V8 Scripts Used to
Create the V$ Views

### View Name: GV$ENABLEDPRIVS

```
select     inst_id,-indx
from       x$kzspr
where      x$kzspr.kzsprprv=1
/
```

### View Name: GV$ENQUEUE_LOCK

```
select     /*+ ordered use_nl(l), use_nl(s),
           use_nl(r)+*/.inst_id,l.addr,
           l.ksqlkadr,s.ksusenum,r.ksq rsidt,
           r.ksqrsid1,r.ksqrsid2,l.ksqlkmod,
           l.ksqlkreq,l.ksqlkctim,l.ksqlklblk
from       x$ksqeq l,x$ksuse s,x$ksqrs r
where      l.ksqlkses=s.addr
and        bitand(l.kssobflg,1)!=0
and        (l.ksqlkmod!=0
or         l.ksqlkreq!=0)
and        l.ksqlkres=r.addr
/
```

### View Name: GV$EVENT_NAME

```
select     inst_id, indx, kslednam, ksledp1, ksledp2, ksledp3
from       x$ksled
/
```

### View Name: GV$EXECUTION

```
select     inst_id, pid, val0, func,
           decode(id,1,'call',2,'return',3,'longjmp'),
           nvals, val2, val3, seqh, seql
from       x$kstex
where      op=10
/
```

### View Name: GV$FILESTAT

```
select     k.inst_id, k.kcfiofno,k.kcfiopyr,k.kcfiopyw,
           k.kcfiopbr,k.kcfiopbw, k.kcfioprt, k.kcfiopwt
from       x$kcfio k,x$kccfe f
where      f.fedup <> 0
and        f.fenum=k.kcfiofno
/
```

### View Name: **GV$FILE_PING**

```
select     inst_id, kcfiofno, KCFIOX2N, KCFIOX2NC, KCFIOX2NFWC,
           KCFIOX2NFSC,  KCFIOX2SC, KCFIOX2SFWC, KCFIOX2SSXC,
           KCFIOX2SSXFWC, KCFIOS2NC, KCFIOS2NFSC, KCFIOSS2NC,
           KCFIOWRBC, KCFIOWRBFWC, KCFIORBRC, KCFIORBRFWC,
           KCFIORBRFSC, KCFIOCBRC, KCFIOCBRFWC, KCFION2XC, KCFIOS2XC,
           KCFIOSSX2XC, KCFION2SC, KCFION2SSC
from       x$kcfio x
/
```

### View Name: **GV$FIXED_TABLE**

```
select     inst_id,kqftanam, kqftaobj, 'TABLE', indx
from       x$kqfta union all select inst_id,kqfvinam, kqfviobj, 'VIEW', 65537
from       x$kqfvi union all select inst_id,kqfdtnam, kqfdtobj, 'TABLE', 65537
from       x$kqfdt
/
```

### View Name: **GV$FIXED_VIEW_DEFINITION**

```
select     i.inst_id,kqfvinam,kqftpsel
from       x$kqfvi i, x$kqfvt t where i.indx = t.indx
/
```

### View Name: **GV$GLOBAL_TRANSACTION**

```
select     nst_id,   K2GTIFMT, K2GTITID_EXT, K2GTIBID, K2GTECNT,
           K2GTERCT, K2GTDPCT,      decode (K2GTDFLG, 0, 'ACTIVE',
           1, 'COLLECTING', 2, 'FINALIZED', 4, 'FAILED', 8, 'RECOVERING',
           16, 'UNASSOCIATED', 32, 'FORGOTTEN', 64, 'READY FOR RECOVERY',
           'COMBINATION'), K2GTDFLG, decode (K2GTETYP, 0, 'FREE', 1,
           'LOOSELY COUPLED', 2, 'TIGHTLY COUPLED')
from       X$K2GTE2
/
```

### View Name: **GV$INDEXED_FIXED_COLUMN**

```
select     c.inst_id,kqftanam, kqfcoidx, kqfconam, kqfcoipo
from       x$kqfco c, x$kqfta t
where      t.indx = c.kqfcotab
and        kqfcoidx != 0
/
```

**V8 Scripts Used to Create the V$ Views**

### View Name: GV$INSTANCE

```
select    inst_id,ksuxsins,ksuxssid,ksuxshst,ksuxsver,ksuxstim,
          decode(ksuxssts, 0,'STARTED',1,'MOUNTED',2,'OPEN','UNKNOWN'),
          decode(ksuxsshr,0,'NO',1,'YES',2,NULL),ksuxsthr,
          decode(ksuxsarc,0,'STOPPED',1,'STARTED','FAILED'),
          decode(ksuxslsw,0,NULL,2,'ARCHIVE LOG',3,'CLEAR LOG',4,'CHECKPOINT'),
          decode(ksuxsdba,0,'ALLOWED', 'RESTRICTED'),decode(ksuxsshp,0,'NO','YES')
from      x$ksuxsinst
/
```

### View Name: GV$LATCH

```
select    d.inst_id,d.kslldadr,la.latch#,d.kslldlvl,d.kslldnam,
          la.gets,la.misses,la.sleeps,la.immediate_gets,
          la.immediate_misses,la.waiters_woken,
          la.waits_holding_latch,la.spin_gets,
          la.sleep1,la.sleep2,la.sleep3, la.sleep4,la.sleep5,la.sleep6,
          la.sleep7,la.sleep8,la.sleep9,la.sleep10, la.sleep11
from      x$kslld d,
   (select        kslltnum latch#,sum(kslltwgt) gets,
                  sum(kslltwff)misses,sum (kslltwsl)
                  sleeps,sum(kslltngt)immediate_gets,
                  sum(kslltnfa) immediate_misses,
                  sum(kslltwkc) waiters_woken,
                  sum(kslltwth) waits_holding_latch,
                  sum(ksllthst0) spin_gets,sum(ksllthst1) sleep1,
                  sum(ksllthst2) sleep2,sum(ksllthst3) sleep3,
                  sum(ksllthst4) sleep4,sum(ksllthst5) sleep5,
                  sum(ksllthst6) sleep6,sum(ksllthst7) sleep7,
                  sum(ksllthst8) sleep8,sum(ksllthst9) sleep9,
                  sum(ksllthst10) sleep10,sum(ksllthst11) sleep11
   from           x$ksllt
   group by       kslltnum) la  where la.
latch# = d.indx
/
```

### View Name: GV$LATCHHOLDER

```
select    inst_id,ksuprpid,ksuprsid,ksuprlat,ksuprlnm
from      x$ksuprlat
/
```

### View Name: GV$LATCHNAME

```
select    inst_id,indx,kslldnam
from      x$kslld
/
```

## View Name: GV$LATCH_CHILDREN

```
select      t.inst_id,t.addr,t.kslltnum,t.kslltcnm,n.kslldlvl,
            n.kslldnam,t.kslltwgt,t.kslltwff,t.kslltwsl,t.kslltngt,
            t.kslltnfa,t.kslltwkc,t.kslltwth,t.kslthst0,t.kslthst1,
            t.kslthst2,t.kslthst3,t.kslthst4,t.kslthst5,
            t.kslthst6,t.kslthst7,t.kslthst8,t.kslthst9,
            t.kslthst10, t.kslthst11
from        x$ksllt t, x$kslld n
where       t.kslltcnm > 0
and         t.kslltnum = n.indx
/
```

## View Name: GV$LATCH_MISSES

```
select      t1.inst_id,t1.ksllasnam, t2.ksllwnam, t1.kslnowtf, t1.kslsleep
from        x$ksllw t2, x$kslwsc t1
where       t2.indx = t1.indx
/
```

## View Name: GV$LATCH_PARENT

```
select      t.inst_id,t.addr,t.kslltnum,n.kslldlvl,n.kslldnam,
            t.kslltwgt,t.kslltwff,t.kslltwsl,t.kslltngt,t.kslltnfa,
            t.kslltwkc,t.kslltwth,t.kslthst0,t.kslthst1,t.kslthst2,
            t.kslthst3,t.kslthst4,t.kslthst5,t.kslthst6,t.kslthst7,
            t.kslthst8,t.kslthst9,t.kslthst10, t.kslthst11
from        x$ksllt t, x$kslld n
where       t.kslltcnm = 0
and         t.kslltnum = n.indx
/
```

## View Name: GV$LIBRARYCACHE

```
select      inst_id,decode(indx,0,'SQLAREA',1,'TABLE/PROCEDURE',2,
            'BODY',3,'TRIGGER', 4,'INDEX',5,'CLUSTER',6,'OBJECT',7,'PIPE','?'),
            kglstget, kglstght, decode(kglstget,0,1,kglstght/kglstget),
            kglstpin,kglstpht, decode(kglstpin,0,1,kglstpht/kglstpin),
            kglstrld,kglstinv, kglstlrq,kglstprq,kglstprl,kglstirq,kglstmiv
from        x$kglst
where       indx<8
```

## View Name: GV$LICENSE

```
select      inst_id,ksullms,ksullws,ksullcs,ksullhs,ksullmu
from        x$ksull
/
```

### View Name: GV$LOADCSTAT

```
select     inst_id,kllcntnrd,kllcntnrj,kllcnttds,kllcntnds
from       x$kllcnt
/
```

### View Name: GV$LOADPSTAT

```
select     inst_id,klcpxtn,klcpxpn,klcpxrld
from       x$klpt
/
```

### View Name: GV$LOADTSTAT

```
select     inst_id,klltabnld,klltabnrj,klltabnfw,klltabnan,klltabnls,klltabpld
from       x$klltab
/
```

### View Name: GV$LOCK

```
select     /*+ ordered use_nl(l), use_nl(s), use_nl(r) +*/
           s.inst_id,l.laddr, l.kaddr,s.ksusenum,r.ksqrsidt,r.ksqrsid1,
           r.ksqrsid2,l.lmode, l.request, l.ctime,l.block
from       v$_lock l,x$ksuse s,x$ksqrs r
where      l.saddr=s.addr
and        l.raddr=r.addr
/
```

### View Name: GV$LOCKED_OBJECT

```
select     x.inst_id,x.kxidusn, x.kxidslt, x.kxidsqn, l.ktadmtab,
           s.indx, s.ksuudlna, s.ksuseunm, s.ksusepid, l.ksqlkmod
from       x$ktcxb x, x$ktadm l, x$ksuse s
where      x.ktcxbxba = l.kssobown
and        x.ktcxbses = s.addr
/
```

### View Name: GV$LOCKS_WITH_COLLISIONS

```
select     inst_id, lock_element_addr
from       gv$bh
where      (forced_writes + forced_reads) > 10
group by   lock_element_addr, inst_id
having count(*) > = 2
/
```

### View Name: **GV$LOCK_ELEMENT**

```
select    inst_id, addr, indx, le_class, name, le_mode, le_blks,
          le_rls, le_acq, le_inv, le_flags
from      x$le
/
```

### View Name: **GV$LOG**

```
select    le.inst_id,le.lenum,le.lethr,le.leseq,le.lesiz*le.lebsz,
          ledup, decode(bitand(le.leflg,1),0,'NO','YES'),
          decode(bitand(le.leflg,24), 8, 'CURRENT',16,'CLEARING',24,
          'CLEARING_CURRENT',decode(sign(leseq),0,'UNUSED',
          decode(sign((to_number(rt.rtckp_scn)-to_number
          (le.lenxs))* bitand(rt.rtsta,2)),-1,'ACTIVE','INACTIVE'))),
          to_number(le.lelos), to_date(le.lelot,'MM/DD/RR HH24:MI:SS')
from      x$kccle le, x$kccrt rt
where     le.ledup!=0
and       le.lethr=rt.rtnum
and       le.inst_id = rt.inst_id
/
```

### View Name: **GV$LOGFILE**

```
select    inst_id,fnfno, decode(fnflg,0,'',1,'INVALID',2,
          'STALE',4,'DELETED', 'UNKNOWN'), fnnam
from      x$kccfn
where     fnnam is not null
and       fntyp=3
/
```

### View Name: **GV$LOGHIST**

```
select    inst_id,lhthp,lhseq,to_number(lhlos),
          to_date(lhlot,'MM/DD/RRHH24:MI:SS'), to_number(lhnxs)
from      x$kcclh
/
```

### View Name: **GV$LOG_HISTORY**

```
select    inst_id,lhrid,lhstm,lhthp,lhseq,to_number(lhlos),
          to_date(lhlot,'MM/DD/RR HH24:MI:SS'),to_number(lhnxs)
from      x$kcclh
/
```

### View Name: GV$MTS

```
select      inst_id,kmmsgcmx,kmmsgsta+kmmsgutr,kmmsgtrm,kmmsgsmx
from        x$kmmsg
/
```

### View Name: GV$MYSTAT

```
select      inst_id,ksusenum,ksusestn,ksusestv
from        x$ksumysta
where       bitand(ksspaflg,1)!=0
and         bitand(ksuseflg,1)!=0
and         ksusestn<
  (select    count(*)
   from      x$ksusd)
/
```

### View Name: GV$NLS_PARAMETERS

```
select      inst_id,parameter, value
from        x$nls_parameters
where       parameter != 'NLS_SPECIAL_CHARS'
/
```

### View Name: GV$NLS_VALID_VALUES

```
selepect    inst_id,parameter, value
from        x$ksulv
/
```

### View Name: GV$OBJECT_DEPENDENCY

```
select      d.inst_id,d.kglhdpar, d.kglnahsh, o.kglnaown,
            o.kglnaobj, o.kglhdadr, o.kglnahsh, o.kglobtyp
from        x$kglob o, x$kgldp d
where       o.kglnahsh = d.kglrfhsh
and         o.kglhdadr = d.kglrfhdl
/
```

### View Name: GV$OFFLINE_RANGE

```
select      inst_id,orrid,orstm,ordfp,to_number(orofs),
            to_number(orons), to_date(oront,'MM/DD/RR HH24:MI:SS')
from        x$kccor
/
```

## View Name: GV$OPEN_CURSOR

```
select      inst_id,kgllkuse, kgllksnm, user_name, kglhdpar, kglnahsh, kglnaobj
from        x$kgllk
where       kglhdnsp = 0
and         kglhdpar != kgllkhdl
/
```

## View Name: GV$OPTION

```
select      inst_id,parameter, value
from        x$option
/
```

## View Name: GV$PARAMETER

```
select      x.inst_id,x.indx+1,ksppinm,ksppity,ksppstvl,ksppstdf,
            decode(bitand (ksppiflg/256,1),1,'TRUE','FALSE'),
            decode(bitand(ksppiflg/65536,3),1,'IMMEDIATE',2,'DEFERRED',
            3,'IMMEDIATE','FALSE'),decode(bitand(ksppstvf,7),1,'MODIFIED',
            4,'SYSTEM_MOD','FALSE'),decode(bitand(ksppstvf,2),2,
            'TRUE','FALSE'),ksppdesc
from        x$ksppi x, x$ksppcv y
where       x.indx = y.indx
and         translate(ksppinm,'_','#') not like '#%'
/
```

## View Name: GV$PQ_SESSTAT

```
select      inst_id, kxfpssnam, kxfpssval, kxfpsstot
from        x$kxfpsst
/
```

## View Name: GV$PQ_SLAVE

```
select      inst_id,kxfpdpnam, decode(bitand(kxfpdpflg, 16), 0,
            'BUSY', 'IDLE'), kxfpdpses, floor(kxfpdpit / 6000),
            floor(kxfpdpcbt / 6000), floor(kxfpdpcct / 100), kxfpdpclsnt
            + kxfpdpcrsnt, kxfpdpclrcv + kxfpdpcrrcv, floor((kxfpdptit
            + kxfpdpcit) / 6000), floor((kxfpdptbt + kxfpdpcbt) / 6000),
            floor((kxfpdptct + kxfpdpcct) / 100), kxfpdptlsnt + kxfpdpclsnt
            + kxfpdptrsnt + kxfpdpcrsnt, kxfpdptlrcv + kxfpdpclrcv +
            kxfpdptrrcv + kxfpdpcrrcv
from        x$kxfpdp
where       bitand(kxfpdpflg, 8) != 0
/
```

V8 Scripts Used to Create the V$ Views

### View Name: **GV$PQ_SYSSTAT**

```
select    inst_id, rpad(kxfpysnam,30), kxfpysval
from      x$kxfpys
/
```

### View Name: **GV$PQ_TQSTAT**

```
select    inst_id, kxfqsqn, kxfqsid, rpad(kxfqsty,10),
          kxfqscnt, kxfqslen, kxfqset, kxfqsavl, kxfqsdw,
          kxfqsdt, rpad(kxfqssid,10), kxfqsiid
from      x$kxfqsrow
/
```

### View Name: **GV$PROCESS**

```
select    inst_id, addr,indx,ksuprpid,ksuprunm,ksuprser,
          ksuprtid,ksuprpnm, decode(bitand(ksuprflg,2),0,null,1),
          decode(ksllawat,hextoraw('00'), null,ksllawat),
          decode(ksllaspn,hextoraw('00'),null,ksllaspn)
from      x$ksupr
where     bitand(ksspaflg,1)!=0
/
```

### View Name: **GV$PWFILE_USERS**

```
select    inst_id,username,decode(sysdba,1,'TRUE','FALSE'),
          decode(sysoper,1, 'TRUE','FALSE')
from      x$kzsrt
where     valid=1
/
```

### View Name: **GV$QUEUE**

```
select    inst_id,kmcqspro,decode(indx,0,'COMMON',1,'OUTBOUND',
          'DISPATCHER'), kmcqsncq,kmcqswat,kmcqstnc
from      x$kmcqs
where     indx in (0,1)
or        kmcqspro!=hextoraw('00')
/
```

### View Name: **GV$RECOVERY_FILE_STATUS**

```
select    fn.inst_id, fn.fnfno, fn.fnnam, decode(nvl(mf.cps, 0),
          0, 'NOT RECOVERED', 281474976710655, 'CURRENT', 'IN RECOVERY')
from      x$kcrmx mx, x$kccfn fn, x$kccfe fe, x$kcrmf mf
where     fn.fntyp = 4
```

```
and        mf.fno(+) = fn.fnfno
and        ((bitand(mx.flg,2) != 0
and        fe.fedup != 0)
or         mf.fno = fn.fnfno)
and        fe.fenum = fn.fnfno
/
```

## View Name: GV$RECOVERY_LOG

```
select     inst_id,lhthp,lhseq,to_date(lhlot,'MM/DD/RR HH24:MI:SS'),lhnam
from       x$kcclh
where      to_number(lhnxs) >
   (select       min(to_number(fhscn))
    from         x$kcvfhmrr
    where        hxerr = 0)
and              lhseq not in
   (select leseq
    from         x$kccle
    where        lethr = lhthp)
and              to_number(lhlos) <
   (select   max(to_number(hxsts))
    from         x$kcvfhmrr
    where        hxerr = 0)
/
```

## View Name: GV$RECOVERY_STATUS

```
select     fx.inst_id, to_date(mx.ckptim,'MM/DD/RR HH24:MI:SS'),
           mx.thr, mx.seq, mx.los, to_date(mx.tim, 'MM/DD/RR HH24:MI:SS'),
           nvl(mx.nam, 'NONE'), decode(bitand(mx.mrs, 256 + 128 + 64 + 8),
           8, 'RELEASE', 64, 'WRONG LOG', 128, 'MISSING NAME', 256,
           'UNNEEDED NAME', 'NONE'), decode(nvl(fx.err, 3), 1,'NEED LOG',
           3, 'END OF THREAD', 4, 'LOG REUSED', 'UNKNOWN')
from       x$kcrmx mx, x$kcrfx fx
where      fx.thr(+) = mx.thr
/
```

## View Name: GV$RECOVER_FILE

```
select     inst_id,hxfil, decode(hxons, 0, 'OFFLINE', 'ONLINE'),
           decode(hxerr, 0,'',1,'FILE MISSING', 2,'OFFLINE NORMAL',
           3,'NOT VERIFIED', 4,'FILE NOT FOUND',5,'CANNOT OPEN FILE',
           6,'CANNOT READ HEADER', 7,'CORRUPT HEADER',8,'WRONG FILE TYPE',
           9,'WRONG DATABASE', 10,'WRONG FILE NUMBER',11,'WRONG FILE CREATE',
           12,'WRONG FILE CREATE', 13,'WRONG FILE SIZE','UNKNOWN ERROR'),
           to_number(fhscn), to_date(fhtim,'MM/DD/RR HH24:MI:SS')
from       x$kcvfhmrr
/
```

### View Name: GV$REQDIST

```
select      inst_id,kmmrdbuc,sum(kmmrdcnt)
from        x$kmmrd
where       kmmrdpro!=hextoraw('00')
group by    inst_id,kmmrdbuc
/
```

### View Name: GV$RESOURCE

```
select      inst_id,addr,ksqrsidt,ksqrsid1,ksqrsid2
from        x$ksqrs
where       bitand(ksqrsflg,2)!=0
/
```

### View Name: GV$RESOURCE_LIMIT

```
select      inst_id, ksurlmnm, ksurlmcv, ksurlmmv,
            LPAD(decode(bitand(ksurlmfg, 1), 0, to_char(ksurlmia),
            'UNLIMITED'),10),  LPAD(decode(bitand(ksurlmfg, 2),
            0, to_char(ksurlmlv), 'UNLIMITED'),10)
from        x$ksurlmt
/
```

### View Name: GV$ROLLSTAT

```
select      inst_id,kturdusn,kturdext,kturdsiz,kturdwrt,kturdnax,
            kturdget,kturdwat, decode(kturdopt, -1,to_number(null),
            kturdopt), kturdhwm, kturdnsh, kturdnwp, kturdnex, kturdash,
            kturdaae, decode(kturdflg, 0,'ONLINE', 2,'PENDING OFFLINE',
            3,'OFFLINE', 4, 'FULL', 'UNKNOWN'), kturdcex, kturdcbk
from        x$kturd
where       kturdsiz!=0
and         kturdflg != 3
/
```

### View Name: GV$ROWCACHE

```
select      inst_id,kqrstcid,decode(kqrsttyp,1,'PARENT',
            'SUBORDINATE'), decode(kqrsttyp,2,kqrstsno,null),kqrsttxt,kqrstcsz,
            kqrstusg,kqrstfcs,kqrstgrq,kqrstgmi,kqrstsrq,kqrstsmi,
            kqrstsco,kqrstmrq,kqrstmfl,kqrstilr,kqrstifr,kqrstisr
from        x$kqrst
/
```

## View Name: GV$SESSION

```
select     inst_id,addr,indx,ksuseser,ksuudses,ksusepro,ksuudlui,
           ksuudlna,ksuudoct, ksusesow,decode(ksusetrn,hextoraw('00'),
           null,ksusetrn),decode(ksqpswat,hextoraw ('00'),null,ksqpswat),
           decode(bitand(ksuseidl,11),1,'ACTIVE',0,
           decode(bitand(ksuseflg,4096),0,'INACTIVE','CACHED'),
           2,'SNIPED',3,'SNIPED', 'KILLED'),
           decode(ksspatyp,1,'DEDICATED',2,'SHARED',3,'PSEUDO','NONE'),
           ksuudsid,ksuudsna,ksuseunm, ksusepid,ksusemnm,
           ksusetid,ksusepnm, decode(bitand(ksuseflg,19),17,'BACKGROUND',1,
           'USER',2,'RECURSIVE','?'), ksusesql, ksusesqh, ksusepsq,
           ksusepha, ksuseapp, ksuseaph,  ksuseact, ksuseach, ksusecli,
           ksusefix,  ksuseobj, ksusefil, ksuseblk, ksuseslt, ksuseltm,
           ksusectm,  decode(bitand(ksuseflg, 32768),0,'NO','YES'),
           decode(ksuseft, 2,'SESSION', 4,'SELECT',8,'TRANSACTIONAL','NONE'),
           decode(ksusefm,1,'BASIC',2,'PRECONNECT',4,'PREPARSE','NONE'),
           decode(ksusefs, 1, 'YES', 'NO')
from       x$                                        ksuse
where      bitand(ksspaflg,1)!=0
and        bitand(ksuseflg,1)!=0
/
```

## View Name: GV$SESSION_CONNECT_INFO

```
select     distinct inst_id,trunc(indx/5, 0), decode(ksuseaty,
           0, 'DATABASE', 1, 'PROTOCOL', 2, 'NETWORK SERVICE',
           '?'), ksuseunm, ksuseban
from       x$ksusecon
where      bitand(ksuseflg,1)!=0
and        bitand(ksuseflg,16)=0
/
```

## View Name: GV$SESSION_CURSOR_CACHE

```
select     inst_id,kgiccmax,kgicccnt,kgiccopd,kgiccope,
           kgiccopn,kgicchit, decode(kgiccopn,0,1,kgicchit/kgiccopn)
from       x$kgicc
/
```

## View Name: GV$SESSION_EVENT

```
select     s.inst_id, s.kslessid, d.kslednam, s.ksleswts,
           s.kslestmo, s.kslestim,  s.kslestim / s.ksleswts
from       x$ksles s, x$ksled d
where      s.ksleswts != 0
and        s.kslesenm = d.indx
/
```

### View Name: GV$SESSION_LONGOPS

```
select    inst_id,ksulosno, ksulosrn, ksulosuc, ksulocna,
          ksuloobj, ksuloctx, ksulostp, ksulomsg, ksulossf,
          ksulosto, ksulosfr, ksulotot, ksuloap1, ksuloap2,
          ksuloap3, to_date(ksulostm,'MM/DD/RR HH24:MI:SS'),
          to_date(ksulortm,'MM/DD/RR HH24:MI:SS'),
          (to_date(ksulortm,'MM/DD/RR HH24:MI:SS')-
          to_date(ksulostm,'MM/DD/RR HH24:MI:SS'))*86400
from      x$ksulop
/
```

### View Name: GV$SESSION_OBJECT_CACHE

```
select    inst_id,kocstpin,kocsthit,kocsttht,
          decode(kocstpin,0,1, kocsthit/kocstpin),
          decode(kocstpin,0,1,kocsttht/kocstpin),
          kocstorf,kocstrfs,kocstofs,kocstfls,kocstshr,
          kocstcnt,kocstpnd,kocstsiz,kocstopt, kocstmax
from      x$kocst
/
```

### View Name: GV$SESSION_WAIT

```
select    s.inst_id,s.indx,s.ksussseq,e.kslednam,e.ksledp1,
          s.ksussp1,s.ksussp1r, e.ksledp2,s.ksussp2,s.ksussp2r,
          e.ksledp3,s.ksussp3,s.ksussp3r,s.ksusstim,s.ksusewtm,
          decode(s.ksusstim, 0, 'WAITING', -2, 'WAITED UNKNOWN TIME',
          -1, 'WAITED SHORT TIME', 'WAITED KNOWN TIME')
from      x$ksusecst s, x$ksled e
where     bitand(s.ksspaflg,1)!=0
and       bitand(s.ksuseflg,1)!=0
and       s.ksussseq!=0
and       s.ksussopc=e.indx
/
```

### View Name: GV$SESSTAT

```
select    inst_id,indx,ksusestn,ksusestv
from      x$ksusesta
where     bitand(ksspaflg,1)!=0
and       bitand(ksuseflg,1)!=0
and       ksusestn<
   (select   count(*)
    from     x$ksusd)
/
```

## View Name: **GV$SESS_IO**

```
select     inst_id,indx, ksusesbg, ksusescg, ksusespr, ksusesbc, ksusescc
from       x$ksusio
where      bitand(ksspaflg,1)!=0
and        bitand(ksuseflg,1)!=0
/
```

## View Name: **GV$SGA**

```
select     inst_id,ksmsdnam,ksmsdval
from       x$ksmsd
/
```

## View Name: **GV$SGASTAT**

```
select     inst_id,'',ksmssnam,ksmsslen
from       x$ksmfs
where      ksmsslen>1
union      all
select     inst_id, 'shared pool',ksmssnam,ksmsslen
from       x$ksmss
where      ksmsslen>1
union      all
select     inst_id, 'large pool',   ksmssnam,ksmsslen
from       x$ksmls
where      ksmsslen>1
/
```

## View Name: **GV$SHARED_POOL_RESERVED**

```
select     avg(x$ksmspr.inst_id),sum(decode(ksmchcls,
           'R-free',ksmchsiz,0)), avg(decode(ksmchcls,
           'R-free',ksmchsiz,0)), sum(decode(ksmchcls,
           'R-free',1,0)), max(decode(ksmchcls,'R-free',
           ksmchsiz,0)), sum(decode(ksmchcls,'R-free',0,
           ksmchsiz)), avg(decode(ksmchcls,'R-free',0,ksmchsiz)),
           sum(decode(ksmchcls,'R-free',0,1)), max(decode
           (ksmchcls,'R-free',0,ksmchsiz)), avg(kghlurcn),
           avg(kghlurmi), avg(kghlurmz), avg(kghlurmx), avg(kghlunfu),
           avg(kghlunfs), avg(kghlumxa), avg(kghlumer), avg(kghlumes)
from       x$ksmspr, x$kghlu
where      ksmchcom not like '%reserved sto%'
/
```

**V8 Scripts Used to
Create the V$ Views**

V8 Scripts Used to Create the V$ Views

### View Name: GV$SHARED_SERVER

```
select      inst_id,kmmsinam,kmmsiprp,kmmsista,kmmsinmg,kmmsinmb,
            kmmsibrk,kmmsivcp, kmmsiidl,kmmsibsy,kmmsitnc
from        x$kmmsi
where       bitand(kmmsiflg,1)!=0
/
```

### View Name: GV$SORT_SEGMENT

```
select      inst_id, tablespace_name, segment_file, segment_block,
            extent_size, current_users, total_extents, total_blocks,
            used_extents, used_blocks, free_extents, free_blocks,
            added_extents, extent_hits,freed_extents, free_requests,
            max_size, max_blocks, max_used_size, max_used_blocks,
            max_sort_size, max_sort_blocks, relative_fno
from        x$ktstssd
/
```

### View Name: GV$SORT_USAGE

```
select      x$ktsso.inst_id, username, ktssoses, ktssosno,
            prev_sql_addr, prev_hash_value, ktssotsn, decode
            (ktssocnt, 0, 'PERMANENT', 1, 'TEMPORARY'), ktssofno,
            ktssobno, ktssoexts, ktssoblks, ktssorfno
from        x$ktsso, v$session
where       ktssoses = v$session.saddr
and         ktssosno = v$session.serial#
/
```

### View Name: GV$SQL

```
select      inst_id,kglnaobj,kglobhs0+kglobhs1+kglobhs2+kglobhs3
            +kglobhs4+kglobhs5+kglobhs6+kglobt16,kglobt08+kglobt11,
            kglobt10, kglobt01, decode(kglobhs6, 0,0,1), decode
            (kglhdlmd,0,0,1), kglhdlkc, kglhdexc, kglobpc6, kglhdldc,
            substr (to_char(kglnatim,'YYYY-MM-DD/HH24:MI:SS'),1,19),
            kglhdivc, kglobt12,kglobt13, kglobt14, kglobt15, kglobt02,
            decode(kglobt32,0, 'NONE', 1, 'ALL_ROWS',2, 'FIRST_ROWS', 3,
            'RULE', 4, 'CHOOSE', 'UNKNOWN'), kglobtn0, kglobt17, kglobt18,
            kglhdkmk, kglhdpar, kglobtp0, kglnahsh, kglobt09, kglobts0,
            kglobt19, kglobts1, kglobt20, kglobt21
from        x$kglcursor
where       kglhdadr != kglhdpar
and         kglobt02 != 0
/
```

## View Name: GV$SQLAREA

```
select     inst_id,kglnaobj, sum(kglobhs0+kglobhs1+kglobhs2+
           kglobhs3+kglobhs4+kglobhs5+kglobhs6), sum(kglobt08+kglobt11),
           sum(kglobt10), sum(kglobt01), count(*)-1, sum(decode
           (kglobhs6,0,0,1)), decode(sum(decode(kglhdlmd,0,0,1)),0,0,
           sum(decode(kglhdlmd,0,0,1))-1), sum(kglhdlkc)/2, sum(kglhdexc),
           sum(kglobpc6), sum(kglhdldc)-1, substr(to_char(kglnatim,
           'YYYY-MM-DD/HH24:MI:SS'),1,19), sum(kglhdivc), sum(kglobt12),
           sum(kglobt13), sum(kglobt14), sum(kglobt15), sum(decode
           (kglobt09,0, kglobt02,0)) , decode(count(*)-1, 1, decode(sum
           (decode(kglobt09, 0, kglobt32, 0)), 0, 'NONE', 1, 'ALL_ROWS',
           2, 'FIRST_ROWS', 3, 'RULE', 4, 'CHOOSE','UNKNOWN'),
           'MULTIPLE CHILDREN PRESENT'), sum(decode(kglobt09,0, kglobt17,0)),
           sum(decode(kglobt09,0,kglobt18,0)), decode(sum(decode
           (kglhdkmk,0,0,1)),0,0,sum(decode(kglhdkmk,0,0,1))-1), kglhdpar,
           kglnahsh, kglobts0, kglobt19, kglobts1, kglobt20, sum(kglobt21)
from       x$kglcursor
group by   inst_id,kglnaobj,kglhdpar,kglnahsh,kglnatim,
           kglobts0, kglobt19, kglobts1, kglobt20
having     sum(decode(kglobt09,0,kglobt02,0)) != 0
/
```

## View Name: GV$SQLTEXT

```
select     inst_id,kglhdadr, kglnahsh, kgloboct, piece, name
from       x$kglna
where      kgloboct != 0
/
```

## View Name: GV$SQLTEXT_WITH_NEWLINES

```
select     inst_id,kglhdadr, kglnahsh, kgloboct, piece, name
from       x$kglna1
where      kgloboct != 0
/
```

## View Name: GV$SQL_BIND_DATA

```
select     inst_id,kxsbdcur, kxsbdbnd, kxsbddty, kxsbdmxl,
           kxsbdpmx, kxsbdmal, kxsbdpre, kxsbdscl, kxsbdofl,
           kxsbdof2, kxsbdbfp, kxsbdbln, kxsbdavl, kxsbdbfl,
           kxsbdind, kxsbdval
from       x$kxsbd
/
```

V8 Scripts Used to Create the V$ Views

### View Name: GV$SQL_BIND_METADATA

```
select      inst_id,kglhdadr, position, kkscbndt, kkscbndl, kkscbnda, kksbvnnam
from        x$kksbv
/
```

### View Name: GV$SQL_CURSOR

```
select      inst_id,kxscccur, kxscccfl, decode(kxsccsta, 0,
            'CURNULL', 1, 'CURSYNTAX', 2, 'CURPARSE', 3, 'CURBOUND',
            4, 'CURFETCH', 5, 'CURROW', 'ERROR'), kxsccphd, kxsccplk,
            kxsccclk, kxscccpn, kxscctbm, kxscctwm, kxscctbv, kxscctdv,
            kxsccbdf, kxsccflg, kxsccfl2
from        x$kxscc
/
```

### View Name: GV$SQL_SHARED_MEMORY

```
select      /*+use_nl(h,c)*/ c.inst_id,kglnaobj, kglnahsh, kglobhd6,
            rtrim(substr(ksmchcom, 1, instr(ksmchcom, ':', 1, 1) - 1)),
            ltrim(substr(ksmchcom, -(length(ksmchcom) - (instr(ksmchcom,
            ':', 1, 1))), (length(ksmchcom) - (instr(ksmchcom, ':', 1, 1))
            + 1))), ksmchcom, ksmchptr, ksmchsiz, ksmchcls, ksmchtyp, ksmchpar
from        x$kglcursor c, x$ksmhp h
where       ksmchds = kglobhd6
and         kglhdadr != kglhdpar
/
```

### View Name: GV$STATNAME

```
select      inst_id,indx,ksusdnam,ksusdcls
from        x$ksusd
/
```

### View Name: GV$SUBCACHE

```
select      inst_id,kglnaown, kglnaobj, kglobtyp, kqlfshpn,
            kqlfscid, kqlfsscc, kqlfsesp, kqlfsasp, kqlfsusp
from        x$kqlset
/
```

### View Name: GV$SYSSTAT

```
select      inst_id,indx,ksusdnam,ksusdcls,ksusgstv
from        x$ksusgsta
/
```

### View Name: **GV$SYSTEM_CURSOR_CACHE**

```
select      inst_id,kgicsopn,kgicshit,decode(kgicsopn,0,1,kgicshit/kgicsopn)
from        x$kgics
/
```

### View Name: **GV$SYSTEM_EVENT**

```
select      d.inst_id, d.kslednam, s.ksleswts, s.kslestmo,
            s.kslestim,s.kslestim / s.ksleswts
from        x$kslei s, x$ksled d
where       s.ksleswts != 0
and         s.indx = d.indx
/
```

### View Name: **GV$SYSTEM_PARAMETER**

```
select      x.inst_id,x.indx+1,ksppinm,ksppity,ksppstvl,ksppstdf,
            decode(bitand (ksppiflg/256,1),1,'TRUE','FALSE'),
            decode(bitand(ksppiflg/65536,3),1,'IMMEDIATE',2,
            'DEFERRED','FALSE'),decode(bitand(ksppstvf,7),1,
            'MODIFIED','FALSE'),   decode(bitand(ksppstvf,2),2,
            'TRUE','FALSE'),   ksppdesc
from        x$ksppi x, x$ksppsv y
where       x.indx = y.indx
and         translate(ksppinm,'_','#') not like '#%'
/
```

### View Name: **GV$TABLESPACE**

```
select      inst_id,tstsn,tsnam
from        x$kccts
where       tstsn != -1
/
```

### View Name: **GV$THREAD**

```
select      inst_id,rtnum,decode(bitand(rtsta,1),1,'OPEN',
            'CLOSED'),  decode(bitand(rtsta,6),0,'DISABLED',2,'PRIVATE',6,
            'PUBLIC','UNKNOWN'),  rtnlf,rtsid,to_date(rtots,'MM/DD/RR
            HH24:MI:SS'),rtcln,rtseq, to_number(rtckp_scn),
            to_date(rtckp_tim,'MM/DD/RR HH24:MI:SS'),
            to_number(rtenb),to_date(rtets,'MM/DD/RR HH24:MI:SS'),
            to_number(rtdis),to_date(rtdit,'MM/DD/RR HH24:MI:SS')
from        x$kccrt
where       rtnlf!=0
/
```

V8 Scripts Used to
Create the V$ Views

### View Name: GV$TIMER

```
select      inst_id,ksutmtim
from        x$ksutm
/
```

### View Name: GV$TRANSACTION

```
select      inst_id,ktcxbxba,kxidusn,kxidslt,kxidsqn,ktcxbkfn,
            kubablk, kubaseq,kubarec,decode(ktcxbsta,0,'IDLE',1,
            'COLLECTING',2,'PREPARED',3,'COMMITTED',4,'HEURISTIC ABORT',
            5,'HEURISTIC COMMIT', 6,'HEURISTIC DAMAGE',7,'TIMEOUT',9,'
            INACTIVE', 10,'ACTIVE',11,'PTX PREPARED',12,'PTX COMMITTED',
            'UNKNOWN'), ktcxbstm,ktcxbssb,ktcxbssw, ktcxbsen,ktcxbsfl,
            ktcxbsbk,ktcxbssq,ktcxbsrc, ktcxbses,ktcxbflg, decode(bitand
            (ktcxbflg,16),0,'NO','YES'),decode(bitand(ktcxbflg,32),0,'NO',
            'YES'), decode(bitand(ktcxbflg,64),0,'NO','YES'), decode
            (bitand(ktcxbflg, 8388608),0,'NO','YES'), ktcxbpus,ktcxbpsl,
            ktcxbpsq, ktcxbpxu,ktcxbpxs, ktcxbpxq, ktcxbdsb, ktcxbdsw,
            ktcxbubk,ktcxburc,ktcxblio,ktcxbpio, ktcxbcrg,ktcxbcrc
from        x$ktcxb
where       bitand(ksspaflg,1)!=0
and         bitand(ktcxbflg,2)!=0
/
```

### View Name: GV$TRANSACTION_ENQUEUE

```
select      /*+ ordered use_nl(l), use_nl(s), use_nl(r)
            +*/s.inst_id,l.addr, l.ksqlkadr,s.ksusenum,r.ksqrsidt,
            r.ksqrsid1,r.ksqrsid2, l.ksqlkmod, l.ksqlkreq,l.ksqlkctim,
            l.ksqlklblk
from        x$ktcxb l,x$ksuse s,x$ksqrs r
where       l.ksqlkses=s.addr
and         bitand(l.ksspaflg,1)!=0
and         (l.ksqlkmod!=0
or          l.ksqlkreq!=0)
and         l.ksqlkres=r.addr
/
```

### View Name: GV$TYPE_SIZE

```
select      inst_id,kqfszcom,kqfsztyp,kqfszdsc,kqfszsiz
from        x$kqfsz
/
```

### View Name: GV$VERSION

```
select     inst_id, banner
from       x$version
/
```

### View Name: GV$WAITSTAT

```
select     inst_id,decode(indx,1,'data block',2,'sort block',3,
           'save undo block', 4,'segment header',5,'save undo header',
           6,'free list',7,'extent map', 8,'bitmap block',9,'bitmap
           index block',10,'unused',11,'system undo header', 12,
           'system undo block',13,'undo header',14,'undo block'),
           count,time
from       x$kcbwait
where      indx!=0
/
```

### View Name: GV$_LOCK

```
select     USERENV('Instance'),laddr,kaddr,saddr,raddr,lmode,request,
           ctime,  block
from       v$_lock1
union      all
select     inst_id,addr,ksqlkadr,ksqlkses,ksqlkres,ksqlkmod,ksqlkreq,
           ksqlkctim, ksqlklblk
from       x$ktadm
where   .  bitand(kssobflg,1)!=0
and        (ksqlkmod!=0 or ksqlkreq!=0)
union      all
select     inst_id,addr,ksqlkadr,ksqlkses,ksqlkres,ksqlkmod,
           ksqlkreq, ksqlkctim,ksqlklblk
from       x$ktcxb
where      bitand(ksspaflg,1)!=0
and        (ksqlkmod!=0
or         ksqlkreq!=0)
/
```

### View Name: GV$_LOCK1

```
select     inst_id,addr,ksqlkadr,ksqlkses,ksqlkres,ksqlkmod,
           ksqlkreq, ksqlkctim, ksqlklblk
from       x$kdnssf
where      bitand(kssobflg,1)!=0
```

```
and        (ksqlkmod!=0 or ksqlkreq!=0)
union      all
select     inst_id,addr,ksqlkadr,ksqlkses,ksqlkres,ksqlkmod,
           ksqlkreq,ksqlkctim, ksqlklblk
from       x$ksqeq
where      bitand(kssobflg,1)!=0
and        (ksqlkmod!=0 or ksqlkreq!=0)
/
```

## View Name: GV$_SEQUENCES

```
select     inst_id, KGLNAOWN,KGLNAOBJ,KGLOBT08,decode(bitand
           (KGLOBT00,1),0,'N','Y'), decode(bitand(KGLOBT00,2),0,'N','Y'),
           decode(bitand(KGLOBT00,16),0,'N','Y'),KGLOBTN0,
           KGLOBTN2,KGLOBTN3,KGLOBTN1,decode(bitand(KGLOBT09,1),0,'N','Y'),
           decode(bitand(KGLOBT09,2),0,'N','Y'),KGLOBTN4,KGLOBTN5,
           decode(KGLOBT10,1,'Y','N'),decode(KGLOBT10,1,KGLOBT02,null)
from       X$KGLOB
where      KGLOBTYP = 6
and        KGLOBT11 = 1
/
```

## View Name: V$ACCESS

```
select     ID , OWNER , OBJECT , TYPE
from       GV$ACCESS
where      inst_id = USERENV('Instance')
/
```

## View Name: V$ACTIVE_INSTANCES

```
select     INST_NUMBER , INST_NAME
from       GV$ACTIVE_INSTANCES
where      inst_id = USERENV('Instance')
/
```

## View Name: V$ARCHIVE

```
select     GROUP# , THREAD# , SEQUENCE# , "CURRENT" , FIRST_CHANGE#
from       GV$ARCHIVE
where      inst_id = USERENV('Instance')
/
```

V8 Scripts Used to Create the V$ Views

## View Name: **V$ARCHIVED_LOG**

```
select     RECID , STAMP , NAME , THREAD# , SEQUENCE# ,
           RESETLOGS_CHANGE# , RESETLOGS_TIME , FIRST_CHANGE# ,
           FIRST_TIME , NEXT_CHANGE# , NEXT_TIME , BLOCKS ,
            BLOCK_SIZE , ARCHIVED , DELETED , COMPLETION_TIME
from       GV$ARCHIVED_LOG
where      inst_id = USERENV('Instance')
/
```

## View Name: **V$ARCHIVE_DEST**

```
select     ARCMODE, STATUS, DESTINATION
from       GV$ARCHIVE_DEST
where      inst_id = USERENV('Instance')
/
```

## View Name: **V$BACKUP**

```
select     FILE# , STATUS , CHANGE# , TIME
from       GV$BACKUP
where      inst_id = USERENV('Instance')
/
```

## View Name: **V$BACKUP_CORRUPTION**

```
select     RECID , STAMP , SET_STAMP , SET_COUNT , PIECE# ,
           FILE# , BLOCK# , BLOCKS , CORRUPTION_CHANGE# , MARKED_CORRUPT
from       GV$BACKUP_CORRUPTION
where      inst_id = USERENV('Instance')
/
```

## View Name: **V$BACKUP_DATAFILE**

```
select     RECID , STAMP , SET_STAMP , SET_COUNT , FILE# ,
           CREATION_CHANGE# , CREATION_TIME , RESETLOGS_CHANGE# ,
           RESETLOGS_TIME , INCREMENTAL_LEVEL , INCREMENTAL_CHANGE# ,
           CHECKPOINT_CHANGE# , CHECKPOINT_TIME , ABSOLUTE_FUZZY_CHANGE# ,
           MARKED_CORRUPT , MEDIA_CORRUPT , LOGICALLY_CORRUPT ,
           DATAFILE_BLOCKS , BLOCKS , BLOCK_SIZE, OLDEST_OFFLINE_RANGE,
           COMPLETION_TIME
from       GV$BACKUP_DATAFILE
where      inst_id = USERENV('Instance')
/
```

V8 Scripts Used to Create the V$ Views

### View Name: V$BACKUP_DEVICE

```
select    DEVICE_TYPE, DEVICE_NAME
FROM      GV$BACKUP_DEVICE
where     inst_id = USERENV('Instance')
/
```

### View Name: V$BACKUP_PIECE

```
select    RECID , STAMP , SET_STAMP , SET_COUNT , PIECE# ,
          DEVICE_TYPE , HANDLE , COMMENTS , MEDIA , CONCUR ,
          TAG , DELETED , START_TIME , COMPLETION_TIME ,
          ELAPSED_SECONDS
from      GV$BACKUP_PIECE
where     inst_id = USERENV('Instance')
/
```

### View Name: V$BACKUP_REDOLOG

```
select    RECID , STAMP , SET_STAMP , SET_COUNT , THREAD# ,
          SEQUENCE# , RESETLOGS_CHANGE# , RESETLOGS_TIME ,
          FIRST_CHANGE# , FIRST_TIME , NEXT_CHANGE# , NEXT_TIME ,
          BLOCKS , BLOCK_SIZE
from      GV$BACKUP_REDOLOG
where     inst_id = USERENV('Instance')
/
```

### View Name: V$BACKUP_SET

```
select    RECID , STAMP , SET_STAMP , SET_COUNT , BACKUP_TYPE ,
          CONTROLFILE_INCLUDED , INCREMENTAL_LEVEL , PIECES , START_TIME ,
          COMPLETION_TIME , ELAPSED_SECONDS , BLOCK_SIZE
from      GV$BACKUP_SET
where     inst_id = USERENV('Instance')
/
```

### View Name: V$BGPROCESS

```
select    paddr,name,description,error
from      gv$bgprocess
where     inst_id = USERENV('Instance')
/
```

## View Name: **V$BH**

```
select    file#, block#, class#, status, xnc, forced_reads,
          forced_writes, lock_element_addr, lock_element_name,
          lock_element_class, dirty, temp, ping, stale, direct,
          new, objd
from      gv$bh
where     inst_id = USERENV('Instance')
/
```

## View Name: **V$BUFFER_POOL**

```
select    id, name, lo_setid, hi_setid, set_count, buffers, lo_bnum, hi_bnum
from      gv$buffer_pool
where     inst_id = USERENV('Instance')
/
```

## View Name: **V$CIRCUIT**

```
select    CIRCUIT , DISPATCHER , SERVER , WAITER , SADDR ,
          STATUS , QUEUE , MESSAGE0 , MESSAGE1 , MESSAGES ,
          BYTES , BREAKS
from      GV$CIRCUIT
where     inst_id = USERENV('Instance')
/
```

## View Name: **V$CLASS_PING**

```
select    class, x_2_null, x_2_null_forced_write,
          x_2_null_forced_stale, x_2_s,  x_2_s_forced_write,
          x_2_ssx, x_2_ssx_forced_write, s_2_null,
          s_2_null_forced_stale,  ss_2_null,  null_2_x, s_2_x,
          ssx_2_x, null_2_s, null_2_ss
from      gv$class_ping
where     inst_id = USERENV('Instance')
/
```

## View Name: **V$COMPATIBILITY**

```
select    TYPE_ID , RELEASE , DESCRIPTION
from      GV$COMPATIBILITY
where     inst_id = USERENV('Instance')
/
```

V8 Scripts Used to
Create the V$ Views

### View Name: **V$COMPATSEG**

```
select    TYPE_ID , RELEASE , UPDATED
from      GV$COMPATSEG
where     inst_id = USERENV('Instance')
/
```

### View Name: **V$CONTROLFILE**

```
select    STATUS , NAME
from      GV$CONTROLFILE
where     inst_id = USERENV('Instance')
/
```

### View Name: **V$CONTROLFILE_RECORD_SECTION**

```
select    TYPE , RECORD_SIZE , RECORDS_TOTAL , RECORDS_USED ,
          FIRST_INDEX , LAST_INDEX , LAST_RECID
from      GV$CONTROLFILE_RECORD_SECTION
where     inst_id = USERENV('Instance')
/
```

### View Name: **V$COPY_CORRUPTION**

```
select    RECID , STAMP , COPY_RECID , COPY_STAMP , FILE# ,
          BLOCK# , BLOCKS , CORRUPTION_CHANGE# , MARKED_CORRUPT
from      GV$COPY_CORRUPTION
where     inst_id = USERENV('Instance')
/
```

### View Name: **V$DATABASE**

```
select    DBID , NAME , CREATED , RESETLOGS_CHANGE# ,
          RESETLOGS_TIME , PRIOR_RESETLOGS_CHANGE#,
          PRIOR_RESETLOGS_TIME,LOG_MODE , CHECKPOINT_CHANGE# ,
          ARCHIVE_CHANGE# , CONTROLFILE_TYPE , CONTROLFILE_CREATED ,
          CONTROLFILE_SEQUENCE# , CONTROLFILE_CHANGE# , CONTROLFILE_TIME ,
          OPEN_RESETLOGS, VERSION_TIME
from      GV$DATABASE
where     inst_id = USERENV('Instance')
/
```

### View Name: **V$DATAFILE**

```
select    FILE# , CREATION_CHANGE# , CREATION_TIME , TS# , RFILE# ,
          STATUS , ENABLED, CHECKPOINT_CHANGE# , CHECKPOINT_TIME,
          UNRECOVERABLE_CHANGE#, UNRECOVERABLE_TIME, LAST_CHANGE# ,
```

```
          LAST_TIME , OFFLINE_CHANGE# , ONLINE_CHANGE# , ONLINE_TIME ,
          BYTES, BLOCKS , CREATE_BYTES , BLOCK_SIZE , NAME
from      GV$DATAFILE
where     inst_id = USERENV('Instance')
/
```

## View Name: **V$DATAFILE_COPY**

```
select    RECID , STAMP , NAME , TAG , FILE# , RFILE# ,
          CREATION_CHANGE# , CREATION_TIME , RESETLOGS_CHANGE# ,
          RESETLOGS_TIME , INCREMENTAL_LEVEL, CHECKPOINT_CHANGE# ,
          CHECKPOINT_TIME , ABSOLUTE_FUZZY_CHANGE# , RECOVERY_FUZZY_CHANGE# ,
          RECOVERY_FUZZY_TIME , ONLINE_FUZZY , BACKUP_FUZZY ,
          MARKED_CORRUPT, MEDIA_CORRUPT , LOGICALLY_CORRUPT , BLOCKS ,
          BLOCK_SIZE , OLDEST_OFFLINE_RANGE, DELETED, COMPLETION_TIME
from      GV$DATAFILE_COPY
where     inst_id = USERENV('Instance')
/
```

## View Name: **V$DATAFILE_HEADER**

```
select    FILE# , STATUS , ERROR , FORMAT, RECOVER , FUZZY,
          CREATION_CHANGE#, CREATION_TIME , TABLESPACE_NAME ,
          TS# , RFILE# , RESETLOGS_CHANGE# , RESETLOGS_TIME ,
          CHECKPOINT_CHANGE# , CHECKPOINT_TIME ,CHECKPOINT_COUNT ,
          BYTES , BLOCKS , NAME
from      GV$DATAFILE_HEADER
where     inst_id = USERENV('Instance')
/
```

## View Name: **V$DBFILE**

```
select    FILE# , NAME
from      GV$DBFILE
where     inst_id = USERENV('Instance')
/
```

## View Name: **V$DBLINK**

```
select    DB_LINK , OWNER_ID , LOGGED_ON , HETEROGENEOUS ,
          PROTOCOL , OPEN_CURSORS , IN_TRANSACTION , UPDATE_SENT ,
          COMMIT_POINT_STRENGTH
from      GV$DBLINK
where     inst_id = USERENV('Instance')
/
```

V8 Scripts Used to Create the V$ Views

### View Name: V$DB_OBJECT_CACHE

```
select    OWNER , NAME , DB_LINK , NAMESPACE , TYPE , SHARABLE_MEM ,
          LOADS , EXECUTIONS , LOCKS , PINS , KEPT
from      GV$DB_OBJECT_CACHE
where     inst_id = USERENV('Instance')
/
```

### View Name: V$DB_PIPES

```
select    OWNERID , NAME , TYPE , PIPE_SIZE
from      GV$DB_PIPES
where     inst_id = USERENV('Instance')
/
```

### View Name: V$DELETED_OBJECT

```
select    RECID , STAMP , TYPE , OBJECT_RECID , OBJECT_STAMP
from      GV$DELETED_OBJECT
where     inst_id = USERENV('Instance')
/
```

### View Name: V$DISPATCHER

```
select    NAME , NETWORK , PADDR , STATUS , ACCEPT , MESSAGES ,
          BYTES , BREAKS , OWNED , CREATED , IDLE , BUSY , LISTENER
from      GV$DISPATCHER
where     inst_id = USERENV('Instance')
/
```

### View Name: V$DISPATCHER_RATE

```
select    NAME, ADDR,CUR_LOOP_RATE,CUR_EVENT_RATE,
          CUR_EVENTS_PER_LOOP,CUR_MSG_RATE,
          CUR_SVR_BUF_RATE,CUR_SVR_BYTE_RATE,
          CUR_SVR_BYTE_PER_BUF,CUR_CLT_BUF_RATE,
          CUR_CLT_BYTE_RATE,CUR_CLT_BYTE_PER_BUF,
          CUR_BUF_RATE,CUR_BYTE_RATE,CUR_BYTE_PER_BUF,
          CUR_IN_CONNECT_RATE,CUR_OUT_CONNECT_RATE,
          CUR_RECONNECT_RATE,MAX_LOOP_RATE,MAX_EVENT_RATE,
          MAX_EVENTS_PER_LOOP,MAX_MSG_RATE,MAX_SVR_BUF_RATE,
          MAX_SVR_BYTE_RATE,MAX_SVR_BYTE_PER_BUF,
          MAX_CLT_BUF_RATE,MAX_CLT_BYTE_RATE,
          MAX_CLT_BYTE_PER_BUF,MAX_BUF_RATE,MAX_BYTE_RATE,
```

```
          MAX_BYTE_PER_BUF,MAX_IN_CONNECT_RATE,
          MAX_OUT_CONNECT_RATE,MAX_RECONNECT_RATE,AVG_LOOP_RATE,
          AVG_EVENT_RATE,AVG_EVENTS_PER_LOOP,AVG_MSG_RATE,
          AVG_SVR_BUF_RATE,AVG_SVR_BYTE_RATE,AVG_SVR_BYTE_PER_BUF,
          AVG_CLT_BUF_RATE,AVG_CLT_BYTE_RATE,AVG_CLT_BYTE_PER_BUF,
          AVG_BUF_RATE,AVG_BYTE_RATE,AVG_BYTE_PER_BUF,
          AVG_IN_CONNECT_RATE,AVG_OUT_CONNECT_RATE,
          AVG_RECONNECT_RATE,NUM_LOOPS_TRACKED,NUM_MSG_TRACKED,
          NUM_SVR_BUF_TRACKED,NUM_CLT_BUF_TRACKED,NUM_BUF_TRACKED,
          NUM_IN_CONNECT_TRACKED,NUM_OUT_CONNECT_TRACKED,
          NUM_RECONNECT_TRACKED,SCALE_LOOPS,SCALE_MSG,SCALE_SVR_BUF,
          SCALE_CLT_BUF,SCALE_BUF,SCALE_IN_CONNECT,SCALE_OUT_CONNECT,
          SCALE_RECONNECT
from      GV$DISPATCHER_RATE
where     inst_id = USERENV('Instance')
/
```

## View Name: V$DLM_CONVERT_LOCAL

```
select    INST_ID, CONVERT_TYPE, AVERAGE_CONVERT_TIME, CONVERT_COUNT
from      GV$DLM_CONVERT_LOCAL
where     inst_id = USERENV('Instance')
/
```

## View Name: V$DLM_CONVERT_REMOTE

```
select    INST_ID, CONVERT_TYPE, AVERAGE_CONVERT_TIME, CONVERT_COUNT
from      GV$DLM_CONVERT_LOCAL
where     inst_id = USERENV('Instance')
/
```

## View Name: V$DLM_LATCH

```
select    LATCH_TYPE, IMM_GETS, TTL_GETS
from      GV$DLM_LATCH
where     inst_id = USERENV('Instance')
/
```

## View Name: V$DLM_MISC

```
select    STATISTIC#, NAME, VALUE
from      GV$DLM_MISC
where     inst_id = USERENV('Instance')
/
```

V8 Scripts Used to
Create the V$ Views

### View Name: V$ENABLEDPRIVS

```
select      PRIV_NUMBER
from        GV$ENABLEDPRIVS
where       inst_id = USERENV('Instance')
/
```

### View Name: V$ENQUEUE_LOCK

```
select      ADDR , KADDR , SID , TYPE , ID1 , ID2 , LMODE , REQUEST ,
            CTIME , BLOCK
from        GV$ENQUEUE_LOCK
where       inst_id = USERENV('Instance')
/
```

### View Name: V$EVENT_NAME

```
select      event#,name,parameter1,parameter2,parameter3
from        gv$event_name
where       inst_id = USERENV('Instance')
/
```

### View Name: V$EXECUTION

```
select      PID , DEPTH , FUNCTION , TYPE , NVALS , VAL1 , VAL2 ,
            SEQH , SEQL
from        GV$EXECUTION
where       inst_id = USERENV('Instance')
/
```

### View Name: V$FILESTAT

```
select      FILE# , PHYRDS , PHYWRTS , PHYBLKRD , PHYBLKWRT , READTIM , WRITETIM
from        GV$FILESTAT
where       inst_id = USERENV('Instance')
/
```

### View Name: V$FILE_PING

```
select      file_number, frequency, x_2_null, x_2_null_forced_write,
            x_2_null_forced_stale, x_2_s, x_2_s_forced_write, x_2_ssx,
            x_2_ssx_forced_write,s_2_null, s_2_null_forced_stale,
            ss_2_null, wrb, wrb_forced_write, rbr, rbr_forced_write,
```

```
                rbr_forced_stale, cbr, cbr_forced_write, null_2_x, s_2_x,
                ssx_2_x, null_2_s, null_2_ss
from            gv$file_ping
where           inst_id = USERENV('Instance')
/
```

## View Name: V$FIXED_TABLE

```
select          NAME , OBJECT_ID , TYPE , TABLE_NUM
from            GV$FIXED_TABLE
where           inst_id = USERENV('Instance')
/
```

## View Name: V$FIXED_VIEW_DEFINITION

```
select          VIEW_NAME , VIEW_DEFINITION
from            GV$FIXED_VIEW_DEFINITION
where           inst_id = USERENV('Instance')
/
```

## View Name: V$GLOBAL_TRANSACTION

```
select          FORMATID, GLOBALID, BRANCHID, BRANCHES, REFCOUNT,
                PREPARECOUNT, STATE, FLAGS, COUPLING
from            GV$GLOBAL_TRANSACTION
where           inst_id = USERENV('Instance')
/
```

## View Name: V$INDEXED_FIXED_COLUMN

```
select          TABLE_NAME , INDEX_NUMBER , COLUMN_NAME , COLUMN_POSITION
from            GV$INDEXED_FIXED_COLUMN
where           inst_id = USERENV('Instance')
/
```

## View Name: V$INSTANCE

```
select          INSTANCE_NUMBER , INSTANCE_NAME , HOST_NAME , VERSION ,
                STARTUP_TIME , STATUS , PARALLEL , THREAD# , ARCHIVER ,
                LOG_SWITCH_WAIT , LOGINS , SHUTDOWN_PENDING
from            GV$INSTANCE
where           inst_id = USERENV('Instance')
/
```

V8 Scripts Used to
Create the V$ Views

## View Name: V$LATCH

```
select    addr,latch#,level#,name,gets,misses,sleeps,immediate_gets,
          immediate_misses,waiters_woken,waits_holding_latch,spin_gets,
          sleep1,sleep2,sleep3,sleep4,sleep5,sleep6,sleep7,sleep8,sleep9,
          sleep10,sleep11
from      gv$latch
where     inst_id = USERENV('Instance')
/
```

## View Name: V$LATCHHOLDER

```
select    PID , SID , LADDR , NAME
from      GV$LATCHHOLDER
where     inst_id = USERENV('Instance')
/
```

## View Name: V$LATCHNAME

```
select    latch#,name
from      gv$latchname
where     inst_id = USERENV('Instance')
/
```

## View Name: V$LATCH_CHILDREN

```
select    ADDR , LATCH# , CHILD# , LEVEL# , NAME , GETS , MISSES ,
          SLEEPS , IMMEDIATE_GETS , IMMEDIATE_MISSES , WAITERS_WOKEN ,
          WAITS_HOLDING_LATCH , SPIN_GETS , SLEEP1 , SLEEP2 , SLEEP3 ,
          SLEEP4 , SLEEP5 , SLEEP6 , SLEEP7 , SLEEP8, SLEEP9 , SLEEP10 ,
          SLEEP11
from      GV$LATCH_CHILDREN
where     inst_id = USERENV('Instance')
/
```

## View Name: V$LATCH_MISSES

```
select    PARENT_NAME , "WHERE" , NWFAIL_COUNT , SLEEP_COUNT
from      GV$LATCH_MISSES
where     inst_id = USERENV('Instance')
/
```

## View Name: **V$LATCH_PARENT**

```
select    ADDR , LATCH# , LEVEL# , NAME , GETS , MISSES , SLEEPS ,
          IMMEDIATE_GETS , IMMEDIATE_MISSES , WAITERS_WOKEN ,
          WAITS_HOLDING_LATCH , SPIN_GETS , SLEEP1 , SLEEP2 , SLEEP3 ,
          SLEEP4 , SLEEP5 , SLEEP6 , SLEEP7 , SLEEP8 , SLEEP9 , SLEEP10 ,
          SLEEP11
from      GV$LATCH_PARENT
where     inst_id = USERENV('Instance')
/
```

## View Name: **V$LIBRARYCACHE**

```
select    NAMESPACE , GETS , GETHITS , GETHITRATIO , PINS , PINHITS ,
          PINHITRATIO , RELOADS , INVALIDATIONS , DLM_LOCK_REQUESTS ,
          DLM_PIN_REQUESTS , DLM_PIN_RELEASES, DLM_INVALIDATION_REQUESTS ,
          DLM_INVALIDATIONS
from      GV$LIBRARYCACHE
where     inst_id = USERENV('Instance')
/
```

## View Name: **V$LICENSE**

```
select    sessions_max,sessions_warning,sessions_current,
          sessions_highwater, users_max
from      gv$license
where     inst_id = USERENV('Instance')
/
```

## View Name: **V$LOADCSTAT**

```
select    READ , REJECTED , TDISCARD , NDISCARD
from      GV$LOADCSTAT
where     inst_id = USERENV('Instance')
/
```

## View Name: **V$LOADPSTAT**

```
select    TABNAME , PARTNAME , LOADED
from      GV$LOADPSTAT
where     inst_id = USERENV('Instance')
/
```

V8 Scripts Used to
Create the V$ Views

### View Name: V$LOADTSTAT

```
select    LOADED , REJECTED , FAILWHEN , ALLNULL , LEFT2SKIP , PTNLOADED
from      GV$LOADTSTAT
where     inst_id = USERENV('Instance')
/
```

### View Name: V$LOCK

```
select    ADDR , KADDR , SID , TYPE , ID1 , ID2 , LMODE , REQUEST ,
          CTIME , BLOCK
from      GV$LOCK
where     inst_id = USERENV('Instance')
/
```

### View Name: V$LOCKED_OBJECT

```
select    xidusn,xidslot,xidsqn,object_id,session_id,oracle_username,
          os_user_name,process,locked_mode
from      gv$locked_object
where     inst_id = USERENV('Instance')
/
```

### View Name: V$LOCKS_WITH_COLLISIONS

```
select    lock_element_addr
from      v$bh
where     (forced_writes + forced_reads) > 10
group by  lock_element_addr
          having count(*) >= 2
/
```

### View Name: V$LOCK_ELEMENT

```
select    lock_element_addr, indx, class, lock_element_name,
          mode_held, block_count, releasing, acquiring, invalid,
          flags
from      gv$lock_element
where     inst_id = USERENV('Instance')
/
```

### View Name: V$LOG

```
select    GROUP# , THREAD# , SEQUENCE# , BYTES , MEMBERS , ARCHIVED ,
          STATUS , FIRST_CHANGE# , FIRST_TIME
```

```
from      GV$LOG
where     inst_id = USERENV('Instance')
/
```

## View Name: **V$LOGFILE**

```
select    GROUP# , STATUS , MEMBER
from      GV$LOGFILE
where     inst_id = USERENV('Instance')
/
```

## View Name: **V$LOGHIST**

```
select    THREAD# , SEQUENCE# , FIRST_CHANGE# , FIRST_TIME , SWITCH_CHANGE#
from      GV$LOGHIST
where     inst_id = USERENV('Instance')
/
```

## View Name: **V$LOG_HISTORY**

```
select    RECID , STAMP , THREAD# , SEQUENCE# , FIRST_CHANGE# ,
          FIRST_TIME , NEXT_CHANGE#
from      GV$LOG_HISTORY
where     inst_id = USERENV('Instance')
/
```

## View Name: **V$MTS**

```
select    MAXIMUM_CONNECTIONS , SERVERS_STARTED , SERVERS_TERMINATED ,
          SERVERS_HIGHWATER
from      GV$MTS
where     inst_id = USERENV('Instance')
/
```

## View Name: **V$MYSTAT**

```
select    SID , STATISTIC# , VALUE
from      GV$MYSTAT
where     inst_id = USERENV('Instance')
/
```

## View Name: **V$NLS_PARAMETERS**

```
select    PARAMETER , VALUE
from      GV$NLS_PARAMETERS
where     inst_id = USERENV('Instance')
/
```

V8 Scripts Used to
Create the V$ Views

### View Name: V$NLS_VALID_VALUES

```
select    PARAMETER , VALUE
from      GV$NLS_VALID_VALUES
where     inst_id = USERENV('Instance')
/
```

### View Name: V$OBJECT_DEPENDENCY

```
select    FROM_ADDRESS, FROM_HASH, TO_OWNER, TO_NAME, TO_ADDRESS,
          TO_HASH, TO_TYPE
from      GV$OBJECT_DEPENDENCY
where     inst_id = USERENV('Instance')
/
```

### View Name: V$OFFLINE_RANGE

```
select    RECID , STAMP , FILE# , OFFLINE_CHANGE# , ONLINE_CHANGE# ,
          ONLINE_TIME
from      GV$OFFLINE_RANGE
where     inst_id = USERENV('Instance')
/
```

### View Name: V$OPEN_CURSOR

```
select    SADDR , SID , USER_NAME , ADDRESS , HASH_VALUE , SQL_TEXT
from      GV$OPEN_CURSOR
where     inst_id = USERENV('Instance')
/
```

### View Name: V$OPTION

```
select    PARAMETER , VALUE
from      GV$OPTION
where     inst_id = USERENV('Instance')
/
```

### View Name: V$PARAMETER

```
select    NUM , NAME , TYPE , VALUE , ISDEFAULT , ISSES_MODIFIABLE ,
          ISSYS_MODIFIABLE , ISMODIFIED , ISADJUSTED , DESCRIPTION
from      GV$PARAMETER
where     inst_id = USERENV('Instance')
/
```

### View Name: **V$PQ_SESSTAT**

```
select    STATISTIC , LAST_QUERY , SESSION_TOTAL
from      GV$PQ_SESSTAT
where     inst_id = USERENV('Instance')
/
```

### View Name: **V$PQ_SLAVE**

```
select    SLAVE_NAME , STATUS , SESSIONS , IDLE_TIME_CUR ,
          BUSY_TIME_CUR , CPU_SECS_CUR , MSGS_SENT_CUR , MSGS_RCVD_CUR ,
          IDLE_TIME_TOTAL , BUSY_TIME_TOTAL , CPU_SECS_TOTAL ,
          MSGS_SENT_TOTAL , MSGS_RCVD_TOTAL
from      GV$PQ_SLAVE
where     inst_id = USERENV('Instance')
/
```

### View Name: **V$PQ_SYSSTAT**

```
select    STATISTIC , VALUE
from      GV$PQ_SYSSTAT
where     inst_id = USERENV('Instance')
/
```

### View Name: **V$PQ_TQSTAT**

```
select    FO_NUMBER , TQ_ID , SERVER_TYPE , NUM_ROWS , BYTES ,
          OPEN_TIME , AVG_LATENCY , WAITS , TIMEOUTS , PROCESS , INSTANCE
from      GV$PQ_TQSTAT
where     inst_id = USERENV('Instance')
/
```

### View Name: **V$PROCESS**

```
select    addr, pid,spid,username,serial#,terminal,program,background,
          latchwait,latchspin
from      gv$process
where     inst_id = USERENV('Instance')
/
```

### View Name: **V$PWFILE_USERS**

```
select    USERNAME , SYSDBA , SYSOPER
from      GV$PWFILE_USERS
where     inst_id = USERENV('Instance')
/
```

V8 Scripts Used to Create the V$ Views

### View Name: **V$QUEUE**

```
select    PADDR , TYPE , QUEUED , WAIT , TOTALQ
from      GV$QUEUE
where     inst_id = USERENV('Instance')
/
```

### View Name: **V$RECOVERY_FILE_STATUS**

```
select    FILENUM , FILENAME , STATUS
from      GV$RECOVERY_FILE_STATUS
where     inst_id = USERENV('Instance')
/
```

### View Name: **V$RECOVERY_LOG**

```
select    THREAD# , SEQUENCE# , TIME , ARCHIVE_NAME
from      GV$RECOVERY_LOG
where     inst_id = USERENV('Instance')
/
```

### View Name: **V$RECOVERY_STATUS**

```
select    RECOVERY_CHECKPOINT , THREAD , SEQUENCE_NEEDED , SCN_NEEDED ,
          TIME_NEEDED , PREVIOUS_LOG_NAME , PREVIOUS_LOG_STATUS , REASON
from      GV$RECOVERY_STATUS
where     inst_id = USERENV('Instance')
/
```

### View Name: **V$RECOVER_FILE**

```
select    FILE# , "ONLINE" , ERROR , CHANGE# , TIME
from      GV$RECOVER_FILE
where     inst_id = USERENV('Instance')
/
```

### View Name: **V$REQDIST**

```
select    BUCKET , COUNT
from      GV$REQDIST
where     inst_id = USERENV('Instance')
/
```

### View Name: **V$RESOURCE**

```
select    ADDR , TYPE , ID1 , ID2
from      GV$RESOURCE
where     inst_id = USERENV('Instance')
/
```

## View Name: **V$RESOURCE_LIMIT**

```
select     RESOURCE_NAME, CURRENT_UTILIZATION, MAX_UTILIZATION,
           INITIAL_ALLOCATION, LIMIT_VALUE
from       GV$RESOURCE_LIMIT
where      inst_id = USERENV('Instance')
/
```

## View Name: **V$ROLLSTAT**

```
select     USN , EXTENTS , RSSIZE , WRITES , XACTS , GETS , WAITS ,
           OPTSIZE , HWMSIZE, SHRINKS , WRAPS , EXTENDS , AVESHRINK ,
           AVEACTIVE , STATUS , CUREXT , CURBLK
from       GV$ROLLSTAT
where      inst_id = USERENV('Instance')
/
```

## View Name: **V$ROWCACHE**

```
select     cache#,type,subordinate#,parameter,count,usage,fixed,
           gets,getmisses, scans,scanmisses,scancompletes,modifications,
           flushes,dlm_requests,dlm_conflicts,dlm_releases
from       gv$rowcache
where      inst_id = USERENV('Instance')
/
```

## View Name: **V$SESSION**

```
select     SADDR , SID , SERIAL# , AUDSID , PADDR , USER# ,
           USERNAME , COMMAND , OWNERID, TADDR , LOCKWAIT ,
           STATUS , SERVER , SCHEMA# , SCHEMANAME , OSUSER ,
           PROCESS , MACHINE , TERMINAL , PROGRAM , TYPE ,
           SQL_ADDRESS , SQL_HASH_VALUE , PREV_SQL_ADDR ,
           PREV_HASH_VALUE , MODULE , MODULE_HASH , ACTION ,
           ACTION_HASH , CLIENT_INFO , FIXED_TABLE_SEQUENCE ,
           ROW_WAIT_OBJ# , ROW_WAIT_FILE#, ROW_WAIT_BLOCK# ,
           ROW_WAIT_ROW# , LOGON_TIME , LAST_CALL_ET , PDML_ENABLED ,
           FAILOVER_TYPE , FAILOVER_METHOD , FAILED_OVER
from       GV$SESSION
where      inst_id = USERENV('Instance')
/
```

## View Name: **V$SESSION_CONNECT_INFO**

```
select     sid,authentication_type,osuser,network_service_banner
from       gv$session_connect_info
where      inst_id = USERENV('Instance')
/
```

V8 Scripts Used to
Create the V$ Views

V8 Scripts Used to
Create the V$ Views

### View Name: **V$SESSION_CURSOR_CACHE**

```
select      MAXIMUM , COUNT , OPENED_ONCE , OPEN , OPENS , HITS , HIT_RATIO
from        GV$SESSION_CURSOR_CACHE
where       inst_id = USERENV('Instance')
/
```

### View Name: **V$SESSION_EVENT**

```
select      sid,event,total_waits,total_timeouts,time_waited,average_wait
from        gv$session_event
where       inst_id = USERENV('Instance')
/
```

### View Name: **V$SESSION_LONGOPS**

```
select      SID , SERIAL# , UPDATE_COUNT, COMPNAM , OBJID , CONTEXT ,
            STEPID , MSG , STEPSOFAR , STEPTOTAL , SOFAR , TOTALWORK ,
            APPLICATION_DATA_1, APPLICATION_DATA_2, APPLICATION_DATA_3,
            START_TIME, CURRENT_TIME, ELAPSED_SECONDS
from        GV$SESSION_LONGOPS
where       inst_id = USERENV('Instance')
/
```

### View Name: **V$SESSION_OBJECT_CACHE**

```
select      pins,hits,true_hits,hit_ratio,true_hit_ratio,
            object_refreshes, cache_refreshes,object_flushes,
            cache_flushes,cache_shrinks,cached_objects,
            pinned_objects,cache_size,optimal_size,maximum_size
from        gv$session_object_cache
where       inst_id = USERENV('Instance')
/
```

### View Name: **V$SESSION_WAIT**

```
select      sid,seq#,event,p1text,p1,p1raw,p2text,p2,p2raw,
            p3text,p3,p3raw, wait_time,seconds_in_wait,state
from        gv$session_wait
where       inst_id = USERENV('Instance')
/
```

## View Name: **V$SESSTAT**

```
select     SID , STATISTIC# , VALUE
from       GV$SESSTAT
where      inst_id = USERENV('Instance')
/
```

## View Name: **V$SESS_IO**

```
select     SID, BLOCK_GETS, CONSISTENT_GETS, PHYSICAL_READS,
           BLOCK_CHANGES, CONSISTENT_CHANGES
from       GV$SESS_IO
where      inst_id = USERENV('Instance')
/
```

## View Name: **V$SGA**

```
select     NAME , VALUE
from       GV$SGA
where      inst_id = USERENV('Instance')
/
```

## View Name: **V$SGASTAT**

```
select     POOL, NAME , BYTES
from       GV$SGASTAT
where      inst_id = USERENV('Instance')
/
```

## View Name: **V$SHARED_POOL_RESERVED**

```
select     FREE_SPACE , AVG_FREE_SIZE , FREE_COUNT , MAX_FREE_SIZE ,
           USED_SPACE , AVG_USED_SIZE , USED_COUNT , MAX_USED_SIZE ,
           REQUESTS , REQUEST_MISSES , LAST_MISS_SIZE , MAX_MISS_SIZE ,
           REQUEST_FAILURES , LAST_FAILURE_SIZE , ABORTED_REQUEST_THRESHOLD ,
           ABORTED_REQUESTS , LAST_ABORTED_SIZE
from       GV$SHARED_POOL_RESERVED
where      inst_id = USERENV('Instance')
/
```

**V8 Scripts Used to Create the V$ Views**

## View Name: **V$SHARED_SERVER**

```
select    NAME , PADDR , STATUS , MESSAGES , BYTES , BREAKS , CIRCUIT ,
          IDLE , BUSY , REQUESTS
from      GV$SHARED_SERVER
where     inst_id = USERENV('Instance')
/
```

## View Name: **V$SORT_SEGMENT**

```
select    TABLESPACE_NAME , SEGMENT_FILE , SEGMENT_BLOCK ,
          EXTENT_SIZE , CURRENT_USERS , TOTAL_EXTENTS , TOTAL_BLOCKS ,
          USED_EXTENTS , USED_BLOCKS , FREE_EXTENTS , FREE_BLOCKS ,
          ADDED_EXTENTS , EXTENT_HITS , FREED_EXTENTS , FREE_REQUESTS ,
          MAX_SIZE , MAX_BLOCKS , MAX_USED_SIZE , MAX_USED_BLOCKS ,
          MAX_SORT_SIZE , MAX_SORT_BLOCKS , RELATIVE_FNO
from      GV$SORT_SEGMENT
where     inst_id = USERENV('Instance')
/
```

## View Name: **V$SORT_USAGE**

```
select    USER , SESSION_ADDR , SESSION_NUM , SQLADDR , SQLHASH ,
          TABLESPACE , CONTENTS , SEGFILE# , SEGBLK# , EXTENTS ,
          BLOCKS , SEGRFNO#
from      GV$SORT_USAGE
where     inst_id = USERENV('Instance')
/
```

## View Name: **V$SQL**

```
select    SQL_TEXT , SHARABLE_MEM , PERSISTENT_MEM , RUNTIME_MEM ,
          SORTS , LOADED_VERSIONS , OPEN_VERSIONS , USERS_OPENING ,
          EXECUTIONS , USERS_EXECUTING , LOADS , FIRST_LOAD_TIME ,
          INVALIDATIONS , PARSE_CALLS , DISK_READS , BUFFER_GETS ,
          ROWS_PROCESSED , COMMAND_TYPE , OPTIMIZER_MODE ,
          OPTIMIZER_COST , PARSING_USER_ID, PARSING_SCHEMA_ID ,
          KEPT_VERSIONS , ADDRESS , TYPE_CHK_HEAP , HASH_VALUE ,
          CHILD_NUMBER , MODULE , MODULE_HASH , ACTION , ACTION_HASH ,
          SERIALIZABLE_ABORTS
from      GV$SQL
where     inst_id = USERENV('Instance')
/
```

## View Name: **V$SQLAREA**

```
select    SQL_TEXT , SHARABLE_MEM , PERSISTENT_MEM , RUNTIME_MEM ,
          SORTS , VERSION_COUNT , LOADED_VERSIONS , OPEN_VERSIONS ,
          USERS_OPENING , EXECUTIONS , USERS_EXECUTING , LOADS ,
          FIRST_LOAD_TIME , INVALIDATIONS , PARSE_CALLS , DISK_READS ,
```

```
            BUFFER_GETS , ROWS_PROCESSED , COMMAND_TYPE , OPTIMIZER_MODE ,
            PARSING_USER_ID , PARSING_SCHEMA_ID , KEPT_VERSIONS , ADDRESS ,
            HASH_VALUE , MODULE , MODULE_HASH , ACTION , ACTION_HASH ,
            SERIALIZABLE_ABORTS
from        GV$SQLAREA
where       inst_id = USERENV('Instance')
/
```

## View Name: V$SQLTEXT

```
select      ADDRESS , HASH_VALUE , COMMAND_TYPE , PIECE , SQL_TEXT
from        GV$SQLTEXT
where       inst_id = USERENV('Instance')
/
```

## View Name: V$SQLTEXT_WITH_NEWLINES

```
select      ADDRESS , HASH_VALUE , COMMAND_TYPE , PIECE , SQL_TEXT
from        GV$SQLTEXT_WITH_NEWLINES
where       inst_id = USERENV('Instance')
/
```

## View Name: V$SQL_BIND_DATA

```
select      CURSOR_NUM , POSITION , DATATYPE , SHARED_MAX_LEN ,
            PRIVATE_MAX_LEN , ARRAY_SIZE , PRECISION , SCALE ,
            SHARED_FLAG , SHARED_FLAG2 , BUF_ADDRESS , BUF_LENGTH ,
            VAL_LENGTH , BUF_FLAG , INDICATOR , VALUE
from        GV$SQL_BIND_DATA
where       inst_id = USERENV('Instance')
/
```

## View Name: V$SQL_BIND_METADATA

```
select      ADDRESS , POSITION , DATATYPE , MAX_LENGTH , ARRAY_LEN , BIND_NAME
from        GV$SQL_BIND_METADATA
where       inst_id = USERENV('Instance')
/
```

## View Name: V$SQL_CURSOR

```
select      CURNO , FLAG , STATUS , PARENT_HANDLE , PARENT_LOCK ,
            CHILD_LOCK , CHILD_PIN , PERS_HEAP_MEM , WORK_HEAP_MEM ,
            BIND_VARS , DEFINE_VARS , BIND_MEM_LOC, INST_FLAG , INST_FLAG2
from        GV$SQL_CURSOR
where       inst_id = USERENV('Instance')
/
```

V8 Scripts Used to
Create the V$ Views

### View Name: V$SQL_SHARED_MEMORY

```
select      SQL_TEXT , HASH_VALUE , HEAP_DESC , STRUCTURE , FUNCTION ,
            CHUNK_COM , CHUNK_PTR , CHUNK_SIZE , ALLOC_CLASS , CHUNK_TYPE ,
            SUBHEAP_DESC
from        GV$SQL_SHARED_MEMORY
where       inst_id = USERENV('Instance')
/
```

### View Name: V$STATNAME

```
select      STATISTIC# , NAME , CLASS
from        GV$STATNAME
where       inst_id = USERENV('Instance')
/
```

### View Name: V$SUBCACHE

```
select      OWNER_NAME , NAME , TYPE , HEAP_NUM , CACHE_ID , CACHE_CNT ,
            HEAP_SZ , HEAP_ALOC , HEAP_USED
from        GV$SUBCACHE
where       inst_id = USERENV('Instance')
/
```

### View Name: V$SYSSTAT

```
select      STATISTIC# , NAME , CLASS , VALUE
from        GV$SYSSTAT
where       inst_id = USERENV('Instance')
/
```

### View Name: V$SYSTEM_CURSOR_CACHE

```
select      OPENS , HITS , HIT_RATIO
from        GV$SYSTEM_CURSOR_CACHE
where       inst_id = USERENV('Instance')
/
```

### View Name: V$SYSTEM_EVENT

```
select      event,total_waits,total_timeouts,time_waited,average_wait
from        gv$system_event
where       inst_id = USERENV('Instance')
/
```

## View Name: **V$SYSTEM_PARAMETER**

```
select    NUM , NAME , TYPE , VALUE , ISDEFAULT , ISSES_MODIFIABLE ,
          ISSYS_MODIFIABLE , ISMODIFIED , ISADJUSTED , DESCRIPTION
from      GV$SYSTEM_PARAMETER
where     inst_id = USERENV('Instance')
/
```

## View Name: **V$TABLESPACE**

```
select    TS# , NAME
from      GV$TABLESPACE
where     inst_id = USERENV('Instance')
/
```

## View Name: **V$THREAD**

```
select    THREAD# , STATUS , ENABLED , GROUPS , INSTANCE , OPEN_TIME ,
          CURRENT_GROUP#, SEQUENCE# , CHECKPOINT_CHANGE# , CHECKPOINT_TIME ,
          ENABLE_CHANGE#, ENABLE_TIME , DISABLE_CHANGE# , DISABLE_TIME
from      GV$THREAD
where     inst_id = USERENV('Instance')
/
```

## View Name: **V$TIMER**

```
select    HSECS
from      GV$TIMER
where     inst_id = USERENV('Instance')
/
```

## View Name: **V$TRANSACTION**

```
select    ADDR , XIDUSN , XIDSLOT , XIDSQN , UBAFIL , UBABLK ,
          UBASQN , UBAREC , STATUS , START_TIME , START_SCNB , START_SCNW ,
          START_UEXT , START_UBAFIL , START_UBABLK , START_UBASQN ,
          START_UBAREC , SES_ADDR , FLAG , SPACE , RECURSIVE , NOUNDO ,
          PTX , PRV_XIDUSN , PRV_XIDSLT , PRV_XIDSQN , PTX_XIDUSN ,
          PTX_XIDSLT , PTX_XIDSQN , "DSCN-B" , "DSCN-W" , USED_UBLK ,
          USED_UREC , LOG_IO , PHY_IO , CR_GET , CR_CHANGE
from      gv$transaction
where     inst_id = USERENV('Instance')
/
```

## View Name: **V$TRANSACTION_ENQUEUE**

```
select    ADDR , KADDR , SID , TYPE , ID1 , ID2 , LMODE , REQUEST ,
          CTIME , BLOCK
from      GV$TRANSACTION_ENQUEUE
where     inst_id = USERENV('Instance')
/
```

## View Name: **V$TYPE_SIZE**

```
select    COMPONENT , TYPE , DESCRIPTION , TYPE_SIZE
from      GV$TYPE_SIZE
where     inst_id = USERENV('Instance')
/
```

## View Name: **V$VERSION**

```
select    BANNER
from      GV$VERSION
where     inst_id = USERENV('Instance')
/
```

## View Name: **V$WAITSTAT**

```
select    class,count,time
from      gv$waitstat
where     inst_id = USERENV('Instance')
/
```

## View Name: **V$_LOCK**

```
select    LADDR , KADDR , SADDR , RADDR , LMODE , REQUEST , CTIME , BLOCK
from      GV$_LOCK
where     inst_id = USERENV('Instance')
/
```

## View Name: **V$_LOCKI**

```
selectLADDR , KADDR , SADDR , RADDR , LMODE , REQUEST , CTIME , BLOCK
from   GV$_LOCK1
where inst_id = USERENV('Instance')
/
```

## View Name: **V$_SEQUENCES**

```
select    SEQUENCE_OWNER , SEQUENCE_NAME , OBJECT# , ACTIVE_FLAG ,
          REPLENISH_FLAG , WRAP_FLAG , NEXTVALUE , MIN_VALUE , MAX_VALUE ,
          INCREMENT_BY , CYCLE_FLAG , ORDER_FLAG , CACHE_SIZE , HIGHWATER ,
          BACKGROUND_INSTANCE_LOCK , INSTANCE_LOCK_FLAGS
from      GV$_SEQUENCES
where     inst_id = USERENV('Instance')
/
```

To obtain an understanding of the creation of x$ tables, V$ and data dictionary views can be crucial to fully comprehend the intricacies of Oracle. While the knowledge of the views and tables is critical to your career, the creation has remained somewhat of a painstaking mystery. The following illustration shows the creation of the underlying tables and the data dictionary views:

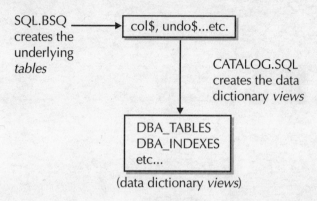

The following illustration shows the creation of the x$ tables and the V$ views:

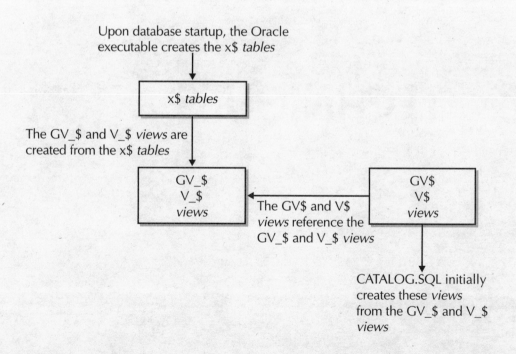

# TIPS

# &

# TECHNIQUES

# APPENDIX C

# The x$ Tables (DBA)

T he x$ tables are usually not mentioned or talked about much in the Oracle documentation or the Oracle user community. For this reason, I am including them in this book as one of the only references available. The x$ tables vary in structure and number based on the database version and release used. Run the queries on your version of the database to get the number of views and structure for your specific version. Areas covered in this appendix are as follows:

- A list of all version 7 x$ tables
- A list of all version 8 x$ tables
- A list of all version 8 x$ indexes
- The version 7 x$ tables cross-referenced to the V$ views
- The version 8 x$ tables cross-referenced to the V$ views
- The version 7 V$ views cross-referenced to the x$ tables
- The version 8 GV$ views cross-referenced to the x$ tables
- A listing of version 7 x$ tables *not* referenced by a V$ view
- A listing of version 8 x$ tables *not* referenced by a GV$ view

# Version 7 x$ Tables Ordered by Name

This is the version 7 query to get this listing:

```
select      name
from        v$fixed_table
where       name like 'X%'
order by    name;
```

These are the version 7 x$ tables ordered by name (126 total):

| | | | |
|---|---|---|---|
| x$bh | x$k2gte | x$k2gte2 | x$kcbcbh |
| x$kcbfwait | x$kcbrbh | x$kcbwait | x$kcccf |
| x$kccdi | x$kccfe | x$kccfn | x$kccle |
| x$kcclh | x$kccrt | x$kcfio | x$kckce |
| x$kckfm | x$kckty | x$kcvfh | x$kcvfhmrr |

| | | | |
|---|---|---|---|
| x$kcvfhonl | x$kdnce | x$kdnssc | x$kdnssf |
| x$kdnst | x$kdxhs | x$kdxst | x$kghlu |
| x$kgicc | x$kgics | x$kglau | x$kglbody |
| x$kglcluster | x$kglcursor | x$kgldp | x$kglindex |
| x$kgllc | x$kgllk | x$kglna | x$kglob |
| x$kglpn | x$kglst | x$kgltable | x$kgltr |
| x$kgltrigger | x$kglxs | x$kksbv | x$kllcnt |
| x$klltab | x$kmcqs | x$kmcvc | x$kmmdi |
| x$kmmdp | x$kmmrd | x$kmmsg | x$kmmsi |
| x$kqdpg | x$kqfco | x$kqfdt | x$kqfsz |
| x$kqfta | x$kqfvi | x$kqrpd | x$kqrsd |
| x$kqrst | x$ksbdd | x$ksbdp | x$ksled |
| x$kslei | x$ksles | x$kslld | x$ksllt |
| x$ksmcx | x$ksmlru | x$ksmsd | x$ksmsp |
| x$ksmss | x$ksppi | x$ksqdn | x$ksqeq |
| x$ksqrs | x$ksqst | x$ksucf | x$ksull |
| x$ksulv | x$ksumysta | x$ksupl | x$ksupr |
| x$ksuprlat | x$ksuru | x$ksusd | x$ksuse |
| x$ksusecst | x$ksusesta | x$ksusgsta | x$ksusio |
| x$ksutm | x$ksuxsinst | x$ktadm | x$ktcxb |
| x$kttvs | x$kturd | x$kvii | x$kvis |
| x$kvit | x$kxfpcds | x$kxfpcms | x$kxfpcst |
| x$kxfpdp | x$kxfpsds | x$kxfpsms | x$kxfpsst |
| x$kxfpys | x$kzdos | x$kzspr | x$kzsro |
| x$kzsrt | x$le | x$le_stat | x$messages |
| x$nls_parameters | x$option | x$trace | x$traces |
| x$uganco | x$version | | |

**Version 7 x$ Tables Ordered by Name**

# Version 8 x$ Tables Ordered by Name

This is the version 8 query to get this listing:

```
select      name
from        v$fixed_table
where       name like 'X%'
order by    name;
```

These are the version 8 x$ tables ordered by name (200 total):

| | | | |
|---|---|---|---|
| x$activeckpt | x$bh | x$ckptbuf | x$class_stat |
| x$dual | x$k2gte | x$k2gte2 | x$kcbbf |
| x$kcbbmc | x$kcbcbh | x$kcbfwait | x$kcbrbh |
| x$kcbsw | x$kcbwait | x$kcbwbpd | x$kcbwds |
| x$kcbwh | x$kccal | x$kccbf | x$kccbl |
| x$kccbp | x$kccbs | x$kcccc | x$kcccf |
| x$kcccp | x$kccdc | x$kccdi | x$kccdl |
| x$kccfc | x$kccfe | x$kccfn | x$kccle |
| x$kcclh | x$kccor | x$kccrs | x$kccrt |
| x$kccts | x$kcfio | x$kckce | x$kckfm |
| x$kckty | x$kclfh | x$kclfi | x$kclfx |
| x$kclls | x$kclqn | x$kcluh | x$kclui |
| x$kcrfx | x$kcrmf | x$kcrmt | x$kcrmx |
| x$kcrrdest | x$kcvfh | x$kcvfhmrr | x$kcvfhonl |
| x$kdnssf | x$kdxhs | x$kdxst | x$kghlu |
| x$kgicc | x$kgics | x$kglau | x$kglbody |
| x$kglcluster | x$kglcursor | x$kgldp | x$kglindex |
| x$kgllc | x$kgllk | x$kglna | x$kglna1 |
| x$kglob | x$kglpn | x$kglrd | x$kglsn |
| x$kglst | x$kgltable | x$kgltr | x$kgltrigger |
| x$kglxs | x$kjicvt | x$kjilft | x$kjisft |
| x$kksai | x$kksbv | x$kllcnt | x$klltab |

| | | | |
|---|---|---|---|
| x$klpt | x$kmcqs | x$kmcvc | x$kmmdi |
| x$kmmdp | x$kmmrd | x$kmmsg | x$kmmsi |
| x$kocst | x$kqdpg | x$kqfco | x$kqfdt |
| x$kqfp | x$kqfsz | x$kqfta | x$kqfvi |
| x$kqfvt | x$kqlset | x$kqrpd | x$kqrsd |
| x$kqrst | x$ksbdd | x$ksbdp | x$ksfhdvnt |
| x$ksfvsl | x$ksfvsta | x$ksimat | x$ksimav |
| x$ksimsi | x$ksled | x$kslei | x$ksles |
| x$kslld | x$ksllt | x$ksllw | x$kslpo |
| x$kslwsc | x$ksmfs | x$ksmfsv | x$ksmhp |
| x$ksmlru | x$ksmls | x$ksmmem | x$ksmpp |
| x$ksmsd | x$ksmsp | x$ksmspr | x$ksmss |
| x$ksmup | x$ksppcv | x$ksppi | x$ksppsv |
| x$ksqdn | x$ksqeq | x$ksqrs | x$ksqst |
| x$kstex | x$ksucf | x$ksull | x$ksulop |
| x$ksulv | x$ksumysta | x$ksupl | x$ksupr |
| x$ksuprlat | x$ksurlmt | x$ksuru | x$ksusd |
| x$ksuse | x$ksusecon | x$ksusecst | x$ksusesta |
| x$ksusex | x$ksusgsta | x$ksusio | x$ksutm |
| x$ksuxsinst | x$ksxafa | x$ktadm | x$ktcxb |
| x$ktsso | x$ktstssd | x$kttvs | x$kturd |
| x$ktuxe | x$kvii | x$kvis | x$kvit |
| x$kxfpcds | x$kxfpcms | x$kxfpcst | x$kxfpdp |
| x$kxfpsds | x$kxfpsms | x$kxfpsst | x$kxfpys |
| x$kxfqsrow | x$kxsbd | x$kxscc | x$kzdos |
| x$kzspr | x$kzsro | x$kzsrt | x$le |
| x$le_stat | x$messages | x$nls_parameters | x$option |
| x$trace | x$traces | x$uganco | x$version |

**Version 8 x$ Tables Ordered by Name**

# Version 8 x$ Indexes

This is the version 8 query to get this listing:

```
select     table_name, column_name, index_number
from       v$indexed_fixed_column
order by   table_name;
```

These are the version 8 x$ indexes ordered by table name (216 total):

| table_name | column_name | index_number |
| --- | --- | --- |
| x$bh | indx | 1 |
| x$class_stat | addr | 1 |
| x$class_stat | indx | 2 |
| x$dual | addr | 1 |
| x$dual | indx | 2 |
| x$kcbbf | addr | 1 |
| x$kcbbf | indx | 2 |
| x$kcbbmc | addr | 1 |
| x$kcbbmc | indx | 2 |
| x$kcbcbh | addr | 1 |
| x$kcbcbh | indx | 2 |
| x$kcbfwait | addr | 1 |
| x$kcbfwait | indx | 2 |
| x$kcbrbh | addr | 1 |
| x$kcbrbh | indx | 2 |
| x$kcbsw | addr | 1 |
| x$kcbsw | indx | 2 |
| x$kcbwait | addr | 1 |
| x$kcbwait | indx | 2 |
| x$kcbwbpd | addr | 1 |
| x$kcbwbpd | indx | 2 |
| x$kcbwds | addr | 1 |

| table_name | column_name | index_number |
|---|---|---|
| x$kcbwds | indx | 2 |
| x$kcbwh | addr | 1 |
| x$kcbwh | indx | 2 |
| x$kccal | alrid | 1 |
| x$kccbf | bfrid | 1 |
| x$kccbl | blrid | 1 |
| x$kccbp | bprid | 1 |
| x$kccbs | bsrid | 1 |
| x$kcccc | ccrid | 1 |
| x$kcccp | cptno | 1 |
| x$kccdc | dcrid | 1 |
| x$kccdl | dlrid | 1 |
| x$kccfc | fcrid | 1 |
| x$kccfe | fenum | 1 |
| x$kccfn | fnnum | 1 |
| x$kccle | lenum | 1 |
| x$kcclh | lhrid | 1 |
| x$kccor | orrid | 1 |
| x$kccrt | rtnum | 1 |
| x$kccts | tsrno | 1 |
| x$kcfio | addr | 1 |
| x$kcfio | indx | 2 |
| x$kcvfh | hxfil | 1 |
| x$kdnssf | addr | 1 |
| x$kdnssf | indx | 2 |
| x$kdxhs | addr | 1 |
| x$kdxhs | indx | 2 |
| x$kdxst | indx | 1 |

| table_name | column_name | index_number |
|---|---|---|
| x$kghlu | addr | 1 |
| x$kghlu | indx | 2 |
| x$kgicc | addr | 1 |
| x$kgicc | indx | 2 |
| x$kgics | addr | 1 |
| x$kgics | indx | 2 |
| x$kgldp | kglnahsh | 1 |
| x$kgllc | addr | 1 |
| x$kgllc | indx | 2 |
| x$kgllk | kglnahsh | 1 |
| x$kglna | kglnahsh | 1 |
| x$kglna1 | kglnahsh | 1 |
| x$kglob | kglnahsh | 1 |
| x$kglrd | kglnachv | 1 |
| x$kglst | addr | 1 |
| x$kglst | indx | 2 |
| x$kllcnt | addr | 1 |
| x$kllcnt | indx | 2 |
| x$klltab | addr | 1 |
| x$klltab | indx | 2 |
| x$kmcqs | addr | 1 |
| x$kmcqs | indx | 2 |
| x$kmcvc | addr | 1 |
| x$kmcvc | indx | 2 |
| x$kmmdi | addr | 1 |
| x$kmmdi | indx | 2 |
| x$kmmdp | addr | 1 |
| x$kmmdp | indx | 2 |

| table_name | column_name | index_number |
|---|---|---|
| x$kmmrd | addr | 1 |
| x$kmmrd | kmmrdbuc | 3 |
| x$kmmrd | indx | 2 |
| x$kmmsg | addr | 1 |
| x$kmmsg | indx | 2 |
| x$kmmsi | addr | 1 |
| x$kmmsi | indx | 2 |
| x$kocst | addr | 1 |
| x$kocst | indx | 2 |
| x$kqdpg | addr | 1 |
| x$kqdpg | indx | 2 |
| x$kqfdt | addr | 1 |
| x$kqfdt | indx | 2 |
| x$kqfp | addr | 1 |
| x$kqfp | indx | 2 |
| x$kqfsz | addr | 1 |
| x$kqfsz | indx | 2 |
| x$kqfta | addr | 1 |
| x$kqfta | indx | 2 |
| x$kqfvi | addr | 1 |
| x$kqfvi | indx | 2 |
| x$kqfvt | addr | 1 |
| x$kqfvt | indx | 2 |
| x$kqrpd | addr | 1 |
| x$kqrpd | indx | 2 |
| x$kqrsd | addr | 1 |
| x$kqrsd | indx | 2 |
| x$kqrst | addr | 1 |

**Version 8 x$ Indexes**

| table_name | column_name | index_number |
|---|---|---|
| x$kqrst | indx | 2 |
| x$ksbdd | addr | 1 |
| x$ksbdd | indx | 2 |
| x$ksbdp | indx | 1 |
| x$ksimat | addr | 1 |
| x$ksimat | indx | 2 |
| x$ksled | addr | 1 |
| x$ksled | indx | 2 |
| x$kslei | addr | 1 |
| x$kslei | indx | 2 |
| x$ksles | indx | 1 |
| x$kslld | addr | 1 |
| x$kslld | jndx | 2 |
| x$ksllw | addr | 1 |
| x$ksllw | indx | 2 |
| x$kslpo | addr | 1 |
| x$kslpo | indx | 2 |
| x$kslwsc | addr | 1 |
| x$kslwsc | indx | 2 |
| x$ksmfs | addr | 1 |
| x$ksmfs | indx | 2 |
| x$ksmfsv | addr | 1 |
| x$ksmfsv | indx | 2 |
| x$ksmhp | ksmchds | 1 |
| x$ksmls | addr | 1 |
| x$ksmls | indx | 2 |
| x$ksmmem | addr | 1 |
| x$ksmmem | indx | 2 |

| table_name | column_name | index_number |
|---|---|---|
| x$ksmsd | addr | 1 |
| x$ksmsd | indx | 2 |
| x$ksmss | addr | 1 |
| x$ksmss | indx | 2 |
| x$ksppcv | addr | 1 |
| x$ksppcv | indx | 2 |
| x$ksppi | addr | 1 |
| x$ksppi | indx | 2 |
| x$ksppsv | addr | 1 |
| x$ksppsv | indx | 2 |
| x$ksqdn | addr | 1 |
| x$ksqdn | indx | 2 |
| x$ksqrs | addr | 1 |
| x$ksqrs | indx | 2 |
| x$ksqst | addr | 1 |
| x$ksqst | indx | 2 |
| x$kstex | addr | 1 |
| x$kstex | indx | 2 |
| x$ksucf | addr | 1 |
| x$ksucf | indx | 2 |
| x$ksucf | ksuplstn | 3 |
| x$ksumysta | addr | 1 |
| x$ksumysta | indx | 2 |
| x$ksumysta | ksusestn | 3 |
| x$ksupl | addr | 1 |
| x$ksupl | ksuplstn | 3 |
| x$ksupl | indx | 2 |
| x$ksupr | addr | 1 |

**Version 8 x$ Indexes**

| table_name | column_name | index_number |
|---|---|---|
| x$ksupr | indx | 2 |
| x$ksuru | indx | 1 |
| x$ksuru | ksurind | 3 |
| x$ksusd | addr | 1 |
| x$ksusd | indx | 2 |
| x$ksuse | indx | 1 |
| x$ksusecst | indx | 1 |
| x$ksusesta | indx | 1 |
| x$ksusesta | ksusestn | 3 |
| x$ksusex | sid | 1 |
| x$ksusgsta | addr | 1 |
| x$ksusgsta | indx | 2 |
| x$ksusio | indx | 1 |
| x$ksutm | addr | 1 |
| x$ksutm | indx | 2 |
| x$ktadm | addr | 1 |
| x$ktadm | indx | 2 |
| x$kttvs | addr | 1 |
| x$kttvs | indx | 2 |
| x$kvii | addr | 1 |
| x$kvii | indx | 2 |
| x$kvis | addr | 1 |
| x$kvis | indx | 2 |
| x$kvit | addr | 1 |
| x$kvit | indx | 2 |
| x$kxfpcds | addr | 1 |
| x$kxfpcds | indx | 2 |
| x$kxfpcms | addr | 1 |

| table_name | column_name | index_number |
| --- | --- | --- |
| x$kxfpcms | indx | 2 |
| x$kxfpcst | addr | 1 |
| x$kxfpcst | indx | 2 |
| x$kxfpdp | addr | 1 |
| x$kxfpdp | indx | 2 |
| x$kxfpsds | addr | 1 |
| x$kxfpsds | indx | 2 |
| x$kxfpsms | addr | 1 |
| x$kxfpsms | indx | 2 |
| x$kxfpsst | addr | 1 |
| x$kxfpsst | indx | 2 |
| x$kzdos | addr | 1 |
| x$kzdos | indx | 2 |
| x$kzspr | addr | 1 |
| x$kzspr | indx | 2 |
| x$kzsro | addr | 1 |
| x$kzsro | indx | 2 |
| x$le | le_addr | 1 |
| x$le_stat | addr | 1 |
| x$le_stat | indx | 2 |
| x$messages | addr | 1 |
| x$messages | indx | 2 |
| x$trace | addr | 1 |
| x$trace | indx | 2 |
| x$traces | addr | 1 |
| x$traces | indx | 2 |

**Version 8 x$ Indexes**

# Version 7 x$ Tables Cross-Referenced to the V$ Views

These are the V$ views ordered by the x$ table names:

| x$ Tables | V$ Views |
|---|---|
| x$kcbwait | V$WAITSTAT |
| x$kcccf | V$CONTROLFILE |
| x$kccdi | V$ARCHIVE, V$DATABASE |
| x$kccfe | V$DATAFILE, V$FILESTAT |
| x$kccfn | V$DATAFILE, V$DBFILE, V$LOGFILE |
| x$kccle | V$ARCHIVE, V$LOG, V$RECOVERY_LOG |
| x$kcclh | V$LOGHIST, V$LOG_HISTORY, V$RECOVERY_LOG |
| x$kccrt | V$LOG, V$THREAD |
| x$kcfio | V$FILESTAT |
| x$kckce | V$COMPATSEG |
| x$kckty | V$COMPATIBILITY |
| x$kcvfhmrr | V$RECOVERY_LOG, V$RECOVER_FILE |
| x$kcvfhonl | V$BACKUP |
| x$kdnssc | V$_LOCK1 |
| x$kdnssf | V$_LOCK1 |
| x$kgicc | V$SESSION_CURSOR_CACHE |
| x$kgics | V$SYSTEM_CURSOR_CACHE |
| x$kglcursor | V$SQLAREA |
| x$kgldp | V$ACCESS |
| x$kgllk | V$OPEN_CURSOR |
| x$kglna | V$SQLTEXT |
| x$kglob | V$ACCESS, V$DB_OBJECT_CACHE |

| x$ Tables | V$ Views |
|-----------|----------|
| x$kglst | V$LIBRARYCACHE |
| x$kllcnt | V$LOADCSTAT |
| x$klltab | V$LOADTSTAT |
| x$kmcqs | V$QUEUE |
| x$kmcvc | V$CIRCUIT |
| x$kmmdi | V$DISPATCHER |
| x$kmmrd | V$REQDIST |
| x$kmmsg | V$MTS |
| x$kmmsi | V$SHARED_SERVER |
| x$kqfdt | V$FIXED_TABLE |
| x$kqfsz | V$TYPE_SIZE |
| x$kqfta | V$FIXED_TABLE |
| x$kqfvi | V$FIXED_TABLE |
| x$kqrst | V$ROWCACHE |
| x$ksbdd | V$BGPROCESS |
| x$ksbdp | V$BGPROCESS |
| x$ksled | V$SESSION_WAIT, V$SYSTEM_EVENT |
| x$kslei | V$SYSTEM_EVENT |
| x$ksles | V$SESSION_EVENT |
| x$kslld | V$LATCHNAME |
| x$ksllt | V$LATCH |
| x$ksmsd | V$SGA |
| x$ksmss | V$SGASTAT |
| x$ksppi | V$PARAMETER |
| x$ksqeq | V$_LOCK1 |

x$ Tables Cross-Referenced to the V$ Views

| x$ Tables | V$ Views |
| --- | --- |
| x$ksqrs | V$LOCK, V$RESOURCE |
| x$ksull | V$LICENSE |
| x$ksulv | V$NLS_VALID_VALUES |
| x$ksumysta | V$MYSTAT |
| x$ksupr | V$PROCESS |
| x$ksuprlat | V$LATCHHOLDER |
| x$ksusd | V$MYSTAT, V$SESSTAT, V$STATNAME |
| x$ksuse | V$ACCESS, V$LOCK, V$SESSION |
| x$ksusecst | V$SESSION_WAIT |
| x$ksusesta | V$SESSTAT |
| x$ksusgsta | V$SYSSTAT |
| x$ksusio | V$SESS_IO |
| x$ksutm | V$TIMER |
| x$ksuxsinst | V$INSTANCE |
| x$ktadm | V$_LOCK |
| x$ktcxb | V$TRANSACTION, V$_LOCK |
| x$kturd | V$ROLLNAME, V$ROLLSTAT |
| x$kxfpdp | V$PQ_SLAVE |
| x$kxfpsst | V$PQ_SESSTAT |
| x$kxfpys | V$PQ_SYSSTAT |
| x$kzspr | V$ENABLEDPRIVS |
| x$kzsrt | V$PWFILE_USERS |
| x$nls_parameters | V$NLS_PARAMETERS |
| x$option | V$OPTION |
| x$uganco | V$DBLINK |
| x$version | V$VERSION |

# Version 8 x$ Tables Cross-Referenced to the V$ Views

These are V$ views ordered by x$ table names:

| x$ Tables | V$ Views |
|-----------|----------|
| x$bh | GV$BH |
| x$kcbwait | GV$WAITSTAT |
| x$kcbwbpd | GV$BUFFER_POOL |
| x$kccal | GV$ARCHIVED_LOG |
| x$kccbf | GV$BACKUP_DATAFILE |
| x$kccbl | GV$BACKUP_REDOLOG |
| x$kccbp | GV$BACKUP_PIECE |
| x$kccbs | GV$BACKUP_SET |
| x$kcccc | GV$COPY_CORRUPTION |
| x$kcccf | GV$CONTROLFILE |
| x$kccdc | GV$DATAFILE_COPY |
| x$kccdi | GV$ARCHIVE, GV$DATABASE |
| x$kccdl | GV$DELETED_OBJECT |
| x$kccfc | GV$BACKUP_CORRUPTION |
| x$kccfe | GV$FILESTAT, GV$DATAFILE, GV$RECOVERY_FILE_STATUS |
| x$kccfn | GV$DBFILE, GV$LOGFILE, GV$DATAFILE, GV$RECOVERY_FILE_STATUS |
| x$kccle | GV$ARCHIVE, GV$LOG, GV$RECOVERY_LOG |
| x$kcclh | GV$LOGHIST, GV$LOG_HISTORY, GV$RECOVERY_LOG |
| x$kccor | GV$OFFLINE_RANGE |
| x$kccrs | GV$CONTROLFILE_RECORD_SECTION |
| x$kccrt | GV$THREAD, GV$LOG |
| x$kccts | GV$TABLESPACE |
| x$kcfio | GV$FILE_PING, GV$FILESTAT |

| x$ Tables | V$ Views |
| --- | --- |
| x$kckce | GV$COMPATSEG |
| x$kckty | GV$COMPATIBILITY |
| x$kcrfx | GV$RECOVERY_STATUS |
| x$kcrmf | GV$RECOVERY_FILE_STATUS |
| x$kcrmx | GV$RECOVERY_STATUS, GV$RECOVERY_FILE_STATUS |
| x$kcvfh | GV$DATAFILE, GV$RECOVER_FILE, GV$BACKUP, GV$RECOVERY_LOG, GV$DATAFILE_HEADER |
| x$kdnssf | GV$_LOCK1 |
| x$kghlu | GV$SHARED_POOL_RESERVED |
| x$kgicc | GV$SESSION_CURSOR_CACHE |
| x$kgics | GV$SYSTEM_CURSOR_CACHE |
| x$kgldp | GV$ACCESS, GV$OBJECT_DEPENDENCY |
| x$kgllk | GV$ACCESS, GV$OPEN_CURSOR |
| x$kglna | GV$SQLTEXT, GV$SQLTEXT_WITH_NEWLINES |
| x$kglna1 | GV$SQLTEXT_WITH_NEWLINES |
| x$kglob | GV$ACCESS, GV$OBJECT_DEPENDENCY, GV$DB_OBJECT_CACHE, GV$DB_PIPES |
| x$kglst | GV$LIBRARYCACHE |
| x$kjicvt | GV$DLM_CONVERT_LOCAL, GV$DLM_CONVERT_REMOTE |
| x$kjilft | GV$DLM_LATCH |
| x$kjisft | GV$DLM_MISC |
| x$kksbv | GV$SQL_BIND_METADATA |
| x$kllcnt | GV$LOADCSTAT |
| x$klltab | GV$LOADTSTAT |
| x$klpt | GV$LOADPSTAT |
| x$kmcqs | GV$QUEUE |
| x$kmcvc | GV$CIRCUIT |
| x$kmmdi | GV$DISPATCHER, GV$DISPATCHER_RATE |
| x$kmmrd | GV$REQDIST |

| x$ Tables | V$ Views |
|---|---|
| x$kmmsg | GV$MTS |
| x$kmmsi | GV$SHARED_SERVER |
| x$kocst | GV$SESSION_OBJECT_CACHE |
| x$kqfco | GV$INDEXED_FIXED_COLUMN |
| x$kqfdt | GV$FIXED_TABLE |
| x$kqfsz | GV$TYPE_SIZE |
| x$kqfta | GV$FIXED_TABLE, GV$INDEXED_FIXED_COLUMN |
| x$kqfvi | GV$FIXED_TABLE, GV$FIXED_VIEW_DEFINITION |
| x$kqfvt | GV$FIXED_VIEW_DEFINITION |
| x$kqlset | GV$SUBCACHE |
| x$kqrst | GV$ROWCACHE |
| x$ksbdd | GV$BGPROCESS |
| x$ksbdp | GV$BGPROCESS |
| x$ksimsi | GV$ACTIVE_INSTANCES |
| x$ksled | GV$SESSION_WAIT, GV$SESSION_EVENT, GV$SYSTEM_EVENT, GV$EVENT_NAME |
| x$kslei | GV$SYSTEM_EVENT |
| x$ksles | GV$SESSION_EVENT |
| x$kslld | GV$LATCH, GV$LATCH_CHILDREN, GV$LATCH_PARENT, GV$LATCHNAME |
| x$ksllt | GV$LATCH, GV$LATCH_CHILDREN, GV$LATCH_PARENT |
| x$ksllw | GV$LATCH_MISSES |
| x$kslwsc | GV$LATCH_MISSES |
| x$ksmfs | GV$SGASTAT |
| x$ksmhp | GV$SQL_SHARED_MEMORY |
| x$ksmls | GV$SGASTAT |
| x$ksmsd | GV$SGA |
| x$ksmsp | GV$SHARED_POOL_RESERVED |
| x$ksmspr | GV$SHARED_POOL_RESERVED |

| x$ Tables | V$ Views |
| --- | --- |
| x$ksmss | GV$SGASTAT |
| x$ksppcv | GV$PARAMETER |
| x$ksppi | GV$PARAMETER, GV$SYSTEM_PARAMETER |
| x$ksppsv | GV$SYSTEM_PARAMETER |
| x$ksqeq | GV$_LOCK1, GV$ENQUEUE_LOCK |
| x$ksqrs | GV$RESOURCE, GV$LOCK, GV$ENQUEUE_LOCK, GV$TRANSACTION_ENQUEUE |
| x$kstex | GV$EXECUTION |
| x$ksull | GV$LICENSE |
| x$ksulop | GV$SESSION_LONGOPS |
| x$ksulv | GV$NLS_VALID_VALUES |
| x$ksupr | GV$PROCESS, GV$LATCHHOLDER |
| x$ksurlmt | GV$RESOURCE_LIMIT |
| x$ksusd | GV$SESSTAT, GV$MYSTAT, GV$STATNAME |
| x$ksuse | GV$SESSION, GV$SESSION_CONNECT_INFO, GV$SESSION_WAIT, GV$LOCKED_OBJECT, GV$LOCK, GV$ENQUEUE_LOCK, GV$TRANSACTION_ENQUEUE, GV$SESSTAT, GV$ACCESS |
| x$ksusio | GV$SESS_IO |
| x$ksutm | GV$TIMER |
| x$ktadm | GV$LOCKED_OBJECT, GV$_LOCK |
| x$ktcxb | GV$TRANSACTION, GV$LOCKED_OBJECT, GV$_LOCK, GV$TRANSACTION_ENQUEUE |
| x$ktsso | GV$SORT_USAGE |
| x$ktstssd | GV$SORT_SEGMENT |
| x$kturd | GV$ROLLSTAT |
| x$kxfpdp | GV$PQ_SLAVE |
| x$kxfpsst | GV$PQ_SESSTAT |
| x$kxfpys | GV$PQ_SYSSTAT |
| x$kxsbd | GV$SQL_BIND_DATA |

| x$ Tables | V$ Views |
|-----------|----------|
| x$kxscc | GV$SQL_CURSOR |
| x$kzspr | GV$ENABLEDPRIVS |
| x$kzsrt | GV$PWFILE_USERS |
| x$le | GV$BH, GV$LOCK_ELEMENT |
| x$option | GV$OPTION |
| x$uganco | GV$DBLINK |
| x$version | GV$VERSION |

# Version 7 V$ Views Cross-Referenced to the x$ Tables

These are x$ tables ordered by the V$ view names:

| V$ Views | x$ Tables |
|----------|-----------|
| V$ACCESS | x$kgldp, x$kglob, x$ksuse, x$kgllk |
| V$ARCHIVE | x$kccdi, x$kccle |
| V$BACKUP | x$kcvfhonl |
| V$BGPROCESS | x$ksbdd, x$ksbdp |
| V$CIRCUIT | x$kmcvc |
| V$COMPATIBILITY | x$kckty |
| V$COMPATSEG | x$kckce |
| V$CONTROLFILE | x$kcccf |
| V$DATABASE | x$kccdi |
| V$DATAFILE | x$kccfe, x$kccfn, x$kcvfh |
| V$DBFILE | x$kccfn |
| V$DBLINK | x$uganco |
| V$DB_OBJECT_CACHE | x$kglob |
| V$DISPATCHER | x$kmmdi |
| V$ENABLEDPRIVS | x$kzspr |

| V$ Views | x$ Tables |
| --- | --- |
| V$FILESTAT | x$kccfe, x$kcfio |
| V$FIXED_TABLE | x$kqfdt, x$kqfta, x$kqfvi |
| V$INSTANCE | x$ksuxsinst |
| V$LATCH | x$ksllt |
| V$LATCHHOLDER | x$ksuprlat |
| V$LATCHNAME | x$kslld |
| V$LIBRARYCACHE | x$kglst |
| V$LICENSE | x$ksull |
| V$LOADCSTAT | x$kllcnt |
| V$LOADTSTAT | x$klltab |
| V$_LOCK1 | x$kdnssc, x$kdnssf, x$ksqeq |
| V$_LOCK | v$_lock1, x$ktadm, x$ktcxb |
| V$LOCK | v$_lock, x$ksqrs, x$ksuse |
| V$LOG | x$kccle, x$kccrt |
| V$LOGFILE | x$kccfn |
| V$LOGHIST | x$kcclh |
| V$LOG_HISTORY | x$kcclh |
| V$MLS_PARAMETERS | v$nls_parameters |
| V$MTS | x$kmmsg |
| V$MYSTAT | x$ksumysta, x$ksusd |
| V$NLS_PARAMETERS | x$nls_parameters |
| V$NLS_VALID_VALUES | x$ksulv |
| V$OPEN_CURSOR | x$kgllk |
| V$OPTION | x$option |
| V$PARAMETER | x$ksppi |
| V$PQ_SESSTAT | x$kxfpsst |
| V$PQ_SLAVE | x$kxfpdp |
| V$PQ_SYSSTAT | x$kxfpys |

| V$ Views | x$ Tables |
|----------|-----------|
| V$PROCESS | x$ksupr |
| V$PWFILE_USERS | x$kzsrt |
| V$QUEUE | x$kmcqs |
| V$RECOVERY_LOG | x$kccle, x$kcclh, x$kcvfhmrr, x$kcvfhmrr |
| V$RECOVER_FILE | x$kcvfhmrr |
| V$REQDIST | x$kmmrd |
| V$RESOURCE | x$ksqrs |
| V$ROLLNAME | x$kturd, undo$ |
| V$ROLLSTAT | x$kturd |
| V$ROWCACHE | x$kqrst |
| V$SESSION | x$ksuse |
| V$SESSION_CURSOR_CACHE | x$kgicc |
| V$SESSION_EVENT | x$ksles |
| V$SESSION_WAIT | x$ksled, x$ksusecst |
| V$SESSTAT | x$ksusd, x$ksusesta |
| V$SESS_IO | x$ksusio |
| V$SGA | x$ksmsd |
| V$SGASTAT | x$ksmss |
| V$SHARED_SERVER | x$kmmsi |
| V$SQLAREA | x$kglcursor |
| V$SQLTEXT | x$kglna |
| V$STATNAME | x$ksusd |
| V$SYSSTAT | x$ksusgsta |
| V$SYSTEM_CURSOR_CACHE | x$kgics |
| V$SYSTEM_EVENT | x$ksled, x$kslei |
| V$THREAD | x$kccrt |
| V$TIMER | x$ksutm |
| V$TRANSACTION | x$ktcxb |

| V$ Views | x$ Tables |
|---|---|
| V$TYPE_SIZE | x$kqfsz |
| V$VERSION | x$version |
| V$WAITSTAT | x$kcbwait |

# Version 8 GV$ Views Cross-Referenced to the x$ Tables

Note that the V8 V$ views are the same as the GV$ views. These are the x$ tables ordered by the V$ view names:

| V$ Views | x$ Tables |
|---|---|
| GV$ACCESS | x$kgldp, x$kglob, x$ksuse, x$kgllk |
| GV$ACTIVE_INSTANCES | x$ksimsi |
| GV$ARCHIVE | x$kccdi, x$kccle |
| GV$ARCHIVED_LOG | x$kccal |
| GV$ARCHIVED_DEST | x$kcrrdest |
| GV$BACKUP | x$kcvfhonl |
| GV$BACKUP_CORRUPTION | x$kccfc |
| GV$BACKUP_DATAFILE | x$kccbf |
| GV$BACKUP_DEVICE | x$ksfhdvnt |
| GV$BACKUP_PIECE | x$kccbp |
| GV$BACKUP_REDOLOG | x$kccbl |
| GV$BACKUP_SET | x$kccbs |
| GV$BGPROCESS | x$ksbdd, x$ksbdp |
| GV$BH | x$bh, x$le |
| GV$BUFFER_POOL | x$kcbwbpd |
| GV$CIRCUIT | x$kmcvc |
| GV$CLASS_PING | x$class_stat |
| GV$COMPATIBILITY | x$kckty |

| V$ Views | x$ Tables |
|---|---|
| GV$COMPATSEG | x$kckce |
| GV$CONTROLFILE | x$kcccf |
| GV$CONTROLFILE_RECORD_SECTION | x$kccrs |
| GV$COPY_CORRUPTION | x$kcccc |
| GV$DATABASE | x$kccdi |
| GV$DATAFILE | x$kccfe, x$kccfn, x$kcvfh |
| GV$DATAFILE_COPY | x$kccdc |
| GV$DATAFILE_HEADER | x$kcvfh |
| GV$DBFILE | x$kccfn |
| GV$DBLINK | x$uganco |
| GV$DB_OBJECT_CACHE | x$kglob |
| GV$DB_PIPES | x$kglob |
| GV$DELETED_OBJECT | x$kccdl |
| GV$DISPATCHER | x$kmmdi |
| GV$DISPATCHER_RATE | x$kmmdi |
| GV$DLM_CONVERT_LOCAL | x$kjicvt |
| GV$DLM_CONVERT_REMOTE | x$kjicvt |
| GV$DLM_LATCH | x$kjilft |
| GV$DLM_MISC | x$kjisft |
| GV$ENABLEDPRIVS | x$kzspr |
| GV$ENQUEUE_LOCK | x$ksqeq, x$ksuse, x$ksqrs |
| GV$EVENT_NAME | x$ksled |
| GV$EXECUTION | x$kstex |
| GV$FILESTAT | x$kccfe, x$kcfio |
| GV$FILE_PING | x$kcfio |
| GV$FIXED_TABLE | x$kqfdt, x$kqfta, x$kqfvi |
| GV$FIXED_VIEW_DEFINITION | x$kqfvt, x$kqfvi |
| GV$GLOBAL_TRANSACTION | x$k2gte2 |

| V$ Views | x$ Tables |
| --- | --- |
| GV$INDEXED_FIXED_COLUMN | x$kqfco, x$kqfta |
| GV$INSTANCE | x$ksuxsinst |
| GV$LATCH | x$kslld, x$ksllt |
| GV$LATCHHOLDER | x$ksuprlat |
| GV$LATCHNAME | x$kslld |
| GV$LATCH_CHILDREN | x$kslld, x$ksllt |
| GV$LATCH_MISSES | x$kslwsc, x$ksllw |
| GV$LATCH_PARENT | x$kslld, x$ksllt |
| GV$LIBRARYCACHE | x$kglst |
| GV$LICENSE | x$ksull |
| GV$LOADCSTAT | x$kllcnt |
| GV$LOADPSTAT | x$klpt |
| GV$LOADTSTAT | x$klltab |
| GV$_LOCK | v$_lock1, x$ktadm, x$ktcxb |
| GV$_LOCK1 | x$kdnssf, x$ksqeq |
| GV$LOCK | v$_lock, x$ksqrs, x$ksuse |
| GV$LOCKED_OBJECT | x$ktcxb, x$ktadm, x$ksuse |
| GV$LOCKS_WITH_COLLISIONS | gv$bh |
| GV$LOCK_ELEMENT | x$le |
| GV$LOG | x$kccle, x$kccrt |
| GV$LOGFILE | x$kccfn |
| GV$LOGHIST | x$kcclh |
| GV$LOG_HISTORY | x$kcclh |
| GV$MTS | x$kmmsg |
| GV$MYSTAT | x$ksumysta, x$ksusd |
| GV$NLS_PARAMETERS | x$nls_parameters |
| GV$NLS_VALID_VALUES | x$ksulv |
| GV$OBJECT_DEPENDENCY | x$kglob, x$kgldp |

| V$ Views | x$ Tables |
|---|---|
| GV$OFFLINE_RANGE | x$kccor |
| GV$OPEN_CURSOR | x$kgllk |
| GV$OPTION | x$option |
| GV$PARAMETER | x$ksppi, x$ksppcv |
| GV$PQ_SESSTAT | x$kxfpsst |
| GV$PQ_SLAVE | x$kxfpdp |
| GV$PQ_SYSSTAT | x$kxfpys |
| GV$PQ_TQSTAT | x$kxfqsrow |
| GV$PROCESS | x$ksupr |
| GV$PWFILE_USERS | x$kzsrt |
| GV$QUEUE | x$kmcqs |
| GV$RECOVERY_FILE_STATUS | x$kcrmx, x$kccfn, x$kccfe, x$kcrmf |
| GV$RECOVERY_LOG | x$kccle, x$kcclh, x$kcvfhmrr, x$kcvfhmrr |
| GV$RECOVERY_STATUS | x$kcrmx, x$kcrfx |
| GV$RECOVER_FILE | x$kcvfhmrr |
| GV$REQDIST | x$kmmrd |
| GV$RESOURCE | x$ksqrs |
| GV$RESOURCE_LIMIT | x$ksurlmt |
| GV$ROLLSTAT | x$kturd |
| GV$ROWCACHE | x$kqrst |
| GV$_SEQUENCES | x$kglob |
| GV$SESSION | x$ksuse |
| GV$SESSION_CONNECT_INFO | x$ksusecon |
| GV$SESSION_CURSOR_CACHE | x$kgicc |
| GV$SESSION_EVENT | x$ksles, x$ksled |
| GV$SESSION_LONGOPS | x$ksulop |
| GV$SESSION_OBJECT_CACHE | x$kocst |

Version 8 GV$ Views Cross-Referenced to the x$ Tables

Version 8 GV$ Views Cross-Referenced to the x$ Tables

| V$ Views | x$ Tables |
| --- | --- |
| GV$SESSION_WAIT | x$ksled, x$ksusecst |
| GV$SESSTAT | x$ksusd, x$ksusesta |
| GV$SESS_IO | x$ksusio |
| GV$SGA | x$ksmsd |
| GV$SGASTAT | x$ksmss, x$ksmfs, x$ksmls |
| GV$SHARED_POOL_RESERVED | x$ksmspr, x$kghlu |
| GV$SHARED_SERVER | x$kmmsi |
| GV$SORT_SEGMENT | x$ktstssd |
| GV$SORT_USAGE | x$ktsso, v$session |
| GV$SQL | x$kglcursor |
| GV$SQLAREA | x$kglcursor |
| GV$SQLTEXT | x$kglna |
| GV$SQLTEXT_WITH_NEWLINES | x$kglna1 |
| GV$SQL_BIND_DATA | x$kxsbd |
| GV$SQL_BIND_METADATA | x$kksbv |
| GV$SQL_CURSOR | x$kxscc |
| GV$SQL_SHARED_MEMORY | x$kglcursor, x$ksmhp |
| GV$STATNAME | x$ksusd |
| GV$SUBCACHE | x$kqlset |
| GV$SYSSTAT | x$ksusgsta |
| GV$SYSTEM_CURSOR_CACHE | x$kgics |
| GV$SYSTEM_EVENT | x$ksled, x$kslei |
| GV$SYSTEM_PARAMETER | x$ksppi, x$ksppsv |
| GV$TABLESPACE | x$kccts |
| GV$THREAD | x$kccrt |
| GV$TIMER | x$ksutm |
| GV$TRANSACTION | x$ktcxb |
| GV$TRANSACTION_ENQUEUE | x$ktcxb, x$ksuse, x$ksqrs |

| V$ Views | x$ Tables |
|---|---|
| **V$ Views** | **x$ Tables** |
| GV$TYPE_SIZE | x$kqfsz |
| GV$VERSION | x$version |
| GV$WAITSTAT | x$kcbwait |

# Version 7 x$ Tables *Not* Referenced by a V$ View

The following tables are ordered by x$ table name (53 total):

| | | | |
|---|---|---|---|
| x$bh | x$k2gte | x$k2gte2 | x$kcbcbh |
| x$kcbfwait | x$kcbrbh | x$kckfm | x$kcvfh |
| x$kdnce | x$kdnst | x$kdxhs | x$kdxst |
| x$kghlu | x$kglau | x$kglbody | x$kglcluster |
| x$kglindex | x$kgllc | x$kglpn | x$kgltable |
| x$kgltr | x$kgltrigger | x$kglxs | x$kksbv |
| x$kmmdp | x$kqdpg | x$kqfco | x$kqrpd |
| x$kqrsd | x$ksmcx | x$ksmlru | x$ksmsp |
| x$ksqdn | x$ksqst | x$ksucf | x$ksupl |
| x$ksuru | x$kttvs | x$kvii | x$kvis |
| x$kvit | x$kxfpcds | x$kxfpcms | x$kxfpcst |
| x$kxfpsds | x$kxfpsms | x$kzdos | x$kzsro |
| x$le | x$le_stat | x$messages | x$trace |
| x$traces | | | |

# Version 8 x$ Tables *Not* Referenced by a GV$ View

This is the version 8 query to get this listing:

```
select      name
from        v$fixed_table ft
```

```
where       not exists
    (select    'x'
     from       v$fixed_view_definition fv
     where      instr(fv.view_definition,lower(ft.name)) > 0)
and       name like 'X%'
order     by name;
```

These are the ordered by x$ table names (76 total):

| | | | |
|---|---|---|---|
| x$activeckpt | x$ckptbuf | x$dual | x$k2gte |
| x$k2gte2 | x$kcbbf | x$kcbbmc | x$kcbcbh |
| x$kcbfwait | x$kcbrbh | x$kcbsw | x$kcbwds |
| x$kcbwh | x$kcccp | x$kckfm | x$kclfh |
| x$kclfi | x$kclfx | x$kclls | x$kclqn |
| x$kcluh | x$kclui | x$kcrmt | x$kdxhs |
| x$kdxst | x$kglau | x$kglbody | x$kglcluster |
| x$kglindex | x$kgllc | x$kglpn | x$kglrd |
| x$kglsn | x$kgltable | x$kgltr | x$kgltrigger |
| x$kglxs | x$kksai | x$kmmdp | x$kqdpg |
| x$kqfp | x$kqrpd | x$kqrsd | x$ksfvsl |
| x$ksfvsta | x$ksimat | x$ksimav | x$kslpo |
| x$ksmfsv | x$ksmlru | x$ksmmem | x$ksmpp |
| x$ksmup | x$ksqdn | x$ksqst | x$ksucf |
| x$ksupl | x$ksuru | x$ksusex | x$ksxafa |
| x$kttvs | x$ktuxe | x$kvii | x$kvis |
| x$kvit | x$kxfpcds | x$kxfpcms | x$kxfpcst |
| x$kxfpsds | x$kxfpsms | x$kzdos | x$kzsro |
| x$le_stat | x$messages | x$trace | x$traces |

# Index